THE COMPLETE OFFICIAL MGB

Model Years 1975-1980

THE COMPLETE OFFICIAL MGB

Model Years 1975–1980

Comprising the official

Driver's Handbook

Workshop Manual

[B] BentleyPublishers
.com

Bentley Publishers, a division of Robert Bentley, Inc.
1734 Massachusetts Avenue
Cambridge, MA 02138 USA
800-423-4595 / 617-547-4170

Information that makes the difference®

BentleyPublishers™ .com

Technical contact information

We welcome your feedback. Please submit corrections and additions to our technical discussion forum at:

`http://www.BentleyPublishers.com`

Updates and corrections

We will evaluate submissions and post appropriate editorial changes online as updates or tech discussion. Appropriate updates and corrections will be added to the book in future printings. Check for updates and corrections for this book before beginning work on your vehicle. See the following web address for additional information:

`http://www.BentleyPublishers.com/updates/`

WARNING—Important Safety Notice

Do not use this manual for repairs unless you are familiar with basic automotive repair procedures and safe workshop practices. This manual illustrates the workshop procedures for some maintenance and service work. It is not a substitute for full and up-to-date information from the vehicle manufacturer or for proper training as an automotive technician. Note that it is not possible for us to anticipate all of the ways or conditions under which vehicles may be serviced or to provide cautions as to all of the possible hazards that may result.

We have endeavored to ensure the accuracy of the information in this manual. Please note, however, that considering the vast quantity and the complexity of the service information involved, we cannot warrant the accuracy or completeness of the information contained in this manual.

FOR THESE REASONS, NEITHER THE PUBLISHER NOR THE AUTHOR MAKES ANY WARRANTIES, EXPRESS OR IMPLIED, THAT THE INFORMATION IN THIS MANUAL IS FREE OF ERRORS OR OMISSIONS, AND WE EXPRESSLY DISCLAIM THE IMPLIED WARRANTIES OF MERCHANTABILITY AND OF FITNESS FOR A PARTICULAR PURPOSE, EVEN IF THE PUBLISHER OR AUTHOR HAVE BEEN ADVISED OF A PARTICULAR PURPOSE, AND EVEN IF A PARTICULAR PURPOSE IS INDICATED IN THE MANUAL. THE PUBLISHER AND AUTHOR ALSO DISCLAIM ALL LIABILITY FOR DIRECT, INDIRECT, INCIDENTAL OR CONSEQUENTIAL DAMAGES THAT RESULT FROM ANY USE OF THE EXAMPLES, INSTRUCTIONS OR OTHER INFORMATION IN THIS MANUAL. IN NO EVENT SHALL OUR LIABILITY WHETHER IN TORT, CONTRACT OR OTHERWISE EXCEED THE COST OF THIS MANUAL.

Before attempting any work on your MGB, read the Warnings and Cautions on page vi and any warning or caution that accompanies a procedure in the manual. Review the warnings and cautions each time you prepare to work on your MGB.

Your common sense and good judgment are crucial to safe and successful service work. Read procedures through before starting them. Think about whether the condition of your car, your level of mechanical skill, or your level of reading comprehension might result in or contribute in some way to an occurrence which might cause you injury, damage your car, or result in an unsafe repair. If you have doubts for these or other reasons about your ability to perform safe repair work on your car, have the work done at an authorized MGB dealer or other qualified shop.

Part numbers listed in this manual are for identification purposes only, not for ordering. Always check with your authorized MGB dealer to verify part numbers and availability before beginning service work that may require new parts.

Special tools required to perform certain service operations are identified in the manual and are recommended for use. Use of improper tools may be detrimental to the car's safe operation as well as the safety of the person servicing the car.

The vehicle manufacturer will continue to issue service information updates and parts retrofits after the editorial closing of this manual. Some of these updates and retrofits will apply to procedures and specifications in this manual. We regret that we cannot supply updates to purchasers of this manual.

ACKNOWLEDGEMENT

Special thanks are due David G. Head, New England Parts Representative, Leyland Motor Sales, Leonia, N.J.

This manual is prepared, published and distributed by Bentley Publishers, 1734 Massachusetts Avenue, Cambridge, Massachusetts 02138 USA. All information contained in this manual is based on the information available to the publisher at the time of editorial closing. MGB has not reviewed and does not vouch for the accuracy or completeness of the technical specifications and work procedures described and given in this manual.

ISBN 978-0-8376-0112-0 **Bentley Stock No. X112** **Mfg. code: X112-15-P1-1108**

Library of Congress Catalog Card No. 75-7766

The paper used in this publication is acid free and meets the requirements of the National Standard for Information Sciences-Permanence of Paper for Printed Library Materials. ♾

Manufactured in the United States of America.

Preface

This Manual has been compiled in order to provide complete, accurate, and comprehensive maintenance and repair data to both car owners and professional mechanics. The *Driver's Handbook*, which comprises the first part of this Manual, is similar to the handbook provided with every new MGB. The *Workshop Manual*, which comprises the second — and largest — portion of this Manual, is the official factory manual and was originally intended for use by dealer service departments. The Publisher has added new material to the factory data so that the present Manual is suitable both for persons of limited mechanical experience and for those trained mechanics who may not be altogether familiar with MG cars.

Home Maintenance and Repair

Though professional mechanics will find this Manual indispensable as a source of specifications, testing procedures, and precision fitting data, such mechanics usually carry out basic assembly and disassembly work guided mainly by their years of training and experience. For example, professional mechanics know without being told that engine, transmission, and rear axle parts must be properly pre-lubricated when they are reassembled following an overhaul. Therefore, such information is not commonly included in factory workshop manuals. On the other hand, non-professionals often need to be reminded of such things since mechanical work may not be a part of their daily routine. Wherever possible, the Publisher has included *Notes* and *Cautions* to alert the non-professional mechanic to those additional considerations that a professional mechanic would take into account as a matter of course.

Though simple maintenance procedures — such as those described in the *Driver's Handbook* portion of this Manual — require only a minimum of tools, the car owner will sooner or later find it desirable to obtain a fairly complete set. The basic tools include an assortment of open- and box-end wrenches and a selection of screwdrivers, pliers, one or two adjustable wrenches and other miscellaneous items such as feeler gauges, a spark plug socket, etc. A socket wrench set — preferably ⅜-in. drive — will speed up many common jobs and may be indispensable to others. A quality set of tools can be a good investment; they will last a lifetime if not abused. Cheaply made tools will not last long without wear and breakage and often damage bolts and fittings which cost more to replace than the money saved in buying inferior tools.

Liberal reference is made in this Manual to the special service tools which are recommended by the factory. Such special tools are not supplied by British Leyland Motors but can be ordered from Messrs. V. L. Churchill & Company Limited, P. O. Box No. 3, London Road, Daventry, Northants, England — information that may prove of little value to a car owner in the U.S. who must repair his car by the next weekend! Fortunately, generic equivalents for most of these special tools are available from American tool manufacturers that supply professional mechanics. Do not, however, overlook the possibility of obtaining the needed tool from a tool rental agency. In many U.S. cities, there are also do-it-yourself garages that rent or loan special tools to those who patronize the shop.

This Manual describes certain precision reconditioning jobs which even Authorized Dealers commonly farm out — either to an automative machine shop or to a specialty shop. These jobs include cylinder reboring, crankshaft reconditioning, valve grinding, starter rebuilding, sheet metal repair, etc. Instead of delivering the entire car to a professional mechanic, who may take the parts to an outside machine shop, you can save considerable money by removing the worn or damaged components and taking them to the machine shop yourself.

Advice for Professionals and Car Owners Alike

Assembly work on small, highly-tuned machines such as the MG sports cars must be carried out with greater precision than is commonly practiced on large American cars. Particular emphasis must be given to the proper use of torque wrenches and to the strict adherance to tightening torque specifications which are given in this Manual. Though all of the torque specifications may fall within the range of a 0–100 ft. lb. (0–14 mkg) torque wrench, torque wrenches operate most efficiently when used in the middle two quarters of their scales. Thus, a small torque wrench with a range of 0–50 ft. lb. (0–7 mkg) is recommended in addition to a larger torque wrench with a 150 ft. lb. (21 mkg) capacity. A fastener that is too tight can be worse than one which is too loose — especially on a lightweight sports car. Stretched or broken bolts and distorted parts, which result from overtightening by muscle-bound mechanics, become a serious concern where the precision fitting of light alloy and thin-wall iron castings is involved.

Lastly, the importance of cleanliness cannot be overemphasized. Under no circumstances should an engine or gearbox be repaired on the ground or on a garage floor. Thoroughly clean the exteriors of major components prior to disassembly in order to keep road dirt and other grime out of the working parts. No more than a pinch of abrasive dust in a gearbox can cause rapid failure of the synchronizers and bearings.

During the final assembly of an engine or gearbox, the cleaned parts should be laid out on a clean workbench which has been covered with clean sheets of new carboard or wrapping paper. The engine or gearbox itself, if not mounted on a special stand, should likewise be placed on a clean workbench. Sandpapering, valve grinding, or the use of bench grinders should not be permitted near the area where final assembly is taking place. If assembly cannot be completed in a day, enclose the partially-assembled engine or gearbox in a large plastic bag — such as a new trash bag or a dry cleaner's garment return bag — so that dust and dirt will be excluded until assembly work resumes.

David N. Wenner
Automotive Editor
Robert Bentley, Inc.

Please read these warnings and cautions before proceeding with maintenance and repair work.

WARNING—

● Do not re-use any fasteners that are worn or deformed in normal use. Many fasteners are designed to be used only once and become unreliable and may fail when used a second time. This includes, but is not limited to, nuts, bolts, washers, self-locking nuts or bolts, circlips, cotter pins. For replacements always use new parts.

● Never work under a lifted car unless it is solidly supported on stands designed for the purpose. Do not support a car on cinder blocks, hollow tiles, or other props that may crumble under continuous load. Do not work under a car that is supported solely by a jack.

● If you are going to work under a car on the ground, make sure that the ground is level. Block the wheels to keep the car from rolling. Never work under the car while the engine is running. Disconnect the battery ground strap to prevent others from starting the car while you are under it.

● Never run the engine unless the work area is well ventilated. Carbon monoxide kills.

● Friction materials such as brake or clutch discs may contain asbestos fibers. Do not create dust by grinding, sanding, or by cleaning with compressed air. Avoid breathing asbestos fibers and asbestos dust. Breathing asbestos can cause serious diseases such as asbestosis or cancer, and may result in death.

● Tie long hair behind your head. Do not wear a necktie, a scarf, loose clothing, or a necklace when you work near machine tools or running engines. If your hair, clothing, or jewelry were to get caught in the machinery, severe injury could result.

● Disconnect the battery ground strap whenever you work on the fuel system or the electrical system. When you work around fuel, do not smoke or work near heaters or other fire hazards. Keep an approved fire extinguisher handy.

● Illuminate your work area adequately but safely. Use a portable safety light for working inside or under the car. Make sure the bulb is enclosed by a wire cage. The hot filament of an accidentally broken bulb can ignite spilled fuel or oil.

● Catch draining fuel, oil, or brake fluid in suitable containers. Do not use food or beverage containers that might mislead someone into drinking from them. Store flammable fluids away from fire hazards. Wipe up spills at once, but do not store the oily rags, which can ignite and burn spontaneously.

● Finger rings should be removed so that they cannot cause electrical shorts, get caught in running machinery, or be crushed by heavy parts.

● Keep sparks, lighted matches, and open flame away from the top of the battery. If hydrogen gas escaping from the cap vents is ignited, it will ignite gas trapped in the cells and cause the battery to explode.

● Always observe good workshop practices. Wear goggles when you operate machine tools or work with battery acid. Gloves or other protective clothing should be worn whenever the job requires it.

● Do not attempt to work on your car if you do not feel well. You increase the danger of injury to yourself and others if you are tired, upset or have taken medicine or any other substance that may impair you from being fully alert.

● Some aerosol tire inflators are highly flammable. Use extreme caution when repairing a tire that may have been inflated using an aerosol tire inflator. Keep sparks, open flame or other sources of ignition away from the tire repair area. Inflate and deflate the tire at least four times before breaking the bead from the rim. Completely remove the tire from the rim before attempting any repair.

● Greases, lubricants and other automotive chemicals contain toxic substances, many of which are absorbed directly through the skin. Read manufacturer's instructions and warnings carefully. Use hand and eye protection. Avoid direct skin contact.

CAUTION—

● If you lack the skills, tools and equipment, or a suitable workshop for any procedure described in this Manual, we suggest you leave such repairs to an authorized dealer or other qualified shop. We especially urge you to consult an authorized dealer before beginning repairs on any car that may still be covered wholly or in part by the new-car warranty.

● British Leyland Motors is constantly improving its cars and sometimes these changes, both in parts and specifications, are made applicable to earlier models. Therefore, part numbers listed in this manual are for reference only. Always check with your authorized parts department for the latest information.

● Before starting a job, make certain that you have all the necessary tools and parts on hand. Read all the instructions thoroughly, do not attempt shortcuts. Use tools appropriate to the work and use only replacement parts meeting specifications. Makeshift tools, parts, and procedures will not make good repairs.

● Use pneumatic and electric tools only to loosen threaded parts and fasteners. Never use these tools to tighten fasteners, especially on light alloy parts.

● Be mindful of the environment and ecology. Before you drain the crankcase, find out the proper way to dispose of the oil. Do not pour oil onto the ground, down a drain, or into a stream, pond, or lake. Consult local ordinances that govern the disposal of wastes.

Special Note

The Editor's Notes that have been provided in Part 2 of this Manual supply additional information that is helpful to the reader's understanding of the material. These notes are found at the end of each individual section of The Workshop Manual. The reference "(See Editor's Notes at the end of section)" will appear in the text at points where the reader will find it informative to take into account the data given in one of the notes

English-American Equivalents

English	*American*
GENERAL	
L.H.S.	left hand side (viewed from drivers seat)
R.H.S.	right hand side (viewed from drivers seat)
L.H.D.	left hand drive (viewed from drivers seat)
R.H.D.	right hand drive (viewed from drivers seat)
bush	bushing (bronze, rubber, etc.)
circlip	snap ring
distance piece	spacer
end float	end clearance
engine revolution counter	tachometer
extractor	gear or bearing puller
fraze	burr from cutting, drilling, etc.
grub screw	dog screw, locating screw
joint washer	gasket
jointing compound	gasket cement, sealing compound
laden	loaded
methylated spirits	denatured alcohol
paraffin	kerosene
perished	rotted (from oil, etc.)
petrol	gasoline
renew	replace
set screw	bolt
spanner	end wrench
spigot	pilot
split pin	cotter pin
spring washer	lock washer
swarf	chips from cutting, drilling, etc.
ENGINE	
choke tube	venturi
cotters	split valve locks
float chamber	carburetor bowl
gudgeon pin	piston pin, wrist pin
oil sump	oil pan
silencer	muffler
valve crash speed	valve float rpm, redline
welch plug	water jacket plug, core plug, freeze plug
CLUTCH	
clutch housing	bellhousing
clutch release bearing	throwout bearing
clutch withdrawal fork	throwout arm
spigot bearing	pilot bearing
GEARBOX	
baulk ring	synchronizing ring, synchro cone
first motion shaft	input shaft
laygear	counter gear, cluster gear
layshaft	countershaft, cluster gear shaft
propeller shaft	driveshaft
third motion shaft	output shaft
REAR AXLE	
crown wheel	ring gear

English	*American*
ELECTRICAL	
control box	voltage regulator
distributor suction advance	vacuum advance
dynamo	generator
earth	ground (positive earth = positive ground)
H.T.	high tension
Megger	ohmmeter
micro adjuster	octane selector (changes vacuum advance)
SUSPENSION AND STEERING	
hydraulic damper	shock absorber
swivel axle	spindle, stub axle
swivel pin	pivot pin, kingpin
BODY	
bonnet	hood, engine compartment cover
boot	trunk compartment
bulkhead	firewall
fascia	dashboard
hood	top, roof
mono construction body	unit construction body (no frame)
overrider	bumperette
seat squab	seat back, upright portion of seat
wing	fender

Contents

MGB
CONVERTIBLE
DRIVER'S HANDBOOK

PART 1

FOREWORD

This Handbook provides an introduction to your car, together with information on the care and periodic maintenance required to combine trouble-free motoring with minimal running costs.

Claims for the replacement of parts under warranty must be submitted to the supplying authorized Austin MG Dealer, or when this is not possible, to the nearest authorized Austin MG Dealer. informing them of the vendor's name and address. Except in emergency, warranty work should always be carried out by an appointed authorized Austin MG Dealer.

By keeping the Passport to Service, signed by the authorized Austin MG Dealer, or vendor in the vehicle, you can quickly establish the date of purchase and provide the necessary details if adjustments are required to be carried out under warranty.

Regular use of the Passport to Service Maintenance Scheme is the best safeguard against the possibility of abnormal repair bills at a later date. Failure to have your car correctly maintained could invalidate the terms of the warranty and may result in unsatisfactory operation of the emission control systems.

Safety features embodied in the car may be impaired if other than genuine parts are fitted. In certain territories, legislation prohibits the fitting of parts not to the vehicle manufacturer's specification. Owners purchasing accessories while travelling abroad should ensure that the accessory and its fitted location on the car conform to mandatory requirements existing in their country of origin.

Your Authorized Austin MG Dealer is provided with the latest information concerning special service tools and workshop techniques. This enables him to undertake your service and repairs in the most efficient and economic manner. The operations carried out by your authorized Austin MG Dealer will be in accordance with current recommendations and may be subject to revision from time to time.

Further details on service parts will be found under "Service" on page 50. **Please note that references to right- or left-hand in this Handbook are made as if viewing the car from the rear.**

Specification details set out in this Handbook apply to a range of vehicles and not to any particular vehicle. For the specification of any particular vehicle owners should consult their authorized Austin MG Dealer.

During running-in from new, certain adjustments vary from specification figures detailed. They will be set to specification by your authorized Austin MG Dealer at the After-Sales Service and should be maintained throughout your car's life.

The Manufacturers reserve the right to vary their specifications with or without notice, and at such times and in such manner as they think fit. Major as well as minor changes may be involved in accordance with the Manufacturer's policy of constant product improvement.

Whilst every effort is made to ensure the accuracy of the particulars contained in this Handbook, neither the Manufacturer nor the authorized Austin MG Dealer, by whom this Handbook is supplied, shall in any circumstances be held liable for any inaccuracy or the consequences thereof.

Emission Controls

Your car is fitted with emission controls and devices required by the United States Clean Air Act.

Please read carefully the **'EMISSION CONTROL SYSTEMS'** section of the Handbook which contains information on the emission control systems fitted to your car and recognition of symptoms of malfunctions which could affect emissions.

It is imperative that you familiarize yourself with the contents of this section and ensure that the car you have purchased will remain in compliance with the intentions of the above Acts.

All **EMISSION CONTROL** maintenance checks and adjustments should be entrusted to your authorized Austin MG Dealer.

[NOTE: Part 1 of this book is a compilation of Driver's Handbooks for model years 1975 through 1980.]

CATALYTIC CONVERTER PRECAUTIONS

Fig. 1

1. **Use unleaded fuel** only. This is essential to maintain the efficiency of the emission control system. Unleaded fuel has the additional advantage that it minimizes spark plug fouling, thereby giving improved engine performance.

2. Have your car maintained in accordance with the Maintenance Summary outlined in this handbook. A correctly tuned engine minimizes exhaust emissions and achieves the optimum performance and fuel economy.

3. Do not continue to operate your car if you detect any engine malfunction. Misfire, or engine run-on may cause unusually high catalytic converter temperatures. Damage to the catalytic converter (1) may occur if any such engine malfunctions are not rectified immediately.

4. DO NOT LEAVE YOUR CAR UNATTENDED WITH THE ENGINE RUNNING AT ANY TIME as an unobserved rise in engine temperature may cause damage to the engine and catalytic converter.

5. The use of a catalytic converter increases exhaust system temperatures. Do not operate or park your car in areas where combustible materials such as dry grass or leaves may come in contact with the exhaust system. The exhaust system could ignite such materials under certain weather conditions.

6. Do not run the engine with a spark plug lead disconnected or a spark plug removed or use any device that requires an insert into a spark plug hole in order to generate air pressure (e.g. tyre pump, paint spray attachment, etc.) as this could also result in catalytic converter damage.

7. Do not push or tow your car to start it. Use jumper cables. Under certain conditions, pushing or towing could damage the catalytic converter.

8. The catalytic converter (1) contains a ceramic material. Avoid heavy impacts on the converter casing.

Fig. 1

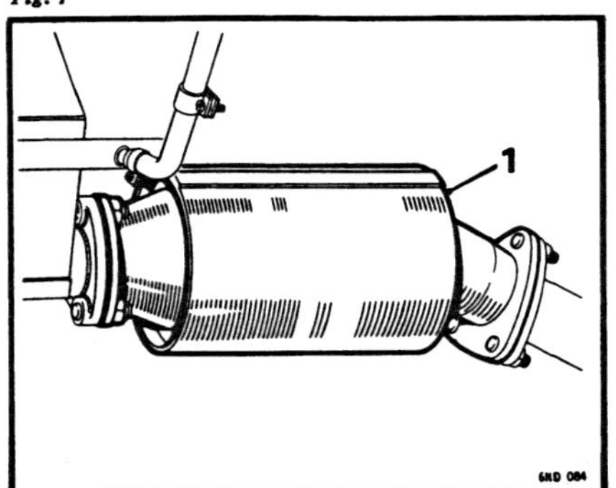

CONTROLS

Fig. 2

Pedals (1) (2) (3) — The pedals are arranged in the conventional positions.

The brake pedal operates the dual hydraulic braking system applying the brakes on all four wheels, also when the ignition is switched on, bringing the stop warning lights into operation.

Gear lever (4) — The gear positions are indicated on the lever knob. To engage reverse gear move the lever to the left in the neutral position until resistance is felt, apply further side pressure to overcome the resistance and then pull the lever back to engage the gear. The reverse lights operate automatically when reverse is selected with the ignition switched on.

Synchromesh engagement is provided on all forward gears.

Overdrive switch (when fitted) (5) — A slide switch incorporated in the gear lever knob operates the overdrive. To engage the overdrive move the switch rearward; to disengage, move the switch forward. For operating instructions see page 11.

Hand brake (6) — The hand brake is of the pull-up lever type, operating mechanically on the rear wheels only. To release the hand brake pull the lever up slightly, depress the button on the end of the lever and push the lever down.

Fig. 2

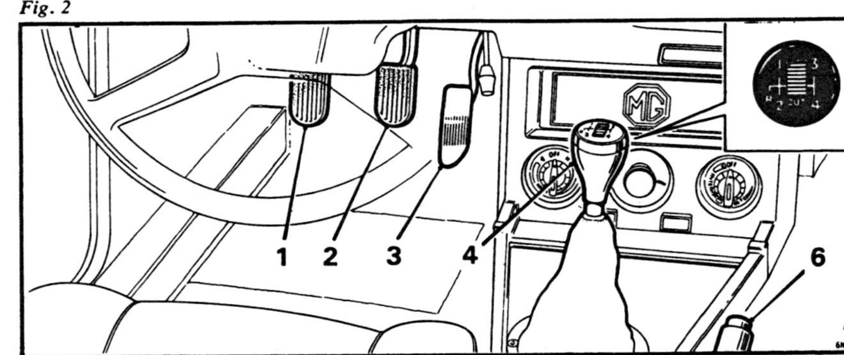

IGNITION/STARTER SWITCH AND STEERING LOCK *Fig. 3*

Key number The key number appears on the key, on the number tag supplied or on a label attached to the windscreen of a new car.

NOTE THE KEY NUMBER in your **DIARY** and in a reference book at **HOME** and then **REMOVE THE LABEL with the key number FROM THE CAR.** Consult your Austin MG Dealer regarding key replacements for the steering-column lock.

The steering-column lock (4), if used properly, will greatly reduce the possibility of the car being stolen.

Unlocking To unlock the steering, insert the key and turn it to position 'I'. If the steering-wheel has been turned to engage the lock, slight movement of the steering-wheel will assist disengagement of the lock plunger.

With the key in the position marked 'I' the ignition is switched off and the steering lock disengaged. The radio may be operated with the key in this position. The key must be in this position when towing the car for recovery.

Ignition and start To switch on the ignition, turn the key to position 'II'. Further movement against spring resistance to position 'III' operates the starter motor. Release the key immediately the engine starts.

Locking To lock the steering, turn the key anti-clockwise to the position marked 'I', press the button (5), turn the key to the 'O' position and withdraw it.

WARNING: The steering lock/ignition/starter switch and its electrical circuits are designed to prevent the ignition system and starter from being energized while the steering lock is engaged. Serious consequences could result from alterations or substitution of the steering lock/ignition switch or its wiring. In no circumstances must the ignition switch be separated from the steering lock.

Do not lubricate the steering lock.

Fig. 3

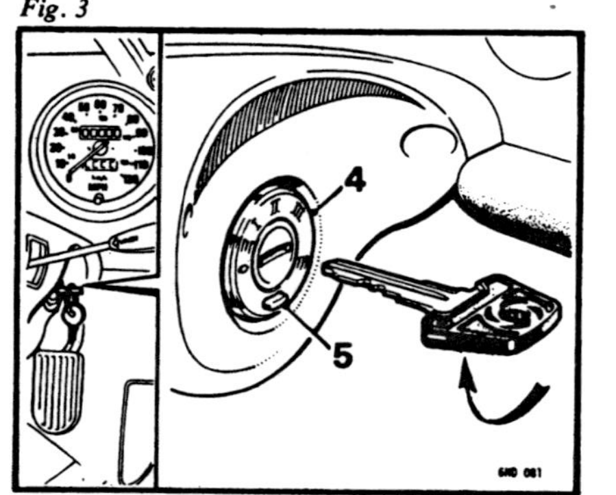

INSTRUMENTS AND SWITCHES

INSTRUMENTS (1975 and 1976) *Fig. 4*

(1) **Speedometer.** In addition to recording the road speed this instrument also records the total distance (3), and the distance travelled for any particular trip (2). To reset the trip recorder, push the knob (4) upwards and turn it clockwise; ensure that all the counters are returned to zero.

(5) **Tachometer.** The instrument indicates the revolutions per minute of the engine and assists the driver to use the most effective engine speed range for maximum performance in any gear.*

(6) **Oil.** The gauge indicates the pressure of the oil in the engine lubrication system.*

(7) **Water.** The gauge is marked 'C' (cold), 'N' (normal), and 'H' (hot), indicating the temperature of the coolant as it leaves the cylinder head.*

(8) **Fuel.** When the ignition is switched on the gauge indicates approximately the amount of fuel in the tank.*

* Also see 'RUNNING INSTRUCTIONS'.

Fig. 4

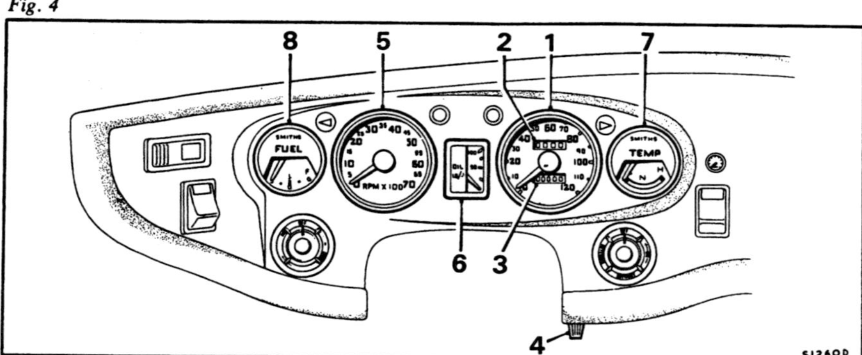

INSTRUMENTS *Fig. 5*
(1977 and later)

Speedometer (1) In addition to indicating the road speed this instrument also records the total distance (3) and the distance travelled for any particular trip (2). To reset the trip recorder, press the knob (4) and all the counters will return to zero.

Tachometer (5) This instrument indicates the revolutions per minute of the engine and assists the driver to use the most effective engine speed range for maximum performance in any gear (see page 11).

Fuel gauge (6) When the ignition is switched on the fuel gauge indicates approximately the amount of fuel in the tank. An important note on filling with fuel is given on pages 10 and 38.

Oil pressure gauge (7) The gauge registers the pressure of the oil in the engine lubricating system. Important notes on its indications are given on page 11.

Clock (8) To start the clock or reset the hands, press and turn the button until the hands are at the correct time.

Coolant temperature gauge (9) The gauge indicates the temperature of the coolant as it leaves the engine cylinder head. An important note about temperature is on page 11.

Fig. 5

WARNING LIGHTS AND SYSTEMS *Fig. 6*
(1977 and later)

Direction indicator (1) GREEN. The warning light flashes when the direction indicators are operating. Additional warning is also given by the audible 'clicking' of the flasher unit.

Main beam (2) BLUE. The light glows when the headlights are switched on with the beams in the raised position. The light goes out when the beams are dipped.

Ignition (3) RED. This light serves the dual purpose of reminding the driver to switch off the ignition and of being a no-charge indicator.

Hazard (4) RED. The warning light will flash when the hazard warning lights are operating, and the direction indicator warning lights will flash when the hazard warning lights are operating.

Brake (5) RED. The warning light serves two separate functions. Firstly, if the brake system hydraulic pressure fails the lamp glows; secondly, the lamp glows as a hand brake 'on' indicator. The warning light will only operate when the ignition is switched on—see NOTE.

Seat belt (6) RED. The warning light will glow for eight seconds each time the ignition starter switch is operated, irrespective of whether the driver's seat belt is fastened—see NOTE.

Further information on the seat belt warning system will be found on page 17.

NOTE: As an automatic check the 'BRAKE' and 'SEAT BELT' warning lamps will glow each time the ignition key is turned to position 'III' (starter motor operating). Consult your authorized Austin MG Dealer if any of these warning lamps fail to glow when the starter is operating.

Fig. 6

Instruments and Switches

SWITCHES (1975 and 1976) *Fig. 7*

(1) **Lighting switch.** Press the lower end of the switch rocker to the first position to operate the parking and tail lamps and to the second position to operate the headlamps. The marking on the switch is illuminated when the panel lamps are switched on.

(2) **Headlamp low beam—(4) Flasher.** With the headlamps switched on at the lighting switch, move the lever down away from the steering-wheel to operate the high beam (3). Lifting the lever towards the steering-wheel from the low-beam position will flash (4) the headlamp high-beams irrespective of whether the lighting switch is on or off.

(5) **Headlamp main-beam warning lamp (blue).** The warning lamp glows when the headlamps are switched on and the beam is in the raised position. The lamp goes out when the beam is lowered.

(6) **Panel lamp switch.** With the parking lamps switched on, illumination of the instruments and switches may be varied by rotating the panel lamp switch knob. Turning the switch knob clockwise from the off position immediately illuminates the panel lamps and further clockwise movement will increase the light brilliance.

Reverse lamps. The reverse lamps operate automatically if reverse gear is selected and the ignition switch is at position 'II' (ignition).

Fig. 7

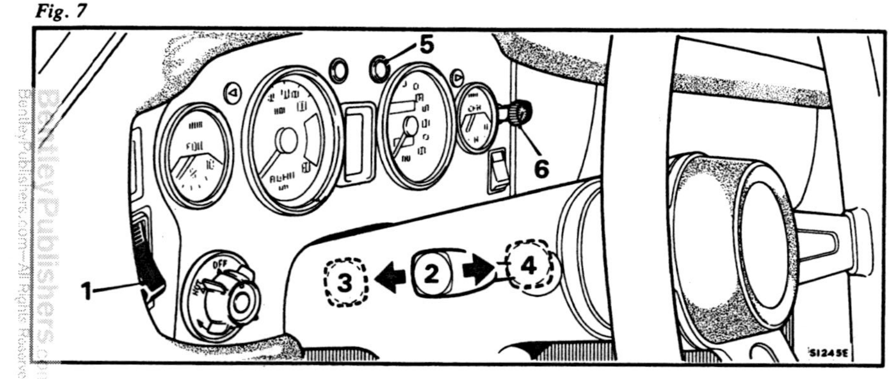

SWITCHES (1975 and 1976) *Fig. 8*

(1) **Direction indicators.** The switch is self-cancelling and operates the indicators only when the ignition is switched on. A visual warning of a front or rear bulb failure is given when, after switching on an indicator, the warning lamp and the serviceable bulb on the affected side give a continuous light.

(2) **Direction indicator warning lamps (green).** The arrow-shaped lamps show the direction selected and each operates with the appropriate flashing direction indicators.

(3) **Horn.** The horn is sounded by pressing the centre motif of the steering-wheel.

(4) **Overdrive.** Move the lever towards the steering-wheel to engage overdrive; move the lever away from the steering-wheel to return to direct drive.

(5) **Windscreen wiper.** Move the switch lever down to operate the windscreen wipers at slow speed; further movement in the same direction will operate the wipers at fast speed. The wiper blades park automatically when the switch lever is returned to the off position.

(6) **Windscreen washer.** Press the knob on the end of the switch lever to operate the windscreen washer. When the windscreen is dirty, operate the washer before setting the wipers in motion.

In cold weather the washer reservoir should be filled with a mixture of water and a recommended washer solvent to prevent the water freezing. On no account should radiator anti-freeze or methylated spirits (denatured alcohol) be used in the windscreen washer.

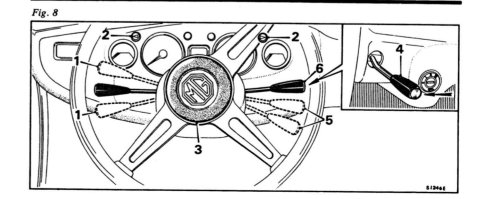

Fig. 8

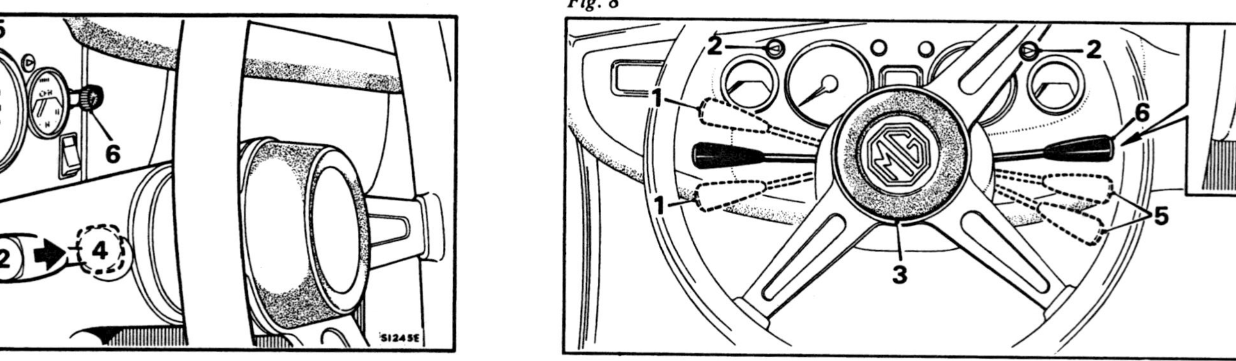

Instruments and Switches

SWITCHES (1975 and 1976) *Fig. 9*

(1) **Courtesy lamp.** The courtesy lamp is controlled by a switch (2) on the lamp and also by switches operated by the doors. With both doors closed the lamp may be switched on or off using the switch on the lamp. Opening either door switches on the lamp and closing the door extinguishes it.

(4) **Hazard warning.** To use the direction indicators as hazard warning lights, press the lower end of the switch rocker; all direction indicators and the warning lamp (3) will operate together, irrespective of whether the ignition is switched on or off. The marking on the switch is illuminated when the panel lamps are switched on.

(5) **Cigar-lighter.** To operate, press the knob inwards. When ready for use the lighter will partially eject itself and may then be withdrawn. The rim of the cigar-lighter is illuminated when the panel lamps are switched on.

Radio (if fitted). Full operating instructions are supplied with the radio.

SWITCHES (1977 and later) *Fig. 10*

Lighting (1) Press the switch lever downwards to the central position to switch on the side and tail lights, and fully down for the headlights.

Panel lamps (2) The panel lights will function only when the side lamps are switched on. Turning the switch knob clockwise switches on the panel lights; further clockwise movement of the knob increases the light brilliance.

Hazard warning (3) To use the direction indicators as a hazard warning to other road users, press the lower end of the switch rocker, when all the direction indicators, their warning lights and the hazard warning light will operate together, irrespective of whether the ignition is on or off. The green illumination light on the face of the switch glows when the panel lights are switched on.

Return the switch to the off position to cancel the warning.

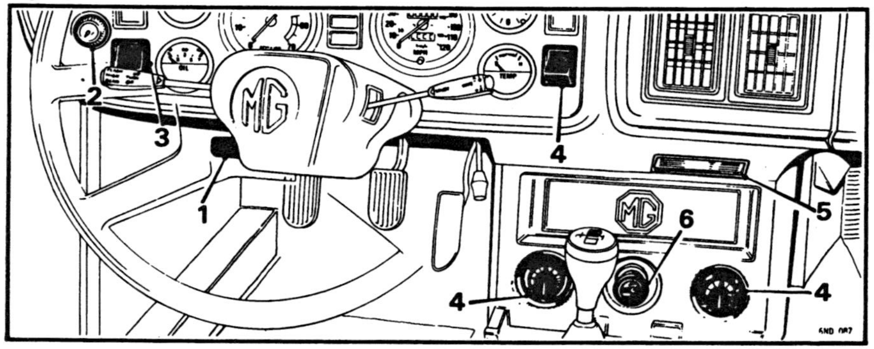

Fig. 9

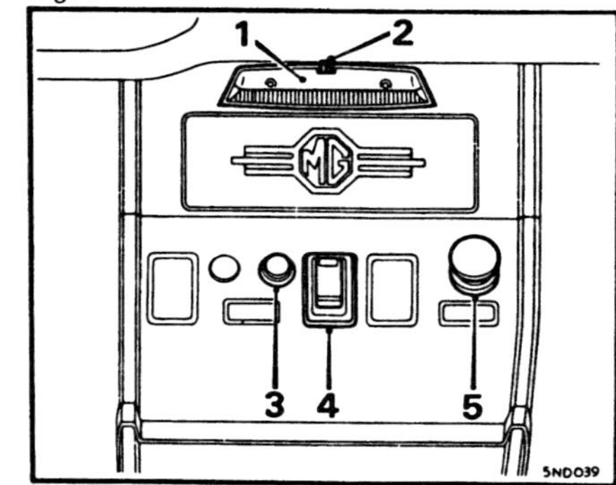

Fig. 10

Instruments and Switches

Blower switch and heater controls (4) For operating instructions see **'HEATING AND VENTILATING'**.

Courtesy light (5) The courtesy light is controlled by a switch in the light and by a switch fitted to each door pillar. With the doors closed the light may be switched on by pressing the front edge of the lens which acts as a rocker switch. Press the rear edge of the lens to switch off the light. Opening either door will switch on the light, and closing the door will extinguish the light.

Cigar-lighter (6) To operate, press the knob inwards and release. When the element has become sufficiently heated the lighter will be partially ejected, and may be withdrawn for use. The rim of the cigar-lighter is illuminated when the panel lights are switched on.

COLUMN SWITCH

Direction indicators, main beam and horn control *Fig. 11*

Direction indicators The switch operates the indicators only when the ignition is switched on.

Move the lever to position **'A'** when turning left and to position **'B'** when turning right.

After making a turn the signal is self-cancelled when the steering-wheel is returned to the straight-ahead position.

The switch lever may be held against spring pressure to select either left or right indicator and will cancel the indication immediately it is released without movement of the steering-wheel.

A visual warning of a front or rear bulb failure is given when, after switching on an indicator, the warning lamp and the serviceable bulb on the affected side give a continuous light.

Headlamp dipper With the headlamps switched on at the lighting switch, move the lever forward (**'C'**) to use the main beams; the warning light will glow (BLUE). Return the lever to the midway position to dip the beams.

Headlamp flasher Lift the lever towards the steering-wheel (**'D'**) to flash the headlamps irrespective of whether they have been switched on at the lighting switch or not.

Horns Press the end of the lever inwards (**'E'**) to sound the horns.

Fig. 11

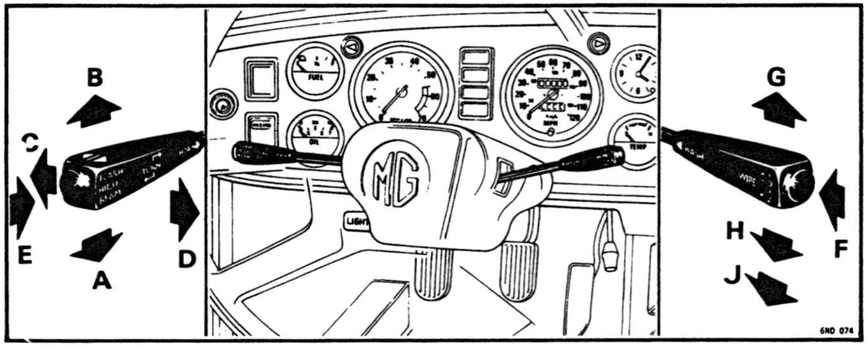

Windscreen washer and wiper control *Fig. 11*

Windscreen washer

Press the end of the lever inwards ('F') to operate the washer jets.

In cold weather the washer reservoir should be filled with a mixture of water and a recommended washer solvent to prevent the water freezing.

To avoid possible damage to paintwork **do not** use radiator anti-freeze in the windscreen washer.

Windscreen wiper

Move the lever upwards ('G') and then release it to obtain a single wipe. The lever will return to the 'off' position and the blades will park automatically at the completion of the wipe.

To operate the wipers at normal speed move the lever down to the first position ('H') and to the second position ('J') when a higher wiping speed is required.

NOTE: Neither the windscreen wiper nor the washer can operate until the ignition has been switched on.

Braking system (all models)

The hydraulic brake system has two independent circuits. If hydraulic pressure fails in one circuit, the remaining circuit will provide an emergency brake condition on the other two wheels and allow the car to be brought to rest by brake pedal application. This would be accompanied by the warning lamp (5) glowing on the instrument panel.

IF THE WARNING LAMP (5) GLOWS AT ANY TIME EXCEPT WHEN STARTING OR WHEN THE IGNITION IS SWITCHED ON AND THE HAND BRAKE IS APPLIED, THE CAUSE MUST BE INVESTIGATED IMMEDIATELY.

Unless as a result of your investigation you are satisfied that it is safe to proceed, you should leave the vehicle where it is and call for assistance. Even if you are satisfied that it is safe to proceed, the car should only be driven in cases of real emergency, extreme care should be taken and heavy braking avoided. In deciding whether it is safe to proceed you should consider whether you will be infringing the law.

Anti-theft warning buzzer (all models)

A combined ignition and steering lock with warning buzzer is fitted to the car. The warning buzzer will sound if the driver's door is opened while the key is in the lock. The buzzer will not operate if the key is removed from the lock.

When leaving the car unattended always:

Set the hand brake.

Lock the steering by removing the key from the ignition steering lock.

Lock the car doors and remove the key.

STARTING AND RUNNING INSTRUCTIONS

ENERGY CONSERVATION

It is essential that owners wishing to achieve the best possible degree of fuel economy ensure, as a first priority, that their vehicle is tuned to its optimum level of performance by regular maintenance in accordance with Leyland recommendations.

Apart from regular maintenance there are a number of areas where deliberate and conscious actions on the part of the owner can achieve further quite marked improvements. The following are recommended:

- After starting from cold, quickly depress and release the throttle pedal to set the automatic choke to its correct position.
- Switch off the ignition if the vehicle is expected to be stationary for more than half a minute.
- Avoid short stop-start journeys.
- Anticipate obstructions, junctions and sharp corners and adjust speed as necessary. Do not generate unnecessary speed.
- Accelerate gently through the gears.
- Decelerate gently whenever possible and avoid heavy braking.
- Stay in top gear as long as possible without labouring the engine.
- Ensure tyres are correctly inflated.
- Remove any unnecessary weight.

CAUTION: **Carburetter piston damper**

An incorrectly fitted or lubricated carburetter piston damper **can cause a marked increase in fuel consumption.** The cautionary note and instructions on carburetter damper topping up given on page 41 MUST be observed.

The following instructions are a guide for starting, running and loading the car, and include notes on the use of the controls and the indications of the instruments.

WARNING: Exhaust fumes will be drawn into the car if it is driven with the boot lid open, causing a health hazard to the passenger and driver.

If it is imperative that the car be driven with the boot lid open, adverse effects can be minimized by adopting the following procedure:

1. Close all windows.
2. Open the face vents fully.
3. Set the heater controls to circulate the maximum amount of cold or hot air.
4. Switch on the blower motor.
5. Do not travel at high speed.

Running in

The treatment given to a new car will have an important bearing on its subsequent life, and engine speeds during this early period must be limited. The following instructions should be strictly adhered to.

During the first 500 miles:

DO NOT exceed 45 m.p.h.

DO NOT operate at full throttle in any gear.

DO NOT allow the engine to labour in any gear.

Exhaust catalytic converter (when fitted)

1. The catalytic converter contains ceramic material. Avoid heavy impacts on the converter casing.
2. **Use unleaded fuel only.** The use of leaded fuel will seriously impair the efficiency of the emission control system.
3. The reaction in the catalytic converter increases exhaust system temperatures. Care must be taken to avoid exhaust system contact with easily combustible materials such as dry grass.
4. If the engine misfires, the cause must be immediately rectified to prevent catalytic converter damage.
5. The use of any device which requires an insert into a spark plug hole in order to generate an air pressure, i.e. tyre pump or paint spray attachment, could also result in catalytic converter damage.

Choice of fuel (1975)

The engine has been designed to operate on 'Regular' fuel and has not been developed for the regular use of unleaded or low lead fuels. The use of such fuels cannot be recommended as they could have a detrimental effect on engine components, resulting in loss of performance, excess exhaust emissions and, possibly, complete engine failure.

Choice of fuel (1976 and later)

The engine has been designed to operate only on unleaded fuel. It is essential that **unleaded fuel is used** otherwise serious damage can be caused in the catalytic converter.

Filling with fuel

The filler neck of the fuel tank is designed to accept fuel dispenser nozzles of the type specified only for unleaded fuel. The dispenser nozzle must be inserted into the filler neck sufficiently to open the trap door for fuel to flow into the fuel tank.

Starting

Sit in the car, then wear and fasten the seat belts; this applies to both driver and passenger.
Switch on the ignition and check:
That the ignition warning light glows.
That the fuel gauge registers.

Depress the throttle pedal fully and release.

Operate the starter. Do not depress the throttle pedal while the starter is operated.

As soon as the engine is started check:
That the oil pressure gauge registers.
That the ignition warning light has gone out.

Within thirty seconds of starting the engine, quickly depress and release the throttle pedal to set the automatic choke to its correct position.

Induction chamber heater *Fig. 12*

An induction chamber heater is fitted and operates below 4°C (40°F). When starting below this temperature it is necessary to allow a warming-up period of thirty seconds between switching on the ignition and starting the engine.

Never leave the ignition switched on in excess of the recommended periods with the engine at rest.

Fuel pump inertia switch *Fig. 13*

The electrical supply to the fuel pump is switched off by an inertia switch if the car is subjected to a moderate impact. The switch (1), shown in the off position, is located under the fascia on the left-hand side. To reset the switch unscrew the three screws (2) to release the bottom panel (3) push the plunger (4) into the switch body and refit the bottom panel.

Fuel cut-off valve (1977 and later) *Fig. 14*

The supply of fuel to the carburetter is mechanically cut off by an inertia valve if the car is subjected to a moderate impact. The valve (1) shown in the off position (fuel flowing), is located in the engine compartment. To reset the valve push the plunger (2) into the valve body.

Starter

Do not operate the starter for longer than five to six seconds.

If after a reasonable number of attempts the engine should fail to start, switch off the ignition and investigate the cause. Continued use of the starter when the engine will not start not only discharges the battery but may also damage the starter.

Ignition warning lamp *Fig. 15(3)*

The light (3) should glow when the engine is switched on, and go out and stay out at all times when the engine is running above normal idling speed. Failure to do so indicates a fault in the battery charging system. Check that the alternator drive belt is correctly tensioned before consulting your authorized Austin MG Dealer.

Fig. 12

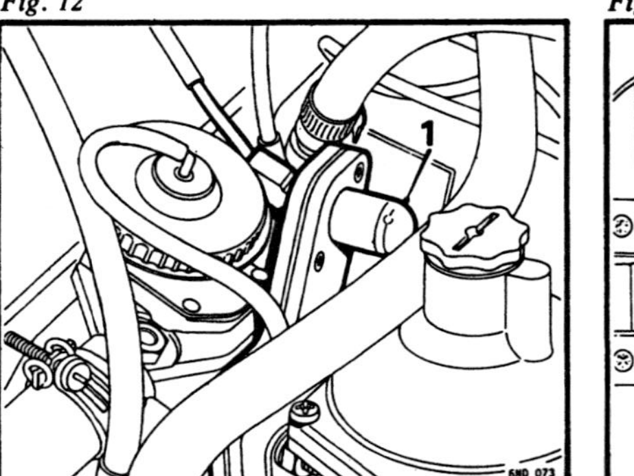

Fig. 13

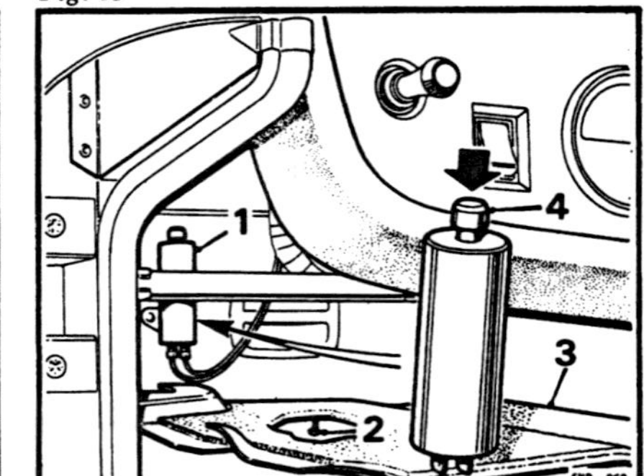

Oil pressure gauge *Fig. 15(1)*

The gauge (1) should register a pressure as soon as the engine is started up. The pressure may rise above 80 lbf/in² when the engine is started from cold, and as the oil is circulated and warmed the pressure should then drop to between 50 and 80 lbf/in² at normal running speeds and to between 10 and 25 lbf/in² at idling speed.

Should the gauge fail to register any pressure, stop the engine immediately and investigate the cause. Start by checking the oil level.

Temperature gauge *Fig. 15(4)*

Normal operating temperature is reached when the pointer is at 'normal'.

Overheating may cause serious damage. Should the pointer reach 'H' (hot), stop the engine and investigate the cause. Check the cooling fan operation (see page 45), the drive belt tension, and when the system has cooled, check the coolant level.

When the ignition is switched off the needle returns to the 'cold' position.

Tachometer *Fig. 15(2)*

For normal road work, and to obtain the most satisfactory service from your engine, select the appropriate gear to maintain engine speeds of between 2,000 and 4,500 rev/min.

When maximum acceleration is required upward gear selections should be made when the needle reaches the shaded sector (5,500–6,000 rev/min). Prolonged or excessive use of the highest engine speeds will tend to shorten the life of the engine. Allowing the engine to pull hard at low engine speeds must be avoided as this also has a detrimental effect on the engine.

The beginning of the red sector (6,000 rev/min) indicates the maximum safe speed for the engine.

Never allow the needle to enter the red sector.

Fig. 14

Fig. 15

Gear change speeds

Under normal driving conditions, it is recommended that to maintain the most favourable exhaust emissions and fuel economy, the gears are selected at the following speeds:

1st to 2nd	15 m.p.h. (24 km/h)
2nd to 3rd	25 m.p.h. (40 km/h)
3rd to 4th	40 m.p.h. (64 km/h)

Overdrive *Fig. 15*

A slide switch (5) incorporated in the gear lever knob operates the overdrive and provides a higher driving ratio for use with fourth gear.

To engage the overdrive move the slide switch rearward; to disengage, move the slide switch forward. Accelerator pedal pressure should be maintained and it is not necessary to depress the clutch pedal during engagement or disengagement.

Overdrive can be engaged at any throttle opening when in fourth gear. In certain driving conditions, if increased acceleration is required the overdrive can be 'switched out' without alteration to the throttle setting or manually moving the gear lever.

DO NOT switch out the overdrive when travelling at speeds exceeding the maximum obtainable in direct drive in fourth gear.

For maximum fuel economy use overdrive when cruising in fourth gear above 40 m.p.h. (64 km.p.h.).

If for any reason the overdrive does not disengage, do not reverse the car otherwise extensive damage may result.

Wet brakes

If the car has been washed, driven through water, or over wet roads for prolonged periods full braking power may not be available. Dry the brakes by applying the foot brake lightly several times while the car is in motion. Keep the hand brake applied while using high-pressure washing equipment.

On-tow for recovery

Should it become necessary to tow the car, use the towing eyes provided.

For recovery the car should be towed with the key in the ignition/steering lock at position 'I'. For tow starting the key should be at position 'II'.

Vehicle loading

Due consideration must be given to the overall weight carried when fully loading the car. Any loads carried on a luggage rack or downward load from a towing hitch must also be included in the maximum loading, see **'GENERAL DATA'**.

Towing

The towing weight of 1,680 lb (762 kg) is the maximum that is permissible. When using bottom gear a gradient of up to 1 in 8 can be ascended from rest while towing a weight not exceeding this figure. It may be necessary to adjust the maximum towing weight to comply with local conditions and regulations. The recommended downward load of a trailer or caravan on the towing hitch is 75 to 100 lb (34 to 45 kg), but this may be reduced or exceeded at the discretion of the driver.

Tyres

The tyre loads and pressures must comply with regulations where such exist.

LOCKS, FITTINGS AND BODY

Keys Three keys and a duplicate set are provided, the large key for the steering lock/ignition switch, the larger all metal key for the glovebox, and the small all metal key for the doors and luggage compartment.

To reduce the possibility of theft, locks are not marked with a number. **NOTE THE KEY NUMBERS IMMEDIATELY** on taking delivery of the car. See page 4.

Window regulators *Fig. 16* To open a door window, turn the handle regulator (1) to obtain the opening required.

Door locks *Fig. 16* Both front doors may be locked from outside the car with the small key provided, and locked from inside the car with the door locking latch.

To unlock the front doors from the outside, insert the key into the lock and turn it towards the front of the car, return it to the upright position and withdraw it. Grasp the handle and depress the button (2) to open the door.

To lock the front doors from the outside, turn the key towards the rear of the car, return it to the upright position and withdraw it.

To lock the doors from inside the car, close the door and move the locking latch (3) towards the rear of the car. To open the doors, move the locking latch towards the front of the car and pull the release lever (4) rearwards. The doors can be opened from the outside when the locking latch is in the forward position. The locking latch cannot be set to the lock position while the door is open.

Fig. 16

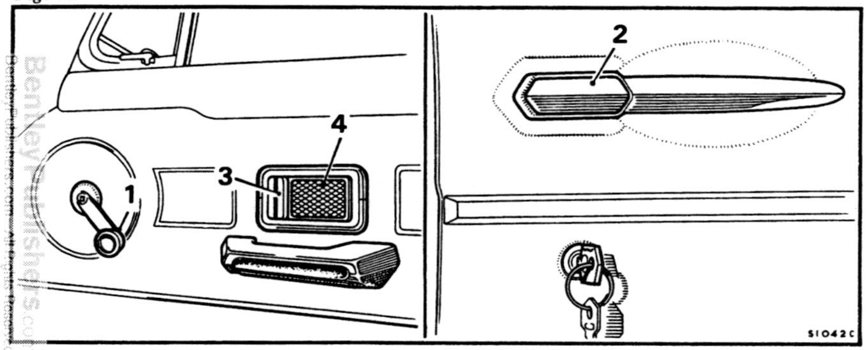

Front ventilator windows *Fig. 17* **To open,** move the catch lever (1) upwards and push the window outwards.

To close, pull the catch inwards, and then push it forward until the catch is in the locked position.

Glovebox *Fig. 18* **To unlock,** insert the key, turn it clockwise, and depress the lock plunger to open the glovebox.

To lock, close the glovebox, turn the key anti-clockwise and withdraw the key from the lock.

Luggage compartment *Fig. 19* **To open,** insert the key and turn it anti-clockwise, depress the lock plunger and raise the lid. When fully raised the support stay will automatically spring into engagement and the lid will be held in the open position. Raising the luggage compartment lid automatically switches on the light.

To close, raise the lid slightly, push the catch (1) on the bonnet stay forward to release the locking mechanism, and lower the lid. To lock insert the key and turn clockwise (arrowed) and withdraw the key.

Fig. 17

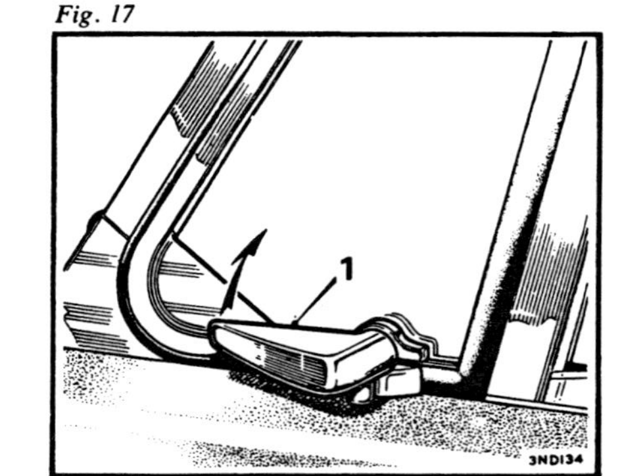

Fig. 18

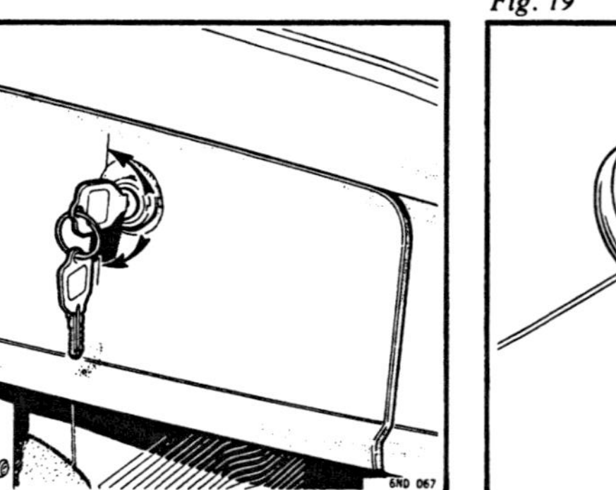

Fig. 19

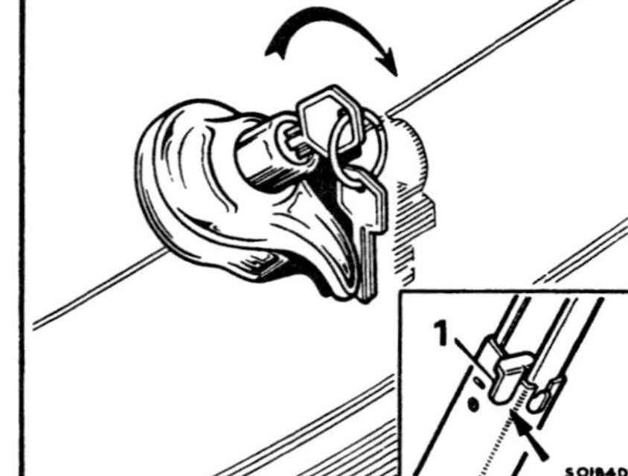

Locks, Fittings and Body

WARNING: Exhaust fumes will be drawn into the car if it is driven with the luggage compartment lid open, causing a health hazard to passengers and driver.

If it is imperative that the car be driven with the luggage compartment lid open, adverse effects can be minimised by adopting the following procedure:

1. Close all windows.
2. Open the face vents fully.
3. Set the heater controls to circulate the maximum amount of cold or hot air
4. Switch on the blower motor to maximum speed.
5. Do not travel at high speed.

Bonnet *Fig. 20* To raise the bonnet, pull the knob (1) located inside the car on the left hand side below the fascia panel.

Press up the safety catch (2) under the front of the bonnet. Raise the bonnet and when fully raised the support stay will automatically spring into engagement and the bonnet will be held in the open position.

To close, raise the bonnet slightly, push the catch (3) on the bonnet stay rearwards to release the locking mechanism, and lower the bonnet. Apply light pressure with the palms of the hands at the front corners of the bonnet and press down quickly; undue force is not necessary and may cause damage. The safety catch and lock will be heard to engage.

Fig. 20

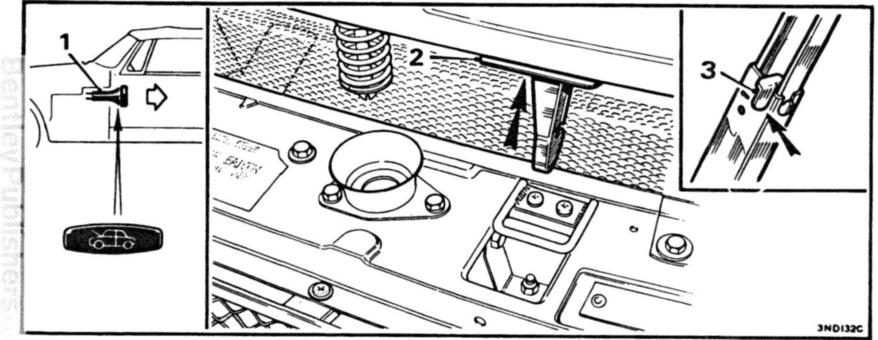

Mirrors **External** (Fig. 21). The mirror head may be adjusted from the seat position when the window is open.

Interior (Fig. 22). The mirror stem with anti-dazzle head is designed to break away from the mounting bracket on impact. The stem may be refitted in the mounting bracket as follows. Align the stem ball (1) with the bracket cup (2) ensuring that the small protrusion (3) on the stem aligns with the indent of the mounting bracket. Give them a smart tap with a soft instrument to join the two components.

Anti-dazzle. To reduce mirror dazzle, press the lever (4) towards the windscreen.

Arm-rest and ashtray *Fig. 23* To gain access to the compartment below the arm-rest, raise the forward end of the arm-rest. To empty the ashtray, raise the lid (1) and remove the ashtray by lifting under the stubber (2).

Do not attempt to remove the ashtray by pulling on the lid.

Fig. 21

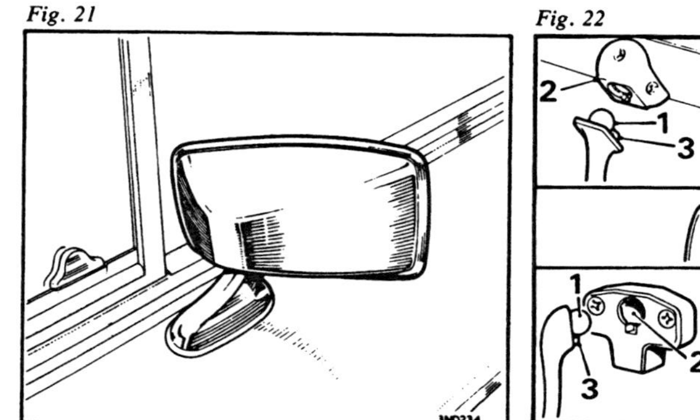

Fig. 22

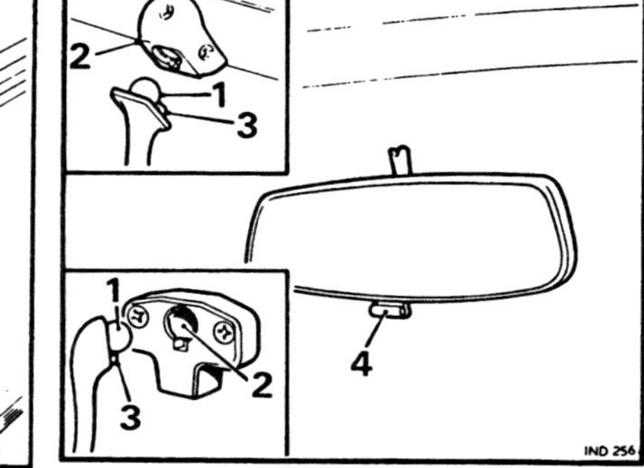

Fig. 23

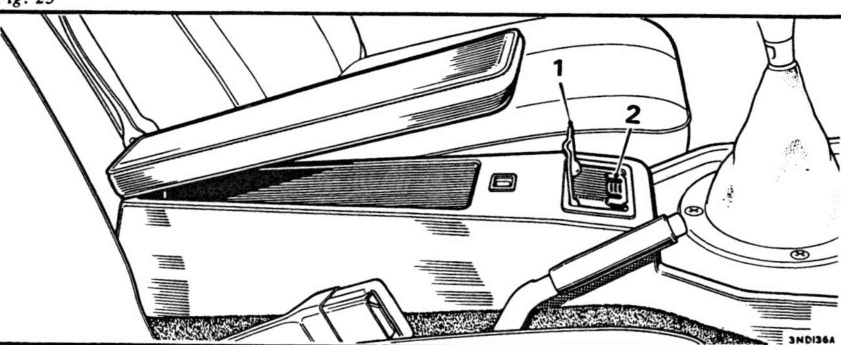

Locks, Fittings and Body

Bumpers Spilling fuel on the bumper may cause temporary local swelling of the rubber. Remove stains by lightly wiping the whole of the bumper with petrol (gasoline) or warm water and liquid detergent.

Body and door drainage points *Fig. 24* Periodic examination of the drain holes should be made to ensure that they are clear of obstruction; use a piece of stiff wire to probe the apertures.

Careless application of underseal can result in restricted drainage. Masking tape or plugs used when underseal is being applied must be removed immediately the operation is completed.

Jacking up beneath the underfloor may deform the drain apertures; always use the jacking points provided.

Lubrication To ensure trouble-free operation it is essential that the locks, hinges and catches are adequately lubricated.

Locks. Inject a small quantity of thin oil, through the key slots and around the push-buttons. **Do not oil the steering lock.**

Hinges. Apply grease or oil to the joints of the hinges.

Bonnet catches. Apply grease to the moving surfaces of the bonnet release mechanism and oil to the release lever and safety-catch pivot points.

Fig. 24

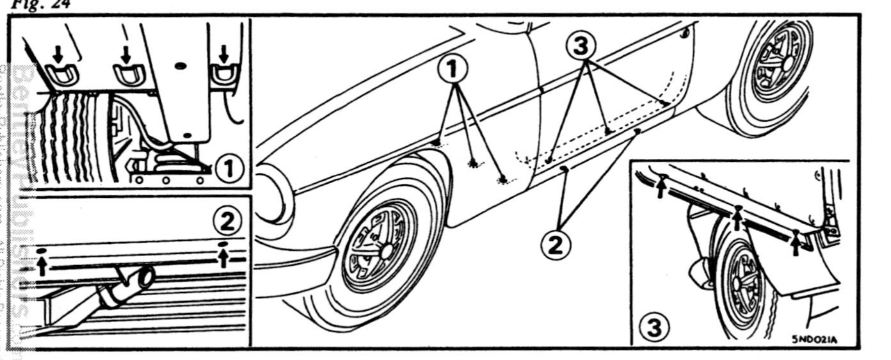

It is most important that the instructions for raising, lowering and folding the hood are followed. Do not fold when the hood is wet or damp.

Lowering the hood *Fig. 25* CAUTION: **Always ensure that the rear window is zipped in position before attempting to lower the hood.**

Unclip the sun visors (1) and move them to one side.

Release both windscreen frame toggle catches (2).

Release the two fasteners (3) on the windscreen rails, the two fasteners (4) on the cant rails and the two fasteners (5) on the hood mounting brackets.

Fig. 26 Release the four fasteners from each rear quarter panel (6) and pull the hood slightly forward to disengage the hook (7) from the socket (8) on the body side panel.

Move the seat tilt catch forward and incline the seat backs towards the front of the car.

Fig. 27 Raise the hood header rail (11) until it is poised approximately midway over the door aperture.

Disengage the hood rear rail from the anchor plates (9) on the tonneau panel.

Fold each quarter-light (10) onto the back-light and continue the fold in the material forward to the header rail (11). **ENSURE THAT THE FOLD IS MADE IN THE HOOD MATERIAL BETWEEN THE QUARTER-LIGHT AND THE BACK-LIGHT. FAILURE TO DO THIS MAY CAUSE PERMANENT DAMAGE TO THE BACK-LIGHT MATERIAL.**

Push the header rail (11) rearwards, and at the same time draw the back-light and hood material (12) out over the luggage compartment lid ensuring that the hood material does not become trapped between the hood sticks.

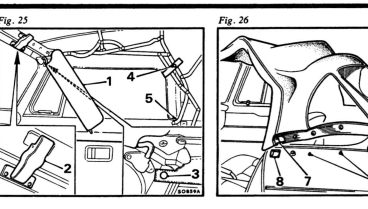

Fig. 25 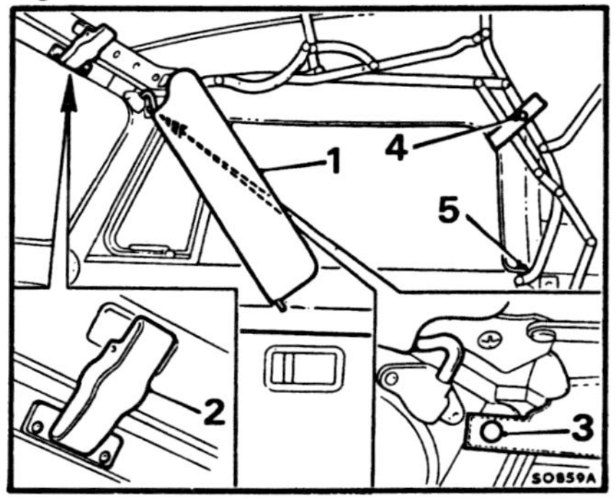 *Fig. 26*

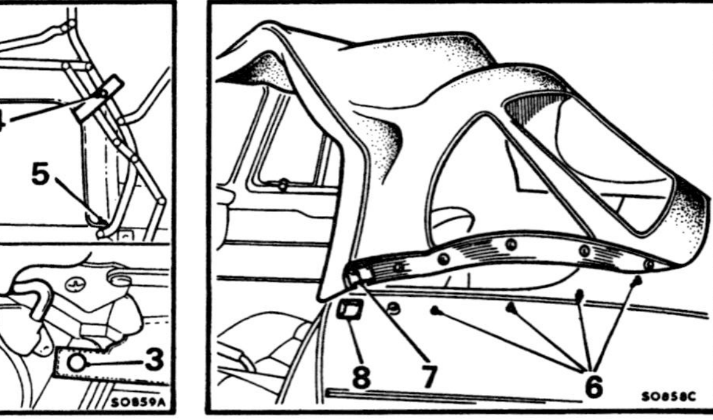

Fig. 28 Fully lower the hood. Fold the two windscreen frame toggle catches (13) rearwards to prevent them damaging the back-light.

Roll the rear window and hood material forward over the folded hood. Position and secure the two retaining straps (14).

Replace the sun visors and return the seat back-rests to their original positions.

Fit the hood cover or tonneau cover.

Raising the hood
Figs. 25, 26, 27, and 28

Remove the hood cover or tonneau cover.

Move the seat catch forward and incline the seat back towards the front of the car.

Unclip the sun visors (1) and move to one side.

Release the two retaining straps (14) and unfold the rear window and hood material rearwards over the luggage compartment.

Raise the header rail (11) and unfold the hood. Engage the rear rail in the anchor plates (9). Pull the hood slightly forwards and engage each hook (7) in its socket (8) on the body side panel. Position the header rail on the windscreen ensuring the rail seal is forward of the seal flange. Secure the windscreen frame toggle catches and fasteners (3), (4), and (5) inside the car.

Secure the fasteners (6) at each rear quarter.

Reposition the seats and sun visors.

Rear window

The rear window may be folded down when extra ventilation is required with the hood in the raised position.

Undo the zip, moving it around the rear window to the left-hand side of the hood.

Fold the window panel down, avoiding creasing or buckling the transparent window material.

CAUTION: It is important that the rear window is zipped in position before lowering the hood. Failure to do this may cause permanent damage to the rear window material.

Fitting the hood cover
Figs. 29 and 30

Assemble the hood cover rail (15) and fit it into the hood support sockets with the cross-rod towards the rear.

Lay the hood cover over the support rail.

Engage the hood cover rear rails in the anchor plates (16) on the tonneau panel.

Pull the cover slightly forwards and engage each side hook in its socket (17) on the body panel.

Secure the fasteners (18) at each quarter side panel.

Secure the fasteners (19) on the heel board.

Removing the hood cover

Reverse the fitting procedure.

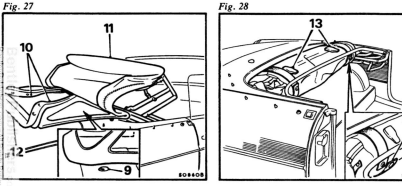

Fig. 27

Fig. 28

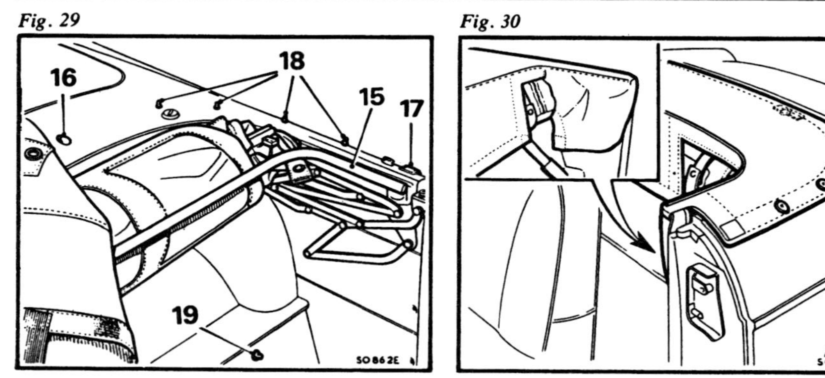

Fig. 29

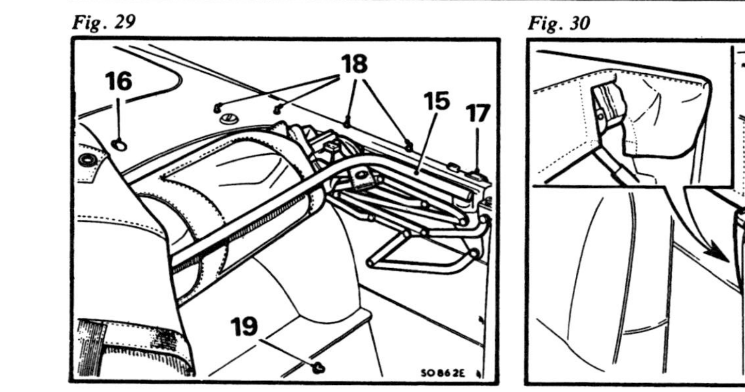

Fig. 30

Locks, Fittings and Body

Tonneau cover
Figs. 29 and 31

Fitting. Assemble the hood cover rail (15) and fit it into the hood support sockets with the cross-rod towards the rear.

Lay the tonneau cover over the cockpit.

Engage the tonneau cover rear rails in the anchor plates on the tonneau panel. Place the pockets in the tonneau cover over the head restraints on the seats; it may be necessary to adjust the seat back (see page 28) to align the pockets in the cover with the head restraints.

Secure the tonneau cover to each rear quarter with the four fasteners (18), and the fastener (20) on the cover at the side zips.

With the centre zip undone, extend the tonneau cover forward, fitting the forward pocket over the steering-wheel and securing to the fasteners (21) on each windscreen pillar, and the fastener (22) on the fascia panel top. Zip up the cover.

Fig. 31

Usage. The centre zip allows the cover to be folded down to give access to the driving seat or both seats. Undo the centre zip, release the press-studs on the fascia (21 and 22), and the press stud (20) at the side zips. Fold the cover down and inwards behind the seat. Move the seat tilt catch forward, and incline the seat back towards the front of the car. Secure the tonneau cover to the heel board, using the fastener on the flap. Return the seat back-rests to their original position.

The side zips allow the seat belt to be used.

Removing. Reverse the fitting procedure.

Stowage

Stowage bags are provided to protect the hood cover and hood cover rail. The stowage bags together with the tool bag are stowed in the luggage compartment and secured with the straps provided.

Fig. 31

Hard top

Fitting. Remove the hood. Fit the hard top side brackets into the hood support sockets and secure with the bolts and spring washers.

Position the hard top on the car, engaging the rear securing plates with the slotted anchor plates on the tonneau panel (inset, Fig. 32), ensuring that the sealing rubber does not foul the slots.

Line up the hard top drip moulding with the rear wing top beading. Push the hard top forwards and engage the toggle catch tongues in the sockets on the windscreen frame.

Fit the bolts into the side fixing brackets; screw in but do not tighten. Ensure that the front sealing rubber is correctly positioned forward of the windscreen frame. Adjust the toggle catches to give adequate tension (when fastened the securing bolt slots allow movement), tighten the securing bolts, fasten the catches and lock them with the securing clips (inset, Fig. 33).

Check that the sealing rubbers are correctly positioned, then slowly and evenly tighten the side fixing bolts until the hard top seals evenly to the body. **AVOID OVERTIGHTENING.** Measure the gap between the hard top and body side fixing brackets (arrowed, Fig. 32). Remove the bolts and fit washers between the brackets to the thickness of the gap. Refit and tighten the bolts.

Wind up both windows and check that a gap of approximately $\frac{1}{16}$ in. exists between the rear edge of the window and the hard top quarter channel. Adjust if necessary by loosening the side fixing bolts and repositioning the hard top. Ensure that there is an adequate seal between the window and hard top rubber and that the doors, when opened with the windows up, do not foul the opening surround.

Removing. Unlock and release the windscreen toggle fasteners. Remove the side fixing bolts. Raise the front of the hard top to disengage the toggle fastener tongues from the windscreen sockets, move the hard top to the rear to disengage the anchor plates, then lift it clear of the car. Remove the side fixing brackets from the hood support sockets. Assemble the fittings loosely to the hard top to prevent loss.

Fig. 32

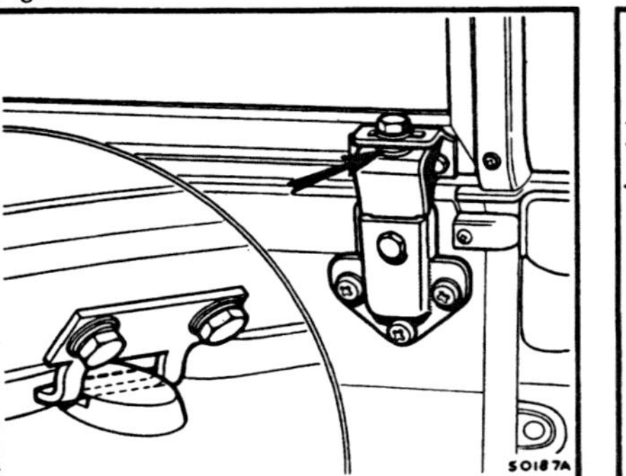

Fig. 33

SEATS

Seat adjustment *Fig. 34* — Front seats can be moved forwards or backwards if the lever (1) located beneath the front of each seat is pressed outwards; hold the lever in this position while the seat position is adjusted. The locking pin is spring-loaded and will automatically lock the seat in the required position when the lever is released.

Adjustable back-rest *Fig. 34* — The angle of the seat back-rest may also be adjusted by easing the body weight from the seat back-rest, and moving the lever (2) in the direction of the arrow. Release the lever and ensure the seat is locked in position by applying back pressure.

Access to rear seats *Fig. 34* — Move the seat catch (3) forward, and fold the back of the front seat forwards. The catch will automatically re-engage when the rear of the seat is moved back to the correct driving position.

Head restraint *Fig. 34* — The head restraint (4) may be raised or lowered as desired.

To remove, lift the head restraint to its stop and withdraw by rocking it from side to side whilst pulling upwards.

SEAT BELTS

Warning system — The seat belt warning system functions when the ignition/starter switch is operated.

The **'FASTEN BELTS'** warning lamp will be switched on for eight seconds each time the ignition/starter switch is operated. The warning buzzer will sound for eight seconds if the ignition/starter switch is operated before the driver's seat belt is fastened.

Wearing — **Always wear a belt as a complete lap and diagonal assembly** and never at any time wear it loosely, as this reduces its protection. Ensure that the belt is lying flat and is not twisted. Always stow a seat belt that is not in use.

Never attempt to use a seat belt for more than one person, even for small children.

Fig. 34

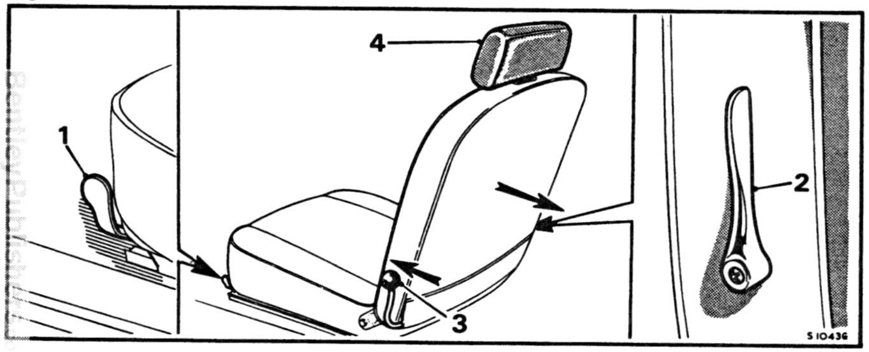

To fasten *Fig. 35* — Lift the engagement tongue (1) and draw the belt from the automatic reel over the shoulder and across the chest, and push it into the locking clip (3) of the short belt nearest the wearer.

To release and stow *Fig. 35* — Depress the release button (4) marked 'PRESS' on the locking device. After releasing the belt, allow the webbing to retract into the automatic reel. Depending on the type of belt fitted, hook the engagement tongue onto the parking device (2B) or fit it into the parking pocket (2A). To prevent the tongue sliding down the belt ensure that the slide (5) is close to the tongue when the belt is stowed.

Testing — **WARNING: This test must be carried out under safe road conditions, i.e. on a dry, straight, metalled road, during a period when the road is free from traffic.** With the belts in use, drive the car at 5 m.p.h. (8 km/h) and brake sharply. The automatic locking device should operate and lock the belt. It is essential that the driver and passenger are sitting in a normal relaxed position when making the test. The retarding effect of the braking must not be anticipated.

If a belt fails to lock, consult your authorized Austin MG Dealer.

Care of the belts — No unauthorized alterations or additions to the belts should be made. Do not bleach or re-dye the belt webbing. Inspect the webbing periodically for signs of abrasion, cuts, fraying, and general wear; pay particular attention to the fixing points and adjusters.

Do not attempt to bleach the belt webbing or re-dye it. If the belts become soiled, sponge with warm water using a non-detergent soap and allow to dry naturally.

Do not use caustic soap, chemical cleaners or detergents for cleaning: do not dry with artificial heat or by direct exposure to the sun.

Renew a seat belt assembly that has withstood the strain of a severe impact.

Fig. 35

HEATING AND VENTILATING (1975 and 1976)

Fresh air *Fig. 36* Fresh air is admitted to the car for cooling and ventilation through an adjustable vent mounted behind the centre console.

Air enters the car interior through the two doors located one each side of the gearbox tunnel in the foot wells.

The flow of air may be adjusted by moving the control knob (1) backwards to one of the three open positions; move the knob to the most forward position to close the vent.

Face-level vents *Fig. 36* Air flow for cooling and ventilation from the face-level vents mounted on the fascia panel may be adjusted by turning the serrated control wheels (2) to open the vents.

The direction of the air flow is adjusted by moving the shutter control knob (3) mounted in the centre of each vent.

Fresh-air heater The heating and ventilating system is designed to provide fresh air either heated by the engine cooling system or at outside temperature to the car at floor level and for demisting and defrosting to the windscreen. Full heat output is not available until the engine has reached normal operating temperature.

Air distribution for heating is independent of the fresh-air system; the control knob (1, Fig. 36) should be in the closed position when heated air is being distributed.

Fig. 36

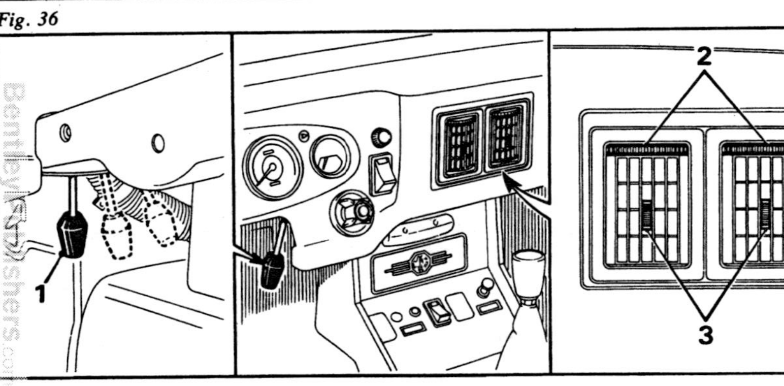

Heater controls *Fig. 37* **Air temperature.** Turn the knob (1) in the direction of the arrow to raise the air temperature.

Air flow. Turn the knob (2) in the direction of the arrow to direct the air distribution.

Booster. Press the lower end of the switch rocker (3) to boost the air flow.

Use the booster when the car is stationary, moving at a slow speed, or to augment the air supply in adverse weather conditions.

Usage The heater and air flow controls may be set at the position marked on the control knobs or to any other intermediate positions. By varying the control settings, and utilizing the booster blower, a wide range of settings can be obtained to suit prevailing conditions.

Illumination The markings on the booster switch and the control dials and the position indicators on the rotary control knobs are illuminated when the panel lamps are switched on.

Fig. 37

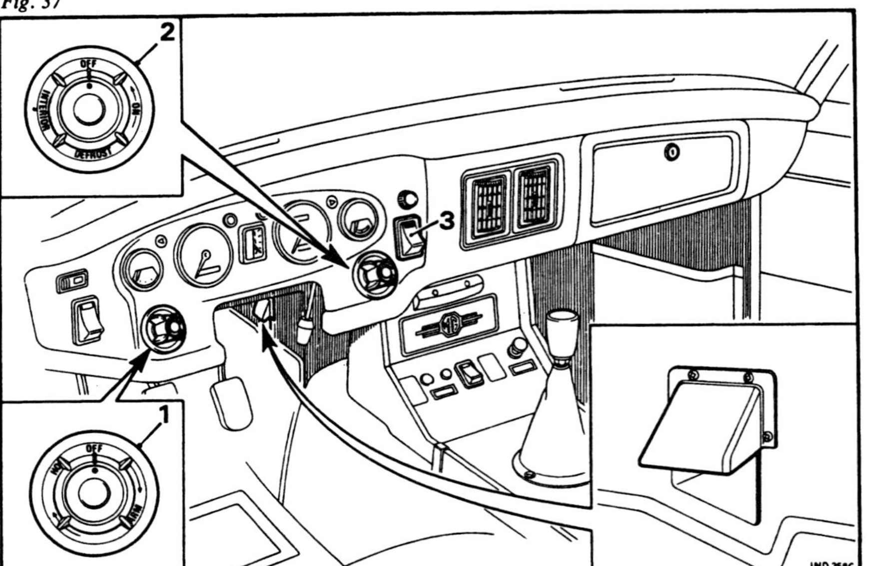

HEATING AND VENTILATING (1977 and later)

Fresh air
Fig. 38

Fresh air is admitted to the car for cooling and ventilation through an adjustable vent mounted behind the centre console.

Air enters the car interior through the two doors (1) located one each side of the gearbox tunnel in the foot wells.

The flow of air may be adjusted by moving the control knob (2) backwards to one of the three open positions; move the knob to the most forward position to close the vent.

Face-level vents
Fig. 38

Fresh unheated air for cooling and ventilation from the face-level vents on the fascia can be obtained by turning the serrated control wheels (3) of each vent away from the centre of the car to open the vents.

Move the shutter control knob (4) mounted in the centre of each vent horizontally and vertically to direct the air flow as required.

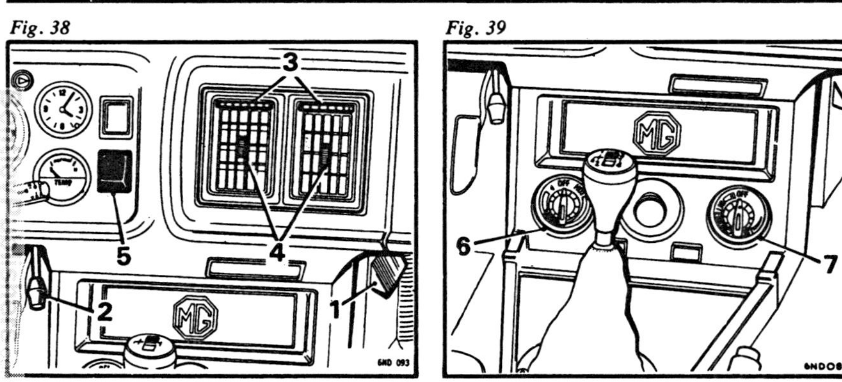

Fig. 38 *Fig. 39*

Fresh-air heater
Fig. 38

The heating and ventilating system is designed to provide fresh air either heated by the engine cooling system or at outside temperature to the car at floor level and for demisting and defrosting to the windscreen. Full heat output is not available until the engine has reached normal operating temperature.

Air distribution for heating is independent of the fresh-air system; the control knob (2) should be in the closed position (fully forward) when heated air is being distributed.

Heater controls
Figs. 38 and 39

Air temperature. Turn the knob (6) anti-clockwise to the arrow end of the blue sector for unheated air supply. Further anti-clockwise movement will progressively increase the temperature, with maximum heat output at the 'HOT' end of the red sector.

Air distribution. Turn the knob (7) anti-clockwise to 'INTERIOR'; air supply is distributed to the car interior at the foot wells, with reduced air flow to the windscreen. Further anti-clockwise movement of the knob to 'DEFROST', all air is directed to the windscreen.

Booster blower. The booster blower operates when the ignition is switched on. Press the lower end of the switch rocker (5) to the central position to operate the blower at slow speed. Press the switch rocker fully down to operate the blower at fast speed.

Usage

The heater and air flow controls may be set at the position marked on the control knobs or to any other intermediate positions. By varying the control settings, and utilising the booster blower, a wide range of settings can be obtained to suit prevailing conditions.

Illumination

The control dials and the position indicators on the rotary control knobs together with the green illumination light on the face of the blower switch are illuminated when the panel lights are switched on.

CLEANING

Interior

Carpets: Clean with a semi-stiff brush or a vacuum cleaner, preferably before washing the outside of the car. Occasionally give the carpets a thorough cleaning with a suitable upholstery cleaner. Carpets must not be 'dry-cleaned'.

Plastic faced upholstery: Clean with diluted upholstery cleaner. Spot clean with upholstery cleaner spread thinly over the surface with a brush or cloth, leave for five minutes, then wipe over with a damp sponge or cloth.

Nylon faced upholstery: Remove loose dirt with a brush or vacuum cleaner. The nylon pile has been chemically treated to resist soiling and care must be taken when cleaning. To remove a stain, apply a nylon cleaner, then pat and wipe with a clean cloth in the direction of the pile until the stain is removed. **DO NOT RUB.** When dry, gently brush against the pile, then with the pile.

Body

Regular care of the body finish is necessary if the new appearance of the car exterior is to be maintained against the effects of air pollution, rain, and mud.

Wash the bodywork frequently, using a soft sponge and plenty of water containing car shampoo. Large deposits of mud must be softened with water before using the sponge. Smears should be removed by a second wash in clean water, and with the sponge if necessary. When dry, clean the surface of the car with a damp chamois-leather. In addition to the regular maintenance, special attention is required if the car is driven in extreme conditions such as sea spray or on salted roads. In these conditions and with other forms of severe contamination an additional washing operation is necessary which should include underbody hosing. Any damaged areas should be immediately covered with paint and a complete repair effected as soon as possible. Before touching-in light scratches and abrasions with paint, thoroughly clean the surface. Use petrol/white spirit (gasoline/hydrocarbon solvent) to remove spots of grease or tar.

Bright trim

Never use an abrasive on stainless, chromium, aluminium, or plastic bright parts and on no account clean them with metal polish. Remove spots of grease or tar with petrol/white spirit (gasoline/hydrocarbon solvent) and wash frequently with water containing car shampoo. When the dirt has been removed polish with a clean dry cloth or chamois-leather until bright. Any slight tarnish found on stainless or plated components which have not received regular attention may be removed with chrome cleaner. An occasional application of light mineral oil or grease will help to preserve the finish, particularly during winter when salt may be used on the roads, but these protectives must not be applied to plastic finishes.

COOLING SYSTEM (1975 and 1976)

Radiator filler cap *Fig. 40* (1)

The system is pressurized to 10 lb./sq. in. when hot, and the pressure must be released gradually when the filler cap is removed. It is advisable to protect the hands against escaping steam and turn the cap slowly anti-clockwise until the resistance of the safety stops is felt. Leave the cap in this position until all pressure is released. Press the cap downwards against the spring to clear the safety stops, and continue turning until it can be lifted off.

Draining the cooling system

To drain the cooling system, slacken the hose clip and remove the bottom hose at its connection to the radiator. Remove the drain plug (2) on the engine cylinder block.

When draining in freezing weather, do so when the engine is hot. Run the engine slowly for one minute when the water has ceased flowing to clear any water from the pump and other places where it might collect. Finally, leave a reminder on the vehicle to the effect that the cooling system has been drained.

Collect the coolant in a clean container if it is to be used again, as cars are filled with a 50% solution of anti-freeze before they leave the factory.

Filling the cooling system

To avoid wastage by overflow add just sufficient coolant to cover the bottom of the header tank. Run the engine until it is hot and add sufficient coolant to bring the surface to the level of the indicator positioned inside the header tank below the filler neck.

NOTE.—The heater control must be set to 'HOT' when draining or filling the cooling system.

Fig. 40

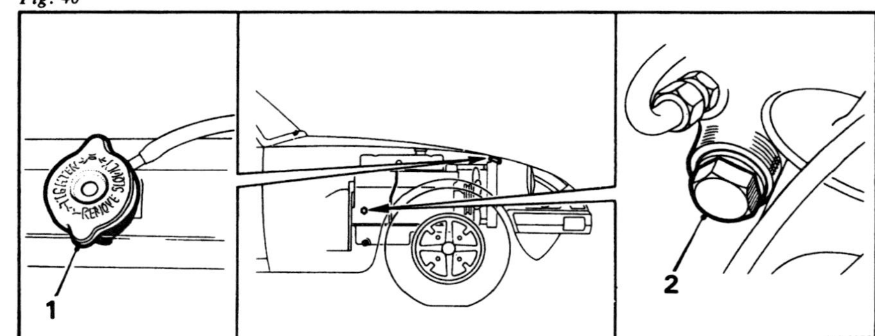

Cooling System (1975 – 1976)

Frost precautions Water expands when it freezes, and if precautions are not taken there is considerable risk of bursting the radiator, cylinder block, or heater. Such damage may be avoided by adding anti-freeze to the water.

Do not use radiator anti-freeze solution in the windscreen washer.

Anti-freeze solutions Anti-freeze can remain in the cooling system for two years provided that the specific gravity of the coolant is checked periodically and anti-freeze added as necessary. The specific gravity check should be carried out by an authorized Austin MG Dealer.

Top up only when the cooling system is at its normal running temperature in order to avoid losing anti-freeze due to expansion.

After the second winter the system should be drained and flushed. Refer to the instructions given for draining the cooling system, then clean out the system thoroughly by flushing water through the radiator passages using a hose inserted in the radiator filler orifice.

Before adding the recommended anti-freeze make sure that the cooling system is watertight; examine all joints and replace any defective hose with new.

We recommend owners to use **anti-freeze** with an ethlyene glycol base which conforms to specification S.A.E. J1034, or B.S.3151/2 to protect the cooling system during frosty weather and reduce corrosion to the minimum.

The correct quantities of anti-freeze for different degrees of frost protection are:

Anti-freeze	*Commences to freeze*		*Frozen solid*		*Amount of anti-freeze*
%	°C.	°F.	°C.	°F.	*U.S. Pts.*
25	−13	9	−26	−15	3
33⅓	−19	− 2	−36	−33	4
50	−36	−33	−48	−53	6

COOLING SYSTEM (1977 and later)

Fig. 41 **The pressurized cooling system incorporates an expansion tank, making the need for regular topping-up unnecessary. The expansion tank, connected to the top of the radiator, receives the normal overflow of coolant when the system is in the process of heating up. When the temperature of the system drops, the pressure in the radiator is reduced and the overflow then returns to the radiator.**

WARNING: The cooling fans can operate when the engine is switched off. To prevent possible injury, remove the fuse from the fans (see page 28) before commencing any work within the engine compartment.

Cooling fans For information on the electrically driven cooling fans, see page 27.

Checking **The coolant level should only be checked when the system is COLD. Remove the expansion tank cap to check the coolant level which must be maintained to the half-full point of the tank.**

If coolant is not displaced or the level in the expansion tank has fallen appreciably since the last periodical check, a leak in the cooling system or overheating must be suspected.

Topping-up *Fig. 41* **WARNING: As injury could be caused while the system is hot by escaping steam or coolant the filler plug (1) must not be removed before the pressure relief cap (2).**

Fig. 41

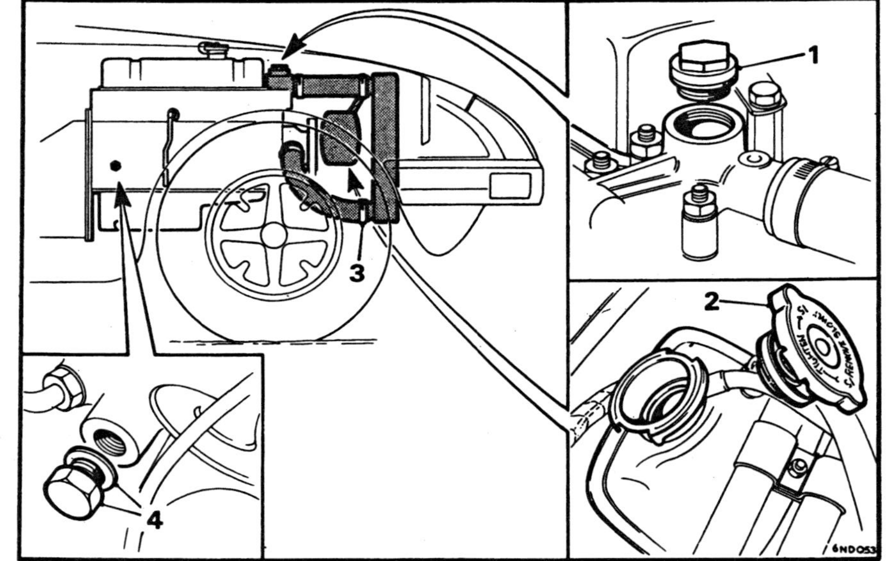

If the system is hot, protect the hands against escaping steam, turn the expansion tank pressure relief cap (2) slowly until the stop is felt and allow the pressure in the system to escape gradually, then remove the cap. Add coolant to the expansion tank to the half-full point, and refit the cap. Remove the filler plug (1) and add coolant to bring the level to the top of the filler neck; refit the plug.

Draining *Fig. 42* To drain the cooling system, stand the car on level ground, remove the expansion tank cap (2), and the filler plug (1) from the coolant outlet elbow. Slacken the hose clip and disconnect the bottom hose (3) at its connection to the radiator. Remove the drain plug (4) on the cylinder block.

Collect the coolant in a clean container if it is to be used again as cars are filled with a 50 per cent solution of anti-freeze before they leave the factory.

Leave a reminder on the vehicle to the effect that the cooling system has been drained.

Owing to the location of the car heater and the expansion tank they cannot be drained with the cooling system. Anti-freeze must be used in the cooling system when freezing conditions are likely to be encountered.

Filling *Fig. 42* Refit the bottom hose and the engine drain plug. Check that **all** hose connections are **tight**. Turn the heater temperature control knob to 'HOT' to open the heater valve.

Top up the coolant in the expansion tank so that the tank is half-full. Refit the cap (2).

Fill the system through the filler plug hole and bring the level up to the bottom of the threads. Refit the filler plug (1).

Start up and run the engine until the top radiator hose is warm and switch off the engine. Allow the system to cool.

Fig. 42

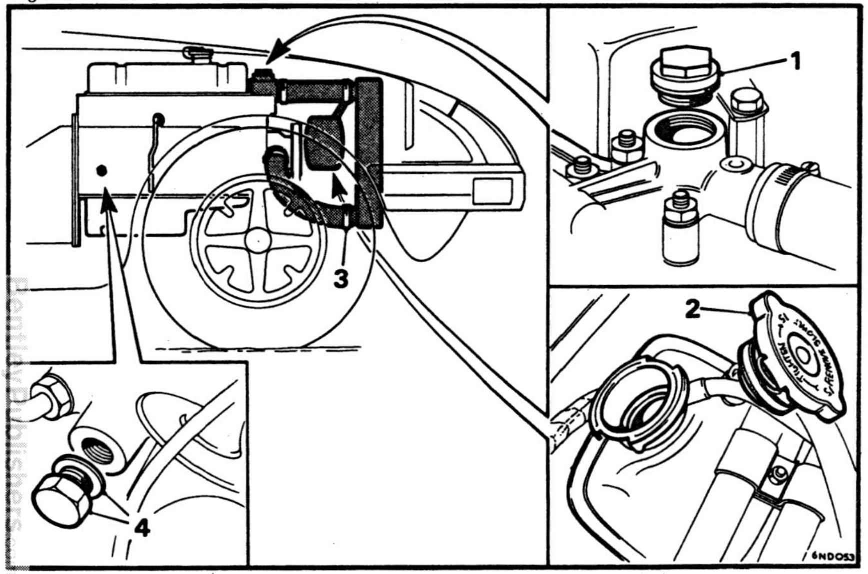

Turn the expansion tank cap to its safety stop to release the pressure. Top up the expansion tank to half-full, and refit the cap.

Remove the radiator filler plug and top up once more to the bottom of the threads. Refit the filler plug.

CAUTION: The system operates at a pressure of 15 lb/in² (1 kg/cm²) and the figure **15** is marked on the expansion tank cap (2).

Frost precautions Water expands when it freezes, and if precautions are not taken there is considerable risk of bursting the radiator, cylinder block, or heater. The heater unit cannot be drained with the cooling system; it is therefore essential to use anti-freeze in the cooling system in freezing conditions.

We recommended owners to use **anti-freeze** with an ethylene glycol base which conforms to specification S.A.E. J1034, or B.S. 3151/2 to protect the cooling system during frosty weather and reduce corrosion to the minimum.

After filling with anti-freeze solution, attach a warning label to a prominent position on the car stating the type of anti-freeze contained in the cooling system to ensure that the correct type is used for topping-up.

Anti-freeze can remain in the cooling system for two years provided that the specific gravity of the coolant is checked periodically and anti-freeze added as necessary. The specific gravity check should be carried out by an authorized Distributor or Dealer. After the second year the system should be drained and flushed by inserting a hose in the filling orifice and allowing water to flow through until clean. Make sure that the cooling system is water-tight, examine all joints and replace any defective hose with a new one. Refill with the appropriate anti-freeze solution, and add 0·25 pint (0·2 litre) of neat anti-freeze to the expansion tank.

The recommended quantities of anti-freeze solution are given below.

Do not use radiator anti-freeze solution in the windscreen-washing equipment. Use the correct washer solvent, which will not damage the paintwork.

Anti-freeze	*Commences to freeze*		*Frozen solid*		*Amount of anti-freeze*
%	*°C*	*°F*	*°C*	*°F*	*U.S. Pts*
25	−13	9	−26	−15	3½
33⅓	−19	− 2	−36	−33	4⅜
50	−36	−33	−48	−53	7

WHEELS AND TYRES

Jacking up *Fig. 43* The jack is designed to lift one side of the car at a time. Apply the hand brake and block the wheels on the opposite side to that being jacked; use a wood block jammed tight against the tyre tread.

Remove the jack socket plug. Insert the lifting arm (1) of the jack into the socket located in the door sill panel. **Make certain that the jack lifting arm is pushed fully into the socket and that the base of the jack is on firm ground.** The jack should lean slightly outwards at the top to allow for the radial movement of the car as it is raised.

WARNING: Do not work beneath the vehicle with the lifting jack as the sole means of support. Place suitable supports under the front side-members or rear axle to give adequate support and safety while working.

Jack maintenance If the jack is neglected it may be difficult to use in a roadside emergency. Examine it occasionally, clean off accumulated dust, and lightly oil the thread to prevent the formation of rust.

ROAD WHEELS

Wheel nuts Owners are recommended to check the wheel nuts for tightness each week in addition to checking the other items listed. Take care not to overtighten. Torque wrench setting 60 to 65 lbf ft (8·3 to 9 kgf m).

Pressed type *Removing and refitting* *Fig. 43* Slacken the four nuts securing the road wheel to the hub; turn anti-clockwise to loosen and clockwise to tighten. Raise the car with the jack to lift the wheel clear of the ground and remove the nuts. Withdraw the road wheel from the hub.

When refitting the road wheel locate the wheel on the hub, lightly tighten the nuts (2) with the wheel nut spanner (securing nuts must be fitted with the **taper side towards the wheel**), and lower the jack. Fully tighten the wheel nuts, tightening them diagonally and progressively, at the same time avoid over-tightening.

The wheel centre trim (3) must be removed and fitted to the wheel in use.

Replace the wheel disc and the jack socket plug.

Fig. 43

Wire type (if fitted) *Removing and refitting* *Fig. 44* Use the spanner and hammer to slacken and tighten the octagonal hub nuts.

Always jack up a wheel before using the tools, and always tighten the hub nuts fully.

Hub nuts are marked 'LEFT' or 'RIGHT' to show which side of the car they must be fitted, and also with the word 'UNDO' and an arrow.

Before replacing a wheel wipe all serrations, threads, and cones of the wheel and hub and then lightly coat them with grease. If a forced change is made on the road, remove, clean, and grease as soon as convenient.

Maintenance When the car is new, after the first long run or after 50 miles of short runs, jack up the wheels and use the hammer and spanner to make sure that the nuts are tight.

Spare wheel *Fig. 45* The spare wheel is stowed in the well of the luggage compartment.

Unscrew the clamp plate (3) to release the spare wheel.

When refitting, position the wheel face down in the well of the luggage compartment and retain in position with the clamp plate.

The spare wheel tyre on new cars is inflated above the recommended running pressure. The pressure must be checked and adjusted before use.

TYRES

Markings Tyres are marked with the maximum load and inflation pressure figures. When fitting replacement tyres ensure that they are to the same specification and marking. **The permissible load and tyre pressures are shown on pages 43 and 44 of this handbook.**

Fig. 44

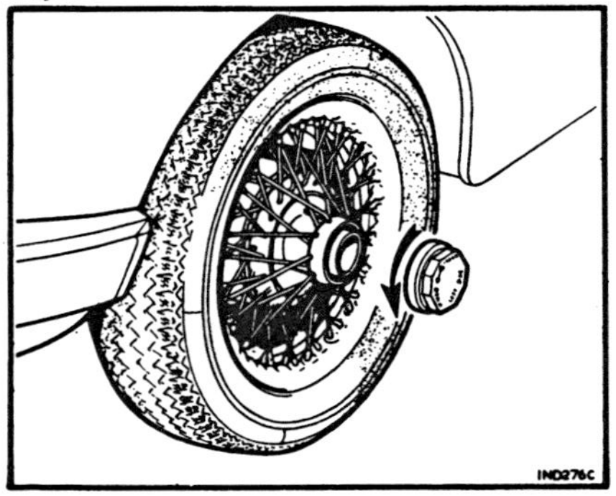

Fig. 45

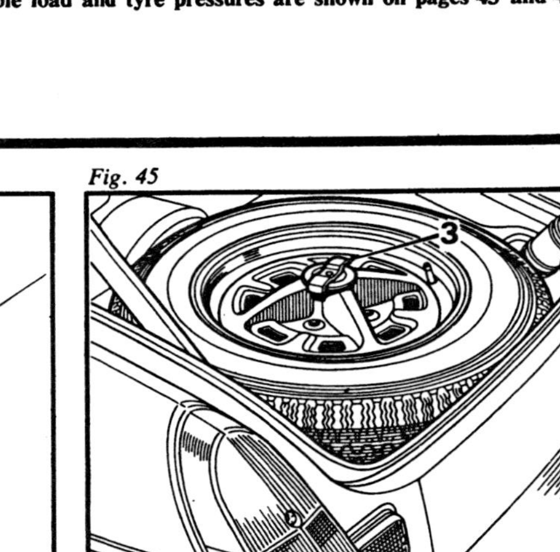

Wheels and Tyres

Tyre pressures Owners are reminded that tyre wear and inflation pressures may be subject to legal requirements; check the tyre pressures weekly, including the spare, and adjust if necessary to the recommendations given in **'GENERAL DATA'**. The spare tyre should be maintained at the highest recommended pressure and adjusted before use.

Pressures should be checked with a **Tyre Pressure Gauge** when the tyres are cold, and should not be reduced in warm tyres where the increase above normal pressure is due to temperature. Tyres are permeable and a natural pressure loss will occur with time. The pressure loss in a week should be no more than 2 lbf in² (0·14 kgf cm²); any unusual pressure loss should be investigated. **If necessary increase the pressure.**

Driving with under-inflated tyres can be hazardous and causes rapid tyre wear and possible permanent damage to the cords of the tyre casing.

Valves and caps See that the valve caps are screwed down firmly by hand. Do not use tools as too much force will damage the rubber seating. The cap prevents the entry of dirt into the valve mechanism and forms an additional seal on the valve.

Tyre care The tyres should also be inspected at frequent intervals for damage and wear. Excessive local distortion as a result of striking a kerb, a loose brick, a deep pothole, etc., may cause the casing cords to fracture. Every effort should be made to avoid such obstacles.

Any oil or grease which may get onto the tyres should be cleaned off by using petrol (fuel) sparingly. Do not use paraffin (kerosene), which has a detrimental effect on rubber.

Flints and other sharp objects should be removed with a penknife or similar tool. If neglected, they may work through the tyre.

Tubeless tyres Normally a tubeless tyre will not leak as a result of penetration by a nail or other puncturing object, provided that it is left in the tyre. At a convenient time have the tyre removed for vulcanizing. If a small diameter puncture has been made a temporary repair can be carried out with the tyre manufacturer's plugging kit.

NOTE: The insertion of a plug to repair a puncture in a tubeless tyre must be regarded as a temporary measure and a **permanent vulcanized repair must be made as soon as possible.** In no circumstances should a plug repair be made to the side wall of a tyre.

The instructions given for the temporary repair of tubeless tyres must be disregarded when tubes are fitted. If in any doubt, consult your authorized Austin MG Dealer.

When repairing tubes, have punctures or injuries vulcanized. Ordinary patches should only be used for emergencies. Vulcanizing is absolutely essential for tubes manufactured from synthetic rubber.

Wheel and tyre balance Unbalanced wheel and tyre assemblies may be responsible for abnormal wear of the tyres and vibration in the steering. Consult your authorized Austin MG Dealer.

Wheel assemblies should always be refitted on the same axle and in the position in which they were balanced.

BRAKES AND MASTER CYLINDERS

Front brake pads *Fig. 46* Wear on the disc brake friction pads (arrowed) is automatically compensated for during braking operations and manual adjustment is therefore not required.

If the wear on one pad is greater than on the other their operating positions should be changed over by your authorized Austin MG Dealer.

Remove the road wheel to gain clear access to the pads for inspection.

The pads must be renewed when the lining material has worn to the minimum permissible thickness of $\frac{1}{16}$ in (1·6 mm) or will have done so before the next regular inspection is due. Special equipment is required to renew the brake pads; this work should be entrusted to your authorized Austin MG Dealer.

After fitting new pads, within the limits of safety, heavy braking should be avoided for a few days to allow the pads to bed-in.

Rear brakes *Fig. 47* Excessive brake pedal travel is an indication that the rear brake-shoes require adjusting. The brake-shoes on both rear wheels must be adjusted to regain even and efficient braking.

Adjusting. Chock the front wheels, fully release the hand brake and jack up each rear wheel in turn, placing suitable supports beneath the vehicle—see "**WARNING**" on page 23. Turn the adjuster (1) in a clockwise direction (viewed from the centre of the car), using a **Brake Adjusting Spanner** until the brake-shoes lock the wheel, then turn the adjuster back until the wheel is free to rotate without the shoes rubbing. Repeat the adjustment on the other rear brake.

Hand brake *Fig. 47* The hand brake is automatically adjusted with the rear brakes. If there is excessive movement of the hand brake lever, consult your authorized Austin MG Dealer. To lubricate, charge the nipple (2) on the hand brake cable with one of the recommended greases (lubrication is unnecessary on 1977 and later cars).

Fig. 46

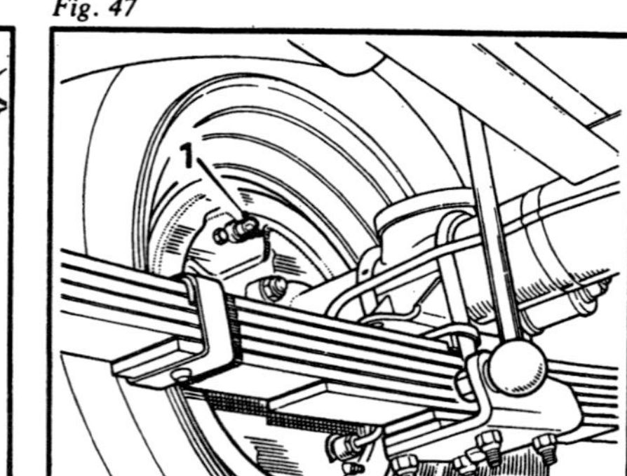

Fig. 47

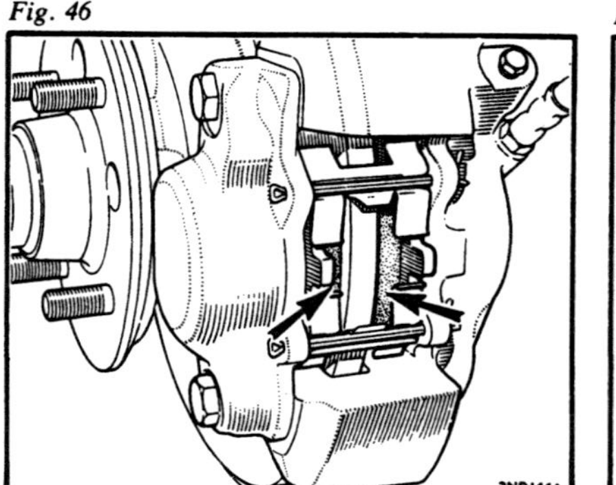

Brakes and Master Cylinders

Replacing brake-shoes or pads

When it becomes necessary to renew brake-shoes or pads it is essential that only genuine replacements, with the correct grade of lining, are used. Always fit new shoes or pads as complete axle sets, never individually or as a single wheel set. Serious consequences could result from out-of-balance braking due to mixing of linings.

Replacement brake-shoes or pads are obtainable from your authorized Austin MG Dealer.

Inspecting rear brake linings
Fig. 48

Chock the front wheels and release the hand brake. Jack up each rear wheel in turn, placing suitable supports beneath the vehicle—see **'WARNING'** on page 23.

Remove the road wheel and slacken the brake-shoe adjuster fully.

Remove the two countersunk screws (1) (pressed wheels) or four nuts (wire wheels) and withdraw the brake-drum (2).

Inspect the linings (3) for wear, and clean the dust from the backplate assembly and drum, preferably using methylated spirit (denatured alcohol). Brake lining dust is dangerous to health if inhaled and therefore should not be blown from the drums. Make certain that sufficient lining material remains to allow the car to run until the next regular inspection is due without the thickness falling below the safe limit.

Refit the brake drums and the road wheels and adjust the brake-shoes (see page 24).

Brake and clutch master cylinder
Figs. 49 and 50

To check the level of the fluid in the clutch master cylinder reservoir (1), remove the plastic filler cap. The fluid level must be maintained at the bottom of the filler neck.

The level of the fluid in the brake master cylinder reservoir is visible through the plastic reservoir (2); the level must be maintained up to the bottom of the filler neck.

Use only **Lockheed Disc Brake Fluid (Series 329S)** or **Castrol Girling Brake Fluid;** alternatively, use a brake fluid conforming to **F.M.V. S.S. D.O.T.3 specification with a minimum boiling-point of 260°C (500°F).**

Before refitting the filler caps, separate the dome (3) from the filler cap and check that the breather holes, indicated by arrows, are clear. Snap fit the dome onto the filler cap.

NOTE: Brake fluid can have a detrimental effect on paintwork. Ensure that fluid is not allowed to contact paint-finished surfaces.

Brake servo

Filter renewing. The filter is located in the servo housing where the push-rod passes through from the brake pedal. Renewing of the filter should be entrusted to your authorized Austin MG Dealer.

Brake pedal
Fig. 51

A free movement of $\frac{1}{8}$ in (A), measured at the pedal pad must be maintained on the pedal. To adjust the free movement, disconnect the stop light switch wiring (1), slacken the locknut (2), and turn the switch (3) clockwise to decrease or anti-clockwise to increase the clearance. Tighten the stop light switch locknut and connect the wiring.

Fig. 48

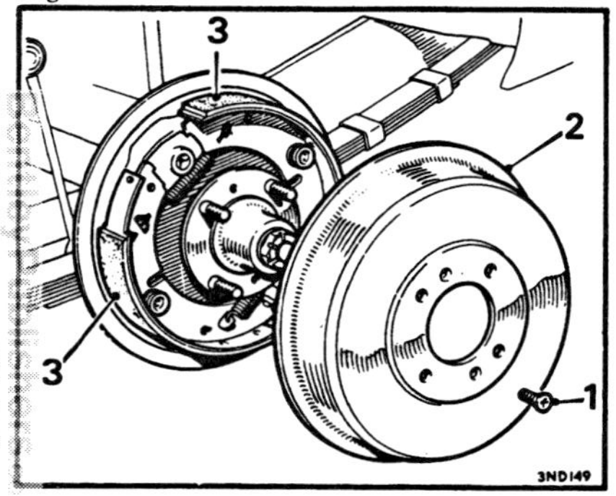

Fig. 49

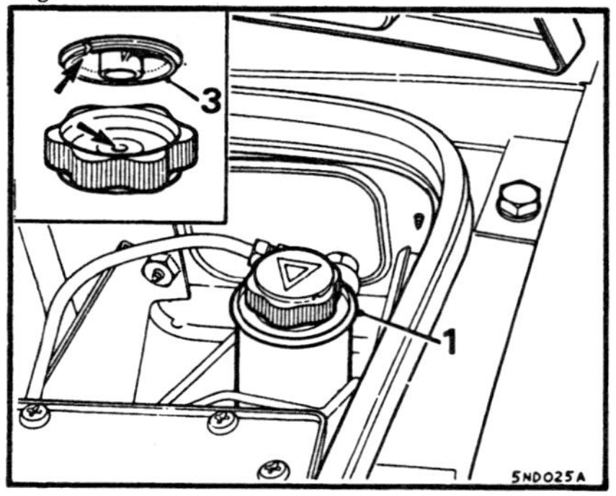

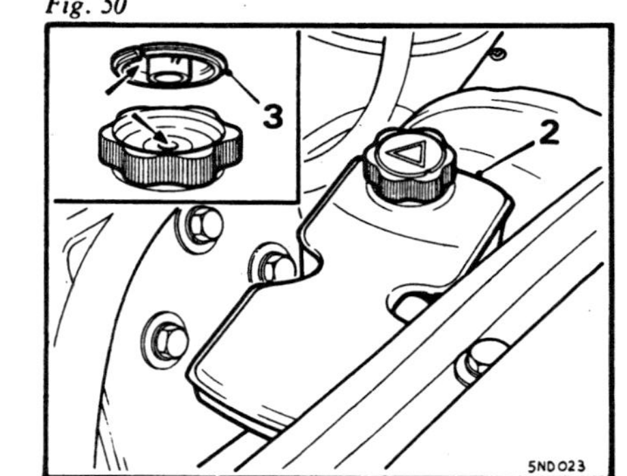

Fig. 50

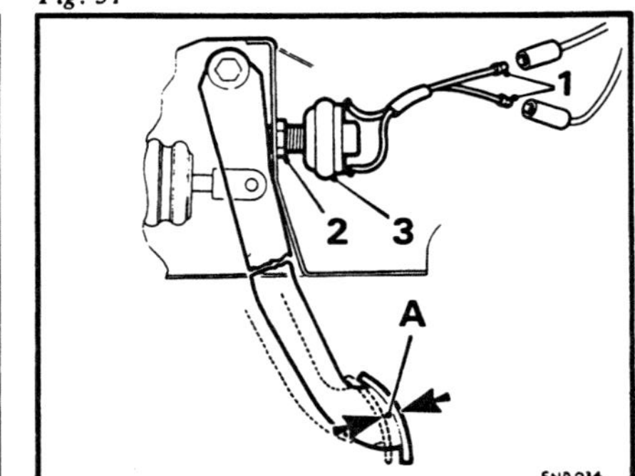

Fig. 51

Brakes and Master Cylinders

Visual check Examine the clutch and brake hoses, pipes, unions, and joints for tightness and general condition. It is most important to ensure that no chafing of connections or pipes develops at any time, and that leakages are rectified immediately.

Preventive maintenance In addition to the recommended periodical inspection of brake components it is advisable as the car ages, and as a precaution against the effects of wear and deterioration, to make a more searching inspection and renew parts as necessary.

It is recommended that:

(1) Disc brake pads, drum brake linings, hoses, and pipes should be examined at intervals no greater than those laid down in the Maintenance Summary.

(2) Brake fluid should be changed completely every 18 months or 19,000 miles whichever is the sooner.

(3) All fluid seals in the hydraulic system and all flexible hoses should be renewed every 3 years or 37,500 miles whichever is the sooner. At the same time the working surface of the piston and of the bores of the master cylinders, wheel cylinders, and other slave cylinders should be examined and new parts fitted where necessary. The brake servo filter should also be renewed.

Care must be taken always to observe the following points:

(*a*) At all times use the recommended brake fluid.

(*b*) Never leave fluid in unsealed containers. It absorbs moisture quickly and this can be dangerous, if used in the braking system in this condition.

(*c*) Fluid drained from the system or used for bleeding is best discarded.

(*d*) The necessity for absolute cleanliness throughout cannot be over-emphasized.

ELECTRICAL

POLARITY The electrical installation on this car is **NEGATIVE (−)** earth return and the correct polarity must be maintained at all times. Reversed polarity will permanently damage semi-conductor devices in the alternator and tachometer, and the radio transistors (when fitted). Never use an ohmmeter of the type incorporating a hand-driven generator for checking semi-conductor components.

Before fitting a radio or any other electrical equipment, make certain that it has the correct polarity for installation in this car.

BATTERY

Access *Fig. 52* Release the rear seat cushion securing straps from the fasteners, and pull the cushion forward.

Remove the carpet covering the rear compartment floor. Turn the three quick-release fasteners (1) anti-clockwise one half turn and remove the battery compartment cover panel (2).

Checking topping-up *Fig. 52* The car must be on level ground when the electrolyte is being checked.

DO NOT USE A NAKED LIGHT WHEN CHECKING THE LEVELS and do not use tap water for topping-up.

Remove the battery vent cover; use the grip at the centre of the cover (3), this will ensure that the filling valves are operated correctly. If no electrolyte is visible inside the battery, pour distilled or de-ionised water into the filling trough until the six tubes (4), and the connecting trough (5), are filled. Refit the vent cover.

The above operations should not be carried out within half an hour of the battery having been charged, other than by the car's own generating system, lest it floods. In extremely cold conditions run the engine immediately after topping-up so as to mix the electrolyte.

IMPORTANT: The vent cover must be kept closed at all times, except when topping-up. The electrolyte will flood if the cover is removed for long periods during or within thirty minutes of the battery being normal (6·5 amp) charged. Single-cell discharge testers cannot be used on these batteries. Operation of the filling device will be destroyed if the battery case is drilled or punctured.

Fig. 52

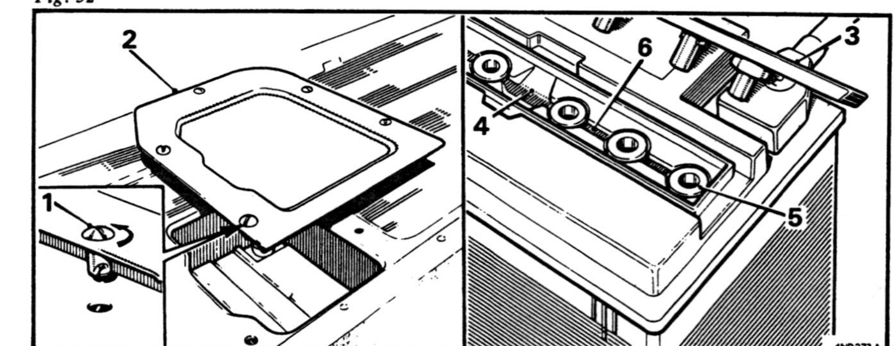

General maintenance The batteries must be kept dry and clean; cable and battery terminals should be smeared with petroleum jelly.

Do not leave the battery in a discharged state for any length of time. When not in regular use have the battery fully charged, and every four weeks give a short refresher trickle charge to prevent permanent damage to the battery plates.

BATTERY BOOSTING AND CHARGING

CAUTION: The following precautions must be observed to avoid the possibility of serious damage to the charging system or electrical components of the vehicle. The factory recommends that you do not use booster batteries at all and that batteries be charged only after removing them. Instead of boosting, replace the discharged battery with a charged battery in order to start the car.

Battery boosting *Fig. 53* A high speed battery charger must not be used as a starting aid.

When connecting an additional battery to boost a discharged battery in the vehicle, ensure that:

—the booster battery is of the same nominal voltage as the vehicle battery;

—the interconnecting cables are of sufficient capacity to carry starting current;

—the cables are interconnected one at a time and to the booster battery first;

—the cables are connected between the battery terminals in the following order: first, + (positive) to + (positive) and then — (negative) to — (negative);

—the engine speed is reduced to 1,000 rev/min or below before disconnecting the boost battery. The vehicle battery must never be disconnected while the engine is running.

Battery charging A high speed charger may only be used if the battery has been completely disconnected from the vehicle electrical system. Certain types of maintenance-free batteries, for example the lead–calcium type, can be damaged by high speed chargers. If in doubt, consult your authorized Austin MG Dealer.

When charging the battery in the vehicle from an outside source such as a trickle charger, ensure that:

—the charger voltage is the same as the nominal voltage of the battery;

—the charger positive (+) lead is connected to the positive (+) terminal of the battery;

—the charger negative (—) lead is connected to the negative (—) terminal of the battery.

ALTERNATOR The following precautions must be observed to prevent inadvertent damage to the alternator and its control equipment.

Polarity. Ensure that the correct battery polarity is maintained at all times; reversed battery or charger connections will damage the alternator rectifiers.

Battery connections. The battery must never be disconnected while the engine is running.

For drive belt tension and alternator cleaning, see page 35.

STARTER The starter motor is mounted on the right-hand side of the engine on the flywheel housing. It requires no lubrication.

FUEL PUMP Fuel is delivered to the carburetters by an S.U. electric fuel pump.

The pump is situated inside the luggage compartment on the right-hand side.

RADIATOR COOLING FANS *Fig. 54* **WARNING: The cooling fans can operate when the engine is switched off. To prevent possible injury, remove the fuse from the fans (see page 28) before commencing any work within the engine compartment.**

The electrically driven cooling fans mounted in front of the radiator are controlled by a thermostatic switch (1) on the radiator top tank. During normal driving the fans will operate intermittently, but when driving slowly or running the engine when stationary they will operate more frequently.

Checking Pull the connector (2) from the thermostatic switch, press the leads (3) together and the fans should operate.

Re-connect the leads, start and run the engine until normal operating temperature is reached and continue running the engine until the fans operate; this should occur before the temperature gauge pointer has reached 'H' (hot).

Should the fans not operate in the manner described in either of the above two checks consult your authorized Austin MG Dealer.

Fig. 53

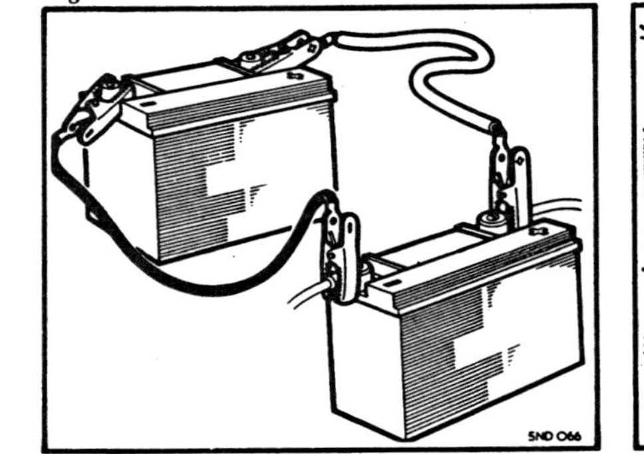

Fig. 54

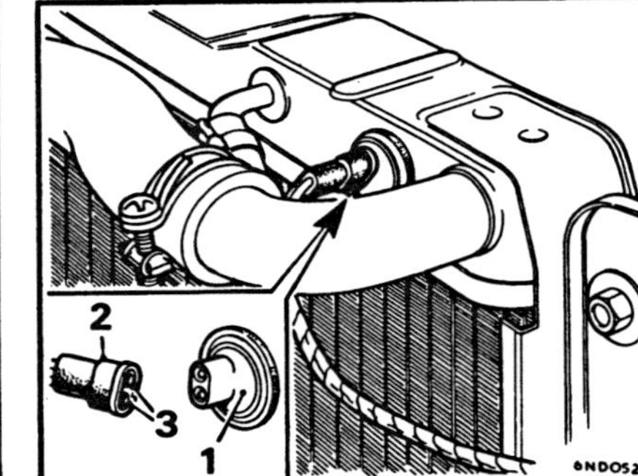

FUSES (1975 and 1976) *Fig. 55*

The fuses are housed in a fuse block (1) mounted in the engine compartment body on the oil filter side of the engine.

Fuse connecting 1–2. The fuse (2) protects one parking lamp, one tail lamp, one number-plate lamp, and one front and rear side marker lamp.

Fuse connecting 3–4. The fuse (3) protects one parking lamp, one tail lamp, one number-plate lamp, and one front and rear side-marker lamp.

Fuse connecting 5–6. The fuse (4) protects the circuits which operate only when the ignition is switched on. These circuits are for the direction indicators, brake stop lamps, reverse lamps and seat belt warning. The heated back-light (when fitted) on GT models is also protected by this fuse.

Fuse connecting 7–8. The fuse (5) protects the equipment which operates independently of the ignition switch, namely horns, interior and luggage compartment lamps, headlamp flasher, brake failure warning lamp, and the cigar-lighter.

Two spare fuses (6) are provided and it is important to use the correct replacement fuse. The fusing value, current rated 17 amp. continuous (35 amp. blow rated), is marked on a coloured slip of paper inside the glass tube of the fuse.

Line fuses *Fig. 55*

Running-on control valve. The 17 amp. continuous current rated (35 amp. blow rated) line fuse (7) protects the running-on control valve circuit which operates when the ignition is switched off.

Seat belt warning control unit. The 500 mA continuous current rated line fuse (8) protects the circuits within the control unit. **Under no circumstances** must any alteration be made to the specified fuse rating.

Hazard warning. The 17 amp. continuous current rated (35 amp. blow rated) line fuse (9) protects the hazard warning lamps and is located behind the hazard warning switch. It is accessible only when the centre console is withdrawn (see page 30).

Radio. A separate additional line fuse protects the radio (if fitted). See the instructions supplied with the radio for the correct fuse ratings.

To change a line fuse, hold one end of the cylindrical fuse holder (10), push in and twist the other end (11). Remove the fuse (12) from the cylindrical holder.

Fig. 55

FUSES (1977 and later) *Fig. 56*

The fuses are housed in a fuse block (1) mounted in the engine compartment body on the right-hand wing valance.

Fuse connecting 1–2. The fuse (2) protects one parking lamp, one tail lamp, one number-plate lamp, and one front and rear side-marker lamp.

Fuse connecting 3–4. The fuse (3) protects one parking lamp, one tail lamp, one number-plate lamp, and one front and rear side-marker lamp.

Fuse connecting 5–6. The fuse (4) protects the circuits which operate only when the ignition is switched on. These circuits are for the direction indicators, brake stop lamps, reverse lamps, seat belt warning, and brake warning lamp.

Fuse connecting 7–8. The fuse (5) protects the equipment which operates independently of the ignition switch, namely horns, interior and luggage compartment lamps, headlamp flasher, and the cigar-lighter.

Line fuses *Fig. 56*

Running-on control valve—slate and slate/purple wiring. The 17 amp continuous current rated (35 amp blow rated) line fuse (7) protects the running on control valve circuit which operates when the ignition is switched off.

Fan thermostat—white/brown and green wiring. The 17 amp continuous current rated (35 amp blow rated) line fuse (8) protects the fan thermostat circuit.

Hazard warning—brown wiring. The 17 amp continuous current rated (35 amp blow rated) line fuse (9) protects the hazard warning lamps.

Radio. A separate additional line fuse protects the radio (if fitted). See the instructions supplied with the radio for the correct fuse ratings.

To change a line fuse, hold one end of the cylindrical fuse holder (10), push in and twist the other end (11). Remove the fuse (12) from the cylinder holder.

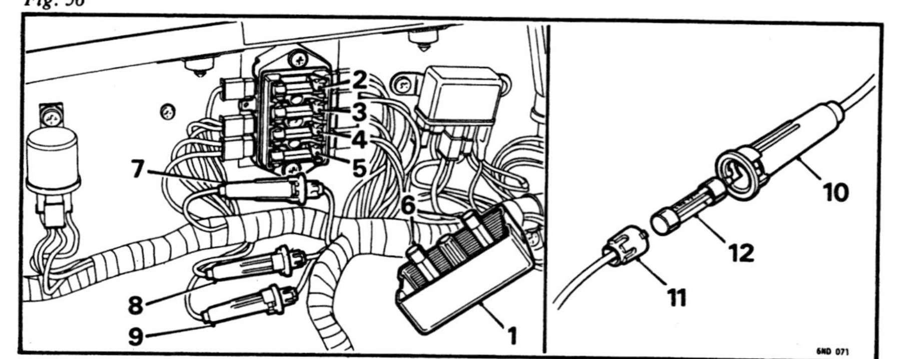

Fig. 56

Spare fuses *Fig. 56* Two spare fuses (6) are provided and it is important to use the correct replacement fuse. The fusing value, current rated 17 amp continuous (35 amp blow rated), is marked on a coloured slip of paper inside the glass tube of the fuse.

Blown fuses A blown fuse is indicated by the failure of all the units protected by it, and is confirmed by examination of the fuse when withdrawn. Before renewing a blown fuse inspect the wiring of the units that have failed for evidence of a short-circuit or other fault.

HEADLAMPS

Light unit *Fig. 57* To remove a light unit, ease the bottom of the outer rim (1) forwards away from the lamp. Unscrew the three inner rim retaining screws (2), remove the inner rim (3), withdraw the light unit (4), and disconnect the three-pin plug (5).

To fit a light unit, connect the three-pin plug, position the light unit in the headlamp body ensuring that the three lugs formed on the outer edge of the light unit engage in the slots formed in the body, and fit the inner retaining rim. Position the outer rim on the retaining lugs with the cut-away portion of the rim at the bottom of the lamp, and press the rim downwards and inwards.

Beam setting *Fig. 57* Two adjusting screws are provided on each headlamp for setting the main beams. The screw (6) is for adjusting the beam in the vertical plane, and the screw (7) is for horizontal adjustment. The beams must be set in accordance with local regulations; resetting and checking should be entrusted to your authorized Austin MG Dealer, who will have special equipment available for this purpose.

Fig. 57

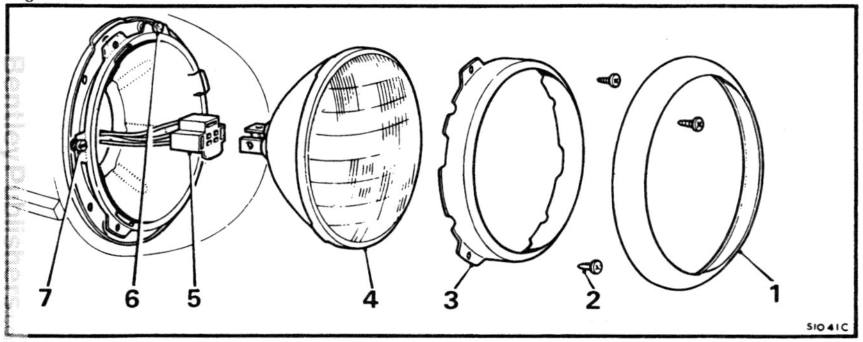

LAMPS

Parking and direction indicator *Fig. 58* To gain access to the parking and direction indicator bulb (1), unscrew the two retaining screws (2) and withdraw the rim and lens.

Stop, tail and direction indicator *Fig. 59* Remove the lens retaining screws (1) and slide the lens upwards to gain access to the stop/tail (2) and direction indicator (3) bulbs.

The direction indicator lamps have a single-filament bulb (3) which may be fitted either way round in the socket. The tail and stop lamp bulb (2) has a twin filament and offset peg bayonet fixing to ensure correct fitment.

Number-plate *Fig. 60* To change a bulb, remove the two screws (1), pull the lens (2) clear of the lamp body and unclip the bulb (3) from its contacts. When refitting, ensure that the lens engages in the seal lip and that the connectors are correctly fitted.

Side-marker *Fig. 61* To renew a bulb, remove the securing screw (1) and lift off the lamp lens, noting that one end is secured by a locating tab (2). When refitting, ensure that the sealing rubber is positioned correctly and that the lens tab (2) is located beneath the lamp body rim before refitting the securing screw.

Fig. 58

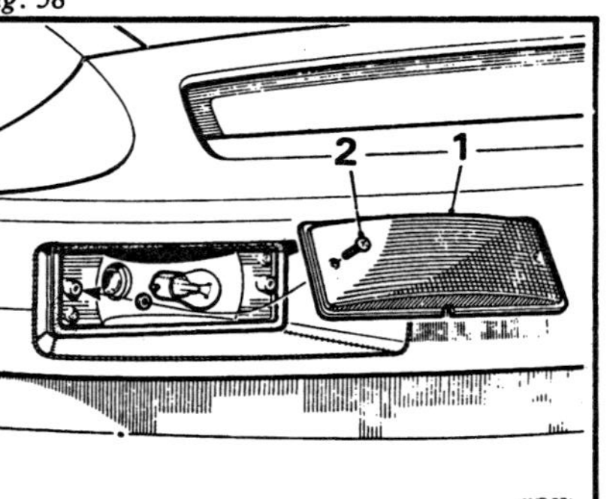

Fig. 59

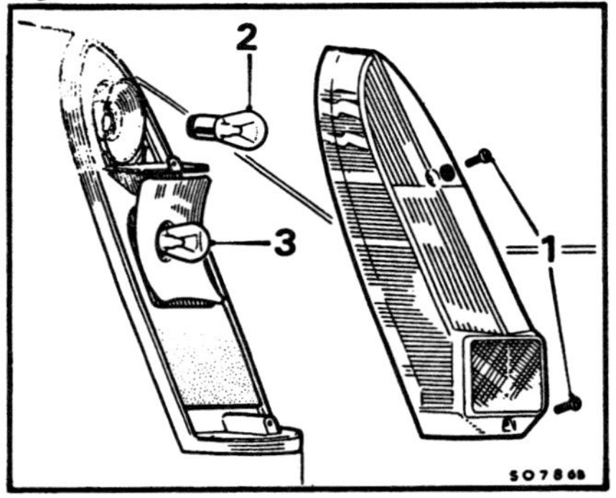

Fig. 60

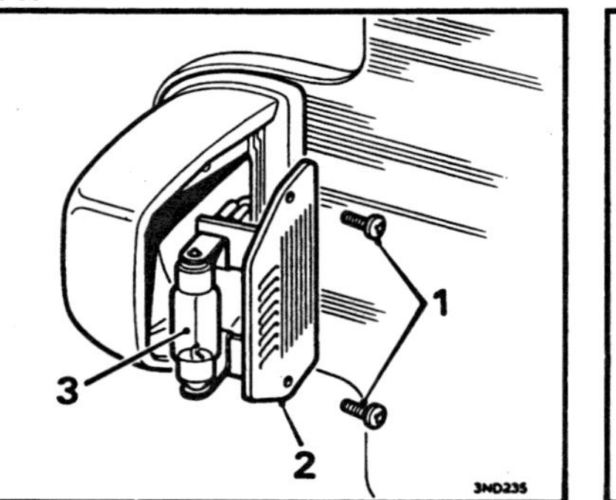

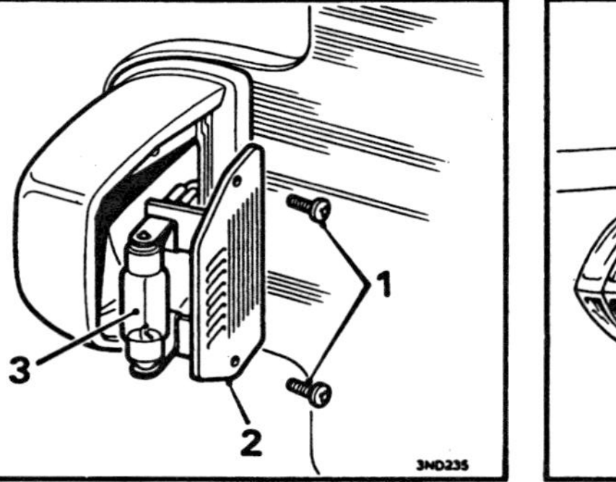

Fig. 61

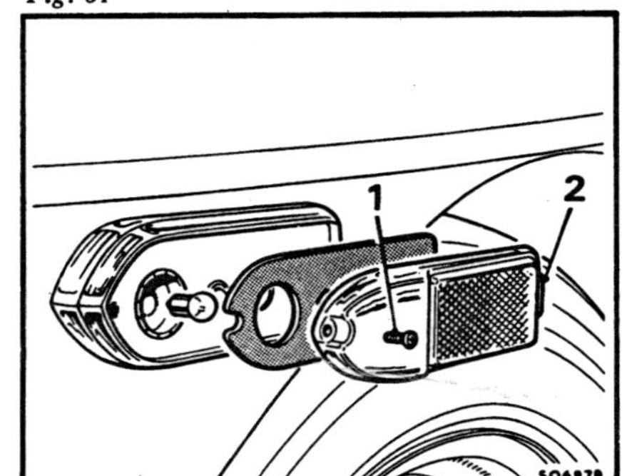

Reverse
Fig. 62
To renew a bulb, remove the two securing screws (1) and withdraw the lens. Press the bulb (2) down towards the lower contact and withdraw it from the lamp.

Fit one end of the new bulb into the hole in the lower contact, then press the top of the bulb into the lamp until the point of the cap engages the hole in the upper contact.

Luggage compartment
Fig. 63
The lens is held in the lamp by four locating lugs. To gain access to the bulb, gently squeeze the sides of the lens together and withdraw it from the lamp. Remove the bulb from its contacts.

Courtesy (1975 and 1976)
Fig. 64
To renew a bulb, remove the two screws (1) retaining the lamp bezel and remove the bezel and lens. The bulb may then be withdrawn from its contacts.

Courtesy (1977 and later)
Fig. 65
To gain access to the bulb, carefully prise the light (1) downwards from the fascia. Withdraw the festoon type bulb (2) from its contacts.

Fig. 62

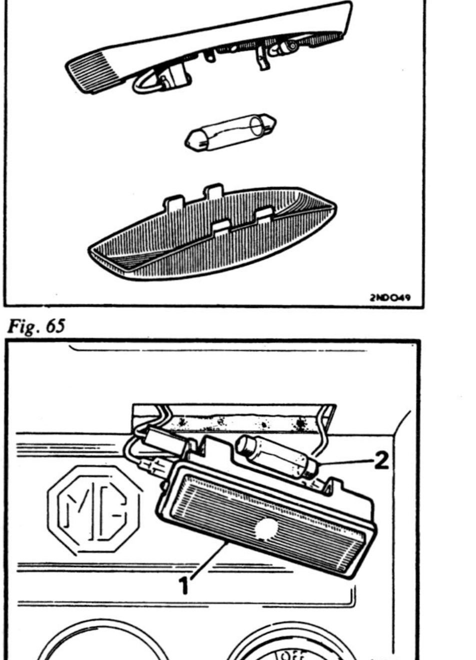

Fig. 63

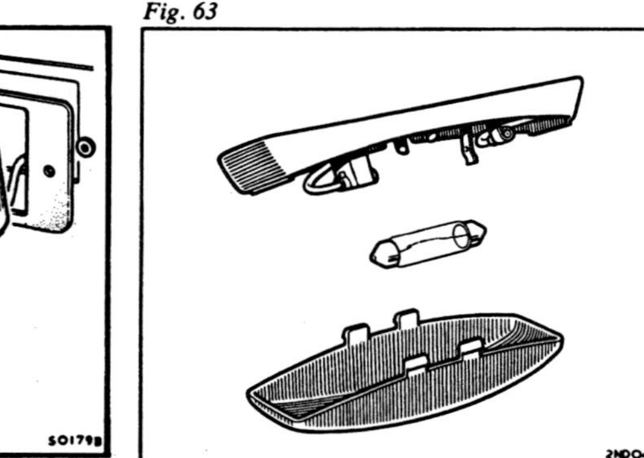

Fig. 64

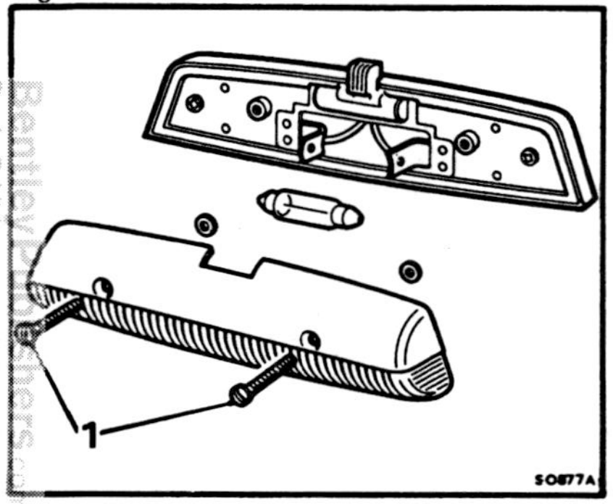

Fig. 65

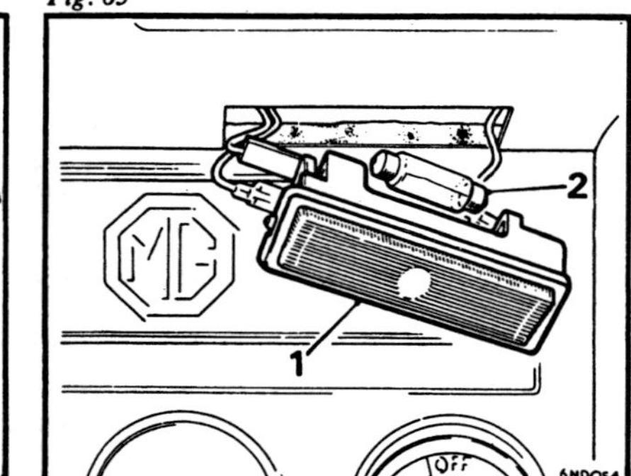

Warning, Panel and Illumination (1975 and 1976)
Figs. 66 and 67
To gain access to the bulbs the fascia bottom panel must be removed and/or the centre console withdrawn.

Fascia bottom panel. Unscrew the three screws (1) securing the bottom panel (2) and pull the panel forward from its retaining clips (3) at the rear.

Centre console. Remove the gear-lever knob and locknut (15). Unscrew the four screws (16) securing the gaiter retaining ring, noting that the front screw is the shorter of the four screws. Raise the hinged arm-rest, unscrew the retaining screw (17) and remove the arm-rest complete with the gaiter. Unscrew the four screws (18) retaining the console and withdraw the console rearwards.

Heater control lamp bulbs. Remove the fascia bottom panel. Remove the push-fit bulb holders (4) from the controls and remove the bayonet fixing type bulb (5). To remove the air flow control illumination bulb the centre console must also be withdrawn.

Instrument panel lamp bulbs. Remove the fascia bottom panel. Remove the push-fit bulb holders (6) from the instruments and unscrew the bulbs (7).

Lights and heater booster switch bulbs. Remove the fascia bottom panel. Remove the push-fit bulb holders (8) from the switches and remove the bayonet fixing type bulbs (9). To remove the heater booster switch bulb the centre console must also be withdrawn.

Warning lamp bulbs. Remove the fascia bottom panel. Remove the push-fit bulb holders (10) from the lamps and remove the bayonet fixing type bulbs (11).

Fig. 66

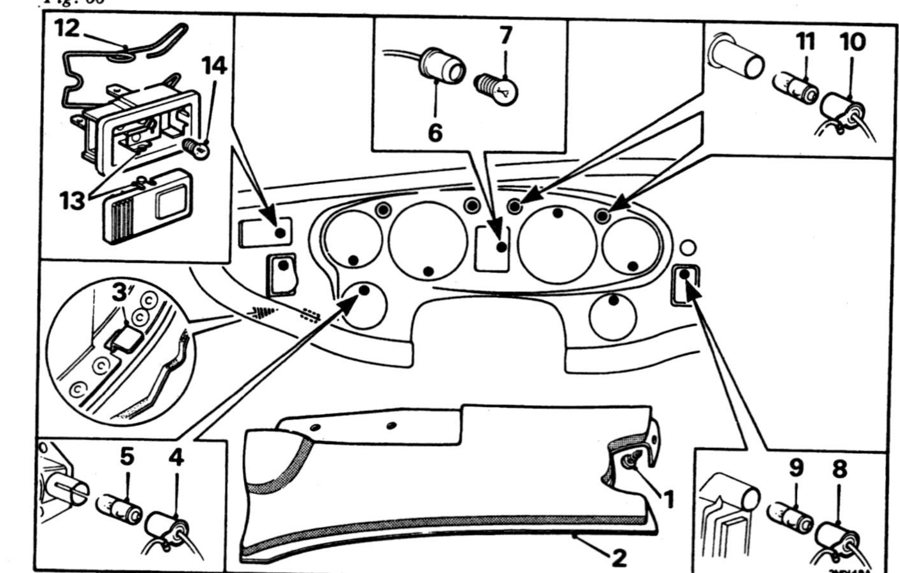

Brake failure warning lamp bulb. Remove the fascia bottom panel. Remove the retaining spring clip (12) and withdraw the holder/test-push assembly from the fascia. Through the two pivot holes in the holder depress the pivot legs (13) and remove the test-push rocker from its holder. Unscrew and remove the bulb (14).

Hazard switch bulb. Withdraw the centre console. Remove the push-fit bulb holder (19) from the switch, and remove the bayonet fixing type bulb (20).

Hazard and seat belt warning lamp bulbs. Withdraw the centre console. Remove the push-fit bulb holders (21) from the lamps and remove the bayonet fixing type bulbs (22).

Cigar-lighter illumination bulb. Withdraw the centre console Squeeze the sides of the bulb hood (23) and remove the hood. Remove the bulb holder (24) from the hood clip and remove the bayonet fixing type bulb (25).

Fig. 67

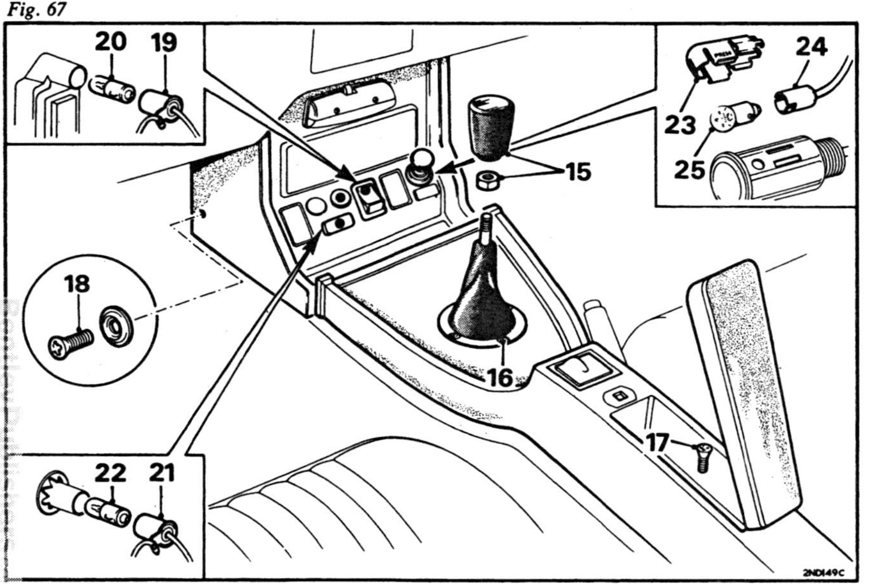

Fascia warning and illumination lamps (1977 and later) *Fig. 68*

The warning instrument panel and switch illumination lamps on the fascia are located in the positions shown.

To gain access to the instrument and warning bulbs the fascia bottom panel must be removed. The warning and instrument bulb holders can be reached from underneath the fascia.

To remove the fascia bottom panel. Unscrew the three screws (1) securing the bottom panel (2) and pull the panel forward from its retaining clips (3) at the rear.

Instrument panel lamps. To change a bulb, remove the fascia bottom panel. Remove the push-fit bulb holder (4) or (5) or (6) from the back of the instrument and unscrew the bulb (7).

Warning lamp bulbs. To change a bulb, remove the fascia bottom panel. Remove the push-fit bulb holder (8) from the back of the warning lamp and remove the bulb (9) which has a bayonet type fitting.

Switch illumination. To change a bulb remove the switch cover (10) by engaging a suitable wire clip into the forward recess on each side of the cover and pull the cover from the switch. To remove the blower switch bulb (12) use a wiring harness connector or a suitable length of rubber tube (11) and unscrew the bulb. To remove the hazard switch bulb (14) release the spring clip (13) and remove the bulb.

Fig. 68

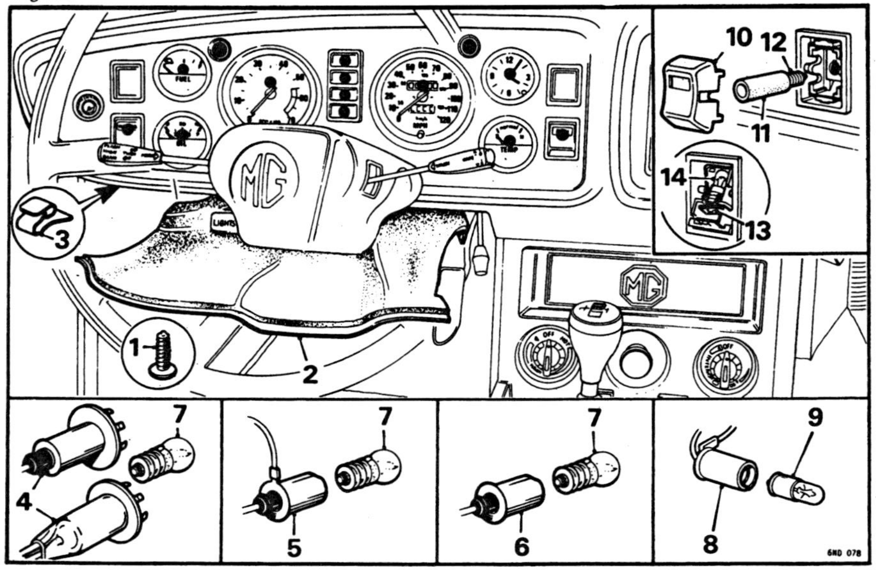

Centre console warning and illumination lamps
Fig. 69

To gain access to the bulbs the centre console must be withdrawn.

To withdraw the centre console. Unscrew the four screws (15), noting that the front screw is the shortest, and remove the gaiter retaining ring (16). Raise the hinged arm-rest and unscrew the retaining screw (17). Remove the arm-rest (18) by easing it up over the gaiter and the gear lever. Remove the four screws (19) retaining the console and remove the console (20) rearwards to give the required access to change a bulb.

Heater control illumination. To change a bulb withdraw the centre console for access. Remove the push-fit bulb holder (21) from the back of the control and remove the bayonet fixing type bulb (22).

Cigar-lighter illumination. To change a bulb, withdraw the centre console for access. Squeeze the sides of the bulb hood (23) and remove the hood. Remove the bulb holder (24) from the hood clip and remove the bayonet fixing type bulb (25).

Seat belt warning lamp. To change a bulb, withdraw the centre console for access. Remove the push-fit bulb holder (26) and remove the bayonet fixing type bulb (27).

Fitting the centre console. Secure the console in position with the four screws (19). Refit the arm-rest, threading the gaiter through the hole in the arm-rest, ensuring that the screw holes of the gaiter are aligned with the holes in the arm-rest. Secure the retaining ring with the four screws (15), ensuring that the short screw is at the front. Lift the arm-rest and fit the rear securing screw (17).

Fig. 69

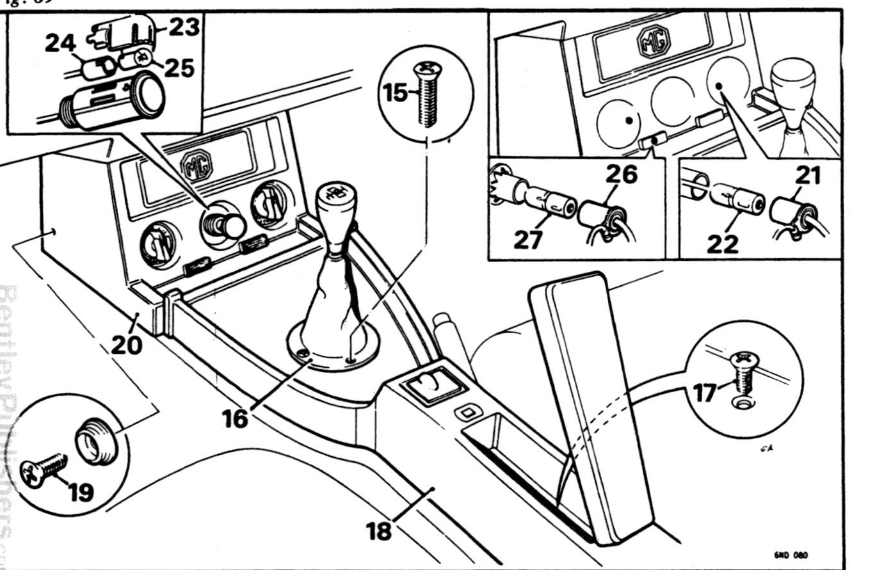

		Volts	*Watts*	*Part No.*
Replacement bulbs	Sidelamp (with flasher)	12	5/21	GLB 380
	Stop/tail	12	5/21	GLB 380
	Reverse	12	18	BFS 273
	Number-plate lamp	12	5	GLB 254
	Direction indicator	12	21	GLB 382
	Side marker lamp, front and rear	12	5	BFS 222
	Luggage compartment lamp (1975–1976)	12	6	GLB 254
	Courtesy lamp (1975–1976)	12	6	GLB 254
	Luggage compartment lamp (1977 and later)	12	5	GLB 254
	Courtesy lamp (1977 and later)	12	10	GLB 272
	Ignition warning	12	2	GLB 281
	Main beam	12	2	GLB 281
	Direction indicator warning lamp	12	2	GLB 281
	Brake warning lamp (1975–1976)	12	1.5	GLB 280
	Brake warning lamp (1977 and later)	12	2	GLB 281
	Hazard warning lamp	12	2	GLB 281
	Seat belt warning lamp	12	2	GLB 281
	Switch illumination (1975–1976)	12	2	GLE 281
	Switch illumination (1977 and later)	12	0·75	GLB 284
	Heater rotary control illumination	12	2	GLB 281
	Panel illumination lamp	12	2·2	GLB 987
	Cigar-lighter illumination	12	2·2	GBS 643
Sealed beam unit	Headlamp (1975–1976)	12	50/40	
	Headlamp (1977 and later)	12	60/50	GLU 133

WINDSCREEN WIPER AND WASHER

Wiper arms
Fig. 71

To re-position a wiper arm on the spindle, hold the spring clip (1) clear of the retaining groove in the spindle and withdraw the arm. Position the arm on the spindle (2).

Fig. 70

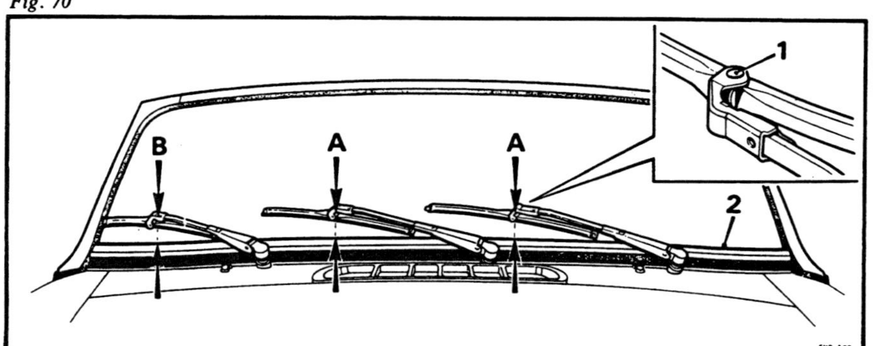

Electrical

Fig. 70 Ensure that there is a distance between the top wiper blade pivot (1) and the windscreen rubber (2) in the position shown as follows:

'A'—Centre and left-hand arm 1 to 1½ in.

'B'—Right-hand arm 1½ to 2 in.

Press the arm down onto the spindle until it is retained in position by the clip.

Wiper blade *Fig. 71* To renew a wiper blade pull the arm away from the windscreen. Hold the fastener (3) and the spring retainer (4) away from the wiper arm (5) and withdraw the blade assembly from the arm.

Insert the end of the wiper arm into the spring fastener of the new blade and push the blade into engagement (6) with the arm.

To ensure efficient wiping it is recommended that wiper blades are renewed annually.

Windscreen washer *Fig. 71* The windscreen washer system should be checked for correct operation and the reservoir refilled if necessary every week, and before a long journey in addition to the mileage intervals given in **'MAINTENANCE SUMMARY'.**

Washer reservoir. To fill the reservoir (7), remove the cap (8).

In cold weather the washer reservoir should be filled with a mixture of water and a recommended washer solvent to prevent the water freezing.

On no account should radiator anti-freeze or methylated spirits (denatured alcohol) be used in the windscreen washer.

Jet adjusting. Turn the jet (9) using a small screwdriver, to adjust the height of the spray. The spray should strike the top of the windscreen.

Fig. 71

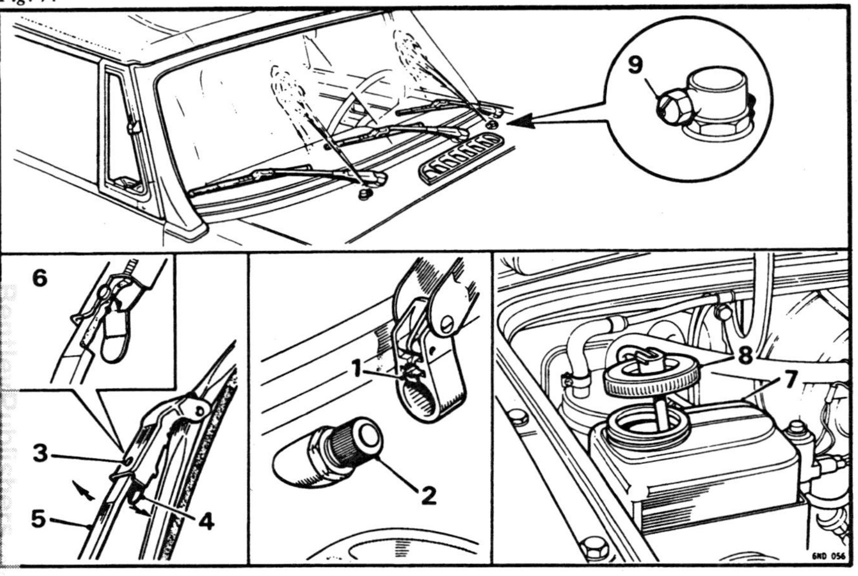

IGNITION

Ignition timing The ignition timing is set dynamically to give optimum engine performance with efficient engine emission control. Electronic test equipment must be used to check the ignition timing setting and the automatic advance (see **'GENERAL DATA'**). Checking and adjustment of the ignition timing setting should be carried out by your authorized Austin MG Dealer control service station.

The dynamic ignition timing must be checked after cleaning, re-setting, or renewing of the distributor contacts.

Basic tuning data will be found on the Vehicle Emission Control Information Label located in the engine compartment.

Distributor (1975) *Fig. 72* Release the retaining clips and remove the distributor cover. Remove the rotor arm (1).

Lubrication. Very lightly smear the cam (2) and pivot post (3) with grease. Add a few drops of oil to the felt pad (4) in the top of the cam spindle and through the gap (5) between the contact plate and the cam spindle to lubricate the centrifugal weights. Do **not** oil the cam wiping pad.

Every 25,000 miles in addition to the routine maintenance lubricate the contact breaker assembly centre bearing with a drop of oil in each of the two holes (6) in the base plate.

Carefully wipe away all surplus lubricant and see that the contact breaker points are perfectly clean and dry.

Cleaning distributor cover. With a nap free cloth wipe the rotor arm and the inside of the distributor cover. Refit the rotor arm and the distributor cover.

Fig. 72

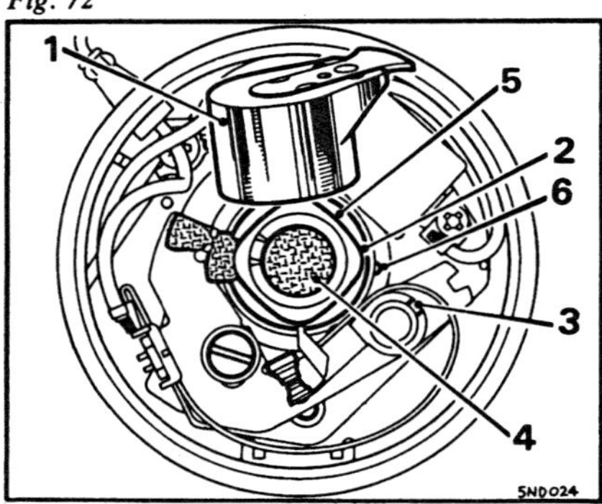

Distributor (1976 and later) *Fig. 73*

Release the retaining clips and remove the cover (1). Remove the rotor arm (2) and the anti-flash shield (3).

Lubrication. Add a few drops of oil to the felt pad (4) in the top of the timing rotor carrier.

Remove the anti-flash shield and lubricate the pick-up plate centre bearing with a drop of oil in each of the two holes (5) in the base plate.

Apply a few drops of oil through the aperture (6) to lubricate the centrifugal timing control.

CAUTION: **Do not** disturb the screw (7) securing the base plate.

Cleaning. With a clean nap-free cloth wipe the inside of the distributor cover, the rotor arm and the anti-flash shield. Refit the anti-flash shield, ensuring that the cut-outs are aligned with the distributor cover retaining clips. Refit the rotor arm and the cover.

Fig. 73

Spark plugs *Fig. 74*

Disconnect the H.T. lead from each plug, and partly unscrew each plug. Clean the area of the cylinder head surrounding the seating of each plug, then unscrew each plug.

The spark plugs should be cleaned, preferably with an air-blast service unit.

When fitting new spark plugs ensure that only the recommended type and grade are used (see **'GENERAL DATA'**).

Check the plug gaps, and reset if necessary to the recommended gap (see **'GENERAL DATA'**). To reset, use a special Champion spark plug gauge and setting tool; move the side electrode, never the centre one.

Screw the plug down by hand as far as possible, then use a spanner for tightening only. Always use a tubular box spanner to avoid possible damage to the insulator, and do not under any circumstances use a movable wrench. Never overtighten a plug, but ensure that a good joint is made between the plug body, washer, and cylinder head. Wipe clean the outside of the plugs before reconnecting the H.T. leads.

Ignition cables

The high-tension cables connecting the distributor to the sparking plugs may, after long use, show signs of perishing. They must then be renewed using the correct type of ignition cable.

Fig. 74

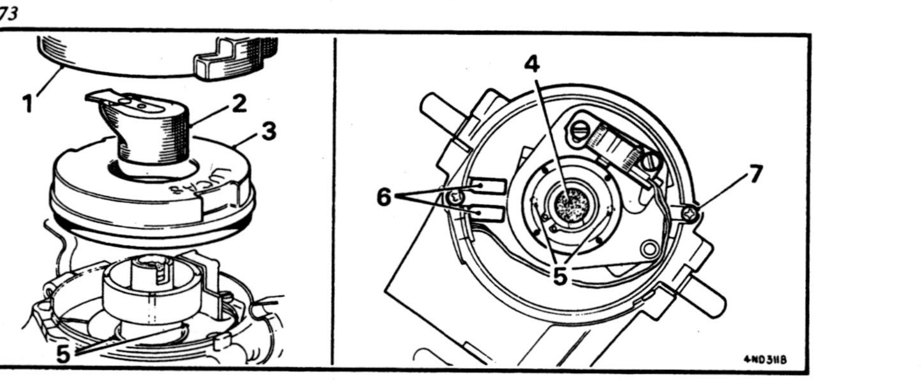

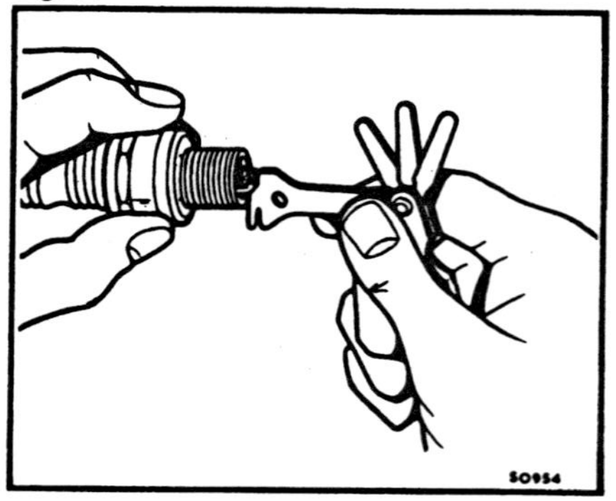

LUBRICATION

Checking *Fig. 75*

The level of the oil in the engine sump is indicated by the dipstick (1) on the right-hand side of the engine. Maintain the level between the 'MIN' and 'MAX' mark on the dipstick and never allow it to fall below the 'MIN' mark.

The filler (2) is on the forward end of the rocker cover and is provided with a quick-action cap.

Ensure that the dipstick is correctly refitted.

The oil level should always be checked before a long journey.

Draining *Fig. 75*

To drain the engine oil, remove the drain plug (3) located on the right-hand side at the rear of the sump. This operation should be carried out while the engine is warm.

Clean the drain plug; check that its copper sealing washer is in a satisfactory condition, and refit.

Filling

Fill the engine with the correct quantity (see 'GENERAL DATA') of a recommended oil. Run the engine for a short while then allow it to stand for a few minutes before checking the level with the dipstick.

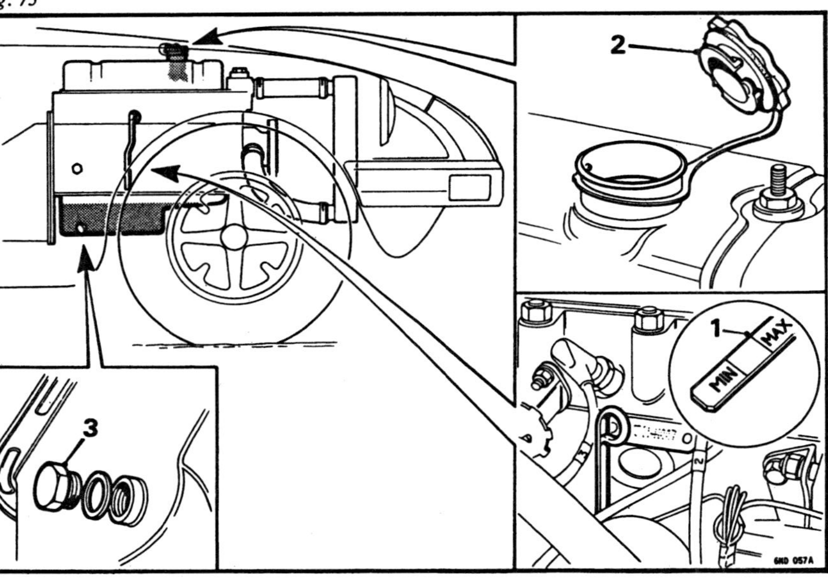

Fig. 75

Oil filter changing *Fig. 76*

The oil filter is a disposable cartridge type.

To renew, unscrew the cartridge (1) from the filter head (2) and discard the cartridge.

NOTE: If difficulty in unscrewing the cartridge is experienced, consult your authorized Austin MG Dealer.

Smear the new seal (3) with engine oil and fit it into its groove in the new cartridge. Screw the cartridge to the filter head using hand force only.

Refill the engine with the correct quantity of a recommended lubricant, start the engine and check for oil leakage.

DRIVE BELT

Alternator *Fig. 77*

Tension. When correctly tensioned, a total deflection of $\frac{1}{2}$ in. under moderate hand pressure, should be possible at the midway point of the longest belt run between the pulleys.

Adjusting. To adjust the belt tension, slacken the securing bolts (1) and adjusting link nuts (2), and move the alternator to the required position. Apply any leverage necessary to the alternator end bracket (3) only and not to any other part; to avoid damaging the drive-end bracket the lever should preferably be of wood or soft metal. Tighten the bolts and re-check the belt tension. **DO NOT OVERTIGHTEN** as this will impose an excess loading on the drive bearings.

Cleaning. Keep the slots in the plastic end-cover (4) clean.

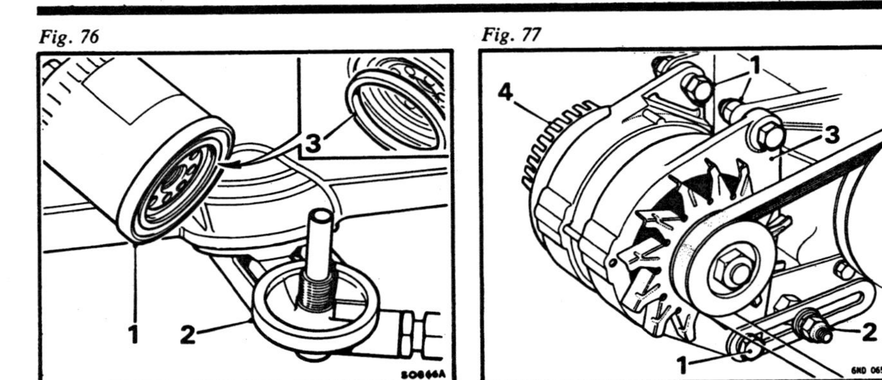

Fig. 76

Fig. 77

VALVE ROCKER CLEARANCE

Checking *Fig. 78* Disconnect the purge pipe (1) from the rocker cover. Unscrew the nut and remove the vapour pipe (2), and disconnect the lead (3) from the induction heater. Remove the rocker cover (4) and insert a 0·013 in. feeler gauge (5) between the valve rocker arms and the valve stem. The gauge should be a sliding fit, when the engine is warm. Check each clearance in the following order:

Check No. 1 valve with No. 8 fully open. Check No. 8 valve with No. 1 fully open.
" " 3 " " " 6 " " " " 6 " " " 3 " "
" " 5 " " " 4 " " " " 4 " " " 5 " "
" " 2 " " " 7 " " " " 7 " " " 2 " "

Adjusting *Fig. 78* Slacken the adjusting screw locknut (6) on the opposite end of the rocker arm and rotate the screw (7) clockwise to reduce the clearance or anti-clockwise to increase it. Re-tighten the locknut when the clearance is correct, holding the screw against rotation with a screwdriver.

Cleaning *Fig. 78* Clean the rocker cover sealing face. Examine the orifice (8) of the restrictor for obstruction. Clean any dirt or deposit from the restrictor orifice, using a length of soft wire.

Refitting *Fig. 78* Check the rocker cover gasket (9) for damage. Fit a new gasket if necessary. Refit the cover, the vapour pipe, and connect the purge pipe. Connect the lead to the induction heater. Check that the oil filler cap (10) seals correctly; renew it if necessary.

Fig. 78

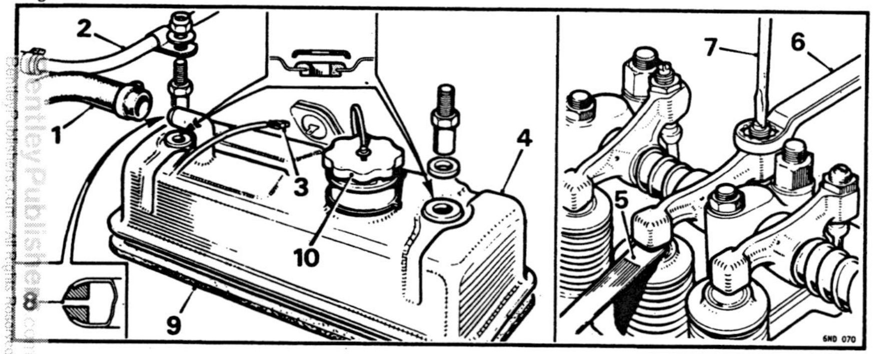

EMISSION CONTROL SYSTEMS

You and each subsequent owner of the car are urged to make sure that the recommended maintenance procedures are carried out at the intervals specified. For the emission controls to continue to function effectively, it is strongly recommended that you arrange for regular maintenance inspections to be carried out by your authorized Austin MG Dealer or by any other qualified service outlet which regularly performs such service on British Leyland cars.

You have been provided with a Passport to Service which contains a facility to record that maintenance has been carried out at the recommended mileages.

You should have the maintenance record completed by your authorized Austin MG Dealer (or by other dealer or station equipped to render such service) at the regular mileage intervals indicated in the Maintenance Summary. The Handbook and Passport to Service should be handed to subsequent purchasers of the vehicle at the time of sale so that the maintenance instructions are available and that the record of maintenance can be continued.

You are also urged to study with care the section covering **'MALFUNCTION IDENTIFICATION'**. Study of this section will be of aid to you in detecting possible malfunctions of the emission controls so that necessary service measures can immediately be taken.

IMPORTANT

Your attention is particularly drawn to the following:

1. Maintenance and service charges applicable to the emission control system are not covered by the warranty and are not reimbursable, unless shown to have been caused by defects in materials and workmanship covered by the warranty.

2. The engine has been designed for the regular use of **unleaded fuel.** Leaded fuel or low lead fuel must not be used as such fuels will seriously impair the efficiency of the emission control system and cause permanent damage to the catalytic converter.

General description This section gives a general description of the crankcase, exhaust and fuel evaporative emission control systems fitted to this vehicle and the function of their individual components. It must be emphasized that correct carburetter adjustment and ignition timing which have been pre-set at the factory are essential for the efficient functioning of the exhaust emission controls. Should it become necessary to check these settings this work should be carried out by an authorized Austin MG or British Leyland Dealer who has the specialist equipment and training to undertake these adjustments.

The basic engine tuning data will be found on the emission control information label located in the front of the engine compartment.

Crankcase emission control The engine crankcase breather outlet incorporates an oil separator flame-trap which is connected by hoses to the controlled depression chamber between the piston and the throttle disc valve of the carburetter. Piston blowby fumes are drawn into the depression chamber where they combine with the engine inlet charge for combustion in the engine cylinders in the normal way. Fresh filtered air is supplied to the engine crankcase through a hose connected between the engine valve rocker cover and the charcoal canister of the fuel evaporative emission control system.

THE EMISSION CONTROL COMPONENTS

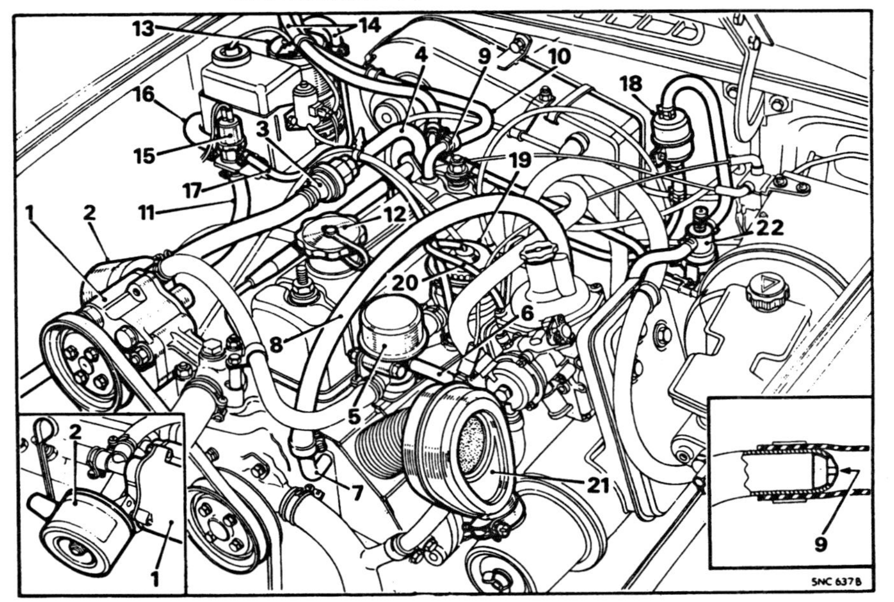

1. Air pump
2. Air pump air cleaner
3. Check valve
4. Air manifold
5. Gulp valve
6. Sensing pipe
7. Oil separator/flame trap
8. Breather pipe
9. Restricted connection
10. Purge line
11. Air vent pipe
12. Sealed oil filler cap
13. Charcoal adsorption canister
14. Vapour lines
15. Running-on control valve
16. Running-on control hose
17. Running-on control pipe
18. Fuel filter.
19. Exhaust gas recirculation (E.G.R.) valve
20. E.G.R. valve hose
21. Air temperature control valve
22. Fuel cut-off valve. (1977 and later)

THE EMISSION CONTROL COMPONENTS
(1975–1978)

NOTE: [For a diagram of emission control components for 1979 and later models, see page 282.]

Exhaust emission control The exhaust emission control system is designed to give the required degree of control of the carbon monoxide, unburnt hydrocarbons and oxides of nitrogen content of exhaust gases.

The exhaust emission control system is a combination of engine components and air injection techniques and consists of a special carburetter, air injection into the exhaust ports and exhaust gas recirculation.

The quantity of air-polluting elements in the gases leaving the exhaust pipe is reduced by adding air to the hot gases immediately they leave the combustion chambers of the engine. The injection of air into the exhaust gases promotes a continued conversion of the undesirable hydrocarbon and carbon monoxide components of the exhaust gases to relatively harmless carbon dioxide and water.

The exhaust gas recirculation valve mounted on the exhaust manifold will recirculate a controlled quantity of the exhaust gases to reduce combustion chamber temperature.

The catalytic converter is fitted into the exhaust system in order to reduce carbon monoxide and hydrocarbon emissions (not used on 1975 cars).

An air pump mounted on the front of the engine, and belt-driven from the water pump pulley, supplies air under pressure through hoses and a check valve and distribution manifold to injectors in each exhaust port in the engine cylinder head. The check valve prevents high pressure exhaust gases from blowing back into the air pump due to, for example, pump drive failure.

Air from the pump is also supplied to a gulp valve, the outlet of which is connected to the engine inlet manifold. A small-bore sensing pipe connected between the inlet manifold and the diaphragm chamber of the gulp valve relays changes in manifold depression to the valve which will open under certain conditions such as those created by deceleration or engine overrun.

When the gulp valve opens, a small quantity of air is admitted directly into the inlet manifold to lean off the rich air/fuel mixture which is present in the manifold under conditions immediately following throttle closure. This mixture, having been reduced to a burnable condition, combines with engine inlet charge for combustion in the engine cylinders in the normal way.

The carburetter is manufactured to a special exhaust emission specification and is tuned to give the maximum emission control consistent with retaining vehicle performance and drivability. The metering needle is arranged in such a manner that it is always lightly spring loaded against the side of the jet to ensure consistency of fuel metering. A throttle by-pass valve limits the inlet manifold depression and ensures that during conditions of engine overrun the air/fuel mixture enters the engine cylinders in a burnable condition consistent with low emission levels.

Fuel evaporative loss control

To prevent air pollution by vapours from the fuel tank and carburetter vents, the control equipment stores the vapour in a charcoal-filled canister while the engine is stopped and disposes of it via the engine crankcase emission control system when the engine is running.

The fuel tank venting is designed to ensure that no liquid fuel is carried to the storage canister with the vapours and that vapours are vented through the control system.

The capacity of the fuel tank is limited by a specially positioned filler vent tube and ensures sufficient volume is available after filling to accommodate fuel which would otherwise be displaced as a result of a high temperature rise.

Warning: When filling with fuel do not attempt to add more than the capacity given in **'GENERAL DATA'.** Slow filling, or allowing the level to drop and then adding more fuel, is not recommended and **can result in spillage due to expansion.**

MALFUNCTION IDENTIFICATION

Check the following items regularly for visual signs of a malfunction and also if any of the Driving Symptoms listed should persistently occur. **If you are unable to locate and/or correct the malfunction you are advised to contact your authorized Austin MG Dealer immediately.**

Visual checks

1. Condition and adjustment of drive belts.
2. Baked or overheated hose between air pump and check valve.
3. All hoses for security, damage and deterioration.
4. Fuel leakage.
5. Oil filler cap for sealing.

Driving symptoms

1. Violent backfire in exhaust system.
2. Hesitation to accelerate on re-opening the throttle after sudden throttle closure.
3. Engine idles erratically or stalls.
4. Noisy air pump.
5. Ignition warning light on above idle speed (slack or broken drive belt).
6. Smell of fuel vapours.
7. Engine stops after short running periods (fuel starvation).
8. Lack of power.
9. High fuel consumption.
10. Engine misfire.
11. High temperature indicated (overheating of coolant).

THE LAYOUT OF THE FUEL EVAPORATIVE LOSS CONTROL SYSTEM

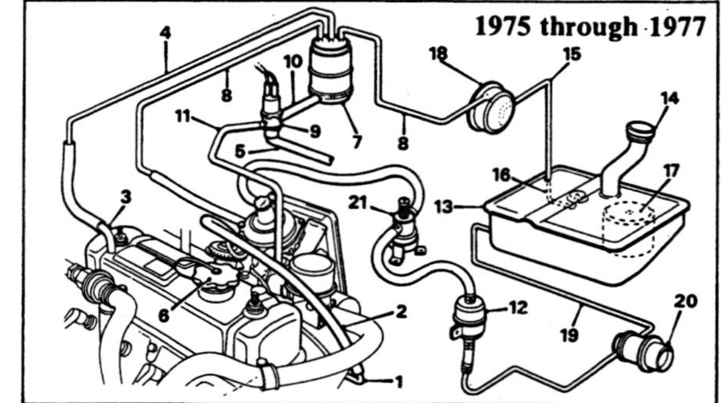

1. Oil separator/flame trap
2. Breather pipe
3. Restrictor connection
4. Purge line
5. Air vent pipe
6. Sealed oil filler cap
7. Charcoal adsorption canister
8. Vapour lines
9. Running-on control valve
10. Running-on control hose
11. Running-on control pipe
12. Fuel filter
13. Fuel tank
14. Sealed fuel filler cap
15. Vapour line
16. Vapour tube
17. Capacity limiting tank
18. Separation tank
19. Fuel pipe
20. Fuel pump
21. Fuel cut-off valve (1977 only)

THE LAYOUT OF THE FUEL EVAPORATIVE LOSS CONTROL SYSTEM

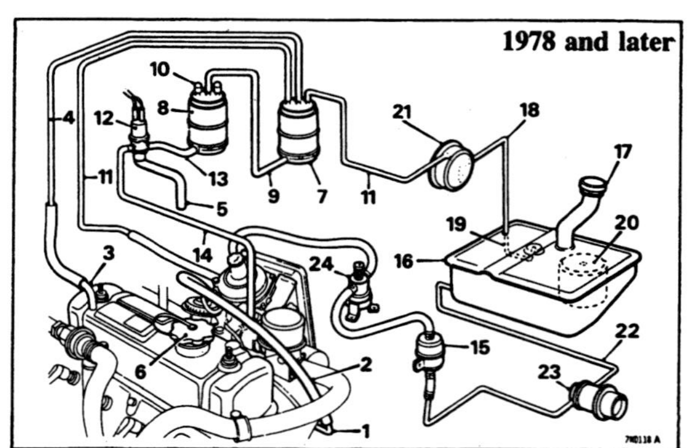

1. Oil separator/flame trap
2. Breather pipe
3. Restrictor connection
4. Purge line
5. Air vent pipe
6. Sealed oil filler cap
7. Primary charcoal adsorption canister
8. Secondary charcoal adsorption canister
9. Canister inter-connecting pipe
10. Sealing cap
11. Vapour lines
12. Running-on control valve
13. Running-on control hose
14. Running-on control pipe
15. Fuel filter
16. Fuel tank
17. Sealed fuel filler cap
18. Vapour line
19. Vapour tube
20. Capacity limiting tank
21. Separation tank
22. Fuel pipe
23. Fuel pump
24. Fuel cut-off valve

MAINTENANCE OPERATIONS

All items marked† in the "**MAINTENANCE SUMMARY**" given on pages 44 to 47 are emission control related.

Adsorption canister (1975–1977) *Fig. 79A*

The adsorption canister (5) must be renewed every 25,000 miles.

To remove the canister. Unscrew the windscreen washer reservoir cap (1), withdraw the tube from the reservoir and remove the reservoir (2) from its mounting. Disconnect the air vent pipe (3), vapour lines (4) and purge pipe (5) from their connections on the canister. Remove the securing bracket, nut and bolt (6), collecting the spacer, and remove the canister (7).

Adsorption canister (1978 and later) *Fig. 79B*

The adsorption canisters (7) and (8) must be renewed every 25,000 miles.

To remove the canisters. Unscrew the windscreen washer reservoir cap, withdraw the tube from the reservoir and remove the reservoir from its mounting. Disconnect the vapour lines (1) and purge pipe (2) from the primary canister. Disconnect the inter-connecting pipe (3) from the primary and secondary canister. Remove the sealing caps (4) and disconnect the air vent pipe (5) from the secondary canister. Unscrew each securing bracket nut and bolt (6) and remove the primary (7) and secondary (8) canisters.

Refitting. When refitting, ensure that all connections to the canister are secure. Locate the windscreen washer reservoir on its mounting, insert the tube and fit the cap.

To prevent the engine running on after the ignition has been switched off a control valve is fitted to the air vent pipe of the adsorption canister. The valve is a self-contained unit and requires no regular maintenance. Care should be taken when renewing the adsorption canister not to disturb the valve or its connections.

Fuel filter *Fig. 80*

The filter assembly must be renewed every 12,500 miles.

Removing. Squeeze the ends of the clip and remove the carburetter feed hose (1), and the fuel tank delivery hose (2) from the filter (4). Slacken the screw (3) clamping the filter in position. Withdraw the filter from the clip and discard it.

Refitting. Fit the new filter into the clip, with the end marked 'IN' towards the fuel tank delivery hose (2). Tighten the clamp screw, and fit the hoses to the filter.

Fig. 79A

Fig. 79B

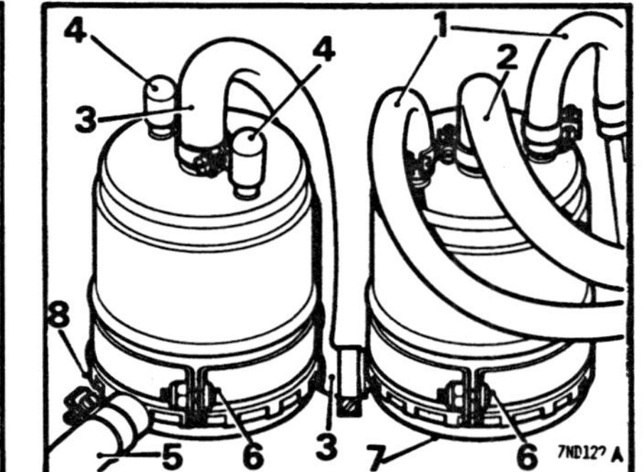

Purge line restrictor

To check, disconnect the purge line from the rocker cover elbow. Examine the orifice of the restriction formed in the elbow for obstruction. Clear any dirt or deposits from the restrictor orifice, using a length of wire. See page 41.

Air pump

The element of the air pump air cleaner must be renewed every 12,500 miles or 12 months; more frequent changes may be necessary in dusty operating conditions.

Air cleaner element changing (Fig. 81). Remove the nut and washer (1). Withdraw the cover (2) and discard the element (3). Clean the inside of the cover thoroughly and reassemble using a new element.

Drive belt tension. When correctly tensioned, a total deflection of ½ in. under moderate hand pressure, should be possible at the midway point of the belt run.

Adjusting (Fig. 82). Slacken the securing bolt (1) and the two adjusting link bolts (2), move the air pump to the required position. Tighten the bolts and re-check the belt tension. **DO NOT OVERTIGHTEN.**

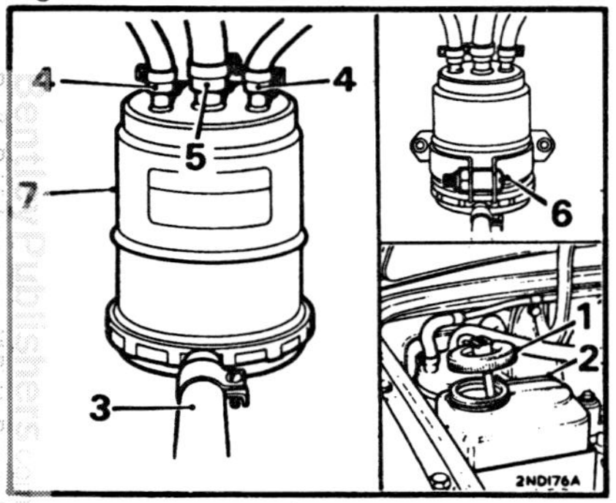

Fig. 80

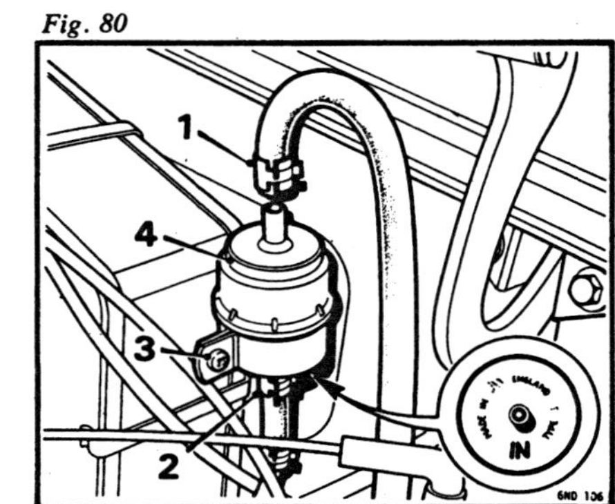

Fig. 81

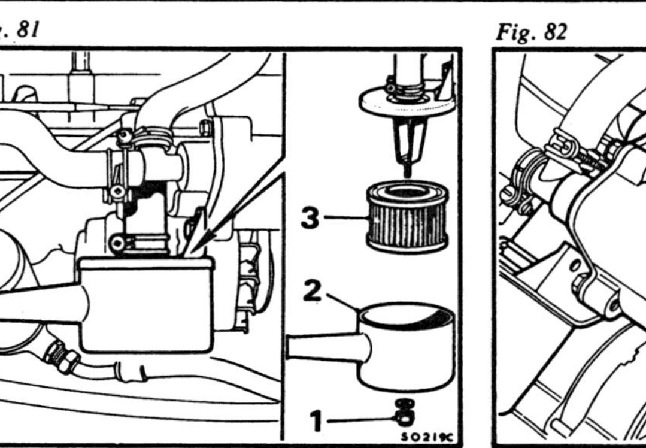

Fig. 82

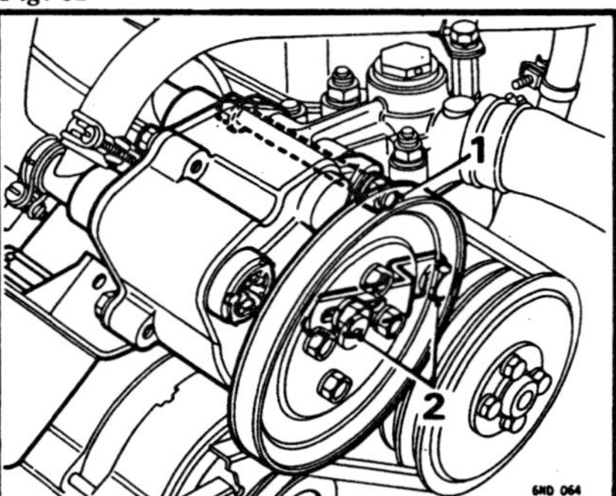

Emission Control Systems

Filler caps
Fig. 83

Both the engine oil filler cap (1) and the fuel tank filler cap (2) are non-venting and form a seal on the filling apertures.

IT IS ESSENTIAL TO THE SATISFACTORY OPERATION OF THE EVAPORATIVE LOSS SYSTEM THAT BOTH CAPS ARE ALWAYS REFITTED CORRECTLY AND TIGHTENED FULLY. A DEFECTIVE CAP OR CAP SEAL (3) MUST BE REPLACED.

Exhaust gas recirculation valve
Fig. 84

The E.G.R. valve warning light (1) will glow when the car has completed a distance of 25,000 miles, indicating to the driver that the valve (2) should be serviced. At the same time the service interval counter will show the mileage percentage that has elapsed in a 25,000 mile period.

Servicing the E.G.R. valve should be carried out by your authorized Austin MG Dealer who on completion will reset the service interval counter to zero, and cancel the warning light illumination.

NOTE: No. E.G.R. service is necessary on 1977 and later cars.

Fig. 83

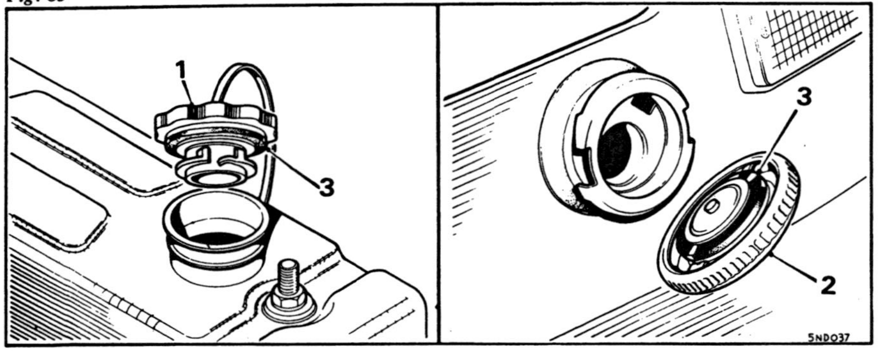

Fig. 84

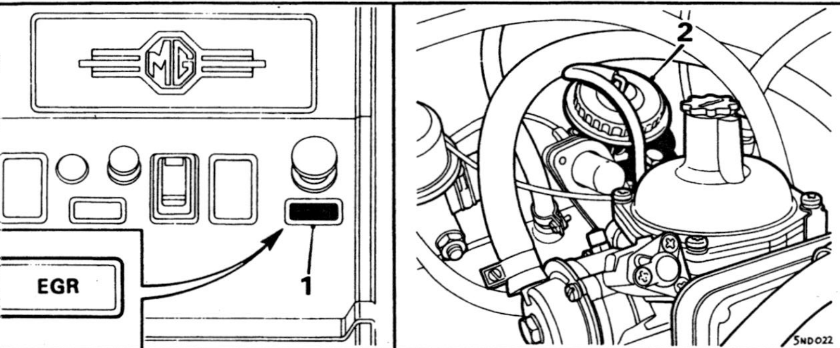

FUEL SYSTEM

AIR CLEANER

The element of the air cleaner must be renewed every 12,500 miles; more frequent changes may be necessary in dusty operating conditions.

Element changing
Fig. 85

Unscrew the wing nut (1), pivot the end cover away from the engine to release the air temperature control valve from the hot air hose (2), and remove the end cover (3). Withdraw the element (4) and discard it.

Thoroughly clean the air cleaner cover and the casing (6). Fit a new element. Locate the end cover in position, ensuring that its lip (6) supports the inside of the filter element. Connect the air temperature control valve to the hot air hose, fit and tighten the wing nut.

Air intake temperature control
Fig. 85

The temperature of the air entering the carburetter is controlled by a valve fitted to the intake of the air cleaner. The control valve (7) should be inspected for condition and operation by your authorized Austin MG Dealer.

Fig. 85

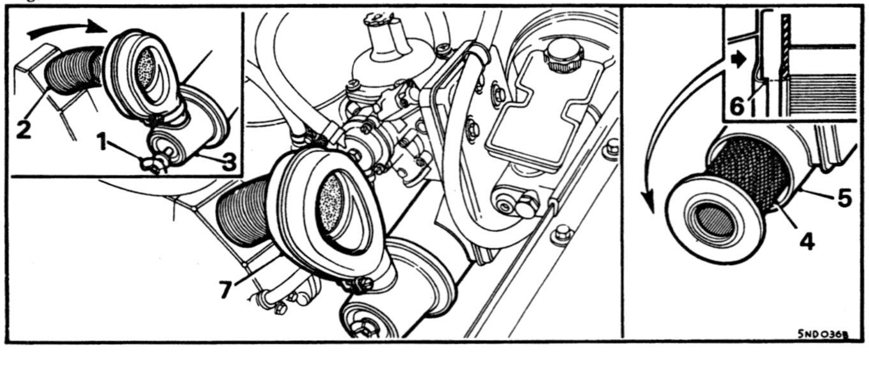

CARBURETTER

Air pollution control The carburetter incorporates features which assist in reducing exhaust emissions. Maladjustment or the fitting of parts not to the required specification may render these features ineffective.

Carburetter damper *Fig. 86*

Checking oil level. Unscrew the damper cap (4) from the carburetter top cover. Carefully raise the damper to the top of its travel. Lower the damper back into the hollow piston rod. If the oil level in the hollow piston rod is correct, resistance should be felt when there is a gap of approximately ¼ in. (A) between the cap and the carburetter top cover. Top up if necessary. Screw the damper cap firmly to the carburetter top cover.

Topping up the oil level. Detach the throttle cam return springs (1) from the air cleaner. Remove the three bolts (2) securing the air cleaner to the carburetter, noting that the top bolt secures the brake servo vacuum hose clip. Detach the air temperature control valve from the hot air hose (3) and manœuvre the air cleaner forwards in the engine compartment.

Unscrew the damper cap (4) from the carburetter top cover. Raise the piston (5) with a finger, and at the same time lift the damper (4) and carefully ease the retaining cap (6) from the hollow piston rod to release the damper assembly from the piston. With the piston raised, top up the hollow piston rod with a recommended engine oil until the level is ¼ in. below the top of the hollow piston rod. Lower the piston. **UNDER NO CIRCUMSTANCES SHOULD A HEAVY BODIED LUBRICANT BE USED.** Ensure the oil level is correct. Raise the piston and carefully press the retaining cup into the hollow piston rod. Screw the damper cap firmly into the carburetter top cover.

Check the condition of the air cleaner gasket, renew if necessary. Connect the air temperature control valve to the hot air hose and secure the air cleaner to the carburetter.

Tuning The tuning of the carburetter is confined to setting the idle speed and mixture strength (CO percentage). Adjustment should only be undertaken by your authorized Austin MG Dealer who will have the essential special equipment for this purpose.

Fig. 86

GEARBOX

Fig. 87

Checking From underneath the car, remove the oil level filler plug (1) and check the oil level. The correct level is at the bottom of the filler level plug hole.

OVERDRIVE

Fig. 87

Draining Remove the plug (2) to drain the oil from the gearbox and overdrive unit.

Sump filter Drain the gearbox and overdrive unit.

Clean the sump cover and its surroundings. Remove the cover securing screws, withdraw the cover (3) and the filter (4). Clean all metallic particles from the two magnets fitted to the inside of the cover, wash the cover and filter in gasoline. Refit the filter and cover.

Relief valve filter Remove the plug and the seal (5); withdraw the relief valve approximately ½ in. and remove the filter (6). Wash the filter, plug and seal in gasoline.

Fit the filter to the relief valve, push the valve fully home and refit the plug and seal.

Filling Fill the gearbox and overdrive unit through the oil level filler plug hole (1) with the correct quantity (see **'GENERAL DATA'**) of one of the recommended oils. Refit the plug. Run the car for a short distance, allow it to stand for a few minutes, then re-check the level. **Anti-friction additives must not be used in the gearbox or overdrive.**

Fig. 87

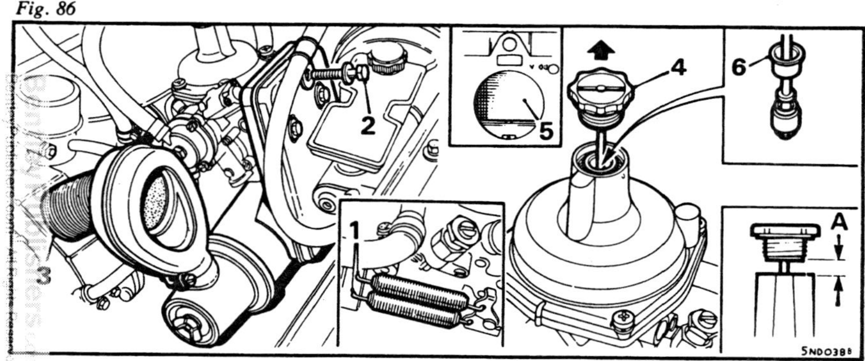

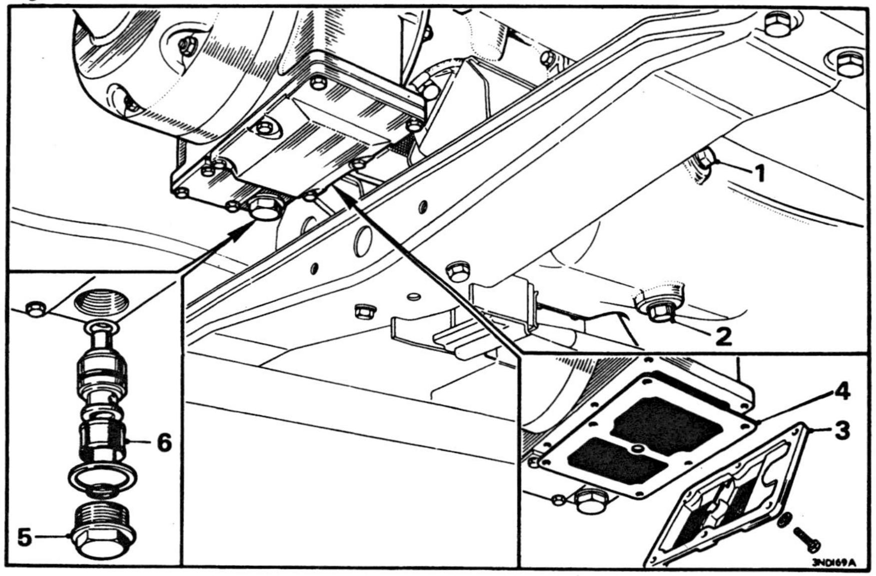

Transmission

REAR AXLE

Checking *Fig. 88* — A combined oil filler and level plug (1) is located on the rear of the axle. The oil level must be maintained at the bottom of the plug aperture; ensure that the car is standing level when checking. After topping-up the oil level, allow sufficient time for any surplus oil which may have been added to run out of the aperture before replacing the plug.

Do not drain the rear axle when the After-sales Service is carried out.

PROPELLER SHAFT

Lubrication *Fig. 89* — A nipple (1) is provided at the front end of the propeller shaft for lubricating the sliding yoke. To lubricate, give three or four strokes of a gun filled with a recommended grease.

Fig. 88

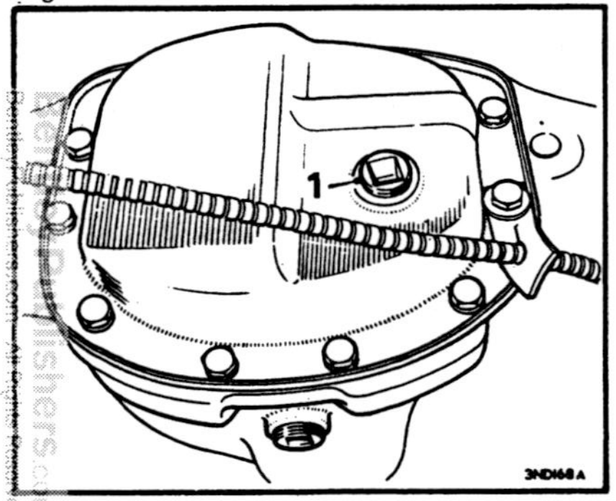

Fig. 89

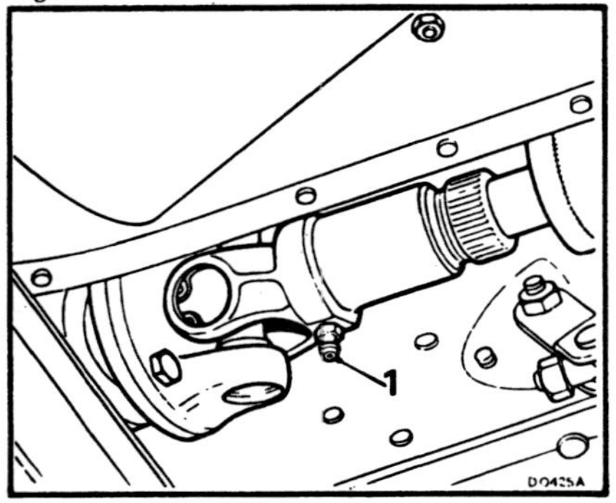

STEERING/SUSPENSION

STEERING

Wheel alignment *Fig. 90* — Incorrect wheel alignment can cause excessive and uneven tyre wear. The front wheels must be set so that the distance 'A' is $\frac{1}{16}$ in. to $\frac{3}{16}$ in. (toe in) less than the distance 'B'.

Wheel alignment requires the use of a special gauge and this work should be entrusted to your authorized Austin MG Dealer.

SUSPENSION

Lubrication *Figs. 91 and 92* — The three lubricating nipples (arrowed) on each of the swivel pins should be charged periodically with one of the recommended greases.

Steering rack — Inspect the gaiters or bellows of the steering rack for leakage of lubricant and deterioration. If leakage of lubricant is evident, consult your authorized Austin MG Dealer.

Fig. 90

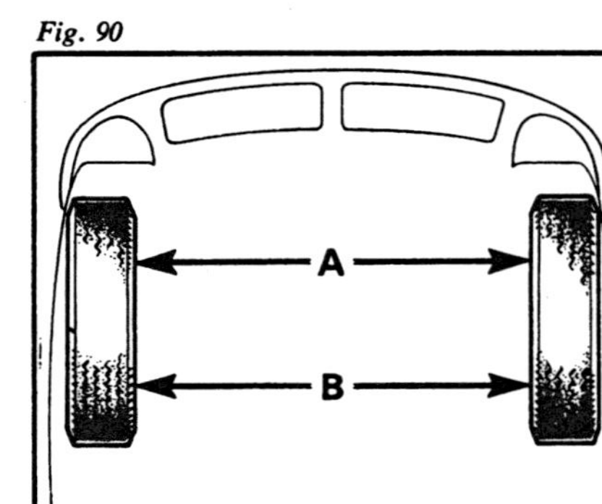

Fig. 91

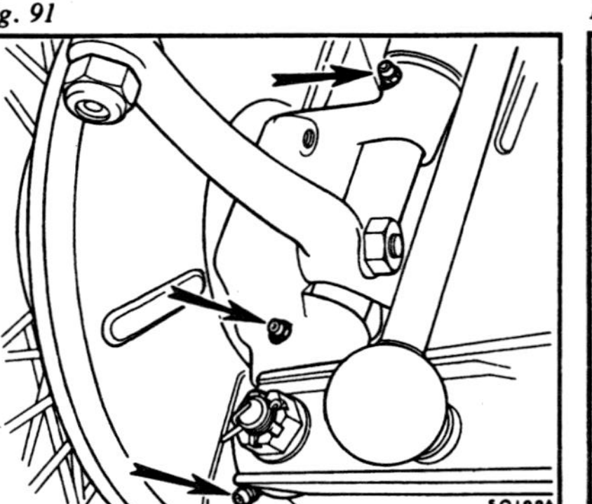

Early cars

Fig. 92

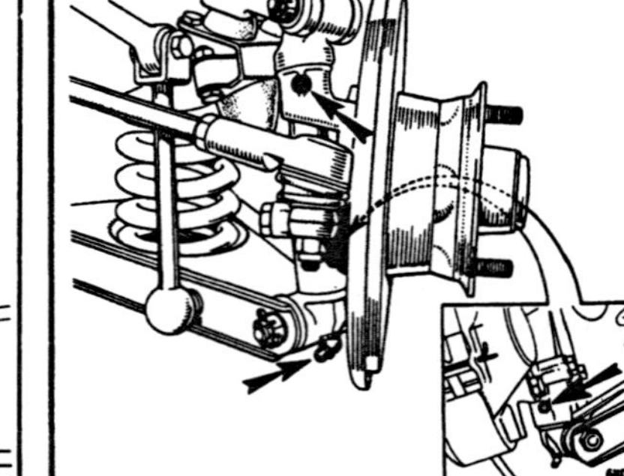

Late cars

GENERAL DATA

During running-in from new certain adjustments vary from the specification figures detailed. They will be set to specification by your authorized Austin MG Dealer at the **After-Sales Service** and should thereafter be maintained throughout the car's life.

Engine

Type (1975)	18V 797AE Standard 18V 798AE Overdrive	
Type (1976)	18V 797AE Standard 18V 798AE Overdrive	
Type (1977 and later)	18V 801AE Standard 18V 802AE Overdrive 18V 883AE, 18V 890AE Standard 18V 884AE, 18V 891AE Overdrive	with catalytic converter (18V 883AE, 18V 890AE, 18V 884AE, 18V 891AE)
Bore	3·16 in	80·3 mm
Stroke	3·5 in	88·9 mm
No. of cylinders	4	
Capacity	110 in³	1798 cc
Compression ratio	8 : 1	
Firing order	1, 3, 4, 2	
Valve rocker clearance—set warm	0·013 in	0·33 mm
Oil pressure: Idling	10 to 25 lbf/in²	0·17 to 1·7 kgf/cm²
Oil pressure: Normal	50 to 80 lbf/in²	3·5 to 5·6 kgf/cm²
Idle speed	850 rev/min	
Exhaust gas content analyser reading at idle speed	5½±1% CO maximum	

Ignition

Distributor (1975–1976)	Lucas type 45D4	
Distributor (1977 and later)	Lucas type 45DE4	
Serial number (1975–1976)	41599	
Serial number (1977 and later)	41693 all States except California 41695 California only	
Stroboscopic ignition timing (cars without catalytic converter)	13° B.T.D.C. at 1500 rev/min	
Stroboscopic ignition timing (cars with catalytic converter)	10° B.T.D.C. at 1500 rev/min	
Timing marks	Notch on crankshaft pulley, pointers on timing chain cover	
Contact breaker gap (1975 and 1976)	0·014–0·016 in	0·36–0·41 mm
Spark plugs	Champion N-9Y	
Plug gap	0·035 in	0·90 mm

Fuel system

Recommended octane rating	See page 10.
Carburetter	Zenith Stromberg type 175 CD5T
Fuel pump	S.U. type AUF 300 electric

Gearbox and overdrive

Overdrive ratio	0·82 : 1	
Overall ratios: First (1975–1976)	11·867 : 1	
First (1977 and later)	13·03 : 1	
Second	8·47 : 1	
Third	5·40 : 1	*Overdrive*
Fourth	3·909 : 1	3·20 : 1
Reverse	12·098 : 1	
Top gear speed per 1,000 rev/min: Standard	18 m.p.h. (29 km/h)	
Overdrive	22 m.p.h. (35 km/h)	

Capacities

Fuel tank (1975–1976)	12 U.S. gal	10 gal	45·4 litres
Fuel tank (1977 and later)	13 U.S. gal	11 gal	50 litres
Cooling system (1975–1976)	11·4 U.S. pt	9½ pt	5·4 litres
Cooling system (1977 and later)	13·8 U.S. pt	11½ pt	6·6 litres
Cooling system with heater (1975–1976)	12 U.S. pt	10 pt	5·6 litres
Cooling system with heater (1977 and later)	14·4 U.S. pt	12 pt	6·8 litres
Engine sump	6 U.S. pt	5¼ pt	3 litres
Engine sump with filter change	7·25 U.S. pt	6 pt	3·4 litres
Gearbox	6 U.S. pt	5 pt	2·84 litres
Gearbox with overdrive	7·25 U.S. pt	6 pt	3·4 litres
Rear axle	2 U.S. pt	1½ pt	0·85 litre

Dimensions

Length	13 ft 2¼ in	4 m
Width	4 ft 11 15/16 in	152·3 cm
Height, hood erected	4 ft 2⅞ in	129·2 cm
Ground clearance (minimum)	4 3/16 in	106 mm
Track: Pressed spoked wheel: Front	4 ft 1½ in	124·7 cm
Rear	4 ft 1¾ in	126·4 cm
Wire wheel: Front	4 ft 1 in	124·4 cm
Rear	4 ft 1¼ in	125 cm
Wheelbase	7 ft 7⅛ in	231·5 cm
Turning circle	32 ft	9·75 m
Toe in	1/16 to 3/32 in	1·5 to 2·3 mm

Wheels and tyres

Wheel size: Pressed spoked	5J FH × 14	
Wire	4½J × 14 (60-spoke)	
Tyres:	*Size*	*Type*
Tourer	165SR—14	Radial-ply (with tube when wire wheels fitted)

Tyre pressures

Condition		Normal driving			Sustained high speed		
		lbf/in²	*kgf/cm²*	*bars*	*lbf/in²*	*kgf/cm²*	*bars*
Normal load	Front	21	1·5	1·45	27	1·9	1·86
	Rear	24	1·7	1·66	30	2·1	2·07
Maximum load	Front	21	1·5	1·45	27	1·9	1·86
	Rear	26	1·8	1·79	32	2·25	2·21

Refer to page 44 for Weights

General Data

Weights (1975–1976)

Loading conditions		Total weight	Distribution	
			Front	*Rear*
Kerbside	Including full fuel tank and all optional extras	2290 lb (1039 kg)	1157 lb (525 kg)	1133 lb (514 kg)
Normal	Kerbside weight including driver and passenger	2590 lb (1174 kg)	1266 lb (574 kg)	1324 lb (600 kg)
Gross	Maximum weight condition, refer to note below	2710 lb (1229 kg)	1242 lb (563 kg)	1468 lb (666 kg)
Maximum permissible towing weight		1680 lb (762 kg)		
Recommended towbar hitch load		100 lb (45 kg)		

Weights (1977 and later)

Loading conditions		Total weight	Distribution	
			Front	*Rear*
Kerbside	Including full fuel tank and all optional extras	2416 lb (1097 kg)	1207 lb (548 kg)	1209 lb (549 kg)
Normal	Kerbside weight including driver and passenger	2716 lb (1234 kg)	1303 lb (591 kg)	1413 lb (641 kg)
Gross	Maximum weight condition, refer to note below	2836 lb (1287 kg)	1279 lb (580 kg)	1557 lb (707 kg)
Maximum permissible towing weight		1680 lb (762 kg)		
Recommended towbar hitch load		100 lb (45 kg)		

NOTE: Due consideration must be given to the overall weight when fully loading the car. Any loads carried on a luggage rack or downward load from a towing hitch must also be included in the maximum loading.

MAINTENANCE SUMMARY

Basic engine tuning data will be found on the Vehicle Emission Control Information label located in the engine compartment.
Detailed maintenance instructions will be found in the appropriate sections of this manual.

The following items should be checked weekly by the driver:
Engine oil level
Brake fluid level
Radiator coolant level
Battery electrolyte level
Windshield washer reservoir fluid level
All tyre pressures
All lights for operation
Horn operation
Windshield wipers operation

MAINTENANCE INTERVALS
†These items are emission related

Service	Mileage × 1000	Monthly intervals
A	1	After Sales Service
B	3, 9, 16, 22, 28, 34, 41, 47	3
C	6, 19, 31, 44	6
D	12·5, 37·5	12
E	25, 50	24

NOTE: The service intervals are based on an annual mileage of approximately 12,500 miles. Should the vehicle complete substantially less miles than this per annum, it is recommended that a 'C' service is completed at six-month intervals, and a 'D' service at twelve-month intervals.

'A' SERVICE

Lubrication
Lubricate all grease points (excluding hubs)
Renew engine oil
Check/top up brake fluid reservoir
Check/top up clutch fluid reservoir
Check/top up battery electrolyte
Check/top up cooling system
Check/top up rear axle
Renew gearbox oil
Gearbox with overdrive, drain, clean filters and refill with new oil
†Lubricate distributor
†Lubricate accelerator control linkage and pedal pivot; check operation
Lubricate all locks and hinges (**not steering lock**)

Engine
†Check driving belts; adjust or renew
Check cooling and heater systems for leaks and hoses for security and condition
†Check crankcase breathing and evaporative loss system. Check hoses/pipes for security
†Check air injection system hoses/pipes for condition and security
Check security of engine mountings
†Check/adjust torque of cylinder head nuts
†Check/adjust valve clearances
†Check security of E.G.R. valve operating line
†Check exhaust system for leaks and security (including manifold nuts)

'A' SERVICE—*continued*

Ignition

†Check ignition wiring for fraying, chafing and deterioration
†Check/adjust ignition timing, using electronic equipment

Fuel system

†Check fuel system for leaks, pipes and unions for chafing and corrosion
†Top up carburetter piston damper
†Check/adjust carburetter idle settings

Safety

Check/adjust operation of all washers and top up reservoir
Check/adjust tyre pressures, including spare
Check tightness of road wheel fastenings
Check condition and security of steering unit, joints and gaiters
Check security of suspension fixings
Check steering rack and suspension for oil/fluid leaks
Check brake servo hose for security and condition
Check/adjust foot and hand brake
Check visually hydraulic pipes and unions for chafing, leaks and corrosion
Check/adjust front wheel alignment
Check function of original equipment, i.e. interior and exterior lamps, horns, wipers and warning indicators
Check/adjust headlamp alignment
Check operation of all door, bonnet and luggage compartment locks
Check operation of window controls
Check condition and security of seats and seat belts

Road test

Road/roller test and check function of all instrumentation

'B' SERVICE

Lubrication

Lubricate all grease points (excluding hubs)
Check/top up engine oil
Check/top up brake fluid reservoir
Check/top up clutch fluid reservoir
Check/top up battery electrolyte
Check/top up cooling system
Check/top up gearbox and rear axle oils

Engine

†Check alternator drive belt; adjust or renew
Check cooling and heater systems for leaks and hoses for security and condition
†Check exhaust system for leaks and security

'B' SERVICE—*continued*

Fuel system

†Check fuel system for leaks, pipes and unions for chafing and corrosion

Safety

Check/adjust operation of all washers and top up reservoir
Check tyres for tread depth and visually for external cuts in fabric, exposure of ply or cord structure, bumps or bulges
Check that tyres comply with manufacturer's specification
Check/adjust tyre pressures, including spare
Check tightness of road wheel fastenings
Check condition and security of steering unit, joints and gaiters
Check steering rack and suspension for oil/fluid leaks
Check/adjust foot and hand brake
Check visually hydraulic pipes and unions for chafing, leaks and corrosion
Check function of original equipment, i.e. interior and exterior lamps, horns, wipers and warning indicators
Check, if necessary renew, wiper blades
Check/adjust headlamp alignment
Check condition and security of seats and seat belts

Road test

Report additional work required

'C' SERVICE

Lubrication

Lubricate all grease points (excluding hubs)
Renew engine oil and filter
Check/top up brake fluid reservoir
Check/top up clutch fluid reservoir
Check/top up battery electrolyte
Check/top up cooling system
Check/top up gearbox and rear axle oils
†Lubricate distributor
†Lubricate accelerator control linkage and pedal pivot; check operation
Lubricate all locks and hinges (**not steering lock**)

Engine

†Check alternator drive belt; adjust or renew
Check cooling and heater systems for leaks and hoses for security and condition
†Check exhaust system for leaks and security

Ignition

†Clean/adjust spark plugs

Fuel system

†Check fuel system for leaks, pipes and unions for chafing and corrosion

'C' SERVICE—*continued*

Safety

Check/adjust operation of all washers and top up reservoir
Check tyres for tread depth, and visually for external cuts in fabric, exposure of ply or cord structure, bumps or bulges
Check that tyres comply with manufacturer's specification
Check/adjust tyre pressures, including spare
Check tightness of road wheel fastenings
Check condition and security of steering unit, joints and gaiters
Check security of suspension fixings
Check steering rack and suspension for oil/fluid leaks
Inspect brake pads for wear, discs for condition
Check brake servo hose for security and condition
Check/adjust foot and hand brake
Check visually hydraulic pipes and unions for chafing, leaks and corrosion
Check/adjust front wheel alignment
Check output of charging system
Check function of original equipment, i.e. interior and exterior lamps, horns, wipers and warning indicators
Check, if necessary renew, wiper blades
Check/adjust headlamp alignment
Check operation of all door, bonnet and luggage compartment locks
Check condition and security of seats and seat belts

Road test

Road/roller test and check operation of all instrumentation
Report additional work required

Brakes

It is further recommended that at 19,000 miles (or 18 months) the brake fluid is renewed. This additional work should be carried out by your authorized Austin MG Dealer

'D' SERVICE

Lubrication

Lubricate all grease points (excluding hubs)
Renew engine oil and filter
Check/top up brake fluid reservoir
Check/top up clutch fluid reservoir
Check/top up battery electrolyte
Check/top up cooling system
Check/top up gearbox and rear axle oils
†Lubricate distributor
Lubricate accelerator control linkage and pedal pivot, check operation
Lubricate all locks and hinges (**not steering lock**)

'D' SERVICE—*continued*

Engine

†Check driving belts, adjust or renew
Check cooling and heater systems for leaks and hoses for security and condition
†Renew carburetter air cleaner element
†Renew air pump air filter element
†Check gulp valve and check valve operation
†Check air injection system hoses/pipes for condition and security
†Check air intake temperature control system
†Check crankcase breathing and evaporative loss systems. Check hoses/pipes and restrictors for blockage, security and condition
†Check/adjust valve clearances
†Check exhaust system for leaks and security

Ignition

†Check ignition wiring for fraying, chafing and deterioration
†Renew spark plugs
†Clean distributor cap; check for cracks and tracking
†Check/adjust ignition timing, using electronic equipment

Fuel system

†Renew fuel filter
†Check fuel system for leaks, pipes and unions for chafing and corrosion
†Top up carburetter piston damper
†Check/adjust carburetter idle settings
†Check condition of fuel filler cap seal

Safety

Check/adjust operation of all washers and top up reservoir
Check tyres for tread depth and visually for external cuts in fabric, exposure of ply or cord structure, bumps or bulges
Check that tyres comply with manufacturers' specification
Check/adjust tyre pressures, including spare
Check tightness of road wheel fastenings
Check condition and security of steering unit, joints and gaiters
Check security of suspension fixings
Check steering rack and suspension for oil/fluid leaks
Inspect brake linings/pads for wear, drums/discs for condition
Check brake servo hose for security and condition
Check/adjust foot and hand brake
Check visually hydraulic pipes and unions for chafing, leaks and corrosion
Check/adjust front wheel alignment
Check output of charging system
Check function of original equipment, i.e. interior and exterior lamps, horns, wipers and warning indicators
Check, if necessary renew, wiper blades
Check/adjust headlamp alignment
Check operation of all door, bonnet and luggage compartment locks
Check operation of window controls
Check condition and security of seats and seat belts

'D' SERVICE—*continued*

Road test
Road/roller test and check function of all instrumentation
Report additional work required

Brakes
It is further recommended that every 37,500 miles (or 3 years) the brake fluid, hydraulic seals and hoses in the brake and clutch hydraulic systems are renewed. Examine working surfaces of pistons and bores in master, slave, and wheel cylinders and renew parts as necessary. Renew brake servo filter. This additional work should be carried out by your authorized Austin MG Dealer.

'E' SERVICE

Lubrication
Lubricate all grease points (excluding hubs)
Renew engine oil and filter
Check/top up brake fluid reservoir
Check/top up clutch fluid reservoir
Check/top up battery electrolyte
Check/top up cooling system
Check/top up gearbox (non-overdrive) and rear axle oils
Gearbox with overdrive, drain, clean filters and refill with new oil
†Lubricate distributor
†Lubricate accelerator control linkage and pedal pivot, check operation
Lubricate all locks and hinges (**not steering lock**)

Engine
†Check driving belts; adjust or renew
Check cooling and heater systems for leaks and hoses for security and condition
†Renew carburetter air cleaner element
†Renew air pump air filter element
†Check gulp valve and check valve operation
†Check air injection system hoses/pipes for condition and security
†Check air intake temperature control system
†Check crankcase breathing and evaporative loss systems. Check hoses/pipes and restrictors for blockage, security and condition
†Check/adjust valve clearances
†Renew adsorption canister
†Check exhaust system for leaks and security

Ignition
†Check ignition wiring for fraying, chafing and deterioration
†Renew spark plugs
†Clean distributor cap; check for cracks and tracking
†Check/adjust ignition timing, using electronic equipment

'E' SERVICE—*continued*

Fuel system
†Renew fuel filter
†Check fuel system for leaks, pipes and unions for chafing and corrosion
†Top up carburetter piston damper
†Check/adjust carburetter idle settings
†Check condition of fuel filler cap seal

Safety
Check/adjust operation of all washers and top up reservoir
Check tyres for tread depth and visually for external cuts in fabric, exposure of ply or cord structure, bumps or bulges
Check that tyres comply with manufacturer's specification
Check/adjust tyre pressures, including spare
Check tightness of road wheel fastenings
Check condition and security of steering unit, joints and gaiters
Check security of suspension fixings
Check steering rack and suspension for oil/fluid leaks
Inspect brake linings/pads for wear, drum/discs for condition
Check brake servo hose for security and condition
Check/adjust front wheel alignment.
Check/adjust foot and hand brake
Check visually hydraulic pipes and unions for chafing, leaks and corrosion
Check output of charging system
Check function of original equipment, i.e. interior and exterior lamps, horns, wipers and warning indicators
Check, if necessary renew, wiper blades
Check/adjust headlamp alignment
Check operation of all door, bonnet and luggage compartment locks
Check operation of window controls
Check condition and security of seats and seat belts

Road test
Road/roller test and check function of all instrumentation
Report additional work required

LUBRICATION

The lubrication systems of your new car are filled with high quality oils. You should always use a high quality oil of the correct viscosity range in the engine, gearbox and rear axle during subsequent maintenance operations or when topping up. The use of oils not to the correct specification can lead to high oil and fuel consumption and ultimately do damage to the engine, gearbox or rear axle components.

Oils to the correct specification contain additives which disperse the corrosive acids formed by combustion and also prevent the formation of sludge which can block oilways. **Additional oil additives should not be used.** Servicing intervals must be adhered to.

Engine Use a well known brand of oil to B.L.S. O.L. O.2 or MIL-L-2104B or A.P.I, SE quality, with a viscosity band spanning the temperature range of your locality.

SAE Viscosity

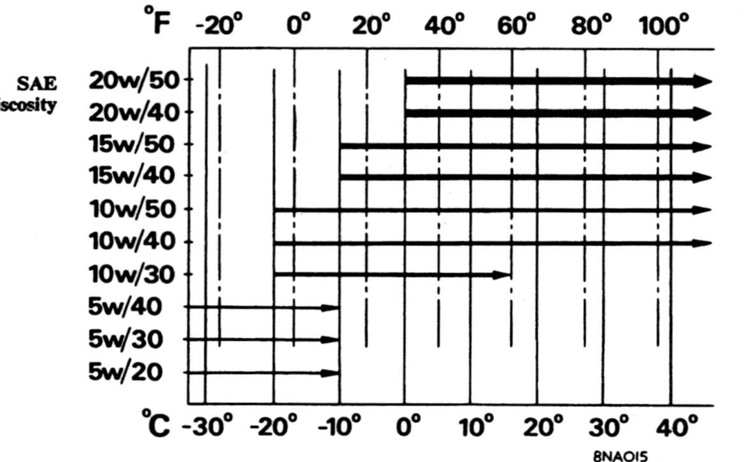

Synchromesh gearbox Use the same oil selected for the engine.

NOTE: SAE 90 Hypoid oil is also suitable for use in the gearbox, with or without overdrive. However, if the gearbox contains one kind of lubricant, for example engine oil, it should be thoroughly drained before Hypoid oil is added to the gearbox.

Rear axle and steering rack Top up and refill with H.D. 90 (MIL-L-2105B) above −10°C (10°F) or H.D. 80 (MIL-L-2105B) below −5°C (20°F).

Grease points Use Multipurpose Lithium Grease N.L.G.I. consistency No. 2.

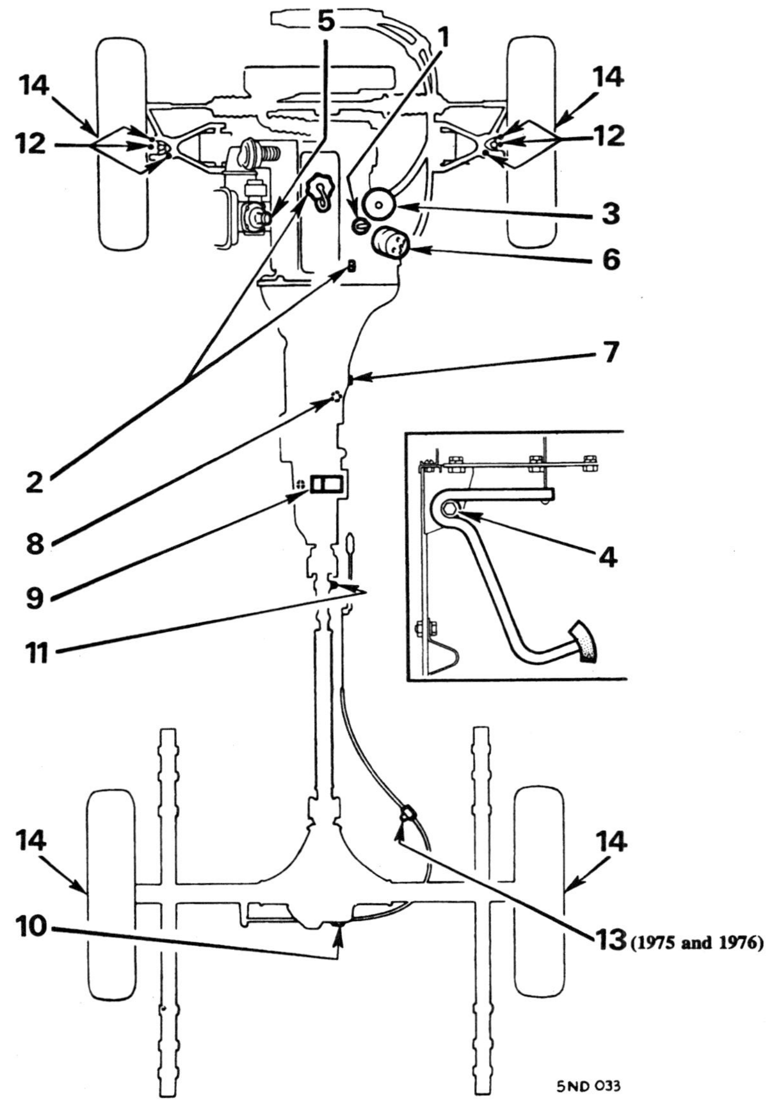

NOTE: Ensure that the vehicle is standing on a level surface when checking the oil levels.

WEEKLY

(1) ENGINE. Check oil level, and top up if necessary.

'A' SERVICE

(2) ENGINE. Drain and refill with new oil.
(4) THROTTLE. Lubricate throttle control linkage, cable and accelerator pedal fulcrum.
(5) CARBURETTER. Top up carburetter piston damper.
(6) DISTRIBUTOR. Lubricate all parts as necessary.
(8) GEARBOX (NON OVERDRIVE). Drain and refill with new oil.
(9) GEARBOX WITH OVERDRIVE. Drain, clean overdrive filters, refill with new oil—refer to page 41.
(10) REAR AXLE. Check oil level, and top up if necessary.
(11) PROPELLER SHAFT (1 nipple)
(12) FRONT SUSPENSION (6 nipples)
(13) HAND BRAKE CABLE (1 nipple) [1975–1976 only]
} Give three or four strokes with a grease gun.
(14) WIRE WHEELS. Lubricate wire wheel and hub splines.
LOCKS, HINGES AND LINKAGES. Lubricate all door, bonnet, boot locks and hinges (not steering lock), and hand brake mechanical linkage.
FRICTION POINTS. Spray lubricant on all friction points.

'B' SERVICE

(1) ENGINE. Check oil level, and top up if necessary.
(7) GEARBOX. Check oil level, and top up if necessary.
(10) REAR AXLE. Check oil level, and top up if necessary.
(11) PROPELLER SHAFT (1 nipple)
(12) FRONT SUSPENSION (6 nipples)
(13) HAND BRAKE CABLE (1 nipple) [1975–1976 only]
} Give three or four strokes with a grease gun.
(14) WIRE WHEELS ONLY. Grease wheel and hub splines.
FRICTION POINTS. Spray lubricant on all friction points.

'C' AND 'D' SERVICES

(2) ENGINE. Drain and refill with new oil.
(3) ENGINE OIL FILTER. Remove disposable cartridge; fit new.
(4) THROTTLE. Lubricate throttle control linkage, cable and accelerator pedal fulcrum.
(5) CARBURETTER. Top up carburetter piston damper—'D' SERVICE only.
(6) DISTRIBUTOR. Lìbricate all parts as necessary.
(7) GEARBOX. Check oil level, and top up if necessary.
(10) REAR AXLE. Check oil level, and top up if necessary.
(11) PROPELLER SHAFT (1 nipple)
(12) FRONT SUSPENSION (6 nipples)
(13) HAND BRAKE CABLE (1 nipple) [1975–1976 only]
} Give three or four strokes with a grease gun.
(14) WIRE WHEELS ONLY. Grease wheel and hub splines.
LOCKS, HINGES AND LINKAGES. Lubricate all door, bonnet, boot locks and hinges (not steering lock); and the hand brake mechanical linkage.
FRICTION POINTS. Spray lubricant on all friction points.

'E' SERVICE

Carry out a 'D' SERVICE in addition to the following:
(9) GEARBOX WITH OVERDRIVE. Drain, clean overdrive filters, refill with new oil—refer to page 41.

SERVICE

Identification *Fig. 93*

When communicating with your Distributor or Dealer always quote the car and engine numbers. When the communication concerns the transmission units or body details it is necessary to quote also the transmission casing and body numbers.

(1) **Car number.** Stamped on a plate secured to the left-hand door post, and to a plate secured to the top of the fascia.

(2) **Engine number.** Stamped on a plate secured to the right-hand side of the cylinder block.

Service parts

Genuine BRITISH LEYLAND and UNIPART parts are designed and tested for your vehicle and have the full backing of the British Leyland Factory Warranty.

Genuine British Leyland and UNIPART parts are supplied in cartons and packs bearing either or both of these symbols.

British Leyland Motors Inc.

600 Willow Tree Road, Leonia

New Jersey 07605

Telephone: (201) 461/7300 *Telex:* 135491

Fig. 93

MGB CONVERTIBLE WORKSHOP MANUAL 1975-1980

PART 2

INTRODUCTION

The purpose of this manual is to assist skilled mechanics in the efficient repair and maintenance of British Leyland vehicles.

MANUAL ARRANGEMENT

The first part of the Manual includes the General Specification Data, Engine Tuning Data, General Fitting Instructions, Service Lubricants and Maintenance.

A Service Tools section is featured towards the end of the Manual.

The remainder of the manual is divided into sections and each section carries a reference letter that identifies the section with an assembly or a major component. Each section is preceded by a contents page and is sub-divided numerically. The pages and illustrations are numbered consecutively within each section and the section title and letter are shown at the top of each page.

REFERENCES

References to the left- or right-hand side in the manual are made when viewing the vehicle from the rear. With the engine and gearbox assembly removed, the water pump end of the engine is referred to as the front.

To reduce repetition, operations covered in this manual do not include reference to testing the vehicle after repair. It is essential that work is inspected and tested after completion and if necessary a road test of the vehicle is carried out particularly where safety related items are concerned.

DIMENSIONS

The dimensions quoted are to design engineering specification. Alternative unit equivalents, shown in brackets following the dimensions, have been converted from the original specification.

REPAIRS AND REPLACEMENTS

When replacements are required it is essential that only genuine **British Leyland** or **Unipart** parts are used.

Attention is particularly drawn to the following points concerning repairs and the fitting of replacement parts and accessories:

Safety features embodied in the car may be impaired if other than genuine parts are fitted. In certain territories, legislation prohibits the fitting of parts not to the vehicle manufacturer's specification.

Torque wrench setting figures given in the Manual must be strictly adhered to.

Locking devices, where specified, must be fitted. If the efficiency of a locking device is impaired during removal it must be renewed.

Owners purchasing accessories while travelling abroad should ensure that the accessory and its fitted location on the car conform to mandatory requirements existing in their country of origin. **The car warranty may be invalidated by the fitting of other than genuine British Leyland parts.**

All **British Leyland** or **Unipart** replacements have the full backing of the factory warranty.

SPECIFICATION

British Leyland UK Limited is constantly seeking ways to improve the specification of its vehicles and alterations take place continually. While every effort is made to produce up-to-date literature this Manual should not be regarded as an infallible guide to current specifications. Further the specification details set out in this Manual apply to a range of vehicles and not to any particular one.

Distributors and Dealers are not agents of British Leyland UK Limited and have absolutely no authority to bind British Leyland UK Limited by any express or implied undertaking or representation.

[**NOTE:** Any material added to this Workshop Manual by Robert Bentley, Inc. has been indicated by use of brackets ([ ]). Updated information has been indicated by the addition of a source reference at the bottom of the appropriate page.]

CONTENTS

ENGINE

Type (1975)	18V 797AE Standard 18V 798AE Overdrive
Type (1976)	18V 797AE Standard 18V 798AE Overdrive
Type (1977 and later)	18V 801AE Standard 18V 802AE Overdrive 18V 883AE, 18V 890AE Standard 18V 884AE, 18V 891AE Overdrive (18V 801AE to 18V 891AE: with Catalytic Converter)
Number of cylinders	4.
Bore	3.16 in. (80.26 mm).
Stroke	3.5 in. (89 mm.).
Capacity	1798 c.c. (109.8 cu. in.).
Firing order	1, 3, 4, 2.
Valve operation	Overhead by push-rod.
Compression ratio	8.0 : 1
Compression pressure	130 lb./sq. in. (9.15 kg./cm.²).
Torque	105 lb. ft. (14.5 kg. m.) at 3,000 r.p.m.
Engine idle speed (approx.)	850 r.p.m.
Oversize bore: First	.010 in. (.254 mm.).
Oversize bore: Max.	.040 in. (1.016 mm.).

Crankshaft

Main journal diameter	2.1262 to 2.127 in. (54.01 to 54.02 mm.).
Crankpin journal diameter	1.8759 to 1.8764 in. (47.648 to 47.661 mm.).
Crankshaft end-thrust	Taken on thrust washers at centre main bearing.
Crankshaft end-float	.004 to .005 in. (.10 to .13 mm.).

Main bearings

Number and type	Five thinwall.
Length: Front, centre and rear	1⅛ in. (28.5 mm.).
Length: Intermediate	⅞ in. (22.23 mm.).
Diametrical clearance	.001 to .0027 in. (.0254 to .068 mm.).
Undersizes	–.010, –.020, –.030 and –.040 in. (–.254, –.508, –.762 and –1.016 mm.).

Connecting rods

Type	Horizontal-split big-end.
Length between centres	6.5 in. (165.1 mm.).
Locking method–big-end	Multi-sided nut.

Big-end bearings

Type	Shell.
Length	.775 to .785 in. (19.68 to 19.94 mm.).
Diametrical clearance	.001 to .0027 in. (0254 to .068 mm.).
Undersizes	–.010, –.020, –.030 and –.040 in. (–.254, –.508, –.762 and –1.016 mm.).
End-float on crankpin (nominal)	.008 to .012 in. (.20 to .30 mm.).

Pistons

Type	Aluminium solid skirt, three rings.
Clearance of skirt in cylinder: Top	.0021 to .0033 in. (.053 to .084 mm.).
Clearance of skirt in cylinder: Bottom	.0006 to .0012 in. (.015 to .030 mm.).
Number of rings	Three; 2 compression. 1 oil control.
Width of ring grooves: Compression	.064 to .065 in. (1.625 to 1.651 mm.).
Width of ring grooves: Oil control	.1578 to .1588 in. (4.01 to 4.033 mm.).
Gudgeon pin bore	.8126 to .8129 in. (20.610 to 20.167 mm.).

Piston rings

Type: Compression: Top	Plain, sintered alloy.
Second	Tapered, sintered alloy—marked 'TOP'.
Oil control	Two chrome-faced rings with expander, Apex.
Fitted gap: Compression	.012 to .022 in. (.305 to .600 mm.).
Oil control	.015 to .045 in. (.38 to 1.14 mm.).
Width: Compression	.0615 to .0625 in. (1.56 to 1.59 mm.).
Oil control	.152 to .158 in. (3.86 to 4.01 mm.).
Thickness: Compression: Top	.124 to .127 in. (3.14 to 3.22 mm.).
Second	.104 to .111 in. (2.64 to 2.81 mm.).
Ring to groove clearance: Compression	.0015 to .0035 in. (.038 to .088 mm.).
Oil control	.0016 to .0036 in. (.04 to .09 mm.).

Gudgeon pin

Type	Press fit in connecting rod.
Fit in: Piston	Hand push-fit at 16°C. (60°F.)
Small end	12 lb. ft. (1.7 kg.m.) minimum using 18G 1150 and adaptor type C.
Diameter (outer)	.7499 to .7501 in. (19.04 to 19.05 mm.).

Camshaft

Journal diameters: Front	1.78875 to 1.78925 in. (45.424 to 45.437 mm.).
Centre	1.72875 to 1.72925 in. (43.910 to 43.923 mm.).
Rear	1.62275 to 1.62325 in. (41.218 to 41.230 mm.).
Bearing liner inside diameter (reamed after fitting): Front	1.79025 to 1.79075 in. (45.472 to 45.485 mm.).
Centre	1.73025 to 1.73075 in. (43.948 to 43.961 mm.).
Rear	1.62425 to 1.62475 in. (41.256 to 41.269 mm.).
Diametrical clearance	.001 to .002 in. (.0254 to .0508 mm.).
End-thrust	Taken on locating plate.
End-float	.003 to .007 in. (.076 to .178 mm.).
Cam lift	.250 in. (6.35 mm.).
Drive	Chain and sprocket from crankshaft.
Timing chain	$\frac{3}{8}$ in. (9.52 mm.). pitch x 52 links.

Tappets

Type	Barrel with flat base.
Outside diameter	$\frac{13}{16}$ in. (20.64 mm.).
Length	2.293 to 2.303 in. (58.25 to 58.5 mm.).

Rocker gear

ROCKER SHAFT	
Length	14$\frac{1}{32}$ in. (.356 mm.).
Diameter	.624 to .625 in. (15.85 to 15.87 mm.).
ROCKER ARM	
Bore	.7485 to .7495 in. (19.01 to 19.26 mm.).
Rocker arm bush inside diameter	.6255 to .626 in. (15.8 to 15.9 mm.).
Ratio	1.4 : 1.

Valves

Seat angle: Inlet and exhaust	45½°
Head diameter: Inlet	1.562 to 1.567 in. (39.67 to 39.80 mm.).
Exhaust	1.343 to 1.348 in. (34.11 to 34.23 mm.).
Stem diameter: Inlet	0.3429 to 0.3434 in. (8.70 to 8.72 mm.).
Exhaust	0.3423 to 0.3428 in. (8.69 to 8.70 mm.).
Stem to guide clearance: Inlet	0.0007 to 0.0019 in. (0.020 to 0.050 mm.).
Exhaust	0.0013 to 0.0025 in. (0.03 to 0.06 mm.).
Valve lift: Inlet and exhaust	0.3645 in (9.25 mm.).

Valve guides

Length: Inlet	$1\frac{7}{8}$ in. (47.63 mm.).
Exhaust	$2\frac{13}{64}$ in. (55.95 mm.).
Outside diameter: Inlet and exhaust	.5635 to .5640 in. (14.30 to 14.32 mm.).
Inside diameter: Inlet and exhaust	.3442 to .3447 in. (8.73 to 8.74 mm.).
Fitted height above head: Inlet	¾ in. (19 mm.).
Exhaust	$\frac{5}{8}$ in. (15.875 mm.).
Interference fit in head: Inlet and exhaust	.0005 to .00175 in. (.012 to .044 mm.).

Valve springs

Free length	1.92 in. (48.77 mm.).
Fitted length	1.44 in. (36.58 mm.).
Load at fitted length	82 lb. (37.2 kg.).
Load at top of lift	142 lb. (64.4 kg.).
Valve crash speed	6,200 r.p.m.

Valve timing

Timing marks	Dimples on camshaft and crankshaft wheels.
Rocker clearance: Running	.013 in. (.33 mm.) warm
Timing	.055 in. (1.4 mm.).
Inlet valve: Opens	16° B.T.D.C.
Closes	56° A.B.D.C.
Exhaust valve: Opens	51° B.B.D.C.
Closes	21° A.T.D.C.

ENGINE LUBRICATION

System	Wet sump, pressure fed.
System pressure: Running	Between 50 and 80 lb./sq. in. (3.51 and 5.6 kg./cm.^{2}).
Idling	Between 10 and 25 lb./sq. in. (.7 and 1.7 kg./cm.^{2}).
Oil pump	Hobourn-Eaton or eccentric rotor.
Capacity	4 U.S. gal./min. at 2,000 r.p.m.
Oil filter	Tecalemit full-flow felt element.
By-pass valve opens	13 to 17 lb./sq. in. (.9 to 1.1 kg./cm.^{2}).
Oil pressure relief valve	70 lb./sq. in. (4.9 kg./cm.^{2}).
Relief valve spring: Free length	3 in. (76.2 mm.).
Fitted length	$2\frac{5}{32}$ in. (54.7 mm.).
Load at fitted length	15.5 to 16.5 lb. (7.0 to 7.4 kg.).

FUEL SYSTEM

Carburetter	See '**ENGINE TUNING DATA**'.
Air cleaner	Paper element.

Fuel pump

Type	S.U. electric AUF 300.
Minimum flow	15 gal./hr. (68.2 litre/hr. 18 U.S. gal./hr.).
Suction head	18 in. (457 mm.).
Delivery head	4 ft. (122 cm.).
Minimum starting voltage	9.5 volts.

COOLING SYSTEM

Type	Pressurized. Pump-impeller- and fan-assisted.
Thermostat setting	
Standard	82°C. (180°F.).
Cold climate	88°C. (190°F.).
Pressure cap	10 lb. (4.54 kg.)—1977 and later: 15 lb. (6.8 kg).
Fan belt: Width	15/32 in. (11.9 mm.).
Length	37.38 in. (94.9 cm.) at ⅜ in. width equivalent.
Thickness	27/64 in. (10.7 mm.).
Tension	½ in. (12.8 mm.) movement at midway of longest run.
Type of pump	Centrifugal.
Pump drive	Belt from crankshaft pulley.

IGNITION SYSTEM

Coil	See 'ENGINE TUNING DATA'.
Distributor	See 'ENGINE TUNING DATA'.

CLUTCH

Make and type	Borg & Beck 8 in. DS.G. diaphragm spring.
Diaphragm spring colour	Dark blue.
Clutch plate diameter	8 in. (20.32 cm.).
Facing material	Wound yarn.
Number of damper springs	6.
Damper spring load	110 to 120 lb. (49.8 to 54.3 kg.).
Damper spring colour	Black/light green.
Clutch release bearing	Graphite (MY3D).

GEARBOX AND OVERDRIVE

Number of forward gears	4.	
Synchromesh	All forward gears.	
Gearbox ratios: Reverse	3.095 : 1.	
First	3.036 : 1—1977 and later: 3.333 : 1.	
Second	2.167 : 1.	
Third	1.382 : 1.	
Fourth	1.000 : 1.	
Overdrive: Type	Laycock L.H.	
Ratio	.82 : 1.	
Overall gear ratios: Reverse	12.098 : 1.	
First	11.867 : 1— 1977 and later: 13.03 : 1.	
Second	8.47 : 1.	OVERDRIVE
Third	5.4 : 1	4.43 : 1.
Fourth	3.909 : 1	3.2 : 1.
Top gear speed per 1,000 r.p.m.: Standard	18 m.p.h. (29 km.p.h).	
Overdrive	22 m.p.h. (35 km.p.h.).	
Speedometer gear ratio: Standard	10 : 26.	
Overdrive	8 : 21.	
Synchromesh hub springs: Free length	.72 in. (18.3 mm.).	
Fitted length	.385 in. (9.8 mm.).	
Load at fitted length	5.5 to 6 lb. (2.5 to 2.7 kg.).	
First and third speed gear end-float	.005 to .008 in. (.13 to .20 mm.).	
Second gear end-float	.005 to .008 in. (.13 to .20 mm.).	
Laygear end-float	.002 to .003 in. (.05 to .08 mm.).	

PROPELLER SHAFT

Type	Open tubular, telescopic.
Universal joints	Hardy Spicer needle roller.
Angular movement	18° to 20°.
Overall length: Fully extended: Standard	30¾ in. (78.1 cm.).
Overdrive	31 7/8 in. (81 cm.).
Fully compressed: Standard	29 1/16 in. (74 cm.).
Overdrive	30 3/16 in. (76.5 cm.).
Length of shaft assembly: Standard	25 11/32 in. (64.3 cm.).
Overdrive	26 15/32 in. (67 cm.).
Tube diameter	2 in. (50.8 mm.).

REAR AXLE

Type	Hypoid, semi-floating.
Ratio	3.909 : 1 (11/43).
Differential bearing preload	.002 in. (.05 mm.) 'nip' per bearing.
Pinion bearing preload	Refer to Section H.
Backlash adjustment: Crown wheel	Shims.
Pinion	Head washer.

STEERING

Type	Rack and pinion.
Steering-wheel diameter	16½ in. (419.10 mm.) 1977 and later: 14½ in. (368.30 mm).
Turns—lock to lock	2.93—1977 and later: 3.57.
Turning circle	32 ft. (9.75 m.).
Universal joint	Hardy Spicer KO518, GB166.
Damper end-float	.0005 to .003 in. (.012 to .076 mm.) (unladen).
Toe-in.	1/16 to 3/32 in. (1.5 to 2.3 mm.) (unladen).
Angle of inner wheel with outer wheel at 20°	19°±1°.

FRONT SUSPENSION

Type	Independent. Coil spring and wishbone.
Spring: Coil diameter (mean)	3.238 in. (82.2 mm.).
Free height	10.20±0.06 in. (259.08±1.5 mm.).
Static length at 1,030 lb. (467.2 kg.) load	7.44 in. (188.98 mm.).
Number of effective coils	9.
Camber angle	Nominal 1° positive (+¼°, −1¼°) =1¼° positive, ¼° negative (unladen).
Castor angle	Nominal 7° (+¼°, −2°)=5° to 7¼° (unladen).
King pin inclination	Nominal 8° (+1°, −¾°)=7¼° to 9° (unladen).
Dampers	Armstrong piston type.
Arm centres	8 in. (203.2 mm.).
Wheel bearing end-float	.002 to .004 in. (.05 to .10 mm.).

REAR SUSPENSION

Type	Semi-elliptic leaf spring.
Number of spring leaves	6+ bottom plate. Interleaving 1/2, 2/3.
Width of spring leaves	1¾ in. (44.4 mm.).
Gauge of leaves	3 at 7/32 in. (5.6 mm.), 3 at 3/16 in. (4.8 mm.).
Working load (± 15 lb. [7 kg.])	450 lb. (204.1 kg.).
Dampers	Armstrong piston type.
Arm centres	5¼ in. (133 mm.).

ELECTRICAL

System	12-volt, NEGATIVE earth.	

Battery

Type	Lucas CP11	Lucas CP13/11
Capacity: 20-hour rate	66 amp.-hour	68 amp.-hour
Plates per cell	11	13
Electrolyte to fill one cell	1 pint (570 c.c., 1.2 U.S. pints).	

Alternator

Type	Lucas 18ACR
Output at 14 volts and 6,000 r.p.m.	43 amps.
Maximum permissible rotor speed	15,000 r.p.m.
Stator phases	3.
Rotor poles	12.
Rotor winding resistance	3.201 ohms ± 5% at 20°C. (68°F.).

Starter motor	2M100 Pre-engaged.
Lock torque	14.4 lb. ft. (2.02 kg. m.) at 463 amps.
Torque at 1,000 r.p.m.	7.3 lb. ft. (1.02 kg. m.) at 300 amps.
Brush spring tension	36 oz. (1.02 kg.).
Minimum brush length	⅜ in. (9.5 mm.).
Minimum commutator thickness	0.140 in. (3.5 mm.).
Light running current	40 amp. at 6,000 r.p.m. (approx.).
Maximum armature end-float	0.010 in. (0.25 mm.).
Solenoid: Closing (series) winding resistance	0.25 to 0.27 ohm.
Hold-on (shunt) winding resistance	0.76 to 0.80 ohm.

Wiper motor	Lucas 14W (two-speed).
Drive to wheelboxes	Rack and cable.
Armature end-float	.004 to .008 in. (.1 to .21 mm.).
Light running current: Normal speed	1.5 amp.
High speed	2.0 amp.
Light running speed: Normal speed	46 to 52 r.p.m.
High speed	60 to 70 r.p.m.

Horns

Type	9H 12-volt.

BRAKES

Type	Lockheed hydraulic. Disc front, drum rear.

Front

Disc diameter	10¾ in. (27.3 cm.).
Pad material	Don 55–FF.
Swept area	203.2 sq. in. (1311 cm.^{2}).

Rear

Drum diameter	10 in. (25.4 cm.).
Lining material	Don 24–FE.
Swept area	106.8 sq. in. (683.9 cm.^{2}).
Lining dimensions	9$\frac{7}{16}$x1¾x $\frac{3}{16}$ in. (240x44.4x4.76 mm.).

WHEELS

Type .. .. Pressed spoked, 4-stud fixing.
Wire (optional).

Size: Pressed spoked .. .. 5J FH x 14.
Wire .. .. 4½J x 14.

TYRES .. .. 165 SR–14 Radial-ply.

TYRE PRESSURES

Condition	Front			Rear		
	lbf/in²	*kgf/cm²*	*bars*	*lbf/in²*	*kgf/cm²*	*bars*
Normal car weight	21	1.48	1.45	24	1.69	1.66
Gross car weight and sustained speed	21	1.48	1.45	26	1.83	1.79

It is recommended that for sustained speeds at near maximum the above tyre pressures are increased by 6 lbf/in² (0.42 kgf/cm², 0.32 bars).

[**NOTE:** Please also refer to the Tyre Pressures Chart given on page 43 of the Driver's Handbook.]

DIMENSIONS

Overall length .. .. 13 ft. 2¼ in. (4 m.).
Overall width .. .. 4 ft. 11 15/16 in. (152.3 cm.).
Overall height (hood erected) .. .. 4 ft. 2⅞ in. (129.2 cm.).
Ground clearance (minimum) .. .. 4 3/16 in. (106 mm.).
Wheelbase .. .. 7 ft. 7⅛ in. (231.5 cm.).
Track: Front .. .. 4 ft. 1 in. (124.4 cm.).
Rear .. .. 4 ft. 1¼ in. (125 cm.).
Toe-in .. .. 1/16 to 3/32 in. (1.5 to 2.3 mm.).

WEIGHTS

1975–1976

Loading conditions		Total weight	Distribution	
			Front	*Rear*
Kerbside	Including full fuel tank and all optional extras	2290 lb (1039 kg)	1157 lb (525 kg)	1133 lb (514 kg)
Normal	Kerbside weight including driver and passenger	2590 lb (1174 kg)	1266 lb (574 kg)	1324 lb (600 kg)
Gross	Maximum weight condition, refer to note below	2710 lb (1229 kg)	1242 lb (563 kg)	1468 lb (666 kg)
Maximum permissible towing weight		1680 lb (762 kg)		
Recommended towbar hitch load		100 lb (45 kg)		

NOTE: Due consideration must be given to the overall weight when fully loading the car. Any loads carried on a luggage rack or downward load from a towing hitch must also be included in the maximum loading.

1977 and later

Loading conditions		Total weight	Distribution	
			Front	**Rear**
Kerbside	Including full fuel tank and all optional extras	2416 lb (1097 kg)	1207 lb (548 kg)	1209 lb (549 kg)
Normal	Kerbside weight including driver and passenger	2716 lb (1234 kg)	1303 lb (591 kg)	1413 lb (641 kg)
Gross	Maximum weight condition, refer to note below	2836 lb (1287 kg)	1279 lb (580 kg)	1557 lb (707 kg)
Maximum permissible towing weight		1680 lb (762 kg)		
Recommended towbar hitch load		100 lb (45 kg)		

NOTE: Due consideration must be given to the overall weight when fully loading the car. Any loads carried on a luggage rack or downward load from a towing hitch must also be included in the maximum loading.

Year: 1975–1976 — Without catalytic converter

ENGINE	
Type	18V 797 AE Standard 18V 798 AE Overdrive
Displacement	110 cu. in. (1800 c.c.)
Firing order	1, 3, 4, 2
Compression ratio	8.0 : 1
Valve rocker clearance: Inlet and exhaust	0.013 in. (0.33 mm) set warm
Idle speed	850 rev/min
Stroboscopic ignition timing	13°B.T.D.C. at 1,500 rev/min
Timing mark location	Pointer on timing case, notch on crankshaft pulley
DISTRIBUTOR	
Make/type	Lucas/45D4
Contact breaker gap	0.014 to 0.016 in. (0.35 to 0.40 mm)
Condenser capacity	0.18 to 0.25 mF
Rotation of rotor	Anti-clockwise
Dwell angle	51°± 5°
Serial number	41599†
Centrifugal advance	
Crankshaft degrees and rev/min	16° to 20° at 2,000 rev/min 30° to 34° at 4,000 rev/min 34° to 38° at 5,000 rev/min
Vacuum advance	Unit fitted but not connected
IGNITION COIL	
Make/type	Lucas/16C6
Resistance: Primary	1.43 to 1.58 ohms at 20°C (68°F)
Consumption at 2,000 rev/min	1 amp
Ballast resistor	1.3 to 1.4 ohms
SPARKING PLUGS	
Make/type	Champion/N9Y
Gap	0.035 in (0.90 mm)
CARBURETTER	
Make/type	Single Zenith 175 CD 5T
Specification No.	3824*
Needle No.	45 G
Air valve spring	Blue
Choke: Needle	K
Fast idle cam No.	CT4
Fast idle setting	0.025 in nominal
EXHAUST EMISSION	
Exhaust gas analyser reading at engine idle speed	5½% ± 1% CO maximum, disconnect air pump and plug injector pipe
Air pump test speed	850 rev/min (crankshaft)

* The carburetter specification number is printed on the identification tag attached to the carburetter suction chamber.

† The distributor serial number is stamped on the side of the distributor body.

Year: 1976 and later — Catalytic converter equipped cars

ENGINE	
Type (1976)	18V 801AE Standard 18V 802AE Overdrive
(1977 and later)	18V 883AE, 18V 890AE Standard 18V 884AE, 18V 891AE Overdrive
Displacement	110 cu. in. (1800 c.c.)
Firing order	1, 3, 4, 2
Compression ratio	8.0 : 1
Valve rocker clearance:	
Inlet and exhaust	0.013 in (0.33 mm) set warm
Idle speed	850 ± 100 rev/min
Stroboscopic ignition timing	10° B.T.D.C. at 1,500 rev/min
Timing mark location	Pointer on timing case, notch on crankshaft pulley
DISTRIBUTOR	
Make/type	Lucas 45DE4
Nominal pick-up air gap	0.010 to 0.017 in (0.25 to 0.43 mm)
Rotation of rotor	Anti-clockwise
Serial number (1976)	41600†
1977 and later—Federal	41693†
1977 and later—California	41695†
Centrifugal advance	
Crankshaft degrees and rev/min	13° to 17° at 2,000 rev/min 28° to 32° at 3,500 rev/min 33° to 37° at 4,500 rev/min
Vacuum advance (1976)	Unit fitted but not connected
Vacuum advance (1977 and later)	**Federal** / **California**
Starts	3 in Hg / 5 in Hg
Finishes	11 in Hg / 11 in Hg
Total advance	24° ± 2° / 14° ± 2°
IGNITION COIL	
Make/type	Lucas/16C6
Resistance: Primary	1.43 to 1.58 ohms at 20°C (68°F)
Consumption at 2,000 rev/min	1 amp.
Ballast resistor	1.3 to 1.4 ohms
SPARKING PLUGS	
Make/type	Champion/N9Y
Gap	0.035 in (0.90 mm)
CARBURETTER	
Make/type	Single Zenith 175 CD 5T—1977-1978: 175 CD-2
Specification No.	*
Needle No. (1976)	45H.
(1977-1978)	Low altitude: 45H; High altitude: 45M
(1979 and later)	45M
Bias of spring-loaded needle	Toward air cleaner
Air valve spring	Blue
Choke: Needle	K
Fast idle cam No.	CT4—1978 and later: C5
Fast idle setting	0.025 in. nominal
EXHAUST EMISSION	
Exhaust gas analyser reading at engine idle speed	5½% ± 1% CO maximum, disconnect air pump and plug injector pipe
Air pump test speed	850 rev/min (crankshaft)
Air pump pressure	4.5-6.5 lb/cu. in.

* The carburetter specification number is printed on the identification tag attached to the carburetter suction chamber.
† The distributor serial number is stamped on the side of the distributor body.

ENGINE

Main bearing nuts	70 lb. ft. (9.7 kg.m.).
Flywheel set screws	40 lb. ft. (5.5 kg.m.).
Big-end nuts	33±2 lb. ft. (4.5±0.3 kg.m.).
Cylinder head nuts	45 to 50 lb. ft. (6.2 to 6.9 kg. m.).
Rocker bracket nuts	25 lb. ft. (3.4 kg.m.).
Oil pump to crankcase	14 lb. ft. (1.9 kg.m.).
Sump to crankcase	6 lb. ft. (.8 kg. m.).
Cylinder side cover screws	2 lb. ft. (.28 kg. m.).
Second type—deep pressed cover	5 lb. ft. (.7 kg. m.).
Timing cover—¼ in. screws	6 lb. ft. (.8 kg. m.).
Timing cover— 5/16 in. screws	14 lb. ft. (1.9 kg. m.).
Rear plate— 5/16 in. screws	30 lb. ft. (4.1 kg.m.).
Rear plate—3/8 in. screws	30 lb. ft. (4.1 kg. m.).
Water pump to crankcase	17 lb. ft. (2.4 kg. m.).
Water outlet elbow nuts	8 lb. ft. (1.1 kg. m.).
Rocker cover nuts	4 lb. ft. (.56 kg. m.).
Manifold nuts	15 lb. ft. (2.1 kg. m.).
Oil filter centre-bolt	15 lb. ft. (2.1 kg. m.).
Clutch to flywheel	25 to 30 lb. ft. (3.4 to 4.1 kg. m.).
Carburetter stud nuts	2 lb. ft. (.28 kg. m.).
Distributor clamp bolt (nut trapped)	4.16 lb. ft. (.57 kg. m.).
Distributor clamp nut (bolt trapped)	2.5 lb. ft. (.35 kg. m.).
Fan blade fixing screws	7.3 to 9.3 lb. ft. (1 to 1.3 kg. m.).
Crankshaft pulley nuts	70 lb. ft. (9.6 kg. m.).
Camshaft nut	60 to 70 lb. ft. (8.3 to 9.6 kg. m.).
Oil pipe banjo	37 lb. ft. max. (5.1 kg. m. max.).
Front plate — 5/16 in screws	20 lb. ft. (2.8 kg. m.).
Rear engine mounting bolt	38 to 40 lb. ft. (5.22 to 5.5 kg. m.).

REAR AXLE

Half-shaft nut (semi-floating axle)	150 lb. ft. (20.75 kg. m.).
Differential bearing cap bolts	50 to 55 lb. ft. (6.9 to 7.6 kg. m.).
Crown wheel bolts	60 to 65 lb. ft. (8.3 to 8.9 kg. m.).
Pinion nut, new spacer only	180 to 220 lb. ft. (28.89 to 30.42 kg. m.).
Pinion nut, oil seal change	Adjust to preload. See Section Ha.
Axle shaft nut	150 lb. ft. (20.6 kg. m.) and aligned to next split pin hole.

REAR SUSPENSION

Rear shock absorber bolts	55 to 60 lb. ft. (7.6 to 8.3 kg. m.).

FRONT SUSPENSION

Front shock absorber bolts	43 to 45 lb. ft. (5.9 to 6.2 kg. m.).
Brake disc to hub	40 to 45 lb. ft. (5.5 to 6.2 kg. m.).
Brake calliper mounting	40 to 45 lb. ft. (5.5 to 6.2 kg. m.).
Bearing retaining nut	40 to 70 lb. ft. (5.5 to 9.7 kg. m.).
Cross-member to body	54 to 56 lb. ft. (7.5 to 7.7 kg. m.).
Shock absorber pinch bolt	28 lb. ft. (3.87 kg. m.).
Wishbone cross-bolt	28 lb. ft. (3.87 kg. m.).

STEERING

Steering arm bolts	60 to 65 lb. ft. (8.3 to 8.9 kg. m.).
Steering wheel nut	27 to 29 lb. ft. (3.73 to 4.01 kg. m.).
Steering tie-rod lock nut	33.3 to 37.5 lb. ft. (4.6 to 5.2 kg. m.).
Steering lever ball joint nut	34 to 35 lb. ft. (4.7 to 4.8 kg. m.).
Steering-column universal joint bolt	20 to 22 lb. ft. (2.8 to 3.0 kg. m.).
Steering-column top fixing bolts	12 to 17 lb. ft. (1.66 to 2.35 kg. m.).

ROAD WHEELS

Road wheel nuts	60 to 65 lb. ft. (8.3 to 9 kg. m.).

GENERAL

Stiffnut to cross-member mounting bolt	44 to 46 lb. ft. (6.08 to 6.36 kg. m.).
Gearbox remote control cover to tunnel	7.5 to 9.5 lb. ft. (1.04 to 1.31 kg. m.).
Alternator shaft nut	25 to 30 lb. ft. (3.46 to 4.15 kg. m.).
Interior mirror special screw	5 lb. in. (.058 kg. m.).
Hydraulic brake pipe connection – $\frac{3}{8}$ in. UNF.	5 to 7 lb. ft. (.69 to .96 kg. m.).
Hydraulic brake pipe connection – $\frac{7}{16}$ in. UNF.	7 to 10 lb. ft. (.96 to 1.38 kg. m.).

Directions for using torque wrenches calibrated in newton meters

[In adopting the SI (*Systeme International*) units of measure, which constitute the Modernized Metric System, tool manufacturers are beginning to introduce torque wrenches that are calibrated in newton meters. As metrication proceeds, torque specifications given in foot pounds (ft. lb., lb. ft., or lbf. ft.) and meter kilograms (mkg, kg. m., or kgf. m.) will eventually be replaced by torque specifications given in newton meters (N·m or Nm).

At present, there are in use too few torque wrenches calibrated in newton meters to justify the inclusion of newton meter torque specifications in this Manual. Nevertheless, if you purchase a new torque wrench, we recommend that you try to obtain one that is calibrated in newton meters. Such a tool can easily be used with this Manual by converting the meter kilogram specifications to newton meters.

To convert meter kilograms (kg. m.) to newton meters, simply disregard the decimal point. For example, 3.5 kg. m. would become 35 Nm. To convert centimeter kilograms (kg. cm.) to newton meters, point-off the one place with a decimal. For example, 50 kg. cm. would become 5.0 Nm. These conversions are not mathematically precise (3.5 kg. m. actually equals 34.3 Nm) but they are adequate for normal workshop purposes.]

Precautions against damage
Always fit wing and seat covers before commencing work.
Avoid spilling brake fluid or battery acid on paintwork. Wash off with water immediately if this occurs.
Disconnect the battery earth lead before starting work.
Always use the recommended Service tool or a satisfactory equivalent where specified.
Protect exposed screw threads from damage.

Safety precautions
Wear protective overalls and use protective barrier creams when necessary.
Ensure the car is on level ground when being lifted or jacked up. Apply the handbrake and chock the wheels.
Never rely on a jack as the sole means of support when working beneath the car. Place additional safety supports beneath the car.
Ensure that any lifting apparatus has adequate load capacity for the work in hand.
Do not leave tools, lifting equipment, spilt oil, etc., around or on the work area.

Cleaning components
Always use the recommended cleaning agent or equivalent.
Wherever possible, clean components and the surrounding area externally before removal.
Always observe scrupulous cleanliness when cleaning dismantled components.
Do not use degreasing equipment for components containing items which could be damaged by the use of this process.

Joints and joint faces
Always use the recommended gaskets and/or jointing compound.
Remove all traces of old jointing material prior to re-assembly. Do not use a tool which will damage the joint faces.
Fit joints dry unless otherwise specified in the Manual.
Smooth out any scratches or burrs on the joint faces with an oil stone.
Do not allow dirt or jointing material to enter any tapped holes.
Blow out any pipes, channels or crevices with compressed air.

Brake and clutch hydraulics
Two types of brake fittings are in use. Refer to the chart for identification and comments.
WARNING: **It is imperative that the correct brake fittings are used. The threads of components must be compatible.**
Containers for hydraulic fluid must be kept absolutely clean.
Do not store hydraulic fluid in an unsealed container. It will absorb water, and fluid in this condition would be dangerous to use.
Do not allow hydraulic fluid to be contaminated with mineral oil, or use a container which has previously contained mineral oil.
Do not re-use fluid bled from the system.
Always use clean brake fluid or a recommended alternative to clean hydraulic components.
Fit a blanking cap to a hydraulic union and a plug to its socket after removal to prevent the ingress of dirt.
Absolute cleanliness must be observed with hydraulic components at all times.

Service tools
Service tools are designed to enable dismantling and assembly to take place without unnecessary damage to components and loss of time.
Always use the correct Service tool if available. Some operations cannot be carried out without the aid of the relevant Service tool.
Where a Service tool is advisable and not available from the tool manufacturers, information is given to enable a tool to be manufactured locally.

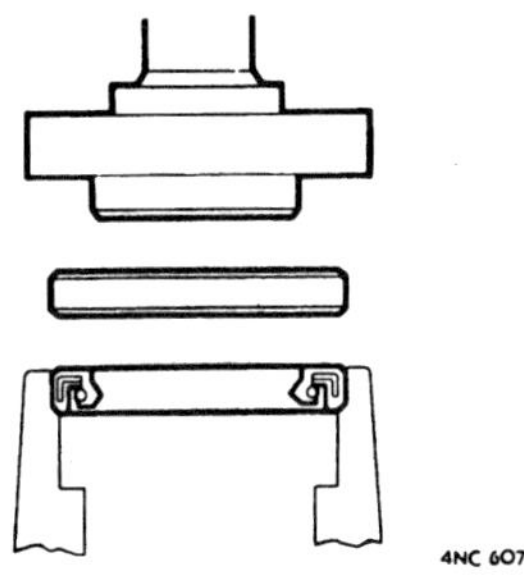

Oil seals
Always renew oil seals which have been removed from their working location, either as an individual component or as part of an assembly.
Lubricate the sealing lips and the outer diameter with a recommended lubricant before assembly to prevent damage on initial use.
Protect the seal from any surface which could cause damage over which it has to pass when being fitted. Use a protective sleeve or tape to cover the relevant surface.
Ensure that oil seals are fitted square in their housings with the sealing lip facing the lubricant to be retained.
Use a press and the recommended Service tool to fit an oil seal. If it is not possible to use a press, a hammer may be used instead.
If the correct Service tool is not available, use a suitable drift approximately 0.015 in (0.4 mm) smaller than the outside diameter of the seal.
Press or drift the seal in to the depth of its housing if the housing is shouldered, or flush with the face of the housing where no shoulder is provided.

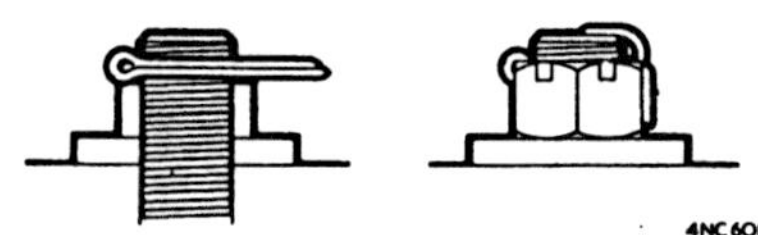

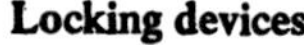

Locking devices

Always fit new locking washers, do not re-use an old one.
Always fit new split pins. Ensure that the split pin is the correct size for the hole in the bolt or stud. Fit as illustrated.
Self-locking nuts can be re-used, providing resistance can be felt when the locking portion passes over the thread of the bolt or stud. DO NOT re-use self-locking nuts in critical locations, e.g. engine bearings and suspension pivots.
Always use the correct replacement self-locking nut and ensure the thread of the bolt, plain washer and nut are clean and dry.

Screw threads

Both U.N.F. and Metric threads to I.S.O. standards are used.
Damaged threads must always be discarded. Cleaning up threads with a die or tap impairs the strength and closeness of fit of the threads and is not recommended.
Castellated nuts must not be slackened back to accept a split pin, except in those recommended cases when this forms part of an adjustment.
Do not allow oil or grease to enter blind threaded holes. The hydraulic action on screwing in the bolt or stud could split the housing.
Always tighten a nut or bolt to the recommended torque figure. Damaged or corroded threads can affect the torque reading.
To check or retighten a bolt or screw to a specified torque figure, first slacken a quarter of a turn, then retighten to the correct figure.
Always oil threads lightly before tightening to ensure a free-running thread, except in the case of self-locking nuts.

Bolt identification

An I.S.O. Metric bolt or screw, made of steel and larger than 6mm in diameter can be identified by either of the symbols ISO M or M embossed or indented on top of the head.

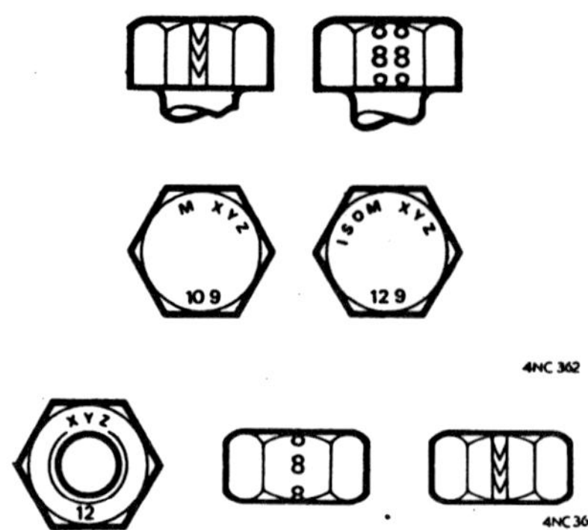

In addition to marks to identify the manufacturer, the head is also marked with symbols to indicate the strength grade e.g. 8.8; 10.9; 12.9 or 14.9. As an alternative some bolts and screws have the M and strength grade symbol on the flats of the hexagon.

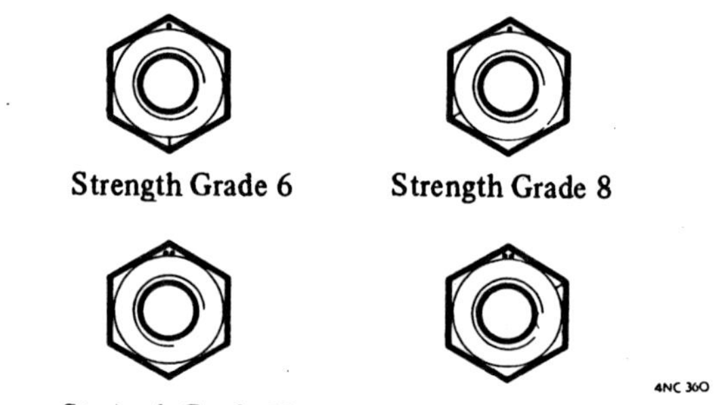

Strength Grade 6 Strength Grade 8

Strength Grade 12 Strength Grade 14

Nut identification

A nut with an I.S.O. metric thread is marked on one face or on one of the flats of the hexagon with the strength grade symbol 8, 12 or 14. Some nuts with a strength 4, 5 or 6 are also marked and some have the metric symbol M on the flat opposite the strength grade marking.
A clock face system is used as an alternative method of indicating the strength grade. The external chamfers or a face of the nut is marked in a position relative to the appropriate hour mark on a clock face to indicate the strength grade.
A dot is used to locate the 12 o'clock position and a dash to indicate the strength grade. If the grade is above 12, two dots identify the 12 o'clock position.

Five Thread Forms Replaced by I.S.O. Metric

BA	B.S.W.	B.S.F	U.N.C.	U.N.F.	Metric Size
2	$\frac{3}{16}$	$\frac{3}{8}$	10	10	M5
1			12	12	
0	$\frac{1}{4}$	$\frac{1}{4}$	$\frac{1}{4}$	$\frac{1}{4}$	M6
	$\frac{5}{16}$	$\frac{5}{16}$	$\frac{5}{16}$	$\frac{5}{16}$	M8
	$\frac{3}{8}$	$\frac{3}{8}$	$\frac{3}{8}$	$\frac{3}{8}$	M10
	$\frac{7}{16}$	$\frac{7}{16}$	$\frac{7}{16}$	$\frac{7}{16}$	
	$\frac{1}{2}$	$\frac{1}{2}$	$\frac{1}{2}$	$\frac{1}{2}$	M12

COMMENTS	UNIFIED	METRIC
The illustrations show metric and the equivalent Unified (U.N.F.) parts for comparison.		
Metric pipe nuts, hose ends, unions and bleed screws are coloured **GOLD** or BLACK and most are also identified with the letter 'M'. The correct Metric or Unified pipe flares must be used.		
Metric parts are not counterbored; some U.N.F. threaded parts also had no counterbore; always check.		
End of a Metric hose is also coloured **GOLD** or **BLACK**.		
If the thread of a component is in doubt, screw the hydraulic connections and bleed screw fully in with the fingers. If they cannot be screwed right in or if they are unduly slack, the threads may not be compatible. Metric hose seals against the bottom of the port, gap between hose hexagon and face of cylinder or calliper.		

Lubrication

The lubrication systems of your new car are filled with high quality oils. You should always use a high quality oil of the correct viscosity range in the engine, gearbox and rear axle during subsequent maintenance operations or when topping-up. The use of oils not to the correct specification can lead to high oil and fuel consumption and ultimately to damage to components.

Oil to the correct specification contains additives which disperse the corrosive acids formed by combustion and also prevent the formation of sludge which can block oilways. **Additional oil additives should not be used.** Servicing intervals must be adhered to.

Engine

Use a well-known brand of oil to B.L.S. OL.02 or MIL-L-2104B or A.P.1, SE quality, with viscosity band spanning the temperature range of your locality.

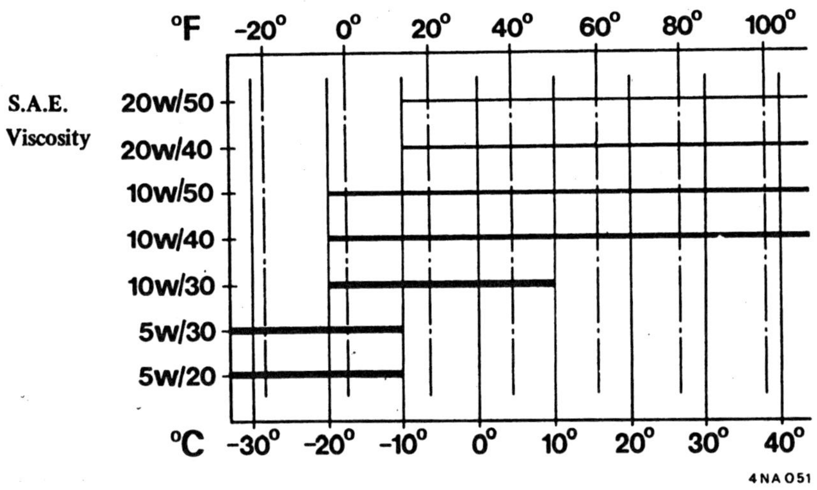

[NOTE: Please also refer to the S.A.E. viscosity chart given on page 48 of the Driver's Handbook.]

Synchromesh gearbox

Use the same oil selected for the engine.

NOTE: SAE 90 Hypoid oil is also suitable for use in the gearbox, with or without overdrive. However, if the gearbox contains one kind of lubricant, for example engine oil, it should be thoroughly drained before Hypoid oil is added.

Rear axle and steering rack

Top up and refill with H.D.90 (MIL-L-2105B) above –10°C (10°F) or H.D.80 (MIL-L-2105B) below –5° (20°F).

Grease points

Use Multipurpose Lithium Grease N.L.G.1 consistency No. 2.

Fuel

Non catalytic converter cars . . . . Regular fuel

Catalytic converter equipped cars . . . . .Unleaded fuel

Brake and Clutch Fluid

Use **Lockheed Universal Brake Fluid (Series 329S)** or **Castrol Girling Brake Fluid**; alternatively, use a brake fluid conforming to **F.M.V.S.S. D.O.T.3 specification with a minimum boiling point of 260°C (500°F). DO NOT use any other type of fluid in the braking system.**

SERVICE LUBRICANTS, FUEL AND FLUIDS – CAPACITIES

Anti-Freeze Solutions

Use an ethylene glycol based anti-freeze conforming to specification B.S. 3151/2 or S.A.E. J1034.
The recommended quantities of anti-freeze for a car fitted with a heater for different degrees of frost protection are:

For 1975 and 1976 cars

Solution	Amount of anti-freeze			Commences freezing		Frozen solid	
%	U.S. pt	Pt	Litres	°C	°F	°C	°F
25	3	2½	1.5	−13	9	−26	−15
33⅓	4	3¼	2	−19	−2	−36	−33
50	6	5	3	−36	−33	−48	−53

For 1977 and later cars

Solution	Amount of anti-freeze			Commences freezing		Frozen solid	
%	U.S. pt	Pt	Litres	°C	°F	°C	°F
25	3½	3	1.65	−13	9	−26	−15
33⅓	4⅝	3¾	2.15	−19	−2	−36	−33
50	7	6	3.32	−36	−33	−48	−53

Capacities (approx.)

Engine sump including filter	7.25 U.S. pt	6 pt	3.4 litres
Gearbox	6 U.S. pt	5 pt	2.84 litres
Gearbox with overdrive	7.25 U.S. pt	6 pt	3.4 litres
Rear axle	2 U.S. pt	1½ pt	0.85 litres
1975–1976 Cooling system (with heater)	12 U.S. pt	10 pt	5.6 litres
1977 and later Cooling system (with heater)	14.4 U.S. pt	12 pt	6.8 litres
Heater	0.6 U.S. pt	½ pt	0.28 litres
Windscreen washer bottle	3.6 U.S. pt	3 pt	1.71 litre
1975–1976 Fuel tank	12 U.S. gal	10 gal	45.4 litres
1977 and later Fuel tank	13 U.S. gal	11 gal	50 litres
Steering rack	0.39 U.S. pt	⅓ pt	0.19 litres

MAINTENANCE

MAINTENANCE SUMMARY

Basic engine tuning data will be found on the Vehicle Emission Control Information label located in the engine compartment.

The following items should be checked weekly by the driver:

Engine oil level.
Brake fluid level.
Radiator coolant level.
Battery electrolyte level.
Windscreen washer reservoir fluid level.
All tyre pressures.
All lights for operation.
Horn operation.
Windscreen wipers operation.

MAINTENANCE INTERVALS

***These items are emission related** 

Service	Mileage x 1000	Monthly intervals
A	1	After Sales Service
B	3, 9, 16, 22, 28, 34, 41, 47	3
C	6, 19, 31, 44	6
D	12.5, 37.5	12
E	25, 50	24

NOTE: The service intervals are based on an annual mileage of approximately 12,500 miles. Should the vehicle complete substantially less miles than this per annum, it is recommended that a 'C' service is completed at six-month intervals, and a 'D' service at twelve-month intervals.

'A' SERVICE

Lubrication

Lubricate all grease points (except hubs).
Renew engine oil.
Check/top up brake fluid reservoir.
Check/top up clutch fluid reservoir.
Check/top up battery electrolyte.
Check/top up cooling system.
Check/top up rear axle.
Drain gearbox, refill with new oil (non-overdrive).
Drain gearbox and overdrive, clean filters and refill with new oil.
Check/top up screen washer reservoir.
*Lubricate distributor.
*Lubricate accelerator control linkage and pedal pivot; check operation.
Lubricate all locks and hinges (not steering lock).

Engine

*Check driving belts; adjust or renew.
Check cooling system hoses/pipes for security and condition.
Check air injection system hoses/pipes for security.
*Check crankcase breathing and evaporative loss systems. Check hoses/pipes for security.
*Check security of engine bolts and mountings.
*Check/adjust torque of cylinder head nuts.
*Check/adjust valve clearances.
*Check security of E.G.R. valve operating lines.
*Check exhaust system for leaks and security.

'A' SERVICE–*continued*

Ignition

*Check ignition wiring for fraying, chafing and deterioration.
*Check/adjust dwell angle and ignition timing, using electronic equipment (Lucas distributor type 45D4).
*Check/adjust ignition timing using electronic equipment (Lucas distributor type 45DE4).

Fuel system

*Check fuel system for leaks.
*Top up carburetter piston damper.
*Check adjust carburetter idle settings.

Safety

Check tyres for tread depth, visually for cuts in tyre fabric, exposure of ply and cord structure, lumps or bulges.
Check/adjust tyre pressures, including spare.
Check tightness of road wheel fastenings.
Check condition and security of steering unit, joints and gaiters.
Check security of suspension fixings.
Check steering and suspension for oil/fluid leaks.
Check brake servo hoses/pipes for security.
Check/adjust foot and hand brake.
Check visually hydraulic pipes and unions for chafing, leaks and corrosion.
Check/adjust front wheel alignment.
Check output of charging system.
Check function of original equipment, i.e. interior and exterior lamps, horns, warning indicators, windscreen wipers and washers.
Check/adjust headlamp alignment.
Check instrumentation.
Check operation of all door locks and window controls.

Road test

Road/roller test and check operation of all instrumentation.
Report additional work required.

'B' SERVICE

Lubrication

Lubricate all grease points (except hubs).
Check/top up engine oils.
Check/top up brake fluid reservoir.
Check/top up clutch fluid reservoir.
Check/top up battery electrolyte.
Check/top up cooling system.
Check/top up gearbox and rear axle oils.
Check/top up screen washer reservoir.

Engine

*Check fan drive belt; adjust or renew.
*Check exhaust system for leaks and security.

Fuel system

*Check fuel system for leaks

'B' SERVICE—*continued*

Safety

Check tyres for tread depth, visually for cuts in tyre fabric, exposure of ply or chord structure, lumps or bulges.
Check that tyres comply with manufacturer's specification.
Check/adjust tyre pressures, including spare.
Check tightness of road wheel fastenings.
Check condition and security of steering unit, joints and gaiters.
Check steering and suspension for oil/fluid leaks.
Check/adjust foot and hand brake.
Check visually hydraulic pipes and unions for chafing, leaks and corrosion.
Check function of original equipment, i.e. interior and exterior lamps, horns, warning indicators, windscreen wipers and washers.
Check, if necessary renew, wiper blades.
Check/adjust headlamp alignment.

'C' SERVICE

Lubrication

Lubricate all grease points (except hubs).
Renew engine oil and filter.
Check/top up brake fluid reservoir.
Check/top up clutch fluid reservoir.
Check/top up battery electrolyte.
Check/top up cooling system.
Check/top up gearbox and rear axle oils.
Check/top up screen washer reservoir.
*Lubricate distributor.
*Lubricate accelerator control linkage and pedal pivot; check operation.
Lubricate all locks and hinges (not steering lock).

Engine

*Check fan drive belt; adjust or renew.
Check cooling system hoses/pipes for security and condition.
*Check exhaust system for leaks and security.

Ignition

*Clean spark plugs.

Fuel system

*Check fuel system for leaks.

Safety

Check tyres for tread depth, visually for cuts in tyre fabric, exposure of ply or cord structure, lumps or bulges.
Check that tyres comply with manufacturer's specification.
Check/adjust tyre pressures, including spare.
Check tightness of road wheel fastenings.
Check condition and security of steering unit, joints and gaiters.
Check security of suspension fixings.
Check steering and suspension for oil/fluid leaks.
Inspect brake pads for wear, discs for condition.
Check brake servo hoses/pipes for security.
Check/adjust foot and hand brake.

'C' SERVICE–*continued*

Safety–*continued*

Check visually hydraulic pipes and unions for chafing and corrosion.
Check/adjust front wheel alignment.
Check output of charging system.
Check function of original equipment, i.e. interior and exterior lamps, horns, warning indicators, windscreen wipers and washers.
Check, if necessary renew wiper blades.
Check/adjust headlamp alignment.
Check instrumentation.
Check condition and security of seats, seat belts and seat belt warning system.

Road test

Road/roller test and check operation of all instrumentation.
Report additional work required.

Brakes

It is further recommended that at 19,000 miles (or 18 months) the brake fluid is renewed. This is additional work.

'D' SERVICE

Lubrication

Lubricate all grease points (except hubs).
Renew engine oil and filter.
Check/top up brake fluid reservoir.
Check/top up clutch fluid reservoir.
Check/top up battery electrolyte.
Check/top up cooling system.
Check/top up gearbox and rear axle oils.
Check/top up screen washer reservoir.
*Lubricate distributor.
*Lubricate accelerator control linkage and pedal pivot; check operation.
*Lubricate all locks and hinges (not steering lock).

Engine

*Check driving belts; adjust or renew.
Check cooling system hoses/pipes for security and condition.
*Renew carburetter air cleaner element.
*Renew air pump air filter.
*Check gulp valve and check valve operation.
*Check air injection system hoses/pipes for security.
*Check air intake temperature control system.
*Check crankcase breathing and evaporative loss systems. Check hoses/pipes and restrictors for blockage, security and condition.
*Check/adjust valve clearances.
*Check exhaust system for leaks and security.

Ignition

*Check ignition wiring for fraying, chafing and deterioration.
*Renew spark plugs.
*Renew distributor points (Lucas distributor type 45D4).
*Clean distributor cap; check for cracks and tracking.
*Check/adjust dwell angle and ignition timing, using electronic equipment (Lucas distributor type 45D4).
*Check/adjust ignition timing, using electronic equipment (Lucas distributor type 45DE4).

'D' SERVICE–*continued*

Fuel system

*Renew fuel line filter.
*Check fuel system for leaks.
*Top up carburetter piston damper.
*Check condition of fuel filler seal.
*Check/adjust carburetter idle settings.

Safety

Check tyres for tread depth, visually for cuts in tyre fabric, exposure of ply or cord structure, lumps or bulges.
Check that tyres comply with manufacturer's specification.
Check/adjust tyre pressures, including spare.
Check tightness of road wheel fastenings.
Check condition and security of steering unit, joints and gaiters.
Check security of suspension fixings.
Check steering and suspension for oil/fluid leaks.
Inspect brake linings pads for wear, drums/discs for condition.
Check brake servo hoses/pipes for security.
Check/adjust foot and hand brake.
Check visually hydraulic pipes and unions for chafing and corrosion.
Check/adjust front wheel alignment.
Check output of charging system.
Check function of original equipment, i.e. interior and exterior lamps, horns, warning indicators, windscreen wipers and washers.
Check, if necessary renew, wiper blades.
Check/adjust headlamp alignment.
Check instrumentation.
Check operation of all door locks and window controls.
Check condition and security of seats, seat belts and seat belt warning system.

Road test

Road/roller test and check operation of all instrumentation.
Report additional work required.

Brakes

It is further recommended that every 37,500 miles (or 3 years), the brake fluid, hydraulic seals and hoses in the brake and clutch hydraulic systems be renewed. Examine working surfaces of pistons and bores in master, slave and wheel cylinders and renew parts as necessary. Renew the brake servo filter.

'E' SERVICE

Lubrication

Lubricate all grease points (except hubs).
Renew engine oil and filter.
Check/top up brake fluid reservoir.
Check/top up clutch fluid reservoir.
Check/top up battery electrolyte.
Check/top up cooling system.
Check/top up gearbox (non-overdrive) and rear axle oils.
Drain gearbox and overdrive, clean filter and refill with new oil.
Check/top up screen washer reservoir.
*Lubricate distributor.
*Lubricate accelerator control linkage and pedal pivot; check operation.
Lubricate all locks and hinges (not steering lock).

'E' SERVICE—*continued*

Engine

*Check driving belts; adjust or renew.
Check cooling system hoses/pipes for security and condition.
*Renew carburetter air cleaner element.
*Renew air pump air filter.
*Check gulp valve and check valve operation.
*Check air injection system hoses/pipes for security.
*Check air intake temperature control system.
*Check crankcase breathing and evaporative loss systems. Check hoses/pipes and restrictors for blockage, security and condition.
*Check/adjust valve clearances.
*Check E.G.R. system.
*Renew catalytic converter (if fitted).
*Renew adsorption canister.
*Check exhaust system for leaks and security.

Ignition

*Check ignition wiring for fraying, chafing and deterioration.
*Renew spark plugs.
*Renew distributor points (Lucas distributor type 45D4).
*Clean distributor cap; check for cracks and tracking.
*Check/adjust dwell angle and ignition timing, using electronic equipment (Lucas distributor type 45D4).
*Check adjust ignition timing using electronic equipment (Lucas distributor type 45DE4).

Fuel system

*Renew fuel line filter.
*Check fuel system for leaks.
*Top up carburetter piston damper.
*Check condition of fuel filler seal.
*Check/adjust carburetter idle settings.

Safety

Check tyres for tread depth, visually for cuts in tyre fabric, exposure of ply or cord structure, lumps or bulges.
Check that tyres comply with manufacturer's specification.
Check adjust tyre pressures, including spare.
Check tightness of road wheel fastenings.
Check condition and security of steering unit, joints and gaiters.
Check steering and suspension for oil/fluid leaks.
Check security of suspension fixings.
Inspect brake linings pads for wear, drums/discs for condition.
Check brake servo hoses/pipes for security.
Check/adjust front wheel alignment.
Check/adjust foot and hand brake.
Check visually hydraulic pipes and unions for chafing and corrosion.
Check output of charging system.
Check function of original equipment, i.e. interior and exterior lamps, horns, warning indicators, windscreen wipers and washers.
Check, if necessary renew, wiper blades.
Check/adjust headlamp alignment.
Check instrumentation.
Check operation of all door locks and window controls.
Check condition and security of seats, seat belts and seat belt warning system.

Road test

Road/roller test and check operation of all instrumentation.
Report additional work required.

LUBRICATION

NOTE: Ensure that the vehicle is standing on a level surface when checking the oil levels.

WEEKLY

(1) ENGINE. Check oil level, and top up if necessary.

'A' SERVICE

(2) ENGINE. Drain and refill with new oil.
(4) THROTTLE. Lubricate throttle control linkage, cable and accelerator pedal fulcrum.
(5) CARBURETTER. Top up carburetter piston damper.
(6) DISTRIBUTOR. Lubricate all parts as necessary.
(8) GEARBOX (NON-OVERDRIVE). Drain and refill with new oil.
(9) GEARBOX WITH OVERDRIVE. Drain, clean overdrive filters, refill with new oil.
(10) REAR AXLE. Check oil level, and top up if necessary.
(11) PROPELLER SHAFT (1 nipple)
(12) FRONT SUSPENSION (6 nipples)
(13) HAND BRAKE CABLE (1 nipple)
} Give three or four strokes with a grease gun.
(14) WIRE WHEELS. Lubricate wire wheel and hub splines.
LOCKS, HINGES AND LINKAGES. Lubricate all door, bonnet, boot locks and hinges (not steering lock); and hand brake mechanical linkage.
FRICTION POINTS. Spray lubricant on all friction points.

'B' SERVICE

(1) ENGINE. Check oil level, and top up if necessary.
(7) GEARBOX. Check oil level, and top up if necessary.
(10) REAR AXLE. Check oil level, and top up if necessary.
(11) PROPELLER SHAFT (1 nipple)
(12) FRONT SUSPENSION (6 nipples)
(13) HAND BRAK CABLE (1nipple)
} Give three or four strokes with a grease gun.
(14) WIRE WHEELS ONLY. Grease wheel and hub splines.
FRICTION POINTS. Spray lubricant on all friction points.

'C' AND 'D' SERVICES

(2) ENGINE. Drain and refill with new oil.
(3) ENGINE OIL FILTER. Remove disposable cartridge; fit new.
(4) THROTTLE. Lubricate throttle control linkage, cable and accelerator pedal fulcrum.
(5) CARBURETTER. Top up carburetter piston damper–'D' SERVICE only.
(6) DISTRIBUTOR. Lubricate all parts as necessary.
(7) GEARBOX. Check oil level, and top if necessary.
(10) REAR AXLE. Check oil level, and top up if necessary.
(11) PROPELLER SHAFT (1 nipple)
(12) FRONT SUSPENSION (6 nipples)
(13) HAND BRAKE CABLE (1 nipple)
} Give three or four strokes with a grease gun.
(14) WIRE WHEELS ONLY. Grease wheel and hub splines.
LOCKS, HINGES AND LINKAGES. Lubricate all door, bonnet, boot locks and hinges **(not steering lock)**; and the hand brake mechanical linkage.
FRICTION POINTS. Spray lubricant on all friction points.

'E' SERVICE

Carry out 'D' SERVICE in addition to the following:
(9) GEARBOX WITH OVERDRIVE. Drain, clean overdrive filters, refill with new oil.

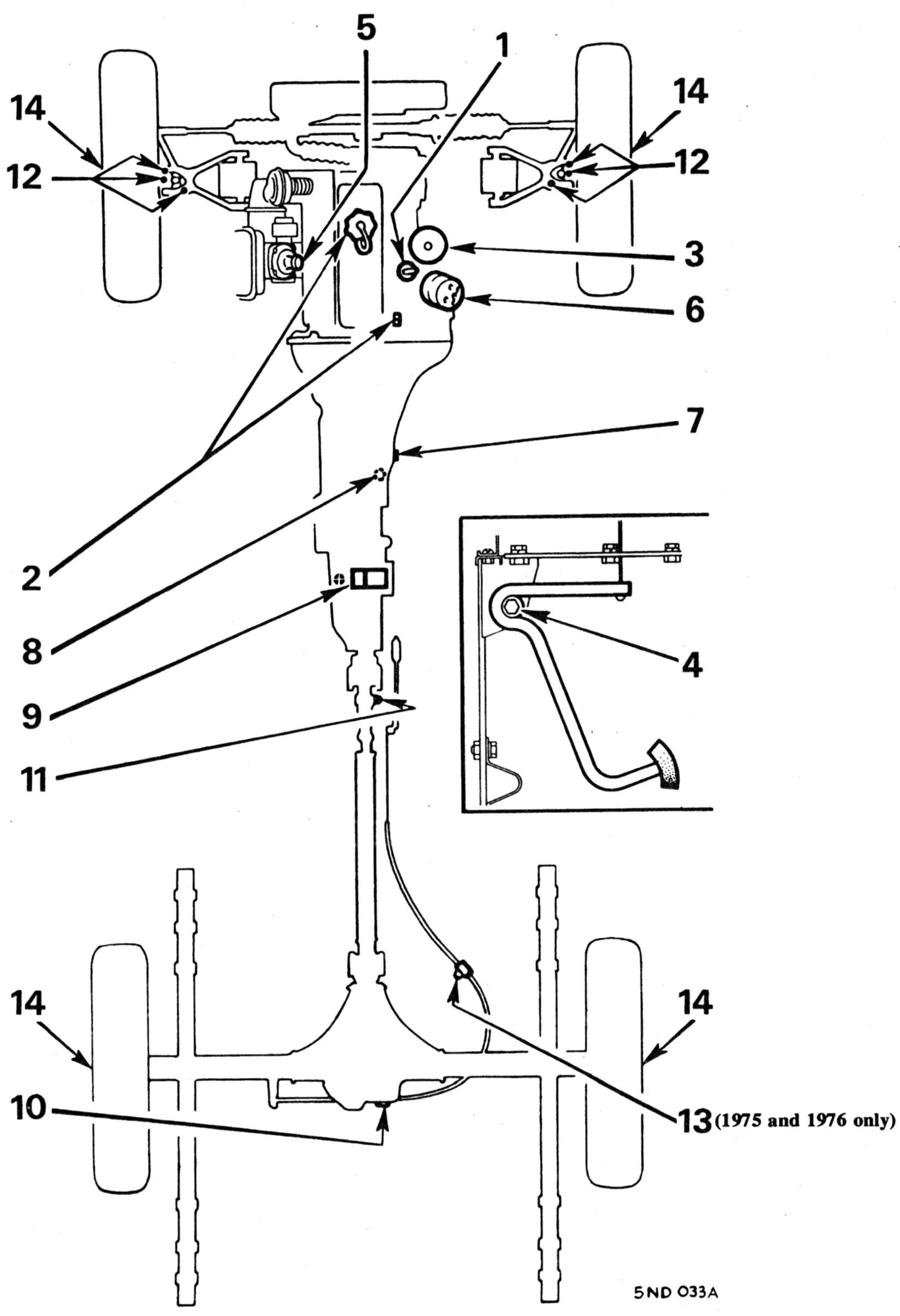
5
1
14
14
12
12
3
6
7
2
8
4
9
11
14
14
10
13 (1975 and 1976 only)
5ND 033A

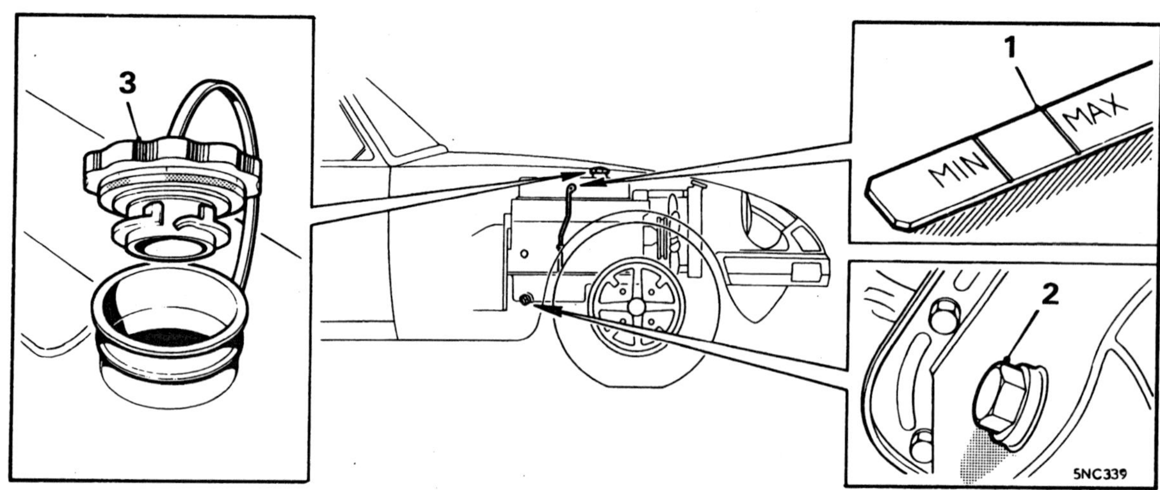

ENGINE

Lubrication

Checking oil level

1. Maintain the level between the 'MIN' and 'MAX' mark on the dipstick. Ensure that the seal of the dipstick contacts the tube when the dipstick is refitted.

Draining and refilling

2. Drain the oil while the engine is warm. Clean the drain plug; check that its copper sealing washer is in satisfactory condition and refit.
3. Refill with the correct quantity and grade of oil. Run the engine for a short while, then allow it to stand for a few minutes before checking the level.

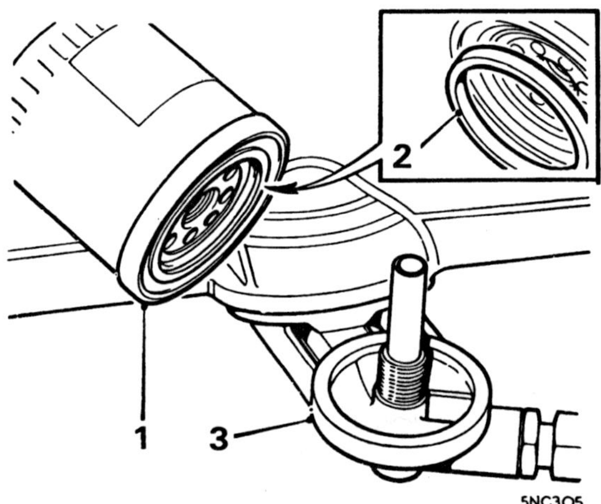

Disposable cartridge filter renewal

1. Unscrew the cartridge from the filter head and discard.
2. Smear the new seal with engine oil and fit it into its groove in the new cartridge.
3. Screw the new cartridge to the filter head, using hand force only.
4. Check the engine oil level, start the engine and check the cartridge for leaks.
5. Re-check the oil level after waiting for a few minutes.

Fan belt tension

When correctly tensioned, a total deflection of 0.5 in (13 mm) under moderate hand pressure, should be possible at the midway point of the longer belt run between the pulleys.

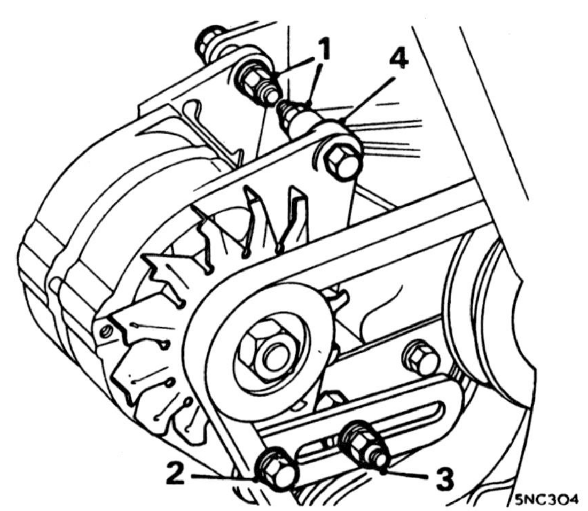

Adjusting

1. Slacken the alternator securing bolts.
2. Slacken the bolt securing the adjusting link to the alternator.
3. Slacken the adjusting link nut.
4. Move the alternator to the required position—avoid over-tightening. Apply any leverage necessary to the alternator drive end bracket only, using a wood or soft metal lever.
5. Tighten the securing bolts and adjusting link nut.

Engine mountings

Check the following fastenings for tightness:

1. The nuts and bolts retaining each engine mounting bracket.
2. The nut retaining each engine mounting rubber.

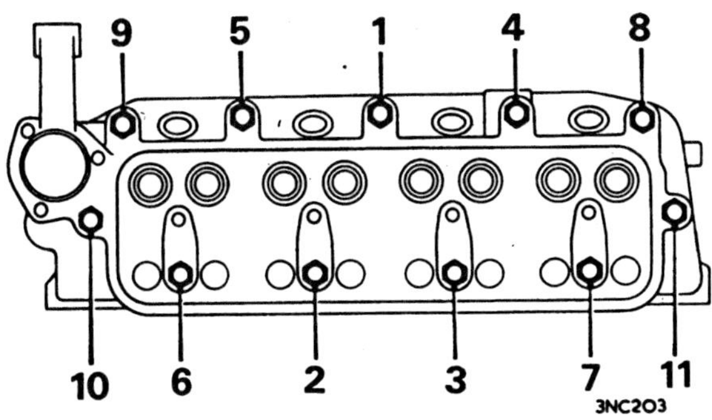

Cylinder head

1. Using a suitable torque wrench, tighten the cylinder head nuts gradually in the sequence illustrated to a torque of 45 to 50 lbf ft (6.2 to 6.9 kgf m).

Valve rocker adjustment

1. Disconnect the purge pipe from the rocker cover.
2. Remove the rocker cover.
3. Check the clearance between the valve rocker arms and valve stems with a feeler gauge. The clearance should be 0.013 in (0.33 mm).

The gauge should be a sliding fit when the engine is warm.

Check the clearance of each valve in the following order:

Check No. 1 valve with No. 8 fully open.

,,	,, 3	,,	,,	,, 6	,,	,,
,,	,, 5	,,	,,	,, 4	,,	,,
,,	,, 2	,,	,,	,, 7	,,	,,
,,	,, 8	,,	,,	,, 1	,,	,,
,,	,, 6	,,	,,	,, 3	,,	,,
,,	,, 4	,,	,,	,, 5	,,	,,
,,	,, 7	,,	,,	,, 2	,,	,,

4. Slacken the locknut.
5. Rotate screw, clockwise to decrease or anti-clockwise to increase the clearance.
6. Retighten the locknut when the clearance is correct, holding the screw against rotation.
7. Clean the rocker cover face of all deposits.
8. Examine the orifice of the restrictor; clean any dirt or deposits from the restrictor, using a piece of soft wire.
9. Check the condition of the rocker cover gasket; renew the gasket if necessary.
10. Check the oil filler cap, ensure that it seals when fitted to the rocker cover. Renew the cap if necessary.
11. Refit the rocker cover.

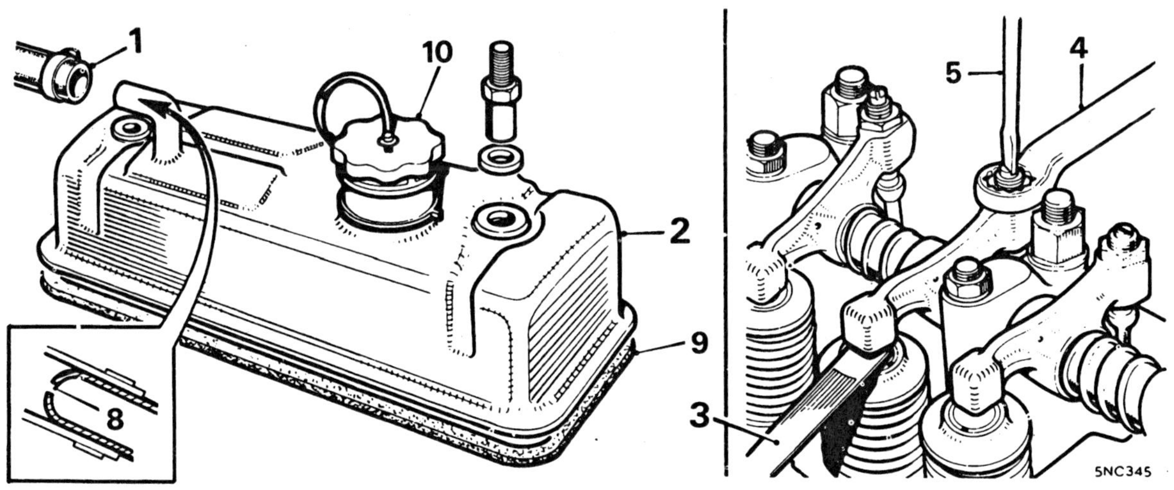

[NOTE: The valves are numbered consecutively 1 through 8, from the front to the rear of the engine.]

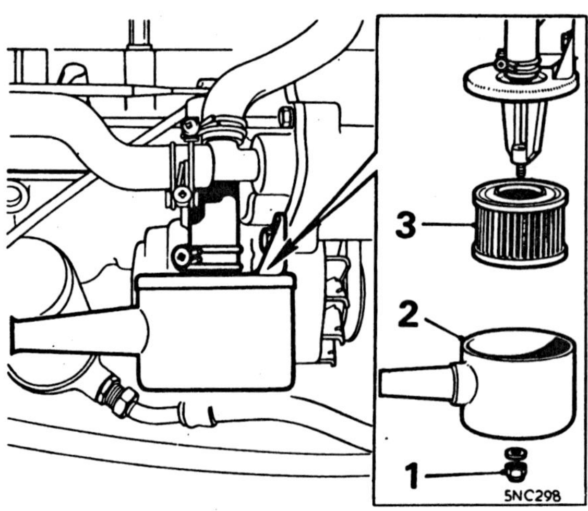

EXHAUST EMISSION

Air pump

Air cleaner element renewal

1. Remove the nut and washer.
2. Detach the cover.
3. Remove the element and discard.
4. Clean the inside of the cover thoroughly and reassemble using a new element.

Drive belt tension

When correctly tensioned, total deflection of 0.5 in (13 mm) under moderate hand pressure, should be possible at the midway point of the belt run.

Adjusting

1. Slacken the mounting bolt.
2. Slacken the two adjusting link bolts.
3. Move the air pump to the required position, tighten the bolts and re-check the belt tension. **DO NOT OVERTIGHTEN.**

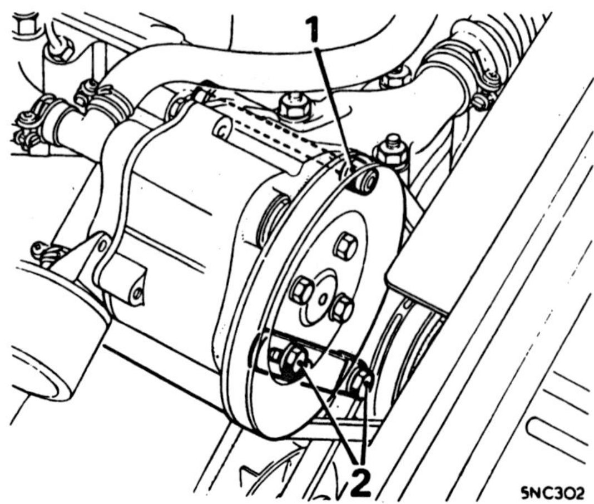

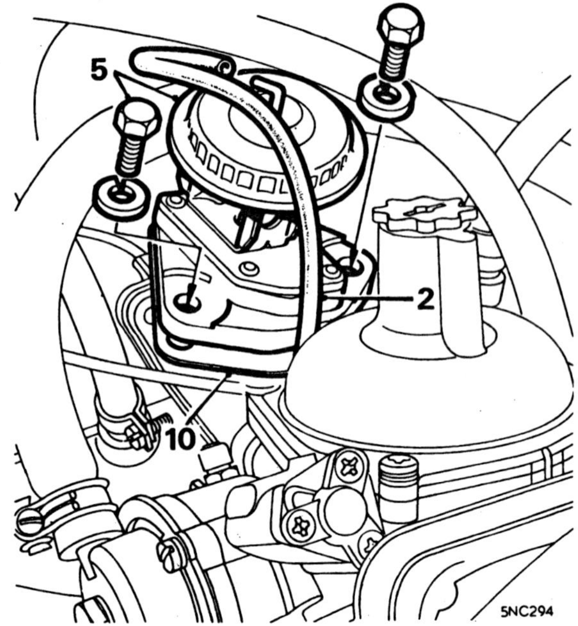

Exhaust gas recirculation (E.G.R.) valve
Servicing

1. Start the engine, and run it until normal operating temperature is attained. Switch off the engine.
2. Disconnect the vacuum hose from the E.G.R. valve. Disconnect the vacuum pipe from the gulp valve and connect it to the E.G.R. valve, using an additional length of pipe.
3. Start the engine and observe the valve spindle. As soon as the engine is started and as engine speed increases the spindle will rise, opening the valve. If the vacuum pipe is now disconnected from the valve the spindle will drop, closing the valve. Stop the engine.
4. Remove the vacuum pipe from the E.G.R. valve and re-connect it to the gulp valve.
5. Remove the retaining bolts and lift the E.G.R. valve unit from the manifold.
6. Visually check that the valve is closed.
7. Renew the valve if faulty.
8. Remove all gasket sealing material from the mating surfaces of the manifold and E.G.R. valve.
9. Clean all deposits from the restrictor, and ports in the manifold, and from the ports within the valve body. Care should be taken to ensure that deposits do not fall into the manifold. When cleaning the circular port in the valve body avoid touching the protruding valve spindle. Do not attempt to clean the valve disc or seat. [**NOTE:** A spark plug cleaner may be used to clean the metering valve. Hold the diaphragm upward with your fingers and blast the valve at 30-second intervals until clean.]
10. Refit the cleaned or new E.G.R. valve, using a new gasket.
11. Re-connect the vacuum hose.
12. Check the E.G.R. valve for correct operation, operations 1 to 4.
13. Re-connect the vacuum hose.

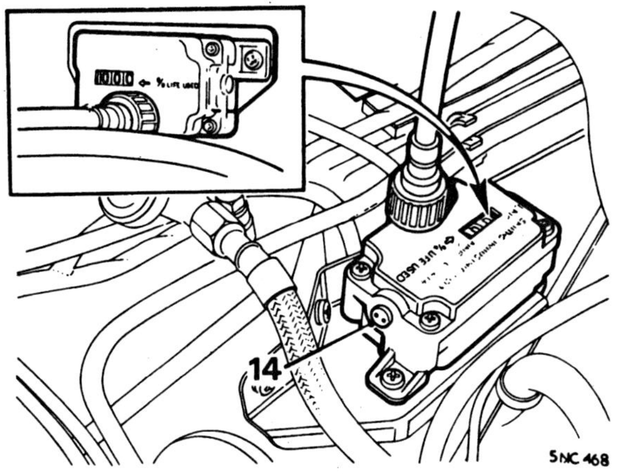

14. Insert the service interval counter (if fitted) resetting key in the reset button located on the side of the unit and turn the key until all the counters return to zero. Remove the key.

Gulp valve

Testing
1. Slacken the clip and remove the air supply hose to the gulp valve at the air pump.
2. Connect a vacuum gauge, with a 'T' (tee) connector, to the disconnected end of the gulp valve air hose.
3. Start the engine and run it at idle speed.
4. Temporarily seal the unused inlet of the 'T' (tee) connector and check that the gauge reads zero for approximately 15 seconds; if a vacuum is registered, renew the gulp valve. It is most important that the engine speed is not increased above idling during this test.
5. With the gauge 'T' (tee) connector sealed, operate the throttle rapidly from closed to open; the gauge should then register a vacuum. Repeat the test several times, temporarily unsealing the connector to destroy the vacuum before each operation of the throttle. If the gauge fails to register a vacuum, renew the gulp valve.
6. Ensure that the restrictor is in position when refitting the hose to the air pump.

NOTE: If a vacuum pump is not available place a finger over the end of the air supply hose, 1, to detect a vacuum.

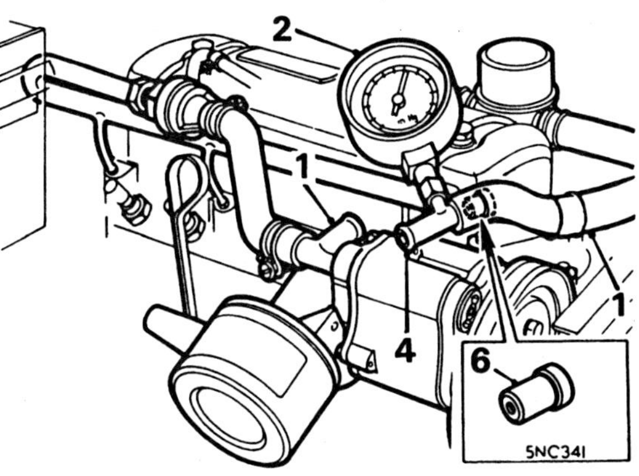

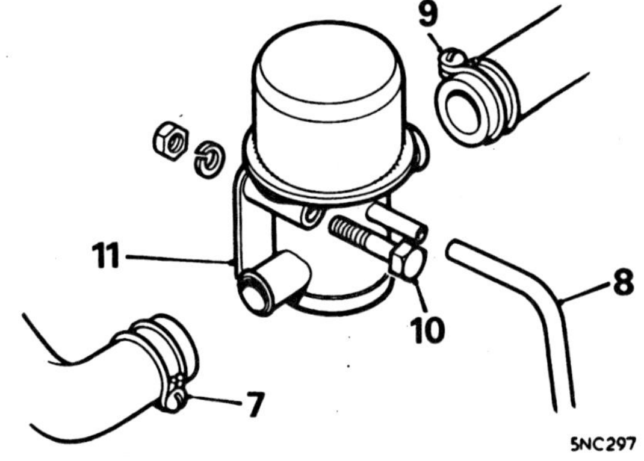

Removing
7. Disconnect the air pump hose from the gulp valve.
8. Disconnect the sensing pipe from the gulp valve.
9. Slacken the clip securing the manifold hose to the gulp valve.
10. Remove the two nuts, bolts, and washers securing the gulp valve to the mounting bracket.
11. Remove the gulp valve.

Refitting
12. Reverse the procedure in 7 to 11.

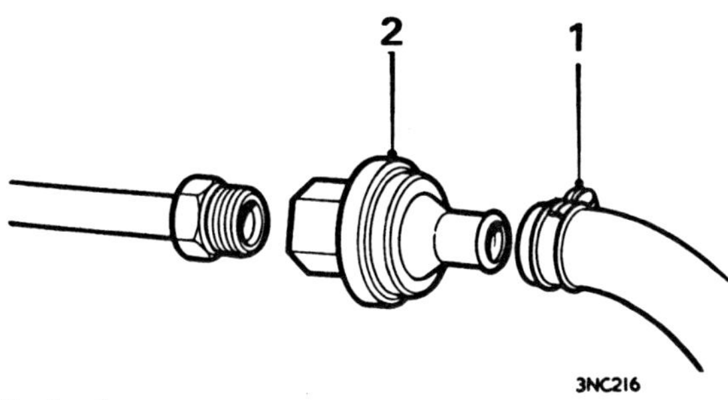

Check valve

Removing
1. Slacken the clip and remove the air supply hose from the check valve.
2. Hold the air manifold connection to prevent it twisting and unscrew the check valve.

Testing

CAUTION: Do not use a pressure air supply for this test.

3. Blow through the valve, orally, in turn from each connection. Air should only pass through the valve when blown from the air supply hose connection. If air passes through the valve when blown from the air manifold connection, renew the check valve.

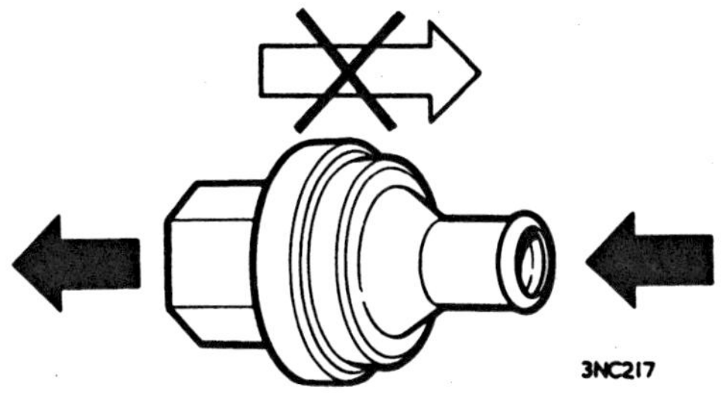

Refitting the check valve

4. Reverse the procedure in 1 and 2. Ensure that the hose is free from restrictions.

Catalytic converter (if fitted)–Renewal

On completion of each 25,000 miles the maintenance operation will be indicated by a warning light on the console.

1. Jack up and support the front of the car.
2. Remove the bolt securing the exhaust pipe to the support bracket.
3. Release the exhaust pipe from the catalytic converter.
4. Remove the olive.
5. Release the carburetter springs from the air cleaner casing.
6. Remove the three bolts securing the air cleaner casing to the carburetter, noting that the top bolt secures the brake servo vacuum hose clip.
7. Disconnect the hot air hose from the air temperature control valve.
8. Remove the air cleaner casing.
9. Remove the two cross-head screws and nut securing the heat shield to the support bracket.
10. Disengage the water rail stud from the heat shield.
11. Remove the heat shield, manoeuvring it rearwards, and turning it anti-clockwise.
12. Remove the three nuts securing the catalytic converter to the exhaust manifold.
13. Remove the catalytic converter, manoeuvring it rearwards around the carburetter.
14. Fit a new catalytic converter by reversing the procedure in 1 to 12, and noting:
    a. Renew the exhaust flange gasket and exhaust pipe olive.
    b. Renew the air cleaner gasket and heat shield if damaged or showing signs of deterioration.
15. Service the E.G.R. valve.
16. Reset the E.G.R. and catalytic converter warning indicator by inserting the key into the button, and rotating it to zero the counter. Remove the key.

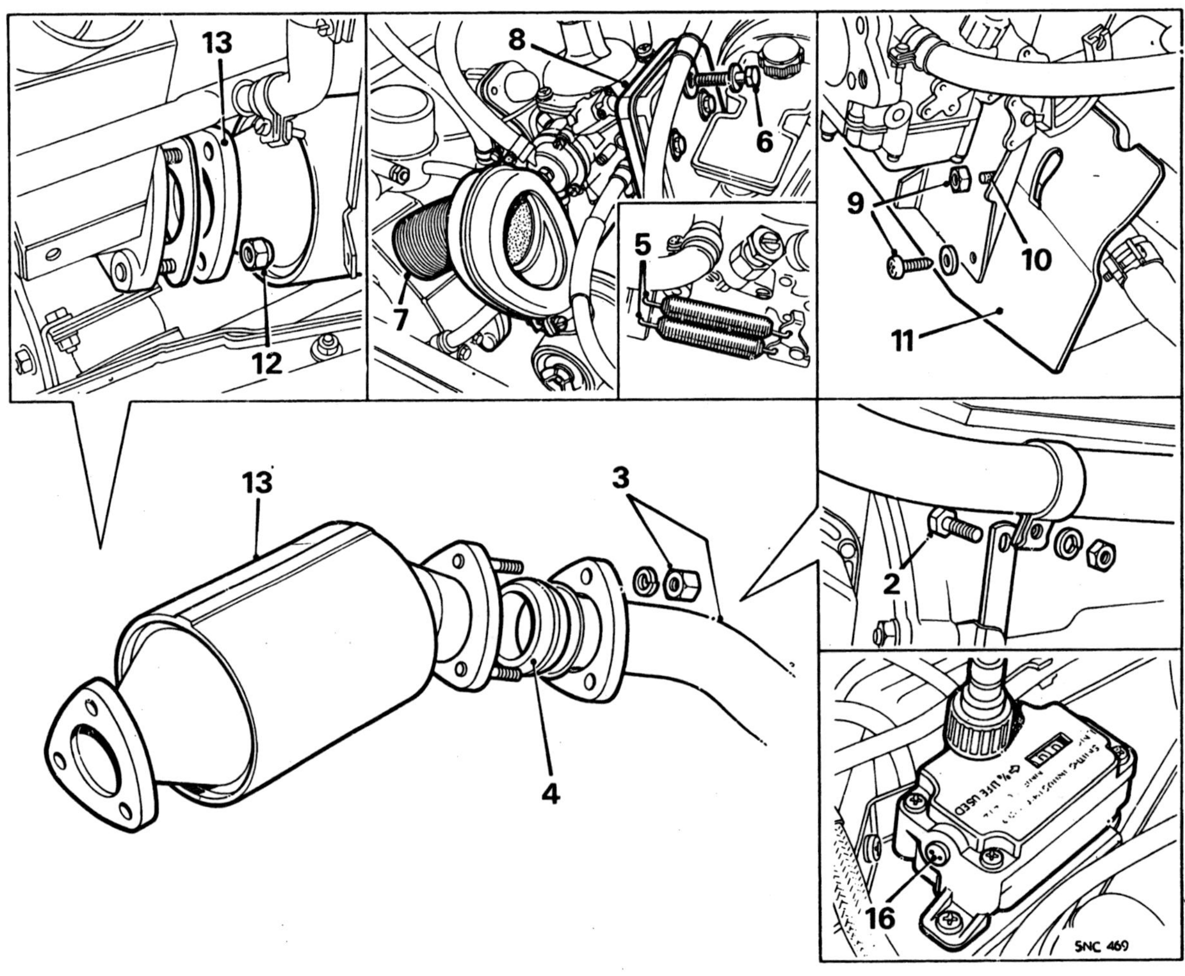

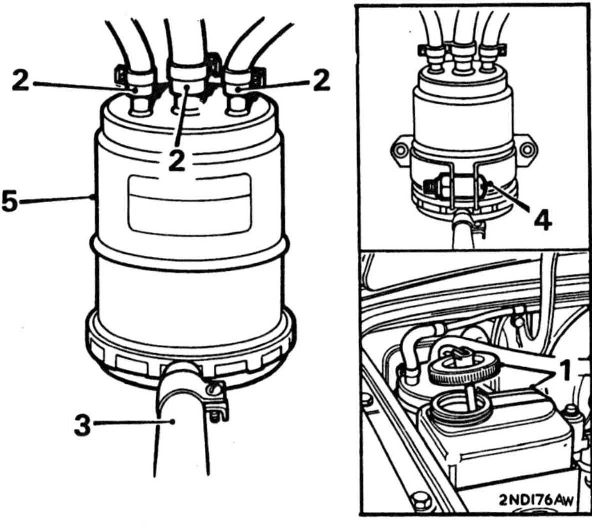

Adsorption canister

Removing

1. Unscrew the windscreen washer reservoir cap, withdraw the tube and remove the reservoir.
2. Disconnect the carburetter and fuel tank vapour lines and the rocker cover purge line from the canister.
3. Disconnect the air vent pipe from the canister.
4. Remove the clamp band nut and bolt and collect the spacer.
5. Remove the canister.

Refitting

6. Reverse the procedure in 1 to 5.

FUEL SYSTEM

Throttle

Lubricate the throttle control linkage, the cable and the accelerator pedal fulcrum.

Air cleaner element renewal

In dusty operating conditions the element may require changing more frequently than recommended.

Removing

1. Undo the wing nut and pivot the air cleaner end cover and air temperature control valve assembly away from the engine to release it from the hot air hose.
2. Remove the end cover together with the air temperature control valve assembly and the end cap from the air cleaner casing.
3. Withdraw the element and discard.
4. Thoroughly clean the air cleaner casing, cover and cap.
5. Fit a new element and refit the end cap ensuring that its lip supports the inside of the filter element.
6. Refit the end cover and air temperature control valve assembly.

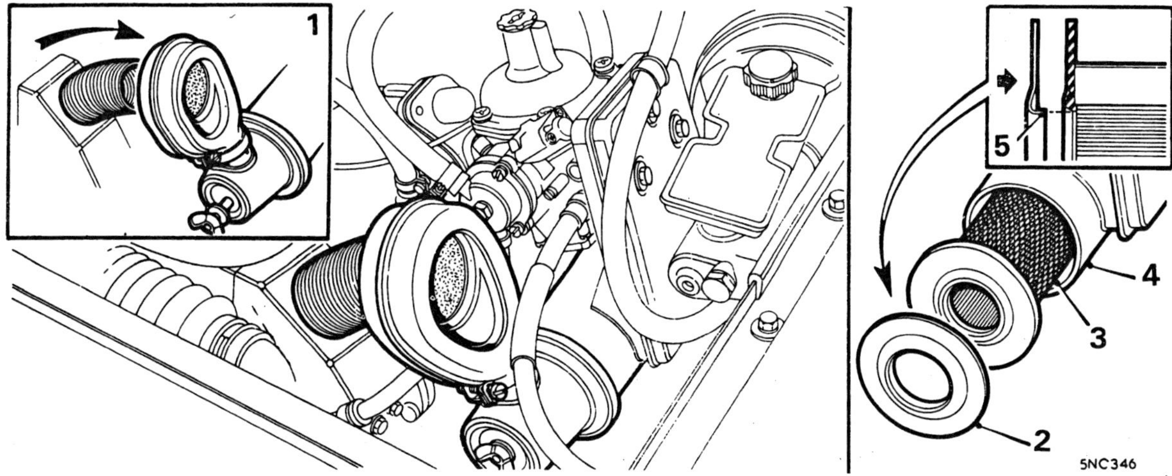

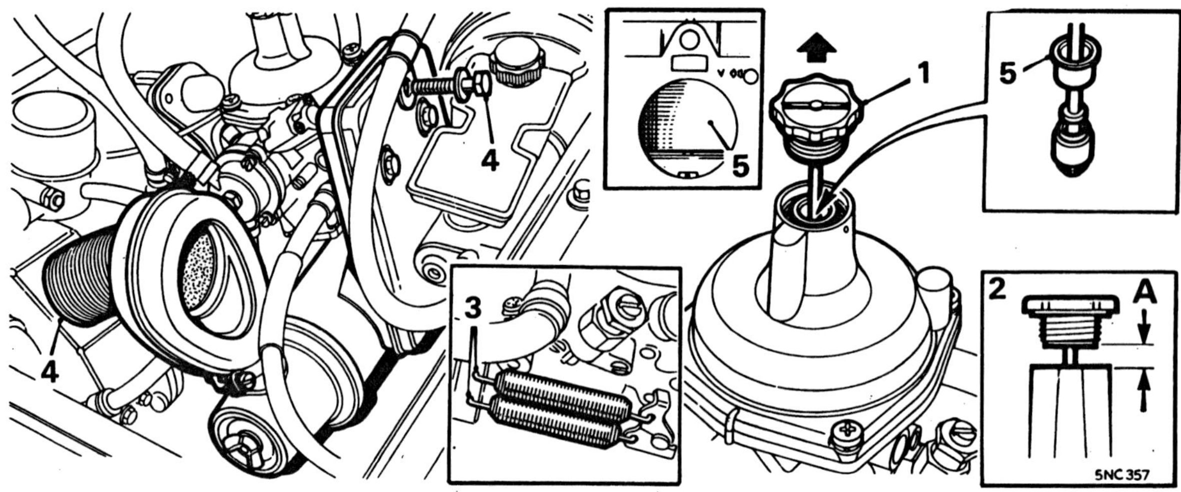

Carburetter

Checking oil level

1. Unscrew the damper cap from the carburetter.
2. Carefully raise the damper and then lower it into the hollow piston rod. If the oil level is correct resistance should be felt when there is a gap 'A' of ¼ in (6 mm) between the cap and the carburetter.

Topping-up

3. Detach the throttle return springs from the air cleaner.
4. Remove the three bolts securing the air cleaner to the carburetter, detach the air temperature control valve from the hot air hose and manoeuvre the air cleaner forwards in the engine compartment.
5. Unscrew the damper cap, raise the carburetter piston, release the damper retaining cup and remove the damper assembly from the piston.
6. With the piston raised, top up the hollow piston rod with a recommended engine oil until the level is ¼ in (6 mm) below the top of the rod.
7. Insert the damper and press the retaining cup into the hollow piston rod. Tighten the damper cap.
8. Refit the air cleaner.

Air pollution control

The carburetter incorporates features which assist in reducing exhaust emissions. Maladjustment or the fitting of parts not to the required specification may render these features ineffective.

Adjustments

Adjustments should only be undertaken if the use of an accurate tachometer, and exhaust gas analyser (CO meter) is available.

The tuning of the carburetter is confined to setting the idle speed and mixture strength (CO percentage). Obtaining the correct carburetter settings depends on correct ignition timing and spark plug gaps, valve rocker clearances, and on good seals at oil filler cap to valve rocker cover, valve rocker cover to cylinder head, side covers to cylinder block, engine oil dipstick to cylinder block, carburetter to induction manifold, induction manifold to cylinder head, all induction manifold tappings and the carburetter spindle seals.

Tuning

1. Check the throttle control for correct functioning.
2. Remove the air cleaner.
3. Unscrew the air valve damper—do not remove.
4. Using a finger, raise the air valve slowly through its full travel and release. The unit should move freely and smoothly and return to the carburetter bridge with an audible 'click'. If the air valve fails to move freely, the carburetter must be overhauled.
5. Top up the carburetter air valve damper with recommended engine oil to the correct level if necessary.
6. Refit the air cleaner.
7. Run the engine until normal operating temperature is reached, then drive the vehicle for a further five minutes on the road.
8. Disconnect the air manifold hose from the air pump and plug the hose.
9. Disconnect the float chamber vent pipe from the carburetter.

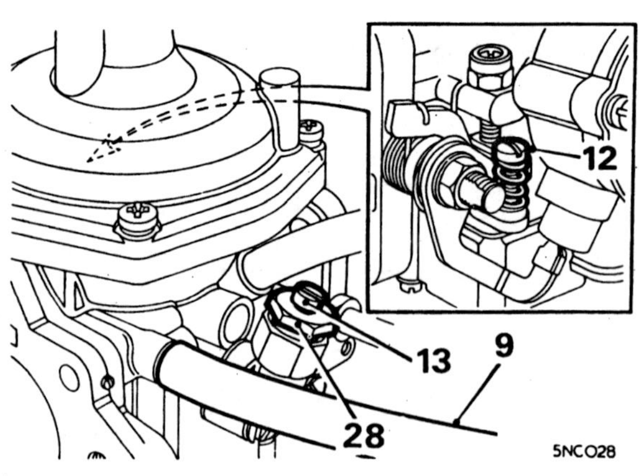

10. Connect an accurate tachometer.
11. Increase the engine speed to 2,500 rev/min for thirty seconds.

NOTE: Tuning must commence immediately. If delay prevents the adjustment being completed within three minutes, increase the engine speed to 2,500 rev/min for thirty seconds and then continue tuning. Repeat this clearing procedure at three-minute intervals until tuning is completed.

12. Check and if necessary adjust the idle speed, see **'ENGINE TUNING DATA'**.
13. Use the exhaust gas analyser in accordance with the manufacturer's instructions to check the percentage CO at idle. If the reading falls outside the prescribed limits, see **'ENGINE TUNING DATA'**, adjust the fine idle screw clockwise to enrich or anti-clockwise to weaken.
14. If the reading is within limits, continue with operations 34 to 37. If the correct CO percentage cannot be attained:
15. Turn the fine idle screw clockwise to the limit of its adjustment, then turn the screw anti-clockwise 2½ turns: this will position the screw in the mid-point of its adjustment range.

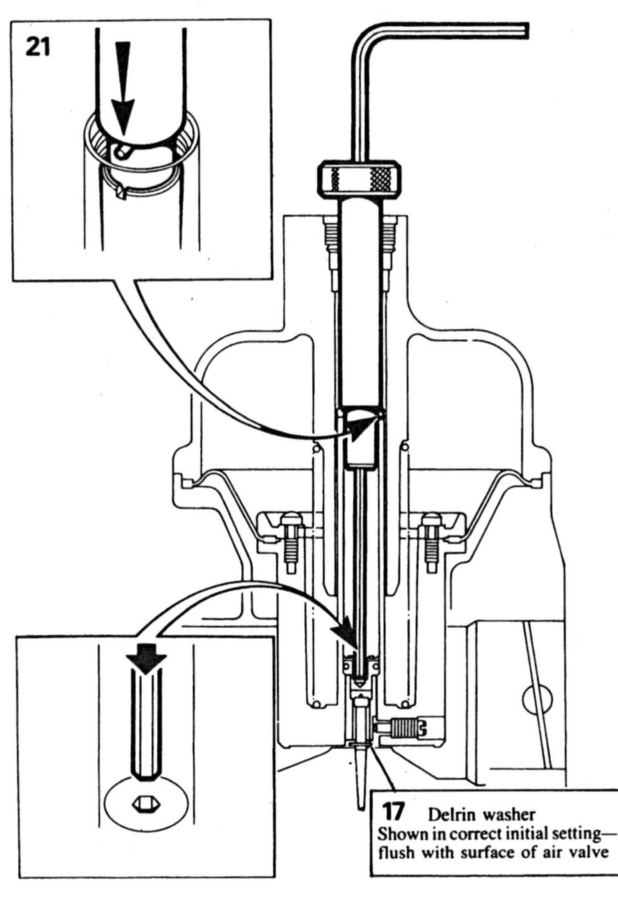

17 Delrin washer
Shown in correct initial setting—flush with surface of air valve

16. Remove the suction chamber and air valve from the carburetter.
17. Check that the initial needle adjustment is correct. [If not, turn the needle adjuster plug one way or the other until the lower surface of the Delrin washer is flush with the adjacent surface of the air valve.]
18. Ensure that the spring loaded needle is biased away from the engine.
19. If the needle is correctly adjusted, continue with tuning at operation 28. If the adjustment is not correct, proceed as follows:
20. Remove the air valve damper from the suction chamber.
21. Carefully insert tool S353 [or BLT2010] into the dashpot until the outer tool engages the air valve and the inner tool engages the hexagon in the needle adjuster plug.

    NOTE: The outer tool must be correctly engaged or the air valve diaphragm may be torn.
22. Hold the outer tool firmly and turn the inner tool to correct the initial needle adjustment.
23. Refit the air valve, ensuring that the moulded tag on the rubber diaphragm locates in the depression in the air valve housing.
24. Refit the suction chamber cover, ensuring that the location mark aligns with the mark on the carburetter body above the air cleaner flange.
25. Top up the carburetter damper and refit the damper.
26. Check the idle speed and percentage CO as before. If necessary, adjust the fine idler screw.
27. If it is still not possible to obtain the required idle CO percentage, reposition the fine idler screw in the midpoint of its adjustment range – operation 15.
28. Adjust the coarse idle nut, clockwise to enrich or anti-clockwise to weaken.
29. If it is not possible to obtain the required CO percentage, screw the coarse idle nut clockwise to the limit of its adjustment (do not apply excessive force as this may damage the thread), then turn the nut anti-clockwise two turns. This will position the nut in the mid-point of its adjustment range.
30. Remove the air valve damper and insert main mixture adjusting tool S353 [or BLT2010] as in operation 21.
31. Hold the outer tool and turn the inner tool clockwise to enrich the mixture or anti-clockwise to weaken the mixture as required.
32. Top up the piston damper and refit the damper.
33. Re-check the CO percentage and repeat operations 30 to 32 as necessary until the required idle CO percentage is obtained.
34. Unplug the air manifold hose and refit the hose to the air pump.
35. Increase the engine speed to 2,500 rev/min for thirty seconds.
36. Readjust the idle screw to give the required idle speed.
37. Re-connect the float chamber vent pipe.
38. If it is not possible to attain the required idle CO percentage, overhaul the carburetter.

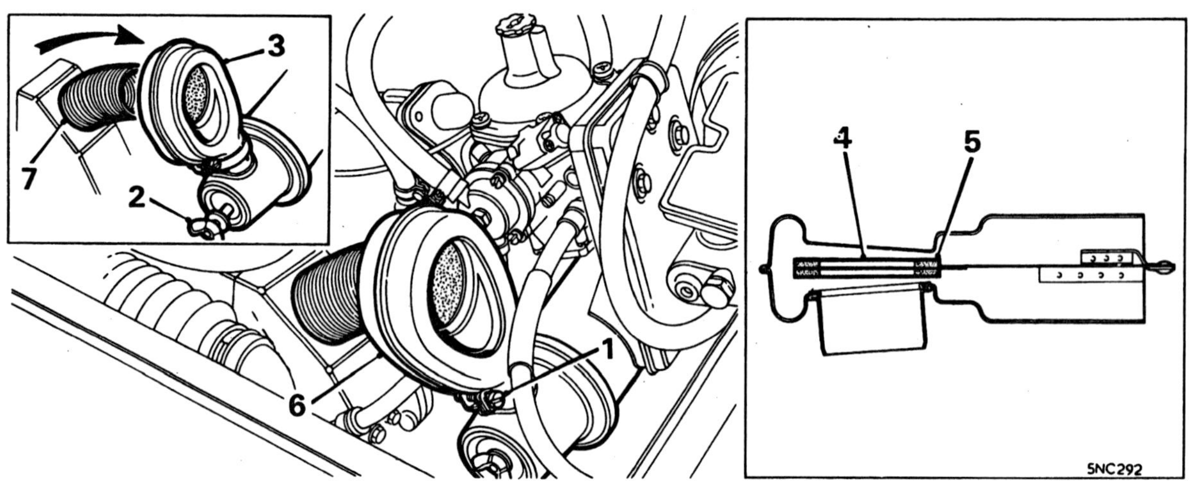

Air temperature control valve

Removing

1. Slacken the clip securing the valve to the air cleaner end cover.
2. Slacken the wing nut and pivot the end cover and valve assembly away from the engine to detach the valve from the hot air hose.
3. Remove the valve.

Inspection

4. Note the position of the valve plate, depress the plate and release it. Check that the valve plate returns to its original position.
5. Check that the foam seats of the valve are in good condition.
6. Renew the valve if it is faulty.
7. Check that the hot air hose is in good condition – renew if necessary.

Refitting

8. Reverse the procedure in 1 to 3.

Testing

1. With engine cold, ensure that flap valve blocks air entry from engine compartment.
2. With engine at normal running temperature, ensure that flap valve blocks air entry from exhaust manifold or pipe.

Fuel filler cap seal

1 The seal must be inspected for damage and wear and renewed if necessary.

IT IS ESSENTIAL TO THE SATISFACTORY OPERATION OF THE EVAPORATIVE LOSS SYSTEM THAT THE CAP IS ALWAYS REFITTED CORRECTLY AND TIGHTENED FULLY. A DEFECTIVE CAP OR SEAL MUST BE REPLACED.

Fuel line filter

1. Remove the screw to release the carburetter hose retaining clip.
2. Disconnect the carburetter hose from the filter.
3. Disconnect the fuel tank delivery hose from the filter.
4. Remove and discard the filter.
5. Fit a new filter ensuring that the flow arrow is directed towards the carburetter feed hose.

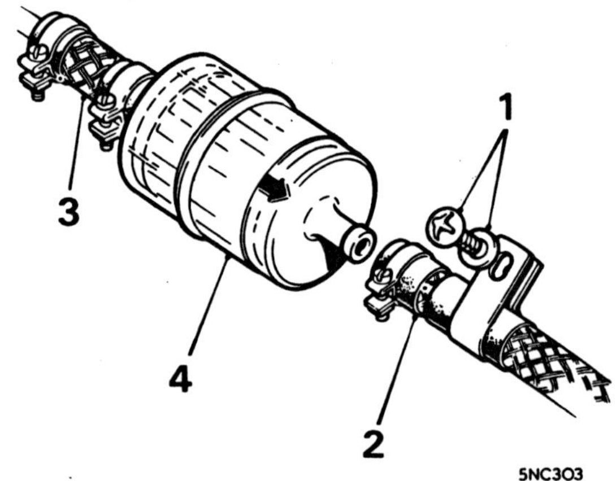

IGNITION

Distributor–Lucas type 45D4

Lubrication

1. Remove the distributor cover and rotor arm.
2. Lightly smear the cam and pivot post with grease.
3. Add a few drops of oil to the felt pad in the top of the cam spindle.
4. Add a few drops of oil through the gap between the cam spindle and base plate to lubricate the centrifugal weights.
5. Every 25,000 miles lubricate the contact breaker assembly centre bearing with a drop of oil in each of the two holes in the base plate.

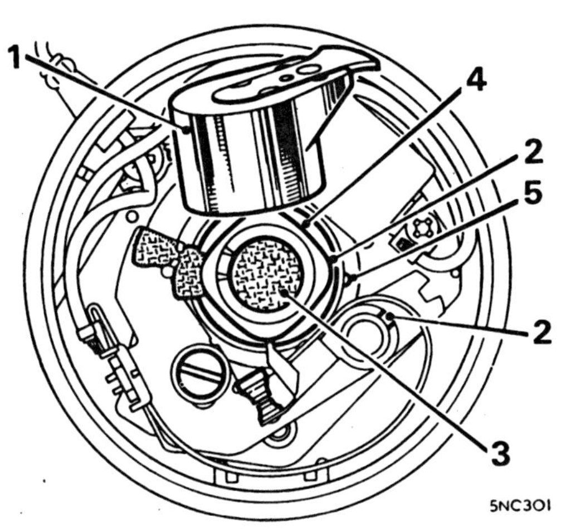

Renewing contact breaker points

6. Remove the securing screw with its spring and flat washer.
7. Lift the contact set.
8. Press the spring and release the terminal plate from the end of the spring.
9. Before fitting new contact points, wipe the points clean with fuel or methylated spirit.
10. Lightly grease the pivot post.
11. Re-connect the terminal plate to the end of the contact breaker spring.
12. Position the contact set on the distributor base plate and lightly tighten the securing screw. Ensure that the contact breaker spring is firmly in its register on the insulator and set the contact breaker gap.

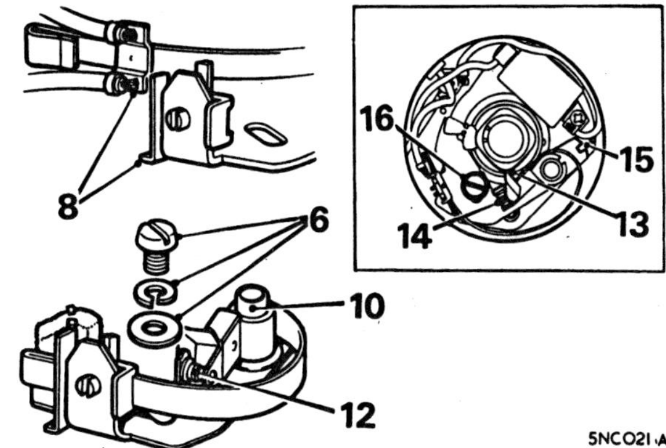

Contact breaker gap–Checking–Adjusting

13. Turn the crankshaft until the heel of the contact point is on the highest point of any one of the cam lobes.
14. Check the contact gap; it should be 0.014 to 0.016 in (0.35 to 0.40 mm).
15. Adjust the gap; to adjust insert a screwdriver in the slot in the contact breaker plate and lever against the pip or cutout provided on the base plate.
16. Tighten the securing screw.
17. Turn the crankshaft until the heel of the contact is on the highest point of an alternative cam lobe.
18. Re-check the contact gap.
19. Repeat 17 and 18 for each remaining cam lobe.

Distributor cap–checking

20. Unclip and remove the distributor cap.
21. Remove the rotor arm.
22. Using a clean, nap-free cloth, wipe the rotor arm and the inside of the distributor cap.
23. Examine the cap and arm for cracks and signs of electrical tracking. Renew if necessary.
24. Check the condition and operation of the carbon brush. Refit the distributor cap.

Distributor dwell angle

25. Using suitable equipment, check the distributor dwell angle.
26. Readjust the contact breaker gap to obtain the correct dwell angle as follows:
    To increase the dwell angle, reduce the contact gap.
    To reduce the dwell angle, increase the contact breaker gap.
27. Re-check the ignition timing, and adjust if necessary.

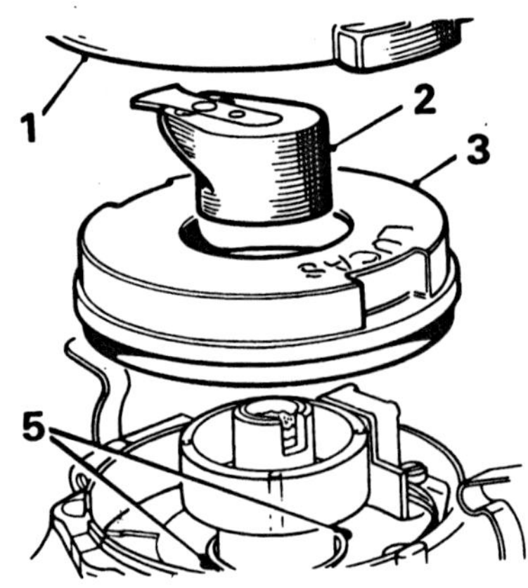

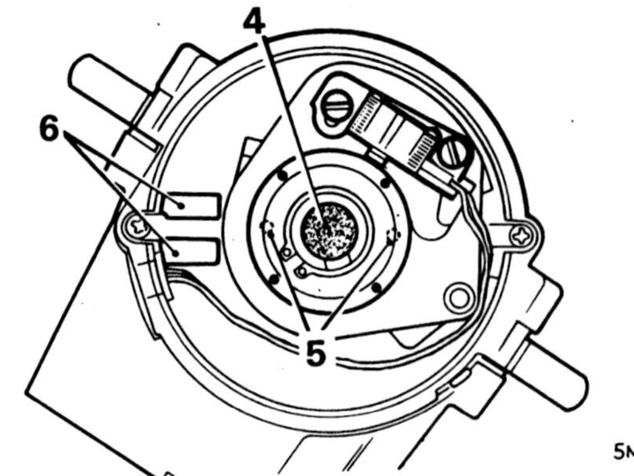

Distributor–Lucas type 45DE4

Lubrication

1. Release the retaining clips and remove the cover.
2. Remove the rotor arm.
3. Remove the anti-flash shield.
4. Add a few drops of oil to the felt pad in the top of the timing rotor carrier.
5. Lubricate the pick-up plate centre bearing with a drop of oil in each of the two holes in the base plate.
6. Apply a few drops of oil through the apertures to lubricate the centrifugal timing control.

Cleaning

7. Wipe the inside of the distributor cover, the rotor arm, and the anti-flash shield with a clean nap-free cloth. Check the carbon brush is free to move in its housing. Inspect the cap and rotor for cracks and any trace of tracking. Renew if necessary.
8. Refit the anti-flash shield ensuring that the cut-outs are aligned with the distributor cover retaining clips.
9. Refit the rotor arm and cover.

Spark plugs – Cleaning – Renewing

1. Mark each spark plug lead with its plug position and remove each lead from its plug.
2. Using a tubular box spanner, partly unscrew each plug.
3. Clean the area surrounding each plug, using compressed air or a brush.
4. Remove the spark plugs.
5. Clean and check the spark plugs, using an air-blast service unit.
   Discard and fit new plugs at the intervals recommended, ensuring that only the recommended type and grade are used.
7. Before fitting, check the gap between the electrodes of each plug and set to the dimension given in **'ENGINE TUNING DATA'**, bending the side electrode only.
8. Screw the plugs into the cylinder head by hand, then use a tubular box spanner to tighten, ensuring that a good joint is made between the plug body, the sealing washer and the cylinder head.
9. Connect the ignition leads onto their respective plugs.

Ignition timing

Checking–Adjusting

1. Start the engine and run it until normal operating temperature is reached.
2. Connect a stroboscopic timing light in accordance with the manufacturer's instructions.
3. Run the engine at timing speed, see **'ENGINE TUNING DATA'**, and position the timing light to illuminate the crankshaft pulley and the timing scale.
4. Adjust the timing, slacken the distributor clamp bolt and rotate the distributor body until the correct setting is achieved.
5. Tighten the distributor clamp bolt.

[**NOTE:** On 1977 and later cars, the vacuum advance is operative, but only in 4th gear or in 4th gear overdrive. See Section Na for a wiring diagram of this transmission-controlled vacuum advance system.]

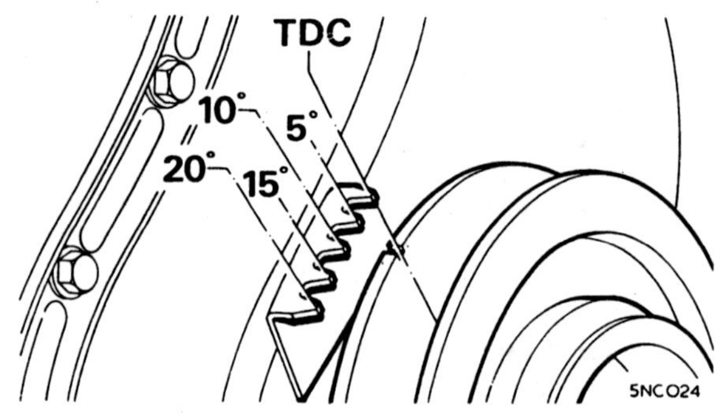

COOLING SYSTEM (1975 and 1976)
[See page 21 for 1977 and later cars.]

Check coolant level

WARNING: The cooling system is under pressure while the engine is hot and the pressure must be released gradually when the filler cap is removed. Add sufficient coolant to cover the bottom of the radiator header tank filler neck.

NOTE: Ensure that the specific gravity of the anti-freeze is maintained.

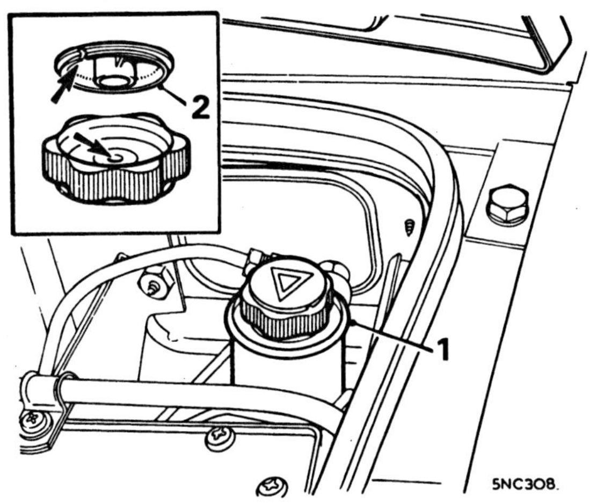

CLUTCH

Topping up clutch master cylinder reservoir

1. The fluid level in the master cylinder should be maintained at the bottom of the filler neck. Top up using a recommended fluid (see **'SERVICE LUBRICANTS FUEL AND FLUIDS–CAPACITIES'**).
2. Before replacing the filler cap separate the dome from the cap and check that the breather holes are clear.

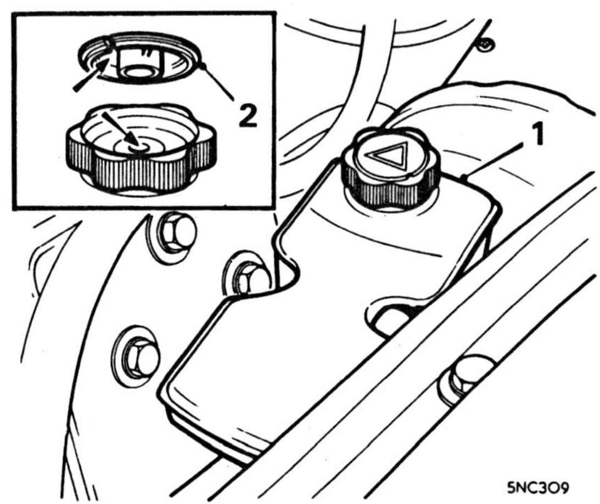

BRAKES

Topping up brake master cylinder reservoir

1. The fluid level in the master cylinder is visible through the plastic reservoir and should be maintained at the bottom of the filler neck. Top up using a recommended fluid (see **'SERVICE LUBRICANTS FUEL AND FLUIDS–CAPACITIES'**).
2. Before replacing the filler cap, separate the dome from the cap and check that the breather holes are clear.

Brake servo air filter renewal

1. Remove the eight screws and one washer securing the pedal box cover.
2. Place the petrol feed pipe clip aside and remove the cover and seal.
3. Pull back the servo dust cover.
4. Detach the end cap from the servo neck.
5. Holding the end cap and dust cover away from the servo neck, remove the air filter and discard.
6. Cut the new filter diagonally, fit over the push-rod and press it into the servo neck.
7. Refit the end cap, dust cover, and pedal box cover.

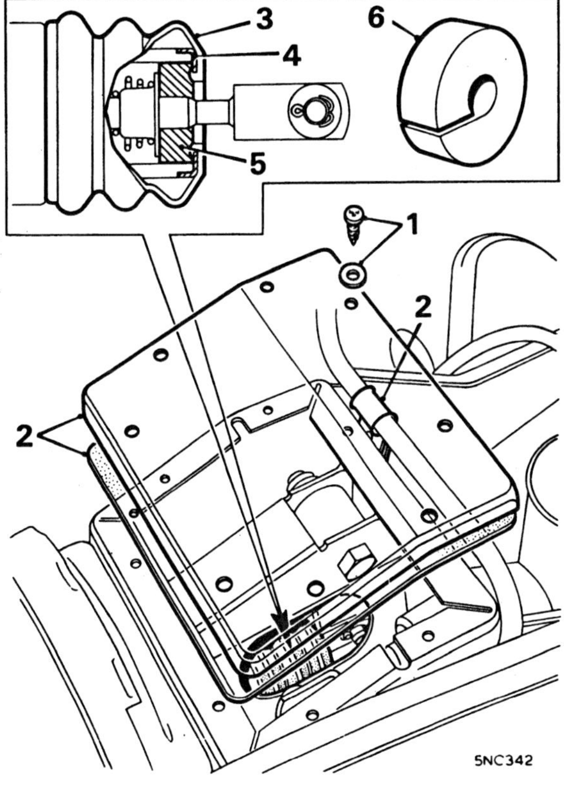

Hand brake

Adjustment

The hand brake is automatically adjusted with the rear brakes. If free play is still excessive the hand brake cable requires adjusting, see Section M.2.

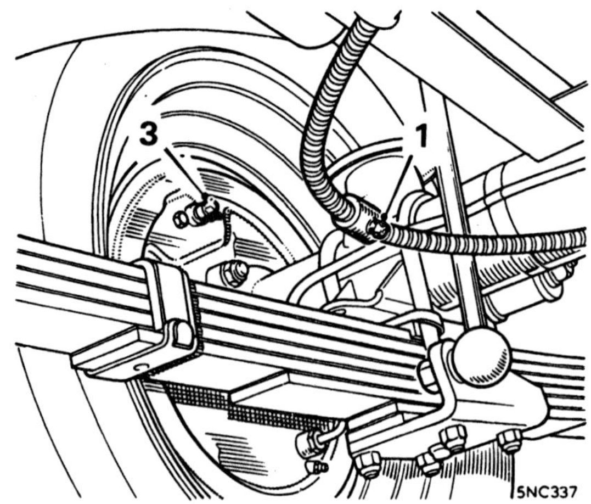

Hand brake lubrication

1. Charge the nipple on the hand brake cable with one of the recommended greases.

Inspecting and adjusting the rear brakes

2. Chock the front wheels, release the hand brake, jack up each rear wheel in turn and place suitable supports beneath the vehicle.
3. Remove the road wheel and slacken the brake-shoe adjuster fully.
4. Remove the two retaining screws and withdraw the brake-drum.
5. Inspect the linings and drums. Ensure that sufficient lining material remains to allow the car to be run until the next check. Clean the dust from the backplate and drum.
6. Refit the brake-drum.
7. Adjust the shoes; turn the adjuster clockwise (viewed from centre of car) until the brake shoes lock the brake-drum, then turn back the adjuster until the drum will rotate without the linings rubbing.
8. Refit the road wheel.

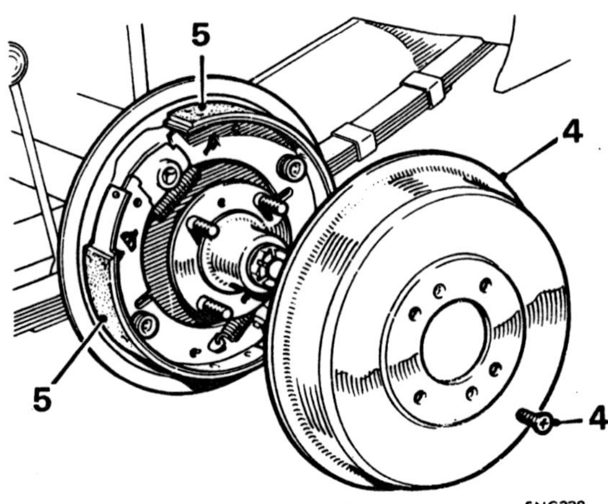

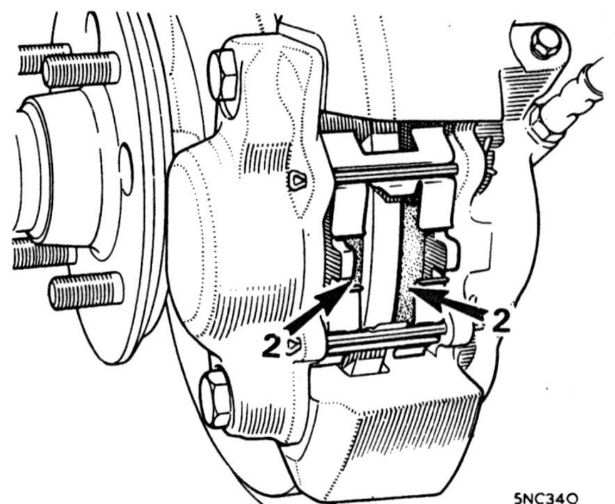

Inspecting front brake disc pads

1. Remove the road wheel to gain clear access to the pads for inspection.
2. Check the thickness of the pads and renew if the lining material has worn to $\frac{1}{16}$ in (1.6 mm) or will have done so before the next regular inspection is due. Change the pads over if wear is not even (see Section M).
   Check the discs for condition and wear.

Brake hoses and pipes

Examine all hoses, pipes and unions for chafing, leaks and corrosion. It is most important that hoses are not subjected to stress and are not positioned near to other components so that chafing can occur. Rectify any leaks and replace hoses and pipes showing signs of damage or deterioration.

Preventive maintenance

In addition to the recommended periodical inspection of brake components it is advisable as the vehicle ages, and as a precaution against the effects of wear and deterioration, to make a more searching inspection and renew parts as necessary.

It is recommended that:

1. Brake linings, hoses and pipes should be examined at intervals no greater than those laid down in the **'MAINTENANCE SUMMARY'**.
2. Brake fluid should be changed completely every 18 months or 19,000 miles (30000 km) whichever is the sooner.
3. All fluid seals and all flexible hoses in the hydraulic system should be renewed every 3 years or 37,500 miles (60000 km) whichever is the sooner. At the same time the working surface of the pistons and of the bores of the master cylinder, wheel cylinders, and other slave cylinders should be examined and new parts fitted where necessary. The brake servo filter should also be changed.

Care must be taken always to observe the following points:
1. At all times use the recommended brake fluid.
2. Never leave fluid in unsealed containers. It absorbs moisture quickly and can be dangerous if used in the braking system in this condition.
3. Fluid drained from the system or used for bleeding is best discarded.
4. The necessity for absolute cleanliness throughout cannot be over-emphasized.

STEERING AND SUSPENSION

Lubrication

Grease each front suspension unit, giving three or four strokes from a grease gun into each of the three nipples.

Steering rack gaiters – shock absorbers

Check for fluid leaks, examine gaiters for damage and deterioration, check tightness of retaining clips.

Front wheel alignment – see Section J.

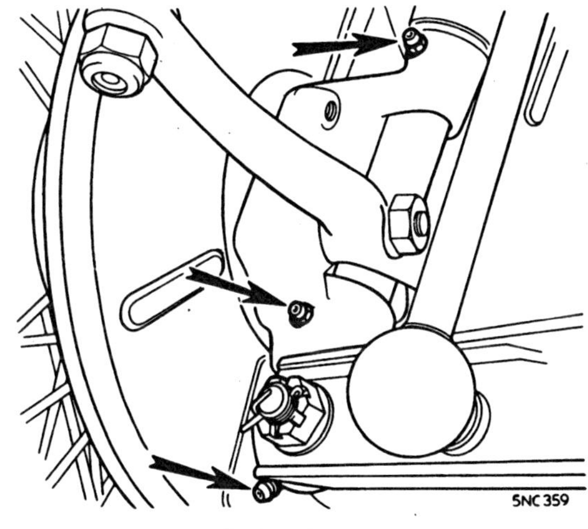

1975–1976 cars

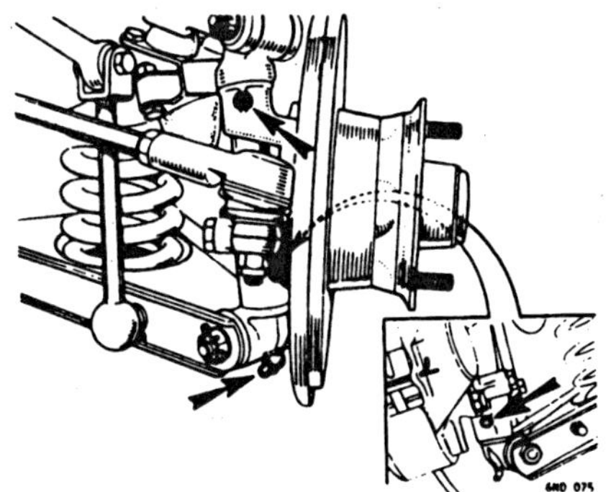
1977 and later

WHEELS AND TYRES

1. Check that tyres are in accordance with the manufacturer's specification: 165SR-14 radial ply.
2. Check and adjust the tyre pressures, including the spare.
   Front: 21 lbf/in², 1.48 kgf/cm², 1.45 bars
   Rear: 24 lbf/in², 1.69 kgf/cm², 1.66 bars
3. Check depth of tread.
4. Check visually for cuts in the tyre fabric, exposure of ply or cord, lumps or bulges.
5. Check tightness of the road wheel nuts: 60 to 65 lbf ft (8.3 to 9 kgf m).

Wire wheels

6. Raise the front of the car and fit suitable safety supports under the chassis front members.
   CAUTION: When the front wheels are clear of the ground, care should be taken to avoid forceful movement of the wheels from lock to lock as damage may occur within the steering mechanism.
7. Remove the road wheel.
8. Smear the splines of the hub and wire wheel with grease.
9. Refit the wire wheel.
10. Lower the car.

Tyre care

Excessive local distortion can cause the casing of a tyre to fracture and may lead to premature tyre failure. Tyres should be examined, especially for cracked walls, exposed cords, etc. Flints and other sharp objects should be removed from the tyre tread, if neglected they may work through the cover. Any oil or grease which may get onto the tyres should be cleaned off by using petrol (gasoline) sparingly. Do not use paraffin (kerosene), which has a detrimental effect on rubber.

Repairs

When repairing tubes, have punctures or injuries vulcanized. Ordinary patches should only be used for emergencies. Vulcanizing is absolutely essential for tubes manufactured from synthetic rubber.

Tubeless tyres

The insertion of a plug to repair a puncture in a tubeless tyre must be regarded as a temporary repair only and a permanent vulcanized repair must be made as soon as possible.

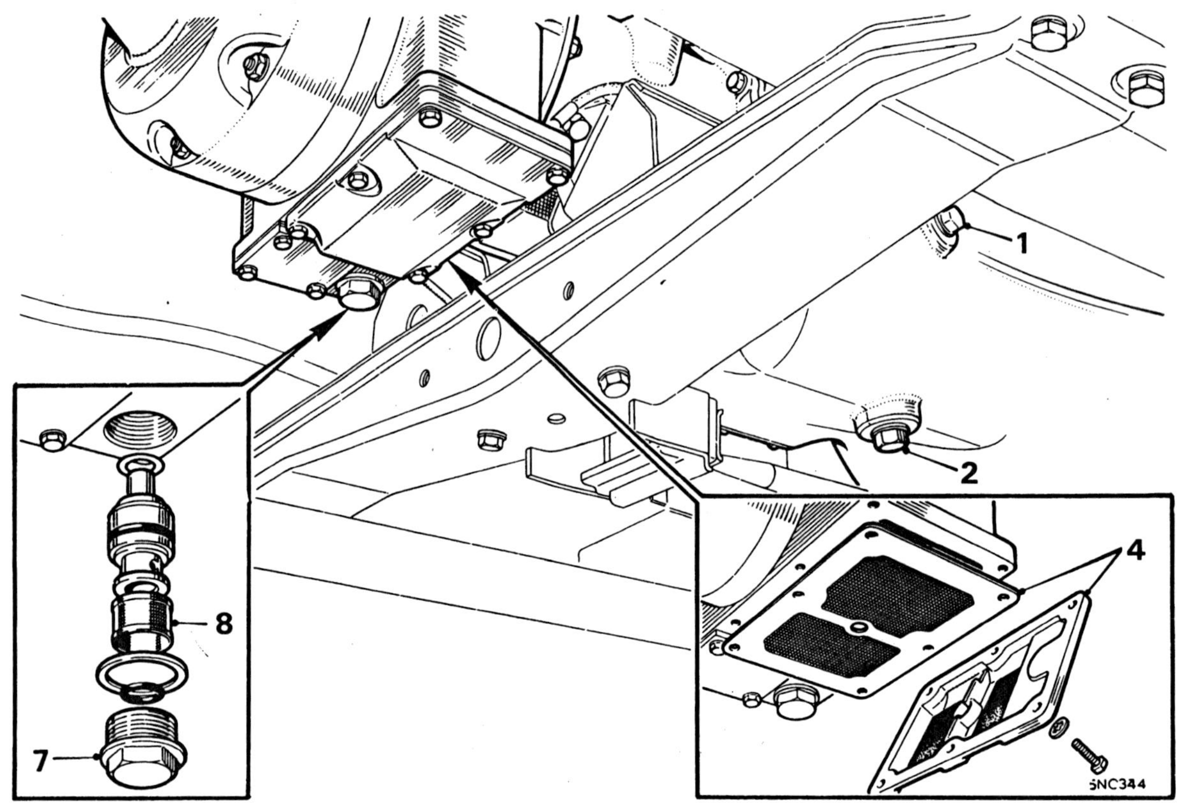

TRANSMISSION

Checking gearbox oil level

1. With the car standing level, check that the oil is level with the bottom of the aperture. Top up using the correct quantity of a recommended oil (see **'SERVICE LUBRICANTS FUEL AND FLUIDS–CAPACITIES'**).

Gearbox with overdrive

Cleaning sump filter

2. Remove the plug to drain the gearbox and overdrive unit.
3. Clean the sump cover and its surroundings.
4. Remove the cover securing screws and withdraw the cover and filter.
5. Clean all metallic particles from the two magnets fitted to the inside of the cover.
6. Wash the filter and cover in petrol (gasoline).

Relief valve filter

7. Remove the plug and seal and withdraw the relief valve approximately ½ in.
8. Remove the filter.
9. Wash the filter, plug and seal in petrol (gasoline).
10. Refit the filter to the relief valve, push the valve fully home and refit the plug and seal.
11. Fill the gearbox and overdrive unit through the combined oil filler with the correct quantity of a recommended oil (see **'SERVICE LUBRICANTS FUEL AND FLUIDS–CAPACITIES'**).
    Run the car for a short distance, allow it to stand for a few minutes, then re-check the level.

NOTE: Anti-friction additives must not be used in the gearbox or overdrive.

Rear axle

Checking oil level

With the car standing level check that the oil is level with the bottom of the plug aperture.

1. Top up with a recommended oil allowing sufficient time for any surplus oil to run out before replacing the plug.

CAUTION: Do not drain the rear axle when the **'After-Sales Service'** is carried out.

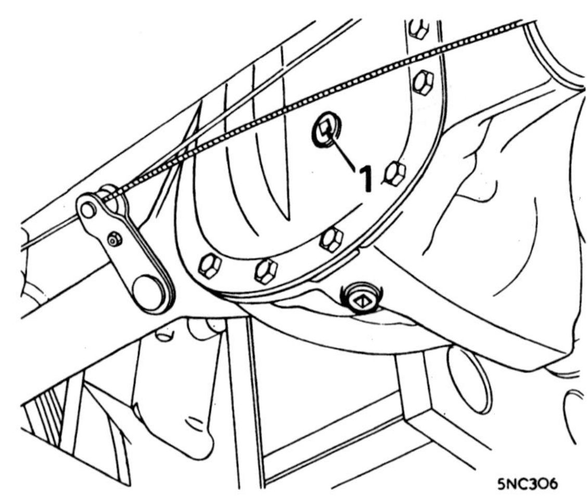

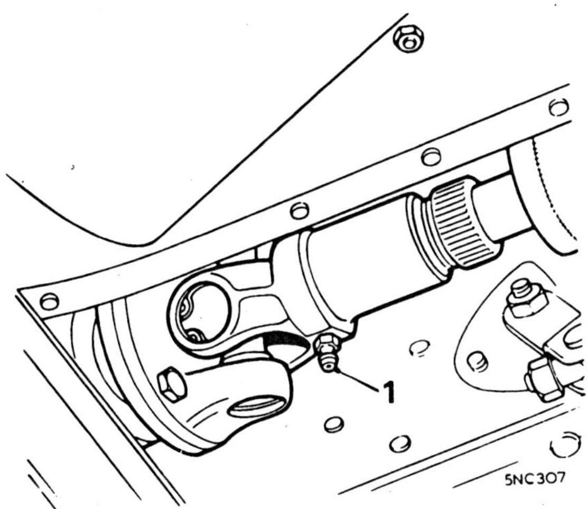

Propeller shaft

1. Lubricate the front end of the propeller shaft giving three or four strokes from a grease gun into the nipple.

Checking electrolyte level

1. Remove the rear compartment carpet, turn the three quick-release fasteners anti-clockwise one half turn and remove the battery compartment cover panel.
2. Lift the vent cover vertically and pull it evenly from the filling valves.
3. Ensure that the filling valves are raised.
4. Top up the battery by pouring distilled water into the filling trough until the valve and connecting trough are filled.
5. Press the vent cover firmly into position; the correct quantity of distilled water will be distributed to each cell.

In freezing conditions run the engine immediately after topping-up to mix the electrolyte.

6. Clean off any corrosion from the battery and its mountings, using diluted ammonia, and then paint affected parts with anti-sulphuric paint.
7. Smear the terminals posts with petroleum jelly and ensure that the terminal screws are secure.

ELECTRICAL

Testing

Check that the lamps, horns, warning indicators, windscreen wipers are functioning correctly.

Battery

CAUTION: Except when topping up, the vent must be kept closed. The electrolyte will flood if the cover is raised while the battery is being trickle or fast charged. Single-cell discharge testers cannot be used on this battery. On no occasion should the vent cover be detached from the battery.

Do not use a naked light when examining the cells.

Checking the charging system output

1. Connect a 0–20V moving coil voltmeter across the battery terminals.
2. Connect a 0–60A test ammeter in series with the main output cable and the '+' terminal of the alternator.
3. Start the engine, increase the engine speed and observe the ammeter.
4. If the reading exceeds 10A, continue running the engine until the reading falls below 10A.
5. The voltmeter reading should be 13.6 to 14.4V indicating that the charging system is working normally.

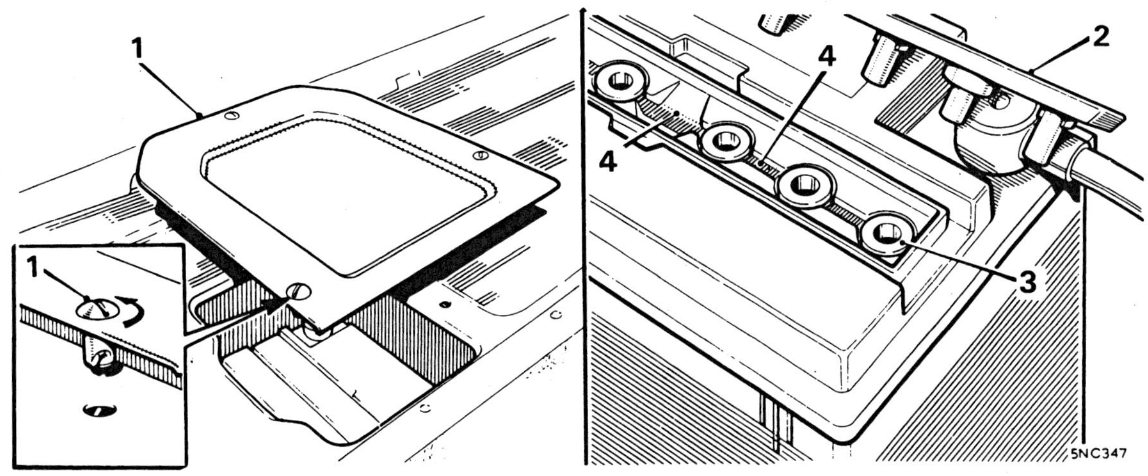

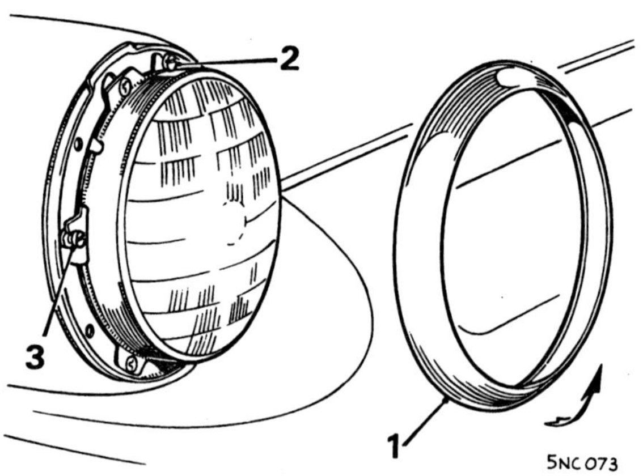

Headlamp beam alignment

Set the beams slightly below horizontal and parallel with each other or in accordance with local regulations.

1. Remove the outer rim by easing the bottom of the rim forwards away from the lamp.
2. Vertical adjustment.
3. Horizontal adjustment.

Windscreen wiper blades

Checking

1. Examine the rubber blades for condition and if they are perished or defective, renew the blade assembly.

Renewing

2. Pull the wiper away from the windscreen.
3. Hold the fastener and spring retainer away from the wiper arm and withdraw the blade assembly from the arm.
4. Insert the end of the arm into the spring fastener of the new blade and push the new blade into engagement with the arm.
5. Lower the wiper onto the windscreen.

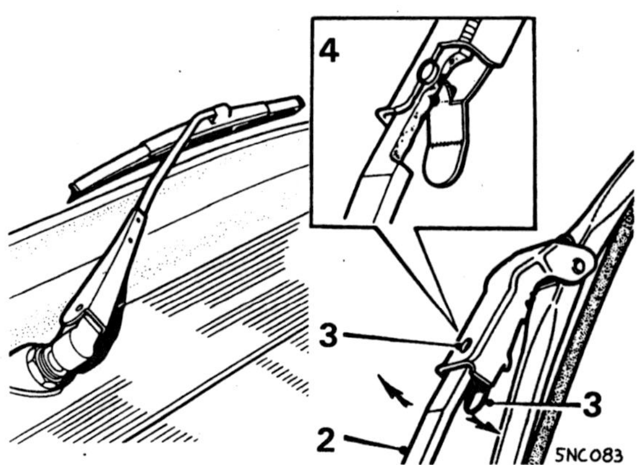

Windscreen washer–checking

1. Switch on the ignition and press the end of the switch lever and check the operation of the washers.
2. If the delivery is incorrect turn the jet using a small screwdriver to adjust the height of the spray.

Windscreen washer–topping up

3. Remove the filler cap and top up as necessary with a mixture of water and a recommended solvent; **do not use radiator anti-freeze.**

BODY

1. Lubricate the bonnet safety catch and release mechanism.
2. Lubricate all hinges and door locks. **Do not oil the steering lock.**
3. Check the condition and security of the seats and seat belts and seat belt interlock.
4. Check operation of all door locks and window controls.

GENERAL

Seat belt warning system

Checking

1. Switch on the ignition and check that the seat belt warning buzzer sounds.
2. Operate the starter, check that the seat belt warning lamp illuminates. Both warnings should cease automatically after eight seconds.

Seat belt testing

WARNING: The following test must only be carried out under safe conditions, i.e. on a dry, straight, metalled road, during a period when the road is free of traffic.

1. With the belts in use, drive the car at 5 m.p.h. and brake sharply.
2. The automatic device should operate and lock the belt. Do not anticipate the retarding effect of braking.

Road/roller test

Road or roller test the vehicle and check that all the instruments function correctly.

NOTE: When checking the tightness of nuts and bolts great care must be taken not to overtighten them. A torque wrench should be used where possible – see **'TORQUE WRENCH SETTINGS'**.

SECTION A

THE ENGINE

† These operations must be followed by an exhaust emission check. 

GENERAL DESCRIPTION

The overhead-valve engine is built in unit construction, with single-plate dry clutch. Cylinder bores are an integral part of the block and are water-jacketed their full length. The valves are set vertically in the detachable cylinder head and are operated through the medium of the rocker gear, push-rods, and tappets from the camshaft in the left-hand side of the cylinder block. Renewable, thinwall bearings support the counterbalanced crankshaft, while end-thrust is taken by the thrust washers fitted to the centre main bearing. The camshaft is driven by a single roller chain which is automatically adjusted by a spring-hydraulic-operated rubber slipper. The oil pump and distributor are driven from the camshaft; each component has its own drive shaft.

Section A.1

LUBRICATION

Engine oil filter

The external oil filter is of the disposable cartridge type and is located on the right-hand side of the engine.

Oil pressure relief valve

The automatic relief valve in the lubrication system deals with any excessive oil pressure when starting from cold. When hot, the pressure drops as the oil becomes more fluid. Should the oil filter become blocked, two relief valves in the filter blow off to enable the oil to by-pass the filter and pass direct into the main gallery.

Continuous cold-running and unnecessary use of the mixture control are often the causes of serious oil dilution by fuel, with a consequent drop in pressure.

Particular attention is called to the recommended changes of oil.

The non-adjustable oil pressure relief valve is situated at the rear of the left-hand side of the cylinder block and is held in position by a domed hexagon nut sealed by two fibre washers or one copper washer. The relief valve spring maintains a valve cup against a seating machined in the block.

The valve should be examined to ensure that the cup is seating correctly and that the relief spring has not lost its tension. The latter can be checked by measuring the length of the spring to give the correct relief pressure (see **'GENERAL SPECIFICATION DATA'**). Fit a new cup and spring if necessary.

Section A.2

MANIFOLDS

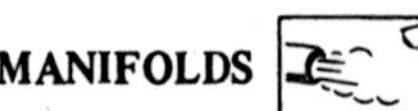

Remove the air cleaner and carburetter as detailed in Section D.

Disconnect the distributor vacuum pipe, the brake servo pipe and the running-on control valve hose from the manifold.

Remove the E.G.R. valve and gulp valve, see **'MAINTENANCE'.**

Remove the hot air duct, see Section T.

Remove the two screws to release the heat shield from the water pipe.

Remove the exhaust pipe to manifold clamp nuts and spring washers and release the pipe.

Six studs and nuts secure the manifolds to the cylinder head.

The four centre nuts have large washers, enabling them to secure both the inlet and exhaust manifolds. The two remaining nuts, one at each end of the manifolds, have small washers and secure the exhaust manifold only.

Replacements of the manifolds is a reversal of these instructions.

Use a new gasket.

Section A.3

ROCKER ASSEMBLY

Drain the cooling system—Section C.

Disconnect the purge pipe from the rocker cover.

Unscrew the two nuts and lift off the rocker cover, taking care not to damage the cork gasket or lose the washers and rubber seals. Notice that under the right-hand rear rocker stud nut is a special locking plate. Unscrew the eight rocker shaft bracket fixing nuts gradually, a turn at a time, in the order shown in Fig. A.3 until all load has been released.

It is neccessary to drain the radiator and slacken the seven external cylinder head securing nuts because four of the rocker shaft bracket fixing nuts also secure the cylinder head, and if the seven external cylinder head fixing nuts are not slackened distortion may result and water find its way from the cooling system into the cylinders and sump.

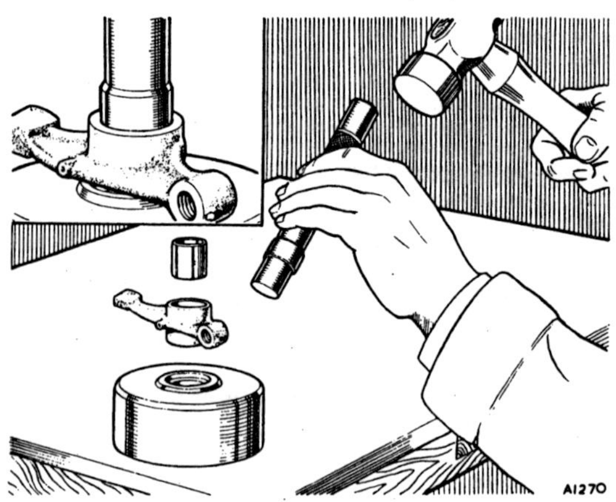

Fig. A.1
Fitting a valve rocker bush, using Service tool 18G 226

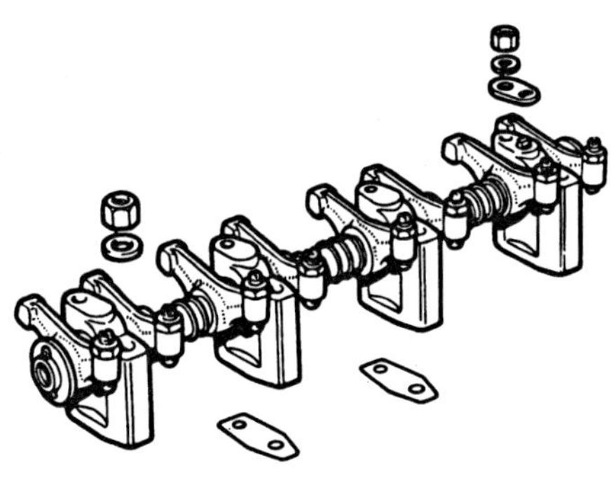

Fig. A.2
Rocker shaft assembly showing shims below the two centre brackets

Completely unscrew the eight rocker shaft bracket nuts and remove the rocker assembly, complete with brackets and rockers. Collect the shims from under the two centre brackets. Withdraw the eight push-rods, storing them carefully so that they may be replaced in the same positions. To dismantle the rocker shaft assembly, first remove the grub screw which locates the rocker shaft in the rear rocker mounting bracket and remove the split pins, flat washers, and spring washers from each end of the shaft. Slide the rockers, brackets, and springs from the shaft.

(See Editor's notes at end of Section A.)

Unscrew the plug from the front end of the shaft and clean out the oilways.

Reassembly and replacement is a reversal of the above procedure replacing the rockers and springs in their original positions on the shaft. Remember to replace the rocker shaft locating screw lock plate. Replace the rocker cover with the vent pipe to the front. Check that the two cap nut rubber bushes and the rocker cover cork gasket are undamaged; if they are found to be faulty, fit new ones or oil leaks may result.

Refitting rocker bushes

To remove and replace worn rocker bushes the use of Service tool 18G 226 is recommended; the bushes and the rockers can be very easily damaged by using improvised drifts. Place the rocker on the anvil and drive out the worn bush.

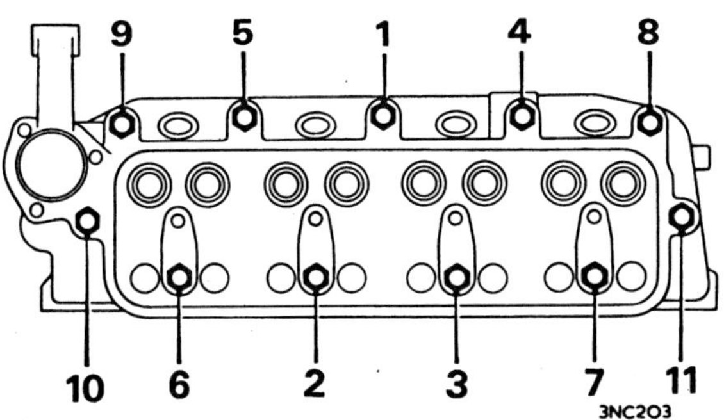

Fig. A3
Cylinder head nut slackening and tightening sequence

Place a new bush on the driver and position the bush with the butt joint at the top of the rocker bore and the oil groove in the bush at the bottom of the rocker bore, as shown in Fig. A.4.

It will be necessary to drill the oil holes in the bush to coincide with the oilways in the rocker.

Use a .093 in. (2.63 mm.) drill to drill out the end plug and to continue the oilway through the bush. Replug the end after this operation with a rivet (Part No. 5C 2436) and weld the plug into position. The oil hole in the top of the rocker barrel must be continued through the bush with a No 47 drill, .0785 in. (1.98 mm.).

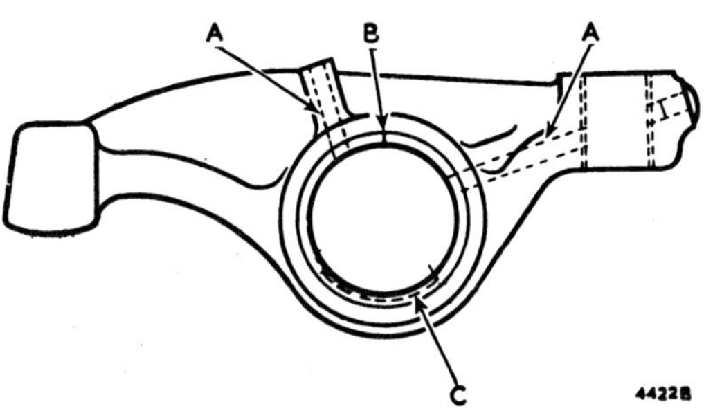

Fig. A.4
Showing the correct position for a valve rocker bush
A. Oilways B. Joint in rocker bush C. Oil groove

Finally, burnish-ream the bush to the dimensions given in the 'GENERAL SPECIFICATION DATA' section.

Section A.4

CYLINDER HEAD ASSEMBLY 

Drain the water from the cooling system–Section C.2. If anti-freeze mixture is being used it should be drained into a suitable clean container and carefully preserved for future use.

Remove the thermostat housing and thermostat, see Section C.

Remove the air cleaner and carburetter as detailed in Section D.

Remove the inlet and exhaust manifolds as detailed in Section A.2.

Remove the rocker assembly as detailed in Section A.3 and remove the seven external cylinder head nuts at the same time. Withdraw the push-rods, keeping them in the order of their removal.

Disconnect the high-tension cables and remove the sparking plugs. Disconnect the heater hose and heater control cable from the water valve.

Disconnect the lead from the thermal transmitter at the front of the cylinder head.

Slacken the clip and disconnect the hose from the water pipe outlet on the left-hand side of the cylinder head. Remove the air manifold assembly, see Section T.

Break the cylinder head joint by levering at one end and withdraw the head evenly up the studs.

Refitting the cylinder head

Make sure that the surfaces of both the cylinder head and the cylinder block are clean. It will be noticed that the cylinder head gasket is marked 'FRONT and 'TOP' to assist in replacing it correctly with the copper side uppermost. Having slipped the gasket over the studs, next lower the cylinder head into position. Fit the seven cylinder head external nuts finger tight.

Replace the push-rods in the positions from which they were taken. Replace the rocker assembly and securing nuts finger tight. Tighten the 11 cylinder head nuts, a turn at a time, in the order given in Fig. A.3. Finally, tighten the four rocker assembly nuts.

Reassembling continues in the reverse order to the dismantling procedure.

Switch on the ignition and check the fuel system for leaks. Start the engine and run it until the normal working temperature is reached. Remove the rocker cover and check the valve clearances (see '**MAINTENANCE**'). Replace the rocker cover and connect the purge pipe.

Section A.5

VALVE GEAR AND VALVES 

Removing

1. Remove the cylinder head – see Section A.4.
2. Compress the valve spring, using 18G 45, and remove the valve cotter.
3. Release the spring compressor and remove the valve collar, valve spring and valve spring cup.
4. Remove the packing ring and withdraw the valve from its guide.
5. Remove each valve assembly in turn and retain in their installed order.

Refitting

6. Insert each valve into its guide in turn and fit the valve spring cup, valve spring and valve collar. Compress the spring. Dip a new packing ring in oil and fit it over the valve stem to just below the cotter groove. Refit the valve cotter and release the spring compressor.

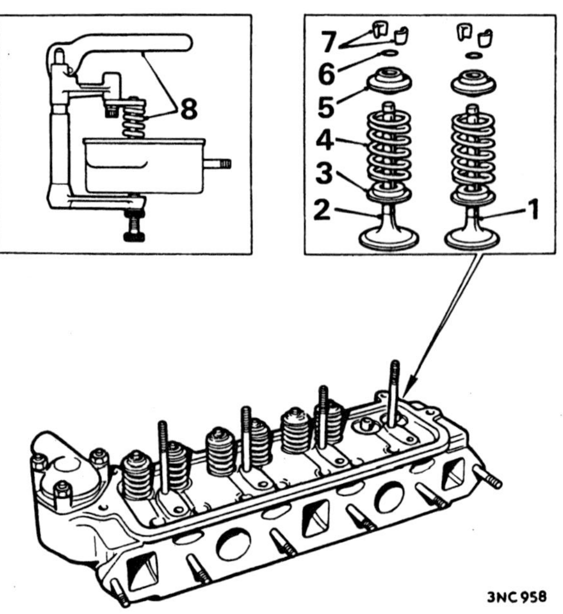

Fig. A.5
Valve Gear

1. Exhaust valve
2. Inlet valve
3. Valve spring cup
4. Valve spring
5. Valve spring collar
6. Packing ring
7. Valve cotter
8. Compress valve spring using tool 18G 45

Removing and replacing valve guides

Rest the cylinder head with its machined face downwards on a clean surface and drive the valve guide downwards into the combustion space with a suitable-sized drift. This should take the form of a hardened steel punch $\frac{9}{16}$ in. (14 mm.) in diameter and not less than 4 in. (10 cm.) in length, with a locating spigot $\frac{5}{16}$ in. (7.9 mm.) diameter machined on one end for a length of 1 in. (2.5 cm.) to engage the bore of the guide.

(See Editor's notes at end of Section A.)

When fitting new valve guides these should be driven in from the top of the cylinder head. The valve guides must be inserted with the end having the largest chamfer at the top. The valve guides should be driven into the combustion spaces until they are the required height above the machined surface of the valve spring seating (see Fig. A.6 and '**GENERAL SPECIFICATION DATA**').

Grinding and testing valves and seatings

Each valve must be cleaned thoroughly and carefully examined for pitting. Valves in a pitted condition should be refaced with a suitable grinder or new valves should be fitted.

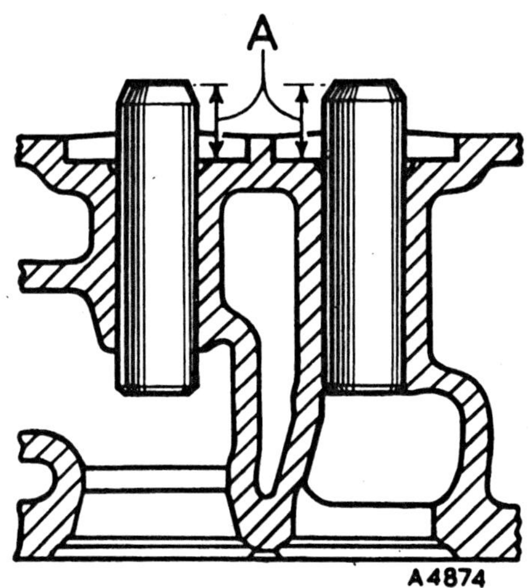

Fig. A.6
When fitting valve guides they must be driven in until they are the required height above the machined surface of the valve spring seating (A)

Pitted or uneven valve seats must be refaced using a grinder or cutter, care being taken that only the minimum quantity of metal necessary to restore the seat is removed. If the seats are very worn or damaged refer to Section A.20.

When grinding a valve onto its seating the valve face should be smeared lightly with fine- or medium-grade carborundum paste and then lapped in with a suction grinder (Service tool 18G 29). Avoid the use of excessive quantities of grinding paste and see that it remains in the region of the valve seating only.

A light coil spring placed under the valve head will assist considerably in the process of grinding. The valve should be ground to its seat with a semi-rotary motion and occasionally allowed to rise by the pressure of the light coil spring. This assists in spreading the paste evenly over the valve face and seat. It is necessary to carry out the grinding operation until a dull, even, mat surface, free from blemish, is produced on the valve seat and valve face.

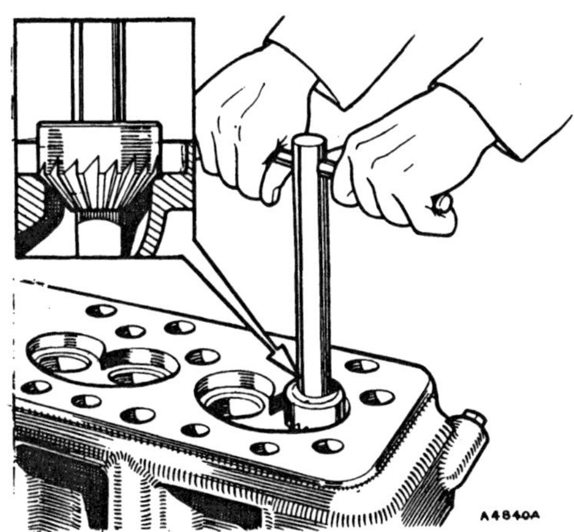

Fig. A.7
Pitted valve seats should be re-faced, using Service tools, 18G 25, 18G 25 A, 18G 174 B, 18G 25 C, 18G 27, 18G 28, 18G 28 A, 18G 28 B, 18G 28 C, and 18G 174 D

On completion, the valve seat and ports should be cleaned thoroughly with a rag soaked in paraffin (kerosene), dried, and then thoroughly cleaned by compressed air. The valves should be washed in paraffin (kerosene) and all traces of grinding paste removed.

Fit a new valve packing ring when refitting the valves (see Fig. A.5).

Checking valve timing

Set No. 1 cylinder inlet valve to .055 in. (1.4 mm.) clearance with the engine cold, and then turn the engine until the valve is about to open.

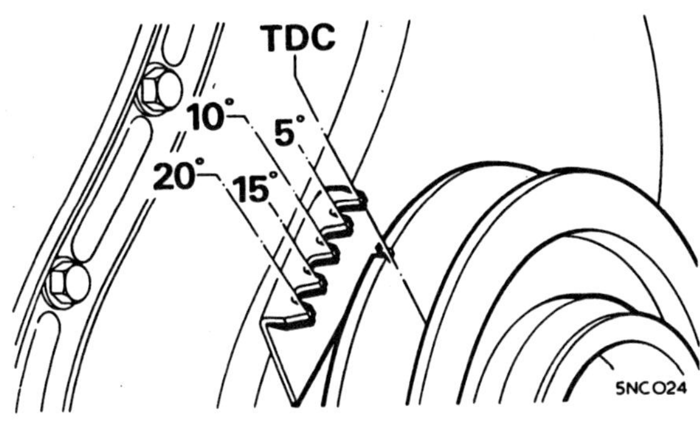

Fig. A.8
The notch in the pulley at the T.D.C. position for pistons 1 and 4

The indicating notch in the flange of the crankshaft pulley should then be opposite the T.D.C. position for pistons 1 and 4, i.e. the valve should be about to open at T.D.C. and No. 4 piston will be at T.D.C. on its compression stroke.

Do not omit to reset the inlet valve clearance to the recommended clearance (see 'GENERAL SPECIFICATION DATA') when the timing check has been completed. The clearance of .055 in. (1.4 mm.) is necessary to bring the opening position of the valve to T.D.C. It is not possible to check the valve timing accurately with the normal running valve clearance.

Adjusting valve rocker clearances – see 'MAINTENANCE'

Section A.6

TAPPETS 

Remove the carburetter (see Section D) and the rocker cover.
Remove the manifolds (see Section A.2).
Disconnect the high-tension leads from the sparking plugs.

Remove the rocker assembly as in Section A.3 and withdraw the push-rods, keeping them in their relative positions to ensure their replacement onto the same tappets. Release the breather pipe, remove the tappet covers, and lift out the tappets, also keeping them in their relative positions.
New tappets should be fitted by selective assembly so that they just fall into their guides under their own weight when lubricated.
Assembly is a reversal of the above procedure, but care should be taken to see that the tappet cover joints are oil-tight and that the rockers are adjusted to give the correct valve clearance.

(See Editor's notes at end of Section A.)

Section A.7

FRONT COVER AND OIL SEAL

Removing

1. Drain the cooling system and remove the radiator – Section C.

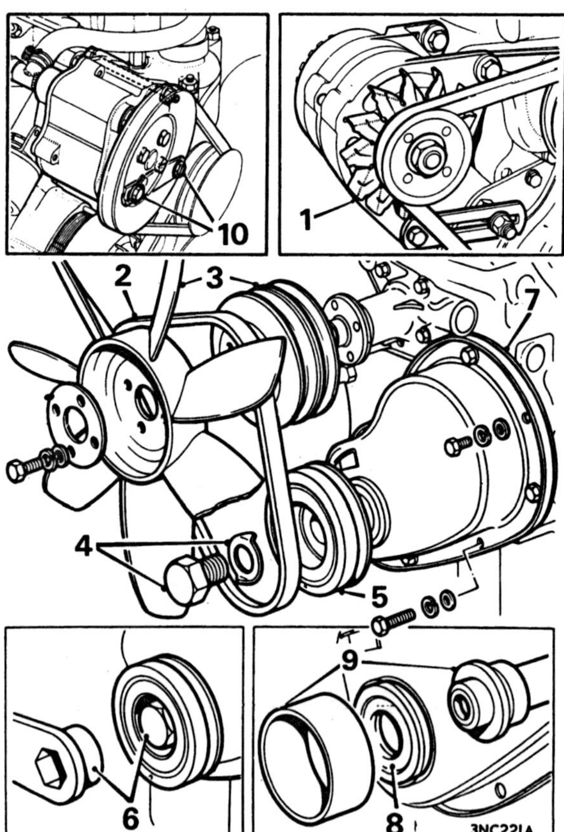

Fig. A.9
Front cover and oil seal

1. Alternator
2. Drive belt–fan
3. Fan and pulley
4. Crankshaft nut and lock washer
5. Crankshaft pulley
6. Crankshaft pulley nut and tool 18G 98 A
7. Front cover and gasket
8. Oil seal
9. Use tool 18G 134 BD to fit oil seal
10. Air pump adjusting link bolts

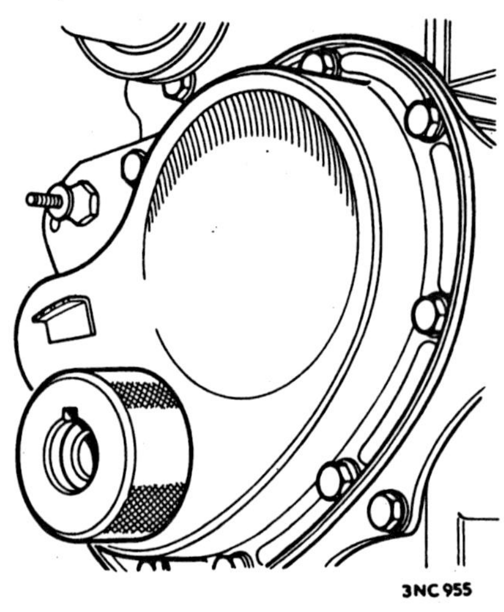

Fig. A.10
Centralize the oil seal on the crankshaft using tool 18G 1046 before tightening the front cover screws

2. Slacken the alternator mounting bolts and adjusting link nut and bolt and remove the drive belt.
3. Slacken the air pump mounting and adjusting link bolts and remove the drive belt.
4. Remove the cooling fan and pulley.
5. Release the locking washer and remove the crankshaft pulley retaining bolt – use tool 18G 98 A.
6. Pull the pulley from the crankshaft.
7. Remove the front cover and gasket; note the screw sizes.
8. Extract the oil seal from the front cover.

Refitting

9. Dip the new oil seal in engine oil and fit the seal into the cover, ensuring that the lips of the seal face inwards, using tool 18G 134 and 18G 134 BD.
10. Clean the front cover and front plate joint faces.
11. Ensure the oil thrower is in position with the 'F' marking showing.
12. Smear the locating faces of tool 18G 1046 with oil and fit into the oil seal.
13. Fit a new joint washer and position the front cover assembly on the crankshaft. Insert all the screws, ensure the seal is centralized and tighten up evenly.
14. Remove tool 18G 1046.
15. Lubricate the hub of the crankshaft pulley, slide the pulley onto the shaft engaging the keyway.
16. Fit a new locking washer. Tighten and lock the retaining bolt.
17. Reverse the procedure in 1 to 4.

Section A.8

TIMING CHAIN AND TENSIONER

Removing

1. Remove the front cover, see Section A.7.

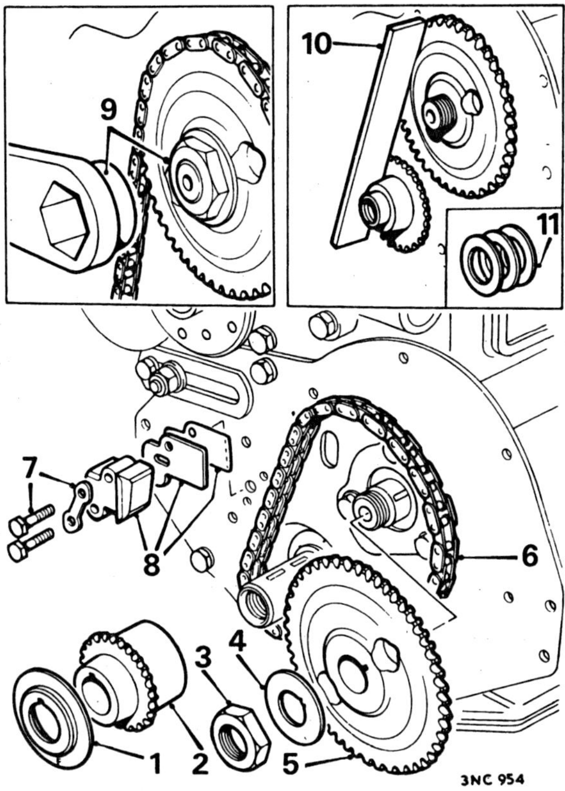

Fig. A.11
Timing chain and gears

1. Oil thrower 'F' marking
2. Crankshaft gear
3. Camshaft nut
4. Lock washer
5. Camshaft gear
6. Timing chain–single
7. Screws and lock washer
8. Chain tensioner assembly and gasket
9. Camshaft nut and tool 18G 98 A
10. Check wheel alignment with a straight-edge
11. Packing washers–crankshaft gear

2. Unlock and remove the tensioner securing screws.
3. Prise the tensioner assembly out of its register in the front plate, taking care to retain the slipper head which is under spring tension, and remove the tensioner and its backplate. Remove the backplate and gasket.
4. Allow the spring tension against the slipper head to relax and withdraw the slipper head, spring and inner cylinder from the tensioner body.
5. Unlock and remove the camshaft nut, using tool 18G 98 A. Note that the lock washer tag fits into the groove of the camshaft wheel.
6. Withdraw the crankshaft and camshaft gears; use suitable levers and ease each gear forward a fraction at a time. Note the packing washers positioned behind the crankshaft gear.

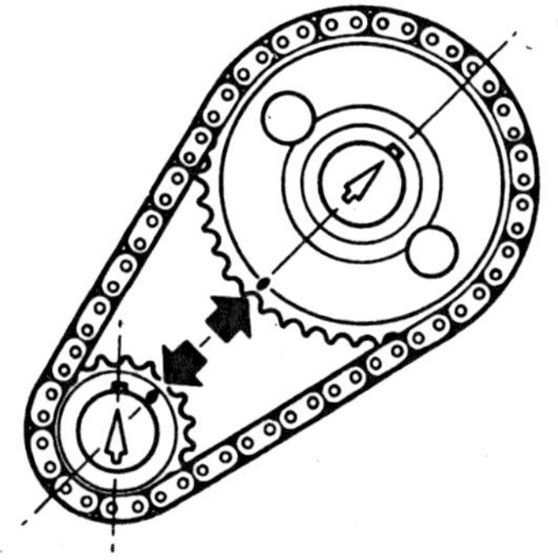

Fig. A.12
Crankshaft keyway at T.D.C. and the timing marks opposite to each other

Refitting

7. Crankshaft gear packing washers: Unless new crankshaft or camshaft components have been fitted use the same number of packing washers as original assembly.
   (i) Fit the crankshaft and camshaft gears hard against the shaft registers.

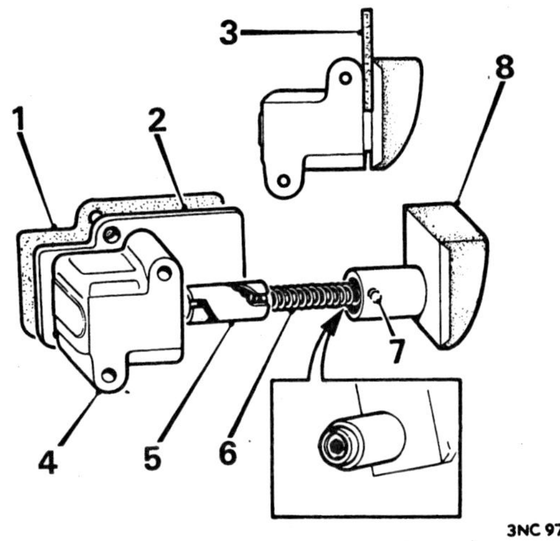

Fig. A.13
Timing chain tensioner assembly

1. Gasket
2. Backplate
3. Spacer to prevent disengagement
4. Tensioner body
5. Inner cylinder
6. Spring
7. Peg.
8. Slipper head

   (ii) Check the alignment of the gear teeth using a straight-edge. Measure the gap with a feeler gauge and subtract 0.005 in. (.013 mm.).
   (iii) Remove the drive keys from the crankshaft and fit packing washers to the thickness calculated in (ii). Packing washers are supplied in a thickness of 0.006 in. (0.15 mm.). Refit the drive keys.
8. Rotate the crankshaft so that its keyways are at T.D.C. and the camshaft with its keyway at two o'clock position.
9. Assemble the timing chain and gear wheels with the timing marks opposite each other, engage the crankshaft key and rotate the camshaft as necessary to engage the camshaft gear keyway.

10. Fit a new lock washer, tighten the nut and lock the camshaft nut.
11. Refit the chain tensioner:
    (i) Refit the inner cylinder and spring into the bore of the slipper head so that the serrated helical slot engages with the peg in the bore.
    (ii) Turn the inner cylinder clockwise against spring tension until the lower serration in the slot engages with the peg and retains the inner cylinder.
    (iii) Refit the slipper assembly into the tensioner body. Insert a 0.06 in. (1.6 mm.) spacer between the slipper head and body to prevent disengagement.
    (iv) Assemble the tensioner and its backplate to the engine.
    (v) Remove the spacer, press the slipper head into the body and release it to disengage the inner cylinder.
12. Position the oil thrower on the crankshaft with the 'F' marking showing.
13. Refit the front cover, see Section A.7.

Section A.9

OIL PUMP

Two bolts secure the oil pump cover and three studs secure the pump to the crankcase. Unscrew the stud nuts and remove the pump and drive shaft.

When refitting the pump use a new joint washer.

Unscrew the two securing screws and carefully withdraw the cover, which is located on the base of the oil pump body by two dowels.

Withdraw the outer rotor, and the inner rotor complete with oil pump shaft, from the pump body.

Thoroughly clean all parts in paraffin (kerosene) and

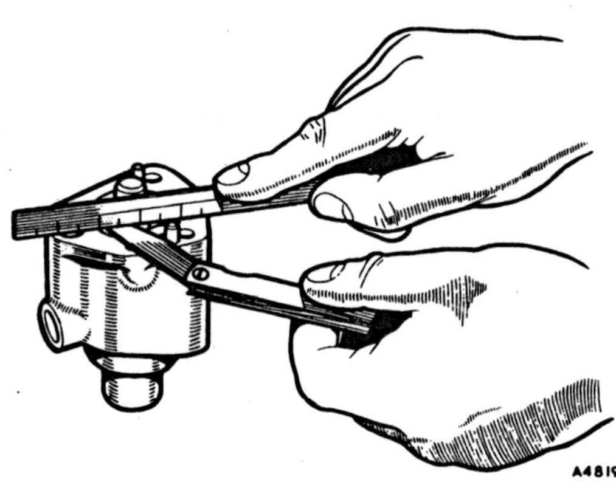

Fig. A.14
Checking the oil pump rotor end-float, which should not exceed .005 in. (.127 mm.)

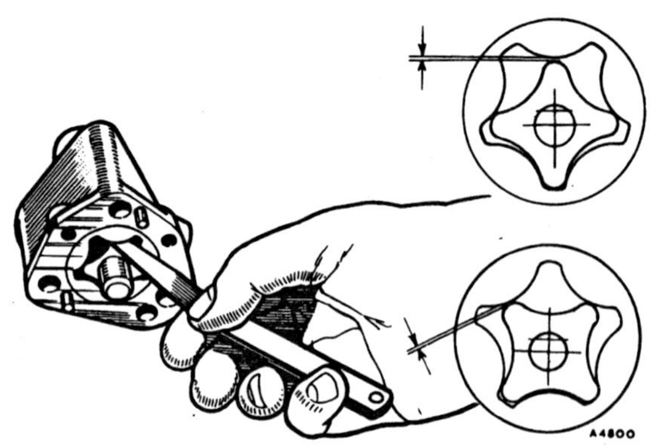

Fig. A.15
The lobe clearance should not exceed .006 in. (.152 mm.) when the oil pump rotors are in the positions illustrated

inspect them for wear. The rotor end-float and lobe clearances should be checked as follows:

1. Install the rotors in the pump body, place a straight-edge across the joint face of the pump body, and measure the clearance between the top face of the rotors and the under side of the straight-edge. The clearance should not exceed .005 in. (.127 mm.). In cases where the clearance is excessive this may be remedied by removing the two cover locating dowels and carefully lapping the joint face of the pump body.
2. Check the diametrical clearance between the outer rotor and the rotor pocket in the pump body. If this exceeds .010 in. (.254 mm.) and cannot be remedied by the renewal of either the pump body or the rotors, then the pump assembly should be renewed.
3. With the rotors installed in the pump body measure the clearance between the rotor lobes when they are in the positions shown in Fig. A.17. If the clearance is in excess of .006 in. (.152 mm.) the rotors must be renewed.

Reassembly is a reversal of the dismantling procedure noting the following points:

1. Lubricate all parts with clean engine oil.
2. Ensure that the outer rotor is installed in the pump body with its chamfered end at the driving end of the rotor pocket in the pump body.
3. After reassembling check the pump for freedom of action.

Section A.10

CAMSHAFT 

Disconnect the battery.
Remove the inlet and exhaust manifold assembly (see Section A.2).
Remove the push-rods and take out the tappets (see Section A.6).
Remove the timing chain and gears (see Section A.8).
Disconnect the suction advance unit pipe from the distributor and take out the two bolts with flat washers securing the distributor to the housing. Do not slacken the clamping plate bolt or the ignition timing setting will be lost.

Remove the distributor driving spindle—Section A.17.

Remove the sump, oil pump, and oil pump drive shaft (see Section A.9).

Take out the three set screws and shakeproof washers which secure the camshaft locating plate to the cylinder block and withdraw the camshaft.

Before reassembly, which is a reversal of the dismantling procedure, assemble the camshaft retaining plate and the chain wheel to the camshaft, and check the camshaft end-float against the dimensions given in the **'GENERAL SPECIFICATION DATA'** section by measuring the clearance between the retaining plate and the thrust face of the camshaft front journal.

If the end-float is excessive the retaining plate should be renewed.

(See Editor's notes at end of Section A.)

Section A.11

RENEWING THE CAMSHAFT BEARINGS

While the camshaft is removed it is advisable to check the bearing liners for damage and wear. If these are not in good condition they must be removed and new ones fitted.

The old bearings can be punched out. The new ones must be tapped into position. These bearings are easily damaged and the use of Service tool 18G 124 A is recommended.

This tool comprises a body with built-in thrust race, screw wing nut, stop plate, 'C' washer and handle, and must be used in conjunction with the following adaptors: 18G 124 B, 18G 124 C, 18G 124 F, 18G 124 H.

Removing the front and rear liners
Insert the small end of the adaptor 18G 124 F into the camshaft front liner from the inside of the cylinder block, thread the body of the tool onto the centre screw, and pass the screw through the adaptor from the front of the block. Place the slotted washer on the flat at the rear of the centre screw and insert the tommy-bar into the centre screw behind the slotted washer.

Tighten up the wing nut to withdraw the worn liner.

The rear liner is withdrawn by the same method, using the adaptor 18G 124 B and withdrawing the liner from the rear of the block.

Removing the centre liner
Insert the stepped pilot adaptor 18G 124 H into the camshaft liner front bore from the inside of the block and the adaptor 18G 124 C into the centre liner from the rear, small end first.

With the body of the tool positioned on the centre screw, pass the screw through the pilot adaptor and the adaptor in the centre liner.

1

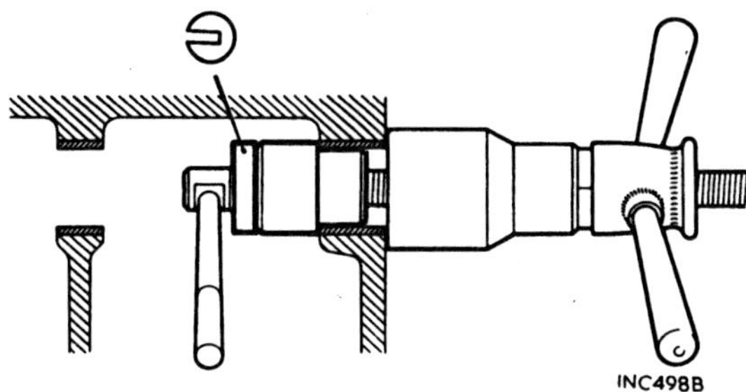

2

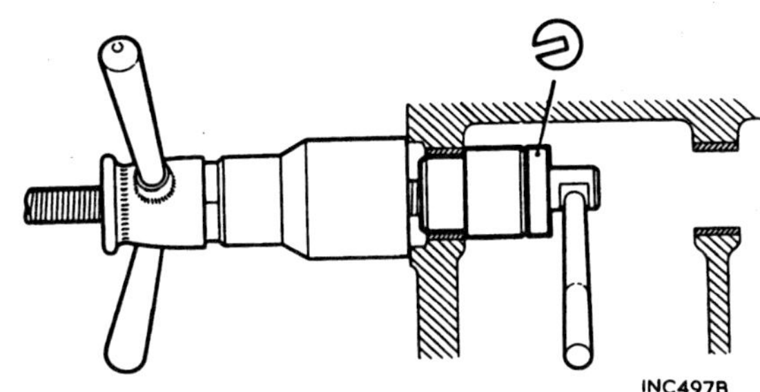

3

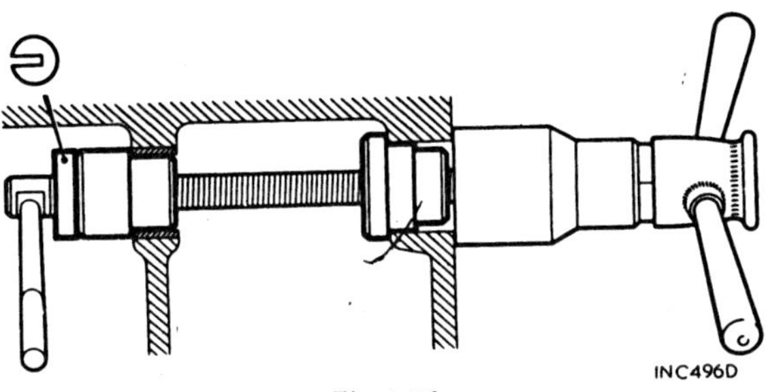

Fig. A.16
Removing the camshaft bearing liners

1. Front liner 2. Rear liner 3. Centre liner

Place the slotted washer on the flat at the rear of the centre screw and insert the tommy-bar into the screw behind the slotted washer.

Tighten up the wing nut to withdraw the liner.

Replacing the front and rear liners
Place the new liner on the smallest diameter of the adaptor 18G 124 F and insert the adaptor into the camshaft front liner bore from the inside of the block, largest diameter first.

Line up the oil holes in the liner and the cylinder block and make certain that they remain correctly positioned during the whole operation.

Thread the body of the tool onto the centre screw and pass the screw through the adaptor located in the front liner from the front of the block.

Position the larger of the two 'C' washers on the centre screw with the cut-away portion turned away from the butt joint of the liner; this joint **must** be covered by the washer.

1

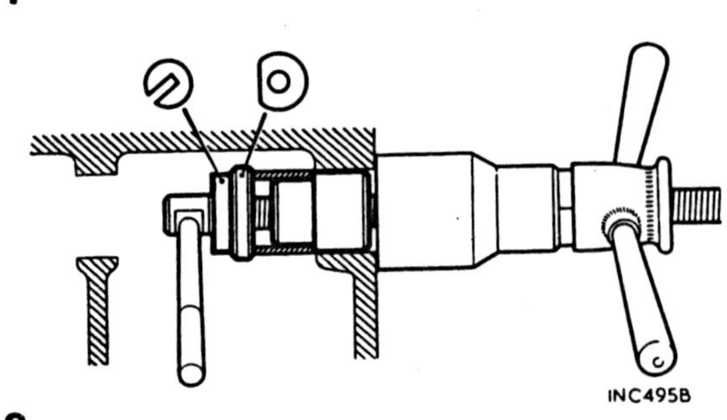

2

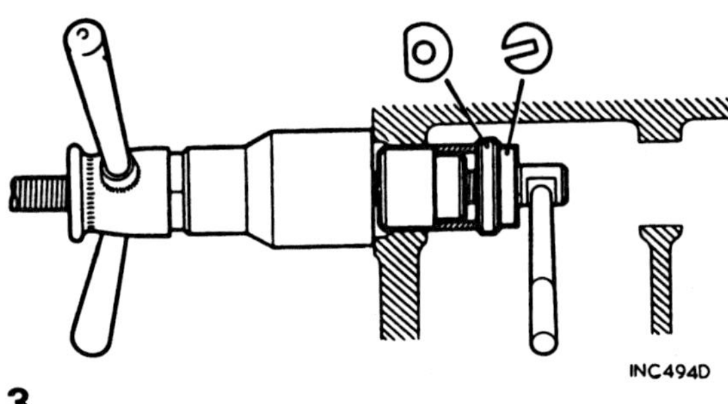

3

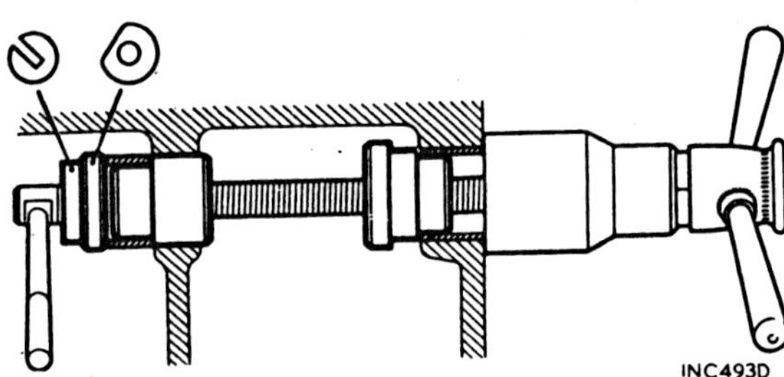

Fig. A.17
Replacing the camshaft bearing liners

1. Front liner 2. Rear liner 3. Centre liner

Place the slotted washer on the flat at the rear of the centre screw and insert the tommy-bar into the screw behind the slotted washer.

Tighten the wing nut to pull the liner squarely into position.

The rear liner is replaced by the same method, using the adaptor 18G 124 B and pulling the liner into position from the rear of the block.

Replacing the centre liner

Insert the stepped pilot adaptor into the camshaft front liner from the inside of the block.

Place a new centre liner on the small end of the adaptor 18G 124 C and position the adaptor in the centre liner bore from the rear, largest diameter first. Ensure that the oil holes in the liner and the cylinder block are lined up and remain so during the whole operation.

With the body of the tool positioned on the centre screw insert the screw through the pilot adaptor and the adaptor in the centre liner bore.

Position the larger of the two 'C' washers on the centre screw with the cut-away portion turned away from the butt joints of the liner; this joint **must** be covered by the washer.

Place the slotted washer and the tommy-bar in the centre screw and tighten up the wing nut to pull the liner into position.

Reaming the liners

Before the camshaft can be reassembled the liners must be reamed in line in order to obtain the correct clearance between the shaft journals and their bearings. For this purpose use tool 18G 123 A, which comprises an arbor with tommy-bar and Allen key, and must be used with the following adaptors: 18G 123 B, 18G 123 E, 18G 123 F, 18G 123 L, 18G 123 T, 18G 123 AB, 18G 123 AC, 18G 123 AD.

Reaming the front and rear liners

Insert the taper pilots 18G 123 AB and 18G 123 AC into the centre and rear liners respectively.

Place the plain pilot 18G 123 L on the arbor, followed by the cutter 18G 123 E.

Locate the cutter 18G 123 B at position '10' (see Fig. A.18) on the arbor.

Pass the arbor through the front liner and the pilot located in the centre liner.

Locate the cutter 18G 123 B at position '6' (see Fig. A.18) on the arbor and push the arbor through the taper on the rear liner.

Ensure that the cutter locating pins are engaged in the correct numbered hole provided in the arbor.

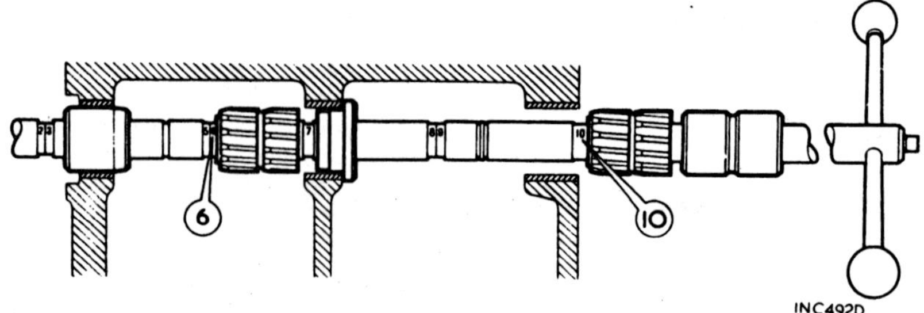

Fig. A.18
Reaming the camshaft front and rear bearing liners

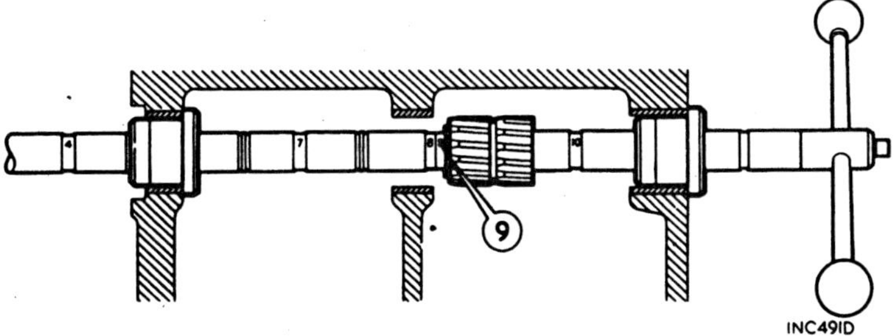

Fig. A.19
Reaming the camshaft centre bearing liner

The cutter for the front liner will cut first with the arbor piloting in the centre and rear liners. Clear away the swarf frequently during the operation. The cutter for the rear liner will follow with the arbor piloting in the front and centre liners. Clear away all the swarf before the plain pilot is allowed to enter the front liner.

When the cut in the rear liner is finished free the cutters and withdraw the arbor.

Reaming the centre liner
Set up for the second part of the operation by inserting the pilots 18G 123 T and 18G 123 AD in the front and rear liners.

Pass the arbor through the pilot in the front liner and place the cutter 18G 123F for the centre liner on the arbor. Push the arbor through the centre liner and the pilot located in the rear liner.

Secure the cutter at position '9' (see Fig. A.19) on the arbor, ensuring that the locating pin of the cutter engages the correct numbered hole in the arbor.

Ream the centre liner, release the cutter, and withdraw the arbor.

IMPORTANT.–It is essential that the cutter flutes are kept clear of swarf at all times during the cutting operation, preferably with air-blast equipment. The cutter should be withdrawn from the liner half-way through the cut and the swarf removed from the cutter and the liner.
Feed the reamer very slowly, and keep the cutters dry.
The arbors should be lightly lubricated before assembling the cutters and pilots.

Section A.12

REMOVING AND REPLACING THE CRANKSHAFT
(Engine Out of Car)

(See Editor's notes at end of Section A.)

Take off the clutch and the flywheel (see Section A.13), the timing wheels and chain (see Section A.8), the sump and the oil pump (see Section A.9). and the rear engine mounting plate.

Remove the camshaft locating plate.
Remove the cylinder block front plate and gasket.
Check the markings of the big-end bearing caps and main bearings.
Remove the big-end caps and bottom half bearing shells.
Remove the main bearing caps, using 18G 284, 18G 284 A and 18G 284 AC, the bottom half bearing shells and the thrust washer halves.
NOTE: Thrust washer halves are fitted each side of the centre main bearing.
Remove the crankshaft.
Remove the main bearing top half shells.
Remove the remaining halves of the thrust washers.
NOTE: Ensure that the bearing shells are retained with their respective caps for correct reassembly.
Thoroughly clean out all the crankshaft oilways.
Fit the top half main bearing shells to the cylinder block.
Fit the crankshaft into the bearings.
Fit the thrust washers with their oilways facing away from the bearings, and the tab on the thrust washer halves locating in th slot on the centre main bearing cap.
Fit the bottom half main bearing shells and main bearing caps, noting:

a. Thoroughly clean the horizontal joint face of the rear main bearing cap.
b. Lightly cover the horizontal joint face of the rear main bearing cap with jointing compound (Hylomar).
c. Renew the sealing corks for Nos. 1 and 5 bearing caps.
d. Soak the sealing corks in engine oil before fitting.

Tighten the main bearing cap nuts to 70 lbf ft. Check the crankshaft end-float; adjust with selective thrust washers.
Tighten the big-end bearing cap nuts to 33 lbf. ft. Check and if necessary renew, the front plate gasket.

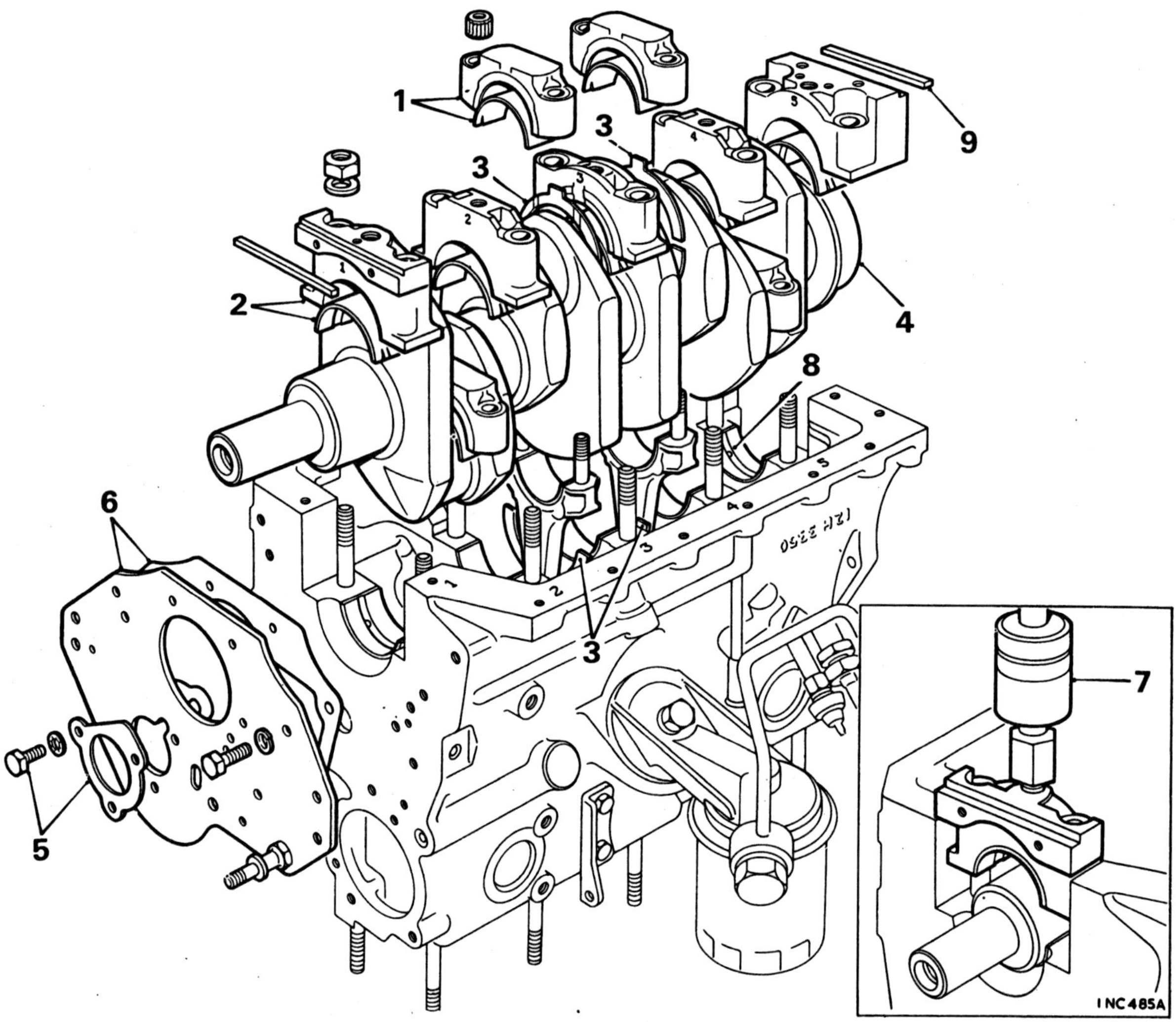

Fig. A.20
Removing the crankshaft

1. Big-end bearing cap and bottom half bearing shell
2. Main bearing cap and bottom half bearing shell
3. Thrust washer halves
4. Crankshaft
5. Camshaft locating plate
6. Cylinder block front plate and gasket
7. Service tool 18G 284 and adaptor.
8. Main bearing top half bearing shell
9. Sealing cork

Section A.13

REMOVING AND REPLACING THE FLYWHEEL (Engine Out of Car)

Remove the clutch by unscrewing the six bolts and spring washers securing it to the flywheel. Release the bolts a turn at a time to avoid distortion of the cover flange. Three dowels locate the clutch cover on the flywheel.

Unlock and remove the six nuts and three lock plates which secure the flywheel to the crankshaft and remove the flywheel.

When replacing the flywheel ensure that the 1 and 4 timing mark on the periphery of the flywheel is in line with and on the same side as the first and fourth throws of the crankshaft.

To assist correct location of the flywheel the depression in the crankshaft flange face is stamped with a similar timing mark which should be in line with the one on the flywheel periphery.

To release the special flywheel bolts the engine sump and rear main bearing cap must also be removed.

(See Editor's notes at end of Section A.)

Section A.14

FITTING THE FLYWHEEL STARTER RING

To remove the old starter ring from the flywheel flange split the ring gear with a cold chisel, taking care not to damage the flywheel. Make certain that the bore of the new rings and its mating surface on the flywheel are free from burrs and are perfectly clean.

To fit the new ring it must be heated to a temperature of 300 to 400° C. (572 to 752° F.), indicated by a light-blue surface colour. If this temperature is exceeded the temper of the teeth will be affected. The use of a thermostatically controlled furnace is recommended. Place the heated ring on the flywheel with the lead of the ring teeth facing the flywheel register. The expansion will allow the ring to be fitted without force by pressing or tapping it lightly until the ring is hard against its register.

This operation should be followed by natural cooling, when the 'shrink fit' will be permanently established and no further treatment required.

(See Editor's notes at end of Section A.)

Section A.15

REMOVING AND REFITTING THE ENGINE AND GEARBOX

Removing the power unit

1. Disconnect the battery.
2. Remove the bonnet–Section R.1.
3. Drain the oil from the engine and gearbox.
4. Drain the coolant from the engine and radiator.
5. Disconnect the oil cooler pipes (if fitted) and oil pressure gauge pipes from the engine.
6. Disconnect the top and bottom radiator hoses from the engine.
7. Remove the oil cooler securing bolts (if fitted).
8. Remove the radiator and diaphragm assembly–Section C.
9. Disconnect the wiring from the alternator and the distributor.
10. Detach the leads from the sparking plugs and remove the distributor cap.
11. Disconnect the heater hoses and control cable.
12. Disconnect the thermometer thermal transmitter from the engine.
13. Remove the cover and disconnect the wiring from the starter.
14. Disconnect the petrol pipe and accelerator cable and remove the air cleaner from the carburetter.
15. Disconnect the purge pipe from the rocker cover.
16. Disconnect the adsorption canister pipe from the carburetter.
17. Disconnect the brake servo vacuum pipe from the manifold.
18. Disconnect the manifold pipe from the running-on control valve.
19. Remove the gear lever surround, raise the rubber boot, unscrew and remove the lever retaining bolts. Remove the gear lever.
20. Disconnect the wiring from the reverse light and overdrive isolation switches and remove the clip securing the wiring harness to the gearbox and starter motor flange.
21. Detach the clutch slave cylinder from the gearbox casing and move it clear of the assembly.
22. Disconnect the speedometer cable from the gearbox.
23. Take the weight of the engine on a crane and support the gearbox.
24. Disconnect the exhaust pipe from the manifold and release the pipe clip from the engine restraint bracket.
25. Disconnect and remove the propeller shaft–Section G.
26. Remove the nuts securing the engine front mountings to the frame.
27. Remove the engine restraint, see Section A.21.
28. Remove the four bolts securing the rear mounting cross-member to the chassis frame.
29. Remove the two bolts securing the bottom tie bracket to the cross-member.
30. Lower the gearbox so that it rests on the fixed cross-member, remove the rear mounting securing nuts and remove the cross-member.
31. Ease the assembly forward until the gearbox is clear of the cross-member, tilt the assembly and lift from the car.
32. Remove the gearbox from the engine as described in Section F.1.

Refitting the engine

33. Reverse the removing procedure, refill the engine and gearbox with a recommended lubricant, and refill the cooling system with coolant.

Section A.16

EXHAUST SYSTEM 

The exhaust system is made up of a front pipe, or catalytic converter (if fitted), an intermediate pipe and silencer, and a rear silencer and tail pipe assembly.

The front pipe support clip is attached to a strap which is bolted to the engine restraint bracket.

A rubber mounting bolted to the rear frame member supports a bushed housing to which is attached the front silencer mounting bracket.

A second rubber mounting bolted to the rear frame embodies a split clamp that secures the tail pipe.

To remove the exhaust assembly remove the nuts from the manifold studs and release the front pipe strap from the engine restraint bracket.

Loosen the rear mounting tail pipe securing bolt, remove the front silencer support clip bolt, and draw the assembly forward and downward.

To refit the assembly reverse the removal sequence but leave the front silencer and tail pipe securing bolts slack until the front pipe has been fitted and tightened. Tighten the silencer clip bolt and finally the split clamp bolt on the tail pipe.

Section A.17

DISTRIBUTOR DRIVING SPINDLE 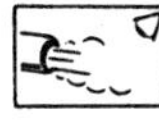

Removing

Remove the distributor as detailed in Section B.

Take out the screw securing the distributor housing to the cylinder block and withdraw the housing.

Screw a $\frac{5}{16}$ in. UNF. bolt approximately 3½ in. (89 mm.) long into the threaded end of the distributor drive spindle and with the crankshaft at 90° or A.T.D.C. (pistons halfway up the bores) withdraw the spindle.

(See Editor's notes at end of Section A.)

Refitting

Turn the crankshaft until No. 1 piston is at T.D.C. on its compression stroke. When the valves on No. 4 cylinder are 'rocking' (i.e. exhaust just closing and inlet just opening) No. 1 piston is at the top of its compression stroke. If the engine is set so that the groove in the crankshaft pulley is in line with the largest pointer on the timing chain cover, or the dimples in the crankshaft and camshaft gears are in line, the piston is exactly at T.D.C.

Enter the spindle with the slot just below the horizontal and the large offset uppermost. As the gear engages with the camshaft the slot will turn in an anti-clockwise direction until it is approximately in the two o'clock position.

Remove the bolt from the gear, insert the distributor housing, and secure it with the special bolt and washer.

Ensure that the correct bolt is used and that the head does not protrude above the face of the housing.

Refit the distributor, referring to Section B, if the clamp plate has been released.

(See Editor's notes at end of Section A.)

Section A.18

OIL COOLER
(If fitted)

Removing

1. Disconnect the oil cooler pipes from the oil filter, cylinder block and oil cooler connections.
2. Remove the four oil cooler securing bolts and remove the cooler.
3. Withdraw the pipes from the radiator diaphragm grommets.

Refitting

4. Reverse the removing procedure.

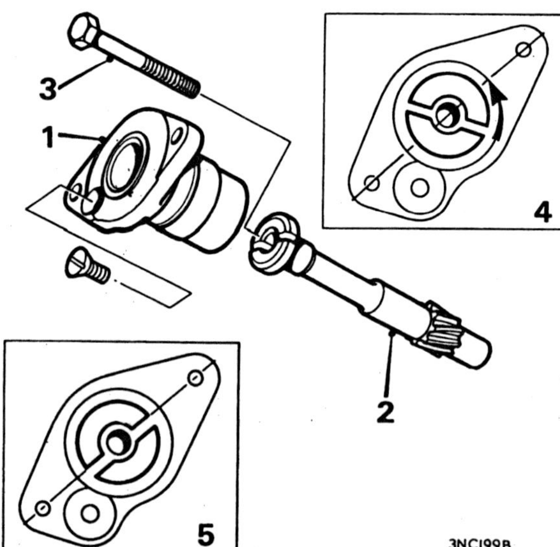

Fig. A.21
Removing and refitting the distributor driving spindle

1. Distributor housing
2. Distributor driving spindle
3. $\frac{5}{16}$ in U.N.F. bolt
4. Refitting position of the distributor driving spindle slot
5. Final position of the distributor driving spindle slot

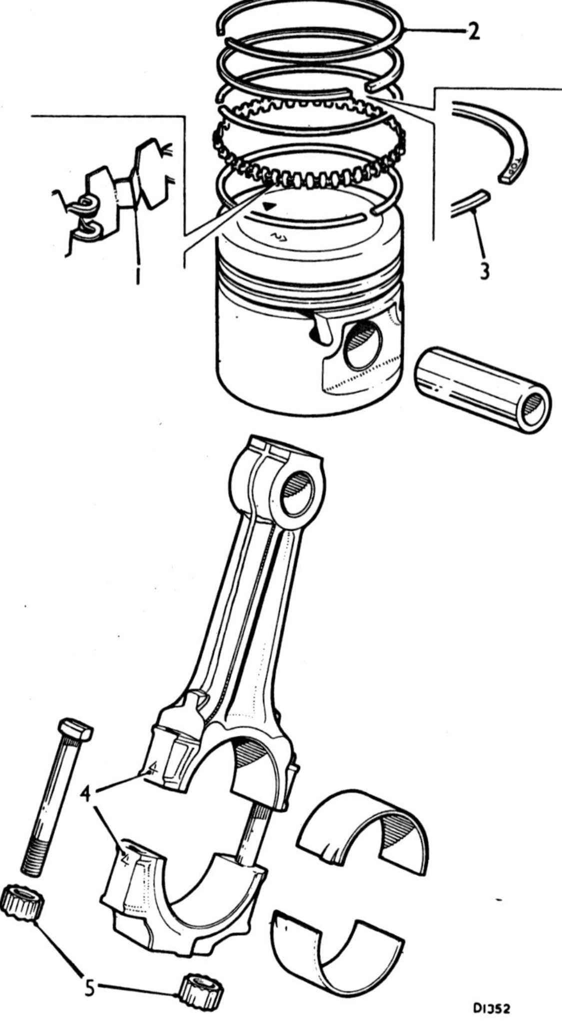

Fig. A.22
A piston and connecting rod assembly with a press fit gudgeon pin

1. Expander rail must butt.
2. Top compression ring.
3. Second compression ring.
4. Connecting rod and cap identification.
5. Multi-sided nut.

Section A.19

PISTONS AND CONNECTING RODS
(See Editor's notes at end of Section A.)

Removing

1. Remove the power unit (Section A.15).
2. Remove the engine sump.
3. Remove the cylinder head assembly (Section A.4).

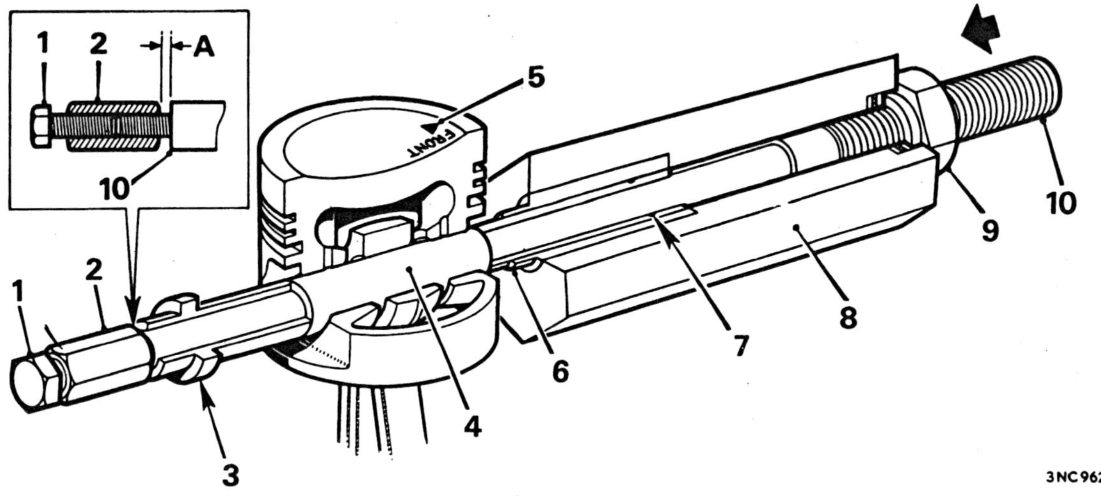

Fig. A.23
Removing a gudgeon pin, using Service tool 18G 1150 and adaptor set 18G 1150 D
'A' = 0.040 in. (1 mm.) end-float

1. Lock screw
2. Stop nut
3. Remover/replacer bush flange away from gudgeon pin.
4. Gudgeon pin
5. Front of piston
6. Piston adaptor
7. Groove in sleeve away from gudgeon pin
8. Hexagon body
9. Large nut
10. Centre screw

4. Mark the bearing caps and connecting rods for reassembly, marking each assembly with the number of the cylinder from which it has been taken. Remove the big-end nuts and withdraw the bearing caps.
5. Withdraw the piston and connecting rod assemblies from the top of the cylinder block and refit the bearing caps.

Dismantling

6. Remove the piston rings over the crown of the piston.
7. Hold the hexagon body of 18G 1150 in a vice.
8. Screw the large nut back until it is flush with the end of the centre screw, ensure the screw and large nut are well lubricated, and push the screw in until the nut contacts the thrust race.
9. Fit adaptor 18G 1150 D on to the centre screw with the piston ring cut-away uppermost.
10. Slide the parallel sleeve, groove end first, onto the centre screw.
11. Fit the piston, 'FRONT' or ▲ towards the adaptor, onto the centre screw.
    IMPORTANT. The gudgeon pin bore is offset and it is essential that the 'FRONT' or ▲ (marked on the piston crown) of the piston is fitted against the adaptor face.
12. Fit the remover/replacer bush on the centre screw, flange end towards the gudgeon pin.
13. Screw the stop nut onto the centre screw and adjust to the correct end-float ('A', Fig. A.23). Lock the stop nut securely with the lock screw.
14. Check that the remover/replacer bush and parallel sleeve are correctly positioned in the bore on both sides of the piston.
15. Screw the large nut up to the thrust race.
16. Hold the lock screw, and turn the large nut (use 18G 587) until the gudgeon pin is withdrawn from the piston.

Reassembling

GUDGEON PIN

17. Check the piston and connecting rod for alignment.
18. Remove the large nut of 18G 1150 and pull the centre screw out of the body a few inches. Ensure the nut and screw are well lubricated, and the piston support adaptor is in place.
19. Slide the parallel sleeve groove end last onto the centre screw and up to the shoulder.
20. Lubricate the gudgeon pin and bores of the connecting rod and piston with graphited oil (Acheson's Colloids 'Oildag').
21. Fit the connecting rod and piston 'FRONT' to the tool, with the connecting rod entered on the sleeve up to the groove.
22. Fit the gudgeon pin into the piston bore up to the connecting rod.
23. Fit the remover/replacer bush flange end towards the gudgeon pin.
24. Screw the stop nut onto the centre screw; adjust to the correct end-float ('A', Fig. A.24). Lock the nut securely with the lock screw.
25. Screw the large nut up to the thrust race.
26. Set the torque wrench 18G 537 to 12 lb. ft. (1.64 kg. m.). This represents the **minimum load for an acceptable fit.**
27. Using the torque wrench and 18G 587 on the large nut, and holding the lock screw, pull the gudgeon pin in until the flange of the remover/replacer bush is the correct distance from the piston skirt ('B', Fig. A.24).

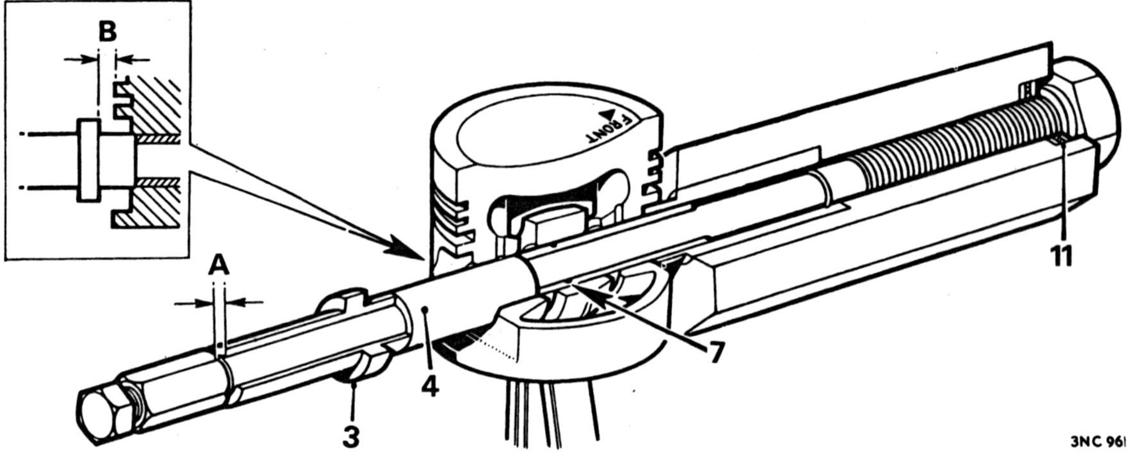

Fig. A.24

Fitting a gudgeon pin, using Service tool 18G 1150 and adaptor set 18G 1150 D

'A' = 0.040 in (1 mm) end float 'B' = 0.080 in (2 mm) from piston

3. Remover/replacer bush flange towards gudgeon pin
4. Gudgeon pin
7. Groove in sleeve towards gudgeon pin
11. Lubricate thrust race and screw thread

Under no circumstances must the flange be allowed to contact the piston.

NOTE.–If the torque wrench **has not broken** throughout the pull, the fit of the gudgeon pin to the connecting rod is not acceptable and necessitates the renewal of components. The large nut and centre screw of the tool must be kept well oiled.

Remove the service tool.

28. Check that the piston pivots freely on the pin, and is free to slide sideways. If stiffness exists, wash the assembly in fuel or paraffin (kerosene), lubricate the gudgeon pin with graphited oil (Acheson's Colloids 'Oildag') and re-check. If stiffness persists dismantle and check for ingrained dirt or damage.

PISTON RINGS

29. Enter the piston rings squarely into the top of the cylinder bore and check the gaps (see **'GENERAL SPECIFICATION DATA'**).
30. Check the ring to piston groove clearances.
31. Fit the bottom rail of the oil control ring to the piston and position it below the bottom groove.
    Fit the oil control expander into the bottom groove and move the bottom oil control ring rail up into the bottom groove. Fit the top oil control rail into the bottom groove.
32. Check that the ends of the expander are butting but not overlapping (see Fig. A.22) and set the gaps of the rails and the expander at 90 degrees to each other.
33. Fit the thinner of the two compression rings into the second groove with the face marked 'TOP' uppermost.
34. Fit the top compression ring.
    Position the ring gaps at 90 degrees to each other and away from the thrust side of the piston.

Refitting

35. Reverse the removal procedure noting the following points.
    (a) Lubricate the piston rings with graphited oil and stagger the compression ring gaps at 90° to each other.
    (b) Compress the piston rings using Service tool 18G 55 A.
    (c) Ensure that each connecting rod and piston is refitted into its original bore, the correct way round.
    (d) Check that the big-end bearings are correctly located in the connecting rods and caps. Use the special multi-sided locknuts and tighten to the torque figure given in **'TORQUE WRENCH SETTINGS'**.

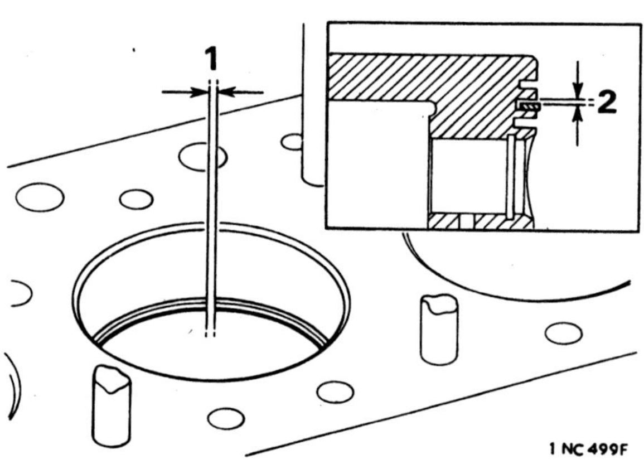

Fig. A.25

1. Piston ring gap in cylinder bore
2. Piston ring to groove clearance

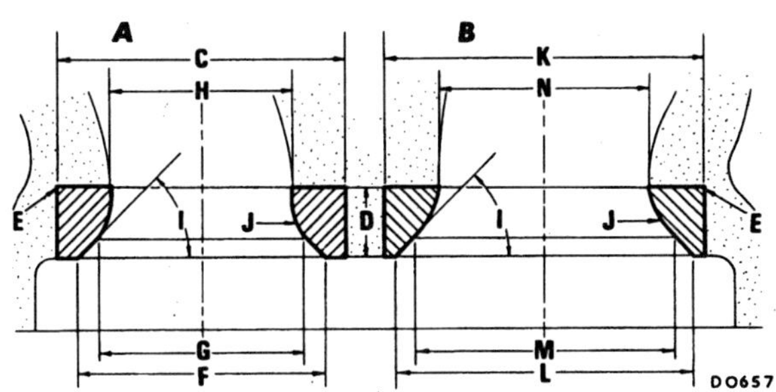

Fig. A.26
Valve seat machining dimensions

Exhaust (A)	Inlet (B)
C. 1.437 to 1.438 in. (36.50 to 36.53 mm.).	K. 1.592 to 1.593 in. (40.43 to 40.46 mm.).
D. .186 to..188 in. (4.72 to 4.77 mm.).	D. .186 to .188 in. (4.72 to 4.77 mm.).
E. Maximum radius .015 in. (.38 mm.)	E. Maximum radius .015 in. (.38 mm.).
F. 1.33 to 1.35 in. (33.78 to 34.29 mm.).	L. 1.552 to 1.572 in. (39.42 to 39.93 mm.).
G. 1.218 to 1.228 in. (30.94 to 31.19 mm.).	M. 1.427 to 1.447 in. (36.25 to 36.75 mm.).
H. Throat diameter 1.146 to 1.166 in. (29.11 to 29.62 mm.).	N. Throat diameter 1.302 to 1.322 in. (33.07 to 33.58 mm.).
I. 45°.	I. 45°.
J. Blend from seating to throat diameter.	J. Blend from seating to throat diameter.

Section A.20

VALVE SEAT INSERTS

Valve seats that cannot be restored to their original standard by normal cutting and refacing should have valve seat inserts fitted.

To fit an insert, machine the cylinder head to the dimensions given (see Fig. A.26). Press in the insert, which will be an interference fit of .0025 to .0045 in. (.06 to .11 mm.). Grind or machine the seats to the dimensions given. Normal valve 'grinding-in' may also be necessary to ensure efficient valve seating.

Section A.21

ENGINE RESTRAINT

Removing

1. Slacken the restraint tube front nut.
2. Remove the restraint tube rear nut and withdraw the rear plate and buffer.
3. Remove the nut and bolt securing the restraint tube to the gearbox bracket and withdraw the restraint tube from the bracket on the rear engine mounting cross-member.
4. Remove the distance tube, front buffer and plate from the restraint tube.

Refitting

5. Reverse the procedure in 1 to 4, noting the following:
   a. Inspect the buffer for damage and deterioration, and renew if necessary.
   b. Tighten the restraint tube rear nut first, then tighten the front nut.

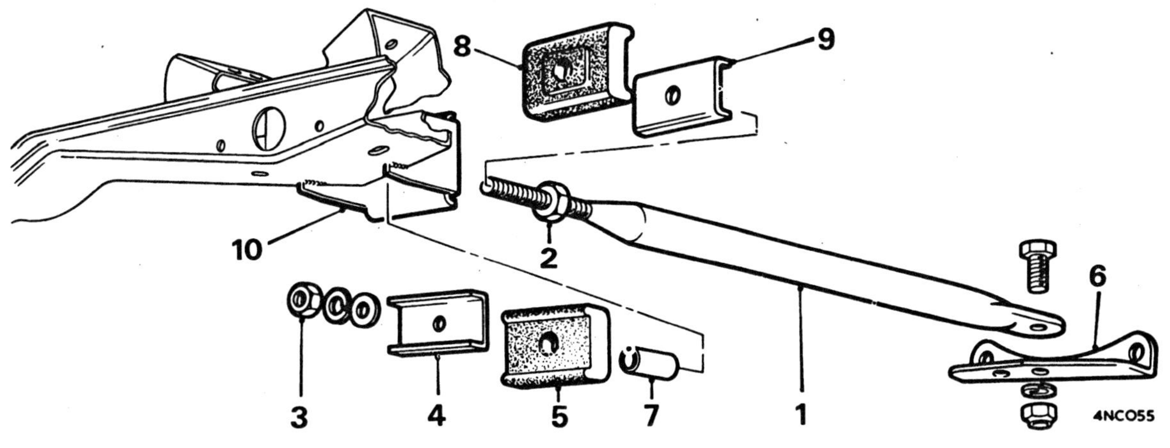

Fig. A.27
The engine restraint

1. Engine restraint tube
2. Front nut
3. Rear nut
4. Rear plate
5. Rear buffer
6. Gearbox bracket
7. Distance tube
8. Front buffer
9. Front plate
10. Engine mounting rear cross-member bracket

Section A.22

CYLINDER BLOCK LINERS

NOTE: Should the condition of the cylinder bores be such that they cannot be cleaned up to accept oversize pistons, dry cylinder liners can be fitted.

Pilots should be made to the dimensions given from case-hardening steel and case-hardened.

The pilot extension should be made from 55-ton hardening and tempering steel, hardened in oil, and then tempered at 1,020°F.

Removing

1. Remove the engine assembly, see Section A.15.
2. Remove the cylinder head, see Section A.4.
3. Remove the crankshaft, see Section A.12.
4. Remove the connecting rods and pistons, see Section A.19.
5. Remove the camshaft, see Section A.10.
6. Remove the cylinder head studs.
7. Remove the oil pump studs.
8. Place the cylinder block on the bed of a press supported on wooden blocks, with the cylinder head face upwards.
9. Screw the pilot extension into the pressing-out pilot, and insert the pressing-out pilot into the top of the cylinder liner.
10. Press the worn liner out of the cylinder block bore, using a power press capable of 5 to 8 tons pressure.

Refitting

11. Machine and hone the cylinder block bores to the dimension given in the table below.
12. Place the cylinder block on the bed of the press, supported on wooden blocks, with the cylinder head face upwards.
13. Position the new liner, with the chamfered end leading, in the top of the cylinder block bore.
14. Insert the pressing-in pilot in the top of the liner.
15. Check that the liner is square with the top of the cylinder block, and the press is over the centre of the bore.

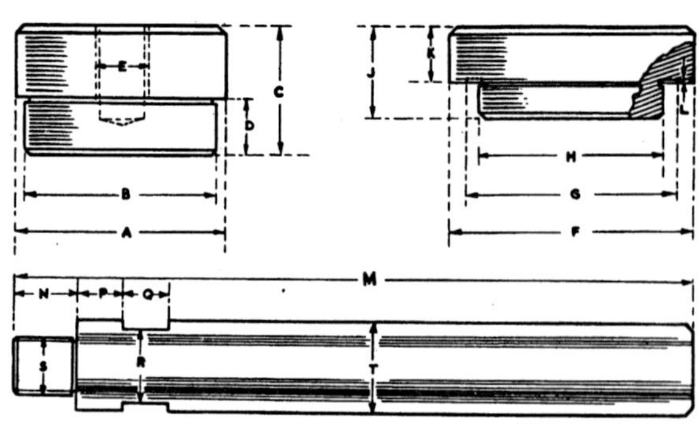

Fig. A.28

Cylinder liner pilot

Pressing-out pilot:

A. $3.25^{+0.005}_{-0.000}$ in (82.55 $^{+0.127}_{-0.000}$ mm)
B. 3.157 $^{+0.000}_{-0.005}$ in (80.17$^{+0.000}_{-0.127}$ mm)
C. 1.75 in (44.45 mm)
D. 0.75 in (19.05 mm)
E. ¾ in B.S.W. thread

Pressing-in pilot

F. 3.625 in (92.08 mm)
G. 3.312 in (84.14.mm)
H. 3.133 $^{+0.000}_{-0.005}$ in (84.66 $^{+0.000}_{-0.127}$ mm)
J. 1.25 in (31.75 mm)
K. 0.75 in (19.05 mm)
L. 0.015 in (.381 mm)

Pilot extension:

M. 14.50 in (368.3 mm)
N. 0.875 in (22.22 mm)
P. 0.625 in (15.87 mm)
Q. 0.625 in (15.87 mm)
R. Two flats 1 in across
S. ¾ in B.S.W. thread
T. 1.25 in (31.75 mm)

16. Press the liner into the cylinder block, using a press capable of 3 tons pressure.
17. Machine and hone the bores of the cylinder liners to the 'standard' bore size given in the table below.
18. Reverse the procedure in 1 to 7.

Bore of cylinder block – machined before fitting liner	Outside diameter of liner	Interference fit of liner	Bore of liner – machined after fitting ('standard')
3.2615 to 3.2620 in (82.84 to 82.85 mm)	3.2635 to 3.2643 in (82.89 to 82.91 mm)	0.0015 to 0.0027 in (0.038 to 0.0684 mm)	3.1591 to 3.1610 in (80.24 to 80.28 mm)

EDITOR'S NOTES

A. The Engine

Rocker assembly

Used pushrods or rockers should never be interchanged. A convenient way to keep pushrods in order is to push them through a piece of cardboard in which you have punched eight holes. If necessary, you can number the holes to identify the location of each pushrod in the engine.

Removing and replacing valve guides

It is always best to drive valve guides in or out with an arbor press or a hydraulic repair press rather than with a hammer.

Tappets

Used tappets should never be interchanged. The best way to identify them for reassembly is to wipe each tappet dry as you remove it. Then use waterproof ink or a waterproof felt-tipped marker to write an identification number on the tappet. During selective assembly, lubricate the tappets with engine oil. However, during final installation lubricate the tappets with assembly lubricant (available from automotive supply stores) or with a thin coat of multipurpose grease.

Camshaft

If you replace the camshaft, you should replace the tappets also. Otherwise, an incorrect wear pattern may be set up on the new cam lobes. During installation of the camshaft, lightly lubricate the cam lobes and camshaft bearing surfaces with assembly lubricant (available from automotive supply stores) or with a thin coat of multipurpose grease. This will prevent cam lobe and tappet wear when the engine is first started following repair.

Removing and replacing the crankshaft (engine out of car)

During refitting of the main bearings and the connecting rod big ends, always check the bearing clearances with Plastigage®. Temporarily reuse the old connecting rod locknuts for this measurement. Plastigage® is a thin plastic string. No lubricant should be used when checking the clearances with Plastigage®. To make this measurement place a piece of Plastigage® on the crankpin or main journal. Install the bearing and bearing cap and torque them down. Next remove the cap and bearing. The width of the flattened Plastigage® indicates the actual clearance. The crankshaft must not be turned during this process, and all traces of Plastigage® should be removed with solvent before reinstalling the bearings and cap. An incorrect clearance reading calls for reconditioning of the crankshaft, the selection of undersize bearings, or both.

During final assembly of the connecting rods and their caps, the bearings should be lubricated. If the engine is to be stored for some time following repairs — or if new bearing shells are being installed — it is advisable to use assembly lubricant (available from automotive supply stores) or a light coating of multipurpose grease on the crankpins and journals rather than ordinary engine oil. Always use NEW multi-sided locknuts (Part No. 13H 5872) during final installation of the connecting rod caps. Do not under any circumstances install the connecting rod caps using the hex nuts installed on new replacement rods for transit purposes. These low-strength, non-locking nuts should always be discarded as they will quickly fail if used in an engine.

Removing and replacing the flywheel (engine out of car)

If the engine is to be used in competion, it is always advisable to have the crankshaft, flywheel, and clutch assembly balanced as a unit by a shop that has precision dynamic balancing equipment.

Fitting the flywheel starter ring

Before you attempt to split the old starter ring gear with a cold chisel, drill a large hole through the gear in a direction parallel to the crankshaft. Drill the hole between two gear teeth. Drill a second large hole on the opposite side of the gear (180° around the flywheel from the first hole). Then break the gear by driving the chisel in between the two gear teeth that flank one of the holes you have drilled. Wear goggles and cover the area around the cold chisel with a cloth in order to protect yourself from flying fragments.

Distributor driving spindle — removing

To prevent abrasive dirt from entering the engine, thoroughly clean the distributor driving spindle housing and the surrounding part of the cylinder block before you remove the housing.

Distributor driving spindle —refitting

To prevent undue wear when the engine is first started, lightly lubricate the driving spindle gear with engine oil during installation.

Pistons and connecting rods

If wear has left ridges of metal around the tops of the cylinders (known as top cylinder ridges), you should not remove the pistons or install new piston rings unless these ridges are first removed with a special ridge reaming tool. If unremoved, the ridges may break the old rings as you remove the pistons, or they may break the new top ring after the engine is returned to service. In severe cases, top cylinder ridges have be even been known to ruin pistons by deforming the ring lands.

Though not specifically mentioned in the work procedures, the pistons and the cylinders should always be checked for wear and for correct clearance whenever the pistons are removed. If necessary, replace worn pistons and rebore worn cylinders to accept new oversize pistons or cylinder block liners.

You should also check the connecting rod alignment. If you lack the micrometers, the skills, or the machinery required for fitting pistons or checking connecting rod alignment, turn this work over to an Authorized Dealer or to a qualified automotive machine shop.

If you install new piston rings, always hone the cylinders lightly with a hone that has 220 grit or finer stones. Move the spinning hone smoothly in and out of the bore to produce a fine crosshatch pattern on the cylinder walls. The object is to remove "glaze" that could keep the new rings from seating. Remove as little metal as possible in order to avoid exceeding the piston clearance specifications. Clean away all abrasive dust with an oil-less solvent or with detergent and water. (The engine block should not have any bearings or moving parts installed in it during cylinder honing.)

You must use a piston ring compressor when you install the pistons in the cylinders. Otherwise, you are likely to break the piston rings. During refitting, lubricate the pistons and the cylinders with engine oil only. Other lubricants may interfere with the proper seating of the new piston rings. Tap the pistons down into their cylinders using a wooden hammer handle. Be careful not to drive the connecting rod big end against the crankpin at an angle. This could damage the crankshaft.

During refitting of the main bearings and the connecting rod big ends, always check the bearing clearances with Plastigage®. Temporarily reuse the old connecting rod locknuts for this measurement. Plastigage® is a thin plastic string. No lubricant should be used when checking the clearances with Plastigage®. To make this measurement place a piece of Plastigage® on the crankpin or main journal. Install the bearing and bearing cap and torque them down. Next remove the cap and bearing. The width of the flattened Plastigage® indicates the actual clearance. The crankshaft must not be turned during this process, and all traces of Plastigage® should be removed with solvent before reinstalling the bearings and cap. An incorrect clearance reading calls for reconditioning of the crankshaft, the selection of undersize bearings, or both.

During final assembly of the connecting rods and their caps, the bearings should be lubricated. If the engine is to be stored for some time following repairs — or if new bearing shells are being installed — it is advisable to use assembly lubricant (available from automotive supply stores) or a light coating of multipurpose grease on the crankpins rather than ordinary engine oil. Always use NEW multi-sided locknuts (Part No. 13H 5872) during final installation of the connecting rod caps. Do not under any circumstance install the connecting rod caps using the hex nuts installed on new replacement rods for transit purposes. These low-strength, non-locking hex nuts should always be discarded as they will quickly fail if used in an engine.

[A.19]

SECTION B

THE IGNITION SYSTEM

† These operations must be followed by an exhaust emission check.

Section B.1

DISTRIBUTOR
(Lucas type 45D4).

Removing

1. Disconnect the battery.
2. Remove the distributor cap.
3. Rotate the crankshaft until the groove in the crankshaft pulley lines up with the static ignition point on the timing indicator (see 'ENGINE TUNING DATA') and at the same time the distributor rotor arm is in the firing position for No. 1 sparking plug.
4. Disconnect the low tension lead from the wiring harness.
5. Disconnect the vacuum pipe from the distributor vacuum advance unit.
6. Remove the two screws securing the distributor clamp plate to the cylinder block.
7. Withdraw the distributor from the engine.

Dismantling

8. Note the relative position of the offset drive dog to the rotor arm lobe. The centre line of the drive dog is parallel with and offset to the centre line of the rotor arm.
9. Remove the rotor arm.
10. Remove the cam oiling pad.
11. Remove the two screws retaining the vacuum unit. (Early cars: Note that two prongs protrude downwards from the base plate and straddle one of the retaining screws.)
12. Disengage the operating arm from the movable plate and remove the assembly.
13. Push the grommet and low tension lead through the body towards the inside of the housing.
14. Remove the base plate retaining screws.
15. Remove the base and bearing plate assembly. (Early cars: Lever the base plate from its retaining groove in the body.)
16. Drive out the parallel pin retaining the drive dog.
17. Remove the drive dog and thrust washer, noting that the raised pips on the washer face the drive dog.
18. Remove the centre spindle complete with the automatic advance weights and springs.
19. Remove the steel washer and nylon spacer from the spindle.
20. Push the moving contact spring inwards and unclip the low tension lead.
21. Remove the screw retaining the earth lead tag and the capacitor.
22. Remove the screw, spring and plain washer retaining the fixed contact and remove the contact assembly.

Inspection

23. Examine the fit of the drive spindle in its bush, and the spindle cam for wear. The automatic advance

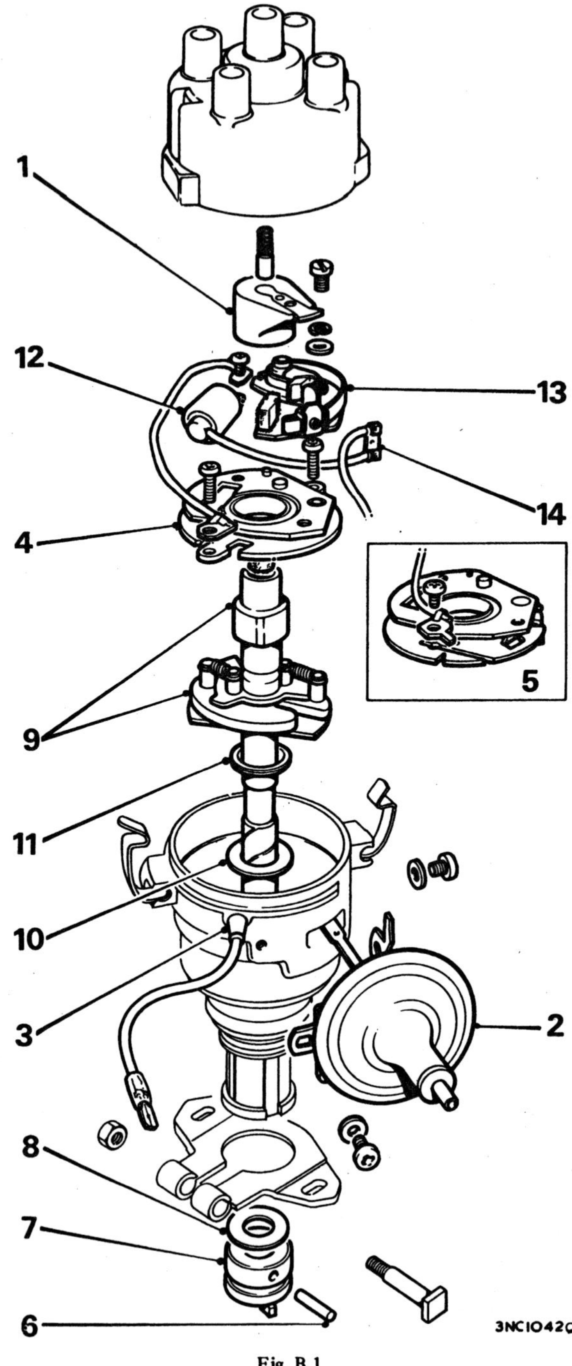

Fig. B.1

The distributor components
(Lucas type 45D4)

1. Rotor arm
2. Vacuum unit
3. Low tension lead
4. Base plate
5. Base plate (early cars)
6. Retaining pin – drive dog
7. Drive dog
8. Thrust washer
9. Cam spindle and automatic advance weights assembly
10. Steel washer
11. Spacer
12. Capacitor
13. Contact set
14. Low tension lead connector

mechanism should not be dismantled other than to remove the control springs. If any of the moving parts are excessively worn or damaged, the complete spindle assembly must be renewed. If the spindle bearing is worn allowing excessive side play, the complete distributor must be replaced.

24. Check the spring between the fixed and movable plates. Operate the plate and examine for freedom of movement and excessive wear. Renew as an assembly.
25. Examine the distributor and cap for cracks and signs of tracking. Examine the pick-up brush for wear and freedom of movement in its holder. Renew as necessary.
26. Check the rotor for damage, electrode security, and burning or tracking. Renew as necessary.

Reassembling

27. During reassembly grease the pivots of the weights and springs and the spindle bearing area with Rocol MP (Molypad).
28. Grease the outside of the contact breaker hollow pivot post and lightly smear the spindle cam, using Retinax 'A' grease.
29. Apply one or two drops of clean engine oil to the oiling pad.
30. Reverse the procedure in 6 to 22, noting:
    a. Set the contact points gap to 0.014 to 0.016 in (0.36 to 0.40 mm).
    b. If a new drive spindle is fitted, tap the drive end of the distributor dog to flatten the pips on the thrust washer and ensure the correct amount of end-float.

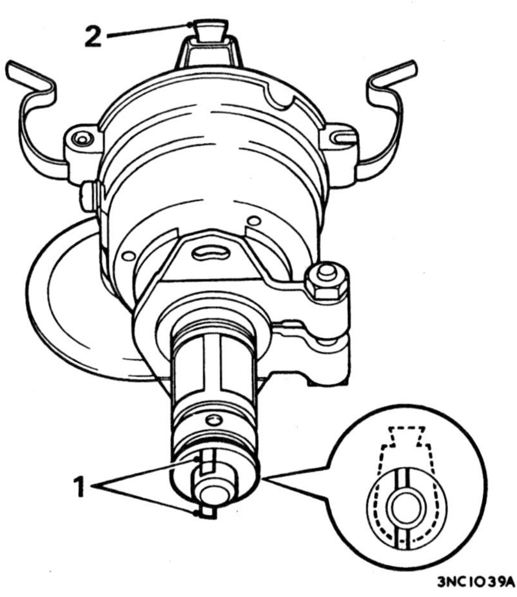

Fig. B.2

Refitting the drive dog
(Lucas type 45D4)

Note the driving tongues (1) are parallel with the centre line of the rotor arm (2)

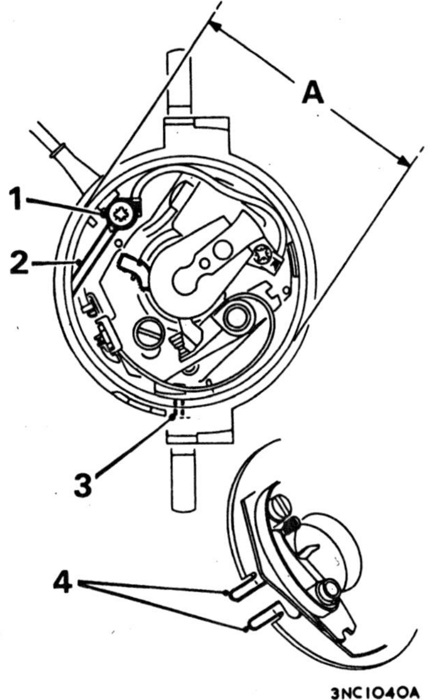

Fig. B.3

Refitting the base plate (early cars)
(Lucas type 45D4)

1. Base plate
2. Slot in base plate
3. Screw hole
4. Prongs

'A' : Diameter checking position

The new spindle should be drilled through the hole in the drive dog. Use a 3/16 in (4.76 mm) drill. During drilling, push the spindle from the cam end, pressing the drive dog and washer against the body shank.

EARLY CARS

c. Ensure the base plate is pressed against the register in the body of the distributor so that the chamfered edge engages the undercut.
d. Measure across the centre of the distributor at a right angle to the slot in the base plate.
e. Tighten the securing screw and re-measure the distance across the body. Unless the measurement has increased by at least 0.006 in (0.152 mm) the contact breaker base plate must be renewed.

Refitting

31. Reverse the procedure in 4 to 7 but do not tighten the flange retaining screws.
32. With the crankshaft and distributor rotor set as in instruction 3, rotate the distributor within the limits of the slotted holes in the flange until the contact breaker points are just opening.
33. Tighten the flange retaining screws to 8 to 10 lbf ft (1.1 to 1.4 kgf m).
34. Refit the distributor cap.
35. Re-connect the battery.
36. Check the ignition timing, see **'MAINTENANCE'**.

Section B.2

DISTRIBUTOR (Lucas type 45DE4)

[Troubleshooting]

CAUTION: Never, during troubleshooting or repair, should you connect the white leads of the amplifier module or the pickup module with either a blue or a black sleeve to a source of positive (+) current supply. (This can easily occur accidentally at the pickup module if caution is not exercised.) Always ensure that the ignition is turned off when you are setting the air gap between the pickup module core and the timing rotor. These precautions are necessary in order to avoid damage to the solid-state components of the ignition system.

Testing to locate cause of misfire

1. Check all electrical connections, both primary (low tension) and secondary (high tension), to ascertain that they are clean and tight-fitting.
2. Test the spark plugs and check their gaps, which should be set at 0.035 in. (0.90 mm).
3. Test the plug cables and the high tension cable for excessive resistance and faulty insulation. Examine the distributor rotor, the distributor cap, and the coil tower for carbon tracking. Replace damaged components.
4. Clean and examine the distributor cap brush and spring and the electrodes.
5. Check the pickup module/timing rotor air gap as described in Section B.3 making sure that the ignition is turned off.
6. If the misfire persists after carrying out the preceding checks and tests, substitute a new ignition coil. If the misfire is still present, substitute a new amplifier module.

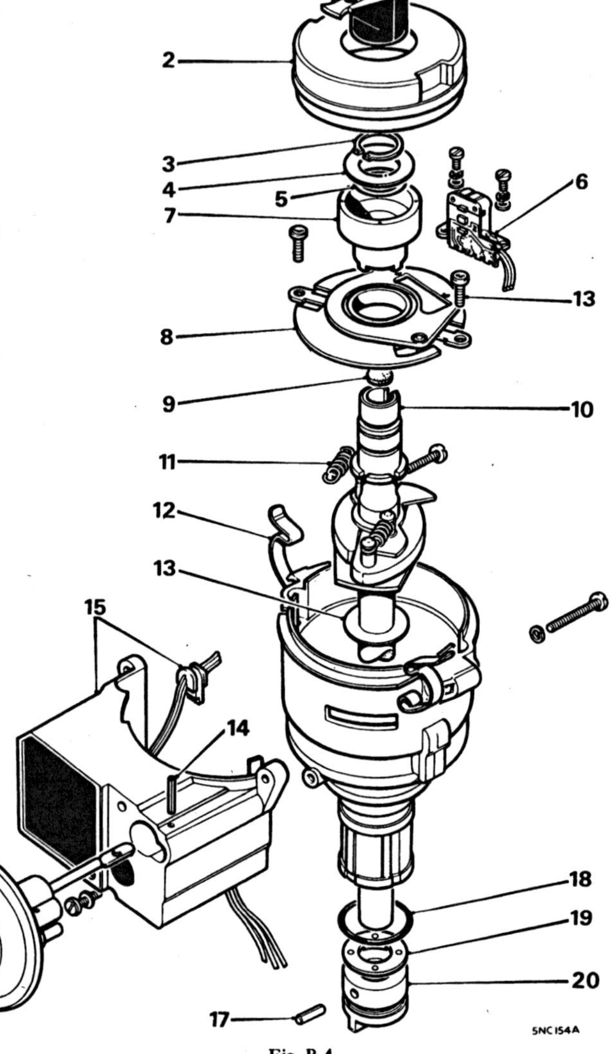

Fig. B.4

The distributor components (Lucas type 45DE4)

1. Rotor
2. Anti-flash shield
3. Circlip
4. Washer
5. 'O' ring
6. Pick-up
7. Timing rotor
8. Base plate
9. Felt pad
10. Spindle
11. Return spring
12. Spring clip
13. Shim
14. Pin
15. Amplifier module
16. Vacuum unit
17. Pin for driving dog
18. 'O' ring
19. Thrust washer
20. Driving dog

[**NOTE:** On 1977 and later cars, the vacuum advance is operative, but only in 4th gear or in 4th gear overdrive. See section Na for a wiring diagram of this system.]

Service Division Dealer Training Aid S 1037

Removing

1. Disconnect the battery.
2. Remove the distributor cap and leads.
3. Disconnect the low tension distributor leads.
4. Turn the engine until the timing notch on the crankshaft pulley is at T.D.C. The distributor rotor arm should be in the firing position for No. 1 sparking plug.
5. Slacken the nut and bolt to release the distributor clamp.
6. Withdraw the distributor assembly .

Dismantling

7. Remove the rotor arm.
8. Remove the anti-flash shield.
9. Remove the felt pad.
10. Remove the two screws, spring washers and plain washers securing the pick-up to the moving plate.
11. Remove the three screws and washers securing the amplifier module to the distributor body.
12. Detach the retard unit link from the pin on the moving plate.
13. Detach the pick-up wiring grommet from the distributor body and remove the amplifier module complete with pick-up and leads.
14. Remove the two spring clips from the distributor body.
15. Drive out the pin securing the retard unit to the amplifier module and withdraw the unit.
16. Remove the circlip and washer securing the timing rotor.
17. Remove the timing rotor and rubber 'O' ring.
18. Remove the two screws securing the base plate to the distributor body.
19. Remove the base plate.
20. Drive out the pin securing the driving dog to the distributor spindle.
21. Remove the driving dog and thrust washer.
22. Ensure that the spindle is free of burrs and withdraw it from the distributor body.
23. Remove the shim.
24. Remove the two return springs.

Reassembling

25. Reverse the procedure in 7 to 24, noting:
    a. Lubricate the centrifugal weights assembly, the distributor spindle and the moving plate pin with Rocol Moly pad or equivalent.
    b. Fit the timing rotor with the large locating lug in the corresponding slot.
    c. Ensure that the amplifier module and the wiring grommet are correctly seated before the three securing screws are tightened.
    d. Adjust the pick up air gap, see Section B.3.
    e. Lubricate the distributor, see 'MAINTENANCE'.

Refitting

26. Set the engine and distributor rotor arm as in instruction 4 and fit the distributor with the clamp.
27. Tighten the distributor clamp nut.
28. Reverse the procedure in 1 to 3.
29. Check the ignition timing, see 'MAINTENANCE'.

Section B.3

PICK-UP AIR GAP ADJUSTMENT (Lucas distributor type 45DE4) 

CAUTION: Do not insert a feeler gauge into the pick-up air gap when the ignition circuit is energised.

1. Disconnect the battery.
2. Remove the distributor cap and leads.
3. Remove the distributor rotor arm.
4. Remove the anti-flash shield.
5. Check the air gap: it should be 0.010 to 0.017 in (0.25 to 0.43 mm).
6. If adjustment is required, slacken the two screws securing the pick-up, and move the pick-up about the pivot screw to give the correct setting.
7. Tighten the two screws and check the air gap.

CAUTION: Ensure that this checking operation is carried out as the air gap may alter substantially when the two screws are tightened.

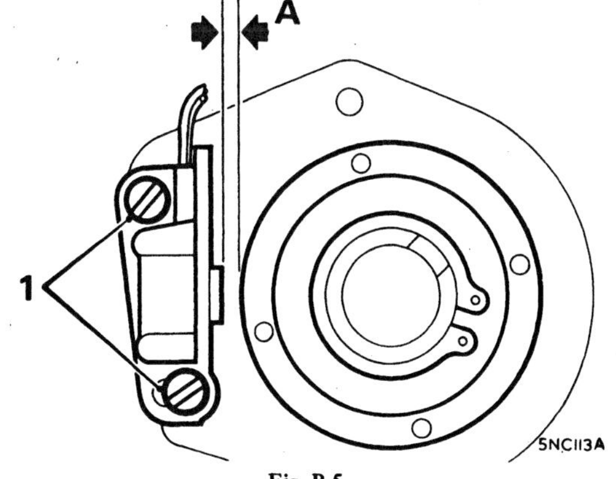

Fig. B.5

The pick-up air gap adjustment (Lucas distributor type 45DE4)

1. Pick-up adjustment screws.
A. 0.010 to 0.017 in (0.25 to 0.43 mm).

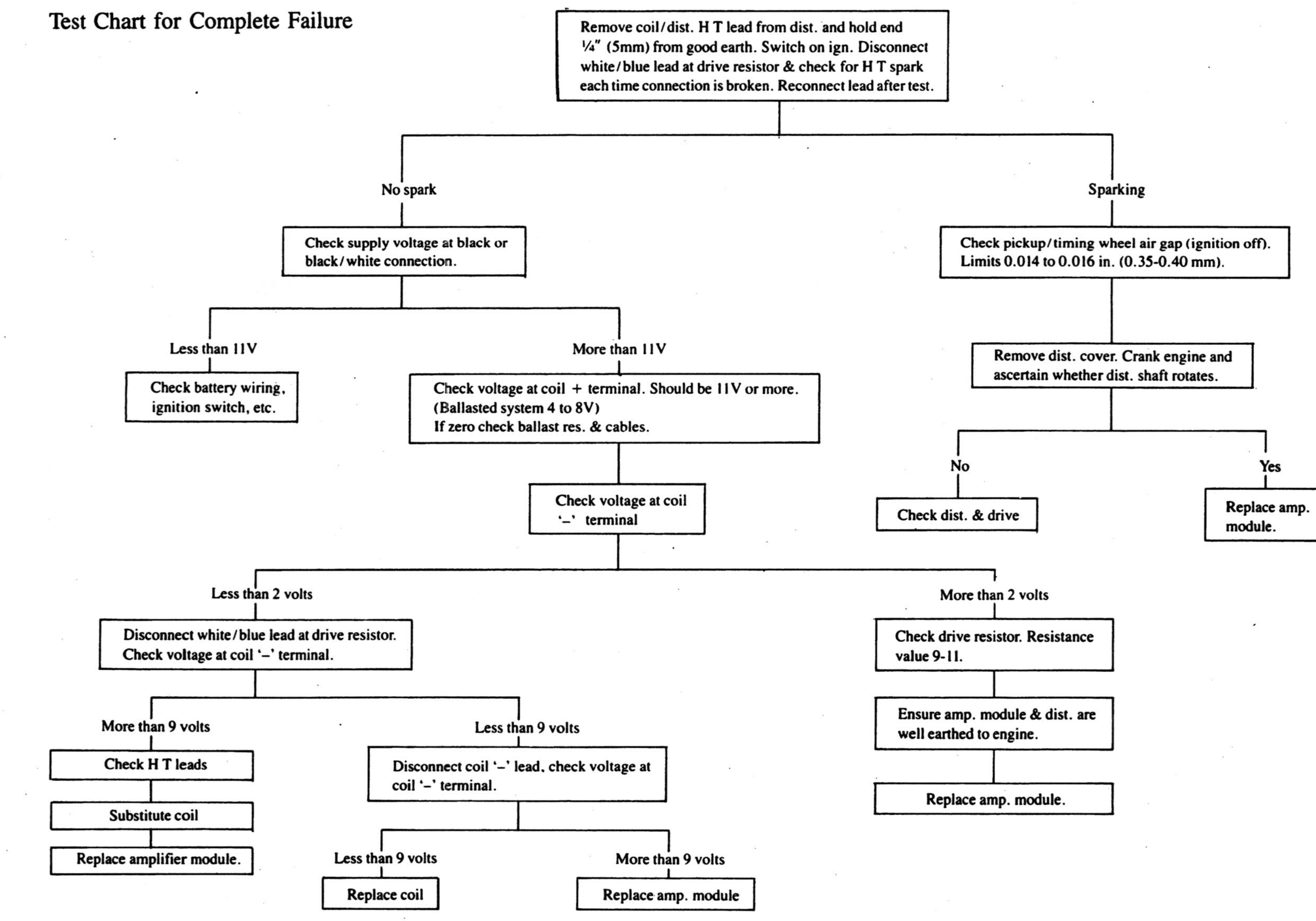

Test Chart for Complete Failure

SECTION C

THE COOLING SYSTEM

GENERAL DESCRIPTION

The cooling system is pressurized and the water circulation is assisted by a pump attached to the front of the engine and driven by a belt from the crankshaft pulley. A relief valve is incorporated into the radiator filler cap which controls the pressure.
The water circulates from the base of the radiator and passes round the cylinders and cylinder head, reaching the header tank of the radiator via the thermostat and top hose. From the header tank it passes down the radiator core to the base tank of the radiator. Air is drawn through the radiator by a fan attached to the water pump pulley.

Section C.1

THERMOSTAT

IMPORTANT.–In hot climates where the thermostat is removed as a permanent measure, it is essential that a thermostat blanking sleeve is fitted. Failure to fit a sleeve will result in higher operating temperatures and possible damage.

Removing

1. Drain the cooling system–Section C.2.
2. Disconnect the radiator top hose from the water outlet elbow.
3. Remove the screw to release the gulp valve hose clip from the thermostat housing retaining nut.
4. Slacken the air pump adjusting link and mounting bolts.
5. Remove the air pump drive belt.
6. Remove the air pump top mounting bolt.
7. Remove the three nuts and washers securing the thermostat housing.
8. Remove the housing and gasket.
9. Remove the thermostat.

Inspection

10. Examine the thermostat for damage and check that the valve is in the closed position. Renew the thermostat if damaged or if the valve is open.
11. Immerse the thermostat in water heated to the temperature marked on the thermostat; the valve will start to open if it is functioning correctly. If the valve fails to open renew the thermostat.

Refitting

12. Reverse the removing procedure using a new joint washer, then refill the cooling system and check that the air pump drive belt is coirectly tensioned.

Section C.2

DRAINING, FLUSHING AND REFILLING THE COOLING SYSTEM

Removing the filler cap

The cooling system is under pressure while the engine is hot, unscrew the cap slowly until the retaining tongues are felt to engage the small lobes on the end of the filler spout cam, and wait until the pressure in the radiator is fully released before finally removing the cap.
It is advisable to protect the hand against escaping steam while removing the cap.

Draining the cooling system

Remove the drain plug located at the rear of the cylinder block on the right-hand side.
Disconnect the bottom hose from the radiator.

NOTE.–Under no circumstances should draining of the cooling system be resorted to as an alternative to the use of anti-freeze mixture, due to the fact that complete draining of the heater unit by means of the cooling system drain taps is not possible.

To ensure sufficient circulation of the coolant and to reduce the formation of scale and sediment in the radiator the system should be periodically flushed out with clear running water, preferably before putting in anti-freeze solution and again after taking it out.

The water should be allowed to run through until it comes out clear from the taps.

This method is adequate under normal conditions, but in extreme cases where excessive 'furring up' is experienced a more efficient method is to completely remove the radiator and flush in the reverse way to the flow, i.e. turn the radiator upside-down and let the water flow in through the bottom hose and out of the top connection.

(See Editor's notes at end of Section C.)

Filling the cooling system

Refit the bottom hose to the radiator and the drain plug to the cylinder block.

Ensure that all hose connections are tight.

Fill up the system through the filler in the radiator header tank until the level of water can just be seen. Run the engine until it is hot and then add sufficient water to raise the level to within 1 in. (25.4mm.) of the bottom of the filler neck.

When possible, soft water, such as clean rain-water, should be used to fill the system.

When using anti-freeze solution avoid overfilling to prevent loss from expansion.

Anti-freeze solutions having an alcohol base are unsuitable for use in the cooling system owing to the high temperatures attained in the top radiator tank. Only anti-freeze solutions of the ethylene glycol type incorporating the correct type of corrosion inhibitor should be employed, see **'SERVICE LUBRICANTS, FUEL and FLUIDS–CAPACITIES'**.

(See Editor's notes at end of Section C.)

Section C.3

RADIATOR AND DIAPHRAGM

The radiator block assembly is supported in a metal diaphragm which is secured to the body sides by screws and washers. The diaphragm has two holes in the right-hand side to permit the oil cooler pipes to pass from the cooler to the engine. A rubber air seal is fitted across the top channel of the diaphragm.

The radiator is supported in the diaphragm by two screws and washers each side and a tie-bar running forward from each top screw to the body sides.

The overflow pipe is secured by two clips that are retained by the radiator fixing screws.

Removing
To remove the radiator drain the coolant–Section C.2, release the top and bottom hose clips, and detach the hoses from their connectors.

Where an oil cooler is not fitted the radiator and diaphragm may be removed as a complete assembly by removing the top radiator to diaphragm screws to release the stays and then removing the screws securing each side of the diaphragm to the body.

If an oil cooler is fitted the pipe connections must be disconnected from the cooler and the engine before removing the radiator and diaphragm assembly.

To remove the radiator without the diaphragm undo the radiator to diaphragm securing screws, slacken the diaphragm to body securing screws, detach the overflow pipe clips, and then lift the diaphragm sufficiently to allow the radiator to be pulled forward and lifted from the car.

Replacing
Replacement is a reversal of the removal sequence, but ensure that the foam seal is correctly positioned at the top of the radiator and that the overflow pipe is secured.

Refit the drain plug, fill with coolant, and check for leaks.

Section C.4

WATER PUMP

Removing
1. Remove the radiator–Section C.3.
2. Remove the fan blades and drive pulley.
3. Remove the screws retaining the air pump adjusting link.

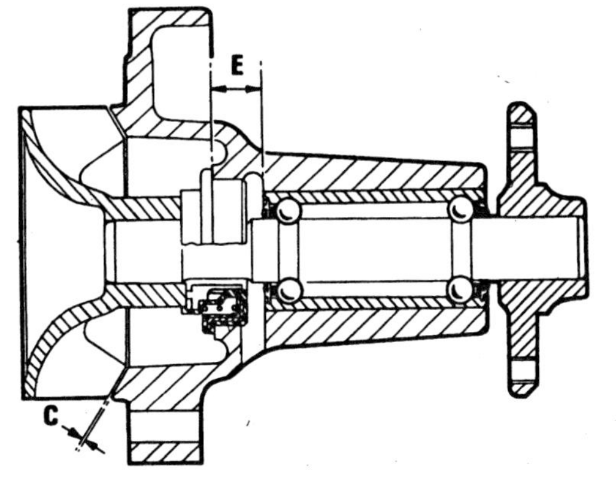

Fig. C.1

A section through the water pump

C. .020 to .030 in (.51 to .76 mm) clearance
E. Distance from rear face of spindle bearing (outer track) to seal housing shoulder should be .534 in ± .005 in (13.56 mm ± 13 mm)

4. Remove the top mounting screw, nut and washers retaining the alternator.
5. Slacken the clip and disconnect the hose from the water pump.
6. Remove the remaining bolts retaining the water pump.
7. Remove the water pump.

Dismantling
8. Withdraw the pulley hub from the spindle.
9. Withdraw the bearing locating wire from the body aperture.
10. Tap the spindle rearwards and remove the spindle complete with the bearing. The bearing cannot be removed from the spindle.
11. Withdraw the impeller from the spindle and remove the seal. (See Editor's notes at end of Section C.)

Reassembling
12. If the interference fit of the fan hub was impaired when the hub was withdrawn from the spindle a new hub must be fitted. The hub must be fitted with its face flush with the end of the spindle.
13. Press the spindle bearing assembly into the pump body and take measurement E, Fig. C.1; adjust the position of the spindle bearing assembly to obtain the correct measurement.
14. Fit a new seal. Smear the jointing face of the seal with a mineral base oil to ensure a watertight joint.
15. Press the impeller onto the spindle, ensuring that the correct running clearance (C, Fig. C.1) is maintained between the impeller vanes and the pump body.

Refitting
16. Reverse the removing procedure in 1 to 7.

[Section C.5]

TWIN ELECTRIC FANS

The 1977 and later models have twin electric fans fitted in front of the radiator. These fans are controlled by a thermal switch located in the top radiator tank close to the water outlet connection. The fans are activated at 93°C (200°F) maximum and are deactivated when the coolant temperature falls to 82°C (180°F) minimum.

(See Editor's notes at end of Section C.)

When correctly installed, the fans turn counterclockwise when viewed from the front of the car. A wiring diagram for the twin electric fan system is given in Section Na. When installing a fan unit on the car, make certain that the wires are at the bottom of the motor. If the motors are installed with the wires uppermost, water may enter the motor housings and cause electrical failure.

EDITOR'S NOTES

C. The Cooling System

Draining the cooling system

Never drain the coolant while the engine is hot. This could warp the engine block or the cylinder head. Also, for best results, the thermostat should be removed when you flush the cooling system. This allows the water to circulate freely throughout the block. In refilling the 1977 and later cooling system, please follow the instruction given on page 22.

Filling the cooling system

Anti-freeze can remain in the cooling system for two years provided that the specific gravity of the coolant is checked periodically and new anti-freeze is added as required. An anti-freeze hydrometer is used to check the specific gravity. With this device a small quantity of the coolant is sucked into a glass cylinder, and the position of a float indicates the specific gravity, usually in terms of the temperature at which ice will begin to form.

Water pump — dismantling

Use a gear puller of suitable size to remove the pulley hub from the spindle. If available, use a hydraulic repair press for this job.

Fuse—fan circuit

The 35 amp fuse in the fan circuit may be replaced with a 20 amp circuit breaker if desired.

Technical Service Bulletin 77-B-6.

SECTION D

THE FUEL SYSTEM

† These operations must be followed by an exhaust emission check. 

Section D.1

FUEL TANK

Removing

1. Disconnect the battery and remove the spare wheel. **NOTE:** Place a clean container beneath the tank if the tank is full.
2. Disconnect the petrol feed pipe from the tank.
3. Remove the four screws, large plain washers and sealing washers securing the tank inside the boot.
4. Slacken the two clips securing the rubber hose to the tank and the fuel filler tube.
5. Disconnect the vapour line from the tank.
6. Remove the screw, nut and washer securing the tank to the R.H. side of the boot floor.
7. Disconnect the electrical lead from the tank gauge unit.
8. Remove the nuts and washers securing the tank to boot floor studs and remove the tank.

Refitting

9. Reverse the procedure in 1 to 8.

Section D.2

FUEL PUMP

Removing

1. Disconnect the battery.
2. Working inside the boot, remove the pump guard, disconnect the electrical lead from the pump and slacken the pump retaining clip.
3. Working beneath the car, disconnect the fuel pipe unions from the pump and support them to prevent loss of fuel.
4. Disconnect the electrical lead from the pump.
5. Disconnect the breather tube from the pump.
6. Remove the pump from the car.

Refitting

7. Reverse the procedure in 1 to 6.

Dismantling

CONTACT BREAKER

1. Remove the insulated sleeve or knob, terminal nut, and connector, together with its shakeproof washer. Remove the tape seal and take off the end cover.
2. Unscrew the 5 B.A. screw which holds the contact blade to the pedestal and remove the condenser from its clip. This will allow the washer, the long coil lead, and the contact blade to be removed.

COIL HOUSING AND DIAPHRAGM

3. Unscrew the coil housing securing screws, using a thick-bladed screwdriver to avoid damaging the screw heads.
4. Remove the earthing screw.
5. ROLLER TYPE. Hold the coil housing over a bench or receptacle to prevent the 11 brass rollers from being damaged or lost as they come free, unscrew the diaphragm assembly anti-clockwise until the armature spring pushes it free of the housing.
   GUIDE PLATE TYPE. Turn the back edge of the diaphragm and carefully lever the two end lobes of the armature guide plate from the recess in the coil housing, unscrew the diaphragm assembly anti-clockwise until the armature spring pushes it free of the housing. Remove the armature guide from the diaphragm assembly.

PEDESTAL AND ROCKER

6. Remove the end cover seal washer, unscrew the terminal nut, and remove the lead washer. This will have flattened on the terminal tag and thread and is best cut away with cutting pliers or a knife. Remove the terminal tag spring washer. Unscrew the two 2 B.A. screws holding the pedestal to the coil housing, remove the earth terminal tag together with the condenser clip. Tip the pedestal and withdraw the terminal stud from the terminal tag. The pedestal may now be removed with the rocker mechanism attached.
7. Push out the hardened steel pin which holds the rocker mechanism to the pedestal.

BODY AND VALVES

8. Unscrew the two Phillips screws securing the valve clamp plate, remove the valve covers, valves, sealing washers, and filter.
   NOTE.–Dismantling of the delivery flow smoothing device should only be undertaken if the operation of it is faulty, and if the necessary equipment for pressure-testing after assembly is available. On this understanding proceed as follows:
9. Remove the four 4 B.A. screws securing the delivery flow smoothing device vent cover, remove the cover, the diaphragm spring, rubber 'O' rings, spring cap, diaphragm, barrier, diaphragm plate, and sealing washer.
10. Remove the single 2 B.A. screw securing the inlet air bottle cover, remove the cover and gasket.
11. Unscrew the inlet and outlet connections.

Inspecting

GENERAL

If gum formation has occurred in the fuel used in the pump, the parts in contact with the fuel will have become coated with a substance similar to varnish. This has a strong, stale smell and will attack the neoprene diaphragm. Brass and steel parts so affected can be cleaned by being boiled in a 20 per cent. solution of caustic soda, dipped in a strong nitric acid solution, and finally washed in boiling

THE FUEL PUMP COMPONENTS

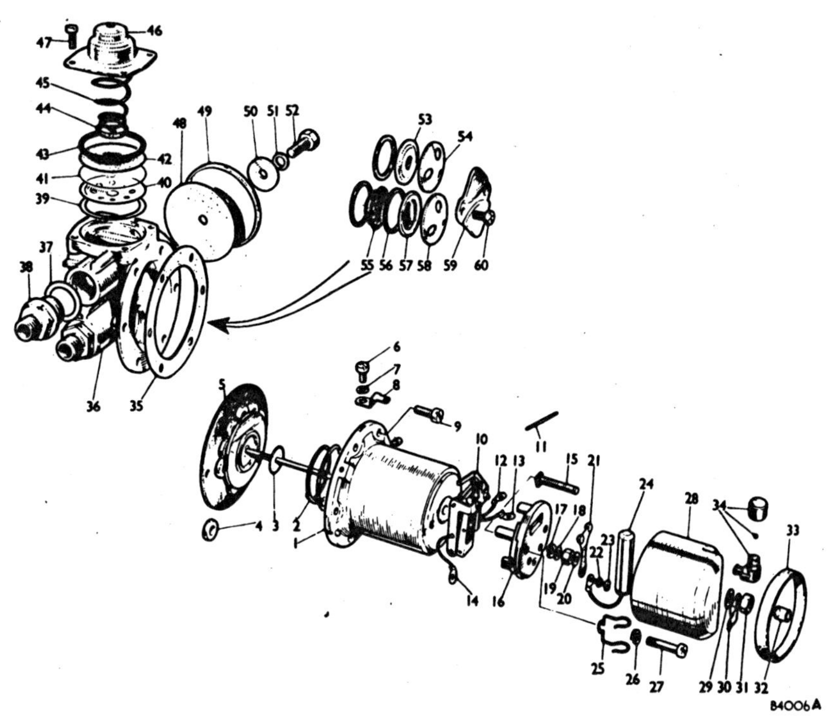

No.	Description	No.	Description	No.	Description
1.	Coil housing.	21.	Contact blade.	41.	Plastic diaphragm barrier.
2.	Armature spring.	22.	Washer.	*42.	Rubber diaphragm.
3.	Impact washer.	23.	Contact blade screw.	43.	Rubber 'O' ring.
4.	Armature centralizing roller.	24.	Condenser.	*44.	Spring end cap.
5.	Diaphragm and spindle assembly.	25.	Condenser clip.	*45.	Diaphragm spring.
6.	Set screw.	26.	Spring washer.	†46.	Delivery flow smoothing device cover.
7.	Spring washer.	27.	Pedestal screw.	47.	Set screw.
8.	Earth connector.	28.	End cover.	48.	Gasket.
9.	Set screw.	29.	Shakeproof washer.	49.	Inlet air bottle cover.
10.	Rocker mechanism.	30.	Lucar connector.	50.	Dished washer.
11.	Rocker pivot pin.	31.	Nut.	51.	Spring washer.
12.	Terminal tag.	32.	Insulating sleeve.	52.	Set screw.
13.	Terminal tag.	33.	Sealing band.	53.	Outlet valve.
14.	Earth tag.	34.	Vent valve.	54.	Valve cap.
15.	Terminal stud.	35.	Gasket.	55.	Filter.
16.	Pedestal.	36.	Pump body.	56.	Sealing washer.
17.	Spring washer.	37.	Fibre washer.	57.	Inlet valve.
18.	Lead washer.	38.	Outlet connection.	58.	Valve cap.
19.	Terminal nut.	39.	Sealing washer.	59.	Clamp plate.
20.	End cover seal washer.	*40.	Diaphragm plate.	60.	Set screw.

* Early pumps. † Delivery air bottle (later pumps).

water. Light alloy parts must be well soaked in methylated spirits and then cleaned.

1. Clean the pump and inspect for cracks, damaged joint faces, and threads.
2. Clean the filter with a brush and examine for fractures. Renew if necessary.
3. Examine the coil lead tags for security and the lead insulation for damage.
4. Examine the contact breaker points for signs of burning and pitting. If this is evident the rockers and spring blade must be renewed.
5. Examine the pedestal for cracks or other damage particularly to the narrow ridge on the edge of the rectangular hole on which the contact blade rests.
6. Examine the diaphragm for signs of deterioration.
7. Examine the non-return vent valve in the end cover for damage, and ensure that the small ball valve is free to move.
8. Examine the plastic valve assemblies for kinks or damage to the valve plates. They can best be checked by blowing or sucking with the mouth.
9. Check that the narrow tongue on the valve cage which prevents the valve being forced out of position, has not been distorted but allows a valve lift of approximately $\frac{1}{16}$ in. (1.6 mm.).
10. Examine the delivery air bottle diaphragm.
11. Examine the inlet air bottle cover and gasket for damage.
12. Examine the valve recesses in the body for damage and corrosion. If it is impossible to remove the corrosion or if the recesses are badly pitted the body must be discarded.

Reassembling

PEDESTAL AND ROCKER

NOTE.–The steel pin which secures the rocker mechanism to the pedestal is specially hardened and must not be replaced by other than a genuine S.U. part.

1. Invert the pedestal and fit the rocker assembly to it by pushing the steel pin through the small holes in the rockers and pedestal struts. Then position the centre toggle so that with the inner rocker spindle in tension against the rear of the contact point the centre toggle spring is above the spindle on which the white rollers run. This positioning is important to obtain the correct 'throw-over' action. It is also essential that the rockers are perfectly free to swing on the pivot pin and that the arms are not binding on the legs of the pedestal. If necessary, rockers can be squared up with a pair of thin-nosed pliers.

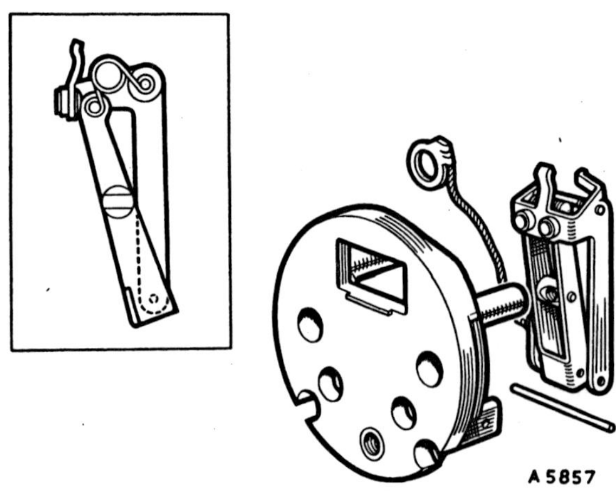

Fig. D.1
Fitting the rocker assembly to the pedestal. (Inset) the correct position of the centre toggle spring

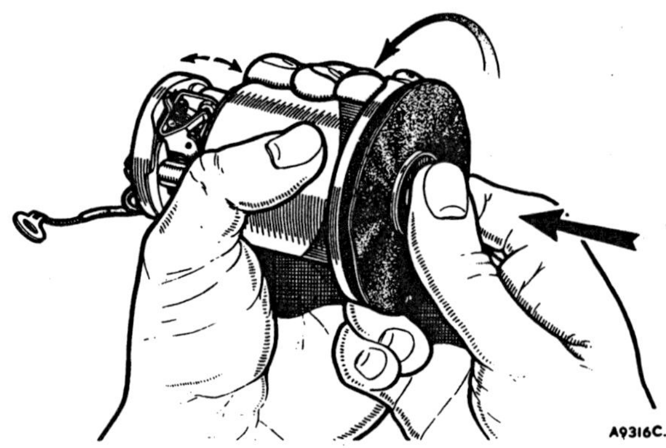

Fig. D.2
Setting the diaphragm. Unscrew until the rocker just 'throws over'

2. Assemble the square-headed 2 B.A. terminal stud to the pedestal, the back of which is recessed to take the square head.
3. Assemble the 2 B.A. spring washer and put the terminal stud through the 2 B.A. terminal tag then fit the lead washer, and the coned nut with its coned face to the lead washer (this makes better contact than an ordinary flat washer and nut). Tighten the 2 B.A. nut and finally add the end cover seal washer.
4. Assemble the pedestal to the coil housing by fitting the two B.A. pedestal screws, ensuring that the condenser wire clip on the left-hand screw (9 o'clock position) is between the pedestal and the earthing tag. The spring washer is not fitted when a condenser is used.
5. Tighten the screws, taking care to prevent the earthing tag from turning as this will strain or break the earthing flex. Do not overtighten the screws or the pedestal will crack. **Do not fit the contact blade at this stage.**

DIAPHRAGM ASSEMBLY

6. Place the armature spring into the coil housing with its large diameter towards the coil.
7. Before fitting the diaphragm make sure that the impact washer (a small neoprene washer that fits in the armature recess) is fitted to the armature. Do not use jointing compound or dope on the diaphragm.
8. Fit the diaphragm by inserting the spindle in the coil and screwing it onto the threaded trunnion in the centre of the rocker assembly.

9. Screw in the diaphragm until the rocker will not 'throw over'. This must not be confused with jamming the armature on the coil housing internal steps.
10. ROLLER TYPE. With the pump held with the rocker end downwards, turn back the edge of the diaphragm and fit the 11 brass rollers into the recess in the coil housing.
On rocker mechanisms with adjustable fingers fit the contact blade and adjust the finger settings as described under those headings, then carefully remove the contact blade.
11. With the pump held horizontally, slowly unscrew the diaphragm while at the same time actuating it, until the rocker just throws over. Unscrew the diaphragm until the holes are aligned, then unscrew it a further quarter of a turn (four holes).
12. ROLLER TYPE. Press the centre of the armature and fit the retaining fork at the back of the rocker assembly.

BODY COMPONENTS

13. GUIDE PLATE TYPE. Turn back the edge of the diaphragm and insert one end lobe of the armature guide plate into the recess between the armature and the coil housing. Progressively position all four lobes, then commencing in the centre and finishing with the two end ones, press the lobes firmly into the recess.
14. Note that the inlet valve recess in the body is deeper than the outlet recess to allow for the filter and extra washer. Screw in the inlet and outlet connections with their sealing rings. Assemble the outlet valve components into the outlet recess in the following order: first a joint washer, then the valve (tongue side downwards), then the valve cover.
15. Assemble the inlet valve into the recess as follows: first a joint washer, then the filter (dome side downwards), then another joint washer, followed by the valve assembly (tongue side uppermost), then the valve cover.
16. Take care that both valve assemblies nest down into their respective recesses, place the clamp plate on top of the valve covers and tighten down firmly on to the body with the two screws. Replace the inlet air bottle cover with its joint washer and tighten down the central screw.
17. **Place the sealing washer in the bottom of the delivery air bottle recess, place the plastic diaphragm, dome side downwards, then add the 'O' section sealing ring and tighten down the cap with its four screws.**

BODY ATTACHMENT

18. Fit the joint washer to the body, aligning the screw holes, and offer up the coil housing to the body, ensuring correct seating between them.
19. Line up the six securing screw holes, making sure that the cast lugs on the coil housing are at the bottom, and insert the six 2 B.A. screws finger tight. Fit the earthing screw with its Lucar connector.
20. ROLLER TYPE. Carefully remove the retaining fork from the rocker assembly and check that the rollers are correctly positioned.
21. Tighten the securing screws in diagonal sequence.

CONTACT BLADE

22. Fit the contact blade and coil lead to the pedestal with the 5 B.A. washer and screw. Place the condenser tag beneath the coil lead tag.

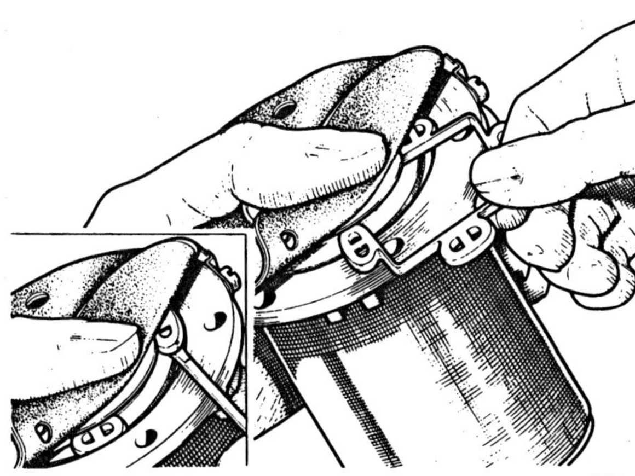

Fig. D.3

Fitting the armature guide plate. (Inset), levering one of the end lobes from the recess

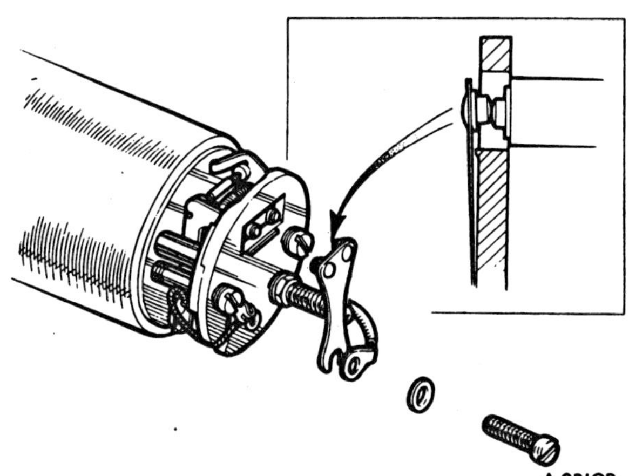

Fig. D.4

Setting the correct relative position of blade and rocker contact points

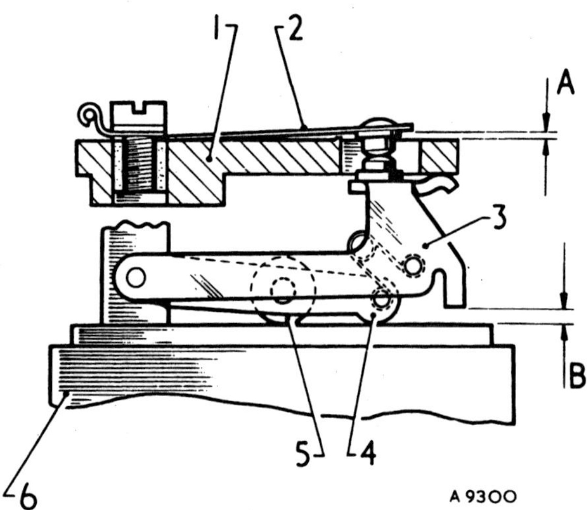

Fig. D.5
The rocker finger settings on modified rocker assemblies

1. Pedestal.
2. Contact blade.
3. Outer rocker.
4. Inner rocker.
5. Trunnion.
6. Coil housing.

A = .035 in. (.9 mm.) B = .070 in. (1.8 mm.).

23. Adjust the contact blade so that the points on it are a little above the contact points on the rocker when the points are closed, also that when the contact points make or break one pair of points wipes over the centre line of the other in a symmetrical manner.
    The contact blade attachment screw slot allows a degree of adjustment.
24. Tighten the contact blade attachment screw when the correct setting is obtained.

CONTACT GAP SETTINGS

25. Check that when the outer rocker is pressed on to the coil housing the contact blade rests on the narrow rib which projects above the main face of the pedestal. If it does not, slacken the contact blade attachment screw, swing the blade clear of the pedestal, and bend it downwards a sufficient amount so that, when re-positioned, it rests against the rib.
26. Check the lift of the contact blade above the top of the pedestal (A) (Fig. D.5) with a feeler gauge, bending the stop finger beneath the pedestal, if necessary, to obtain a lift of .035±.005 in. (.9±.13 mm.).
27. Check the gap between the rocker finger and coil housing (B) (Fig. D.5) with a feeler gauge, bending the stop finger, if necessary, to obtain a gap of .070±.005 in. (1.8±.13 mm.).

END COVER

28. Ensure that the end cover seal washer is in position on the terminal stud, fit the bakelite end cover and shakeproof washer, and secure with the brass nut. Fit the terminal tag or connector and the insulated sleeve. After test, replace the rubber sealing band over the end cover gap and seal with adhesive tape. This must be retained when the pump is not mounted internally in a moisture-free region.

Testing on a test stand

PREPARATION

1. Churchill test rig:
   Secure the pump in the clamping ring, with the outlet connection uppermost. Connect to a 12-volt battery, and with the switch in the 'OFF' position, clip the connector to the pump. Connect the delivery and return of the correct bore to the pump.
   S.U. test rig:
   Mount the pump on the test stand, using the appropriate adaptor set according to the type of pump. Connect the feed and earth terminals to the test battery and check the contact gap setting as described under that heading. Replace the end cover with a cut-away one which allows observation of the rocker assembly while retaining the pivot pin.
   Use paraffin (kerosene) in the test tank. Ensure an adequate supply.

PRIMING

2. Unscrew the regulator valve (Churchill rig only) and switch on: the pump should prime from dry in 10 to 15 seconds. Allow the pump to run for a minute to stabilize the flow.

AIR LEAK CHECK

3. When the pump is first started air bubbles will be mixed with the liquid discharged from the pipe projecting downwards into the flow meter; these bubbles should cease after a minute or so. If they do not, an air leak is indicated either in the pump or the connecting unions, and this must be rectified.

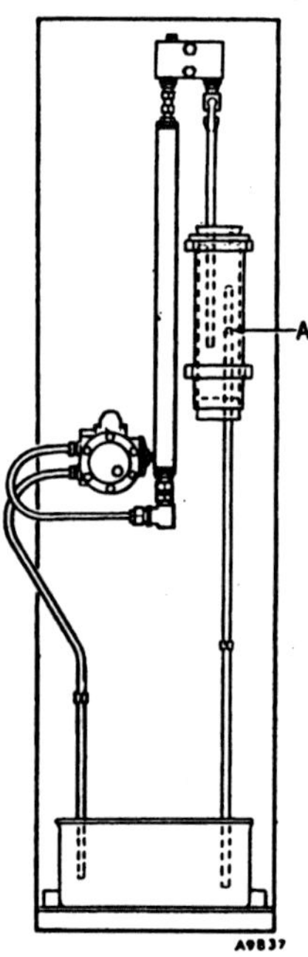

Fig. D.6
The AUF 300 type pump mounted on the S.U. test stand
(A) Hole .187 to .192 in. (4.74 to 4.9 mm.) dia.

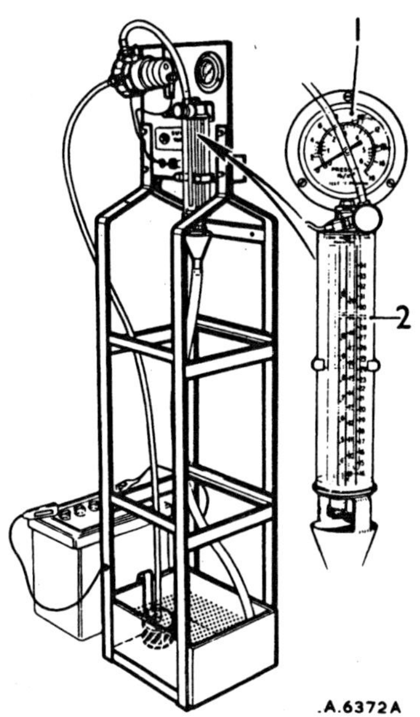

Fig. D.7
A checking rig for S.U. fuel pumps available from V.L. Churchill and Co. Ltd. The rig measures output in gallons of paraffin (kerosene) per hour, against required suction and delivery heads

1. Pressure gauge. 2. Flow glass.

VALVE SEAT CHECK

4. Let the pump run for about 10 minutes and then test as follows:
   With the regulator valve (delivery tap) turned completely off the pump should stand without repeating for a minimum of 20 seconds at the correct delivery head. If it repeats, the inlet valve is not seating correctly. On AUF 300 type pumps malfunction of the inlet valve must be investigated.

DELIVERY CHECK

5. Churchill: Obtain a delivery head reading of 4 feet (1220 mm.) on the gauge by adjusting the regulator valve on top of the flow glass. When correct, the pump flow rate may be read directly from the appropriate colour scale on the flow glass.
   S.U. The paraffin (kerosene) should rise in the glass tube until it flows over the top of the pipe in which a side hole is drilled; if the output is not up to specification, the side hole will carry off all paraffin (kerosene) pumped and none will flow over the top. The maximum delivery should be timed as follows:
   AUF 300 type pump .. 1 pint in 30 sec.

MINIMUM DELIVERY CHECK

6. Check with the tap turned on only slightly, and also by pressing gradually inwards on the tip of the contact blade, so as to reduce the effective stroke, that the pump continues to work with an increasing frequency until it eventually stops because there is no gap left between the points.

REDUCED VOLTAGE

7. Connect a resistance and voltmeter in circuit and test the pump at 9.5 volts with regulator valve open (tap full on); the pump should work satisfactorily although with reduced output.

SPARKING CHECK

8. Check for excessive sparking at the contact points. A moderate degree is permissible; excessive sparking would indicate that the special leak wire incorporated in the coil winding has fractured, necessitating a new coil unit, or that the condenser is faulty.

Fuel pump faults

1. SUSPECTED FUEL FEED FAILURE

Disconnect the fuel line at the carburetter and check for flow.

(a) If normal, examine for obstructed float-chamber needle seating or gummed needle.

(b) If normal initially, but diminishing rapidly and accompanied by slow pump operation, check for correct tank venting by removing the filler cap. Inadequate venting causes a slow power stroke with resultant excessive burning of contact points.

(c) If reduced flow is accompanied by slow operation of the pump, check for any restriction on the inlet side of the pump, such as a clogged filter, which should be removed and cleaned.
In the case of reduced flow with rapid operation of the pump, check for an air leak on the suction side, dirt under the valve, or faulty valve sealing washers.

(d) If no flow, check for:

(i) ELECTRICAL SUPPLY
Disconnect the lead from the terminal and check if current is available.

(ii) FAULTY CONTACT POINTS
If electrical supply is satisfactory, the bakelite cover should be removed to check that the tungsten points are in contact. The lead should then be replaced on the terminal and a short piece of bared wire put across the contacts. If the pump then performs a stroke, the fault is due to dirt or corrosion, or maladjustment of the tungsten points. The points may be cleaned by folding a small piece of fine emery-paper and inserting it between them and sliding it to and fro. To re-adjust the contact points follow the procedure laid down under the appropriate heading.

(iii) OBSTRUCTED PIPELINE BETWEEN FUEL TANK AND PUMP
The inlet pipe should be disconnected. If the pump then operates, the trouble is due to a restriction in the pipeline between the pump and the tank. This may be cleared by the use of compressed air after removing

the fuel tank filler cap. It should be noted, however, that compressed air should not be passed through the pump as this will cause serious damage to the valves.

(iv) FAULTY DIAPHRAGM ACTION
In the event of the previous operations failing to locate the trouble, it may be due to a stiffening of the diaphragm fabric or the presence of abnormal friction in the rocker 'throw-over' mechanism, or a combination of both. To remedy these faults the coil housing should be removed and the diaphragm flexed a few times, taking care not to lose any of the 11 rollers under the diaphragm. Prior to this resetting it is advisable to apply, very sparingly, a little thin oil to the throw-over spring spindles at the point where they pivot in the brass rockers. The diaphragm/armature assembly should then be reassembled in accordance with the instructions given unde that heading.

2. NOISY PUMP
If the pump is noisy in operation, an air leak at the suction line may be the cause. Such a leak may be checked by disconnecting the fuel pipe from the carburetter and allowing the pump to discharge into a suitable containe: with the end of the pipe submerged. The emission of continuous bubbles at this point will confirm the existence of an air leak. The fault should be rectified by carrying out the following procedure:

(a) Check that all connections from the fuel tank to the pump are in good order.
(b) Check that the inlet union is tight and that the sealing 'O' ring is not damaged.
(c) Check that the coil housing securing screws are well and evenly tightened.

Air leaks on the suction side cause rapid operation of the pump and are the most frequent cause of permanent failure.

3. PUMP OPERATES WITHOUT DELIVERING FUEL
If the pump operates continuously without delivery of fuel the most likely causes are:

(a) A very serious air leak on the suction side or,
(b) Foreign matter lodged under one of the valves, particularly the inlet valve.

To remedy (a) see Section 2 (above).

In order to remove any foreign matter lodged under the valves, these should be removed for cleaning and great care taken that the plastic material of the valve disc is not scratched or damaged during this operation.

Section D.3

CARBURETTER 

[CAUTION: Please read the instructions thoroughly before you attempt carburetor repairs. If you lack the necessary skills or tools, we suggest you leave such work to an Authorized Dealer or other qualified shop. Before taking a removed carburetor in for repair, thoroughly clean its exterior, but do not undertake any disassembly.]

Removing

1. Disconnect the petrol feed pipe from the carburetter.
2. Detach the throttle return springs from the carburetter.
3. Remove the air cleaner and air temperature control valve assembly.
4. Disconnect the adsorption canister pipe from the carburetter.
5. Disconnect the crankcase breather pipe from the carburetter.
6. Disconnect the E.G.R. valve pipe from the carburetter.
7. Disconnect the upper water hose from the auto choke unit and slacken the clip securing the lower water hose to the auto choke unit.
8. Remove the nut and washer and detach the throttle quadrant from the carburetter.
9. Remove the four nuts and washers securing the carburetter to the manifold.
10. Detach the carburetter from the manifold studs and the lower water hose and remove from the car.

Dismantling

11. Unscrew the damper cap.
12. Raise the air valve piston; carefully remove the damper retainer and then the damper.
13. Pull the bottom plug from the float chamber.
14. Drain the oil and fuel from the carburetter.
15. Remove the 'O' ring from the plug.
16. Remove the six screws securing the float-chamber to the body.
17. Remove the float-chamber and gasket.
18. Note the metal plate supporting the floats is positioned towards the outside of the float chamber, and press the spindle from the clip.
19. Remove the float chamber needle valve and washer.
20. Remove the four screws securing the top cover to the body.
21. Remove the top cover; note that the cover neck casting offset is positioned facing the air intake.
22. Remove the spring.
23. Note the outer locating tag and position of the air valve diaphragm and remove the air valve assembly.
24. Remove the four screws retaining the diaphragm.
25. Note the inner locating tag and position of the air valve diaphragm and remove the diaphragm, retaining ring and nylon spacer.
26. Slacken the grubscrew fitted on the side of the air valve; do not remove it.

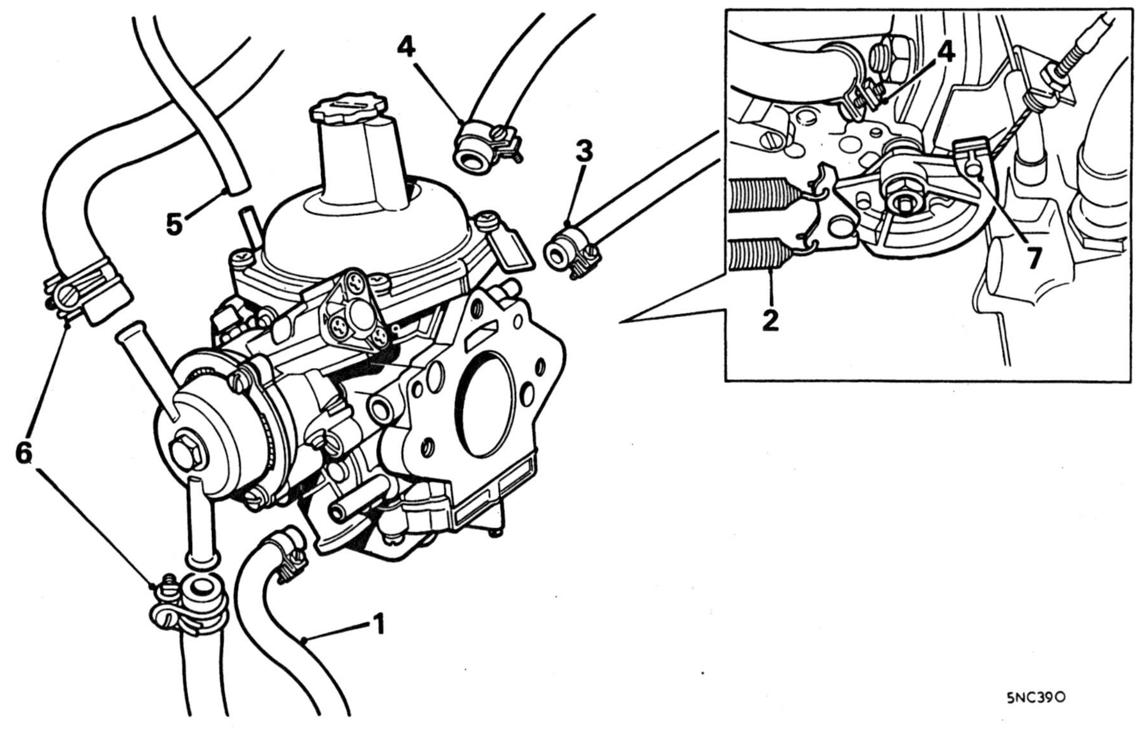

Fig. D.8

Carburetter installation

1. Fuel feed hose
2. Throttle return spring
3. Adsorption canister pipe
4. Crankcase breather pipe
5. E.G.R. valve pipe
6. Water hose
7. Throttle quadrant

27. Insert tool S353 into the stem of the air valve, turn the tool centre spindle anti-clockwise two or three complete turns; the needle housing assembly will be progressively exposed from the air valve as the tool is turned.
28. Remove the grubscrew and pull out the needle and housing assembly. Remove the tool.
    CAUTION: The needle adjuster is a fixed assembly in the stem of the air valve and no attempt should be made to remove it.
29. Unclip and remove the idle air regulator cover, if fitted.
30. Remove the two screws retaining the idle air regulator.
31. Remove the regulator and gasket.
32. Remove the throttle quadrant retaining nut and shakeproof washer.
33. Remove the throttle quadrant and its locating plate.
34. Remove the nut, shakeproof washer and spacer retaining the auto-choke operating lever.
35. Remove the outer lever, bush, and spring.
36. Remove the inner lever and spring.
37. Remove the auto-choke retaining screws.
38. Remove the auto-choke and gasket.
39. Remove the bolt and washer retaining the auto-choke water jacket.
40. Remove the water jacket and sealing ring.
41. Remove the three screws and spring washers retaining the heat mass.
42. Remove the heat mass and its insulator.
43. Remove the vacuum kick piston cover and gasket.

Inspection

44. Clean all components and allow them to dry.
45. Examine all components for wear, damage and deterioration. Examine all castings for cracks, insecure plugs and fittings.
46. The float chamber needle and seat and the air valve diaphragm should be renewed unless the existing components are considered serviceable.
47. Using a low pressure air line, blow through all ports, passages, and the needle valve.

Reassembly

48. Reverse the procedure in 18 to 43.
49. Measure the distance between the float chamber face and the highest point on each float (see 'A', the **CARBURETTER COMPONENTS** illustration). Set the floats parallel to and within the dimensions 0.625 in to 0.672 in (15.87 to 17.07 mm) from the chamber face. Adjust the floats to obtain the specified dimensions by alteration of the selective washer under the needle valve or by bending the float tabs. Ensure that the float tab makes a right angle to the needle valve.

THE CARBURETTER COMPONENTS

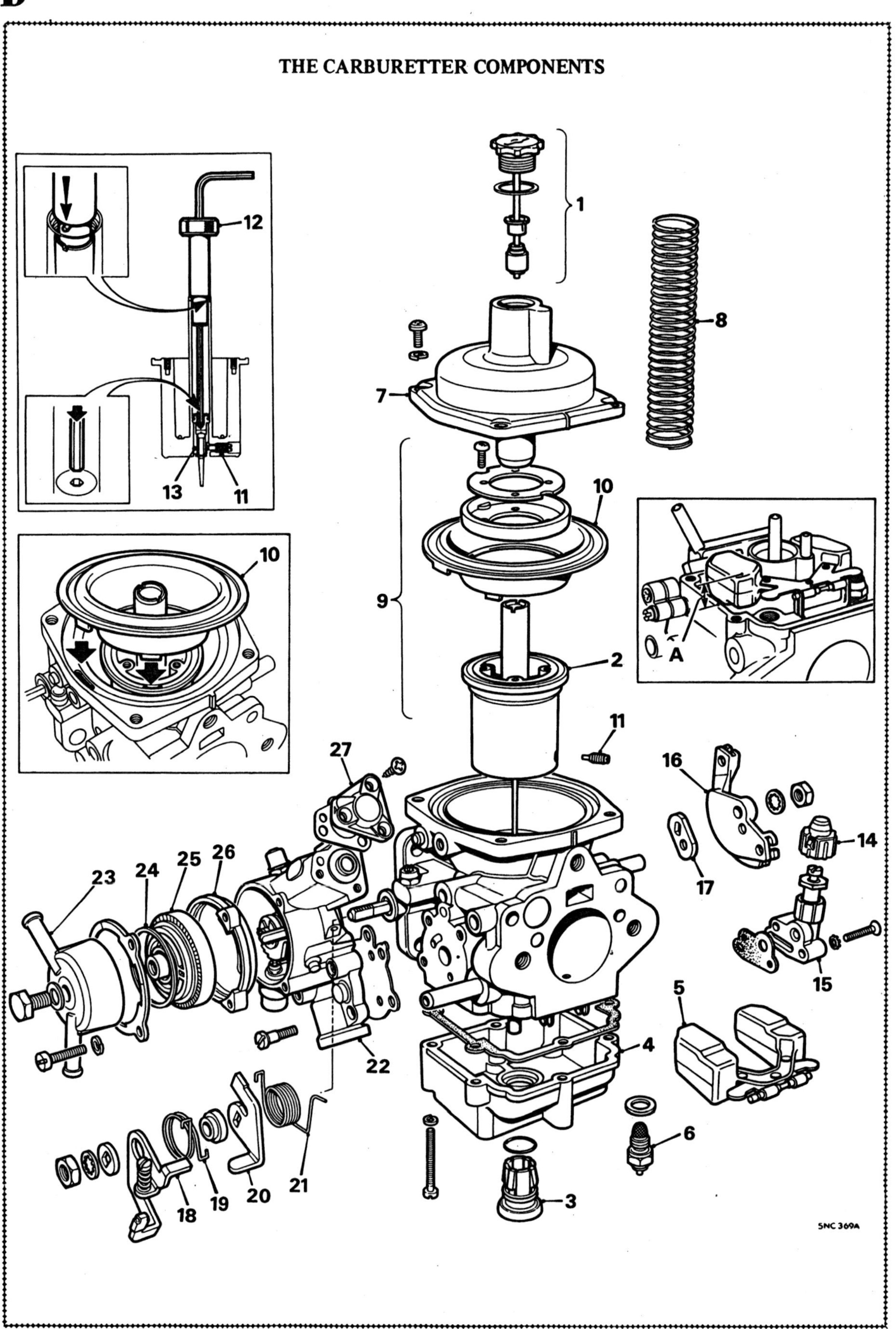

KEY TO THE CARBURETTER COMPONENTS

1. Damper assembly
2. Air valve piston
3. Float chamber plug
4. Float chamber
5. Float
6. Needle valve
7. Top cover
8. Spring
9. Air valve assembly
10. Diaphragm
11. Grubscrew–air valve
12. Tool S 353
13. Needle housing assembly
14. Cover–idle air regulator
15. Idle air regulator
16. Throttle quadrant
17. Locating plate
18. Operating lever assembly–auto choke
19. Spring–outer
20. Operating lever–inner
21. Spring–inner
22. Auto choke
23. Water jacket
24. Sealing rim
25. Heat mass
26. Insulator
27. Cover–vacuum kick piston

A. .625 to .672 in (15.87 to 17.07 mm)

50. Reverse the procedure in 12 to 17.
51. Fill the carburetter dashpot with a recommended oil, see 'MAINTENANCE'.
52 Check and adjust the automatic fuel enrichment unit, see Section D.4.

Refitting

53. Reverse the procedure in 1 to 10, noting:
    a. Fit the rear lower securing nut and washer first.
    b. Top up the cooling system, see 'MAINTENANCE'.
    c. Tune the carburetter, see 'MAINTENANCE'.

Section D.4

AUTOMATIC FUEL ENRICHMENT UNIT 

Checking and adjusting

1. Remove the carburetter, see Section D.3.
2. Open the throttle butterfly and wedge it open.
3. Remove the bolt and washer retaining the auto-choke water jacket.
4. Remove the water jacket and sealing ring.
5. Remove the three screws and spring washers retaining the heat mass.
6. Remove the heat mass and its insulator.
7. Rotate the operating arm and carry out the checks detailed in operations 8, 9 and 10.
8. Check the vacuum kick piston and rod for full and free movement.
9. Check that the fast idle cam and thermostat lever are free on the pivot.
10. Move the cam from the lever and ensure it returns under spring influence to the lever; ensure it remains there when the lever is rotated.
11. Remove the throttle wedge.
12. Set the gap between the choke and throttle levers to $\frac{3}{32}$ in (2.4 mm) ('A' Fig. D.9) by turning the idle speed screw.
13. Adjust the throttle stop screw to obtain a clearance of 0.025 in ('B' Fig. D.9) measured between the end of the fast idle pin and the cam.
14. Lock the adjusting screw by tightening the nut.
15. Reverse the procedure 3 to 6.
16. Align the index mark on the heat mass with the datum mark on the auto-choke body.
17. Tighten the clamp plate screws to 8 to 10 lbf in (0.092 to 0.115 kgf m).

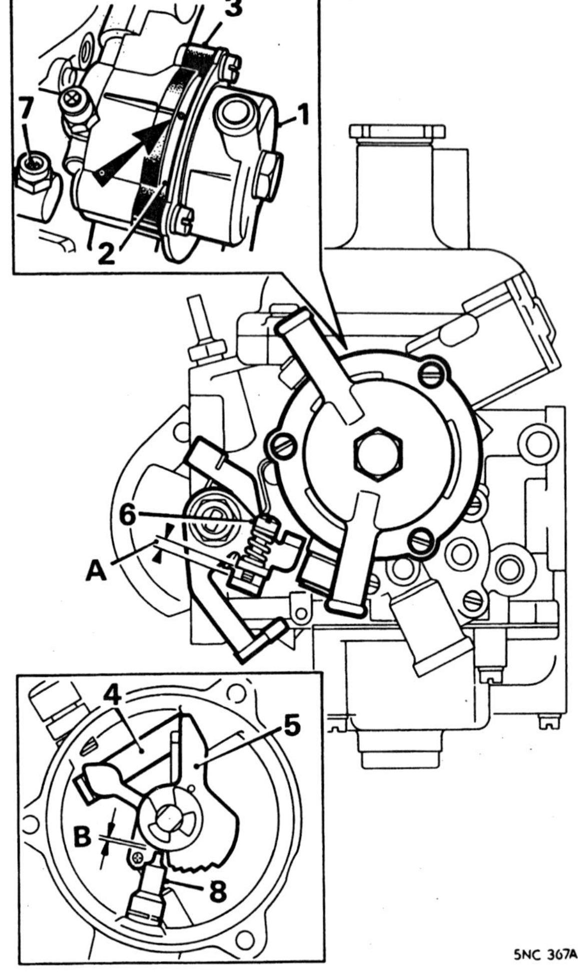

Fig. D.9

Checking and adjusting the automatic fuel enrichment unit

1. Water jacket
2. Heat mass
3. Insulator
4. Rod–vacuum kick piston
5. Fast idle cam
6. Idle speed screw
7. Throttle stop screw
8. Fast idle pin

A. $\frac{3}{32}$ in (2.4 mm)
B. 0.025 in (0.64 mm)

18. Position the water jacket pipe connections in the correct position and tighten the centre bolt to 65 to 75 lbf in (0.749 to 0.865 kgf m).
19. Refit the carburetter, see Section D.3.
20. Tune the carburetter, see 'MAINTENANCE'.

Section D.5

FUEL FILLER SPOUT

Removing

1. Slacken the clip securing the hose to the filler spout, and move the clip forwards along the hose.
2. Withdraw the filler spout.
3. Remove the seal.
4. CATALYTIC CONVERTER CARS: Inspect the restrictor and check that the trap door will open, and that it will also close under its own spring pressure. If the restrictor is faulty rectify as follows:
   Early cars: Fit a new fuel filler spout assembly.
   Later cars: Fit a new restrictor.

Fitting a new restrictor (Catalytic converter cars)

5. Release the three locating tongues.
6. Withdraw the restrictor.
7. Fit the sleeve to the filler spout aligning the vent hole in the sleeve with the stamp mark 'TOP' on the filler spout.
8. Secure the sleeve in position by the three locating tongues.

Refitting

9. Reverse the procedure in 1 to 3, noting:
   a. Fit a new seal if it is showing signs of deterioration.
   b. CATALYTIC CONVERTER CARS: The filler spout must be fitted with the words 'TOP' uppermost.

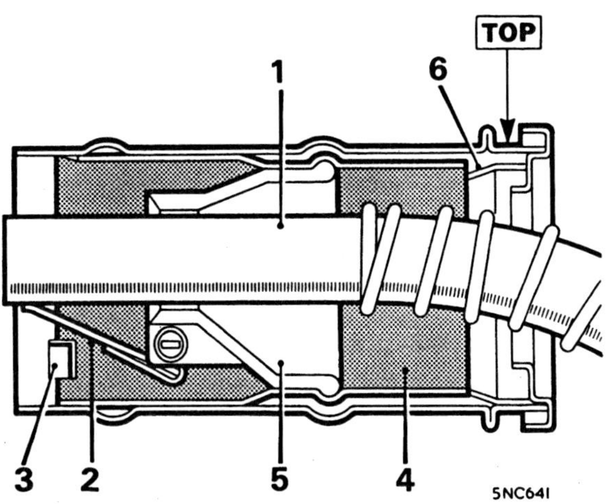

Fig. D.10
The fuel filler spout

1. Fuel dispenser nozzle.
2. Trap door.
3. Locating tongue.
4. Sleeve
5. Restrictor.
6. Vent in sleeve.

SECTION E

THE CLUTCH

THE CLUTCH COMPONENTS

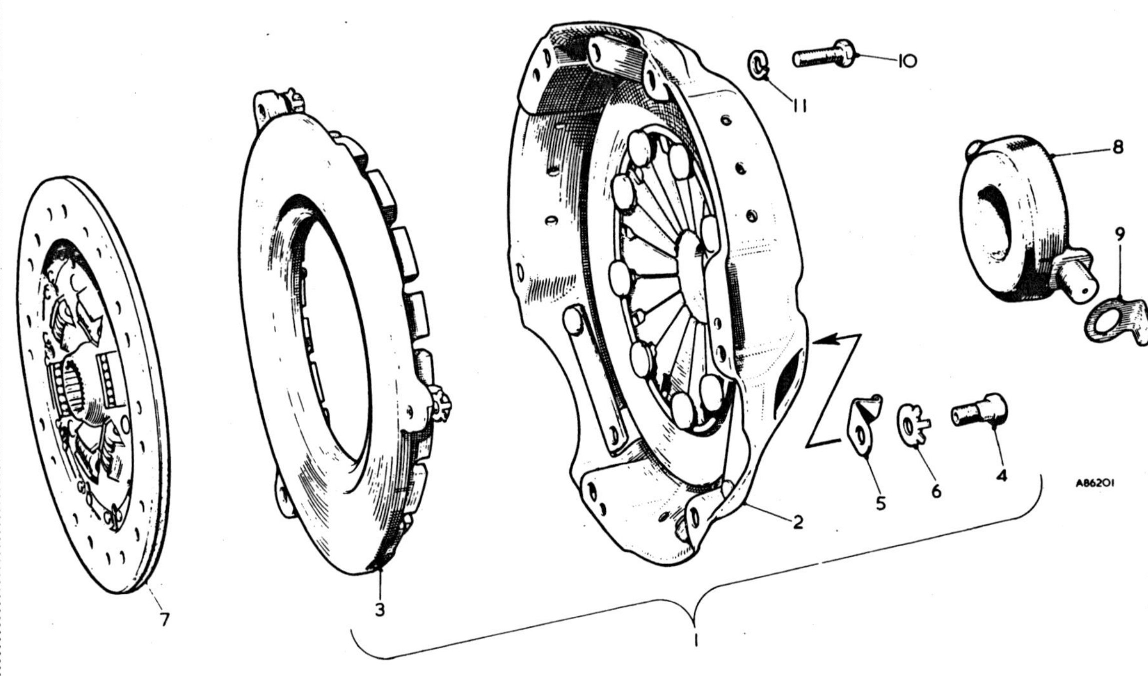

No.	Description
1.	Cover assembly.
2.	Cover with straps, diaphragm spring and release plate.
3.	Plate–pressure.
4.	Bolt–strap.
5.	Clip–pressure plate.

No.	Description
6.	Washer–tab.
7.	Plate assembly–driven.
8.	Bearing assembly–release.
9.	Retainer–bearing.
10.	Screw–clutch to flywheel.
11.	Washer for screw–spring.

GENERAL DESCRIPTION

The clutch mechanism is hydraulically operated and consists of a driven plate, a pressure plate, and a diaphragm spring and cover assembly. The cover is bolted to the flywheel and encloses the driven plate, pressure plate, and diaphragm spring.

The hydraulic system comprises a master cylinder coupled to a slave cylinder which operates the clutch release mechanism.

Section E.1

CLUTCH ASSEMBLY

The driven plate comprises a splined hub connected to a flexible steel plate by a spring mounting. The annular friction facings are riveted to the plate and damper springs are assembled around the hub to absorb power shocks and torsional vibration.

The diaphragm spring is interposed between two annular rings which provide fulcrum points for the diaphragm when it is flexed. The rings and the diaphragm are located and secured to the cover by nine equally spaced rivets. Three clips that engage the outer edge of the diaphragm are bolted to the pressure plate. The bolts pass through three straps which are riveted to the inside of the cover; the straps prevent the diaphragm and the pressure plate from rotating in relation to the cover.

The release plate is secured directly to the diaphragm and is an integral part of the clutch cover assembly. On early cars the release plate is retained with a circlip and can be removed when the circlip is released.

The release bearing is graphite and is mounted in a cup which fits into the fork of the clutch withdrawal lever. The cup is held in position by two spring retainers.

Removing

Remove the engine as described in Section A.15.

Loosen each of the bolts securing the clutch assembly to the flywheel by slackening them a turn at a time until spring pressure is released. The clutch cover can now be disengaged from the dowels on the flywheel and the assembly removed.

Dismantling

Unscrew the three screws securing the clips to the pressure plate, a turn at a time, until the diaphragm contacts the cover. Remove the screws, clips and washers and the pressure plate.

Rotate the release bearing spring retainers through 90° and withdraw the bearing from the withdrawal lever fork.

Assembling

Assembly is a reversal of the dismantling sequence, but ensure that the release bearing retainers are correctly located.

Replacing

Position the driven plate assembly on the flywheel with the large end of the hub away from the flywheel.

Centralize the plate by using Service tool 18G 680, which fits the splined hub of the driven plate and the pivot bearing in the flywheel. As an alternative, a spare first motion shaft can be used.

Locate the cover assembly on the flywheel dowels and secure it with the bolts; tighten the bolts down a turn at a time by diametrical selection. Do not remove the centralizer until all bolts are securely tightened.

Remove the clutch centralizer and refit the engine. The weight of the gearbox must be supported during refitting in order to avoid strain on the first motion shaft and distortion or displacement of the release plate and straps, or driven plate assembly.

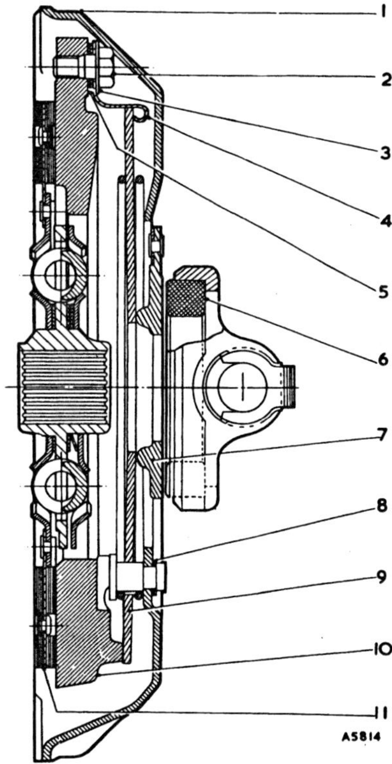

Fig. E.1
A section through the clutch

1. Cover.
2. Strap bolt.
3. Washer–tab.
4. Clip.
5. Strap–diaphragm cover.
6. Release bearing.
7. Release plate.
8. Strap–release plate/cover.
9. Diaphragm spring.
10. Pressure plate.
11. Driven plate.

Section E.2

SERVICING THE CLUTCH

Driven plates
It is important that neither oil nor grease should contact the clutch facings.

It is essential to install a complete driven plate assembly when the renewal of the friction surfaces is required. If the facings have worn to such an extent as to warrant renewal, then slight wear will have taken place on the splines, and also on the torque reaction springs and their seatings. The question of balance and concentricity is also involved. Under no circumstances is it satisfactory to repair or rectify faults in clutch driven plate centres.

Tolerances
Wear on the working faces of the driven plate is about .001 in. (.02 mm.) per 1,000 miles (1600 km.) under normal running conditions. The accuracy of the alignment of the face of the driven plate must be within .015 in. (.38 mm.).

Condition of clutch facings in service
It is natural to assume that a rough surface will give a higher frictional value against slipping than a polished one, but this is not necessarily correct. A roughened surface consists of small hills and dales, only the 'high-spots' of which make contact. As the amount of useful friction for the purpose of taking up the drive is dependent upon the area in actual contact, it is obvious that a perfectly smooth face is required to transmit the maximum amount of power for a given surface area.

Since non-metallic facings of the moulded asbestos type have been introduced in service the polished surface is common, but it must not be confused with the glazed surface which is sometimes encountered due to conditions to be detailed subsequently. The ideally smooth or polished condition will therefore provide proper surface contact, but a glazed surface entirely alters the frictional value of the facing and will result in excessive clutch slip. These two conditions might be simply illustrated by comparison between a piece of smoothly finished wood and one with a varnished surface; in the former the contact is made directly by the original material, whereas in the latter instance a film of dry varnish is interposed between the contact surfaces and actual contact is made by the varnish.

If the clutch has been in use for some time under satisfactory conditions, the surface of the facings assumes a high polish through which the grain of the material can be seen clearly. This polished facing is of light colour when in perfect condition.

Should oil in small quantities gain access to the clutch and find its way onto the facings, it will be burnt off as a result of the heat generated by the slipping occurring under normal starting conditions. The burning of this small quantity of lubricant has the effect of gradually darkening the facings, but provided the polish of the facing remains such that the grain of the material can be distinguished clearly, it has little effect on clutch performance.
Should increased quantities of oil obtain access to the facing, then one of two conditions, or a combination of these, may arise, depending upon the nature of the oil.

1. The oil may burn off and leave a carbon deposit on the surface of the facings, which assume a high glaze, producing further slip. This is a very definite, though very thin, deposit, and in general it hides the grain of the material.
2. The oil may partially burn and leave a resinous deposit on the facings. This has a tendency to produce a fierce clutch, and may also cause excessive 'spinning' due to the tendency of the face of the linings to adhere to the surface of the flywheel or pressure plate.
3. There may be a combination of conditions 1 and 2 which produces a tendency to 'judder' on such engagement.

Still greater quantities of oil produce a dark and soaked appearance of the facings, and the result will be further slip, accompanied by fierceness or 'juddering'.
If the conditions enumerated above are experienced, the clutch driven plate should be replaced by a new one. **The cause of the presence of the oil must be traced and removed.** It is, of course, necessary for the clutch and flywheel to be cleaned out thoroughly before assembly.

Where the graphite release bearing ring is badly worn in service a complete replacement assembly should be fitted, returning the old assembly for salvage of the metal cup. These graphite rings are inserted into their metal cup by heating the metal cup to a cherry red, then forcing the graphite ring into position. Immediately the ring is forced into position the whole should be quenched in oil. Alignment of the thrust pad in relation to its face and the trunnions should be within .005 in. (.12 mm.).
In almost every case of rapid wear on the splines of the clutch driven plate misalignment is responsible.
Looseness of the driven plate on the splined shaft results in noticeable backlash in the clutch. Misalignment also puts undue stress on the driven member, and may result in the hub breaking loose from the plate, with consequent total failure of the clutch.
It may also be responsible for a fierce chattering or dragging of the clutch, which makes gear-changing difficult. In cases of persistent difficulty it is advisable to check the flywheel for truth with a dial indicator. The dial reading should not vary more than .003 in. (.07 mm.) anywhere on the flywheel face.

Section E.3

MASTER CYLINDER

The master cylinder has an integral-type supply tank in which the barrel passes through the tank. A piston contained within the barrel has a rubber main cup and is spring-loaded against its inner end; between the piston and cup is a thin washer which prevents the cup being drawn into the feed holes drilled around the head of the piston. The outer end of the piston carries a secondary cup and is formed with a depression to receive the spherical end of the push-rod assembly. The push-rod has a piston stop that is retained in the body by a circlip. A rubber boot through which the push-rod passes is fitted to the end of the body. At the opposite end of the barrel to the push-rod an end plug screws down against a gasket. This plug forms the outlet connection for the pipe line to the slave cylinder.

Removing
Remove the screws securing the brake and clutch master cylinder cover and take off the cover.
Drain the fluid from the supply tank by attaching a rubber tube in the bleed screws in the clutch slave cylinder, opening the screw one full turn and then depressing the clutch pedal. Hold the pedal down and then tighten the screw and then let the pedal return unassisted. Repeat this operation until the tank is empty.
Remove the split pin, washer, and clevis pin from the push-rod and disengage the clutch pedal lever.
Clean the pipe connection, disconnect the pipe line, and fit a plug to the end of the cylinder to prevent the entry of dirt.
Unscrew the fixing bolts and detach the master cylinder from the box assembly.

Dimantling
Detach the rubber boot from the barrel.
Depress the piston to relieve the load on the circlip, then remove the circlip and the push-rod assembly.
Withdraw the piston, piston washer, main cup, spring retainer, and spring.
Remove the secondary cup by carefully stretching it over the end of the piston.

Examination
Place all metal parts in a tray of clean Clutch and Brake Fluid to soak. Dry them with a clean, non-fluffy cloth. Rubber components are to be examined for swollen or perished cups or other signs of deterioration. Any suspect parts must be renewed.
Swill the main castings in industrial methylated spirit and thoroughly dry out before assembly.
Ensure that the by-pass ports are free of obstruction. The port is drilled with a ⅛ in. (3.17 mm.) drill for half its length and then finished with a .028 in. (.711 mm.) drill.

Assembling
Dip all components in Clutch and Brake Fluid and assemble when wet.
Stretch the secondary cup over the piston with the lip of the cup facing the head of the piston. When the cup is in its groove work it round gently with the fingers to ensure that it is correctly seated.
Insert the return spring, largest diameter first, into the barrel and position the spring seat on the small-diameter end of the spring.
Assemble the main cup, piston washer, piston, and push-rod. When assembling the cups carefully enter the lip edge of the cups into the barrel first.
Depress the piston, position the piston stop, and retain it in the barrel with the circlip.
Place the rubber boot in position and fit the dust excluder.

Replacing
Refit the master cylinder to the master cylinder box and secure it with the bolts. The long bolt passes through the stiffener plate.
Remove the dust excluder and fit the pipe connection to the master cylinder.
Refit the clutch pedal lever to the push-rod and secure it with the clevis pin, washer, and a new split pin.
Refit the master cylinder cover.
Fill the master cylinder and then prime and bleed the system.

Section E.4

SLAVE CYLINDER

The slave cylinder incorporates two threaded connections for the feed hose and the bleed screw and accommodates in the body a piston, a cup, and a spring.
A rubber boot through which passes a push-rod is fitted to the body and is retained by two clips. The push-rod has an eye-end which connects with the clutch withdrawal fork.

Removing
Drain the system as described in Section E.3.
Release the feed pipe from the cylinder and remove the two screws securing the cylinder to the clutch housing. The cylinder may be withdrawn, leaving the push-rod attached to the clutch withdrawal fork, or the rod may be detached from the fork.

Dismantling
Remove the rubber dust cover and with an air line blow out the piston and seal. Extract the spring and cup filler.
Examine all components and renew any that are suspect.

Assembling
Place the spring in the cylinder; followed by the filler, cup, and piston. Depress the piston with the push-rod and refit the rubber boot. Secure the boot to the rod with the small clip and then fit the boot to the cylinder and secure it with the large circlip.

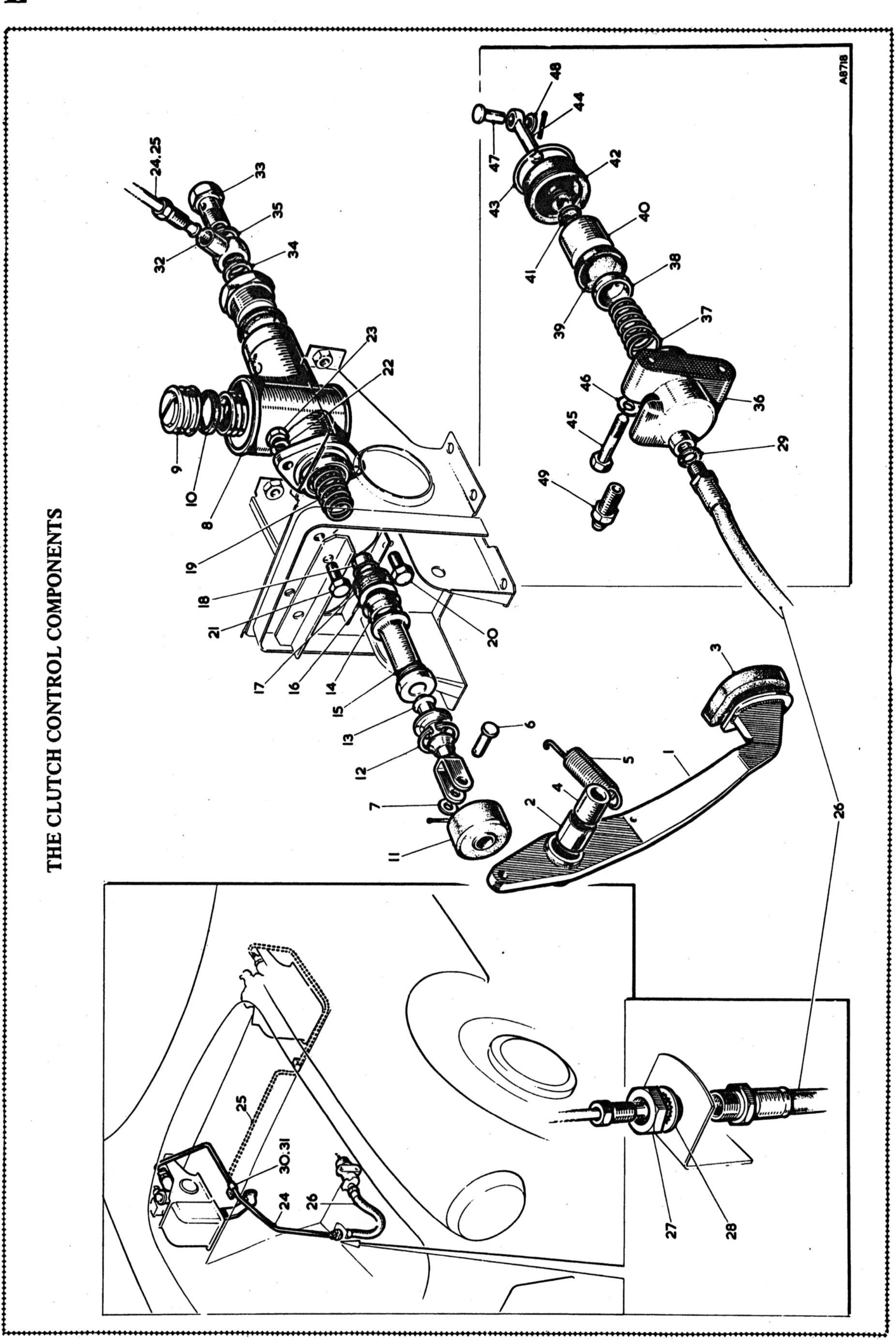

THE CLUTCH CONTROL COMPONENTS

KEY TO THE CLUTCH CONTROL COMPONENTS

No.	Description	No.	Description	No.	Description
1.	Pedal–clutch.	18.	Retainer–spring.	34.	Gasket.
2.	Bush.	19.	Spring.	35.	Gasket.
3.	Pad–pedal (rubber).	20.	Screw–cylinder to box.	36.	Body.
4.	Tube–distance–clutch pedal.	21.	Screw–cylinder and stiffener to box.	37.	Spring–cup filler.
5.	Spring–pedal pull-off.	22.	Washer–spring–for screw.	38.	Filler–piston cup.
6.	Pin–clevis–fork end to pedal.	23.	Nut for screw.	39.	Cup piston.
7.	Washer–plain–for pin.	24.	Pipe–master cylinder to hose.	40.	Piston.
8.	Barrel and tank.	25.	Pipe–master cylinder to hose.	41.	Clip–boot (small).
9.	Cap–filler.	26.	Hose–clutch.	42.	Boot.
10.	Seal–cap.	27.	Locknut for hose.	43.	Clip–boot (large).
11.	Boot.	28.	Washer–shakeproof.	44.	Rod–push.
12.	Circlip.	29.	Gasket–hose to body.	45.	Bolt–cylinder to gearbox.
13.	Rod–push.	30.	Clip–clutch pipe to bulkhead.	46.	Washer–spring–for bolt.
14.	Cup–secondary.	31.	Clip–clutch pipe to bulkhead.	47.	Pin–clevis–cylinder to clutch fork.
15.	Piston.	32.	Connection–banjo.	48.	Washer–plain–for pin.
16.	Washer–piston.	33.	Bolt for banjo connection.	49.	Screw–bleeder.
17.	Cup–main.				

[**CAUTION**: Wash hydraulic cylinder components in brake fluid only. Never use gasoline or other petroleum-based solvents since they will damage rubber parts in the system.]

Replacing
Fit the cylinder to the clutch housing and secure it with the two screws. Assemble the push-rod to the clutch withdrawal fork. Connect the feed line and fill, prime, and bleed the system as described in Section E.5.

Section E.5

BLEEDING THE CLUTCH SYSTEM

Open the bleed screw on the slave cylinder three-quarters of a turn and attach a tube, immersing the open end in a clean receptacle containing a small quantity of the recommended hydraulic fluid. Fill the master cylinder reservoir with the recommended fluid (see **'SERVICE LUBRICANTS, FUEL AND FLUIDS – CAPACITIES'**). Using slow, full strokes, pump the clutch pedal until the fluid entering the container is completely free from air bubbles. On a downstroke of the pedal tighten the bleed screw and remove the bleed tube.

Fig. E.2
Bleeding the clutch hydraulic system at the slave cylinder

SECTION F

THE GEARBOX (ALL SYNCHROMESH)

[**CAUTION**: Please read the instructions thoroughly before you attempt transmission repairs. If you lack the necessary skills or tools, we suggest you leave such work to an Authorized Dealer or other qualified shop. Before taking a removed transmission in for repair, thoroughly clean its exterior, but do not undertake any disassembly.]

Section F.1

GEARBOX ASSEMBLY

Removing

1. Remove the engine and gearbox from the car–Section A.15.
2. Remove the starter.
3. Unscrew the bolts securing the gearbox to the engine and withdraw the gearbox.

Refitting

4. Reverse the removing procedure in 1 to 3 and refill the gearbox with the correct quantity (see 'SERVICE LUBRICANTS, FUEL and FLUIDS – CAPACITIES') of a recommended lubricant.

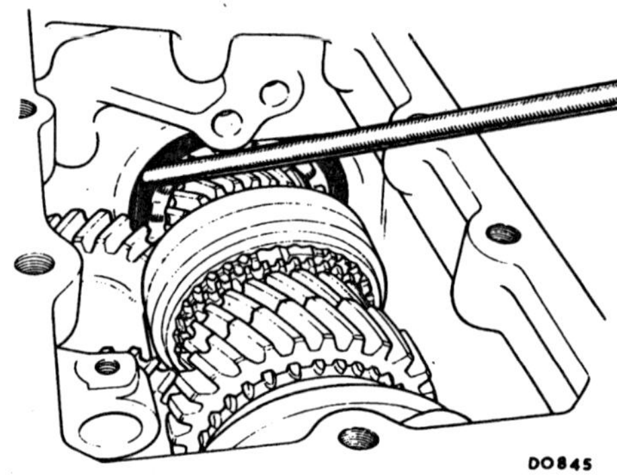

Fig. F.2
Drifting the first motion shaft from the casing

Section F.2

REAR EXTENSION

Removing

1. Drain the gearbox.
2. Using tool 18G 34 A to prevent rotation, unscrew the propeller shaft flange retaining nut and withdraw the flange.
3. Unscrew the bolts securing the remote-control housing to the gearbox and remove the remote control.
4. Withdraw the selector interlocking arm and plate assembly.

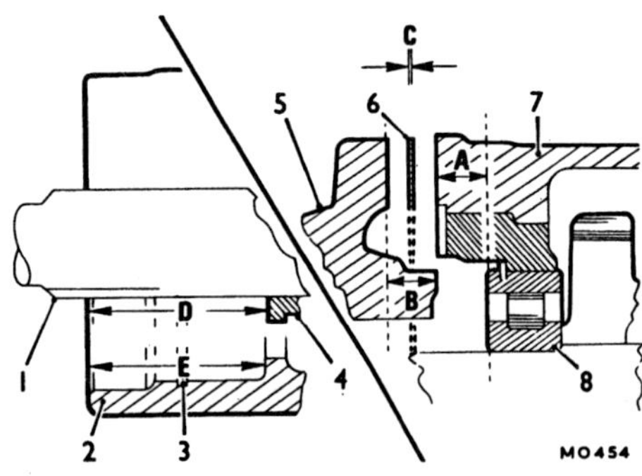

Fig. F.1
Rear extension setting up

1. Third motion shaft.
2. Rear extension.
3. Rear bearing circlip groove.
4. Distance tube.
5. Rear extension.
6. Gasket for rear extension.
7. Gearbox main casing.
8. Bearing.

A. Depth between bearing face and gearbox main casing face.
B. Depth between rear extension face and bearing flange.
C. Thickness of joint washer.
D. Depth from rear extension face to distance tube.
E. Depth from rear extension face to bearing register.

5. Unscrew the nuts securing the rear extension to the gearbox and withdraw the extension, ensuring that the shims fitted to the gearbox third motion shaft are not mislaid.

Dismantling

The following operations are only necessary if the bearing or oil seal are to be renewed.

6. Remove and discard the oil seal.
7. Remove the circlip retaining the bearing.
8. Press the bearing from the extension.

Reassembling

The following procedure must be carried out when fitting a new gearbox extension or if any of the third motion shaft components have been changed.

9. Calculate the thickness of shims required between the third motion shaft front bearing, and the gearbox rear extension case, as follows:
   a. Measure the depth A between the face of the front bearing and its housing, and add the thickness C of the joint washer.
   b. Measure the depth B from the joint face to the bearing register face of the rear extension.
   c. Fit shims between the extension and the face of the front bearing to bring the dimension measured in b .000 to .001 in. (.000 to .025 mm.) less than the dimension in A. Shims of .002 in. (.05 mm.) and .004 in. (.10 mm.) thickness are available.
   d. Fit the rear extension.

10. Calculate the thickness of shims required between the distance tube, and the third motion shaft rear bearing as follows:
    a. Measure the depth D between the rear face of the extension and the rear face of the distance tube.

b. Measure the depth E of the rear bearing register from the rear face of the extension.

c Fit shims between the distance tube and the bearing to bring the dimension measured in A from .000 to .001 in. (.000 to .025 mm) less than the dimension measured in B. Shims of .002 in. (.05 mm.), .005 in. (.13 mm.) and .010 in. (.25 mm.) thickness are available.

d. Press the bearing into the extension using tool 18G 186.

e. Select and fit the thickest circlip that will enter the rear bearing circlip groove from the following range:

.096 to .098 in. (2.43 to 2.49 mm.)
.098 to .100 in. (2.49 to 2.54 mm.)
.100 to .102 in. (2.54 to 2.59 mm.)

11. Using tool 18G 134 with adaptor 18G 134 BK, fit a new oil seal.

Refitting

12. Check that the shims on the third motion shaft are correctly positioned against the distance tube shoulder, and fit the extension.
13. Fit and tighten the extension securing nuts.
14. Reverse the removing procedure 1 to 4.

Section F.3

FRONT COVER

Removing

1. Turn the clutch release bearing retaining clips and withdraw the bearing from the lever.
2. Remove the rubber boot from the clutch lever.
3. Unscrew the front cover retaining nuts and remove the cover, collecting the shims fitted in front of the first motion shaft bearing.

Dismantling

4. Remove the oil seal and gasket.
5. Unscrew the nut retaining the clutch lever pivot bolt, remove the bolt, and withdraw the lever.

Reassembling

The following procedure must be carried out when fitting a new front cover or if any of the first motion shaft components have been changed.

6. Calculate the thickness of shims required between the front cover and the bearing, as follows:

a. Measure the depth A from the face of the cover to the bearing register and add .012 in. (.31 mm.) for the compressed thickness C of the joint washer.

Fig. F.3
Removing the left-handed-threaded first motion shaft nut using tool 18G 48

b. Measure the distance B that the first motion shaft bearing protrudes from the casing.

c. Fit shims between the bearing and cover to bring the dimension measured in B from .000 to .001 in. (.000 to .025 mm.) greater than the dimension in A. Shims of .002 in. (.05 mm.) and .004 in. (.10 mm.) thickness are available.

7. Using tool 18G 134 with adaptor 18G 134 Q, fit a new oil seal to the cover.

8. Position the clutch lever, fit the pivot bolt, screw on and tighten the bolt retaining nut.

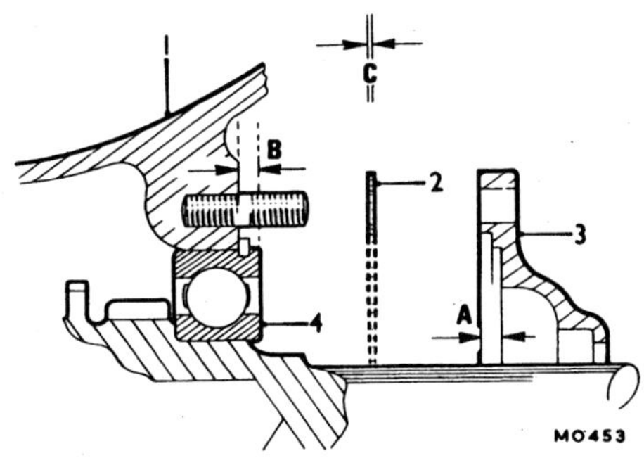

Fig. F.4
Front cover setting up

1. Gearbox main casing.
2. Gasket for front cover.
3. Front cover.
4. Bearing.

A. Depth of front cover to bearing register.
B. First motion shaft bearing protrusion.
C. Compressed thickness of joint washer.

Refitting

9. Reverse the removing procedure noting the following:
   a. Use a new gasket when refitting the cover; ensure that all traces of the old gasket are removed from the cover and gearbox jointing faces before fitting the new gasket.
   b. Check that the first motion shaft bearing shims are correctly positioned.

Section F.4

SELECTOR RODS AND FORKS

Removing

1. Remove the rear extension–Section F.2, 1 to 3–or the overdrive adaptor–Section Fa.9.
2. Unscrew the side cover retaining bolts and remove the cover.
3. Remove the selector detent plunger plugs and springs.
4. Slacken the locknuts on each of the selector fork retaining bolts and remove the bolts.
5. Withdraw the selector rods and remove the selector forks.

Refitting

6. Reverse the removing procedure, noting the following points:
   a. Clean any burrs from the rods at the fork attachment points before refitting the rods.
   b. Check that the detent plungers are clear of the holes before fitting the rods.

Section F.5

REVERSE IDLER GEAR

Removing

1. Remove the rear extension–Section F.2, 1 to 3–or the overdrive adaptor–Section Fa.9.
2. Remove the selector rods and forks–Section F.4, 2 to 5.
3. Knock back the locking tab on the shaft retaining bolt and remove the bolt.
4. Remove the shaft and withdraw the gear.

Inspection

5. Inspect the shaft for signs of excessive wear; renew the shaft if necessary.
6. Examine the gear teeth for wear and damage; renew the gear if necessary.
7. Inspect the gear bushes for signs of excessive wear; worn bushes may be removed and new bushes pressed in.

Refitting

8. Reverse the removing procedure in 1 to 4 using a new locking washer on the shaft retaining bolt.

Section F.6

FIRST MOTION SHAFT

Removing

1. Remove the rear extension–Section F.2, 1 to 5.
2. Remove the front cover–Section F.3, 1 to 3.
3. Remove the selector rods and forks—Section F.4, 2 to 5.
4. Remove the reverse idler gear–Section F.5, 2 to 4.
5. Carefully drift the layshaft from the gearbox.
6. Check that the laygear teeth are clear of the first motion shaft gear teeth.
7. Using a soft metal drift registering against the bearing outer track, carefully drift the shaft assembly forward from the gearbox.

Dismantling

8. Withdraw the needle-roller bearing from inside the rear end of the shaft.
9. Tap back the locking tab on the bearing retaining nut.
10. Fit tool 18G 49 onto the nut and clamp the shaft in a soft-jawed vice.

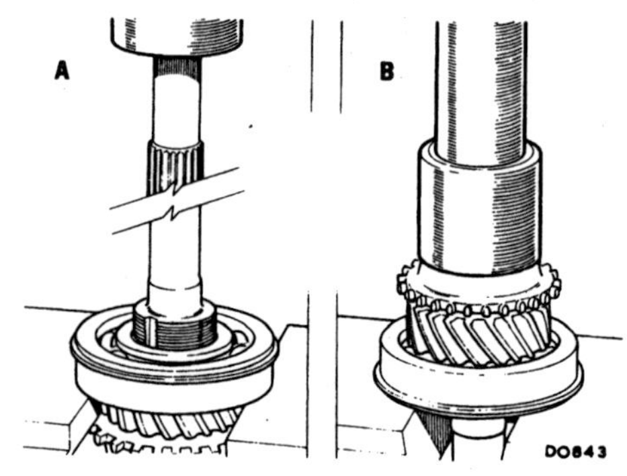

Fig. F.5
First motion shaft bearing

A. Removing the bearing from the shaft.
B. Refitting the bearing.

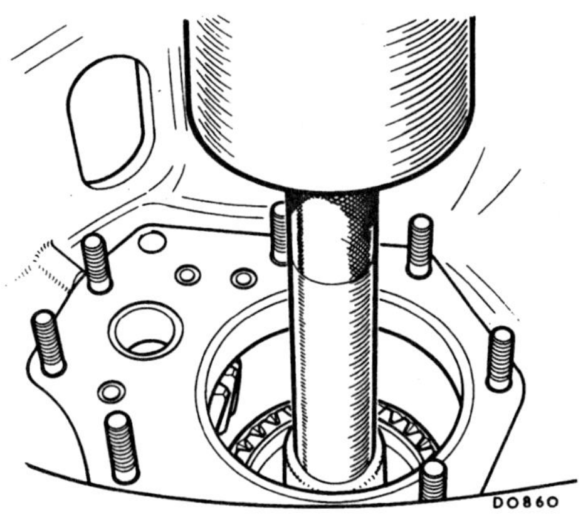

Fig. F.6
Pressing out the third motion shaft using tool 18G 1045

Section F.7

THIRD MOTION SHAFT–NON-OVERDRIVE

Removing

1. Remove the rear extension–Section F.2, 1 to 5.
2. Remove the front cover–Section F.3, 1 to 3.
3. Remove the selector rods and forks–Section F.4, 2 to 5.
4. Remove the reverse idler gear–Section F.5, 2 to 4.
5. Remove the first motion shaft–Section F.6, 5 to 7.
6. Remove the shims and distance tube from the third motion shaft.
7. Unscrew the rear extension securing studs from the gearbox casing.
8. Check that the laygear teeth are clear of the gears and synchronizers.
9. Using tool 18G 1045, press the third motion shaft rearwards from the gearbox.

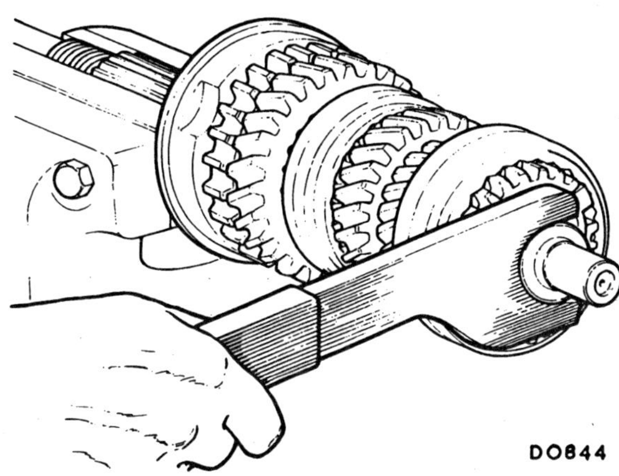

Fig. F.8
Using tool 18G 1024 to remove the front gear locking nut for the third motion shaft

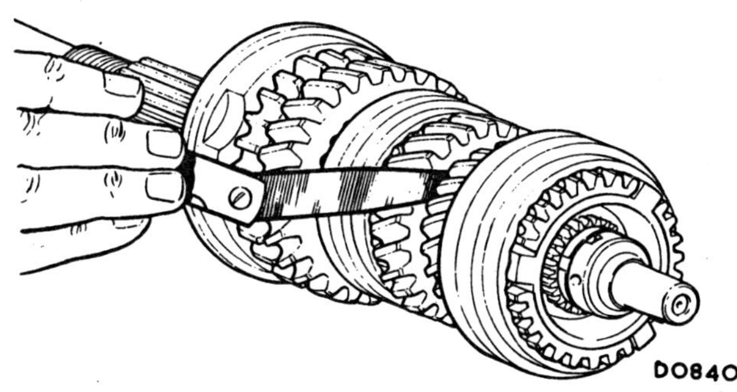

Fig. F.7
Checking the first and second speed gear end-float

Dismantling

SHAFT ASSEMBLY

10. Check the end-float on the first, second, and third speed gears against the figures given in **'GENERAL SPECIFICATION DATA'**.
11. Withdraw the third and fourth speed synchronizer assembly complete with baulk rings.
12. Tap back the locking tabs on front gear locking nut; unscrew the nut using tool 18G 1024 and remove the lock washer.
13. Withdraw the shaft sleeve, third speed gear, and interlocking thrust washer.
14. Withdraw the second speed gear and thrust washer.

11. Unscrew the **left-hand-threaded** nut; remove the nut and lock washer.
12. Press the bearing from the shaft.

Inspection

13. Inspect the shaft for signs of wear and damage to the gear or splines.
14. Examine the bearings for wear and damage; renew the bearing as necessary.

Reassembling

15. Reverse the dismantling procedure in 8 to 12, using a new shaft nut locking washer.

Refitting

16. Carefully drift the assembled shaft into the casing ensuring that the laygear teeth do not foul the shaft gear teeth.
17. Reverse the removing procedure in 1 to 6.

15. Remove the first and second speed synchronizer assembly complete with baulk rings.
16. Withdraw the speedometer gear and remove the gear driving key.
17. Remove the shaft distance piece.
18. Press the first speed gear, reverse gear, and the bearing complete with housing from the shaft (see Fig. F.9).
19. Press the bearing from its housing (see Fig. F.10).

Synchronizers

20. Remove the baulk rings.
21. Wrap a cloth loosely around the assembly to retain the balls and springs and push the synchronizer hub from the sliding coupling.

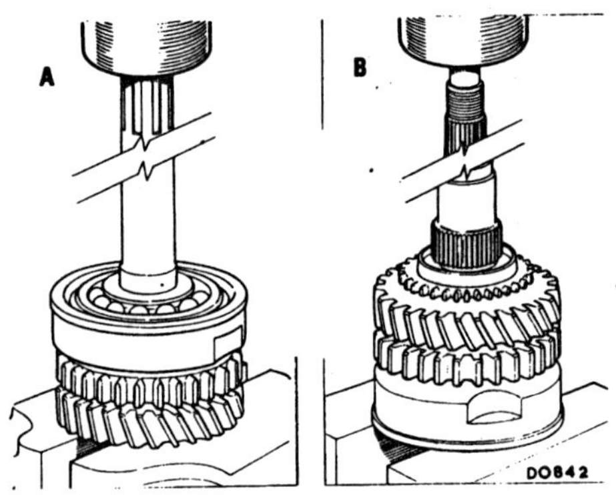

Fig. F.9
Third motion shaft

A. Pressing off the first speed and reverse gears and bearing with housing.
B. Refitting gears and bearing.

Inspection

22. If the end-float on the gears when checked in 10 exceeds the figures given, inspect the relevant gear and thrust washer bearing faces for wear. Renew worn gears and thrust washers as necessary.
23. Examine the gears, hubs, and couplings for wear and damaged or worn parts; replace as necessary.
24. Inspect the shaft for wear and damage to splines and bearing surfaces.
25. Examine the bearing for wear and damage.
26. Check the synchronizer springs against the dimension and pressure given in '**GENERAL SPECIFICATION DATA**'.

Reassembling

SYNCHRONIZERS

27. Fit tool 18G 1026 over the synchronizer hub.

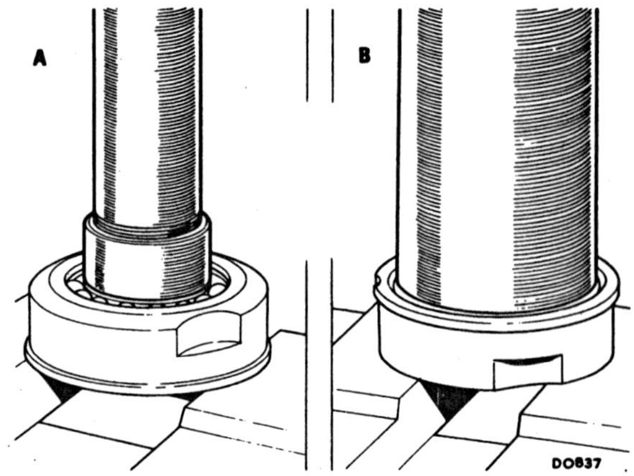

Fig. F.10
Third motion shaft bearing

A. Removing the bearing from its housing.
B. Refitting the bearing.

28. Turn the hub until one of the spring pockets is in line with the hole in the tool.
29. Fit the spring and ball into the pocket; depress the ball and turn the hub so that the ball is retained by the tool.
30. Repeat operations 28 and 29 for the remaining ball and springs.
31. Line up the cut-outs in the coupling with those in the hub and enter the hub into the coupling.
32. Press the hub from the tool into the coupling so that the springs and balls are retained by the coupling as the tool is removed.
33. Fit the baulk rings to the hub.

NOTE.–The baulk rings of the two synchronizer assemblies are not interchangeable. The first and second speed synchronizer baulk rings are identified (see Fig. F.14) by a drill point on one of the baulk ring lugs or by the fillets at the base of the lugs.

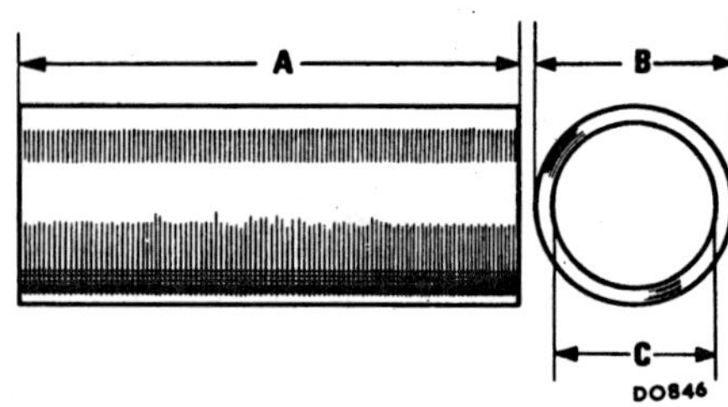

Fig. F.11
Dimensions of tool for refitting the third motion shaft

A = 19 in. (483 mm.) B = 3 in. (76 mm.)
C = 2.75 in. (69 mm.)

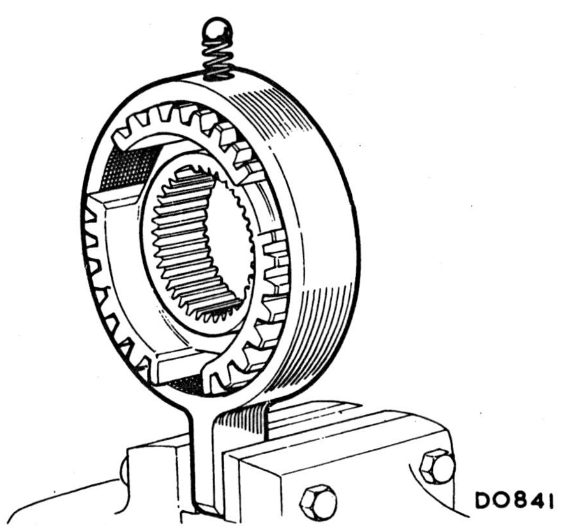

Fig. F.12
Reassembling the synchronizers using tool 18G 1026

SHAFT ASSEMBLY

34. Reverse the dismantling procedure in 10 to 19, noting the following points:
    a. Ensure that the lugs on the shaft sleeve are aligned with the cut-outs in the interlocking thrust washers.
    b. The synchronizer assemblies may be fitted either way round, but their baulk rings or the complete assemblies must not be interchanged with each other.

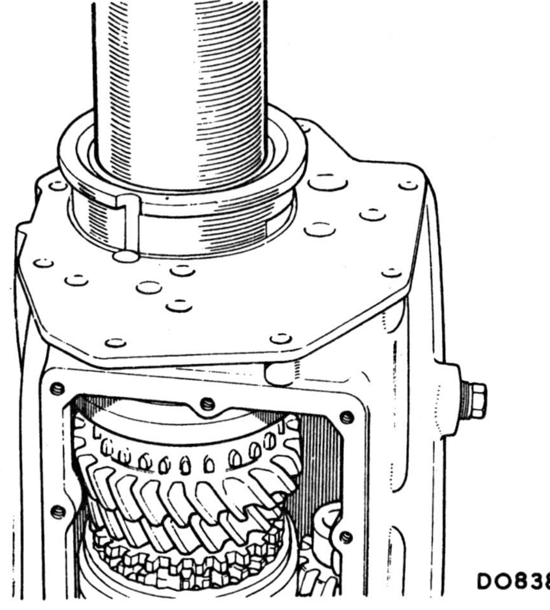

Fig. F.13
Refitting the assembled third motion shaft using the fabricated tool

    c. After reassembly, re-check the end-float on the first, second, and third speed gears.

Refitting

35. Enter the assembled shaft into the gearbox from the rear; ensure that the third and fourth speed synchronizer assembly is fitted to the shaft.
36. Check that the laygear teeth are clear of the shaft gears.
37. Using a fabricated tool to the dimensions shown in Fig. F.11 registering on the outer track of the bearing, press the shaft assembly into the gearbox.
38. Reverse the removing procedure in 1 to 5.

Section F.8

THIRD MOTION SHAFT–WITH OVERDRIVE

Removing

1. Remove the overdrive unit and adaptor–Section Fa.9, 2 to 10.
2. Carry out the operation for removing the non-overdrive third motion shaft given in Section F.7, 2 to 9.

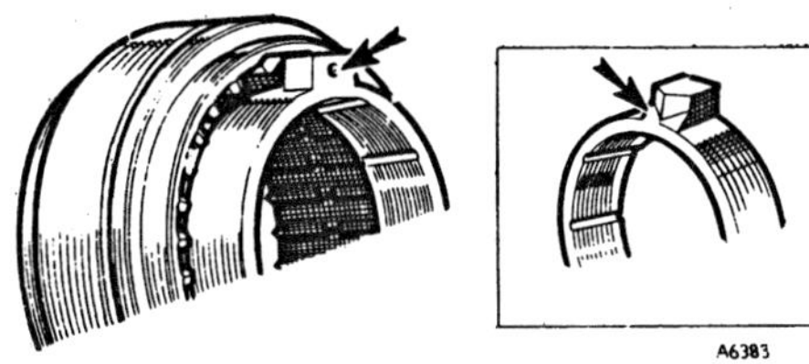

Fig. F.14
The identification drill point or fillets on the lugs of the first and second speed synchronizer baulk rings

Dismantling

3. Carry out operations in Section F.7, 10 to 15.
4. Tap back the locking tab on rear shaft nut.
5. Using tool 18G 391, unscrew the nut and remove the locking washer.
6. Withdraw the distance piece.
7. Carry out operations in Section F.7, 18 to 21.

Inspection

8. Carry out operations in Section F.7, 22 to 26.

Reassembling

9. Carry out operations in Section F.7, 27 to 33.
10. Reverse the dismantling procedure in 3 to 7.

Refitting

11. Reverse the moving procedure in Section F.7, 2 to 9.
12. Refit the overdrive unit and adaptor–Section Fa.9.

Section F.9

LAYGEAR

Removing

1. Remove the rear extension–Section F.2, 1 to 5.
2. Remove the front cover–Section F.3, 1 to 3.
3. Remove the selector rods and forks–Section F.4, 2 to 5.
4. Remove the reverse idler gear–Section F.5, 2 to 4.
5. Remove the first motion shaft–Section F.6, 5 to 7.
6. Remove the third motion shaft–Section F.7, 6 to 9.
7. Temporarily refit the layshaft and check the laygear end-float.
8. Withdraw the layshaft and remove the laygear and its thrust washers.

Dismantling

9. Withdraw the needle-roller bearings from inside the laygear.

Inspection

10. Inspect the layshaft for wear and damage to the bearing surfaces.
11. Examine the roller bearings for wear and damage.
12. Inspect the laygear teeth for damage and the bearing faces and bore for wear.

Reassembling

13. Fit the needle-roller bearings into the laygear.

Refitting

14. Position the laygear and front (large) thrust washer; enter the layshaft through the housing and thrust washer, and into the laygear.
15. If the laygear end-float measured in 7 is outside the limits given, select a rear thrust washer to give the correct end-float.

Fig. F.15
Using tool 18G 391 to unscrew the rear nut on the overdrive gearbox third motion shaft

Rear thrust washers are available in the following thicknesses:

.154 to .156 in. (3.91 to 3.96 mm.)
.157 to .158 in. (3.99 to 4.01 mm.)
.160 to .161 in. (4.06 to 4.08 mm.)
.163 to .164 in. (4.14 to 4.16 mm.)

16. Fit the rear thrust washer and thread a piece of soft wire through the housing, thrust washer, and into the laygear.
17. Withdraw the layshaft, at the same time thread the wire through the laygear and front thrust washer. This will enable the laygear and thrust washers to be retained ready for refitting the layshaft, and at the same time allow sufficient movement of the laygear to prevent the gear teeth obstructing the gears on the first and third motion shafts during refitting.
18. Refit the third motion shaft–Section F.7, 35 to 37.
19. Refit the first motion shaft–Section F.6, 16.
20. Use the wire to align the laygear and thrust washers.
21. Enter the layshaft, plain end first, into the front of the casing; line up the cut-away in the end of the shaft with the front cover recess and press the shaft home.
22. Reverse the removing procedure in 1 to 4.

SECTION Fa

THE OVERDRIVE (TYPE L.H.)

THE OVERDRIVE COMPONENTS (TYPE L.H.)

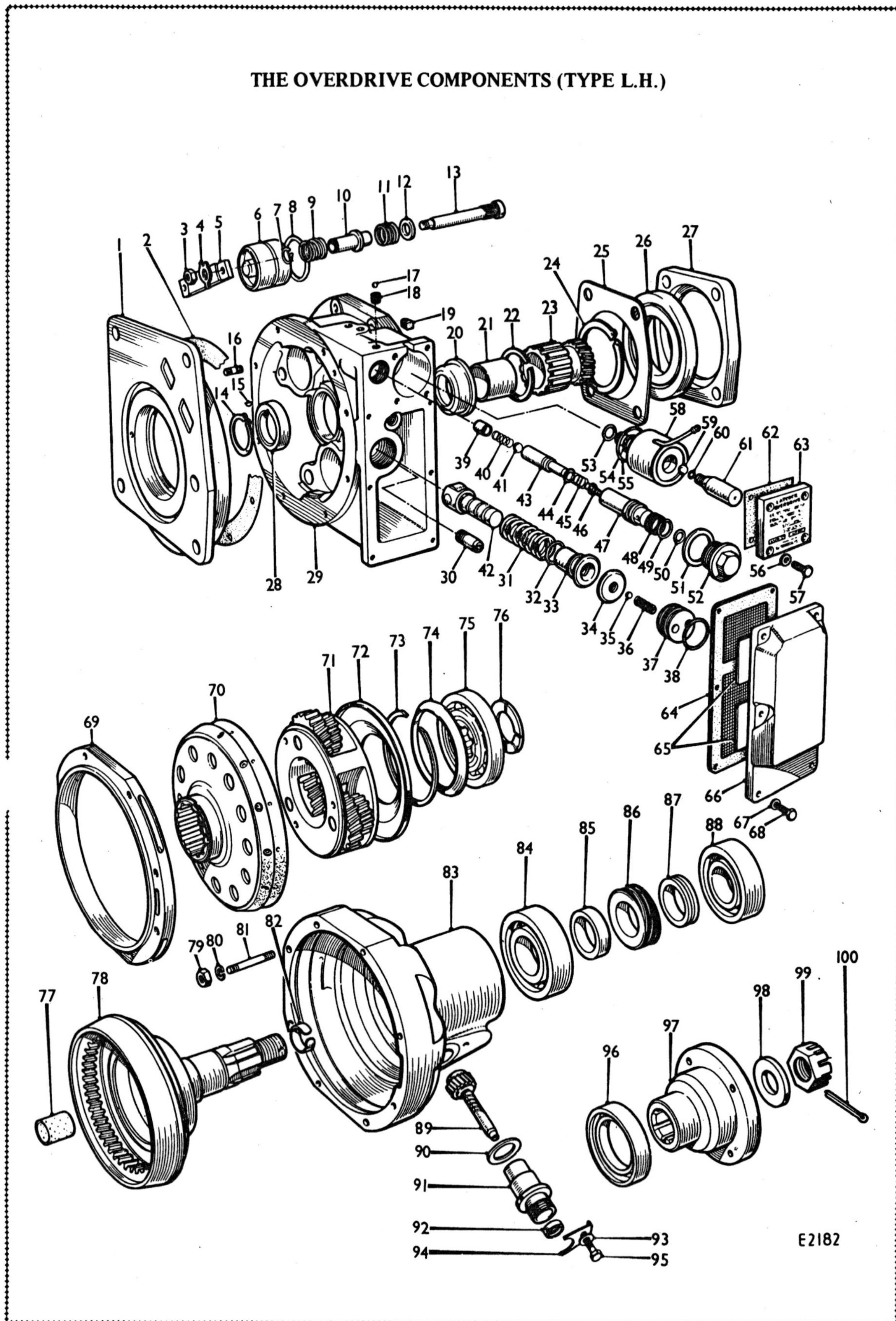

Fa.2

KEY TO THE OVERDRIVE COMPONENTS (TYPE L.H.)

No.	Description	No.	Description	No.	Description
1.	Adaptor plate.	34.	Non-return valve seat.	67.	Washer.
2.	Gasket.	35.	Valve ball.	68.	Screw.
3.	Nut.	36.	Valve spring.	69.	Brake-ring.
4.	Tab washer.	37.	Pump plug.	70.	Clutch sliding member.
5.	Bridge-piece.	38.	'O' ring.	71.	Planet carrier assembly.
6.	Operating piston.	39.	Low pressure valve plug.	72.	Oil catcher.
7.	Circlip.	40.	Valve spring.	73.	Circlip.
8.	'O' ring.	41.	Valve ball.	74.	Oil thrower.
9.	Spring.	42.	Pump plunger.	75.	Uni-directional clutch.
10.	Thrust rod.	43.	Low pressure valve body.	76.	Thrust washer.
11.	Spring.	44.	Washer.	77.	Bush.
12.	Washer.	45.	Relief valve spring.	78.	Annulus.
13.	Thrust housing pin.	46.	Valve plunger.	79.	Nut.
14.	Circlip.	47.	Valve body.	80.	Washer.
15.	Key.	48.	Filter.	81.	Stud.
16.	Stud.	49.	'O' ring.	82.	Spring ring.
17.	Steel ball.	50.	'O' ring.	83.	Rear casing.
18.	Plug.	41.	Washer.	84.	Annulus front bearing.
19.	Grommet.	52.	Plug.	85.	Spacer.
20.	Sun wheel thrust bush.	53.	'O' ring.	86.	Speedometer drive gear.
21.	Sun wheel bush.	54.	Solenoid valve body.	87.	Selective spacer.
22.	Circlip.	55.	'O' ring.	88.	Annulus rear bearing.
23.	Sun wheel.	56.	Washer.	89.	Speedometer driven gear.
24.	Circlip.	57.	Screw.	90.	Sealing washer.
25.	Retainer plate.	58.	Solenoid coil.	91.	Speedometer bearing.
26.	Thrust ball-race.	59.	Valve ball.	92.	Oil seal.
27.	Thrust ring.	60.	'O' ring.	93.	Retaining clip.
28.	Pump cam.	61.	Solenoid plunger.	94.	Washer.
29.	Main casing.	62.	Gasket.	95.	Bolt.
30.	Pump suction tube.	63.	Solenoid cover.	96.	Oil seal.
31.	Spring.	64.	Sump filter and gasket.	97.	Drive flange.
32.	'O' ring.	65.	Filter magnets.	98.	Washer.
33.	Pump body.	66.	Sump.	99.	Nut.
				100.	Split pin.

[**CAUTION**: Please read the instructions thoroughly before you attempt overdrive repairs. If you lack the necessary skills or tools, we suggest you leave such work to an Authorized Dealer or other qualified shop. Before taking a removed overdrive in for repair, thoroughly clean its exterior, but do not undertake any disassembly.]

Section Fa.1

GENERAL DESCRIPTION

The Laycock Type L.H. Overdrive fitted between the gearbox and propeller shaft is a self-contained gear unit which provides a higher overall gear ratio than that given by the final drive.

The overdrive gears consist of a central sun wheel and three planet gears which mesh with an internally toothed annulus. Fitted inside the annulus is a uni-directional clutch. A sliding clutch-member is secured to the sun wheel and is free to move forward and rearward on the sun wheel splines. Attached to a ball bearing, secured on the sliding clutch by a circlip, is a static thrust ring. The thrust ring is actuated by two hydraulic pistons and returned by primary and secondary return springs.

An electrically operated solenoid valve, mechanical pump, relief valve, and low pressure valve comprise the main components of the hydraulic system.

Overdrive engaged

With the overdrive switch selected the solenoid is energized and the ball valve is held in the closed position by the solenoid rod.

The input shaft to the overdrive unit carries a cam which operates the overdrive oil pump. The pump draws oil from

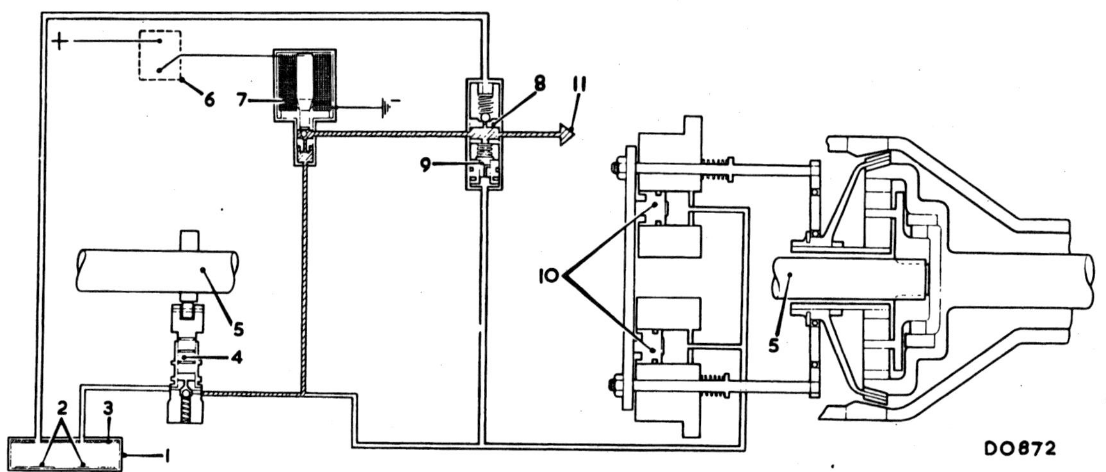

Fig. Fa.1
Direct drive

1. Sump.
2. Magnet filters.
3. Gauze filter.
4. Pump.
5. Third motion shaft (gearbox).
6. Control switch.
7. Solenoid operating valve.
8. Low pressure valve.
9. Relief valve.
10. Operating pistons.
11. Oil return to sump.

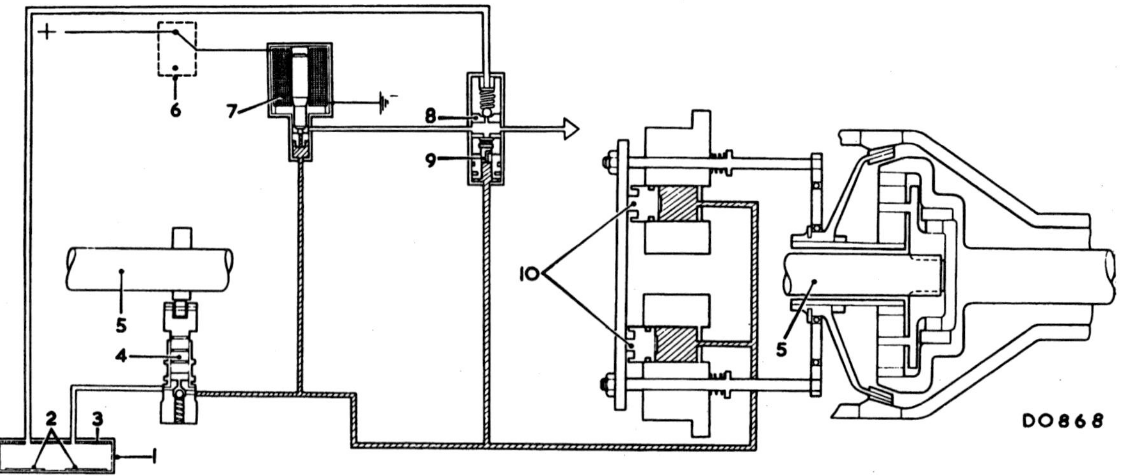

Fig. Fa.2
Overdrive engaged

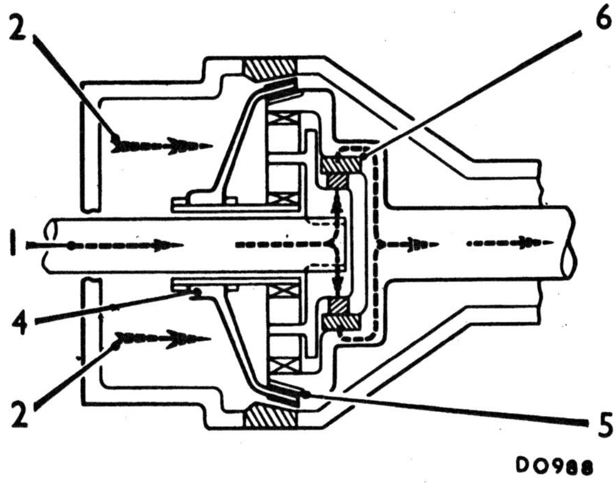

Fig. Fa.3
Direct drive

1. Third motion shaft.
2. Spring pressure.
4. Sun wheel.
5. Cone clutch.
6. Uni-directional clutch.

the sump and the oil from the pump discharge is ducted to the two operating pistons of the clutch sliding member. A build-up of oil pressure operates the two pistons and moves the sliding clutch-member, its outer brake surface contacts the stationary brake ring and the complete sliding member and sun wheel cease to rotate.

At a predetermined spring pressure the relief valve operates and relieves any pressure, in excess of the pressure required to keep the pistons operative, into the low pressure lubricating system. Build-up of pressure in the low pressure lubricating system is relieved by operation of the low pressure valve and the oil relieved returns to the sump.

The planet gear carrier is splined to, and rotates with, the input shaft. The planet gears, forced to turn about their own axis by movement of the carrier, while in mesh with the stationary sun wheel, impart driving force to turn the annulus. Because of the gearing arrangement the annulus turns faster than the input shaft. The propeller shaft, coupled to a flange rigidly secured to the shaft of the annulus, revolves at the same speed as the annulus.

In overdrive the outer bearing surface of the uni-directional clutch inside the annulus, over-rides the rollers, cage, and clutch, attached to the slower-moving input shaft. In this condition the uni-directional clutch is in the unlocked or free condition.

The solenoid valve acts as a safety valve. If the pressure becomes excessive the ball would be blown off its seat against the load of the solenoid.

Overdrive disengaged

CAUTION.–IF OVERDRIVE DOES NOT DISENGAGE, DO NOT REVERSE THE CAR OTHERWISE EXTENSIVE DAMAGE MAY RESULT.

With the overdrive switch in the 'off' position the operating solenoid is de-energized and the valve ball is free to move away from the valve seat. Oil from the pump discharge lifts the valve from its seat, flows to the low pressure valve, and is used for lubrication. This action relieves the oil pressure maintaining the pistons operative. The return springs act to close the pistons and the oil returning from the piston chambers is forced to mix with the pump flow, thus causing a restriction and damping the return movement of the sliding member. Action of the secondary return springs force the clutch sliding member rearward and its inner brake surface contacts the annulus brake ring. The sliding member and annulus commence to revolve in unison. As the sun wheel is splined to the sliding clutch member the complete gear train is locked.

Thrust from the input shaft locks the uni-directional clutch against the outer bearing surface, inside the annulus, and direct drive is applied to the propeller shaft through the annulus extension on which the propeller shaft coupling flange is mounted.

During over-run and reverse, additional load is imparted to the clutch sliding member by the helix thrust of the sun wheel, thus helping to retain direct drive.

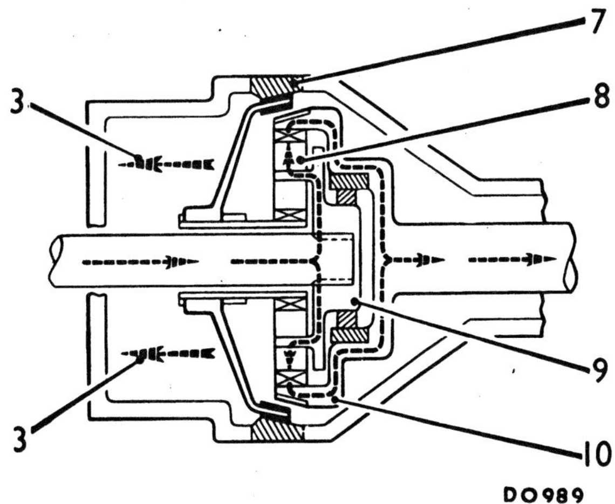

Fig. Fa.4
Overdrive engaged

3. Hydraulic pressure.
7. Brake ring.
8. Planet wheel.
9. Planet carrier.
10. Annulus.

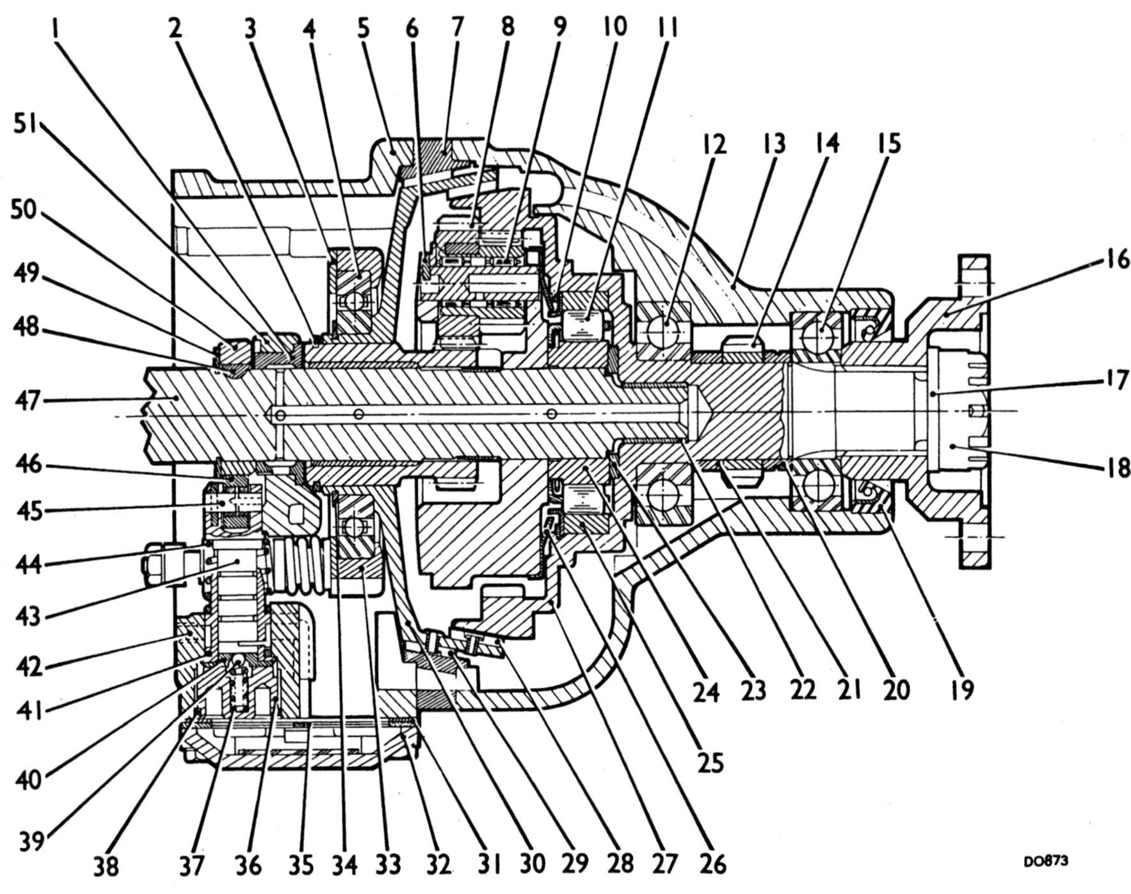

Fig. Fa.5
A section through the overdrive unit

1. Sun wheel thrust bush.
2. Snap ring for sun wheel.
3. Bearing retainer plate.
4. Thrust bearing.
5. Main casing.
6. Grooved pin.
7. Brake ring.
8. Planet wheel.
9. Planet bearing.
10. Circlip.
11. Rollers for uni-directional clutch.
12. Annulus front bearing.
13. Rear casing.
14. Speedometer driving gear.
15. Annulus rear bearing.
16. Drive flange.
17. Washer.
18. Nut.
19. Oil seal.
20. Selective spacer.
21. Spacer.
22. Bush.
23. Thrust washer.
24. Uni-directional clutch, inner member.
25. Uni-directional clutch, outer member.
26. Oil thrower.
27. Annulus.
28. Inner lining of clutch sliding member.
29. Outer lining of clutch sliding member.
30. Clutch sliding member.
31. Sump filter and gasket assembly.
32. Sump.
33. Thrust bearing housing.
34. Circlip.
35. Filter.
36. Pump plug.
37. Non-return valve spring.
38. 'O' ring.
39. Non-return valve ball.
40. Non-return valve seat.
41. Pump body.
42. Main case housing for pump.
43. Pump plunger.
44. Spring for pump plunger.
45. Pin for pump roller.
46. Pump roller.
47. Gearbox third motion shaft.
48. Key for pump cam.
59. Circlip.
50. Pump cam.
51. Main case housing for sun wheel and oil transfer bush.

Section Fa.2

FAULT DIAGNOSIS

OVERDRIVE DOES NOT ENGAGE

(1) Insufficient oil in gearbox .. .. Top up to correct level.
(2) Electrical system fault .. .. Check and rectify fault; check operation of solenoid.
(3) Low hydraulic pressure:
  (a) Pump non-return valve not seating .. .. .. Remove and check the valve; clean or renew.
  (b) Solenoid ball valve not seating .. .. Remove and check the valve; clean or renew.
  (c) Pump filter choked .. .. Remove and clean filter.
(4) Damaged parts within unit .. .. Remove, dismantle, and inspect unit.

OVERDRIVE DOES NOT DISENGAGE

NOTE.– **If the overdrive does not disengage, do not reverse the car as extensive damage may result.**

(5) Electrical control system fault .. .. Check and rectify fault.
(6) Sticking clutch .. .. On a new unit this may be due to insufficient bedding-in of the clutch. The clutch can usually be freed by giving the brake-ring, accessible from beneath the car, several sharp blows with a hide mallet.
(7) Damaged parts within unit .. .. Remove, dismantle, and inspect unit.

OVERDRIVE SLIPS WHEN ENGAGED

(8) Insufficient oil in gearbox .. .. Top up to correct level.
(9) Low hydraulic pressure:
  (a) Pump non-return valve not seating .. .. .. Remove and check the valve; clean or renew.
  (b) Relief valve not seating .. .. Remove and check the valve; clean or renew.
  (c) Solenoid valve not seating .. .. Remove and check the valve; clean or renew.
  (d) Partially blocked pump or relief valve filter .. .. Remove and clean filters.
(10) Worn or glazed clutch lining .. .. Remove, dismantle, and replace faulty parts.

SLIP IN REVERSE OR FREE WHEEL ON OVER-RUN

(11) Worn or glazed clutch lining .. .. Remove, dismantle, and replace faulty parts.
(12) Broken circlip on sun wheel .. .. Remove, dismantle, and replace faulty parts.

Section Fa.3

HYDRAULIC PRESSURE TEST

1. Check the gearbox oil level, and top up as necessary.
2. Raise and support the rear of the car so that the rear wheels are clear of the ground.
3. Securely chock the front wheels.
4. Remove the relief valve plug and its sealing washer.
5. Fit adaptor 18G 251 E, using the relief valve plug sealing washer, into the relief valve orifice.
6. Connect pressure gauge 18G 251.
7. Start the engine, engage top gear and select overdrive.
8. Set the speed to a speedometer reading of 30 m.p.h. (48 km.p.h.) and note the pressure gauge reading; the correct reading is 400 to 420 lb./sq. in. (28 to 29.5 kg./cm.^{2}).
   NOTE.–No pressure reading will be recorded with the overdrive disengaged.

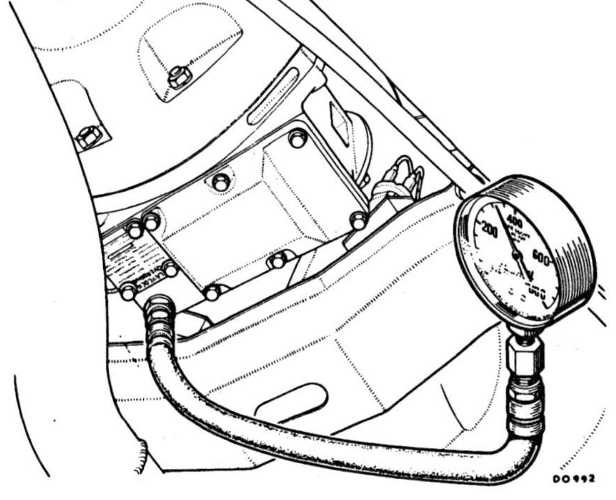

Fig. Fa.6
Pressure gauge 18G 251 and adaptor 18G 251 E connected to check the hydraulic pressure

Section Fa.4

LUBRICATION

IMPORTANT.–Anti-friction additives must not be used in the gearbox and overdrive.

Draining

1. Remove the gearbox drain plug to drain the oil from the gearbox and overdrive unit.

Filling

2. Remove the gearbox dipstick and add the correct quantity (see **'SERVICE LUBRICANTS, FUEL and FLUIDS–CAPACITIES'**) of one of the recommended lubricants.
3. Run the car for a short distance, allow to stand for a few minutes and check the level with the dipstick.

Section Fa.5

FILTERS

Sump

1. Drain the gearbox and overdrive unit.
2. Clean the sump cover and its surroundings.
3. Unscrew the sump cover securing screws and remove the cover and sump filter.
4. Clean all metallic particles from the two magnets fitted inside the cover; wash the cover and filter in petrol (gasoline).
5. Refit the filter and sump cover.
6. Refill the gearbox and overdrive unit with the correct quantity (see **'SERVICE LUBRICANTS, FUEL and FLUIDS–CAPACITIES'**) of one of the recommended lubricants.

Relief valve

7. Drain the gearbox and overdrive unit.
8. Remove the relief valve plug and sealing washer.
9. Withdraw the relief valve body and remove the filter.
10. Clean the filter in petrol (gasoline).
11. Refit the filter to the valve body.
12. Refit the valve body assembly, sealing washer, and plug.
13. Refill the gearbox and overdrive unit with a recommended lubricant.

Section Fa.6

RELIEF AND LOW PRESSURE VALVE

Removing

1. Drain the gearbox and overdrive unit.
2. Remove the relief valve plug and sealing washer.
3. Withdraw the relief valve assembly.

Dismantling

4. Remove the filter, spacer tube, low pressure valve assembly, and relief valve spring.
5. Remove the relief valve plunger.

Inspection

6. Examine the relief valve plunger and seat for pitting, scoring, and wear. Renew worn or damaged parts as necessary.
7. Inspect the relief valve body 'O' rings for signs of deterioration, and renew if necessary.
8. Check the relief valve spring for signs of collapse or weakness against the figures given in **'GENERAL SPECIFICATION DATA'**.
9. Test the low pressure valve for correct setting. The complete valve must be renewed if faulty.

Reassembling

10. Reverse the dismantling procedure in 4 and 5.

Refitting

11. Reverse the removing procedure in 2 and 3, noting that the spacer tube must be fitted with its slotted end farthest from the filter with the slots lining up respectively with the oil outlet hole and locating stud.

Section Fa.7

SOLENOID VALVE

Removing

1. Drain the gearbox and overdrive unit.
2. Unscrew the four screws securing the solenoid cover (name plate) and remove the cover and gasket.
3. Remove the solenoid and valve assembly by carefully pulling on the solenoid lead.

Dismantling

4. Withdraw the solenoid rod and operating valve assembly from the solenoid housing.

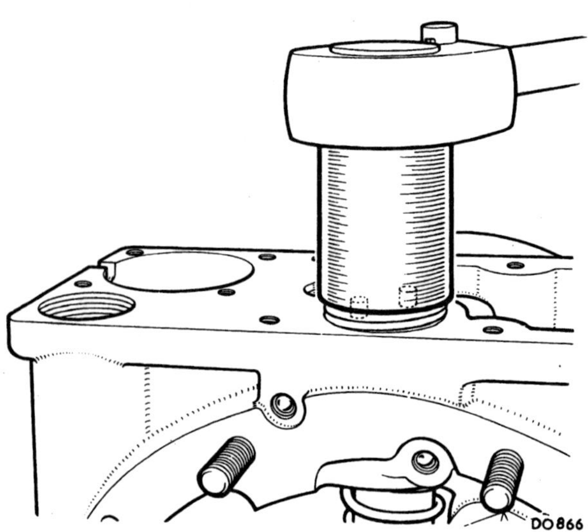

Fig. Fa.7
Removing the pump retaining plug using tool 18G 1118

5. Press the solenoid coil and base cap from the housing.
6. Remove the operating valve plunger and ball by shaking from the solenoid rod.

Inspection

7. Examine the valve ball and seat for pitting and scoring and renew damaged parts; the ball may be reseated by light tapping onto the seat using a suitable drift.
8. Inspect the 'O' ring seals for signs of deterioration, and renew as necessary.

Reassembling

9. Reverse the dismantling procedure 4 to 6.

Refitting

10. Reverse the removing procedure in 2 and 3, ensuring that the lead grommet is pressed fully into its slot, and using a new gasket under the solenoid cover.

Section Fa.8

PUMP AND NON-RETURN VALVE

Removing

1. Drain the gearbox and overdrive unit.
2. Remove the sump filter–Section Fa.5, 2 and 3.
3. Using tool 18G 1118, unscrew the pump retaining plug.
4. Remove the non-return valve spring and ball.
5. Remove the pump body, the pump plunger spring and plunger.

Dismantling

6. Using a suitable drift, separate the non-return valve seat from the pump body taking care not to damage the bore of the pump body.

Inspection

7. Examine the 'O' ring seals for signs of deterioration, and renew where necessary.
8. Examine the non-return valve ball and seat for scoring and pitting, and renew damaged parts; the ball may be reseated by lightly tapping onto its seat using a suitable drift.

Reassembling

9. Carefully refit the non-return valve seat to the pump body.

Refitting

10. Insert the pump plunger into the casing, ensuring that the flat side of the plunger is towards the rear of the overdrive unit and retain in position with tool 18G 1117.
11. Reverse the removing procedure in 2 to 5.

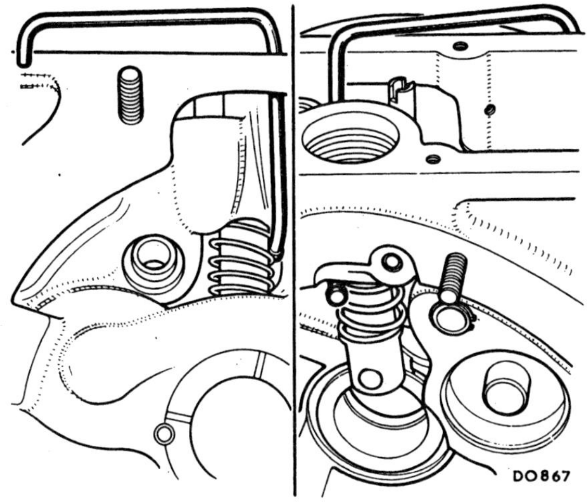

Fig. Fa.8
Using tool 18G 1117 to retain the pump components

Section Fa.9

OVERDRIVE ASSEMBLY

Removing

OVERDRIVE UNIT

1. Remove the engine and gearbox from the car as described in Section A.15.
2. Remove the gearbox drain plug and drain the oil from the gearbox and overdrive.
3. Unscrew the six bolts securing the remote control assembly to the gearbox and remove the remote control.
4. Remove the eight nuts from the studs securing the overdrive unit to the gearbox adaptor.
5. Withdraw the overdrive unit from the gearbox adaptor.

OVERDRIVE ADAPTOR

6. Remove the overdrive unit as in 1 to 5.
7. Slide the overdrive pump driving cam from the gearbox shaft and remove the cam locking ball from its pocket in the shaft.
8. Using tool 18G 1004, remove the pump cam circlip from the shaft.
9. Withdraw the selector interlocking arm and plate assembly.
10. Unscrew the eight nuts securing the adaptor to the gearbox and withdraw the adaptor.

Dismantling

11. Remove the solenoid cover and gasket.
12. Withdraw the solenoid and plunger.
13. Remove the relief valve assembly.
14. Remove the sump and filter.
15. Using tool 18G 1118, unscrew the pump retaining plug and remove the pump components.
16. Remove the speedometer drive retaining clip, drive gear, and sealing washer.

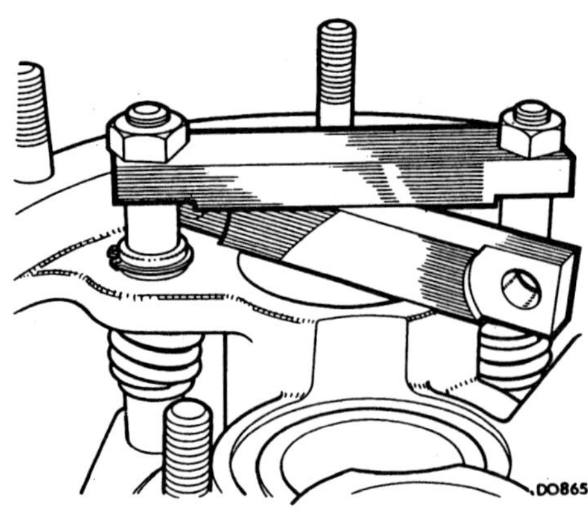

Fig. Fa.9
Using the bridge-pieces to remove the thrust rods

17. Unscrew the s x rear retaining stud nuts and the two front nuts secu ing the rear casing to the main casing assembly.
18. Separate the rear casing from the main casing and remove the planet gear assembly.
19. Unlock and remove the nuts securing the bridge pieces and pistons in the main casing.
20. Remove the bridge piece, pistons, clutch sliding member, brake-ring and sun wheel.
21. Remove the four clutch springs and selective washe .
22. Lever the sun wheel split-ring from the retaining groove and push out the sun wheel.
23. Lift off the bearing retaining plate.
24. Using tool 18G 257, remove the bearing circlip.
25. Drift the clutch sliding member from the bearing.
26. Press the bearing from its housing.
27. Fit the four studs in the thru t ring and insert the studs into the thrust rods from the rear of the main casing.
28. Lay one bridge-piece on its side across one of the piston chambers and fit the remaining bridgepiece, inverted to its normal assembly position, on the two adjacent thrust ring studs and secure with two nuts.
29. Tighten both nuts evenly until the springs are compressed.
30. Remove the circlips securing the thrust rods and springs.
31. Slacken the two nuts evenly until the spring pressure is relieved and remove the nuts.
32. Repeat the operations in 28 to 31 for the remaining thrust rods.
33. Unlock the flange nut, using tool 18G 34A to prevent the shaft turning; remove the nut and washer and withdraw the flange.
34. Press the annulus forward out of the rear casing complete with the front bearing. If the bearing remains in the housing, carefully drift it out with a drift registering on the inner bearing track.
35. Remove the spacer, speedometer driving gear and selective spacer, noting the position of the selective spacer which is identified by a groove cut in its periphery.

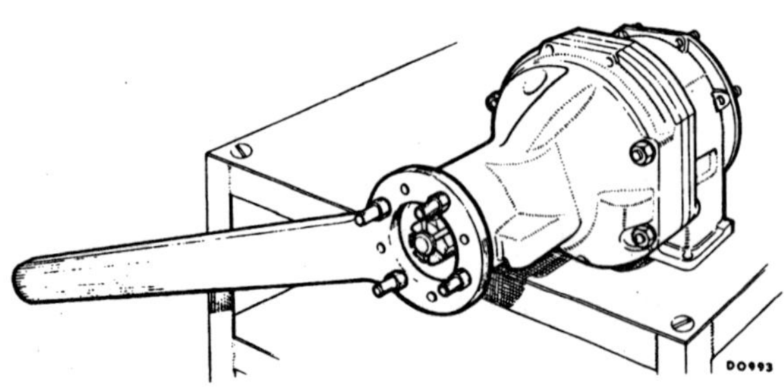

Fig. Fa.10
Using tool 18G 34A to prevent the drive flange from rotating

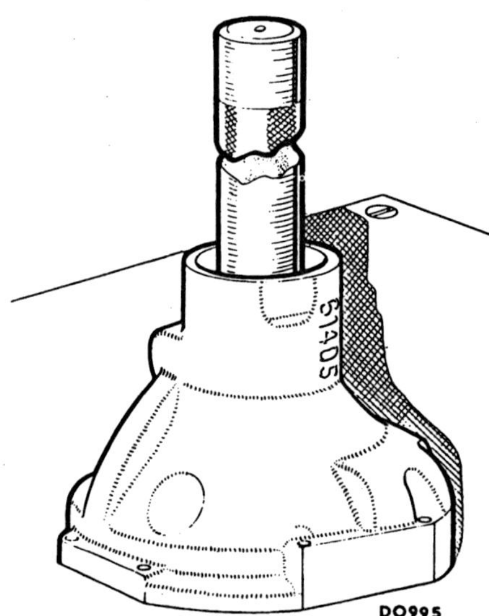

Fig. Fa.11
Fitting the rear bearing using tool 18G 186

36. Press out the rear bearing and oil seal.
37. Remove the front bearing from the annulus if it has been retaining to the shaft.
38. Remove the split ring, oil thrower ring, and uni-directional clutch, collecting the rollers as they come free.
39. Remove the thrust washer.

Inspection

40. Thoroughly clean the components in a cleaning solvent and dry them using lint-free or nylon material or compressed air.
41. Thoroughly examine each component for damage and excessive wear.
42. Examine the bearings for pitting or scoring of the tracks and balls.
43. Check the springs for weakness, collapse or distortion against the following:
44. Inspect the pistons and bores for signs of scoring.
45. Examine the rubber components for signs of deterioration.
46. Inspect the clutch for worn or charred linings and loose rivets. If the clutch is defective a complete new clutch sliding member must be fitted.
47. Examine the shaft splines for signs of wear and damage.
48. Check the condition of the sun wheel bush. If the bush is defective a complete new sun wheel assembly must be fitted.
49. Examine the selective washers for wear. If worn, a new set (four) of washers must be fitted.

Reassembling

50. Press the front bearing into its housing in the rear casing, ensuring that the outer track of the bearing is firmly against the shoulder of the casing.
51. Press the annulus into the front bearing.
52. Fit the spacer, speedometer driving gear, and selective washer.
53. If the rear casing, annulus, speedometer gear, or spacer have been renewed, proceed as follows:
    a. Using dial gauge 18G 191, take a reading from the rear face of the selective washer (Fig. Fa.12).
    b. Take another reading from the shoulder of the rear bearing housing.
    c. The dimension in a should be .010 in. (.254 mm.) $\pm^{0.000}_{0.005}$ in. (.127 mm.) greater than the dimension taken in b. If the correct reading is not obtained, check that the front bearing and annulus are firmly in contact with the shoulders of their respective housings.

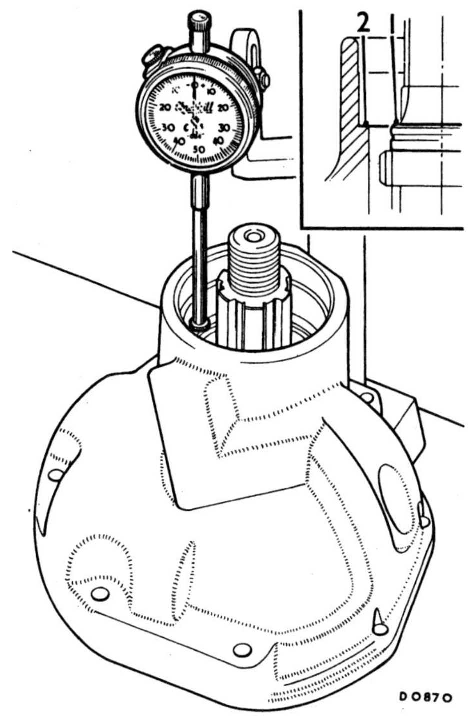

Fig. Fa.12
Using dial gauge 18G 191 to take measurements for the selective washer. Inset shows:
1. Rear face of the selective washer.
2. Shoulder of the bearing housing.

Spring	No. of coils	Wire diameter	Free length	Fitted length	Load at fitted length
Clutch engagement	3¾	.098 in. (2.5 mm.)	.78 in. (19.8 mm.)	.52 in. (13.2 mm.)	65 lb. (29.5 kg.)
Clutch release	4½	.128 in. (3.3 mm.)	.85 in. (21.6 mm.)	.625 in. (15.9 mm.)	150 lb. (68 kg.)
Relief valve	8	.092 in. (2.3 mm.)	1.182 in. (30 mm.)	.995 in. (25.3 mm)	38.35 lb. (17.5 kg.)
Pump	7	.064 in. (1.6 mm.)	1.75 in. (44.5 mm.)	.896 in. (22.8 mm.)	10.99 lb. (5 kg.)

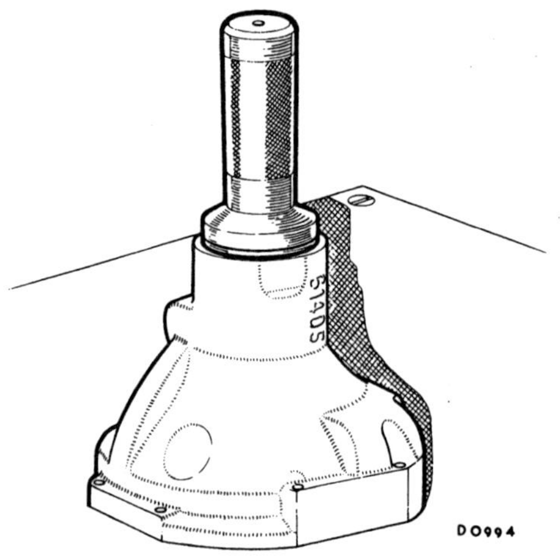

Fig. Fa.13
Fitting the rear oil seal using tool 18G 177

d. If the correct reading is still unobtainable, select a new selective washer to suit. Washers are available in the following thicknesses:

.360 in. (9.1 mm.)	.380 in. (9.7 mm.)
.365 in. (9.3 mm.)	.385 in. (9.8 mm.)
.370 in. (9.4 mm.)	.390 in. (9.9 mm.)
.375 in. (9.5 mm.)	

54. Using tool 18G 186, fit the rear bearing.
55. Smear the outer case of the new rear oil seal with grease, and fit the seal fully into its housing using tool 18G 177.
56. Fit the rear flange, tighten the nut to the torque figure given in **'GENERAL SPECIFICATION DATA'** and lock the nut using a new split pin.
57. Fit the thrust ring.

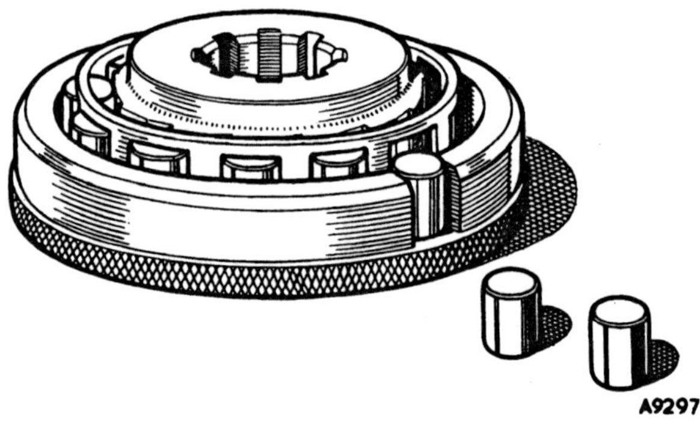

Fig. Fa.14
Assembling the uni-directional clutch using tool 18G 178

58. Fit the spring of the uni-directional clutch to the inner clutch member, and the inner member and spring into the clutch cage, then insert the assembly into tool 18G 178 and fit the clutch rollers.
59. Fit the uni-directional clutch assembly and remove tool 18G 178.
60. Fit the oil thrower and split ring and check that the clutch rotates in an anti-clockwise direction.
61. Rotate each planet wheel until the centre punch mark is radially outwards and in line with the wheel shaft locking pin.
62. Insert the sun wheel into the planet carrier and recheck the alignment of the planet wheel markings.
63. Install the assembled planet carried into the annulus.
64. Remove the sun wheel.
65. Using tool 18G 185, align the splines in the planet carrier and uni-directional clutch.

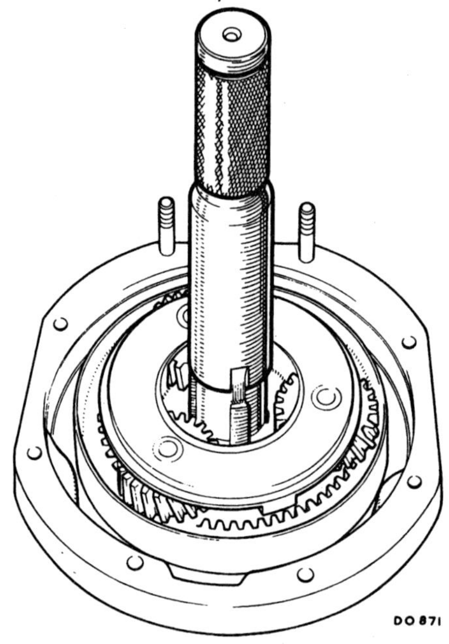

Fig. Fa.15
Using tool 18G 185 to align the splines

66. Refit the four clutch release thrust rods using the dismantling method in 27 to 32; fit new circlips if required.
67. Refit the pistons.
68. Reassemble the clutch sliding member and components by reversing the procedure in 21 to 26, ensuring that the four selective washers fitted are a complete set.

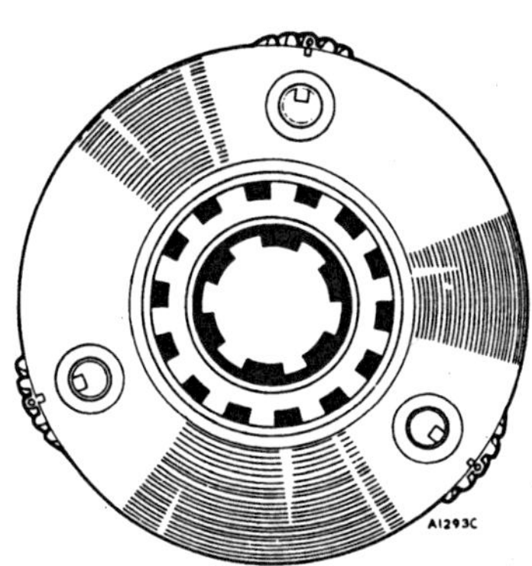

Fig. Fa.16
The planet wheels correctly positioned for fitting the sun wheel and assembling in the annulus

69. Fit the sun wheel, brake ring and clutch sliding member reversing the procedure in 19 to 21 and noting that the jointing faces of the brake ring must be smeared with a liquid jointing compound and the nuts locked using new tab washers.
70. Smear the jointing faces of the two casings with liquid jointing compound and assemble the casings ensuring that the sun wheel meshes with the planet gears.
71. Fit and tighten the retaining nuts and spring washers.
72. Reverse the dismantling procedure in 11 to 16.

Refitting
OVERDRIVE ADAPTOR
73. Reverse the removing procedure in 6 to 10.

OVERDRIVE UNIT
74. Reverse the removing procedure in 1 to 5.

SECTION G

THE PROPELLER SHAFT

THE PROPELLER SHAFT COMPONENTS

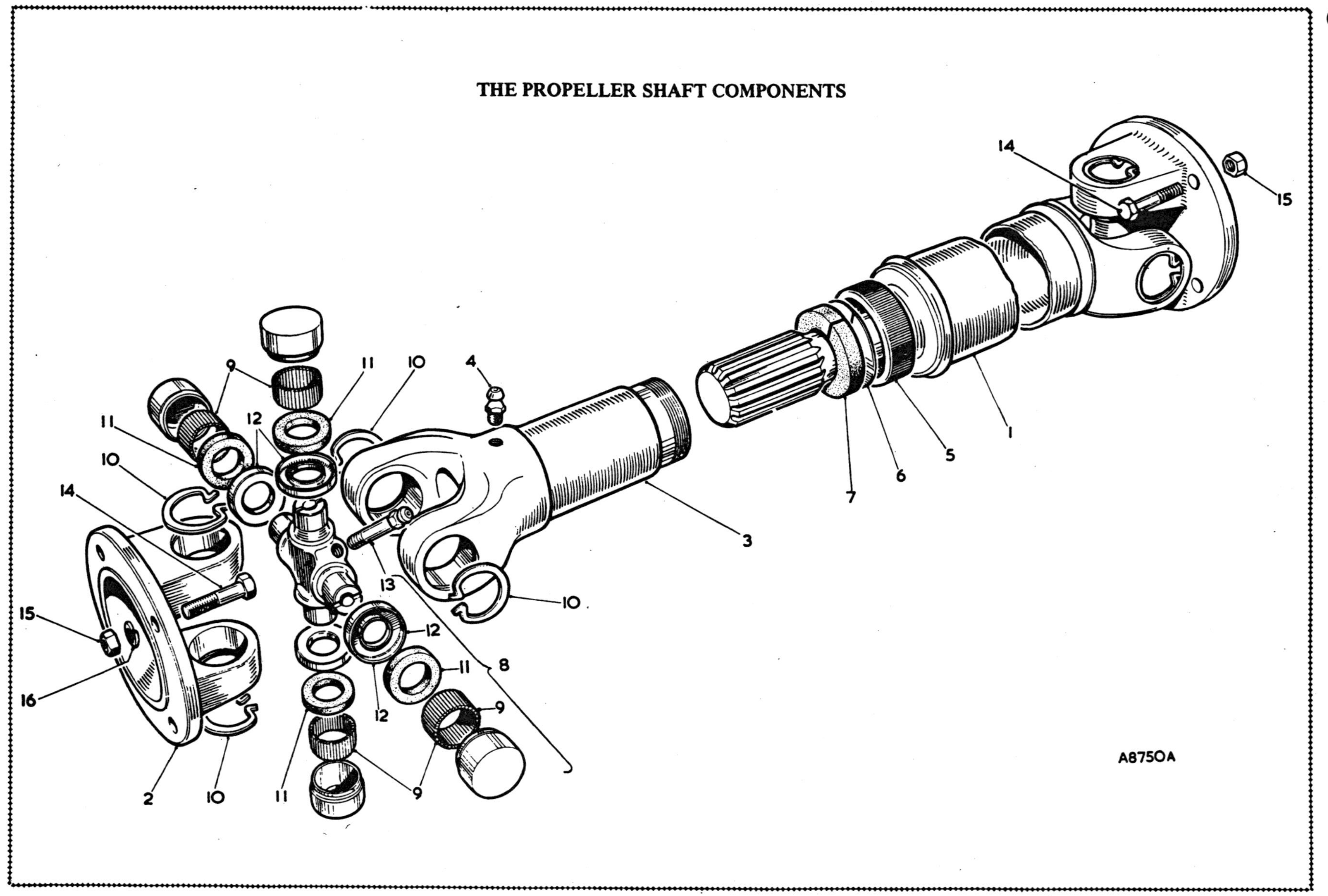

KEY TO THE PROPELLER SHAFT COMPONENTS

No.	Description	No.	Description
1.	Shaft assembly–propeller.	9.	Bearing assembly–needle.
2.	Flange yoke.	10.	Circlip.
3.	Sleeve assembly–yoke.	11.	Gasket.
4.	Lubricator.	12.	Retainer–gasket.
5.	Cap–dust.	13.	Lubricator–journal (if fitted).
6.	Washer–dust cap (steel).	14.	Bolt–shaft to pinion flange (front and rear).
7.	Washer–dust cap (cork).	15.	Nut for bolt.
8.	Journal assembly.	16.	Washer–spring–for front bolt.

GENERAL DESCRIPTION

The propeller shaft and universal joints are of the Hardy Spicer type with needle-roller bearings in the universal joints.

The rear end of the shaft is flanged and carries the rear universal joint flange yoke. The front end of the shaft is splined and engages a sleeve and yoke assembly. In the assembled condition a dust cap, steel washer, and cork washer seal the end of the sleeve and the sliding joint.

Each universal joint is made up of a spider and four gaskets, retainers, and needle bearing assemblies. Each needle bearing assembly is retained in its yoke by a circlip.

The yoke flanges are secured to the pinion and gearbox flanges respectively with eight bolts, spring washers, and Aerotight or Nyloc nuts.

Section G.1

LUBRICATION

A nipple is provided for lubricating the sliding yoke at the fron end of the propeller shaft. Three or four strokes of a grease gun are required when lubricating.

Fig. G.1
When dismantling a universal joint the bearings may be tapped out with a small diameter rod from the inside as shown. Take care not to damage the roller races

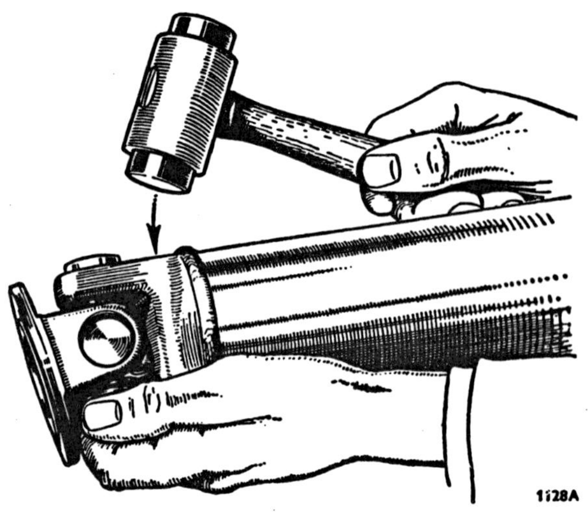

Fig. G.2
Where to apply light blows to the yoke after removing the retaining circlip

Section G.2

REMOVING AND REPLACING THE PROPELLER SHAFT

To remove the propeller shaft proceed as follows:

1. Mark the yoke flanges and the gearbox and rear axle flanges to assist in refitting them in their original positions. **This is most important.**
2. Remove the nuts, washers, and bolts securing the flanges and lower the propeller shaft.

Replacement is a reversal of the removal sequence, but ensure that the joint faces of the flanges are perfectly smooth and clean and that they are correctly aligned with the gearbox and rear axle flanges.

Section G.3

DISMANTLING THE PROPELLER SHAFT

1. Unscrew the dust cap from the sleeve and slide the sleeve off the shaft. Remove the steel washer and the cork washer.
2. Remove all circlips from the universal joints. If a circlip appears to be tight in its groove lightly tap the end of the bearing race to relieve the pressure against the ring.
3. Remove the lubricators from the journals and the sleeve (if fitted).
4. Hold the shaft yoke in one hand and tap the radius of the yoke with a hammer. The bearing should begin to emerge. Turn the yoke over and remove the bearing with the fingers.
5. If necessary, tap the bearing race from inside with a small diameter bar taking care not to damage the bearing face.

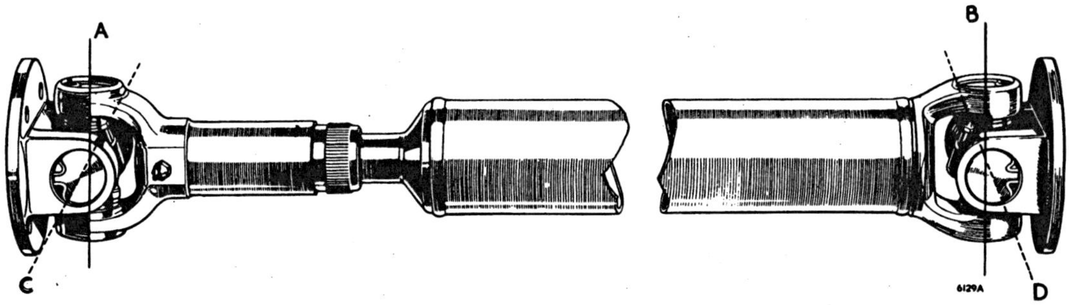

Fig G.3

When the splined shaft is assembled to the drive shaft it is essential to see that the forked yokes on both shafts have their axes parallel to each other. In other words, the yoke (A) must be in alignment with the yoke (B), and the flange yoke (C) must be in alignment with the flange yoke (D)

6. Hold the bearing in a vertical position and remove the race from the bottom side to avoid dropping the needle rollers.
7. Repeat operations 4, 5, and 6 for the opposite bearing.
8. Rest the exposed trunnions on wood blocks and tap the top lug of the flange yoke to remove the bearing race. Turn the yoke over and repeat the operation to remove the remaining bearing.
9. Repeat operations 4 to 8 to remove the bearings from the sleeve and yoke assembly.
10. Remove the gaskets and their retainers from the spider journals.

Section G.4

EXAMINING THE PROPELLER SHAFT

Thoroughly clean, wash, and dry all components prior to examination, paying particular attention to the lubrication passages.

1. Check the splines on the sleeve and shaft for indentation.
2. Examine the bearing races and journals for wear.
3. Examine the holes in the yokes and flanges for ovality.
4. Ensure that the bearing races are a light driving fit in their yokes.
5. Check the flange yoke faces for burrs, cracks, or fractures.

All worn or unserviceable parts must be renewed.

Section G.5

ASSEMBLING THE PROPELLER SHAFT

It is of extreme importance that the assembly of the journals be carried out under absolutely clean, dust-free conditions.

1. Fill the reservoir holes in the journal spider with the recommended grease taking care to exclude all air pockets. Fill each bearing assembly with grease to a depth of ⅛ in. (3 mm.).
2. Fit new seals to the spider journals and insert the spider into the flange yoke, tilting it to engage in the yoke bores.
3. Fit a bearing assembly into the yoke bore in the bottom position, and using a soft-nosed drift slightly smaller in diameter than the hole in the yoke, tap it into the yoke bore until it is possible to fit the circlip. Repeat this operation for the other three bearings starting opposite the bearing first fitted.
4. After assembly, carefully remove all surplus grease with a soft cloth. If the bearing appears to bind, tap lightly with a wooden mallet; this will relieve any pressure of the bearing on the ends of the journals.

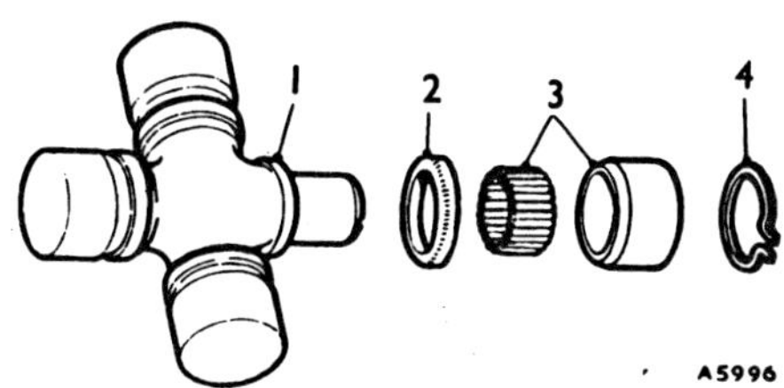

Fig. G.4
A universal joint bearing–sealed type

1. Journal spider.
2. Rubber seal.
3. Needle rollers and bearing.
4. Circlip.

SECTION H

THE REAR AXLE AND REAR SUSPENSION
(SEMI-FLOATING TYPE)

[**CAUTION**: Please read the instructions thoroughly before you attempt rear axle repairs. The precision measurements and adjustments that are described for the setting of the pinion position, the crown wheel position, and the pinion/crown wheel backlash are absolutely essential and require the special tools that are shown. If not correctly adjusted, the final drive gearset will be noisy and will quickly wear out. If you lack the skills, the special tools, or a clean workshop for carrying out the repairs, we suggest that you leave the work to an Authorized Dealer or other qualified shop. Before taking a removed rear axle in for repair, thoroughly clean its exterior, but do not undertake any disassembly.]

GENERAL DESCRIPTION

The rear axle assembly is of the semi-floating type. Adjustment to the bearing is by means of spacers, as also is the position of the pinion in relation to the crown wheel and the backlash between the gears.

Suspension is by semi-elliptic leaf springs, rubber-mounted, and the shackles are fitted with rubber bushes.

Section H.1

LUBRICATION

Oil level

Check the level, and top up if necessary. The filler plug is located on the rear of the axle and also serves as an oil level indicator. After topping up allow time for any surplus oil to run out. This is most important; if the axle is overfilled, the oil may leak through to the brake linings and lessen their efficiency.

NOTE.–It is essential that only Hypoid oil be used.

Draining

The most suitable time for draining is after a long journey while the oil is still warm. Clean the drain plug before it is replaced and tightened.

Refill the axle with fresh oil.

Section H.2

AXLE UNIT

Removing

Raise the rear of the car.

Mark the propeller shaft driving flanges so that they may be replaced in their original relative positions. Remove the four bolts and self-locking nuts and release the rear end of the propeller shaft from the axle. Remove the nuts and spring and flat washers securing each end of each check strap to the anchor pins on the axle and remove the check straps.

Remove the split pin and clevis pin securing the brake cable to each brake operating lever. Remove the set screw securing the hand brake cable clip to the axle casing. Remove the self-locking nut and large flat washer securing the brake balance lever to the pivot on the axle casing.

Remove the nut and spring washer securing the lower end of each damper link to the rear spring clamp plate.

Unscrew the brake fluid supply pipe union and release the flexible pipe from the battery box support bracket.

Release the exhaust pipe from the exhaust manifold and the supporting brackets and lower the exhaust pipe assembly.

Remove the nut and spring washer from each of the spring front anchor pins.

Support the axle casing and remove the rear shackle plates, brackets, and rubbers. Lower the axle support until the axle and spring assembly rests on the road wheels. Withdraw the front anchor pins and roll the assembly from beneath the car.

Refitting

Reverse the removal procedure when refitting.

Bleed and adjust the brakes (see Section M).

Section H.3

HUB AND AXLE SHAFT

Removing

Jack up the car and place blocks under the spring as close as possible to the axle. Remove the wheel. Release the hand brake.

Remove the two countersunk screws (disc wheels) or the four nuts (wire wheels) locating the brake-drum and tap it from the hub. It may be necessary to slacken off the brake adjusters slightly if the shoes hold the drum.

Remove the split pin, unscrew the slotted axle shaft nuts and withdraw the hub. Remove the clevis pin securing the brake cable to the operating lever, and disconnect the hydraulic pipe from the wheel cylinder. Remove the backplate. Remove the oil seal collar, bearing hub cap and oil seal from the axle shaft. Remove the axle shaft using impulse extractor 18G 284 with adaptor 18G 284 D and press the bearing from the shaft.

Refitting

Repack the bearings with grease before refitting.

Reverse the removal procedure, using tool 18G 1067 to drift the axle shaft into position. Lubricate and fit a new oil seal, lip facing inwards. Refit the oil seal collar and bearing hub cap. Tighten the axle shaft nut to the torque figure given in **'TORQUE WRENCH SETTINGS'**. Bleed and adjust the brakes as in Section M.

Section H.4

RENEWING THE PINION OIL SEAL

Removing

1. Raise and support the rear of the car.
2. Remove the rear road wheels and brake drums.
3. Drain the rear axle.
4. Mark the propeller shaft and pinion flanges to ensure correct reassembly and disconnect the propeller shaft.
5. Using 18G 207 (see Fig. H.5) measure and record the torque required to rotate the pinion.
6. Using 18G 34 A to prevent the pinion from rotating, remove the flange retaining nut and washer, and withdraw the pinion flange.
7. Extract and discard the oil seal.

Inspection

8. Examine the pinion flange for damage, paying particular attention to the oil seal track area.

Refitting

9. Grease the periphery and sealing lip of the new oil seal and fit the seal flush with the axle casing.

THE REAR AXLE COMPONENTS

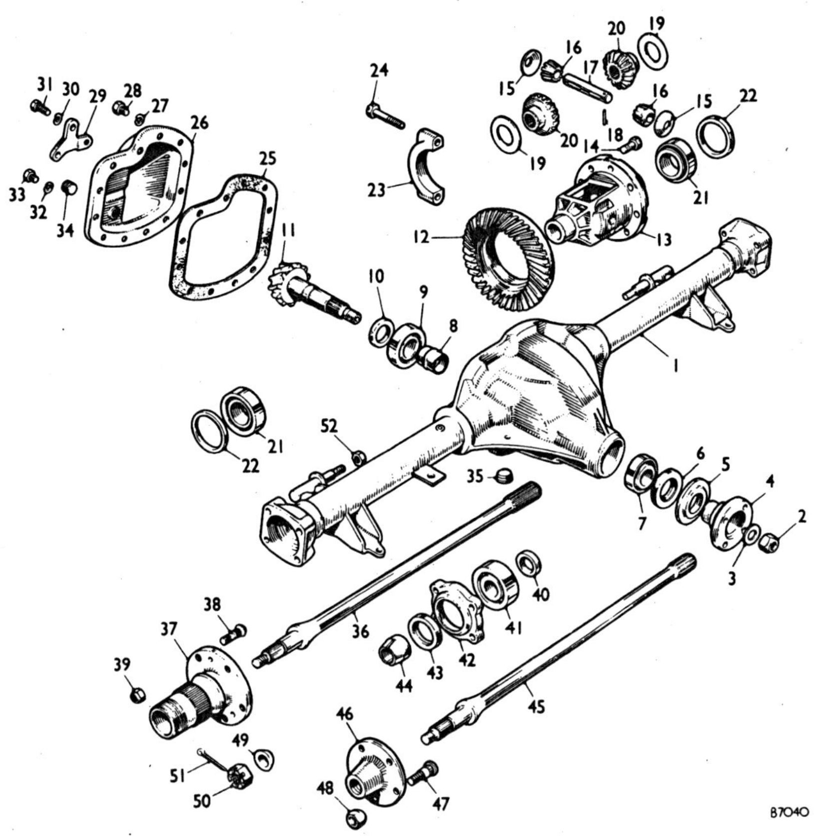

No.	Description	No.	Description	No.	Description
1.	Case assembly.	18.	Roll-pin.	35.	Drain plug.
2.	Nut.	19.	Thrust washer.	36.	Axle shaft. (Wire wheels only.)
3.	Plain washer.	20.	Differential wheels.	37.	Driving flange. (Wire wheels only.)
4.	Universal joint flange.	21.	Differential bearing.	38.	Stud. (Wire wheels only.)
5.	Dust cover.	22.	Distance collars.	39.	Nut. (Wire wheels only.)
6.	Oil seal.	23.	Bearing cap.	40.	Bearing spacer.
7.	Outer pinion bearing.	24.	Bolt.	41.	Bearing.
8.	Bearing spacer.	25.	Joint washer.	42.	Bearing hub cap.
9.	Inner pinion bearing.	26.	Axle case cover.	43.	Oil seal.
10.	Pinion thrust washer.	27.	Spring washer.	44.	Oil seal collar.
11.	Pinion.	28.	Set screws.	45.	Axle shaft. (Disc wheels only.)
12.	Crown wheel.	29.	Compensating lever bracket.	46.	Driving flange. (Disc wheels only.)
13.	Differential cage.	30.	Spring washer.	47.	Wheel stud. (Disc wheels only.)
14.	Bolt.	31.	Set screw.	48.	Wheel nut. (Disc wheels only.)
15.	Thrust washer.	32.	Spring washer.	49.	Axle shaft collar.
16.	Differential pinions.	33.	Set screw.	50.	Axle shaft nut.
17.	Pinion pin.	34.	Filler and level plug.	51.	Split pin.

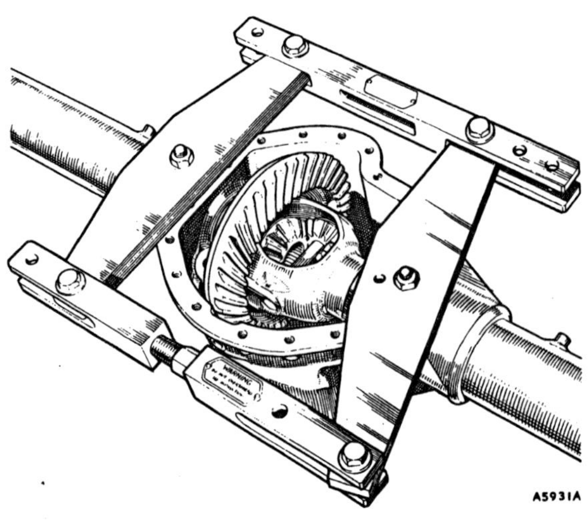

Fig. H.1
Axle stretcher 18G 131 C

10. Refit the pinion flange and washer.
11. Screw on the retaining nut, **tightening the nut gradually** until resistance is felt.
12. Rotate the pinion to settle the bearings and measure the torque required to rotate the pinion.
    If the reading obtained is less than that recorded in Operation 5, before the seal was removed; tighten the nut **A VERY SMALL AMOUNT**, resettle the bearings and recheck the torque reading. Repeat this procedure until a reading equal to that recorded in Operation 5 **BUT NOT LESS THAN 4 to 6 lb. in. (0.04 to 0.07 kg. m.)** is obtained.
    e.g. Reading in Operation 5 = 9 lb. in. (0.10 kg. m.).
    Adjust torque to this figure
    or
    Reading in Operation 5 = 0 lb. in.
    Adjust torque to 4 to 6 lb. in. (0.04 to 0.07 kg. m.).

CAUTION. Preload build up is rapid, tighten the nut with extreme care. IF AN ORIGINAL TORQUE READING, in excess of 6 lb. in. (0.7 kg. m.) is exceeded, THE AXLE MUST BE DISMANTLED AND A NEW COLLAPSIBLE SPACER FITTED.

Section H.5

DIFFERENTIAL AND PINION

Removing the differential

Drain and remove the axle from the car (see Section H.2).

Remove the axle shafts and wheel hubs (see Section H.3).

Remove the differential cover. Mark each differential bearing cap before removal to ensure correct replacement unscrew the two bolts and withdraw both caps.

Before the differential assembly can be withdrawn the axle case must be stretched with Service tool 18G 131 C. When using this tool tighten the turnbuckle one flat at a time until the differential unit can be prised out. Each flat on the turnbuckle is numbered to provide a check on the amount turned on the buckle. Prise the differential assembly out with two levers, one on each side of the differential case opening, using suitable packing between the levers and the gear carrier, and ensure that no leverage is placed upon the axle stretcher.

NOTE.–To prevent the axle case being permanently damaged, it must not be stretched any more than is absolutely necessary.

Maximum stretch is 0.012 in. (.31 mm.) 9 flats.

Release the stretcher.

Dismantling

Bend back the locking tabs and remove the crown wheel securing screws. Remove the crown wheel from the differential cage.

Drive out the pinion pin peg and remove the pin.

Turn the differential wheels by hand until the differential pinions are opposite the openings in the differential cage, remove the differential pinions and the thrust washers fitted behind them.

Remove the differential wheels and their thrust washers.

Should it be necessary to withdraw the differential inner bearing races, Service tool 18G 47 C, adaptor 18G 47 AK and adaptor plug 18G 47 AR must be used.

Reassembling

Use Service tool 18G 134 and adaptor 18G 134 CM to replace the differential bearings.

Fit the differential wheels with the thrust washers in position.

Insert the differential pinions through the opening in the differential cage and mesh them with the differential wheels. Hold the pinion thrust washers in position and install the pinion pin.

Line up the pinion pin with the hole in the differential cage and fit the pinion pin peg.

Bolt the crown wheel to the differential cage but do not knock over the locking tabs. Tighten the bolts to a torque wrench reading of 60 to 65 lb. ft. (8.3 to 8.9 kg. m.).

Mount the assembly on two 'V' blocks and check the amount of run-out of the crown wheel, as it is rotated, by means of a suitably mounted dial indicator. The maximum permissible run-out is .002 in. (.05 mm.) and any greater irregularity must be corrected. If there is excessive run-out, detach the crown wheel and examine the joint faces on the flange of the differential cage and on the crown wheel for any particles of dirt.

When the parts are thoroughly cleaned it is unlikely that the crown wheel will not run true.

Change the position of the crown wheel on the differential cage to correct any misalignment.

Tighten the bolts to the correct torque wrench reading and knock over the locking washers.

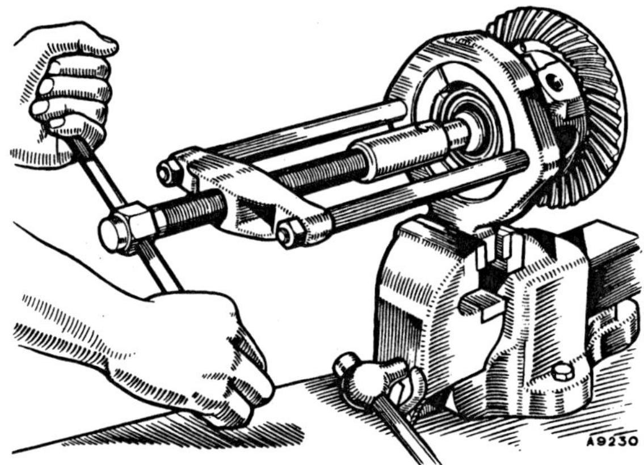
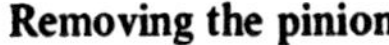

Fig. H.2
Use 18G 47 C, adaptor 18G 47 AK, and adaptor plug 18G 47 AR to remove the differential bearings

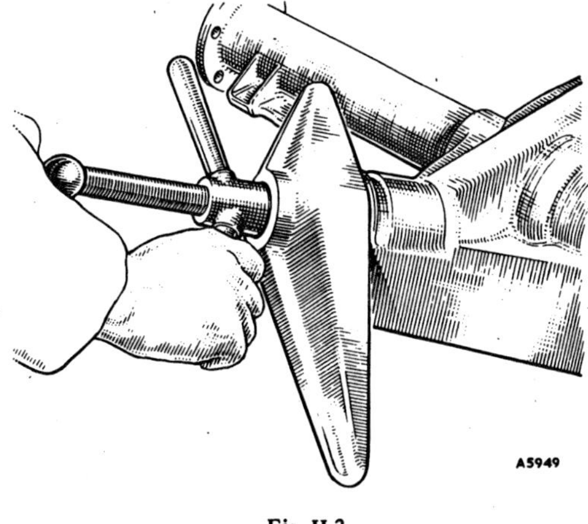

Fig. H.3
Use 18G 264 and adaptors 18G 264 AA, and 18G 264 AD, or 18G 264 AB to remove front and rear bevel pinion outer races

Removing the pinion
Before removing the pinion measure the preload: if this is zero, fit new pinion bearings.
Hold the flange with wrench 18G 34 A and remove the nut and washer.
Withdraw the flange by tapping it with a hide hammer.
Remove the bevel pinion. To prevent damaging the outer bearing the pinion must be pressed and not driven out.

Dismantling
To remove the bevel pinion front and rear outer races from within the gear carrier casing use Service tool 18G 264, with adaptors 18G 264 AA and 18G 264 AD for the front race, and adaptors 18G 264 AA and 18G 264 AB for the rear race. As the front outer race is withdrawn it will carry the pinion oil seal with it.
Use Service tool 18G 47 C and adaptor 18G 47 AS to remove the rear bearing inner race from the bevel pinion.

Reassembling
Refit the pinion front inner race using Service tool 18G 47 C with adaptor 18G 47 AS. With the same tool assemble the rear bearing inner race to the bevel pinion, ensuring that the pressure is exerted on the inner race only.

Refitting the differential and pinion using original parts
Where it is only necessary to fit a new oil seal the differential can be refitted in the reverse order, assuming that the original shim thicknesses are retained, but ensure that the pinion preload figure noted before removing the pinion is achieved when tightening the flange nut.
If any new parts are fitted, i.e. crown wheel and pinion, pinion bearings, etc. the setting of the pinion (its position relative to the crown wheel) must be checked.
Examine the crown wheel teeth. If a new crown wheel is needed, a mated pair–crown wheel and pinion–must be fitted.
Fitting a new crown wheel and pinion involves four distinct operations.

1. Setting the pinion position.
2. Setting the pinion bearing preload.
3. Setting the crown wheel.
4. Setting the backlash.

Refitting

1. SETTING THE PINION POSITION

Fit the bearing outer races to the axle casing using tool 18G 264 and 18G 264 AA with adaptors 18G 264 AD or 18G 264 AB.

The variation in the pinion head thickness is etched on the pinion head and is to be ignored for this setting.

Using the dummy pinion 18G 191 H, fit the inner race of the bearing to the pinion in the gear carrier without the

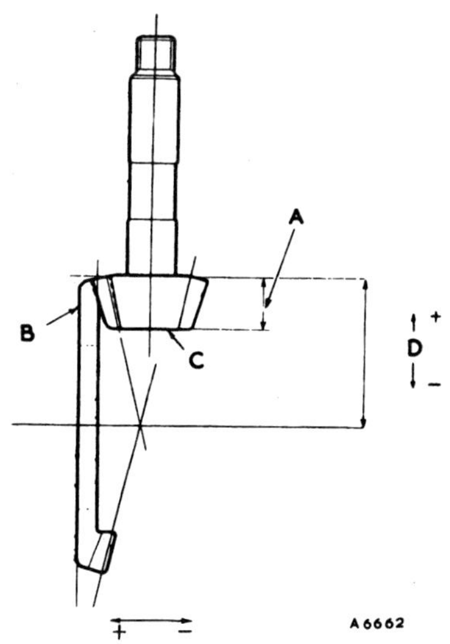

Fig. H.4
Crown wheel and pinion markings

A. Pinion head thickness. Max. –.007 in. (–.178 mm.).
B. Crown wheel marked here.
C. Pinion marked here.
D. Pinion mounting distance. Max. ±.004 in. (±.102 mm.).

collapsible spacer and oil seal. Fit the inner race of the front bearing.

NOTE.–The standard pinion head spacer (0.208 in. (5.3 mm.)) is incorporated in the dummy pinion.

Refit the universal joint driving flange and tighten the nut gradually until a bearing preload figure of 10 to 20 lb. in. (.11 to .2 kg. m.) is obtained.

Clean the dummy pinion head and remove the keep disc from the base of the magnet. Position the dial indicator foot on the pinion head and adjust the dial indicator to zero (see Fig. H.6).

Move the indicator arm until the foot of the gauge rests on the centre of the differential bore at one side and tighten the knurled locking screws. Obtain the maximum depth reading and note any variation from the zero setting. Repeat this check on the opposite bearing bore. Add the two variations together and divide by two to obtain a mean reading.

The reading shown on the clock will be the amount of correction necessary to the spacer which is 0.208 in. (5.3 mm.) thick.

(a) If the clock reading is **negative** (–) reduce the spacer thickness by this amount.

(b) If the clock reading is **positive** (+) increase the spacer thickness by this amount.

Allowance must finally be made for the mounting distance marked on the pinion head in a rectangular bracket. Proceed as follows:
If the marking is **positive** (+) reduce the washer thickness by an equal amount.
If the marking is **negative** (–) increase the washer thickness by an equal amount.

A tolerance of .001 in. is allowed in the thickness of the washer finally fitted.

Remove the dummy pinion.

Available washers for pinion position
Eight washers are available in .002 in. (.051 mm.) steps from 0.208 in. (5.3 mm.) to .222 in. (5.64 mm.).

2. PINION BEARING PRELOAD

A washer of the thickness indicated by the use of the tools and by the calculations should be fitted under the pinion head. Fit the pinion inner bearing race. Using 18G 47 C, and adaptor 18G 47 AS. Insert the pinion into the case and fit the collapsible spacer with the small diameter towards the shoulder of the pinion head.

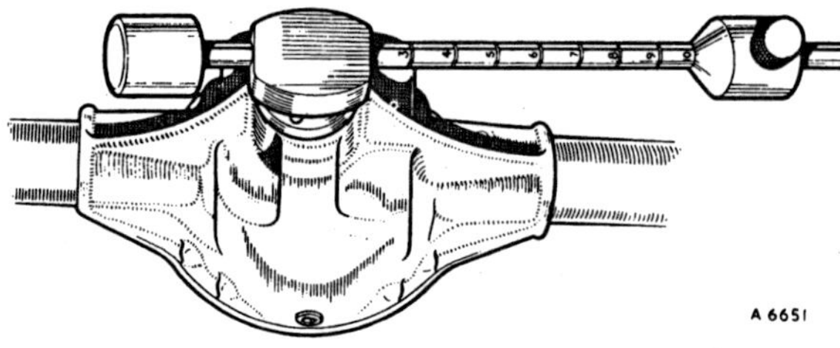

Fig. H.5
Checking the bevel pinion bearing preload (18G 207)

Support the head of the pinion and press the outer bearing onto the pinion; **do not compress the spacer.** Grease the periphery and sealing lip of the seal and fit the seal flush with the axle casing. Fit the universal joint flange, washer and nut.

Tighten the flange nut to 140 lb. ft. (20.7 kg. m.) using 18G 592 and flange wrench 18G 34 A, progressively increase the torque load by 10 lb. ft. (1 kg. m.) until the spacer starts to collapse. Rotate the pinion to settle the bearings and using 18G 207 B check the pinion pre-load. **BEARING PRELOAD IS RAPID. IF THE TORQUE OF 24 LB. IN. (0.3 KG. M.) IS EXCEEDED THE PINION MUST BE DISMANTLED AND A NEW COLLAPSIBLE SPACER FITTED.** In practice the pinion nut will require tightening **A VERY SMALL AMOUNT BETWEEN EACH PINION TORQUE CHECK.** When the nut is correctly tightened it should provide a pre-load of 14 to 18 lb. in. (0.10 to 0.16 kg. m.).

3. SETTING THE CROWN WHEEL POSITION

Assemble each inner and outer bearing race to the differential assembly.

Using crown wheel setting tools (18G 191, 18G 191 F, and 18G 191 J) place the differential assembly onto the jig and load the crown wheel assembly. Spin the unit to settle the bearings.

The standard measurement of the bearing bores is 7.243 in. (183.98 mm.). Any excess machined from the bores will be marked A and B on the axle casing. The A and B tolerances added to the standard measurement will determine the overall dimension (see **Example A**).

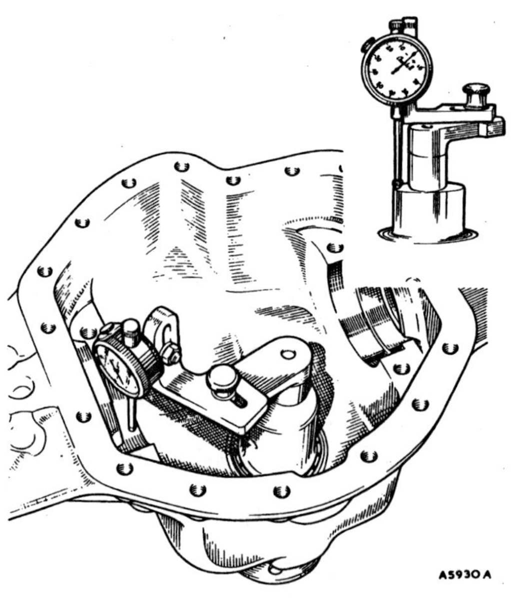

Fig. H.6
Taking a reading of the bearing bore and (inset) the dial gauge set at zero on the dummy pinion

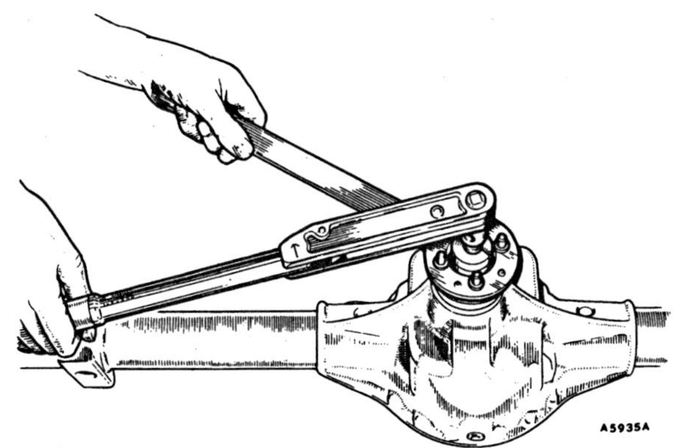

Fig. H.7
Use flange wrench 18G 34 A to hold the flange against rotation when tightening the pinion nut with torque wrench 18G 592

Clean the head of the jig pillar (18G 191 J) and remove the keep disc from the base of the magnet. Position the magnet on the pillar head and adjust the dial gauge to zero when the dial gauge foot is positioned on the pillar head (see Fig. H.9).

NOTE.–The pillar is the standard height of the differential assembly of 6.972 in. (177.10 mm.).

Spin the differential to settle the bearings, move the arm of the dial indicator to the machined face of the jig (see Fig. H.9), and take a reading. Add the variation to the standard height to obtain the total width of the differential assembly (see **Example B**).

Subtract the total width of the differential assembly, and the total distance collar thickness will be found. To this figure a further .004 in. (.102 mm.) must be added to give bearing 'pinch' (see **Example C**). Divide this total by two to obtain the distance collars of equal thickness (see **Example D**).

Example A

Differential case standard ..	7.243 in. (183.98 mm.)
Stamped on case 'A'	.001 in. (.025 mm.)
Stamped on case 'B'	.002 in. (.038 mm.)
Total distance between bores ..	7.246 in. (184.05 mm.)

Example B

Differential assembly standard	6.972 in. (177.10 mm.)
Clock reading (positive) ..	.008 in. (.203 mm.)
Total differential assembly ..	6.980 in. (177.30 mm.)

Example C

Total distance between bores ..	7.246 in. (184.05 mm.)
Minus total differential assembly	6.980 in. (177.30 mm.)
	.266 in. (6.75 mm.)
Plus bearing pre-load	.004 in. (.102 mm.)
	.270 in. (6.86 mm.)

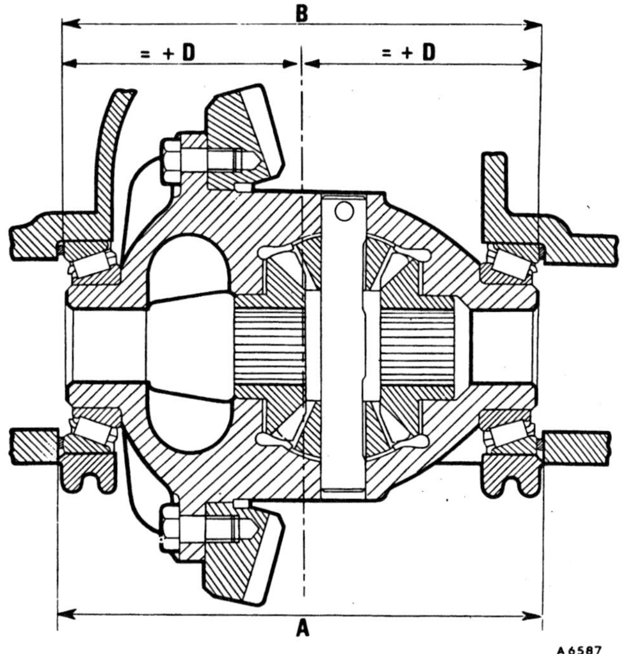

Fig. H.8
Illustrates the points from which the calculations must be made to determine the spacer thickness for the bearings on each side of the carrier

Example D

Spacers each side	.270 in.÷2 (6.86 mm.÷2)	.135 in. (3.43 mm.)

Available spacers for differential assembly

Eighteen spacers are available in .002 in. (.051 mm.) steps from 0.115 in. (2.92 mm.) to .149 in. (3.77 mm.).

Refitting

The correct figure for the backlash to be used with any particular crown wheel and pinion is etched on the rear face of the crown wheel concerned. Increase the spacer thickness on the opposite side of the crown wheel by this amount and decrease the spacer thickness on the crown wheel side by the same amount (see **Example E**).

Example E

Backlash .008

Spacer calculated	.135 in. (3.43 mm.)
Minus backlash	.008 in. (.203 mm.)
Crown wheel side spacer	.127 in. (3.23 mm.)
Spacer calculated	.135 in. (3.43 mm.)
Plus backlash	.008 in. (.203 mm.)
Opposite crown wheel side spacer ..	.143 in. (3.62 mm.)

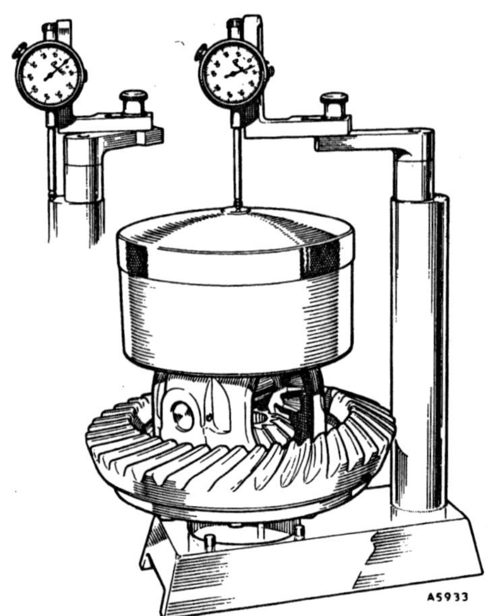

Fig. H.9
Taking a reading on the differential assembly and (inset) the dial gauge set at zero on the jig pillar

Fig. H.10
Checking crown wheel backlash

4. ADJUSTING THE BACKLASH

Fit the differential to the gear carrier. Replace the bearing caps and tighten the bolts to the correct torque wrench reading as given in 'TORQUE WRENCH SETTINGS'. Bolt the special tool surface plate to the gear carrier flange and mount the clock gauge in such a way that an accurate backlash figure may be obtained (see Fig. H.10).
A movement of .002 in. (.051 mm.) shim thickness from one side of the differential cage to the other will produce a variation in backlash of approximately .002 in. (.051 mm.).
Ensure absolute cleanliness during the above operations, as any discrepancies resulting from dirty assembly would affect the setting of the crown wheel or pinion.
Continue refitting by reversing the removing procedure.
Finally, bend back the locating tabs around the bolt heads.
NOTE.—Ensure that the axle case jointing washer is coated with Hylomar Jointing Compound to obtain a perfect oil seal.

Section H.6

REAR ROAD SPRINGS

To remove a rear spring

1. Remove the road wheel adjacent to the spring to be removed.
2. Raise and support the body and support the axle with a hydraulic jack to enable the axle to be lowered to relieve the tension in the spring.
3. Disconnect the shock absorber link from its bracket and the rebound strap from the rebound spindle.
4. Remove the nuts and spring washers from the eyebolt and shackle plate pins and take off the outer shackle plate.
5. Using a suitable drift, tap each shackle plate pin alternately until the plate and pins are free of the spring and the mounting bracket.
6. Withdraw the eyebolt from the front of the spring.
7. From the two 'U' clips remove the locknuts and nuts. Retain the shock absorber bracket, locating plate, and pad which will fall from the under side of the spring.
8. Remove the spring and retain the upper locating plate, pad, pedestal, and 'U' clips.

To refit a rear spring

1. Offer the front of the spring to its bracket, and locate it with the front eyebolt.
2. Fit the shackle plate and pins to the rear eye and the body bracket.
3. Fit the upper locating plate and pad to the spring and locate the hole in the axle spring seat over the head of the centre-bolt.
4. Place the pedestal over the axle, fit the lower pad, locating plate, and shock absorber bracket, and pass the 'U' clips over the axle and through the locating plates. Secure the 'U' clips with the nuts and locknuts.
5. Refit the road wheel, remove the axle and body supports, and refit the washers and nuts to the front eyebolt and the shackle plate, nuts, and washers to the rear shackle plate pins.
6. Refit the shock absorber link and rebound strap.

Section H.7

DISMANTLING AND ASSEMBLING A REAR SPRING

Dismantling

1. Remove the rear spring as detailed in Section H.6.
2. Straighten the ends of the clips on the third and fourth spring leaves.
3. Support the spring in a vice with the top and bottom leaves against the vice jaws and the centre-bolt just clear of the jaws.
4. Remove the locknut and nut from the centre-bolt and withdraw the centre-bolt and distance piece from the spring.
5. Slowly open the vice to relieve the tension in the spring leaves and remove the leaves from the vice.
6. Remove the two rubber bushes from the rear eye of the main leaf and then press out the Silentbloc bush from the front eye.
7. Remove and discard the spring clip rivets and clips.

Clean and examine each leaf for signs of cracks or fractures, particularly around the centre-bolt holes.

Before assembly, cover each leaf with Shell Ensis 260 Fluid.

Assembling

1. Press a new Silentbloc bush into the main leaf front eye and ensure that the outer bush is perfectly central in the eye.
2. Rivet new spring clips to the third and fourth leaves.
3. Use a tapered mandrel having the same maximum diameter as the centre-bolt to align the holes in the spring leaves and assemble the leaves. The longest half of the spring faces the rear of the car.
4. Keep the leaves aligned and slowly compress them in a vice.
5. Remove the mandrel and assemble the distance piece and centre-bolt. Secure the centre-bolt with its nut and locknut.
6. Align the side of the spring and bend the spring clips over the main leaf.

After assembly, refit the spring to the car as detailed in Section H.6.

THE REAR SUSPENSION COMPONENTS

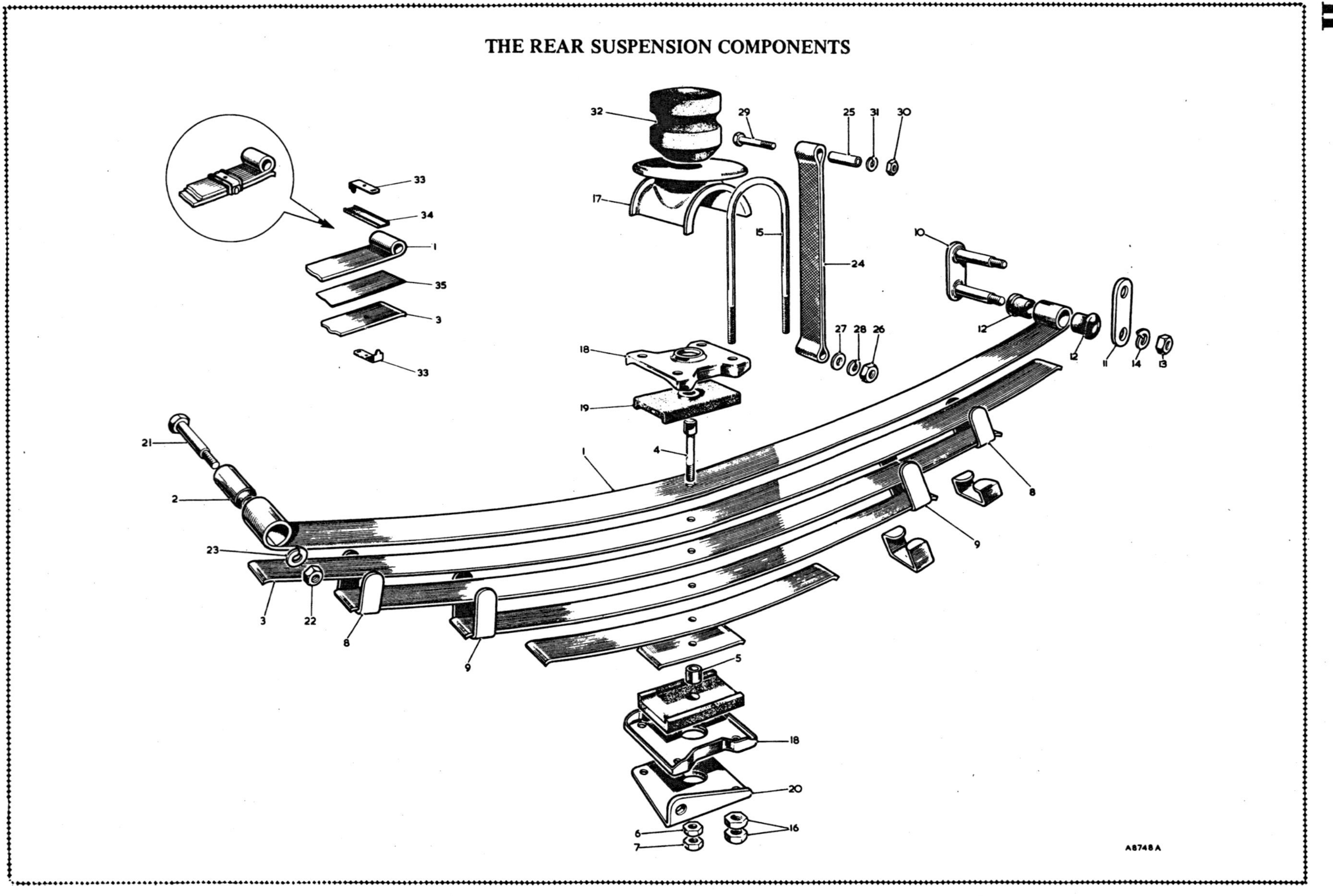

KEY TO THE REAR SUSPENSION COMPONENTS

No.	Description	No.	Description	No.	Description
1.	Leaf assembly–main.	13.	Nut–shackle plate pin.	25.	Distance tube–rebound strap.
2.	Bush.	14.	Washer–spring–nut.	26.	Nut–rebound strap to axle.
3.	Leaf–second.	15.	Clip–'U'–rear spring.	27.	Washer–plain–nut.
4.	Bolt–locating.	16.	Nut–'U' clip.	28.	Washer–spring–nut.
5.	Distance piece.	17.	Pedestal–bump rubber.	29.	Bolt–strap to bracket.
6.	Nut–bolt.	18.	Plate–spring locating.	30.	Nut–bolt.
7.	Locknut–bolt.	19.	Pad–spring seating.	31.	Washer–spring–nut.
8.	Clip–third leaf.	20.	Bracket–shock absorber to rear spring–R.H.	32.	Bump–rubber.
9.	Clip–fourth leaf.	21.	Bolt–spring–front end.	33.	Clip–second leaf } later type only.
10.	Plate–shackle and pins.	22.	Nut–bolt.	34.	Pad–second leaf clip } later type only.
11.	Plate–shackle.	23.	Washer–spring–nut.	35.	Strip–interleaf, 1 2, 2 3, 3 4 } later type only.
12.	Bush–shackle plate (rubber).	24.	Strap–rebound.		

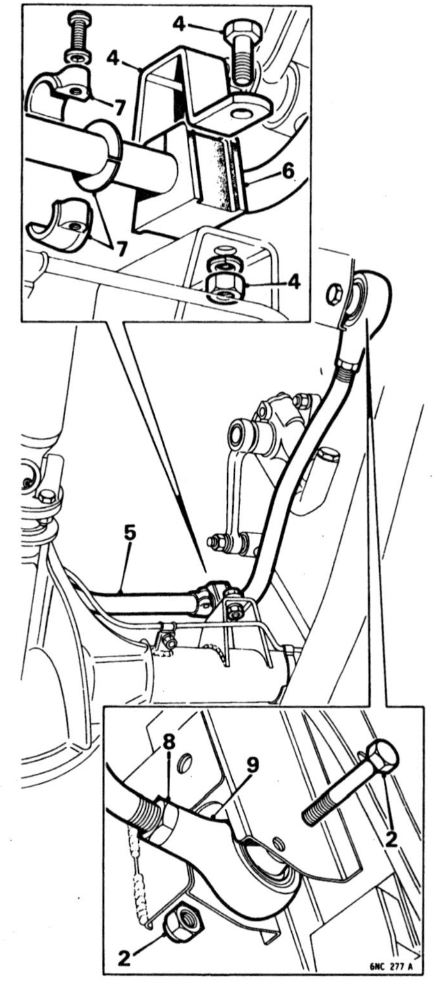

Rear anti-roll bar components
(GHN5 and GHD5 cars from Car No. 410002)

1. Anti-roll assembly
2. Screw
3. Bearing strap
4. Plastic washer
5. Locator
6. Screw
7. Spring washer
8. Nut
9. Spring washer
10. Bearing rubber
11. Bolt
12. End fitting
13. Nut
14. Locknut

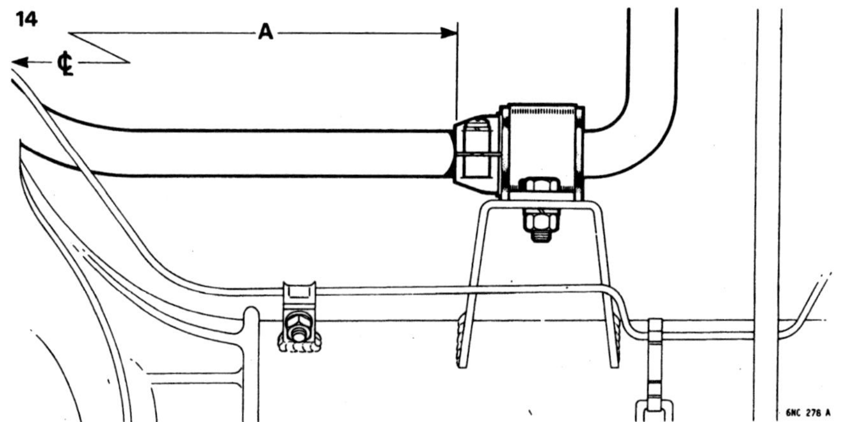

Rear anti-roll bar locator dimension
(GHN5 and GHD5 cars from Car No. 410002)

A = 11 in (279 mm) from locator inner face to centre line of car

SECTION J

THE STEERING GEAR

GENERAL DESCRIPTION

The steering gear is of the direct-acting rack-and-pinion type, providing light and accurate control under all conditions.

It consists of a rack bar and toothed pinion mounted on the front suspension cross-member.

No adjustment for bearing wear in the box is provided, except by fitting of the necessary new parts.

The steering inner column is attached to the pinion by a universal coupling.

CAUTION.—If the vehicle is hoisted with its front wheels clear of the ground care should be taken to avoid forceful movement of the wheels from lock to lock, as damage may occur within the steering mechanism.

Section J.1

FRONT WHEEL ALIGNMENT

The wheels should toe in $\frac{1}{16}$ to $\frac{3}{32}$ in. (1.6 to 2.4 mm.).

See that the tyres are inflated to the correct pressures. Set the wheels in the straight-ahead position.

Set the arms of a suitable trammel to the height of the hub centre on the outside of the wheels.

Place the trammel to the rear of the wheels and adjust the pointers to register with the wheel rims. Chalk the position of the pointers in each wheel rim and push the car forward one half-turn of the wheels. Take the front reading from the same marks on the rims.

If adjustment is necessary, proceed as follows.

Slacken the locknuts at the ends of the short tie-rods and the clips securing the rubber gaiters to the tie-rods.

Use a wrench to rotate each of the tie-rods **equally** in the desired direction. These both have right-hand threads.

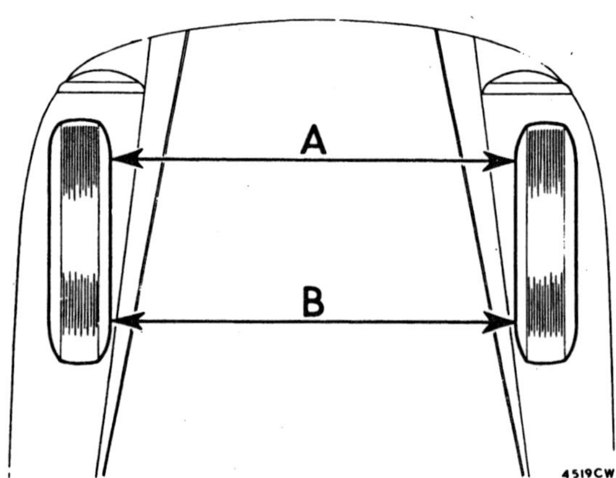

Fig. J.1
The front wheel alignment check must be taken with the front wheels in the straight-ahead position. Dimension (B) is $\frac{1}{16}$ to $\frac{3}{32}$ in. (1.6 to 2.4 mm.) greater than (A)

NOTE.—To ensure that the steering gearbox is in the central position and that the steering geometry is correct, it is important that the tie-rods are adjusted to exactly equal lengths. This can be ascertained by measuring the amount of thread visible behind each locknut, which should be equal.

After adjustment re-tighten the ball joint locknuts and rubber gaiter clips and ensure that the machined under sides of the ball joints are in the same plane.

Section J.2

STEERING-WHEEL

1. Remove the steering-wheel motif and horn-push assembly; it is a press-fit. Remove the horn contact plunger.
2. Turn back the lock ring tabs and remove the bolts, lock ring, and steering-wheel.

HUB

3. Slacken the steering-wheel nut and fit Service tool 18G 1181 to the hub using two $\frac{5}{16}$ U.N.F., $\frac{7}{8}$ in. threaded, $\frac{7}{8}$ in. plain shank bolts. Mark the hub and column to assist correct re-alignment and pull the hub until it is a loose fit on the steering-column. Remove 18G 1181, the steering-wheel nut and hub.
4. When refitting the hub, position it on the column splines in the original position. Fit the nut and tighten to the torque wrench setting given in **'TORQUE WRENCH SETTINGS'**.

Section J.3

STEERING-COLUMN UNIVERSAL JOINT

Removing

Bolts and nuts clamp the universal joint splines on the steering inner column and steering pinion, and the bolts must be withdrawn completely to release the universal joint assembly.

Unscrew the three bolts securing the steering-column to the toe plate.

Slacken the bolts supporting the steering-column below the dash panel.

Withdraw the clamping bolts from the universal joint.

Move the steering-column assembly upwards to withdraw the steering inner column from the universal joint.

Withdraw the universal joint from the steering pinion.

Dismantling and reassembling

The Hardy Spicer joint has four needle-roller bearings retained on a centre spider by circlips. The joints are packed with grease on assembly and there is no further provision for lubrication.

Remove any enamel and dirt from the circlips and bearing races. Remove the circlips by pinching the ears together and prising them out with a screwdriver.
If a ring does not slide readily from its groove, tap the end of the bearing race lightly to relieve the pressure against the bearing.
Hold the joint in one hand with the side of a yoke at the top and tap the radius of the yoke lightly with a copper hammer. The bearing should begin to emerge; turn the joint over and remove the bearing and needle rollers with the fingers. If necessary, tap the bearing race from the inside with a small-diameter bar, taking care not to damage the bearing face, or grip the needle bearing race in a vice and tap the yoke clear.
Repeat this operation for the opposite bearing.
One yoke can now be removed. Rest the two exposed trunnions on wood or lead blocks to protect their ground faces, and tap the top lug of the flange yoke to remove the bearing race.
Turn the yoke over and repeat the operation.
When reassembling, replace the cork gaskets and gasket retainers on the spider journals, using a tubular drift. The spider journal shoulders should be shellacked prior to fitting the retainers to ensure a good oil seal.
Smear the walls of the races with grease and assemble the needle rollers to the bearing races and pack with grease.
Insert the spider in one yoke and, using a soft-nosed drift slightly smaller in diameter than the hole in the yoke, tap the bearings into position. It is essential that the bearing races are a light drive fit in the yoke trunnions.
Repeat this operation for the other bearings and replace the circlips, making sure that they are firmly located in their grooves. If the joint appears to bind, tap lightly with a wooden mallet to relieve any pressure by the bearings on the ends of the journals.

Section J.4

RACK ASSEMBLY

Removing
Raise and support the front of the car and remove both front road wheels.
Remove the tie-rod ball pin locknuts.
Using tool 18G 1063, detach the tie-rod ball pins from the steering arms.

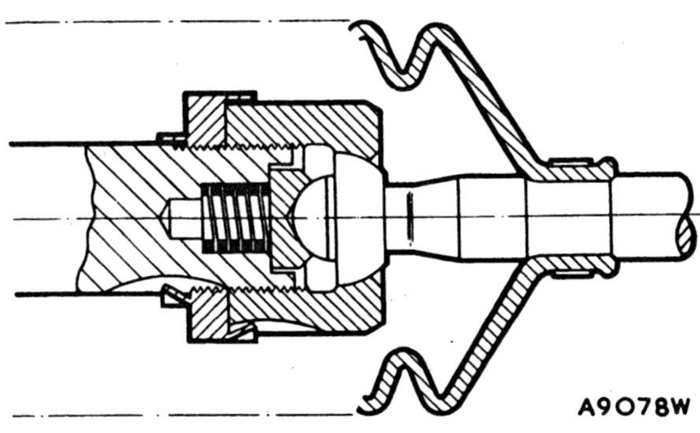

Fig. J.2
The assembly of a tie-rod ball joint

Turn the steering onto the right lock and remove the universal joint lower pinch-bolt.
Remove the nuts and bolts securing the rack assembly to the front cross-member, noting that the front bolts are fitted with self-locking nuts.
Withdraw the rack assembly downwards from the car.

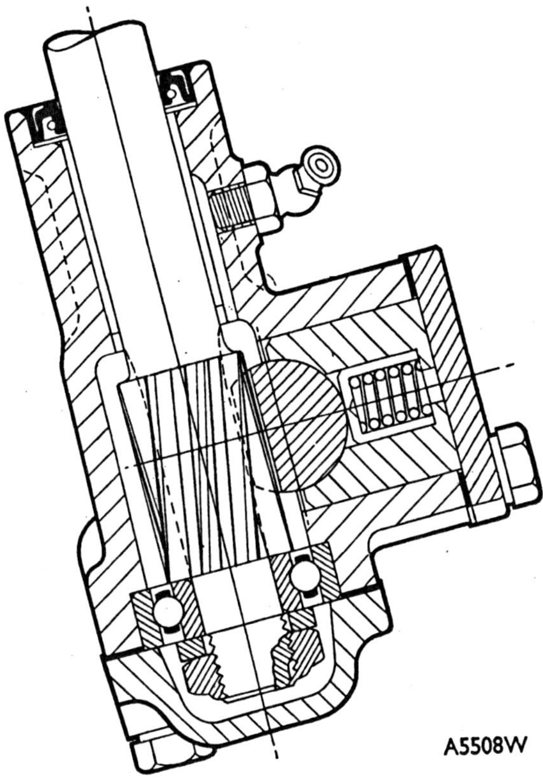

Fig. J.3
A section through the rack and pinion housing, showing the damper and seals

Dismantling
Hold the rack housing between suitable clamps in a vice.
Remove the pinion end cover and joint washer, placing a container to catch the oil that may drain from the housing.
Remove the damper cover and shims, exposing the yoke, damper pad, and spring. After removal of these the pinion, complete with ball race and locknut may be withdrawn.
Unlock the tie-rod ball end locknuts and disconnect the ball end assemblies. Release the rubber gaiter seal clips and withdraw the seals.
Prise up the indentations in the locking rings clear of the slots in the rack and ball housing. Slacken back the locking ring and unscrew the housing to release the tie-rod, ball seat, and seat tension spring.
Withdraw the rack from the pinion end of the housing; if removed from the other end the teeth may damage the rack housing bush.
To remove the rack housing bush unscrew the self-tapping screw retaining it and carefully drive the bush out.

Examining for wear
Thoroughly clean and examine all parts of the assembly; components showing signs of wear must be replaced with

new parts. Fractures, hollows, or roughness in the surfaces of the rack or pinion teeth will render them unserviceable. Take particular note of the rubber gaiters; should they be damaged or show the slightest sign of deterioration, they must be replaced with new ones. The tie-rod ball housing and ball seat should also be subjected to a careful check and new parts fitted if excessive wear is evident.

The outer ball socket assembly cannot be dismantled, and must therefore be renewed complete if it is worn or damaged.

Examine the bush fitted in the end of the rack housing and fit a new one if it shows signs of damage or wear.

Reassembling

Insert the rack housing bush and carefully drive or press it in until the bush is flush with the housing end. Enter a $\frac{7}{64}$ in. (2.78 mm.) diameter drill through the retaining screw hole and drill the outer shell of the bush to receive the retaining screw. A depth of .24 in. (6.3 mm.) will achieve this.

NOTE.—Bushes of sintered iron with an outer shell of pressed steel and rubber injected between the two have superseded the lead-bronze type in earlier use.

Smear the head of the screw with jointing compound before tightening so as to ensure an oil-tight joint.

Replace the rack from the pinion end. Refit the seat spring, seat, tie-rod, and ball housings, smearing the ball seats liberally with S.A.E. 90 oil. Tighten the ball housings until the tie-rod is held firm and without free play. When correctly adjusted a torque of 32 to 52 lb. in. (.359 to .594 kg. m.) must be required on the rod to produce articulation. Relock the housing by tightening up the locking ring to a torque of 33 to 37 lb. ft. (4.60 to 5.63 kg. m.) and secure in the locked position by punching the lips of the locking ring into the slots in the ball housing and rack. It is recommended that new locking rings are fitted whenever these have been disturbed.

Insert the pinion complete with ball race and locking nut into its housing. Replace the pinion end cover and seal, using a sealing compound to make an oil-tight joint. The outer edge of the ball race locknut must be peened into the slot in the pinion shaft if removed and refitted.

To adjust the rack damper replace the plunger in the housing and tighten the cover down without the spring or shims until it is just possible to rotate the pinion shaft by drawing the rack through its housing. With a feeler gauge measure the clearance between the cover and its seating on the rack housing. To this dimension must be added an additional clearance of .0005 to .003 in. (.013 to .076 mm.) to arrive at the correct thickness of shims which must be placed beneath the damper cover-plate.

Remove the damper cover-plate and plunger and replace the assembly, using a sealing compound to make an oil-tight joint.

Refit the rubber gaiters to the housing and the tie-rods. Before securing the gaiter clip on the tie-rod at the pinion end, stand the assembly upright, and pour in $\frac{1}{3}$ pint (.4 U.S. pint, .2 litre) of Extreme Pressure S.A.E. 90 oil through the end of the gaiter, or pump the oil into the rack housing through the nipple provided.

Refit and tighten the gaiter clip.

Refit the ball ends and locknuts.

Refitting

NOTE.—If a new rack assembly is being fitted it must be aligned as described in Section J.8.

Reverse the removing procedure, ensuring that when entering the pinion shaft into the unversal joint both the steering-column and rack are in the straight-ahead position.

Section J.5

NYLON-SEATED BALL JOINTS

Nylon-seated ball joints, which are sealed in manufacture and require no lubrication, are fitted at the steering-arm tie-rod ball joints.

It is essential that no dirt or abrasive matter should enter the nylon ball joint; in the event of a rubber boot being torn or damaged in service it is probable that the ball joint has been left exposed, and it is therefore important to renew both the ball joint and the boot.

If damage to the boot occurs whilst the steering side- or cross-rod is being removed in the workshop, only a new rubber boot need be fitted, provided the ball joints is clean. Smear the area adjacent to the joint with a little Dextragrease Super G.P. prior to assembling the boot.

Section J.6

STEERING LOCK AND IGNITION STARTER SWITCH

Removing

1. Remove the steering-column—Section J.7.
2. Remove the steering-wheel and hub—Section J.2.
3. Remove the direction indicator/headlight flasher/low-high beam switch—Section N.15.
4. Remove the direction indicator switch trip from the inner steering-column.
5. Slide the top clamp bracket off the steering-column.
6. Turn the ignition key to position '1' to ensure that the steering lock is disengaged.
7. Drill out or remove with a suitable proprietary tool, the retaining shear bolts.
8. Unscrew the steering lock locating grub screw.
9. Remove the steering lock and ignition starter switch.

Refitting

10. Reverse the removing procedure in 1 to 9, using new shear bolts and ensuring that the shear bolts are tightened until the bolt heads shear at the waisted point giving a torque tightness of 12 lbf. ft. (1.66 kgf. m.).

Section J.7

STEERING-COLUMN

Removing

1. Disconnect the battery.
2. Remove the carburetter air cleaner.

3. Remove the upper pinch-bolt from the steering-column universal joint.
4. Remove lower panel from under the left-hand side of the fascia panel.
5. Disconnect the steering-column switch wiring at the snap connectors below the fascia.
6. Unscrew the three bolts securing the steering-column to the toe-plate.
7. Note the location, quantity, and thickness of the packing washers between the column upper fixing flanges and the body brackets, remove the securing bolts and collect the packing washers. **If the packing washers are mislaid or their fitting positions are not recorded, the steering must be aligned as described in Section J.8 when refitted.**
8. Withdraw the steering-column complete with steering-wheel and switches.

Dismantling

9. Withdraw the horn-push and contact from the centre of the steering-wheel; unscrew the steering-wheel lock ring bolts and, using tool 18G 1181, remove the hub, see Section J.2
10. Remove the three left-hand switch cowl retaining screws.
11. Unscrew the retaining screws and remove the left-hand switch cowl.
12. Remove the screw retaining the right-hand switch cowl.
13. Unscrew the two screws securing the combined overdrive and windshield wiper/washer switch and remove the switch complete with wiring.
14. Unscrew the two screws securing the combined headlamp flasher and direction indicator switch, and remove the switch complete with wiring.
15. Unscrew the four ignition switch retaining screws and remove the switch complete with wiring.

Reassembling

16. Reverse the dismantling procedure in 9 to 15.

Refitting

NOTE.—If a new steering-column is being fitted it must be aligned as described in Section J.8

17. Fit the column assembly into the car and enter the inner column into the universal joint.
18. Fit the packing washers in their original positions between the column fixing flanges and the body brackets; fit the three securing bolts, tightening them by hand until the packing washers are just pinched.
19. Fit and tighten the three column to toe-plate fixing bolts.
20. Tighten the three upper fixing bolts to the torque figure given in 'TORQUE WRENCH SETTINGS'.
21. Fit and tighten the universal joint pinch-bolt to the torque figure given in 'TORQUE WRENCH SETTINGS'.

Section J.8

ALIGNMENT

1. Fit the toe-plate seal to the steering-column and position the column in the car.
2. Fit one packing washer between each of the two top column fixing flanges and the body brackets.
3. Screw in the two top fixing bolts by hand until the packing washers are just pinched.
4. Check that the column is free to move forwards, backwards and sideways.
5. Screw in the three toe-plate fixing bolts, tightening them by hand only.
6. Check that the lower end of the column is free to move and position it centrally in the aperture.
7. Fit one of the two larger point gauges of tool 18G 1140 on the lower end of the column, positioning it so that the retaining screw tightens onto the flat machined in the splines.
8. Fit the remaining large points gauge of 18G 1140 to the pinion shaft so that the retaining screw tightens onto the radial groove machined in the splines.
9. Fit the rack assembly and tighten the rack fixing bolts.
10. Slacken the screw on the column point gauge and slide the gauge down until the points of both gauges are on the same plane but not overlapping.
11. The steering-column and rack assembly are correctly aligned when the gauges meet exactly at their points (see Fig. J.4).
12. Correct any horizontal misalignment by moving the end of the steering-column.
13. If any vertical misalignment exists between the gauge points, proceed as follows:
    a. Remove the rack fixing bolts.
    b. Add sufficient shims (shim thickness .020 in. (.508 mm.)) to correct the misalignment, between the left-hand and right-hand mounting brackets and the cross-member mounting bosses. Do not rivet the shims to the bosses at this stage.
    c. Refit and tighten the rack mounting bolts.
    d. Recheck the alignment of the gauge points.
    e. If the alignment is still unsatisfactory, adjust the shim thickness.
    f. When correct alignment of the gauge points has been achieved, rivet the shims to the mounting bosses through the holes provided.
14. Remove the rack assembly.
15. Remove the gauges from the pinion and steering-column.
16. Check that the steering-column is in the straight-ahead position, and fit the universal joint on to its splines with the pinch-bolt hole aligned with the machined flat.
17. Check that the rack is in the straight-ahead position.
18. Fit the rack assembly and fully tighten the rack mounting bolts.
19. Tighten the three toe-plate to steering-column securing bolts.

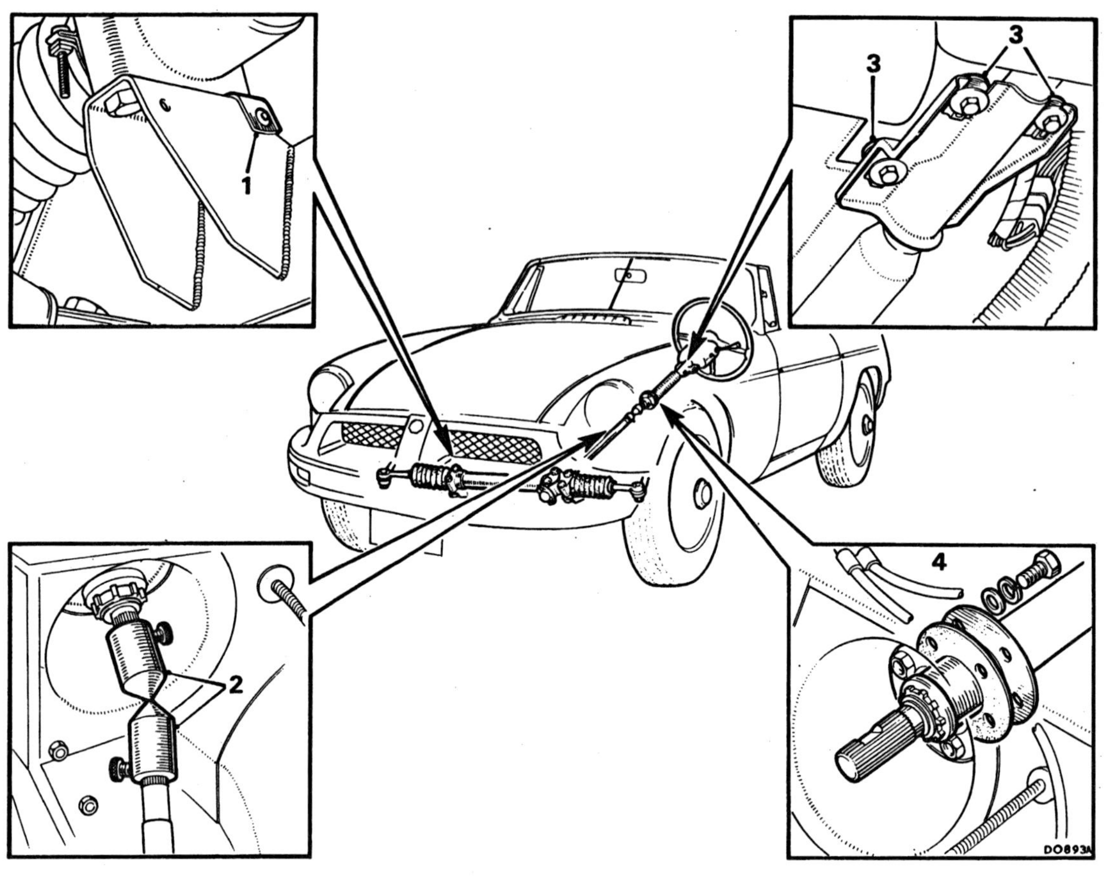

Fig. J.4
Steering alignment

1. Rack shims.
2. Alignment gauge, 18G 1140.
3. Packing washers fitted between column top fixing brackets.
4. Toe-plate fixings.

20. Tighten the two steering-column upper fixing bolts to the torque figure given in **'TORQUE WRENCH SETTINGS'**.
21. Measure the gap between the column upper mounting flange and the body bracket at the third bolt position. Fit packing washers to the thickness of the gap, then fit and tighten the bolt to the torque figure given in **'TORQUE WRENCH SETTINGS'**.
22. Fit the two universal joint pinch-bolts and tighten them to the torque figure given in **'TORQUE WRENCH SETTINGS'**.

SECTION K

THE FRONT SUSPENSION

GENERAL DESCRIPTION

The independent front suspension is of the wishbone and coil type in which the suspension units are mounted one on each end of the cross-member assembly. The cross-member is rubber-mounted and bolted to the body side-members.

This design allows the front suspension to be removed as a complete unit.

The cross-member embodies two mounting brackets for the steering rack, a bracket at each end for the bump rubbers, a towing-eye plate, two front brake hose brackets, and two brake pipe clips.

Each suspension unit comprises a coil spring, a swivel axle unit, a lower wishbone assembly, and an upper assembly formed by the arms of the double-acting dampers mounted on top of the cross-member.

The lower arms are rubber-mounted on a pivot that is bolted to the cross-member; the outer ends of the arms are bolted to the lower end of the swivel pin. The outer ends of the shock absorber arms are secured to the swivel pin upper trunnion link by a fulcrum pin and tapered rubber bushes.

A spring pan secured between the lower wishbone arms supports the coil spring; the upper end of the spring is located by a spigot bolted to the under side of the cross-member.

Both suspension units may be interconnected by a rubber-mounted anti-roll bar.

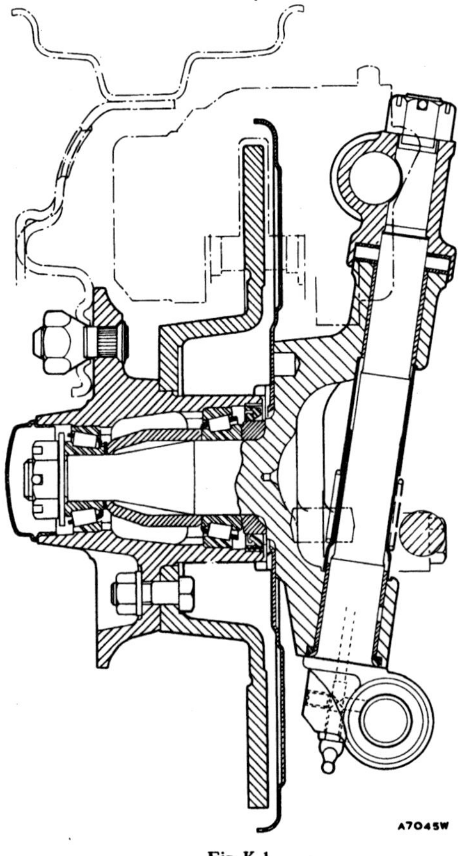

Fig. K.1
Cross-section of a swivel axle and hub

Section K.1

LUBRICATION

Lubrication nipples are provided on the top and bottom swivel pin bushes and in the base of the swivel pin. Each nipple should be charged with grease.

Section K.2

FRONT HUBS

Disc wheels

The front hubs are supported on taper-roller bearings that are mounted on the swivel axles. Four wheel disc studs are pressed into the hub, and the brake disc is secured to the hub by nuts and bolts.

An oil seal is fitted to the inner end of the hub and a spacer and shims are interposed between the inner and outer bearing. The assembly is retained on the swivel axle by a washer, nut, and split pin, and the outer end of the hub is closed by a cap.

Wire wheels

The construction of the wire wheel hubs is similar to that of the disc wheel hubs. Externally the outer end of the hub takes the form of splines, and the grease retainer is fitted inside the hub to close an access hole to the split pin. The outer edge of the hub is threaded externally to permit the fitting of a hub cap.

NOTE.—The right-hand hub is threaded right-hand and the left-hand hub is threaded left-hand.

Removing a hub

To remove a hub apply the hand brake, lift and support the front of the car, and remove the road wheel.

Remove the two studs securing the brake calliper to the swivel axle and support the calliper clear of the hub assembly.

Withdraw the cap and remove the split pin from the stub axle nut. Unscrew the nut.

Using Service tool 18G 363 (wire wheels) or 18G 304 with adaptors 18G 304 B and 18G 304 J (disc wheels), withdraw the hub and disc assembly.

From the hub withdraw the bearing retaining washer, outer bearing, shims, spacer, inner bearing, oil seal collar, and oil seal.

The outer bearing races should be left in the hub unless they are to be renewed.

Inspection of bearings

Wash the bearings in paraffin and thoroughly dry them in an air blast or with a non-fluffy cloth.

Examine the rollers for chips, pitting, or other damage and for security in their cages. Examine also the inner and outer races.

Bearings damaged or suspect must be renewed.

After examination immerse the bearings in mineral oil.

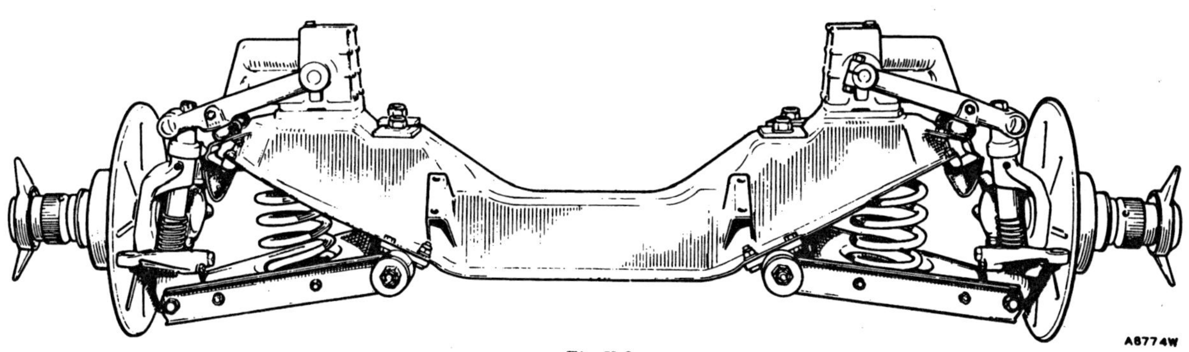

Fig. K.2
The front suspension cross-member and the suspension units

Refitting a hub

If the bearing outer races have been removed refit the new ones by pressing them into the hub.

Fill each bearing with grease ensuring a small protrusion either side of the bearing. Fill the cavity between the bearing and the oil seal and lightly smear the spacer with grease. Do not fill the cavity between the bearings or the cap with grease.

Fit the inner bearing to its race and the collar and seal to the hub, position the spacer and outer bearing, and assemble the hub to the axle.

Adjust the hub bearings as follows to obtain the correct end-float of between .002 and .004 in. (.05 and .10 mm.).

1. Assemble the hub without the shims and mount the assembly on the axle. Fit the retaining washer and nut and tighten the nut until the bearings bind. This will pull the outer races fully against their locating flanges inside the hub.
2. Remove the nut and washer and pull out the roller race of the outer bearing. Insert sufficient shims to produce an excessive end-float and note the thickness of shims used. Refit the bearing, washer, and nut and tighten the nut.
3. Using a clock gauge, measure accurately the end-float in the bearings. Remove the nut, washer, and outer bearing and reduce the number of shims to produce the required end-float.
   The shims are available in thicknesses of .003 in. (.076 mm.), .005 in. (.127 mm.), and .010 in. (.254 mm.).
4. Replace the bearing, washer, and nut and tighten the nut to a torque loading of between 40 and 70 lb. ft. (5.3 and 9.6 kg. m.). Latitude for the torque wrench reading is given so that the nut can be tightened sufficiently to align a slot in the nut with the hole in the axle. Fit a new split pin.
5. Refit the hub caps.

(See Editor's notes at end of Section K.)

Section K.3

COIL SPRINGS

Each coil spring is located between a spring pan bolted to the lower wishbone arms and a spigot bolted to the under side of the cross-member assembly.

To remove a spring fit a spring compressor (Service tool 18G 693) to the lower wishbone arms and take the weight of the spring.

Remove the anti-roll bar link, if fitted, and the bolts securing the spring pan to the wishbone arms.

Unscrew the spring compressor to release the tension in the spring and then remove the spring pan and spring.

Replacement is a reversal of the removal sequence.

Section K.4

SWIVEL AXLES

The swivel axles work on the swivel pins, which are supported at their upper ends by the trunnion links, which are bolted to the shock absorber arms, and at their lower ends by the fulcrum pins, which connect with the lower wishbone arms.

The centre portion of the pins are protected by upper and lower spring-loaded dust shields.

The steering levers and the disc brake dust plates are bolted to the inside of the swivel axles.

Removing and dismantling

To remove the swivel axles jack up and support the car and, dealing with each axle in turn, proceed as follows:

1. Remove the front road wheel.
2. Detach the brake calliper and support it clear of the hub.
3. Remove the hub and brake disc assembly as described in Section K.2.
4. Remove the steering lever bolts and detach the lever and then the disc cover bolts and the cover.
5. Remove the coil spring as described in Section K.3.
6. Extract the split pins from the upper trunnion pin and fulcrum pin and remove the nuts.
7. Unscrew the clamp bolt and centre-bolt of the shock absorber arm, ease the arm outwards, and remove the swivel axle.

THE FRONT SUSPENSION COMPONENTS

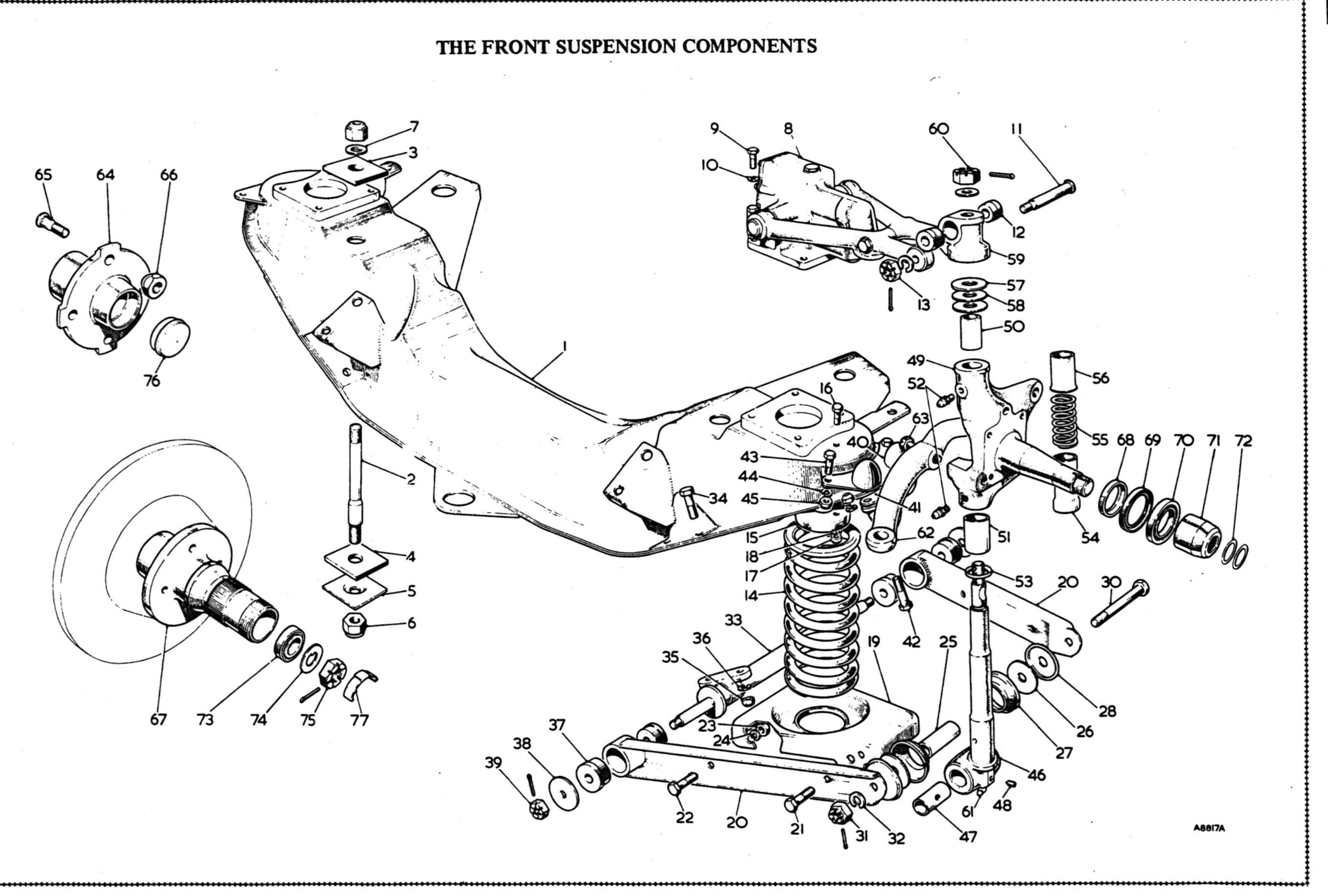

KEY TO THE FRONT SUSPENSION COMPONENTS

No.	Description	No.	Description.	No.	Description
1.	Cross-member.	27.	Seal–link.	53.	Ring–swivel axle pin (cork).
2.	Bolt–cross-member to body.	28.	Support–link seal.	54.	Tube–dust excluder–bottom.
3.	Pad–mounting–upper (rubber).	29.	Nut–wishbone pivot.	55.	Spring–dust excluder.
4.	Pad–mounting–lower (rubber).	30.	Bolt–wishbone to link.	56.	Tube–dust excluder–top.
5.	Plate–clamp.	31.	Nut–bolt.	57.	Washer–thrust.
6.	Nut–mounting bolt.	32.	Washer–spring–nut.	58.	Washer–floating thrust–.052 to .057 in. (1.32 to 1.44 mm.).
7.	Washer–plain–nut.	33.	Pivot–wishbone.	59.	Trunnion–suspension link.
8.	Absorber–shock.	34.	Bolt–pivot to member.	60.	Nut–swivel axle pin.
9.	Screw–shock absorber to cross-member.	35.	Nut–bolt.	61.	Lubricator–swivel pin.
10.	Washer–screw–spring.	36.	Washer–spring–nut.	62.	Lever–steering–R.H.
11.	Pin–fulcrum–top link to shock absorber arm.	37.	Bush–wishbone.	63.	Bolt–steering lever to swivel axle.
12.	Bearing–link.	38.	Washer–wishbone pivot.	64.	Hub assembly.
13.	Nut–fulcrum pin.	39.	Nut–wishbone pivot.	65.	Stud–wheel.
14.	Spring–coil.	40.	Buffer–rebound.	66.	Nut–wheel stud.
15.	Spigot–spring.	41.	Distance piece.	67.	Hub assembly–R.H.
16.	Screw–spigot to cross-member.	42.	Bolt–rebound buffer to cross-member.	68.	Collar–oil seal.
17.	Nut–screw.	43.	Screw–rebound buffer to cross-member.	69.	Seal–oil.
18.	Washer–spring–nut.	44.	Washer–spring.	70.	Bearing for hub–inner.
19.	Pan assembly–spring.	45.	Nut.	71.	Spacer–bearing.
20.	Wishbone assembly–bottom.	46.	Pin–swivel.	72.	Shim–.003 in. (.76 mm.).
21.	Screw–spring pan to wishbone.	47.	Bush–swivel pin.	73.	Bearing–hub–outer.
22.	Screw–spring pan to wishbone.	48.	Screw–grub–swivel pin.	74.	Washer–bearing retaining.
23.	Nut–screw.	49.	Axle assembly–swivel–R.H.	75.	Nut–bearing retaining.
24.	Washer–spring–nut.	50.	Bush–swivel–top.	76.	Cap.
25.	Tube–distance–link.	51.	Bush–swivel–bottom.	77.	Cup–grease-retaining.
26.	Washer–thrust–link.	52.	Lubricator–swivel bush.		

8. Extract the split pin from the swivel axle and remove the nut, upper trunnion suspension link, steel and bronze thrust washers, swivel pin, and dust covers and spring. From the swivel pin remove the cork washer.

Examination

Wash all parts and thoroughly dry them with a non-fluffy cloth. Examine all parts for wear or damage, paying particular attention to the swivel pins, lower fulcrum pins, and all bushes. Check the pins for ovality. Worn or suspect pins or bushes must be renewed.

Assembling and replacing

Reverse the dismantling sequence to reassemble the axles, and, if necessary, renew the thrust washers by selective assembly to produce a condition that will permit the swivel axle to rotate freely on the pin with a minimum amount of end-play. The maximum permissible end-play is .002 in. (.05 mm.).

The thrust washers are available in the following sizes: .052 to .057 in. (1.32 to 1.44 mm.), .058 to .063 in. (1.47 to 1.60 mm.), .064 to .069 in. (1.62 to 1.75 mm.).

After assembly reverse the removal sequence to refit the assembly to the hub.

Section K.5

REMOVING AND REFITTING BUSHES

Swivel pin bush

1. Press out the old bush and ensure that the lubrication channels are clean and free from obstruction.
2. Position the new bush with the split in the bush adjacent to the outer face of the base. This will ensure that the grease channel in the bush is in line with the channel in the pin.
3. Press the bush into the pin squarely and evenly and ream to between .7495 and .7505 in. (19.02 and 19.05 mm.).

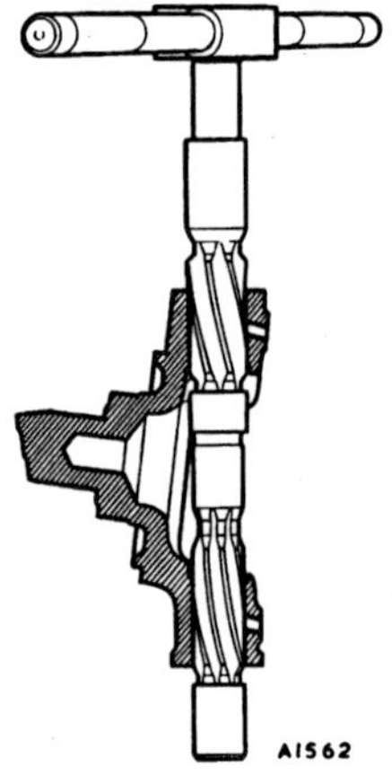

Fig. K.3
Line-reaming a swivel axle

Swivel axle bushes

1. Press out the old bushes from the bottom of the axle.
2. Press in the new upper bushes from the bottom of the axle and ensure that the open end of the oil groove enters the axle first and that the hole in the bush is in line with the lubrication channel in the axle. Press the bush in until its top face is flush with the top face of the axle.
3. Assemble the bottom bush in a similar manner but press it in until the lower face of the bush is flush with the counterbore in the under side of the axle.
4. Line-bore the bushes to the following dimensions:

   Top bush .. .. .7815 to .7820 in. (19.83 to 19.86 mm.).

   Bottom bush .. .9075 to .9080 in. (23.03 to 23.06 mm.).

Section K.6

FRONT SUSPENSION UNIT

Removing

1. Jack up and support the front of the car and remove the road wheels.
2. Disconnect the anti-roll bar links from the spring pans.
3. Remove the steering-rack as described in Section J.5.
4. Drain the hydraulic fluid from the braking system.
5. Disconnect the brake pipes from the flexible hoses and from the clips on the front suspension cross-member.
6. Support the cross-member with a trolley jack positioned under its centre point.
7. Remove the nuts and washers from the tops of the support bolts, lower the cross-member, and remove it from the under side of the car.
8. From the under side of the cross-member remove the bolts, mounting plates, and the upper and lower rubber mounting pads.

Dismantling

1. Remove the coil springs as described in Section K.3, the hubs as described in Section K.2, and the swivel axles as described in Section K.4.
2. Retain the rubber bushes from the upper trunnion link and the distance tube, thrust washers, seals, and supports from the lower end of the swivel pin.
3. Unscrew the shock absorber bolts and remove the shock absorbers.
4. Unscrew the pivot to cross-member securing bolts and remove the pivot and wishbone arms.
5. Unscrew the pivot nuts and from each end of the pivot remove the washer, bush, arm, and inner bush.

6. Remove the two bolts and two screws securing the rebound buffer brackets to the cross-member and remove the brackets.

Examination of components

Thoroughly clean and dry all components and inspect them for cracks, fractures, deterioration, and thread damage. Additionally, carry out the following examinations:

1. Check the hub bearings as described in Section K.2 and the swivel axles and pins as described in Section K.4.
2. Renew rubber bushes or seals that are perished, split, eccentric, or oil-soaked.
3. Examine the holes in the wishbone arms and spring pans for elongation.
4. Examine the coil spring for correct length and weight as given under **'GENERAL SPECIFICATION DATA'**.
5. Check the fulcrum pin distance tubes for scoring or wear. The tubes are 2.337 in. (59.36 mm.) long by .748 in. (19.0 mm.) diameter.
6. Examine the fulcrum pin thrust washers for wear or ridging. The faces should be flat and parallel to within .0005 in. (.01 mm.). The washers are between .065 and .068 in. (1.68 and 1.73 mm.) thick.

Assembling and replacing

Assembly and replacement is a reversal of the dismantling and removal sequence, but attention must be given to the following:

1. The swivel axles must be free to rotate on the pins as described in Section K.4.
2. The fulcrum pin distance tubes, thrust washers, seal supports, and seals should be temporarily assembled and the swivel pin end-float checked. This should be between .008 and .013 in. (.20 and .32 mm.).
3. When assembling the lower wishbone arms the inner pivot must be fully tightened before the coil spring is fitted. This may be done in either the static or rebound position.

EDITOR'S NOTES

K. The Front Suspension

Refitting a hub

A clock gauge is a dial indicator.

THE ANTI-ROLL BAR COMPONENTS

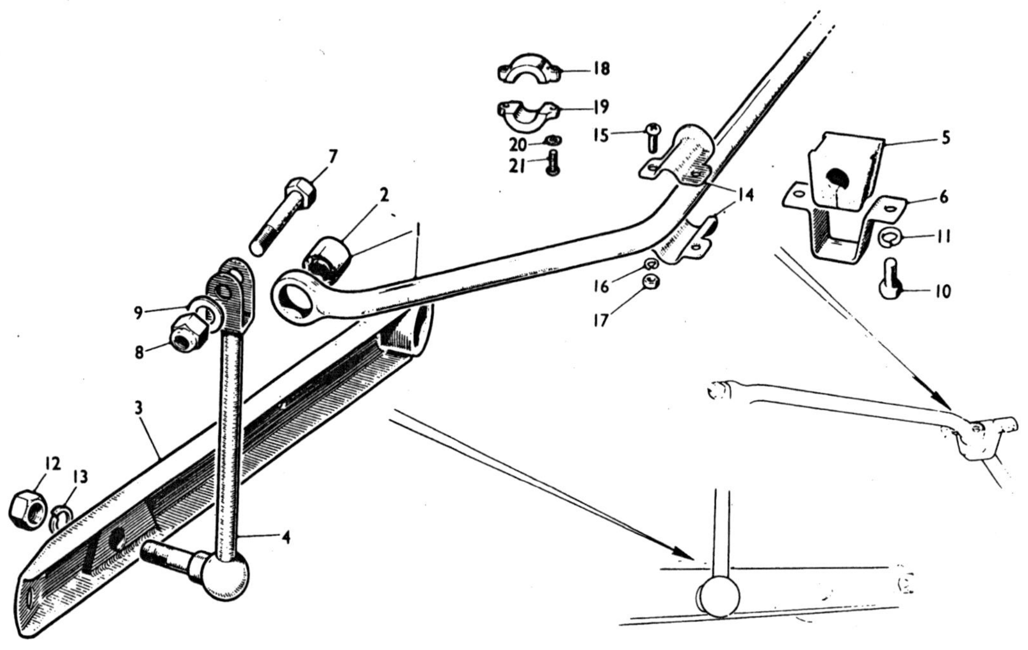

No.	Description
1.	Anti-roll bar assembly.
2.	Bush.
3.	Bottom wishbone assembly–R.H.
4.	Anti-roll bar link–R.H.
5.	Anti-roll bar bearing.
6.	Bearing strap.
7.	Clamping bolt.
8.	Nut.
9.	Plain washer.
10.	Screw.
11.	Spring washer.
12.	Nut.
13.	Spring washer.
14.	Location stop end.
15.	Screw.
16.	Spring washer.
17.	Nut.
18.	Upper locator (if fitted)
19.	Lower locator (if fitted)
20.	Spring washer (if fitted)
21.	Set screws (if fitted)

SECTION M

THE BRAKING SYSTEM

Section M.1

BRAKE PEDAL

Removing

1. Remove the eight screws securing the pedal box cover and remove the cover and seal.
2. Remove the nut securing the brake fluid pipe to the L.H. wing, adjacent to the pedal box.
3. Remove the screw securing the brake fluid pipe clip to the scuttle, adjacent to the L.H. bonnet hinge.
4. Remove the screw securing the brake fluid pipe clip the the L.H. wheel arch below the servo unit.
5. Remove the four nuts and washers securing the servo assembly to the pedal box.
   NOTE: The lower nuts are accessible from the footwell.
6. Detach the return spring from the brake pedal.
7. Remove the split pin and clevis pin securing the brake pedal to the servo push-rod.
8. Remove the brake pedal pivot bolt, nut and washer.
9. Move the servo and master cylinder assembly forward and remove the brake pedal.

Refitting

10. Reverse the procedure in 1 to 9.

Section M.2

HAND BRAKE

The hand brake, which is of the lever type, incorporating a thumb-operated ratchet release in the handle, is located on the right-hand side of the floor tunnel between the seats.
Pulling the handle operates the rear shoes only by means of cable-operated levers. The action of the inner and outer cables is employed through the action of a balance lever mounted on the rear axle to ensure even braking on the rear wheels.
Adjustment of the rear brake-shoes automatically adjusts the hand brake, but excessive movement of the hand brake lever due to cable stretch should be taken up as follows.
Adjust the inner cable length by turning the brass adjusting nut at the lower end of the hand brake lever below the car floor. The adjustment is correct if the hand brake is applied fully when the lever is pulled up three or four notches.
The rear brake-shoes should be adjusted as described in **'MAINTENANCE'** before taking up the hand brake cable stretch.

To remove (lever and cable assembly)

Unscrew and remove the adjusting nut, withdraw the end of the cable from the lower end of the lever, and remove the spring and flat washers.
Remove the nut securing the brake lever to the hand brake spindle and withdraw the spring washer, forked lever, and plain washer. The hand lever may now be withdrawn from inside the car.
Remove the right-hand seat (see Section R). Disconnect the hand brake switch wiring. Unscrew the three screws securing the ratchet plate to the floor tunnel. Lift the carpet and remove the nut and spring washer securing the outer cable front abutment. Disconnect the clips securing the cable assembly to the body and rear axle. Remove the bolt, nut, and spring washer connecting the two halves of the brake compensating lever to each other, slacken fully the self-locking nut securing the lever to the axle bracket, and release the cable abutment trunnion from the lever. Extract the split pins and withdraw the clevis pins to release the cable yokes from the levers on the brake backplates.
On replacement, check the hand brake lever operation as detailed above.

Section M.3

BLEEDING THE BRAKE SYSTEM

(See Editor's notes at end of Section M.)

The following procedure should be adopted either for initial priming of the system or to bleed in service if air has been permitted to enter the system. Air may enter the system if pipe connections become loose or if the level of fluid in the reservoir is allowed to fall below the recommended level. During the bleeding operation it is important to keep the reservoir at least half-full to avoid drawing air into the system.
Check that all connections are tightened and all bleed screws closed. Fill the fluid reservoir with the recommended fluid (see **'SERVICE LUBRICANTS, FUEL and FLUIDS–CAPACITIES'**). Keep it at least half-full throughout the bleeding operation, otherwise air will be drawn into the system, necessitating a fresh start. Attach the bleeder tube to the bleed screw on the near-side rear brake and immerse the open end of the tube in a small quantity of brake fluid contained in a clean glass jar. Disconnect the wiring from the pressure failure switch. Unscrew the pressure failure switch 3½ complete turns, to break the contact between the switch plunger and pressure differential piston. Slacken the bleed screw and depress the brake pedal slowly through its full stroke and allow it to return without assistance. Repeat this pumping action with a slight pause before each depression of the pedal. When fluid entering the jar is completely free of air bubbles hold the pedal firmly against the floorboards and tighten the bleeder screw.
This process must be repeated at each of the three remaining brake assemblies.
Top up the fluid reservoir to its correct level, at the bottom of the filler neck.
When the bleeding operation is completed, tighten the pressure failure switch and re-connect the switch wiring.
If the disc brake callipers have been disturbed it will be necessary to pump the brake pedal several times to restore the automatic adjustment of the friction pads.
Apply a normal working load on the brake pedal for a period of two or three minutes and examine the entire system for leaks.

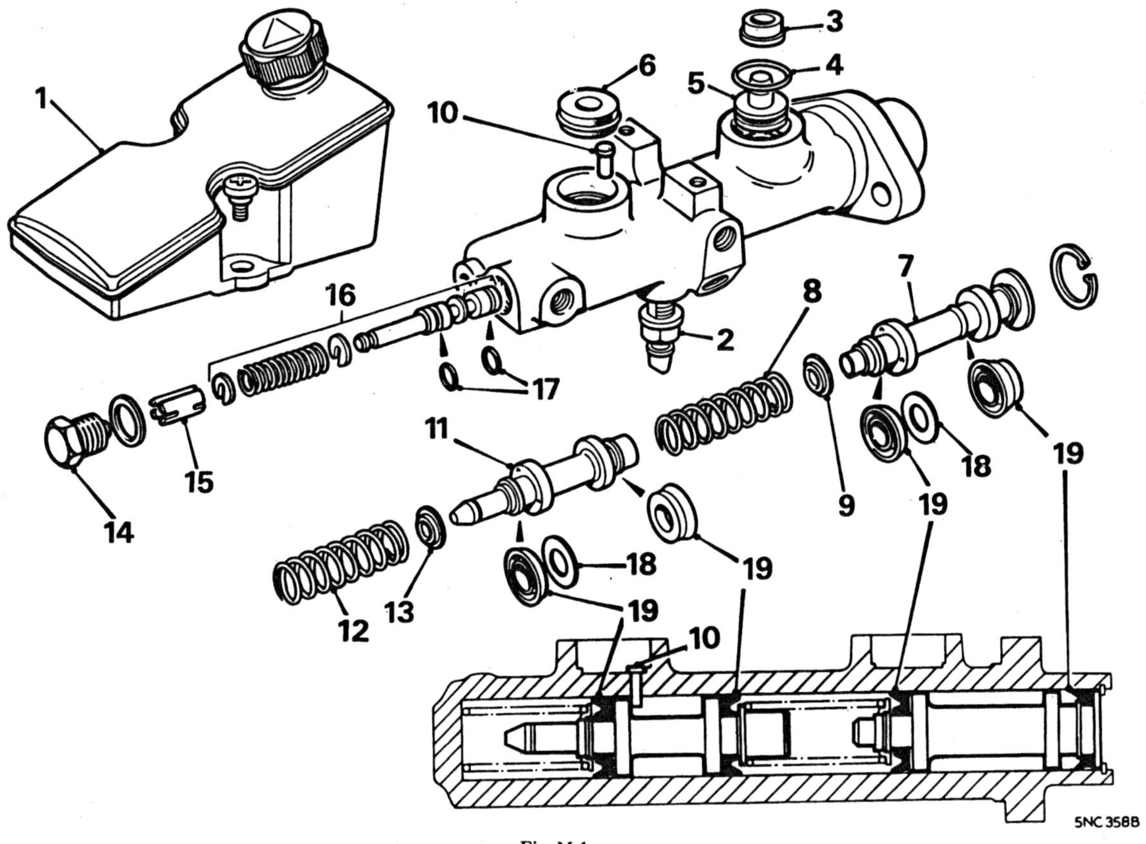

Fig. M.1

The master cylinder components

1. Fluid reservoir.
2. Pressure failure switch.
3. Seal – primary feed port.
4. 'O' ring – primary feed port.
5. Adaptor – primary feed port.
6. Seal – secondary feed port.
7. Primary piston.
8. Return spring.
9. Cup.
10. Stop pin.
11. Secondary piston.
12. Return spring.
13. Cup.
14. End plug.
15. Distance piece.
16. Pressure differential piston assembly.
17. 'O' ring.
18. Shim washer.
19. Seal.

Section M.4

MASTER CYLINDER

Removing

1. Drain the fluid from the reservoir as follows:
   a. Attach rubber tubes to the front brake calliper bleed screw and the rear wheel brake cylinder bleed screw on one side of the car.
   b. Slacken both bleed screws one complete turn.
   c. Depress the brake pedal, hold it in the down position and tighten the bleed screws.
   d. Repeat the operations in (c) until the reservoir is empty.
2. Unscrew the brake pipe unions from the master cylinder.
3. Disconnect the two leads from the master cylinder pressure failure warning switch.
4. Remove the two nuts and washers securing the master cylinder to the servo.
5. Remove the master cylinder assembly.

[CAUTION: Wash hydraulic cylinder components in brake fluid only. Never use gasoline or other petroleum-based solvents since they will damage rubber parts in the system.]

Dismantling

6. Remove the pressure failure switch.
7. Hold the master cylinder in a soft-jawed vice.
8. Remove the two shouldered screws securing the reservoir.
9. Lift the reservoir off the master cylinder.
10. Extract the seal and adaptor assembly from the primary feed port.
11. Extract the seal from the secondary feed port.
12. Extract the circlip from the mouth of the cylinder bore, using tool 18G 1004 or 18G 1112.
13. Withdraw the primary piston, return spring and cup.
14. Insert a soft metal rod into the bore and depress the secondary piston, extract the stop pin from the secondary feed port.
15. Withdraw the secondary piston, return spring and cup, apply air pressure to the secondary outlet port.
16. Remove the end plug and washer. Leave the metal distance piece in place on the end plug spigot.

17. Withdraw the pressure differential piston assembly, apply air pressure to the primary outlet port.
18. Remove the rubber seals from the pistons.

Inspection

19. Clean all components in brake cleaning fluid or industrial alcohol and dry.
    Examine the master cylinder bore: if ridged or scored, renew the unit. Check that the outlet ports are not damaged.

Reassembling

NOTE: Ensure scrupulous cleanliness is observed during assembly.

20. Lubricate the cylinder bores and all rubber seals with unused brake fluid.
21. Fit new 'O' ring seals to the pressure warning piston.
22. Fit a shim washer to the primary and secondary pistons.
23. Select the two piston seals that are identical.
    Use fingers only: fit a piston seal to the primary and secondary pistons with the lip facing away from the shim washer.
24. Fit the seal (thinner of the two remaining) to the secondary piston with its lip towards the primary spring seat.
25. Fit the second seal to the primary piston with its lip towards the first seal.
26. Compare the return springs, the secondary spring is the shorter of the two.
27. Fit the return spring and cup to the secondary piston and insert the assembly, taking care not to turn back the lip of the piston seal.
28. Depress the secondary piston, using a soft metal rod, and insert the stop pin when the piston head has passed the feed port.
29. Fit the return spring and cup to the primary piston and insert the assembly; take care not to turn back the seal lips.
30. Refit the circlip.
31. Enter the pressure differential piston into its bore.
32. Fit the distance piece to the end plug spigot, fit a new sealing washer and tighten the end plug to 33 lbf ft (4.6 kgf m).
33. Fit the 'O' ring and seal to the primary feed port adaptor and fit the assembly into the primary feed port recess.
34. Fit the secondary feed port seal, round edge first.
35. Ensure that the reservoir is clean, locate it on the master cylinder and secure with the shouldered screws—tighten to 6.8 Nm, 5 lbf ft, 0.7 kgf m.
36. Fit the pressure failure switch.

Refitting

37. Fit the master cylinder to the servo. Do not tighten the securing nuts.
38. Start the brake fluid pipe unions in the master cylinder outlets.
39. Tighten the two nuts to secure the master cylinder to the servo.
40. Tighten the brake fluid pipe unions.
41. Reconnect the leads to the pressure failure warning switch.
42. Bleed the hydraulic system, see Section M.3.

Section M.5

DISC BRAKE UNITS

Description

Each front wheel brake unit comprises a hub-mounted disc rotating with the wheel and a braking unit rigidly attached to the swivel axle. The brake unit consists of a calliper manufactured in two halves—the mounting half and the rim half—which are held together by three bolts. A cylinder in each calliper half houses a self-adjusting hydraulic piston, a fluid seal, a dust seal, and a seal retainer. The pistons are interchangeable side for side.

The friction pad assemblies are fitted adjacent to the pistons and are retained in position by a retainer spring and pin.

Fluid pressure generated in the master cylinder enters the mounting half of each calliper and passes through the internal fluid ports into the rim half. An even pressure is therefore exerted on both hydraulic pistons, moving them along the cylinder bores until the friction pad assemblies contact the disc. In order to compensate for wear of the pads the pistons move progressively along each cylinder. The movement of the piston deflects the fluid seal in the cylinder bore, and on releasing the pressure the piston moves back into its original position thus providing the required clearance for the friction pads.

Removing the disc friction pads

Apply the hand brake, jack up the car, and remove the road wheel.

Depress the pad retaining springs and remove the split pins and the retaining springs; lift the pads out of the calliper.

Before the lining material has worn down to a minimum permissible thickness of $\frac{1}{16}$ in. (1.59 mm) the friction pads must be renewed.

Thoroughly clean the exposed end of each piston and ensure that the recesses which are provided in the calliper to receive the friction pads are free from rust and grit.

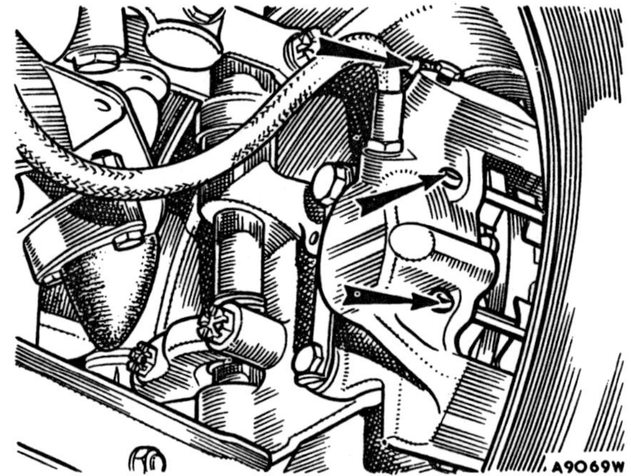

Fig. M.2
Friction pad retaining pins and bleed screw location

THE DISC BRAKE COMPONENTS

[**CAUTION**: Wash hydraulic cylinder components in brake fluid only. Never use gasoline or other petroleum-based solvents since they will damage rubber parts in the system.]

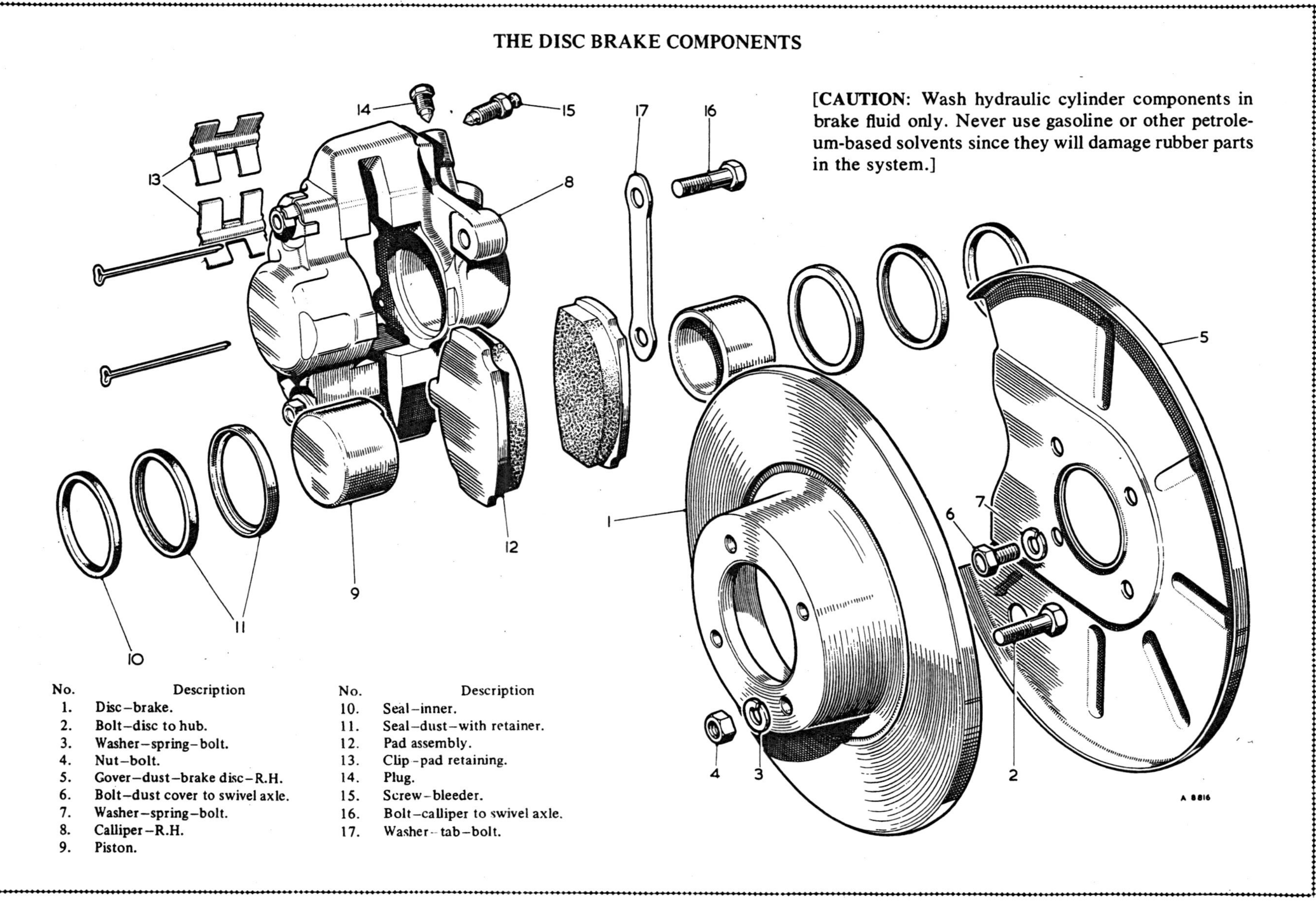

No.	Description
1.	Disc–brake.
2.	Bolt–disc to hub.
3.	Washer–spring–bolt.
4.	Nut–bolt.
5.	Gover–dust–brake disc–R.H.
6.	Bolt–dust cover to swivel axle.
7.	Washer–spring–bolt.
8.	Calliper–R.H.
9.	Piston.
10.	Seal–inner.
11.	Seal–dust–with retainer.
12.	Pad assembly.
13.	Clip–pad retaining.
14.	Plug.
15.	Screw–bleeder.
16.	Bolt–calliper to swivel axle.
17.	Washer–tab–bolt.

Before fitting new friction pads the calliper pistons which will be at their maximum adjustment, must be returned to the base of the bores, using a suitable clamp.

NOTE.—The level of the fluid in the master cylinder supply tank will rise during this operation and it may be necessary to siphon off any surplus fluid to prevent it from overflowing.

Check that the portion that has been machined away from the face of each piston is correctly positioned at the inner end of the calliper (see Fig. M.4). Insert the friction pads (which are interchangeable side for side), replace the retaining springs, and fit the split pins. Ensure that the pad assemblies are free to move easily in the calliper recesses. Remove any high-spots from the pad pressure plate by filing carefully.

Pump the brake pedal several times to readjust the pistons and top up the fluid supply reservoir.

Removing a calliper unit

Apply the hand brake, jack up the car, and remove the road wheel. Withdraw the brake friction pads.

Attach a bleeder tube to the bleed screw and drain the fluid by pumping the brake pedal. Disconnect the flexible hose on the mounting half of the calliper (see Section M.3) and plug the end of the hose to prevent the entry of foreign matter.

Press back the ears of the locking washer, unscrew the two bolts securing the calliper to the swivel axle and withdraw the calliper complete.

Replacing

Reverse the above instructions. Tighten the calliper securing bolts to the torque spanner reading of 40 to 45 lb. ft. (5.6 to 6.2 kg. m.). Finally bleed the system as described in Section M.3.

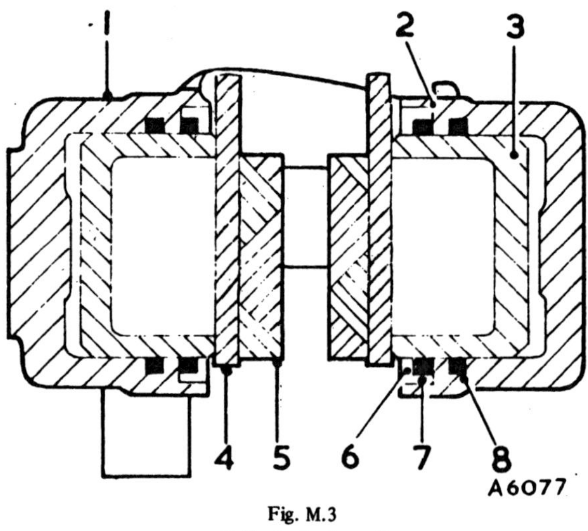

Fig. M.3
A disc brake in section

1. Calliper—mounting half.
2. Calliper—rim half.
3. Hydraulic piston.
4. Pad backing plate.
5. Friction pad.
6. Dust seal retainer.
7. Dust seal.
8. Fluid seal.

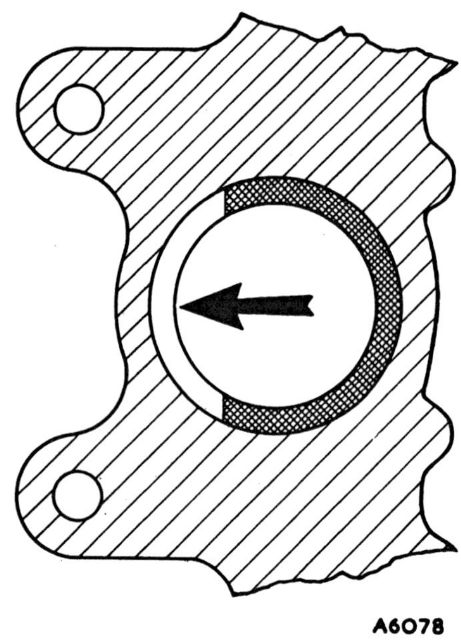

Fig. M.4
The cut-away portion of the piston (arrowed) must be located at the inner edge of the calliper, i.e. towards the hub

Removing the calliper pistons

Unscrew and remove the two bolts securing the calliper to the front hub and withdraw the calliper from the disc and hub. Do not remove the rubber hose, and support the calliper to avoid straining the hose. Remove the friction pads and clean the outside of the calliper, making sure that all dirt and traces of cleaning fluid are completely removed.

Clamp the piston in the mounting half of the calliper and gently apply the foot brake. This operation will force the piston in the rim half of the calliper to move outwards. Continue with gentle pressure on the foot pedal until the piston has emerged sufficiently for it to be removed by hand. Have a clean receptacle ready to catch the fluid as the piston is removed.

With a suitable blunt-nosed tool remove the fluid seal from its groove in the bore of the calliper, taking great care not to damage the bore of the calliper or the seal retaining groove.

The dust seal retainer can be removed by inserting a screwdriver between the retainer and the seal and gently prising the retainer from the mouth of the calliper bore. The rubber seal can then be detached.

Remove the clamp from the mounting-half piston. To remove the mounting-half piston from the calliper it is necessary first to refit the rim-half piston, and thereafter the procedure is as previously detailed.

When cleaning out the calliper it is essential that only methylated spirit or Lockheed Brake Fluid or equivalent be used as a cleaning medium. Other types of cleaning fluid may damage the internal rubber seal between the two halves of the calliper.

Reassembling

Coat a new fluid seal with Lockheed Disc Brake Lubricant or equivalent, making sure that the seal is absolutely dry before so doing, and ease the seal into its groove with the fingers until it is seating correctly in the groove.

Slacken the bleeder screw in the rim half of the calliper one complete turn. Coat the piston with Lockheed Disc Brake Lubricant or equivalent and locate the piston squarely in the mouth of the bore with the cutaway portion of the piston face correctly positioned (see Fig. M.4).

Press in the piston until approximately 5/16 in. (7.94 mm.) of the piston is protruding from the bore. Take great care to prevent the piston tilting during this operation. If the dust seal and retainer have been previously removed, take a new, perfectly dry dust seal, coat it with Lockheed Disc Brake Lubricant or equivalent, and fit the seal into its retainer. Position the seal assembly on the protruding portion of the piston with the seal innermost, ensuring that the assembly is square with the piston. Press home the piston and seal assembly with clamp. Retighten the bleeder screw.

The mounting-half piston is dealt with in the same manner as described for the rim-half piston. The rubber hose must be disconnected to allow the clamp to be used and the bleeder screw must be slackened.

Reconnect the hose and bolt the calliper to the hub. Do not depress the brake pedal. Fit the friction pad assemblies, together with the retaining springs and split pins, and bleed the system.

After bleeding operate the brake pedal several times to adjust the brake.

Dismantling the calliper

Further servicing of the calliper should be confined to removing the bleeder screw and the fluid pipe line and blowing the fluid passages clear with compressed air.

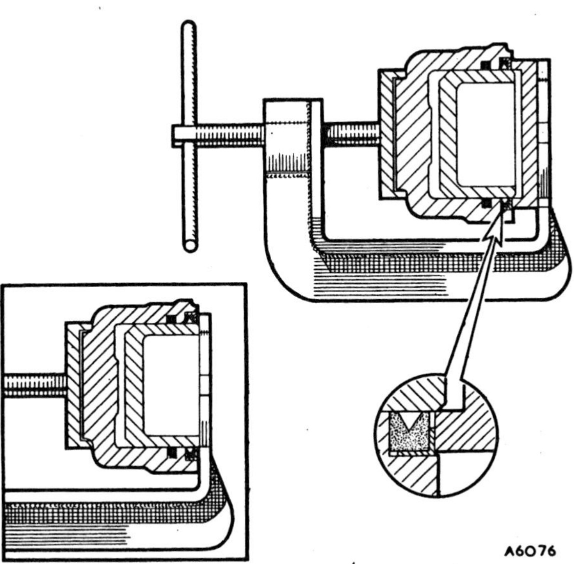

Fig. M.5

Using Service tool 18G590 to install the dust seal and retainer in the recessed mouth of the calliper cylinder. Shown inset is the tool, less the adaptor, being used to reset a piston

Unless it is absolutely unavoidable the calliper should not be separated into two halves. In the event of separation becoming essential, the fluid channel seal, clamping bolts, and lock plates must be renewed when reassembling. Only bolts supplied by British Leyland may be used. On assembly these must be tightened with a torque wrench set at between 35.5 and 37 lb. ft. (4.9 and 5.1 kg. m.).

Ensure that the calliper faces are clean and that the threaded bolt holes are thoroughly dry. Make certain that the new fluid channel seal is correctly located in the recessed face before assembling the two calliper halves.

Section M.6

BRAKE DISCS

Removing

Remove the brake calliper as detailed in Section M.5 without disconnecting the fluid supply and withdraw the hub by the method described in Section K.

Separate the disc from the hub by removing the four securing nuts and washers.

Replacing

Assemble the brake disc to the hub and refit the assembly to the swivel hub.

Check the disc for true rotation by clamping a dial indicator to a suitable fixed point on the vehicle with the needle pad bearing on the face of the hub. Run-out must not exceed .003 in. (.076 mm.) and in the event of this dimension being exceeded the components should be examined for damage and, if necessary, renewed. Damaged disc faces may be rectified by grinding (see below).

Replace the brake calliper as detailed in Section M.5.

A certain amount of concentric and even scoring of the disc faces is not detrimental to the satisfactory operation of the brakes.

If it is found necessary to regrind the disc faces they can be ground up to a maximum of only .040 in. (1.016 mm.) off the original thickness of .350 to .340 in. (8.89 to 8.63 mm.). This may be ground off equally each side, or more on one side than the other, provided that the total reduction does not exceed the maximum limit of .040 in. (1.016 mm.). The reground surface must not exceed 63 micro-in.

After grinding, the faces must run true to within a total clock reading of .002 in. (.05 mm.) and the thickness must be parallel to within .001 in. (.0254 mm.) clock reading.

Section M.7

FLEXIBLE HOSES

Do not attempt to release a flexible hose by turning either end with a spanner. It should be removed as follows:

Unscrew the metal pipe line union nut from its connection to the hose.

Remove the locknut securing the flexible hose union to the bracket and unscrew the hose from the wheel cylinder.

Section M.8

REAR BRAKE ASSEMBLY

The rear brakes are of the leading and trailing shoe type, giving the advantage of equal braking action whether the car is travelling forwards or backwards.

The hand brake lever operates the brakes mechanically through linked levers which apply a force to each shoe. When the foot brake pedal is depressed the master cylinder piston applies pressure to the fluid, thus causing the pistons in the wheel cylinder to operate on the tip of the leading and trailing shoes.

When pressure on the brake pedal is released the brake-shoe springs return the shoes, thrust the pistons back into the wheel cylinders, and the fluid passes back to the master cylinder.

Dismantling

Jack up the car and remove the road wheel.

Remove the brake-drum as described in Section H.

Slacken fully the brake-shoe adjuster.

Depress each shoe steady spring retaining washer and turn to release them from the anchor brackets on the backplate.

Pull the trailing shoe against the load of the springs and disengage at each end; on releasing the tension on the springs the other shoe will fall away.

To remove the wheel cylinder disconnect the brake fluid supply pipe, placing a container to catch the fluid. Withdraw the circlip and retaining washer and remove the cylinder.

Extract the split pin and withdraw the clevis pin to release the hand brake cable from the lever. Detach the rubber dust cover from the brake lever at the rear of the backplate and withdraw the lever.

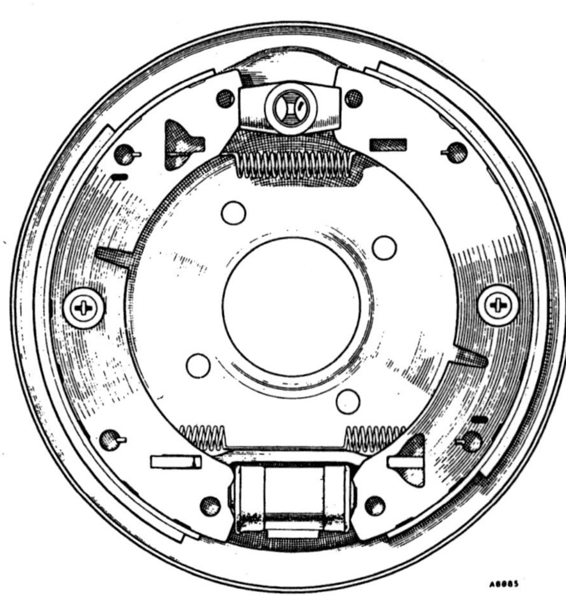

Fig. M.6
The rear brake assembly

Withdraw the tappets from the spindle adjuster and screw the adjusting spindle inwards until clear of the threads. Remove the two nuts and spring washers from the rear of the backplate to release the adjuster body.

Assembling

Thoroughly clean the adjuster body, tappets, and adjuster. Smear the adjuster threads and tappets with Lockheed Expander Lubricant or equivalent. Screw the adjuster fully home and slide the tappets into the body, ensuring that the tapered portion on each is facing inwards.

Examine the rubber seals on both pistons and renew them should they appear damaged or distorted. It is usually advisable to renew the rubbers when rebuilding the cylinders. Smear all internal parts with fluid and reassemble. Replace the dust covers. Hold the cylinder up against the backplate and replace the flat washer and circlip. Reconnect the fluid supply pipe.

Hold the brake lever against the backplate and replace the rubber boot. Reconnect the hand brake cable.

The brake-shoes are interchangeable, but when replacing, the pull-off-springs must be on the backplate side of the shoes and located in the shoes as shown in Fig. M.6.

Replace the steady springs on the shoe web and locate them with the brackets on the backplate by depressing and turning the retaining washer.

Ensure that all adjustments are off and that the shoes are centralized. Fit the drum and the road wheel, bleed the system, and adjust the brakes.

Section M.9

RELINING THE BRAKE-SHOES

Owing to the need for the brake linings to be finished so that they are perfectly concentric with the brake-drums, special precautions must be taken when relining the shoes. **It is imperative that all brake linings should be of the same make, grade, and condition to ensure even braking.**

When brake linings are in need of renewal they must always be replaced in axle sets, and the relining of the shoes in one brake-drum must be avoided.

Any variations from this will give an unequal and unsatisfactory braking performance.

After riveting the new brake linings to the brake-shoes it is essential that any high-spots should be removed before replacement of the backplate assembly.

When new linings are fitted it is necessary to return the spindle adjuster to the fully off position. The hand brake must also be in the fully released position.

Do not allow grease, paint, oil, or brake fluid to come into contact with the brake linings.

Section M.10

REAR BRAKE BACKPLATE

Removing

Jack up the car and remove the road wheel. Remove the brake-drum and withdraw the axle half-shaft and the rear hub (see Section H).

THE REAR BRAKE COMPONENTS

No.	Description	No.	Description
1.	Backplate.	15.	Spring washer.
2.	Backplate to axle case bolt.	16.	Wheel cylinder assembly.
3.	Nut.	17.	Piston.
4.	Spring washer.	18.	Piston seal.
5.	Shoe assembly.	19.	Piston boot.
6.	Pull-off spring–cylinder end.	20.	Wheel cylinder retaining clip.
7.	Pull-off spring–adjustment end.	21.	Bleeder screw.
8.	Brake-shoe steady pin.	22.	Hand brake lever.
9.	Brake-shoe steady spring.	23.	Hand brake lever boot.
10.	Retainer washer.	24.	Brake-drum.
11.	Adjuster assembly.	25.	Drum to hub screw.
12.	Tappet.	26.	Drum retaining nut (wire wheels).
13.	Wedge spindle.		
14.	Adjuster to backplate nut.		

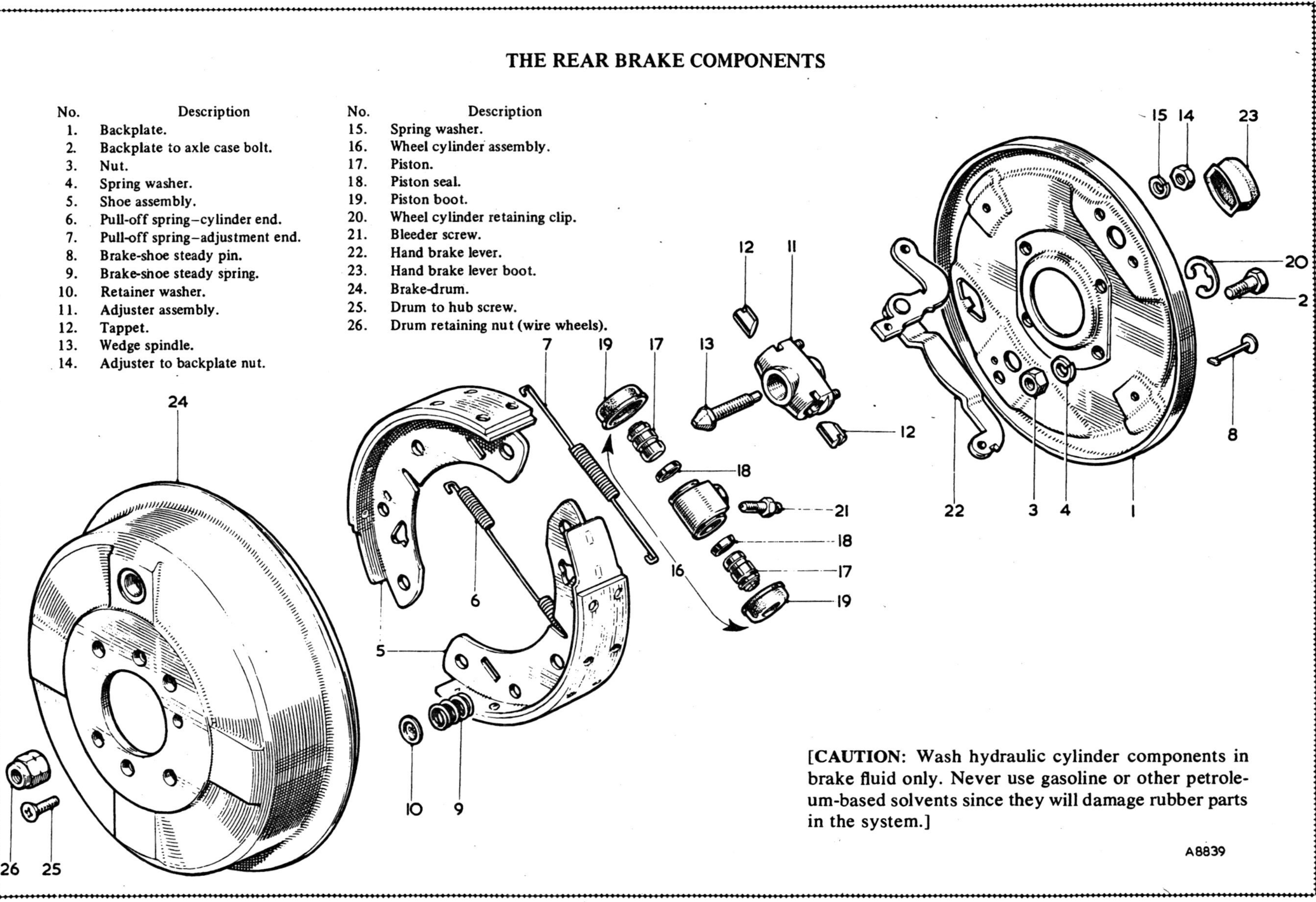

[CAUTION: Wash hydraulic cylinder components in brake fluid only. Never use gasoline or other petroleum-based solvents since they will damage rubber parts in the system.]

Disconnect the brake pipe from the back of the wheel cylinder. Extract the split pin and remove the clevis pin to detach the hand brake cable from the brake lever.
Unscrew the four nuts securing the backplate to the flange on the axle and withdraw the backplate complete with shoes, wheel cylinder, and shoe adjuster.

Replacing
Reverse the above instructions; readjust the brakes (see 'MAINTENANCE') and finally, bleed the hydraulic system as detailed in Section M.3.

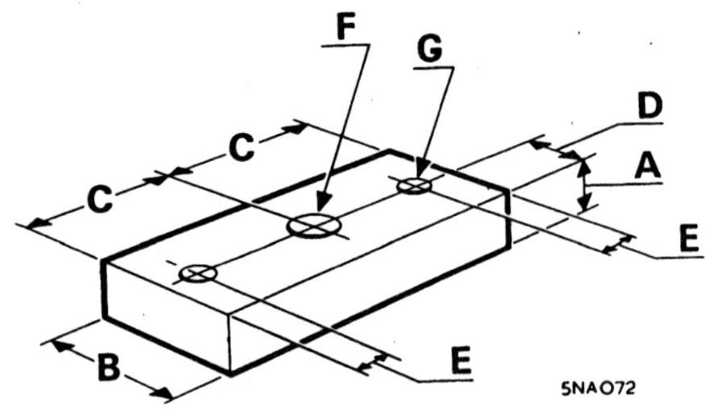

Fig. M.8

Servo dummy flange

A. ½ in (12.70 mm).
B. 1½ in (38.10 mm).
C. 1½ in (38.10 mm).
D. ¾ in (19.05 mm).
E. ⅜ in (9.52 mm).
F. 1 hole ½ in dia. (12.70 mm).
G. 2 holes 0.335 ±.0.005 in dia. (8.51 ± 0.13 mm).

Section M.11

SERVO UNIT

Removing
1. Detach the throttle return springs from the air cleaner.
2. Remove the three bolts and washers securing the air cleaner to the carburetter and remove the air cleaner assembly from the car.
3. Remove the eight screws securing the pedal box cover.
4. Remove the pedal box cover and seal.
5. Remove the nut securing the brake fluid pipe clip to the L.H. wing, adjacent to the pedal box.
6. Remove the screw securing the brake fluid pipe clip to the scuttle, adjacent to the L.H. bonnet hinge.
7. Remove the screw securing the brake fluid pipe clip to the L.H. wheel arch, below the servo unit.

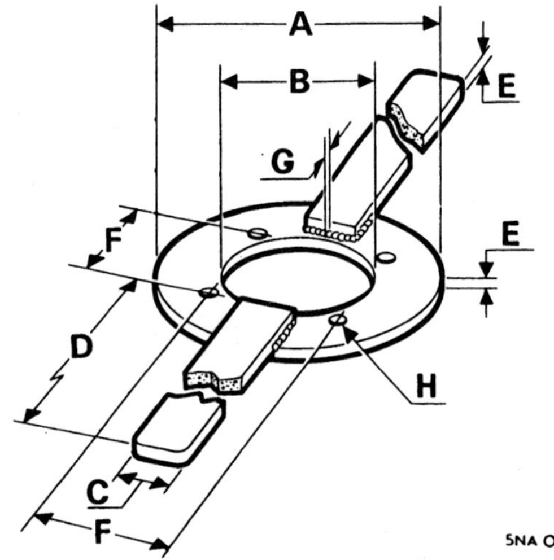

Fig. M.7

Servo end cover removal tool

A. 6⅞ in (174.62 mm).
B. 3⅞ in (98.43 mm)
C. 1½ in (38.10 mm).
D. 12 in (304.80 mm).
E. ¼ in (6.35 mm).
F. 3.40 ± 0.010 in (86.36 ± 0.25 mm).
G. ⅛ in (3.18 mm).
H. 4 holes 11/32 in dia. (8.73 mm).

8. Remove the two nuts and washers securing the brake master cylinder to the servo.
9. Detach the master cylinder from the servo and support it in the engine compartment.
10. Slacken the clip securing the vacuum hose to the servo.
11. Detach the brake pedal return spring from the brake pedal.
12. Remove the split pin and clevis pin securing the brake pedal to the servo push-rod.
13. Remove the four nuts and spring washers securing the servo assembly to the pedal box.
    NOTE: The lower nuts are accessible from the footwell.
14. Detach the servo from the pedal box and disconnect the vacuum hose from the servo.

Dismantling
NOTE: Special tools should be made for the dismantling and assembly of the servo, see Fig. M.7, Fig. M.8, and Fig. M.9.
15. Remove the seal and retainer from the servo shell.
16. Fit the dummy flange (see Fig. M.8) to the two studs on the servo shell and hold the assembly in a vice.
17. Mark the servo cover and shell for correct refitment.
18. Remove the dust cover and end cap and pull out the filter from the end cover.
19. Fit the end cover removal tool (see Fig. M.7).
20. Whilst maintaining downward pressure, turn the removal tool anti-clockwise as far as the stops will allow.
21. Gently release the pressure on the removal tool and remove the cover valve body assembly and return spring.
    NOTE: It may be necessary to lever back the retaining lugs to release the cover from the shell.
22. Remove the seal retainer, bearing, and seal from the cover.
23. Remove the diaphragm from the valve body.

24. Press in the valve rod and plunger to release the retaining key.
25. Remove the valve rod and plunger.
26. Remove the push-rod retainer.
27. Remove the push-rod.
28. Remove the reaction disc.
29. Remove the non-return valve and mounting ring.

Inspection

30. Clean all components in clean brake fluid and dry with a lint-free cloth.
31. Examine all components for faults and wear and be prepared to fit new retainers and rubber parts throughout.
    NOTE: The valve rod and plunger must be renewed as an assembly.

Reassembling

Ensure scrupulous cleanliness is observed during assembly.

32. Reverse the procedure in 15 to 29, noting:
    a. Coat the rubber surfaces of the valve rod and plunger, the rubber reaction disc, the cover seal and bearing and the edge only of the rubber diaphragm with Lockheed Disc Brake Lubricant or equivalent.
    b. Use the setting tool (see Fig. M.9) to press in the seal retainer, flat side first, until the largest shoulder of the tool meets the inside face of the end cover.
    c. Check the distance the push-rod stem protrudes from the servo shell. It should be 0.400 in (10.16 mm). **NOTE**: One complete turn of the adjuster alters the length of the rod by about 0.035 in (0.088 mm).
    d. Check the torque required to turn the adjuster screw; it should not be less than 5 lbf in (0.058 kgf m).

Refitting

33. Reverse the procedure in 1 to 14.

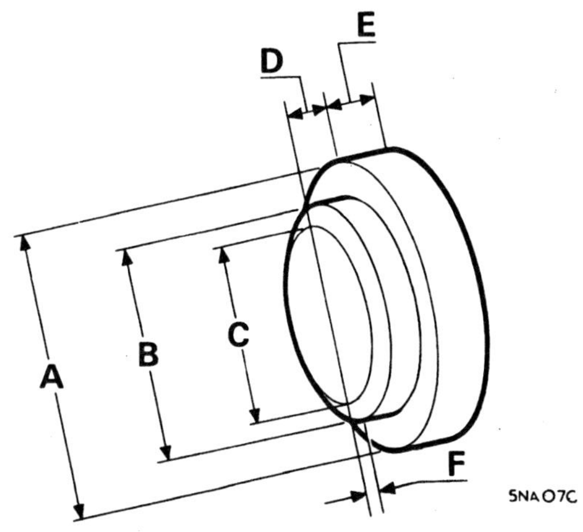

Fig. M.9

Servo cover seal setting tool

A. 2½ in dia. (63.50 mm).
B. 1 31/32 in dia. (50 mm).
C. 1 19/32 in dia. (40.48 mm).
D. 0.270 ± 0.005 in (6.86 ± 0.13 mm).
E. ½ in (12.70 mm).
F. 1/16 in chamfer (1.59 mm).

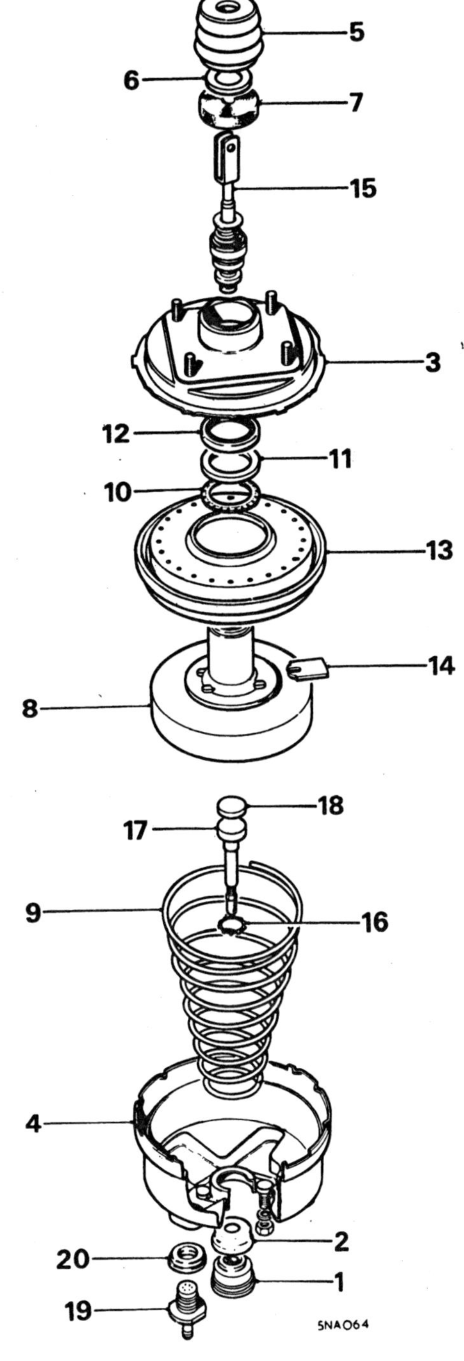

Fig. M.10

The brake servo components

1. Seal.
2. Retainer.
3. Cover.
4. Servo shell.
5. Dust cover.
6. End cap.
7. Filter.
8. Valve body.
9. Return spring.
10. Seal retainer.
11. Bearing.
12. Seal.
13. Diaphragm.
14. Retaining key.
15. Valve rod and plunger.
16. Retainer – push-rod.
17. Push-rod.
18. Reaction disc.
19. Non-return valve.
20. Mounting ring.

Section M.12

PEDAL FREE MOVEMENT

A free movement of $\frac{1}{8}$ in. (3.2 mm.) measured at pedal pad must be maintained on the brake pedal.
To adjust the free movement, slacken the stop light switch locknut and turn the switch clockwise to decrease or anti-clockwise to increase the clearance. Tighten the stop light switch locknut.

(See Editor's notes at end of Section M.)

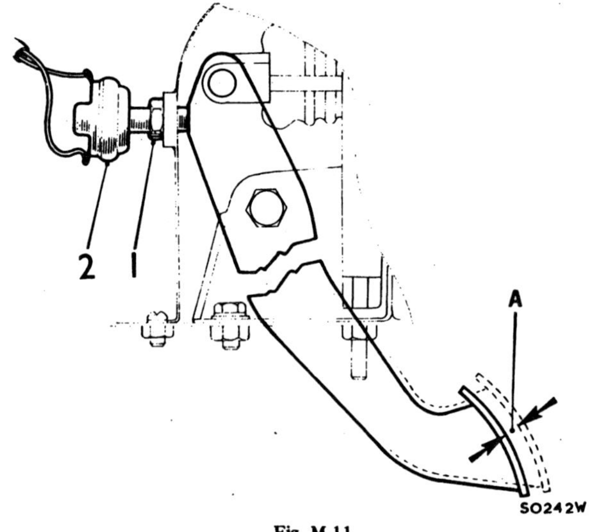

Fig. M.11
Brake pedal adjustment
1 Switch locknut. 2. Stop light switch.
A = $\frac{1}{8}$ in. (3.2 mm.).

Section M.13

HAND BRAKE WARNING SWITCH

Removing

1. Disconnect the battery.
2. Apply the hand brake.
3. Remove the driver's seat.
4. Pull back the carpet and disconnect the switch wiring.
5. Unscrew the locknut and remove the switch.

Refitting

6. Reverse the procedure in 4 to 5.
7. Re-connect the battery and switch on the ignition.
8. Position the hand brake in the off position.
9. Slacken the locknut and position the switch, by turning the bottom locknut, until the light goes out.
10. Tighten the locknuts.
11. Apply the hand brake and check that the warning light operates.
12. Switch off the ignition.
13. If the switch wiring is twisted, disconnect the wiring, straighten it and re-connect.
14. Refit the driver's seat.

EDITOR'S NOTES

M. The Braking System

Bleeding the brake system

In bleeding the brake system, start with the wheel that is farthest from the master cylinder in terms of brake line length; namely, the right-hand rear wheel. Bleed the remaining brake cylinders in the following order: left rear, right front, and left front. This sequence applies to cars with left-hand drive, as used in the U.S.A.

Pedal free movement

If the pedal free movement is not adequate, the pistons in the master cylinder may fail to retract fully when the pedal is released. As a result the compensating ports of the master cylinder will be blocked by the pistons, eventually causing the brakes to drag or lock up.

SECTION N

THE ELECTRICAL SYSTEM

GENERAL DESCRIPTION

The electrical system is 12-volt NEGATIVE earth return. The battery is located in a tray beneath the rear cockpit floor; the battery is retained by a clamp plate and two fixing bolts. A battery access panel is provided in the rear compartment floor and is secured to the floor by three quick-release fasteners.

REPLACEMENT BULBS

	Watts	Part No.
Sidelamp (with flasher)	5/21	GLB 380
Stop/tail	5/21	GLB 380
Reverse	18	BFS 273
Number-plate lamp	6	GLB 254
Direction indicator	21	GLB 382
Side-marker lamp, front and rear ..	5	BFS 222
Ignition warning	2	GLB 281
Main beam	2	GLB 281
Direction indicator warning lamp ..	2	GLB 281
Brake warning lamp	1.5	GLB 280
Panel illumination lamp	2.2	GLB 987
Cigar-lighter illumination	2.2	BFS 643
Luggage compartment lamp	6	GLB 254
Courtesy lamp	6	GLB 254
Hazard warning lamp	2	GLB 281
Seat belt warning lamp	2	GLB 281
Switch illumination	2	GLB 281
Heater rotary control illumination ..	2	GLB 281
E.G.R./catalyst warning lamp (if fitted)	2	GLB 281

SEALED BEAM UNIT

Headlamp	50/40	17H 9472

Section N.1

TESTING THE CHARGING CIRCUIT

Test conditions: Alternator drive belt adjusted correctly, battery terminals clean and tight, battery in good condition (electrolyte specific gravity readings consistent), and cables and terminal connections in the charging circuit in good condition.

Test	Procedure	Remarks
1. To check that battery voltage is reaching the alternator	Remove the cable connector from the alternator. Connect the negative side of a voltmeter to earth. Switch on the ignition. Connect the positive side of the voltmeter to each of the alternator cable connectors in turn.	a. If battery voltage is not available at the 'IND' cable connector, check the no-charge warning lamp bulb and the warning lamp circuit for continuity. b. If battery voltage is not available at the main charging cable connector, check the circuit between the battery and the alternator for continuity. c. If battery voltage is available at the cable connectors mentioned in 'a' and 'b', proceed with Test 2.
2. Alternator test.	Re-connect the cable connector to the alternator. Disconnect the brown cable with eyelet from the terminal on the starter motor solenoid. Connect an ammeter between the brown cable and the terminal on the starter motor solenoid. Connect a voltmeter across the battery terminals. Run the engine at 6,000 alternator rev/min and wait until the ammeter reading is stable.	a. If a zero ammeter reading is obtained, remove and overhaul the alternator. b. If an ammeter reading below 10 amperes and a voltmeter reading between 13.6 and 14.4 volts is obtained, and if battery in a low stage of charge, check the alternator performance on a test bench. The alternator output should be 43 amperes at 14 volts, at 6,000 rev/min. c. If an ammeter reading below 10 amperes and a voltmeter reading below 13.6 volts is obtained, remove the alternator and renew the voltage regulator. d. If an ammeter reading above 10 amperes and a voltmeter reading above 14.4 volts is obtained, renew the voltage regulator.

Section N.2

SERVICE PRECAUTIONS

Polarity
Ensure that the correct battery polarity is maintained at all times: reversed battery or charger connections will damage the alternator rectifiers.

Battery connections
The battery must never be disconnected while the engine is running.

Testing semi-conductor devices
Never use an ohmmeter of the type incorporating a hand-driven generator for checking the rectifiers or the transistors.

Battery boosting and charging
CAUTION: The following precautions must be observed to avoid the possibility of serious damage to the charging system or electrical components of the vehicle.

Battery boosting: When connecting an additional battery to boost a discharged battery in the vehicle, ensure that:

- the booster battery is of the same nominal voltage as the vehicle battery.
- the interconnecting cables are of sufficient capacity to carry starting current.
- **the cables are inter-connected one at a time and to the booster battery first.**
- the cables are connected between the battery terminals in the following order: First, + (Positive) to + (Positive) and then – (Negative) to – (Negative).
- the engine speed is reduced to 1000 rev/min or below before disconnecting the boost battery. The vehicle battery must never be disconnected while the engine is running.

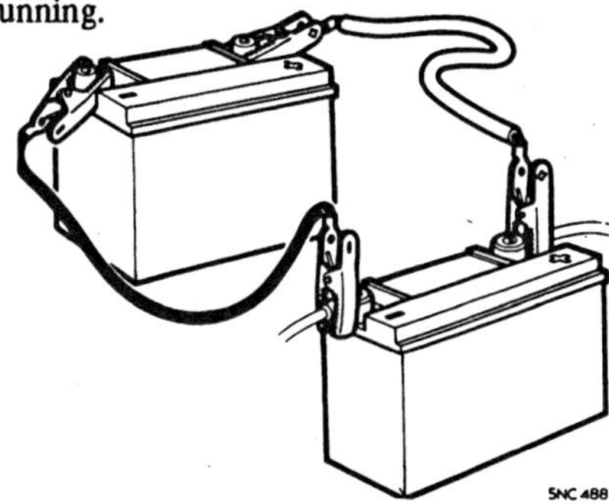

Battery charging: When charging the battery in the vehicle from an outside source such as a trickle charger ensure that:

- the charger voltage is the same as the nominal voltage of the battery.
- the charger positive (+) lead is connected to the positive (+) terminal of the battery.
- the charger negative (–) lead is connected to the negative (–) terminal of the battery.

Section N.3

FUSES

The fuses are mounted in a separate holder located under a large plastic cover on the right-hand wing valance.
Two spare fuses are provided, and it is important that only fuses of the correct value, marked inside the fuse tube, should be used.

Blown fuses
The units which are protected by each fuse can readily be identified by referring to the wiring diagram.
A blown fuse is indicated by the failure of all the units protected by it and is confirmed by examination of the fuse, which can easily be withdrawn from the spring clips. If it has blown the fused state of the wire will be visible inside the glass tube. Before renewing a blown fuse inspect the wiring of the units that have failed for evidence of a short circuit or other faults which may have caused the fuse to blow, and remedy the cause of the trouble.

Section N.4

HEADLAMPS

Removing
1. Disconnect the battery.
2. Disconnect the wiring at the snap connectors in the engine compartment.
3. Feed the wiring through the grommet in the inner wing.
4. Ease the bottom of the outer rim forward away from the lamp and lift it off the retaining lugs at the top of the lamp.
5. Remove the four screws, nuts and washers securing the headlamp unit to the body.
6. Remove the headlamp unit and rubber seal from the body.

Refitting
7. Reverse the procedure in 1 to 6.

Section N.5

SIDE AND DIRECTION INDICATOR LAMPS

Removing
1. Disconnect the battery.
2. Disconnect the feed wires at the snap connectors in the engine compartment and feed the wires through the wing grommet.
3. Remove the two screws securing the lens to the lamp unit.
4. Remove the lens and rubber washers.
5. Remove the two screws securing the lamp unit to the bumper.
6. Pull the unit forward and disconnect the earth lead.
7. Remove the lamp unit.

Refitting

8. Reverse the procedure in 1 to 7, noting:
   a. The lens is marked 'TOP' to ensure correct refitment.

Section N.6

SIDE FRONT MARKER LAMPS

Removing

1. Disconnect the battery.
2. Disconnect the earth lead from the lamp unit and the feed cable at the snap connector in the engine compartment.
3. Remove the two nuts, washers and rubber seals securing the unit to the body.
4. Remove the lamp unit complete with mounting plate and seal.

Refitting

5. Reverse the procedure in 1 to 5.

Section N.7

TAIL LAMPS

Removing

1. Open the luggage compartment lid.
2. Disconnect the lamp leads at the snap connectors.
3. Remove the three nuts securing the lamp assembly to the rear wing.
4. Withdraw the lamp assembly.

Refitting

5. Reverse the procedure in 1 to 4.

Section N.8

REVERSE LAMPS

Removing

1. Open the luggage compartment lid.
2. Disconnect the reverse lamp leads at the multiplug connector.
3. Remove the two screws securing the lens to the lamp.
4. Remove the sealing rubber, withdraw the bulb holder and its sealing rubber.

Refitting

5. Reverse the procedure in 1 to 4.

Section N.9

HORN

Removing the horn

Disconnect the electrical connections, remove the screws and washers securing the horn to the wing valance and withdraw the horn

Refitting

Reverse the removal procedure.

(See Editor's notes at end of Section N.)

Section N.10

NUMBER-PLATE LAMP

Removing

1. Open the luggage compartment lid.
2. Disconnect the lamp leads at the snap connectors.
3. Feed the lamp leads through the grommet in the rear panel.
4. Remove the two nuts securing the lamp assembly to the number-plate.
5. Remove the lamp assembly.

Refitting

6. Reverse the procedure in 1 to 5.

Section N.11

CIGAR LIGHTER

Removing

1. Disconnect the battery.
2. Remove the console, see Section R.
3. Disconnect the wiring from the cigar lighter.
4. Detach the bulb holder from the cigar lighter body.
5. Unscrew the outer shell from the cigar lighter body.
6. Withdraw the cigar lighter body from the front of the console.

Refitting

7. Reverse the procedure in 1 to 6.

Section N.12

ALTERNATOR (Lucas Type 18ACR)

Removing

1. Disconnect the hoses from the air pump discharge connections.
2. Slacken the air pump mounting bolt.
3. Remove the air pump adjusting link bolt from the air pump.
4. Slip the belt from the air pump pulley and raise the air pump.
5. Withdraw the terminal block from the alternator.
6. Remove the adjusting link bolt from the alternator.
7. Slacken the alternator mounting bolts, lower the alternator and slip the fan belt from the alternator pulley.
8. Unscrew the alternator mounting bolts and remove the alternator.

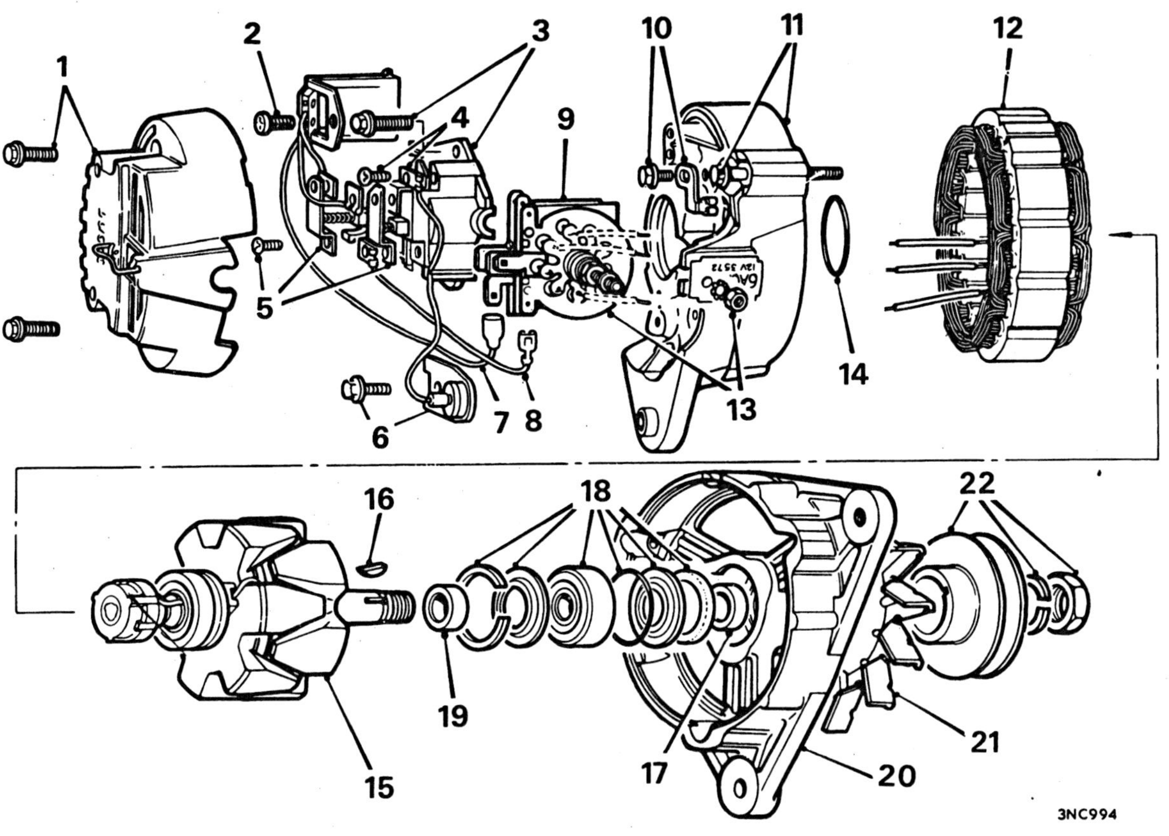

Fig. N.1

Alternator components–Lucas 18ACR

1. End cover and set bolt.
2. Regulator assembly screw.
3. Brush holder and screw.
4. Screw–surge device to bush holder.
5. Bush assemblies and screw.
6. Surge protection device and screw.
7. Terminal–blade between inner and outer rectifier plates.
8. Terminal–blade–outer rectifier plate.
9. Rectifier.
10. Rectifier earth link.
11. Slip-ring end bracket.
12. Stator pack.
13. Rectifier and nut.
14. 'O' ring.
15. Rotor.
16. Pulley key.
17. Distance piece.
18. Bearing assembly.
19. Distance.
20. Drive end bracket
21. Fan.
22. Pulley, spring washer and nut.

Dismantling

9. Remove the two set bolts to release the end cover from the alternator.
10. Detach the cable from the terminal blade on the outer of the three rectifier plates.
11. Detach the cable from the terminal blade between the middle and inner of the three rectifier plates.
12. Remove the four screws to release the two brush assemblies from the brush holder.
13. Remove the screw to release the surge protection device cable from the brush holder.
14. Remove the three set bolts to release the brush holder and regulator assembly from the slip-ring end bracket. Note the leaf spring fitted at the side of the inner brush.
15. Remove the screw to release the regulator assembly from the brush holder.
16. Remove the set bolt securing the surge protection device to the slip-ring end bracket.
17. Remove the set bolt securing the rectifier earthing link to the slip-ring end bracket.
18. Using a pair of pliers as a thermal shunt to avoid overheating the diodes, unsolder each of the three stator cables in turn from the rectifier.
19. Slacken the nut to release the rectifier assembly from the slip-ring end bracket.
20. Mark the drive-end bracket, the stator lamination pack, and the slip-ring end bracket to assist reassembly.
21. Remove the three through-bolts and withdraw the slip-ring end bracket and the stator lamination pack.
22. Remove the 'O' ring from inside the slip-ring end bracket.
23. Remove the nut and withdraw the pulley and fan from the rotor shaft.

24. Remove the pulley key and withdraw the distance piece from the rotor shaft.
25. Press the rotor out of the drive-end bracket bearing.
26. Withdraw the distance piece from the drive end of the rotor.
27. Remove the circlip to release the bearing, bearing cover-plates, 'O' ring, and felt washer from the drive-end bracket.

Inspection

28. Check the bearings for wear and roughness; if necessary, repack the bearings with Shell Alvania RA grease or equivalent. To renew the slip-ring end bearing, unsolder the two field connections from the slip-ring and withdraw the slip-ring and the bearing from the rotor shaft. Reassemble, ensuring that the shielded side of the bearing faces the slip-ring assembly. Use Fry's H.T.3 solder to remake the field connections to the slip-ring.
29. Clean the surfaces of the slip-ring, removing any evidence of burning with very fine glass paper.
    (See Editor's notes at end of Section N.)
30. Check the insulation of the field windings, connecting the test equipment (see 'GENERAL SPECIFICATION DATA') between one of the slip-rings and one of the rotor lobes.
31. Check the field windings against the specification given in 'GENERAL SPECIFICATION DATA', connecting the test equipment (see 'GENERAL SPECIFICATION DATA') between the slip-rings.
32. Check the stator windings for continuity, connecting the test equipment (see 'GENERAL SPECIFICATION DATA') between any two of the stator cables, then repeating the test using the third cable in place of one of the first two.
33. Check the stator winding insulation, connecting the test equipment (see 'GENERAL SPECIFICATION DATA') between any one of the three stator cables and the stator lamination pack.
34. Check the nine rectifying diodes, connecting the test equipment (see 'GENERAL SPECIFICATION DATA') between each diode pin and its associated heatsink in the rectifier pack in turn, and then reverse the test equipment connections. Current should flow in one direction only. Renew the rectifier assembly if a diode is faulty.
35. Check the brush spring pressure and the brush length against the specification given in 'GENERAL SPECIFICATION DATA'.

Reassembling

36. Reverse the procedure in 9 to 27, noting:
    a. Support the inner track of the bearing when refitting the rotor to the drive-end bracket.
    b. Use 'M' grade 45–55 tin–lead solder to re-make the stator to rectifier pack connections, using a pair of pliers as a thermal shunt to avoid overheating of the diodes.
    c. Tighten the alternator pulley nut to 25 lbf. ft. (3.5 kgf. m.).
37. Mount the alternator on the test bench and check its output against the specification given in 'GENERAL SPECIFICATION DATA'.

Refitting

38. Reverse the removal procedure, apply leverage to the drive-end bracket only, and tension the drive belt to allow 0.5 in. (13 mm.) deflection at the centre of its longest run.

Section N.13

WINDSHIELD WIPERS–TWO SPEED

Removing

MOTOR AND GEARBOX ASSEMBLY

1. Disconnect the battery.
2. Remove the wiper arms.
3. Remove the fascia L.H. lower panel cover.
4. Disconnect the wiring from the motor terminals.
5. Unscrew the outer cable retaining nut from the motor housing.
6. Remove the two motor securing bolts.
7. Withdraw the motor and gearbox assembly complete with the inner drive cable. The inner cable will rotate the wiper spindles as it is withdrawn.

WHEELBOXES

8. Remove the motor and gearbox as in 1 to 7.
9. Slacken the cover screws on each wheelbox and detach the cable outer casings.
10. Unscrew the spindle housing retaining nut and remove the front bush and washer from each wheelbox.
11. Remove the wheelboxes complete with rear bushes from beneath the fascia.

Dismantling

MOTOR AND GEARBOX ASSEMBLY

12. Unscrew the four gearbox cover retaining screws and remove the cover.
13. Remove the circlip and flat washer securing the connecting rod to the crankpin.
14. Withdraw the connecting rod taking care not to lose the flat washer fitted under it.
15. Remove the circlip and washer securing the shaft and gear.
16. Clean any burrs from the gear shaft and withdraw the gear, taking care not to lose the dished washer fitted under it.
17. Mark the yoke and gearbox for reassembly.
18. Unscrew the two fixing bolts from the yoke and remove the yoke assembly and armature. The yoke must be kept clear of metallic particles which will be attracted to the pole-piece.
19. Remove the screws securing the brush gear and the terminal end switch assembly, and remove both assemblies.

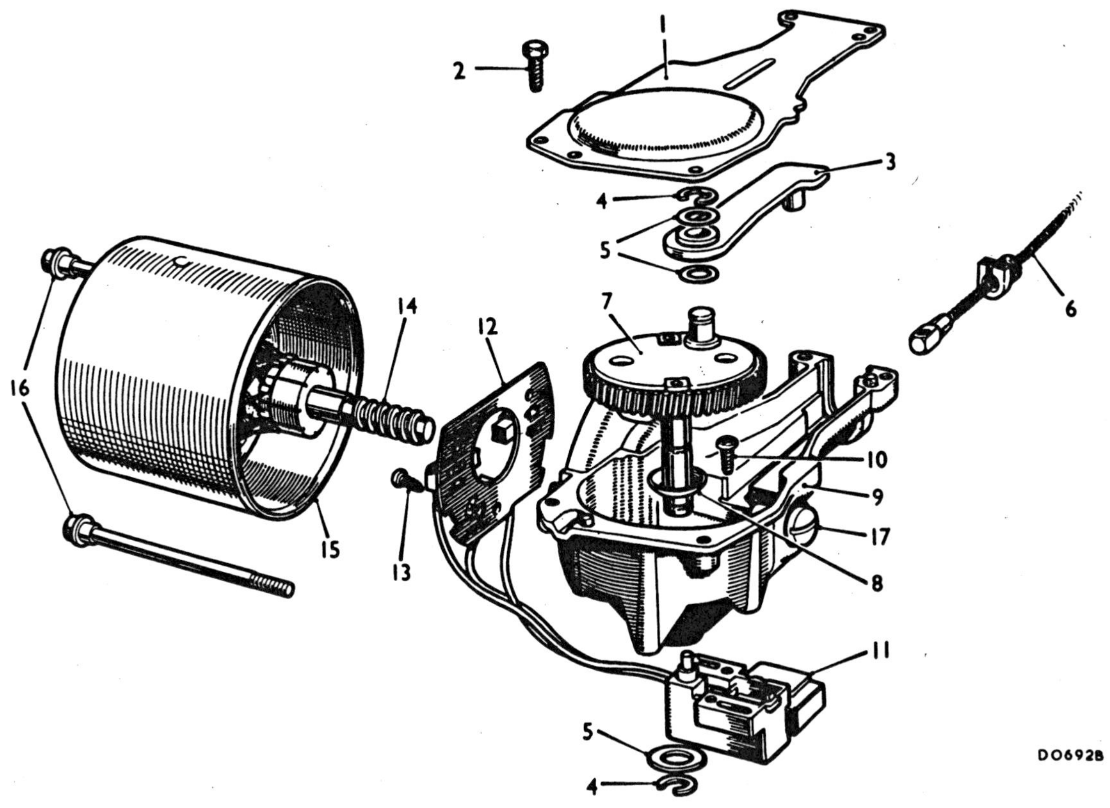

Fig. N.2

The two-speed windshield wiper motor components

1. Gearbox cover.
2. Screw for cover.
3. Connecting rod.
4. Circlip.
5. Plain washer.
6. Cable assembly.
7. Shaft and gear.
8. Dished washer.
9. Gearbox.
10. Screw for limit switch.
11. Limit switch assembly.
12. Brush gear.
13. Screw for brush gear.
14. Armature.
15. Yoke assembly.
16. Armature adjusting screw.

Inspection

MOTOR AND GEARBOX ASSEMBLY

20. Examine the brushes for excessive wear. If the main bushes (diametrically opposite) are worn to $\frac{3}{16}$ in (4.8 mm.) or if the narrow section of the third brush is worn to the full width of the brush the brush gear assembly must be renewed.
21. Check the brush spring pressure with a push-type gauge. The gauge reading should be 5 to 7 oz. (140 to 200 gm.) when the bottom of the brush is level with the bottom of the slot in the brush box. The brush gear assembly must be renewed if the springs are not satisfactory.
22. Test the armature for insulation and open- or short-circuits. Renew the armature if faulty.
23. Examine the gear wheel for damage or excessive wear. Renew if necessary.

Reassembling

MOTOR AND GEARBOX ASSEMBLY

24. Reverse the dismantling procedure in 12 to 19, noting the following points:
    a. Use Ragosine Listate Grease to lubricate the gear wheel teeth and cam armature shaft worm gear, connecting rod and pin, cross-head slide, cable rack, and wheelbase gear wheels.
    b. Use Shell Turbo 41 oil to lubricate the bearing bushes, armature shaft bearing journals (sparingly), gear wheel shaft and crankpin, felt washer in the yoke bearing (thoroughly soak), and the wheelbox spindles.
    c. Tighten the yoke fixing bolts to a torque figure of 20 lb. in. (.23 kg. m.).
    d. If a replacement armature is being fitted, slacken the thrust screw to provide end-float for fitting the yoke.

(See Editor's notes at end of Section N.)

e Fit the thrust disc inside the yoke bearing with its concave side towards the end face of the bearing.

f Fit the dished washer beneath the gear wheel with its concave side towards the gear wheel.

g. When fitting the connecting rod to the crankpin ensure that the larger of the two flat washers is fitted under the connecting rod with the smaller one on top beneath the circlip.

h. With the thrust screw fully tightened against the gearbox casing, an end-float of .004 to .008 in. (.1 to .21 mm.) should exist on the armature. Adjustment of the armature end-float can be achieved by adjustment of the thrust screw.

Refitting

WHEELBOXES

25. Reverse the removing procedure in 8 to 11.

MOTOR AND GEARBOX ASSEMBLY

26. Reverse the removing procedure in 1 to 7 ensuring that the inner cable engages correctly with the wheelbox gear teeth.

Section N.14

STARTER MOTOR (Lucas Type 2M100 Pre-engaged)

Removing

1. Disconnect the battery.
2. Remove the starter motor plastic cover.
3. Remove the starter top securing bolt.
4. Disconnect the wiring from the solenoid terminals.
5. Remove the starter motor lower securing bolt and withdraw the starter.

Dismantling

6. Slacken the nut securing the connecting link to solenoid terminal 'STA'.
7. Remove the two set screws to release the solenoid from the drive-end bracket.
8. Lift the solenoid plunger upwards to separate it from the engagement lever.
9. Withdraw the return spring, spring seat, and dust excluder from the plunger body.
10. Withdraw the block-shaped grommet from between the drive-end bracket and the starter motor yoke.
11. Remove the armature end cap from the commutator end bracket.
12. Using an engineer's chisel, remove a sufficient number of claws from the armature retaining ring to release the retaining ring from the armature shaft.
13. Remove the two through-bolts.
14. Withdraw the commutator end cover and the starter motor yoke from the drive-end bracket.
15. Separate the commutator end cover from the starter motor yoke, disengaging the field coil brushes from the brush box moulding to release the end cover from the yoke.
16. Withdraw the thrust washer from the armature shaft.
17. Remove the Spire nut from the engagement lever pivot pin.
18. Withdraw the engagement lever pivot pin from the drive-end bracket.
19. Withdraw the armature and roller clutch drive assembly from the drive-end bracket.
20. Drive the thrust collar rearwards off its jump ring.
21. Remove the thrust collar jump ring, and withdraw the thrust collar and roller-clutch drive from the armature shaft.
22. Remove the spring ring to release the engagement lever, thrust washers and spring from the roller-clutch drive.
23. Remove the seal from the bore of the drive-end bracket.

Inspection

24. Check for excessive side-play of the armature shaft in the bushes, renewing the bushes if necessary, noting:
    a. Prior to fitting, new bushes must either be immersed in new engine oil for a period of 24 hours, or immersed in new engine oil maintained at a temperature of 100°C (212°F) for two hours, allowing the oil to cool before removing the bush.
    b. Press new bushes into position, using a shouldered, polished mandrel of the dimension given in '**GENERAL SPECIFICATION DATA**'.
25. Check that the roller clutch takes up drive instantaneously in one direction and revolves freely in the other direction. Ensure that the drive assembly moves freely along the armature shaft helices.
26. Check that the brushes move freely in the brush box moulding. Renew brushes that are worn to the dimensions given in '**GENERAL SPECIFICATION DATA**' noting:
    a. Cut the old field coil brush flexibles, leaving approximately ¼ in. (6 mm.) of flexible on each side of the field coil end. Solder new brushes in the position shown to the remaining flexibles on the field coil end.
    b. Renew the other two brushes complete with terminal and rubber grommet.
27. Using a new brush, check the pressure of each brush spring in turn against the specification given in '**GENERAL SPECIFICATION DATA**', renewing the springs if necessary noting:
    a. Extract the old springs using long-nosed pliers.
    b. Fully compress new springs between first finger and thumb.

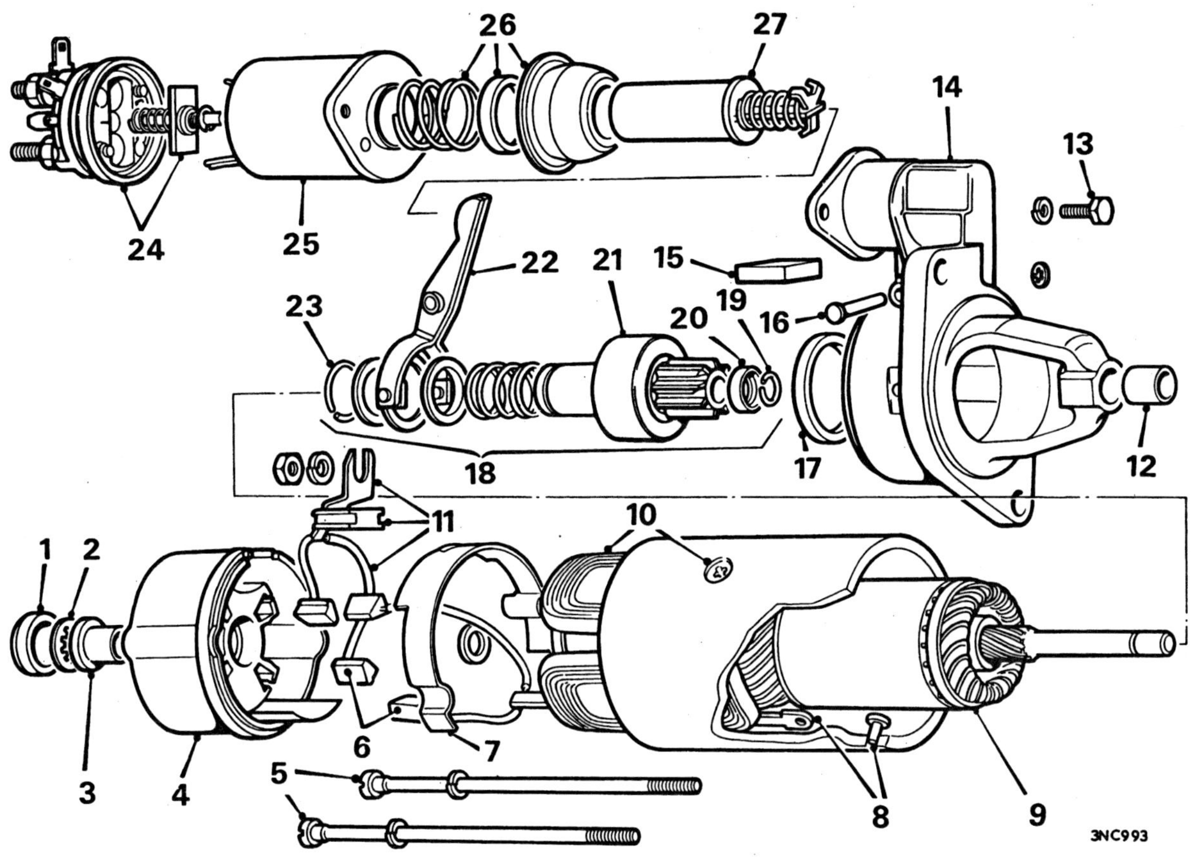

Fig. N.3

Starter motor components–Lucas 2M100 Pre-engaged

1. Armature end cap.
2. Retaining ring.
3. Bearing bush.
4. Commutator end cover.
5. Through-bolts.
6. Brushes–field winding.
7. Seal.
8. Rivet–field winding connection.
9. Armature.
10. Field winding and pole-shoe screw.
11. Brushes–terminal connector.
12. Bearing bush.
13. Screw and apring washer.
14. Drive-end bracket.
15. Sealing block.
16. Pivot pin–engagement lever.
17. Seal–drive end bracket.
18. Drive assembly.
19. Jump ring.
20. Thrust collar.
21. Roller clutch and pinion.
22. Engagement lever and thrust washers.
23. Spring ring.
24. Cover and contacts.
25. Solenoid unit.
26. Spring, seat and dust excluder.
27. Plunger and return spring.

c. Insert the springs horizontally in the brush box moulding and finally locate in position.

28. Check the insulation of each brush spring in turn, connecting the test equipment (see **'GENERAL SPECIFICATION DATA'**) between the brush spring and the commutator end-bracket.
29. Inspect the field coil insulation tape for discolouration due to burning. Ensure that the field coil interconnecting joints and the earthed joint to the yoke are satisfactory.
30. Check the field coil continuity, connecting the test equipment (see **'GENERAL SPECIFICATION DATA'**) between either field coil brush and the yoke.
31. Remove the rivet securing the field coil winding to the yoke. Ensure that neither end of the winding or the brushes are in contact with the yoke, and check the field coil insulation, connecting the test equipment (see **'GENERAL SPECIFICATION DATA'**) between one end of the field coil and the yoke.
32. If the field coils are still suspect, prove them by substitution:
    a. Remove the pole-shoe retaining screws to release the pole-shoes, field coils and through-bolt insulation pieces from the yoke.
    b. Reassemble, using new field coils, ensuring that the through-bolt insulation pieces are in a position 180° apart and 90° each side of the field coil brush connection. Tighten the pole-shoe screws to 30 lbf. ft. (4.15 kgf. m.).
    c. Rivet the field coil earth connection to the yoke.
33. Clean the commutator brush surface, using a flat surface of very fine glass-paper to remove burned

spots or slight grooving. If necessary, skim the commutator in a lathe, ensuring that the finished thickness of the commutator copper is not less than the dimension given in 'GENERAL SPECIFICATION DATA'. After skimming, polish the commutator brush surface with a flat surface of very fine glass-paper.

(See Editor's notes at end of Section N.)

34. Check the armature insulation, connecting the test equipment (see 'GENERAL SPECIFICATION DATA') between one of the commutator segments and the armature shaft.
35. Check the armature for short-circuited windings, using specialized armature testing (Growler) equipment. In the absence of this equipment a suspect armature should be checked by substitution.
36. Check the solenoid windings against the specification given in 'GENERAL SPECIFICATION DATA', connecting the test equipment (see 'GENERAL SPECIFICATION DATA') between the solenoid terminal 'STA' and the solenoid body. If the solenoid windings are satisfactory, this indicates that the contacts of a suspect solenoid are faulty and the terminal box complete with contacts should be renewed.
    a. Remove the two screws securing the terminal box to the solenoid body.
    b. Unsolder the two solenoid winding connectors on the terminal base and withdraw the terminal base and contacts from the solenoid body.
    c. Offer up the new terminal base and contact assembly to the solenoid body, ensuring that the moving contact registers correctly in the terminal base and that the dowel inside the terminal base engages the dowel hole in the solenoid body. Fit the two screws to retain the terminal base in position.
    d. Solder the two solenoid winding connections to the terminal base.

Reassembling

37. Reverse the procedure in 2 to 19, noting:
    a. Ensure that the engagement lever is attached to the roller clutch drive in the position shown.
    b. Attach the solenoid plunger to the engagement lever in the position shown.
    c. Lubricate the armature shaft helices, the moving parts of the engagement lever, the outer surface of the roller-clutch housing and the lip of the seal in the drive-end bracket with Shell SB 2628 Grease (home market and cold climates), Shell Retinax A Grease (hot climates).
    d. Refit the armature Spire nut so that the armature end-float is to the dimension given in 'GENERAL SPECIFICATION DATA'.
38. Mount the starter motor on a test bench and check its performance against the specification given in 'GENERAL SPECIFICATION DATA'.

(See Editor's notes at end of Section N.)

Refitting

39. Reverse the removing procedure in 1 to 5.

Section N.15

STARTER MOTOR SOLENOID

Removing

1. Disconnect the battery.
2. Unscrew the terminal nut and detach the cables terminal post on the solenoid.
3. Detach the cables from the terminal blades on the solenoid.
4. Slacken the nut securing the connecting link to the solenoid.
5. Remove the two screws and withdraw the solenoid from the drive end bracket.

Refitting

6. Reverse the removal procedure.

Section N.16

STARTER MOTOR RELAY

Removing

1. Disconnect the batteries.
2. Disconnect the wiring harness from the termina. blades on the starter motor relay.
3. Remove the two screws to release the starter motor relay from the right-hand wing valance.

Testing

4. Connect a 12-volt direct-current supply between the relay terminals 'W1' and 'W2', and a 12-volt, 2.2-watt test lamp in circuit with a 12-volt direct-current supply between terminals 'C1' and 'C2'.
    a. If the test lamp fails to light check the relay winding resistance, using an ohmmeter connected between terminals 'W1' and 'W2'. Renew the relay if a reading of 76 ohms is not obtained.
    b. If the winding resistance is correct, faulty contact adjustment is indicated which may be corrected as follows:
        i. Uncrimp and remove the cover from the relay.
        ii. Check the air gap between the relay bobbin core and the underside of the armature. The air gap should be 0.030 ± 0.005 in (0.76 ± 0.13 mm) when the contact points are open, and 0.010 ± 0.003 in (0.25 ± 0.08 mm.) when the points are closed. Bend the fixed contact post as necessary.

5. After any adjustment to the air gap, check the relay cut-in and drop-off voltages as follows:
   a. Connect a variable direct current supply between the relay terminals 'W1' and 'W2' and a 12-volt direct-current supply in circuit with a test lamp between terminals 'C1' and 'C2'.
   b. Raise the voltage slowly from zero to 15 volts and check that the test lamp lights at 4.0 to 7.5 volts.
   c. Reduce the voltage slowly from 15 to zero volts and check that the test lamp goes out at 5 volts maximum.
   d. Repeat operation 4 as necessary, and recheck the relay cut-in and drop-off voltages.
6. Refit the relay cover and crimp the cover lip at the points provided.

Refitting

7. Reverse the procedure in 1 to 3.

Section N.17

INSTRUMENTS AND SWITCHES

Removing

IMPORTANT.–Disconnect the battery before attempting to remove any of the switches or instruments.

TACHOMETER

1. Remove the fascia L.H. lower panel cover.
2. Unscrew the two knurled retaining nuts, disconnect the earth cable and remove the retaining brackets.
3. Withdraw the instrument from the fascia and disconnect the wiring.

OIL PRESSURE GAUGE

4. Remove the tachometer as in 1 to 3.
5. Remove the ignition warning lamp and holder.
6. Unscrew the two retaining nuts, withdraw the instrument from the fascia and disconnect the wiring.

SPEEDOMETER

7. Remove the heater air control knob, unscrew the control retaining nut, and disengage the control from its mounting bracket.
8. Unscrew the trip recorder reset knob retaining nut and disengage the reset from its bracket.
9. Unscrew the two knurled retaining nuts remove the retaining brackets and withdraw the instrument from the fascia.
10. Disconnect the drive cable from the back of the speedometer.

TEMPERATURE GAUGE

11. Remove the heater air control as described in 7.
12. Unscrew the knurled retaining nut and withdraw the instrument from the fascia.
13. Disconnect the wiring from the back of the instrument.

FUEL GAUGE

14. Unscrew the knurled retaining nut from the back of the instrument.
15. Withdraw the instrument from the fascia, disconnect the wiring and remove.

BRAKE FAILURE WARNING LAMP ASSEMBLY

16. Remove the speedometer as in 7 to 10.
17. Remove the fuel gauge as in 14 to 15.
18. Disconnect the wiring from the back of the lamp assembly.
19. Disengage the spring retaining clip and withdraw the lamp assembly.

WINDSHIELD WIPER/WASHER AND OVERDRIVE SWITCH

20. Remove the left-hand switch cowl half as in 34 and 35.
21. Remove the screw retaining the right-hand cowl half and remove the cowl.
22. Remove the two switch retaining screws.
23. Disconnect the switch wiring at the snap connectors and remove the switch complete with wiring.

DIRECTION INDICATOR AND HEADLAMP FLASHER SWITCH

24. Detach the windshield wiper/washer switch as in 20 to 23.
25. Remove the two switch retaining screws.
26. Disconnect the switch wiring at the snap connectors and remove the switch complete with wiring.

IGNITION SWITCH

27. Remove both halves of the switch cowl as in 20 and 21.
28. Unscrew the two switch retaining screws.
29. Disconnect the switch wiring at the snap connectors and remove the switch complete with wiring.

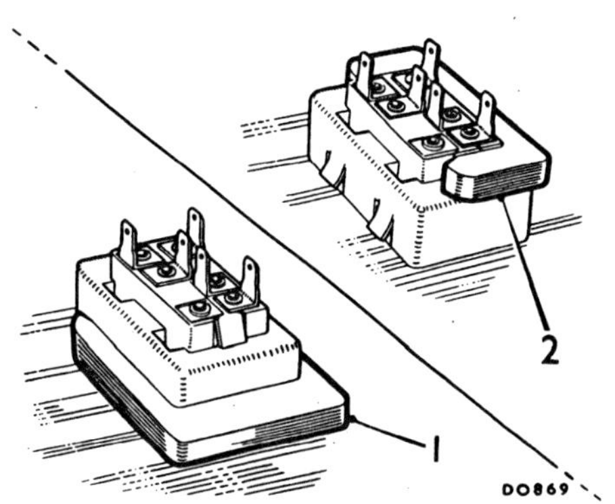

Fig. N.4

Using tool 18G 1145 to remove the switches

1. Switch complete with bezel. 2. Switch interior only.

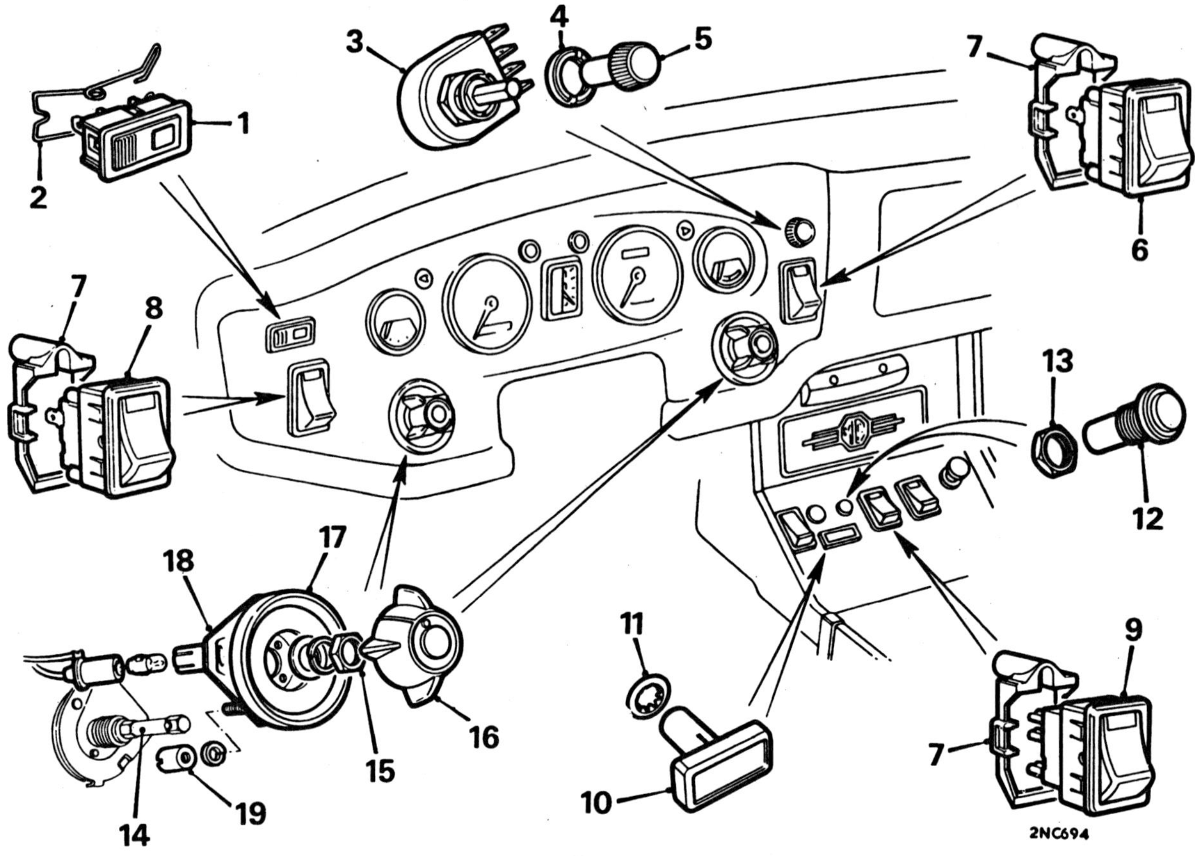

Fig. N.5
The switches, lamps, and controls

1. Brake pressure warning light test-push.
2. Retaining clip.
3. Panel lamp rheostat switch.
4. Retainer.
5. Knob for rheostat switch.
6. Heater blower switch.
7. Retainer for rocker switch.
8. Lighting switch.
9. Hazard warning switch.
10. Seat belt warning lamp.
11. Retainer for seat belt warning lamp.
12. Hazard warning lamp.
13. Retainer for hazard warning lamp.
14. Rotary control.
15. Retaining nut.
16. Rotary control knob.
17. Dial assembly.
18. Light box.
19. Retaining nut.

AUDIBLE WARNING BUZZER

30. Disconnect the electrical leads and remove the screw retaining the buzzer unit. No adjustment is possible and in the event of malfunction the buzzer unit must be replaced.

AUDIBLE WARNING DOOR SWITCH

31. Remove the one self-tapping screw, extract the switch unit and disconnect the leads from the rear of the switch.

HAZARD WARNING SWITCH

32. Remove the console–Section R.
33. Withdraw the bulbholder from the switch retainer.
34. Disconnect the wiring plug from the switch.
35. Remove the retainer from the switch and withdraw the switch from the console.

LIGHTING SWITCH

36. Unscrew the three screws securing the fascia L.H. panel cover and pull the cover forward to release it from its retaining clips at the back of the fascia.
37. Remove the bulb holder from the switch retainer.
38. Disconnect the wiring from the switch.
39. Remove the retainer from the switch and withdraw the switch from the fascia.

HEATER BLOWER SWITCH

40. Remove the glovebox–Section R.
41. Remove the face-level vents–Section R.
42. Disconnect the bulb holder from the switch retainer.
43. Disconnect the wiring from the switch.
44. Remove the retainer from the switch and withdraw the switch from the fascia.

PANEL LAMP RHEOSTAT SWITCH

45. Remove the glovebox–Section
46. Remove the face-level vents–Section
47. Disconnect the wiring from the switch.
48. Depress the pin in the switch knob and withdraw the knob from the switch.
49. Unscrew the switch retainer and remove the switch from the fascia.

SEAT BELT AND EGR/CATALYST WARNING LAMP

50. Remove the console–Section R.
51. Remove the bulb holder from the warning lamp.
52. Remove the warning lamp clip retainer and push the warning lamp out of the centre console.

HAZARD WARNING LAMP

53. Remove the centre console–Section R.
54. Remove the bulb holder from the warning lamp.
55. Unscrew the warning lamp retainer and remove the warning lamp from the centre console.

TEMPERATURE ROTARY CONTROL

56. Unscrew the three screws securing the fascia L.H. lower panel cover and pull the panel forward to release it from its retaining clips at the back of the fascia.
57. Remove the screw retaining the fascia to the cross-tube L.H. bracket.
58. Depress the pin in the switch knob and withdraw the knob from the spindle.
59. Remove the bulb holder from the rotary control light box.
60. Unscrew the nut retaining the rotary control to the fascia and remove the spring and plain washer.
61. Remove the rotary control from the fascia.
62. Unscrew the three nuts and remove the three spring and plain washers to release the light box from the dial assembly.
63. Remove the dial assembly from the fascia.

AIR FLOW ROTARY CONTROL

64. Unscrew the three screws securing the fascia L.H. lower panel cover and pull the cover forward to release it from its retaining clips at the back of the fascia.
65. Depress the pin in the switch knob and withdraw the knob from the spindle.
66. Remove the bulb holder from the rotary control light box.
67. Unscrew the nut retaining the rotary control to the fascia and remove the spring and plain washer.
68. Remove the rotary control from the fascia.
69. Unscrew the three nuts and remove the three spring and plain washers to release the light box from the dial assembly.
70. Remove the dial assembly from the fascia.

Refitting

71. Reverse the removal procedure.

Section N.18

WINDSHIELD WASHER MOTOR

Removing

1. Disconnect the battery.
2. Disconnect the wiring from the motor terminals.
3. Disconnect the water tubes.
4. Unscrew the two pump mounting screws and remove the pump assembly.

Refitting

5. Reverse the removing procedure in 1 to 4.

Section N.19

HAZARD WARNING FLASHER UNIT

Removing

1. Disconnect the battery.
2. Remove the centre console--Section R.
3. Withdraw the flasher unit from its retaining clip.
4. Disconnect the wiring plug from the flasher unit.

Refitting

5. Reverse the removing procedure in 1 to 4.

Section N.20

SEAT BELT WARNING LAMP AND BUZZER– SEAT BELT SWITCH

Removing

1. Disconnect the battery.
2. Remove the bolt to release the seat belt buckle assembly from the floor tunnel.
3. Disconnect the belt switch cables from the wiring harness at the snap connectors under the tunnel carpet.
4. Withdraw the sleeve from the buckle until the sleeve is clear of the switch and the buckle cover.
5. Prise the sides off the belt switch cover at its lower end away from the buckle and withdraw the switch cover.
6. Remove the riveted ends of the switch retaining rivets, using a drill, to release the switch from the seat buckle.
7. Unsolder the cables from the switch.

Refitting

8. Reverse the procedure in 1 to 7.

Section N.21

SEAT BELT WARNING BUZZER TIMER MODULE

Removing

1. Disconnect the battery.
2. Remove the screw securing the module to the bulkhead behind the L.H. side of the fascia.
3. Depress the retaining lever and withdraw the wiring plug from the multi connector on the module.
4. Remove the warning buzzer/timer module from the car.

Refitting

5. Reverse the procedure in 1 to 4.

[Section N.22]

1977 AND LATER INSTRUMENTS

SPEEDOMETER

Removing

1. Disconnect the battery.
2. Unscrew the three screws, securing the fascia left-hand lower panel and remove the panel.

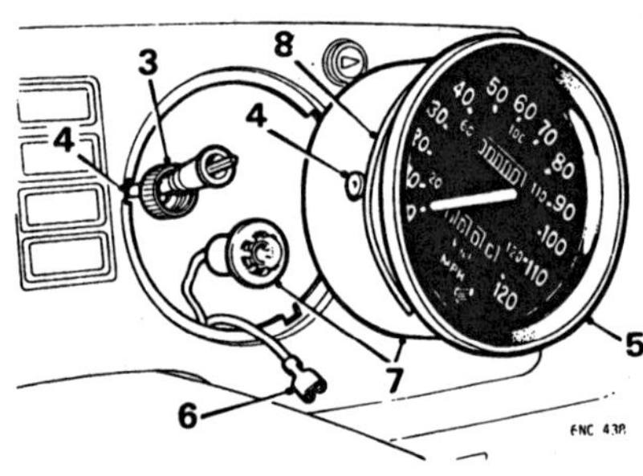

3. Unscrew the knurled nut and disconnect the speedometer cable from the speedometer.
4. Push in and turn the speedometer clockwise for 30° until the three studs located on the body of the speedometer are aligned with the cut-aways in the fascia.
5. Withdraw the speedometer.
6. Disconnect the wiring from the speedometer.
7. Pull the bulb holder from the speedometer, and remove the speedometer.
8. Remove the spring from the speedometer.

Refitting

9. Reverse the procedure in 1 to 8, noting:
   a. Fit the spring with the ends butting and not overlapping.
   b. When refitting the speedometer, first engage the studs on the speedometer body in the fascia and then push in and turn the speedometer anti-clockwise to lock it in the fascia.

SPEEDOMETER CABLE—UPPER

Removing

1. Unscrew the three screws securing the fascia left-hand lower panel and remove the panel.
2. Unscrew the knurled nut and disconnect the cable from the speedometer
3. Remove the screw and nut securing the speedometer cable support clip to the heater unit and remove the clip from the cable.
4. Unscrew the knurled nut and disconnect the upper speedometer cable from the top of the service interval counter (if fitted).
5. Release the grommet from the bulkhead and remove the cable.
6. Remove the grommet from the speedometer cable.

Refitting

7. Reverse the procedure in 1 to 6.

SPEEDOMETER CABLE—LOWER

Removing

1. Unscrew the knurled nut and disconnect the lower speedometer cable from the bottom of the service interval counter (if fitted).
2. Unscrew the knurled nut and disconnect the speedometer cable from the angled drive on the gearbox.
3. Remove the speedometer cable from the car.

Refitting

4. Reverse the procedure in 1 to 3.

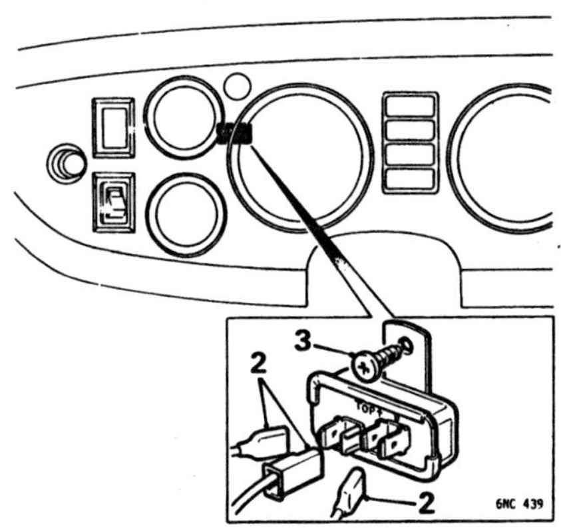

VOLTAGE STABILIZER

Removing

1. Unscrew the three screws securing the fascia left-hand lower panel and remove the panel.
2. From behind the fascia disconnect the wiring from the voltage stabilizer.
3. Remove the screw to release the voltage stabilizer from the bulkhead.

Refitting

4. Reverse the procedure in 1 to 3.

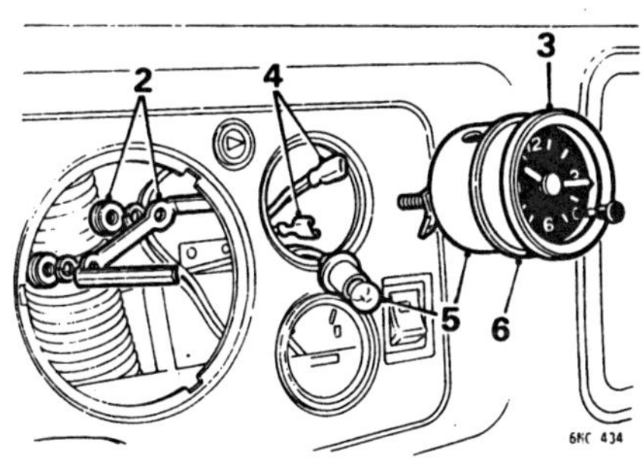

CLOCK

Removing

1. Remove the speedometer.
2. Unscrew the two knurled nuts and washers, and remove the bridge piece from behind the clock.
3. Withdraw the clock from the fascia.
4. Disconnect the wiring from the clock.
5. Pull the bulb holder from the clock, and remove the clock.
6. Remove the seal from the clock.

Refitting

7. Reverse the procedure in 1 to 6.

OIL GAUGE

Removing

1. Disconnect the battery.
2. Unscrew the three screws securing the fascia left-hand lower panel, and remove the panel.
3. Remove the two knurled nuts and washers, and the bridge piece from behind the gauge.
4. Unscrew the oil pressure pipe from the gauge. NOTE—Be careful not to lose the sealing washer for the oil pressure pipe.
5. Withdraw the gauge from the fascia.
6. Pull the bulb holder from the gauge and remove the gauge.

Refitting

7. Reverse the procedure in 1 to 6.

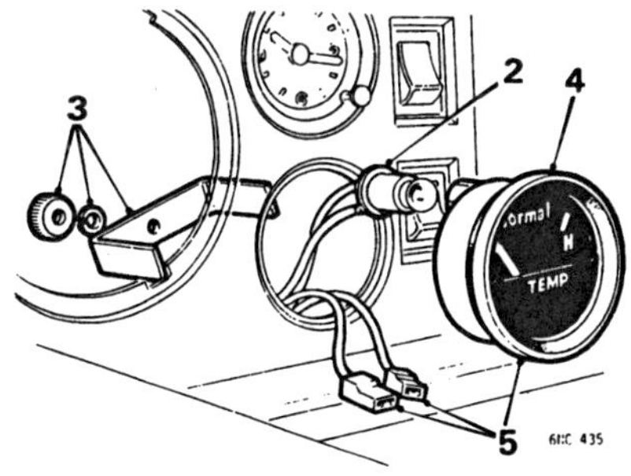

COOLANT TEMPERATURE GAUGE

Removing

1. Remove the speedometer.
2. Pull the bulb holder from the gauge.
3. Remove the knurled nut, washer, and bridge piece from the back of the gauge.
4. Withdraw the gauge from the fascia.
5. Disconnect the wiring from the gauge and remove the gauge.

Refitting

6. Reverse the procedure in 1 to 5.

COOLANT TEMPERATURE TRANSMITTER

Removing

1. Disconnect the wiring from the terminal blade on the transmitter.
2. Unscrew the temperature transmitter from the cylinder head; a quantity of coolant will be released.

Refitting

3. Reverse the procedure in 1 and 2.
4. Refill the cooling system.

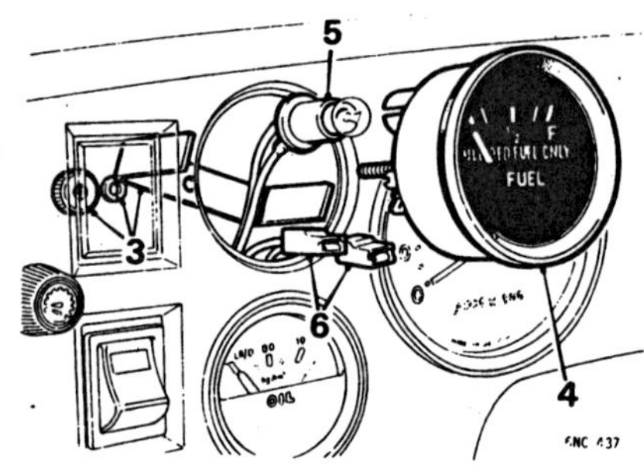

FUEL GAUGE

Removing

1. Disconnect the battery.
2. Unscrew the three screws securing the fascia left-hand lower panel and remove the panel.
3. Remove the knurled nut, spring washer, and bridge piece from behind the gauge.
4. Withdraw the gauge from the fascia.
5. Pull the bulb holder from the gauge.
6. Disconnect the wiring from the gauge.

Refitting

7. Reverse the procedure in 1 to 6.

TACHOMETER

Removing

1. Disconnect the battery.
2. Unscrew the three screws securing the fascia left-hand lower panel and remove the panel.
3. Push in and turn the tachometer clockwise for 30° until the three studs on the body of the tachometer are aligned with the cut-aways in the fascia.
4. Withdraw the tachometer from the fascia.
5. Disconnect the wiring from the tachometer.
6. Pull the bulb holder from the tachometer and remove the tachometer.
7. Remove the spring from the tachometer.

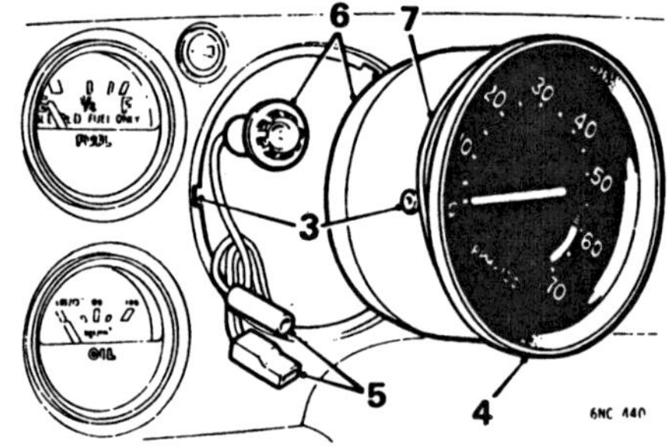

Refitting

8. Reverse the procedure in 1 to 7, noting:
   a. Fit the spring with ends butting and not overlapping.
   b. When refitting the tachometer, first engage the studs on the tachometer body in the fascia and then push in and turn the tachometer anti-clockwise to lock it in the fascia.

EDITOR'S NOTES

N. The Electrical System

Horn

If the "Windtone" horn has a poor tone or fails to sound, it can be adjusted as follows: Turn the serrated screw counterclockwise until the horn just fails to sound. (If the horn already fails to sound, first turn the screw clockwise until a sound is heard.) From the "no sound" position, turn the screw clockwise about one-quarter turn. Do not turn the adjusting screw while the horn is sounding or while electrical current is being delivered to the horn. Turn the screw in small increments, then test the horn between adjustments by applying current or depressing the horn control.

Alternator — inspection

An excellent solder for attaching the alternator rotor's field winding leads to the slip rings is the low melting point silver solder that is commonly sold for soldering stainless steel in food service applications. Though it can be applied with an ordinary soldering iron, it is about five times stronger than lead solder, has a higher melting point, and offers better electrical conductivity. Because an acid flux must be used, neutralize the joints with baking soda solution after the connections have been made. The glass paper mentioned for polishing the slip rings is sandpaper. Do not use emery cloth, which can leave behind conductive particles.

Windshield wipers — reassembling

If you cannot obtain the lubricants mentioned, use any high pressure grease (calcium universal grease). This grease is noted for its resistance to moisture. Where oil is required, use ordinary gear oil of the kind used in the rear axle.

Starter motor — inspection

The glass paper mentioned for polishing the commutator is sandpaper. Do not use emery cloth, which can leave behind conductive particles.

Starter motor — reassembling

If you cannot obtain the lubricants mentioned, use any multipurpose (lithium) grease. Regardless of what grease is used, apply it sparingly. Otherwise, the starter drive may jam in very cold weather.

SECTION Na

WIRING DIAGRAMS

1975 Wiring Diagram (with sequential seat belt control)

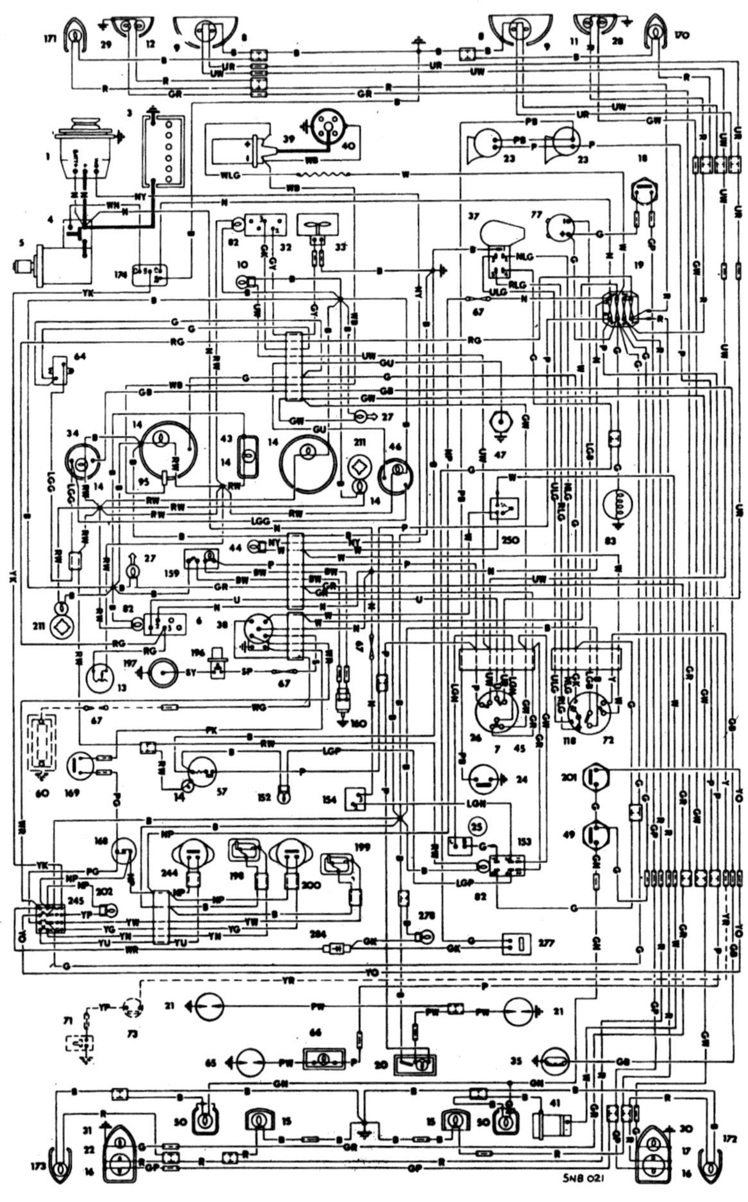

KEY TO THE WIRING DIAGRAM

1. Alternator
3. Battery
4. Starter solenoid
5. Starter motor
6. Lighting switch
7. Headlamp dip switch
8. Headlamp dip beam
9. Headlamp main beam
10. Headlamp main beam warning lamp
11. R.H. parking lamp
12. L.H. parking lamp
13. Panel lamp rheostat switch
14. Panel illumination lamp
15. Number-plate illumination lamp
16. Stop lamp
17. R.H. tail lamp
18. Stop lamp switch
19. Fuse unit (4-way)
20. Interior courtesy lamp
21. Interior lamp door switch
22. L.H. tail lamp
23. Horn
24. Horn-push
25. Flasher unit
26. Direction indicator switch
27. Direction indicator warning lamp
28. R.H. front direction indicator lamp
29. L.H. front direction indicator lamp
30. R.H. rear direction indicator lamp
31. L.H. rear direction indicator lamp
32. Heater motor switch
33. Heater motor
34. Fuel gauge
35. Fuel gauge tank unit
37. Windscreen wiper motor
38. Ignition/statrer switch
39. Ignition coil
40. Distributor
41. Fuel pump
43. Oil pressure gauge
44. Ignition warning lamp
45. Headlamp flasher switch
46. Coolant temperature gauge
47. Coolant temperature transmitter
49. Reverse lamp switch
50. Reverse lamp
57. Cigar lighter—illuminated
60. Radio*
64. Instrument voltage stabilizer
65. Luggage compartment lamp switch
66. Luggage compartment lamp
67. Line fuse
71. Overdrive solenoid*
72. Overdrive manual control switch*
73. Overdrive gear switch*
77. Windscreen washer pump
82. Switch illumination lamp
83. Induction heater
95. Tachometer
118. Combined windscreen washer and wiper switch
152. Hazard warning lamp
153. Hazard warning switch
154. Hazard warning flasher unit
159. Brake pressure warning lamp and lamp test-push
160. Brake pressure failure switch
168. Audible warning buzzer
169. Ignition key audible warning door switch
170. R.H. front side-marker lamp
171. L.H. front side-marker lamp
172. R.H. rear side-marker lamp
173. L.H. rear side-marker lamp
174. Starter solenoid relay
196. Running-on control valve
197. Running-on control valve oil pressure switch
198. Driver's seat belt buckle switch
199. Passenger's seat belt buckle switch
200. Passenger seat switch
201. Seat belt warning gearbox switch
202. 'Fasten belts' warning light
211. Heater control illumination lamp
244. Driver's seat switch
245. Sequential seat belt control unit
250. Inertia switch
277. Service interval counter
278. Service interval counter warning lamp
284. Diode for service interval counter

* Optional fitment circuits shown dotted

CABLE COLOUR CODE

N.	Brown	P.	Purple	W.	White	K.	Pink
U.	Blue	G.	Green	Y.	Yellow	O.	Orange
R.	Red	LG.	Light Green	B.	Black	S.	Slate

When a cable has two colour code letters the first denotes the main colour and the second denotes the tracer colour.

1975 Wiring Diagram (with limited period warning)

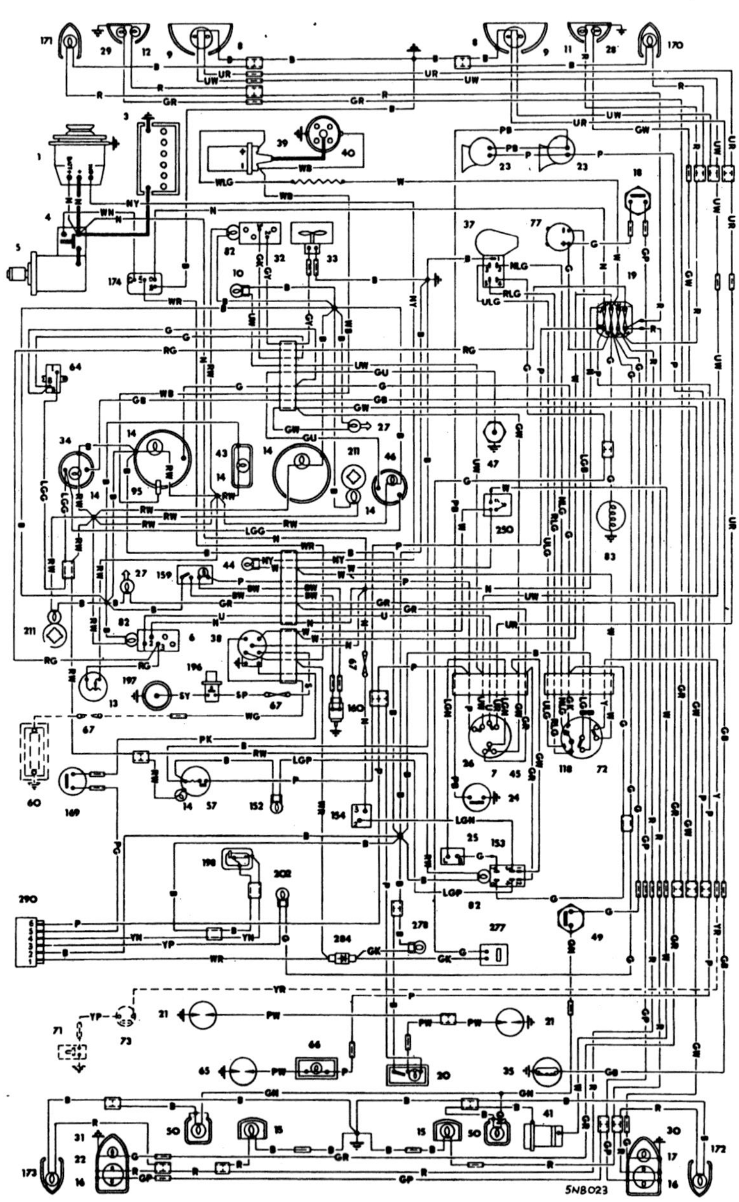

KEY TO THE WIRING DIAGRAM

1. Alternator
3. Battery
4. Starter solenoid
5. Starter motor
6. Lighting switch
7. Headlamp dip switch
8. Headlamp dip beam
9. Headlamp main beam
10. Headlamp main beam warning lamp
11. R.H. parking lamp
12. L.H. parking lamp
13. Panel lamp rheostat switch
14. Panel illumination lamp
15. Number-plate illumination lamp
16. Stop lamp
17. R.H. tail lamp
18. Stop lamp switch
19. Fuse unit (4-way)
20. Interior courtesy lamp
21. Interior lamp door switch
22. L.H. tail lamp
23. Horn
24. Horn-push
25. Flasher unit
26. Direction indicator switch
27. Direction indicator warning lamp
28. R.H. front direction indicator lamp
29. L.H. front direction indicator lamp
30. R.H. rear direction indicator lamp
31. L.H. rear direction indicator lamp
32. Heater motor switch
33. Heater motor
34. Fuel gauge
35. Fuel gauge tank unit
37. Windscreen wiper motor
38. Ignition/starter switch
39. Ignition coil
40. Distributor
41. Fuel pump
43. Oil pressure gauge
44. Ignition warning lamp
45. Headlamp flasher switch
46. Coolant temperature gauge
47. Coolant temperature transmitter
49. Reverse lamp switch
50. Reverse lamp
57. Cigar lighter—illuminated
60. Radio*
64. Instrument voltage stabilizer
65. Luggage compartment lamp switch
66. Luggage compartment lamp
67. Line fuse
71. Overdrive solenoid*
72. Overdrive manual control switch*
73. Overdrive gear switch*
77. Windscreen washer pump
82. Switch illumination lamp
83. Induction heater
95. Tachometer
118. Combined windscreen washer and wiper switch
152. Hazard warning lamp
153. Hazard warning switch
154. Hazard warning flasher unit
159. Brake pressure warning lamp and lamp test-push
160. Brake pressure failure switch
168. Audible warning buzzer
169. Ignition key audible warning door switch
170. R.H. front side-marker lamp
171. L.H. front side-marker lamp
172. R.H. rear side-marker lamp
173. L.H. rear side-marker lamp
174. Starter solenoid relay
196. Running-on control valve
197. Running-on control valve oil pressure switch
198. Driver's seat belt buckle switch
202. 'Fasten belts' warning light
211. Heater control illumination lamp
250. Inertia switch
277. Service interval counter
278. Service interval counter warning lamp
284. Diode for service interval counter
290. Time delay buzzer

* Optional fitment circuits shown dotted

CABLE COLOUR CODE

N. Brown	P. Purple	W. White	K. Pink
U. Blue	G. Green	Y. Yellow	O. Orange
R. Red	LG. Light Green	B. Black	S. Slate

When a cable has two colour code letters the first denotes the main colour and the second denotes the tracer colour.

1976 Wiring Diagram (for cars equipped with catalytic converter)

[See page 246 for 1977 model supplement.]

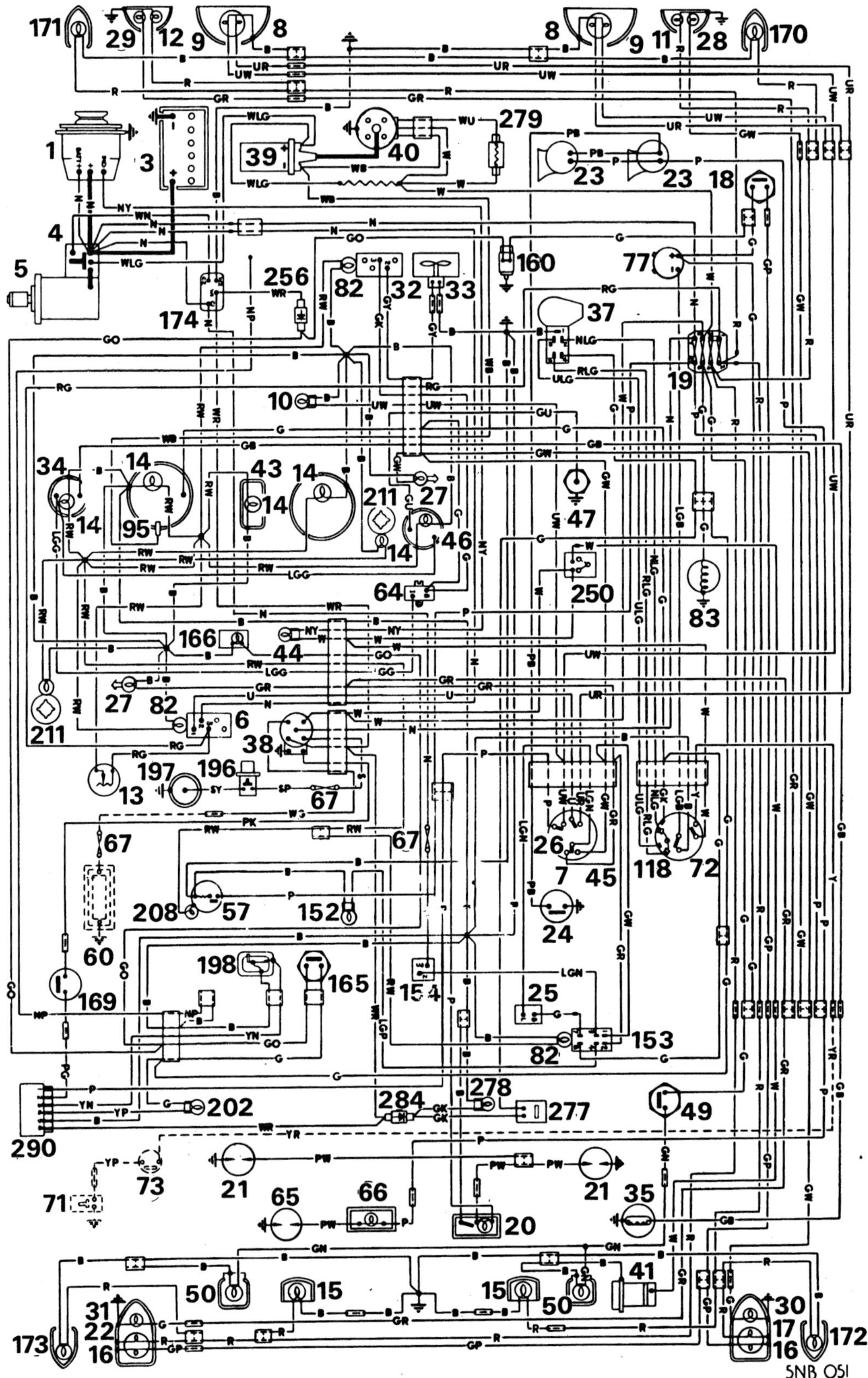

Key to 1976 Wiring Diagram
(for cars equipped with catalytic converter)

No.	Description
1.	Alternator.
3.	Battery.
4.	Starter solenoid.
5.	Starter motor.
6.	Lighting switch.
7.	Headlamp dip switch.
8.	Headlamp dip beam.
9.	Headlamp main beam.
10.	Headlamp main beam warning lamp.
11.	R.H. parking lamp.
12.	L.H. parking lamp.
13.	Panel lamp rheostat switch.
14.	Panel illumination lamp.
15.	Number-plate illumination lamps.
16.	Stop lamp.
17.	R.H. tail lamp.
18.	Stop lamp switch.
19.	Fuse unit (4-way).
20.	Interior courtesy lamp.
21.	Interior lamp door switch.
22.	L.H. tail lamp.
23.	Horn.
24.	Horn-push.
25.	Flasher unit.
26.	Direction indicator switch.
27.	Direction indicator warning lamp.
28.	R.H. front direction indicator lamp.
29.	L.H. front direction indicator lamp.
30.	R.H. rear direction indicator lamp.
31.	L.H. rear direction indicator lamp.
32.	Heater motor switch.
33.	Heater motor.
34.	Fuel gauge.
35.	Fuel gauge tank unit.
37.	Windscreen wiper motor.
38.	Ignition/starter switch.
39.	Ignition coil.
40.	Distributor.
41.	Fuel pump.
43.	Oil pressure gauge.
44.	Ignition warning lamp.
45.	Headlamp flasher switch.
46.	Coolant temperature gauge.
47.	Coolant temperature transmitter.
49.	Reverse lamp switch.
50.	Reverse lamp.
57.	Cigar lighter–illumination lamp.
60.	Radio.*
64.	Instrument voltage stabilizer.
65.	Luggage compartment lamp switch.
66.	Luggage compartment lamp.
67.	Line fuse.
71.	Overdrive solenoid.*
72.	Overdrive manual control switch.*
73.	Overdrive gear switch.*
77.	Windscreen washer pump.
82.	Switch illumination lamp.
83.	Induction heater.
95.	Tachometer.
118.	Combined windscreen washer and wiper switch.
152.	Hazard warning lamp.
153.	Hazard warning switch.
154.	Hazard warning flasher unit.
160.	Brake pressure failure switch.
165.	Hand brake switch.
166.	Hand brake warning lamp.
169.	Ignition key audible warning door switch.
170.	R.H. front side-marker lamp.
171.	L.H. front side-marker lamp.
172.	R.H. rear side-marker lamp.
173.	L.H. rear side-marker lamp.
174.	Starter solenoid relay.
196.	Running-on control valve.
197.	Running-on control valve oil pressure switch.
198.	Driver's seat belt buckle switch.
202.	'Fasten belts' warning light.
208.	Cigar lighter.
211.	Heater control illumination lamp.
250.	Inertia switch.
256.	Diode for brake warning.
277.	Service interval counter.
278.	Service interval counter warning lamp.
279.	Resistor – distributor.
284.	Diode for service interval counter.
290.	Time delay buzzer unit.

* Optional fitment circuits shown dotted.

CABLE COLOUR CODE

N.	Brown.	P.	Purple.	W.	White.	K.	Pink.
U.	Blue.	G.	Green.	Y.	Yellow.	O.	Orange.
R.	Red.	LG.	Light Green.	B.	Black.	S.	Slate.

When a cable has two colour code letters the first denotes the main colour and the second denotes the tracer colour.

1976 Wiring Diagram (for non-catalytic converter cars)

[See page 246 for 1977 model supplement.]

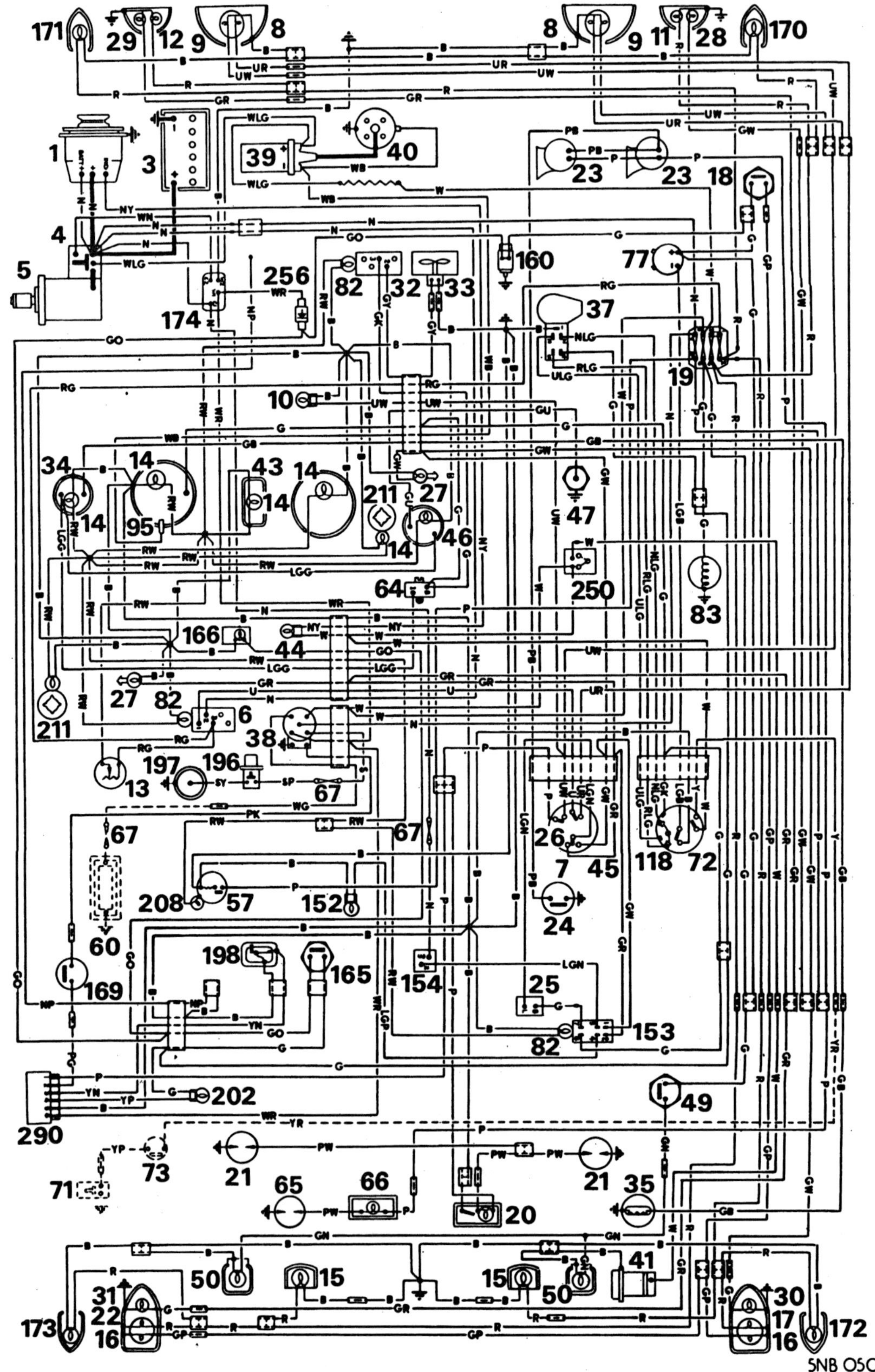

Key to 1976 Wiring Diagram (for non-catalytic converter cars)

No.	Description
1.	Alternator.
3.	Battery.
4.	Starter solenoid.
5.	Starter motor.
6.	Lighting switch.
7.	Headlamp dip switch.
8.	Headlamp dip beam.
9.	Headlamp main beam.
10.	Headlamp main beam warning lamp.
11.	R.H. parking lamp.
12.	L.H. parking lamp
13.	Panel lamp rheostat switch.
14.	Panel illumination lamp.
15.	Number-plate illumination lamps.
16.	Stop lamp.
17.	R.H. tail lamp.
18.	Stop lamp switch.
19.	Fuse unit (4-way).
20.	Interior courtesy lamp.
21.	Interior lamp door switch.
22.	L.H. tail lamp.
23.	Horn.
24.	Horn-push.
25.	Flasher unit.
26.	Direction indicator switch.
27.	Direction indicator warning lamp.
28.	R.H. front direction indicator lamp.
29.	L.H. front direction indicator lamp.
30.	R.H. rear direction indicator lamp.
31.	L.H. rear direction indicator lamp.
32.	Heater motor switch.
33.	Heater motor.
34.	Fuel gauge.
35.	Fuel gauge tank unit.
37.	Windscreen wiper motor.
38.	Ignition/starter switch.
39.	Ignition coil.
40.	Distributor.
41.	Fuel pump.
43.	Oil pressure gauge.
44.	Ignition warning lamp.
45.	Headlamp flasher switch.
46.	Coolant temperature gauge.
47.	Coolant temperature transmitter.
49.	Reverse lamp switch.
50.	Reverse lamp.
57.	Cigar lighter–illumination lamp.
60.	Radio.*
64.	Instrument voltage stabilizer.
65.	Luggage compartment lamp switch.
66.	Luggage compartment lamp.
67.	Line fuse.
71.	Overdrive solenoid.*
72.	Overdrive manual control switch.*
73.	Overdrive gear switch.*
77.	Windscreen washer pump.
82.	Switch illumination lamp.
83.	Induction heater.
95.	Tachometer.
118.	Combined windscreen washer and wiper switch.
152.	Hazard warning lamp.
153.	Hazard warning switch.
154.	Hazard warning flasher unit.
160.	Brake pressure failure switch.
165.	Hand brake switch.
166.	Hand brake warning lamp.
169.	Ignition key audible warning door switch.
170.	R.H. front side-marker lamp.
171.	L.H. front side-marker lamp.
172.	R.H. rear side-marker lamp.
173.	L.H. rear side-marker lamp.
174.	Starter solenoid relay.
196.	Running-on control valve.
197.	Running-on control valve oil pressure switch.
198.	Driver's seat belt buckle switch.
202.	'Fasten belts' warning light.
208.	Cigar lighter.
211.	Heater control illumination lamp.
250.	Inertia switch.
256.	Diode for brake warning.
290.	Time delay buzzer unit.

* Optional fitment circuits shown dotted.

CABLE COLOUR CODE

N.	Brown.	P.	Purple.	W.	White.	K.	Pink.
U.	Blue.	G.	Green.	Y.	Yellow.	O.	Orange.
R.	Red.	LG.	Light-Green.	B.	Black.	S.	Slate.

When a cable has two colour code letters the first denotes the main colour and the second denotes the tracer colour.

Wiring Diagram—1978 and Later

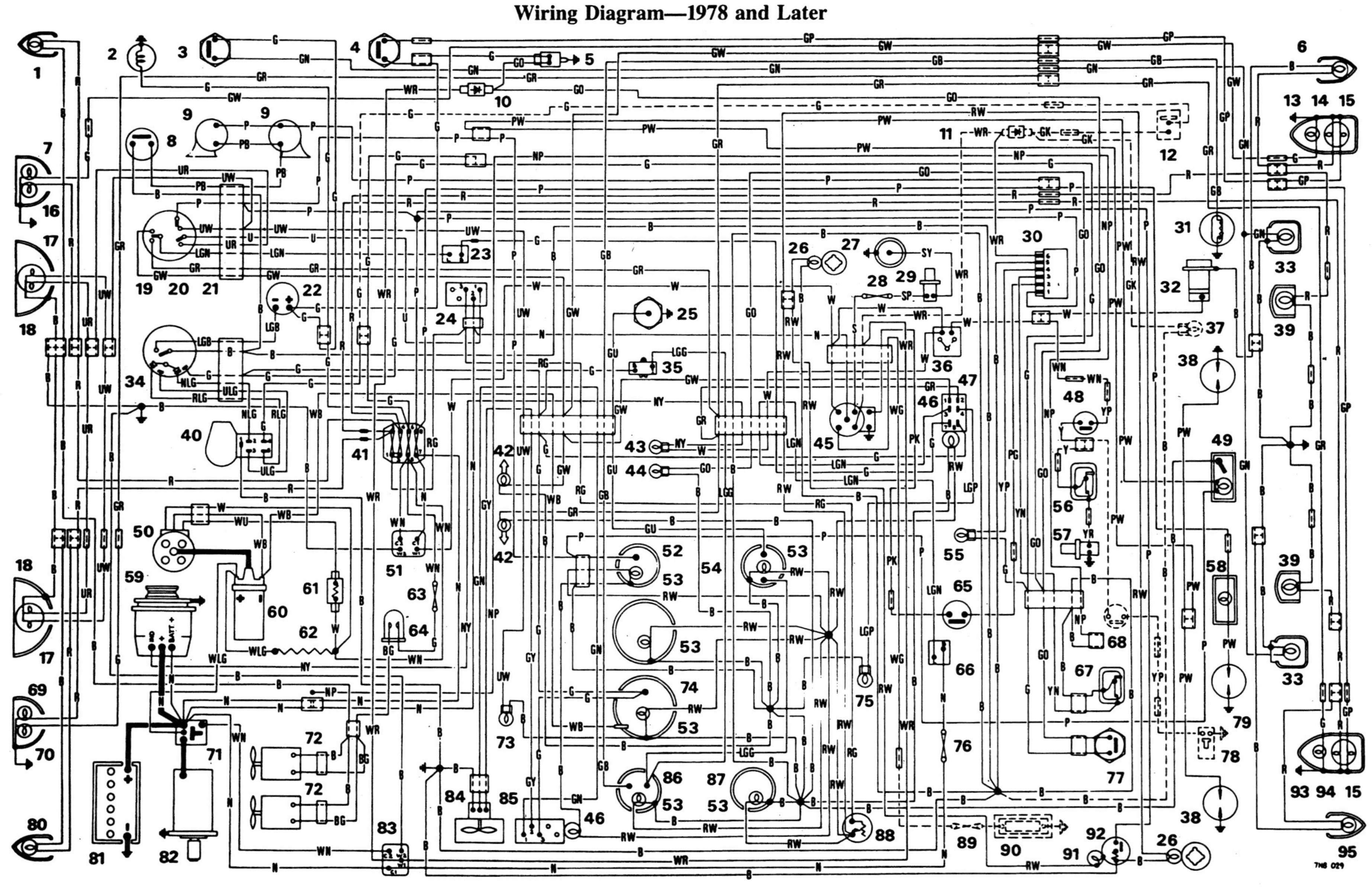

Na.10

Key to Wiring Diagram—1978 and Later

Several of the components listed in this key may not be included in the specification of all models.

1 R.H. front side marker lamp
2 Induction heater
3 Reverse lamp switch
4 Stop lamp switch
5 Brake pressure failure switch
6 R.H. rear side-marker lamp
7 R.H. front flasher lamp
8 Horn-push
9 Horn
10 Diode for brake warning
11 Diode for service interval warning lamp*
12 Service interval counter*
13 R.H. rear flasher lamp
14 R.H. tail lamp
15 Stop lamp
16 R.H. parking lamp
17 Headlamp main beam
18 Headlamp dip beam
19 Direction indicator switch
20 Headlamp dip switch
21 Headlamp flasher switch
22 Windscreen washer pump
23 Flasher unit
24 Lighting switch
25 Coolant temperature transmitter
26 Heater control illumination lamp
27 Running-on control valve oil pressure switch
28 Line fuse for running-on control valve
29 Running-on control valve
30 Time delay buzzer
31 Fuel gauge tank unit
32 Fuel pump
33 Reverse lamp
34 Combined windscreen washer and wiper switch
35 Instrument voltage stabilizer
36 Inertia switch
37 Service interval warning lamp*
38 Interior courtesy lamp door switch
39 Number-plate illumination lamp
40 Windscreen wiper motor
41 Fuse unit
42 Direction indicator warning lamp
43 Ignition warning lamp
44 Handbrake warning lamp
45 Ignition starter switch
46 Switch illumination lamp
47 Hazard warning switch
48 Overdrive gear / T.C.S.A. switch*
49 Interior lamp
50 Distributor
51 Ignition switch relay
52 Clock
53 Panel illumination lamps
54 Coolant temperature gauge
55 Seat belt warning lamp
56 Transmission control spark advance micro-switch
57 Transmission control spark advance solenoid valve
58 Luggage compartment lamp
59 Alternator.
60 Ignition coil
61 Resistor for distributor
62 Resistive cable
63 Line fuse for radiator cooling fan thermostat
64 Radiator cooling fan thermostat
65 Buzzer door switch
66 Hazard warning flasher unit
67 Driver's seat belt buckle switch
68 Overdrive manual control switch*
69 L.H. parking lamp
70 L.H. front flasher lamp
71 Starter solenoid
72 Radiator cooling fan motor
73 Headlamp main beam warning lamp
74 Tachometer
75 Hazard warning lamp
76 Line fuse for hazard warning
77 Handbrake switch
78 Overdrive solenoid
79 Luggage compartment lamp switch
80 L.H. front side-marker lamp
81 Battery
82 Starter motor
83 Starter solenoid relay
84 Heater motor
85 Heater motor switch
86 Fuel gauge
87 Oil pressure gauge
88 Panel lamp switch
89 Line fuse for radio
90 Radio
91 Cigar lighter illumination bulb
92 Cigar lighter
93 L.H. rear flasher lamp
94 L.H. tail lamp
95 L.H. rear side-marker lamp

* If fitted

48 W Y 56 57 YR B 7NA 001

Alternative circuit for Transmission Control Spark Advance (T.C.S.A.) when overdrive is not fitted.

For identification of circuit components refer to the key opposite.

CABLE COLOUR CODE

N	Brown	P	Purple	W	White	K	Pink
U	Blue	G	Green	Y	Yellow	O	Orange
R	Red	LG	Light Green	B	Black	S	Slate

When a cable has two colour code letters the first denotes the main colour and the second denotes the tracer colour

Na.11

1977 Supplementary Wiring Diagram—thermostatically controlled radiator fans

[Use in conjunction with 1976 diagram.]

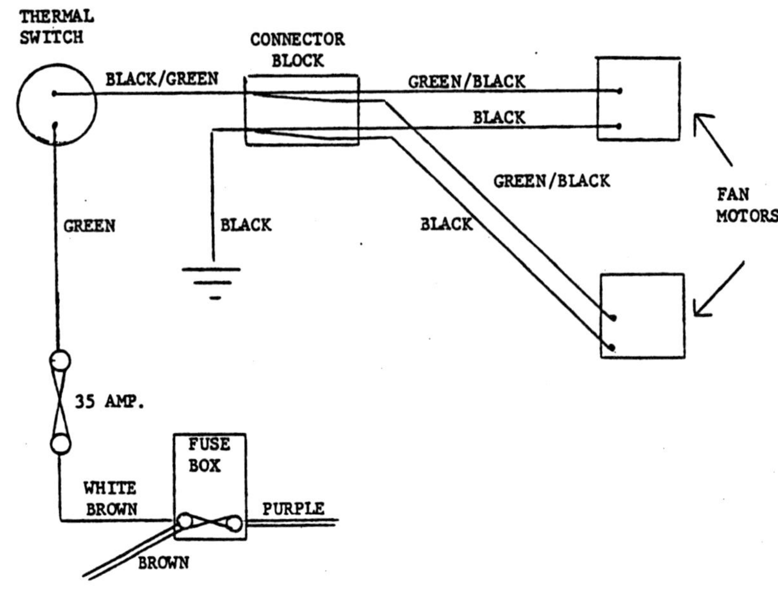

1977 Supplementary Wiring Diagram—transmission-controlled vacuum advance

[Use in conjunction with 1976 diagram.]

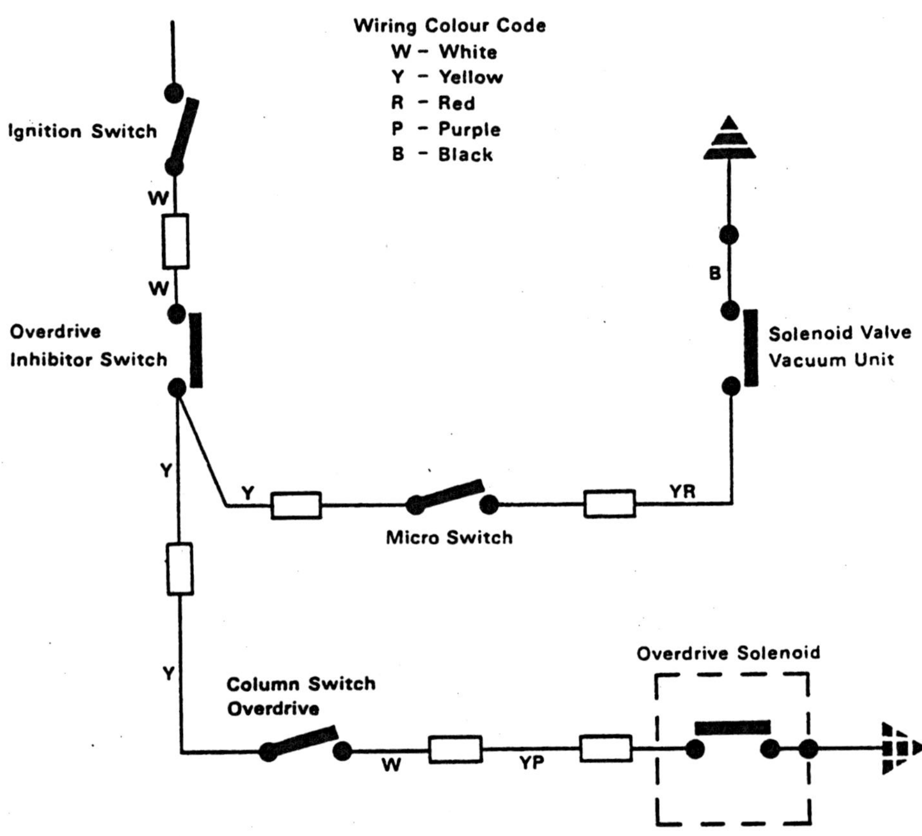

SECTION R

THE BODY

Section R.1

BONNET AND BONNET LOCK

Removing

The bonnet is of light-alloy material. Mark the hinges, support it in the open position and remove the two nuts, washers, and screws that secure each hinge to the bonnet. Remove the nut, screw and spacer to release the stay from the bonnet and lift the bonnet from the car.

Slacken the nut from the bonnet lock pin and withdraw the pin, thimble, and spring. Remove the three screws securing the safety catch to the bonnet and detach the safety catch. From the bonnet lock platform remove the two screws securing the safety catch bracket and take off the bracket. Release the bonnet lock control cable clamp screw and pull the cable from the bonnet lock plate. Unscrew the three screws securing the locating cup and bonnet lock to the platform and remove the cup and lock.

Refitting

Refitting is a reversal of the removal sequence, but ensure that the bonnet lock, safety catch, and the bonnet are correctly aligned before finally tightening the securing screws. After assembly adjust the latch pin to obtain ease of closing, lubricate the lock, catch, hinges and check them for correct operation.

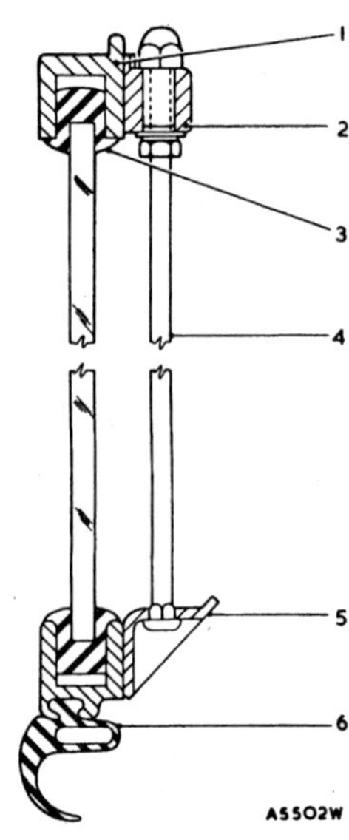

Fig. R.2
A section through the windscreen showing:

1. Top rail.
2. Centre rod upper bracket.
3. Glazing rubber.
4. Centre rod.
5. Bottom bracket.
6. Seal.

Section R.2

WINDSCREEN

Removing

Unscrew the two screws securing the lower centre rod bracket to the body. Remove the fascia (Section R.16) to gain access to the windscreen securing bolts, and then remove the bolts. Lift the windscreen from the car.

Dismantling

Remove the dome nut from the centre rod, draw the rod through the upper bracket, remove the plain washer, spring washer, and nut, and then withdraw the rod from the bottom bracket.

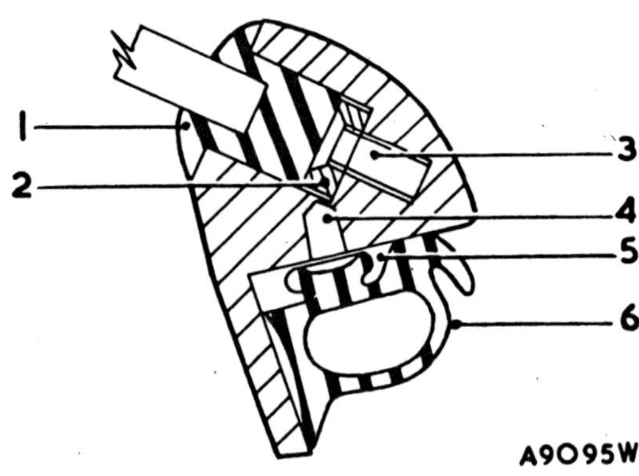

Fig. R.1
A section through a windscreen pillar, showing:

1. Glazing rubber.
2. Bottom reinforcement.
3. Screw–reinforcement to pillar.
4. Rivet–seal retainer.
5. Seal retainer.
6. Seal.

Remove the bottom rail sealing rubber and the two screws securing each corner of the bottom rail to the lower reinforcement pieces. Remove the three screws securing each end of the top rail to the pillars. Gently ease the two side pillars from the top and bottom rails and the rails from the windscreen glass.

Reassembling

Fit the glazing rubber to the screen and then mark the centre of the glass with a wax crayon to align it with the centre of the top and bottom rails. Fit the top and bottom rails and ensure that the centres of the brackets are accurately aligned with the centre-line of the glass screen. Retain the rails in this position by means of a clamp lightly applied or by temporarily assembling the centre rod.

Starting at the bottom of the pillar, carefully tap it into place with the palm of the hand, working alternately from bottom to top. When both pillars have been correctly located refit the securing screws and the lower sealing rubber.

Assemble the centre rod and ensure that the dome nut is not overtightened.

(See Editor's notes at end of Section R.)

Refitting

The foot of each pillar is supported in the body by a metal and a fibre packing piece. The packing pieces are screwed to the side of the body and should not normally be removed.

If a new windscreen is being fitted or extensive body repairs carried out, check the fit of the windscreen by fitting it to the car and checking the clearance between the body and the foot of each pillar. Adjust the fit by inserting or removing the $\frac{3}{32}$ in. (2.38 mm.) fibre packing pieces.
Place the bottom bracket packing piece on the body and the sealing grommets on the windscreen pillars. Fit the windscreen to the body and align the holes in the pillar feet with the packing pieces. Place a special washer on each of the four bolts and screw the bolts through the packing pieces and into the pillars. Spread the bottom rail sealing rubber, secure the centre rod bottom bracket to the body, and finally tighten the windscreen pillar securing bolts. Close the doors and check the fit of the ventilator window against the pillar sealing rubbers.

Section R.3

VENTILATORS

Remove the door glass assembly (Section R.4). Remove the set screws and nuts securing the ventilator top to the door. Remove the ventilator steady set screws and the set screws securing the front door glass channel to the bottom of the door. Lift out the ventilator assembly.

Refitting
Reverse the removing procedure.

Section R.4

DOOR GLASS

Remove the interior door handles and trim pad (Section R.12). Remove the remote control unit (Section R.14). Remove the regulator securing screws and the regulator extension securing screws. Release the window regulator arc from the bottom of the door glass, lift the door glass up to clear the regulator and remove the regulator and extension assembly through the door panel aperture. Remove the nut securing the door glass rear guide channel to the door. Lift out the door glass.

Refitting
Reverse the removing procedure

Section R.5

DOOR GLASS REGULATORS

Removing
Remove the interior door handles and trim pad (Section R.12). Remove the regulator securing screws and the regulator extension securing screws. Release the window regulator arc from the bottom of the door glass, lift the door glass up to clear the regulator and remove the regulator and extension assembly through the door panel aperture.

Refitting
Reverse the removal procedure.

Section R.6

SEATS

Removing
Release the seat catch and push the seat fully back to gain access to the front screws. Remove the screws and push the seat fully forward; remove the rear screws and lift the seat and seat runners from the car. Slide the seat from its runners. Retain the wooden strips and spacers.

Refitting
Refitting is a reversal of the removal sequence. Before finally tightening the front seat runners check the seats for ease of movement and correct alignment.

Section R.7

LUGGAGE COMPARTMENT LOCK

Do not in any circumstances close the luggage compartment lid when the lock mechanism is in the process of being removed or refitted.

Removing
Remove the set screw securing the lock assembly to the luggage compartment lid. Remove the notched locking ring and withdraw the push-button and lock assembly.

Refitting
Reverse the removal procedure.

Section R.8

LUGGAGE COMPARTMENT LID

Removing
Retain the lid in the open position with the stay and mark the hinges to assist when refitting. Remove the lid to hinge securing screws, and the lid to stay securing screw and nut and lift the lid from the body.

Refitting
Refitting is a reversal of the removal procedure. Check the lid for fit to the body and check the operation of the latch before finally tightening the hinge to lid securing screws.

Section R.9

DOORS AND HINGES

Removing
Remove the inner door handles and door trim pad (Section R.12).
Remove the set screws securing the hinge to the door and lift away the door.

THE WINDOW COMPONENTS

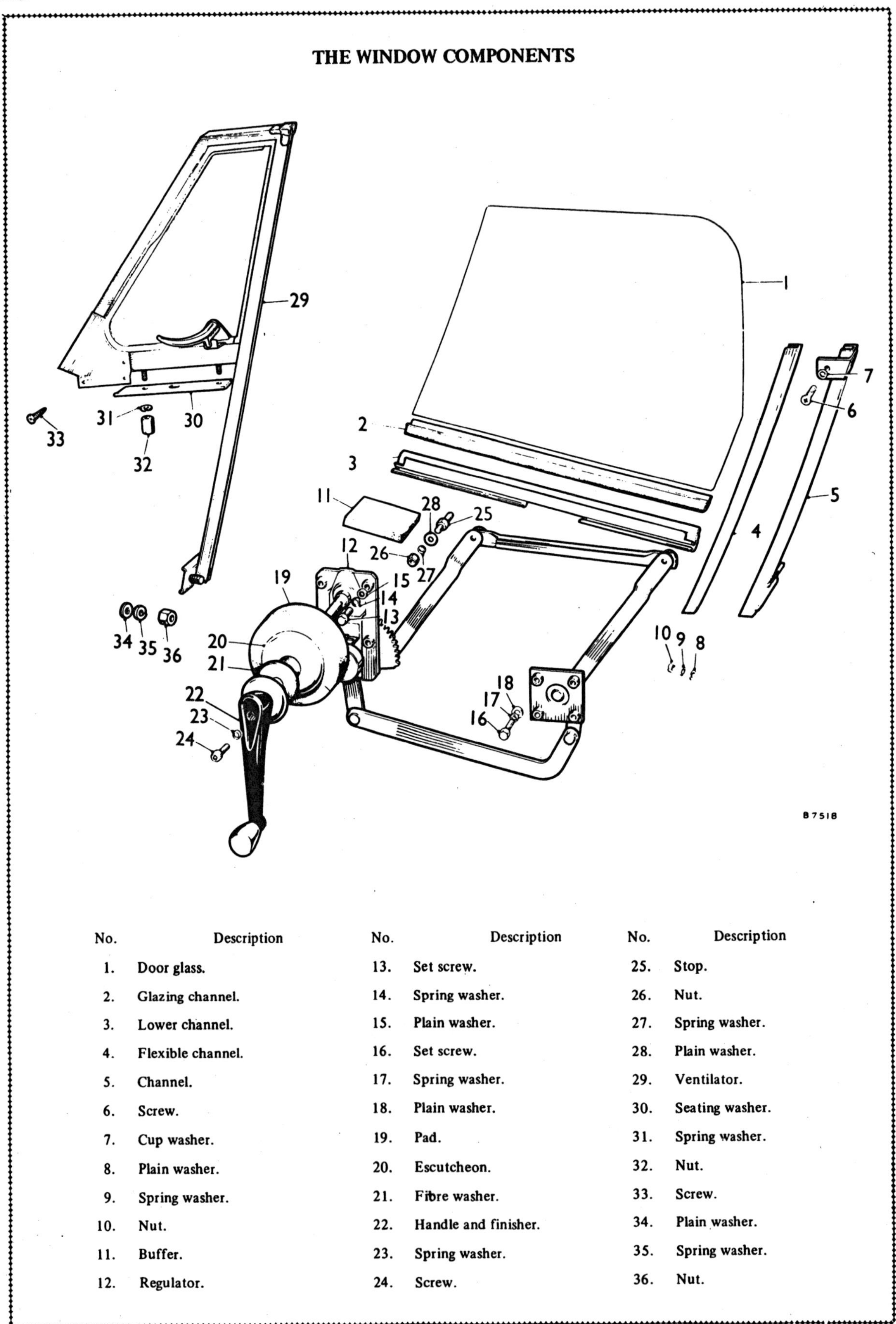

No.	Description	No.	Description	No.	Description
1.	Door glass.	13.	Set screw.	25.	Stop.
2.	Glazing channel.	14.	Spring washer.	26.	Nut.
3.	Lower channel.	15.	Plain washer.	27.	Spring washer.
4.	Flexible channel.	16.	Set screw.	28.	Plain washer.
5.	Channel.	17.	Spring washer.	29.	Ventilator.
6.	Screw.	18.	Plain washer.	30.	Seating washer.
7.	Cup washer.	19.	Pad.	31.	Spring washer.
8.	Plain washer.	20.	Escutcheon.	32.	Nut.
9.	Spring washer.	21.	Fibre washer.	33.	Screw.
10.	Nut.	22.	Handle and finisher.	34.	Plain washer.
11.	Buffer.	23.	Spring washer.	35.	Spring washer.
12.	Regulator.	24.	Screw.	36.	Nut.

To remove the hinge; from the underside of the front wing remove the six screws securing the splash panel to the body and remove the panel to gain access to the hinge bracket nuts; remove the nuts.
Unscrew the four screws securing the hinge bracket to the body and remove the hinge and bracket assembly.

Refitting
Refitting is a reversal of the removal sequence, but before finally tightening the hinge leaf screws ensure that the door lock engages correctly and that the door is correctly positioned with the body.

Section R.10

HEATER

Removing
BLOWER MOTOR ONLY
1. Disconnect the battery.
2. Disconnect the motor wiring at the snap connectors.
3. Drill out the three rivets securing the motor mounting plate and withdraw the motor complete with plate.

HEATER ASSEMBLY
5. Carry out operations 1 and 2.
6. Drain the cooling system.
7. Disconnect the hoses from the heater unit.
8. Remove the screws securing the heater unit to the engine compartment bulkhead.
9. Remove the control console.
10. Unscrew the demister tube retaining clip screws.
11. Withdraw one of the demister tube elbows and remove the tube plate.
12. Withdraw the fibre demister tubes.
13. Detach the heater air control from the fascia panel and disconnect the control cable.
14. Slacken the clip securing the air control cable to the heater unit and slide the outer cable free of the clip.
15. Lift the heater assembly from the car.

Dismantling
16. Remove the securing clips and withdraw the front panel complete with the blower motor and heater matrix.
17. Withdraw the matrix from the plate.
18. Unscrew the blower motor securing screws and remove the motor.
19. Disconnect and remove the air control cable.

Reassembling
20. Reverse the dismantling procedure in 16 to 19.

Refitting
HEATER ASSEMBLY
21. Reverse the removing procedure in 5 to 15 ensuring that the air control cable is correctly routed through the body panel, and the control functions correctly before refitting the demister tubes and speaker panel

BLOWER MOTOR
22. Reverse the removing procedure in 1 to 3.

Section R.11

DOOR LOCK ADJUSTMENT

Checking
1. Wind the window down and close the door.
2. Move the locking latch rearwards to the locked position.
3. Unlock the door by turning the key through 90 degrees towards the rear of the car.
4. Open the door by depressing the outside push-button.
5. Close the door, then open it again using the inside handle.

Adjustments
OUTSIDE PUSH-BUTTON
6. See Section R.13.

REMOTE CONTROL AND CONNECTING RODS
7. See Section R.14.

STRIKER
8. Check that with the door closed a clearance of $\frac{1}{32}$ to $\frac{1}{16}$ in. (1 to 1.6 mm.) exists between the striker and latch faces. Adjust the clearance by adding or removing shims behind the striker.
9. Slacken the striker securing screws sufficiently to permit the striker to move but tight enough to allow the door to be closed to the fully-latched position.
10. Press the door inwards or pull it outwards until it lines up correctly with the body. **Never slam the door while making adjustments.**
11. Open the door and draw a pencil line round the striker to establish its horizontal position.
12. Set the striker at right angles to the hinge axis and tighten the striker securing screws.
13. Open and close the door to check for drop or lift; slacken the securing screws to adjust the striker in the vertical plane until the door can be closed easily without rattling, lifting, or dropping. When correctly adjusted, with the door closed in the fully latched position, a fractional movement should be possible when the door is pressed in against its seals.

Section R.12

INTERIOR DOOR HANDLES AND TRIM PAD

Removing
1. Close the window, remove the screw and spring washer retaining the window regulator handle and remove the handle and its fibre washer.

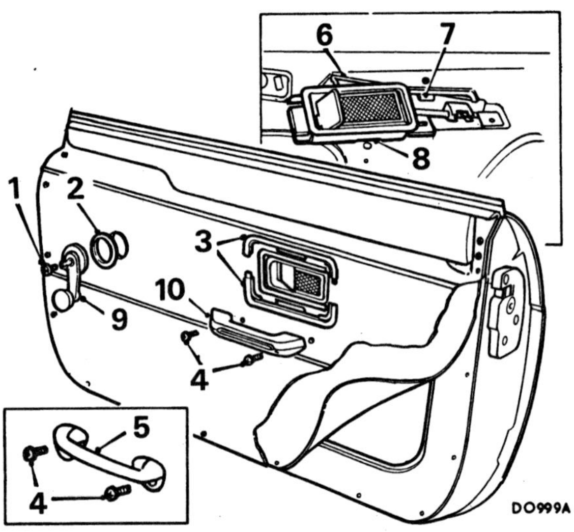

Fig. R.3
Interior door fittings–insert shows remote control being removed

1. Window regulator handle screw.
2. Fibre washer.
3. Remote control unit bezel.
4. Pull handle screw.
5. Pull handle (early models).
6. Lock control rod.
7. Anti-rattle clip.
8. Remote control unit.
9. Window regulator handle.
10. Arm-rest (later models).

2. Withdraw the two-piece plastic bezel from the remote control unit (the top half upwards, bottom half downwards).
3. Unscrew the pull handle/arm-rest securing screws and remove the pull handle/arm-rest.
4. Unscrew the waist rail securing screws and remove the waist rail.
5. Unscrew the screws securing the trim pad and remove the pad.
6. Peel the plastic waterproof cover from the door as required.

Refitting

7. Reverse the removing procedure in 1 to 6 ensuring that the lock and window mechanism is adequately greased and that the door cut-outs and waterproof cover are securely taped.

Section R.13

OUTSIDE DOOR HANDLES

Removing

1. Remove the interior door handles and trim pad–Section R.12.
2. Wind the window fully up, remove the two nuts, spring and plain washers securing the door handle to the door and remove the handle complete with its seating washers.

Refitting

3. Set the latch to the closed position and temporarily fit the handle and seating washers.
4. With access through one of the inner door panel apertures, check the clearance between the push-button plunger bolt and the latch contactor; do not depress the push-button while checking the clearance. The clearance must not be less than $\frac{1}{32}$ in. (1 mm.). Adjust the clearance by slackening the locknut and screwing the plunger bolt in or out as required. Tighten the locknut.
5. Fit the spring and flat washers and screw on and tighten the securing nuts.

Section R.14

DOOR LOCKS

IMPORTANT.–Before removing any part of the door lock mechanism because of unsatisfactory operation, first check that the condition is not caused by incorrect adjustment. See Section R.11

Removing

1. Remove the interior door handles and trim pad–Section R.12.

REMOTE CONTROL UNIT

2. Detach the latch release rod and lock control rod from their retaining clips and bushes on the latch levers.
3. Remove the three remote control retaining screws and washers, and self-tapping screw (later cars).
4. Withdraw the lock control rod from its bush in the top of the locking latch.
5. Remove the remote control unit complete with the latch release rod. If necessary, the lock control rod can be removed after withdrawing it downwards from its anti-rattle clip.

LATCH UNIT

6. Remove the three screws securing the latch to the door and remove the latch.

KEY-OPERATED LOCK

7. From inside the door, compress the legs of the retaining collar and withdraw the lock barrel from outside the door.

Refitting

KEY-OPERATED LOCK

8. Check that the retaining collar is correctly positioned; enter the lock barrel into the door aperture with its operating fork inclined away from the door shut face and press the lock barrel firmly into position.

LATCH UNIT

9. Check that the plastic bushes and spring clips are correctly assembled in their respective holes in the release lever and the locking slide. Each bush must be fitted with its head away from the centre of the latch with the spring clip fitted under the head (see inset A, Fig. R.4).
10. Locate the latch on the door face with the levers entered through the slots provided.

11. Engage the locking lever with the key-operated lock fork.
12. Fit and tighten the latch securing screws.

REMOTE-CONTROL UNIT

13. Check that the latch release rod is fully engaged in its plastic clip attached to the remote-control unit.
14. Check that the lock control rod is fully pressed up into the anti-rattle clip inside the door.
15. Position the remote-control unit in the door and press the end of the lock control rod into the bush in the locking latch.
16. Fit the remote control securing screws and washers but do not tighten.
17. Press the end of the latch release rod into its bush and clip in the latch release lever.
18. Press the lock control rod pivot end into the bush in the locking slide.

Adjusting the remote control

19. With the remote-control unit securing screws slackened, move the control unit towards the latch, without compressing the rod spring, until the latch release lever just contacts its stop, then tighten the

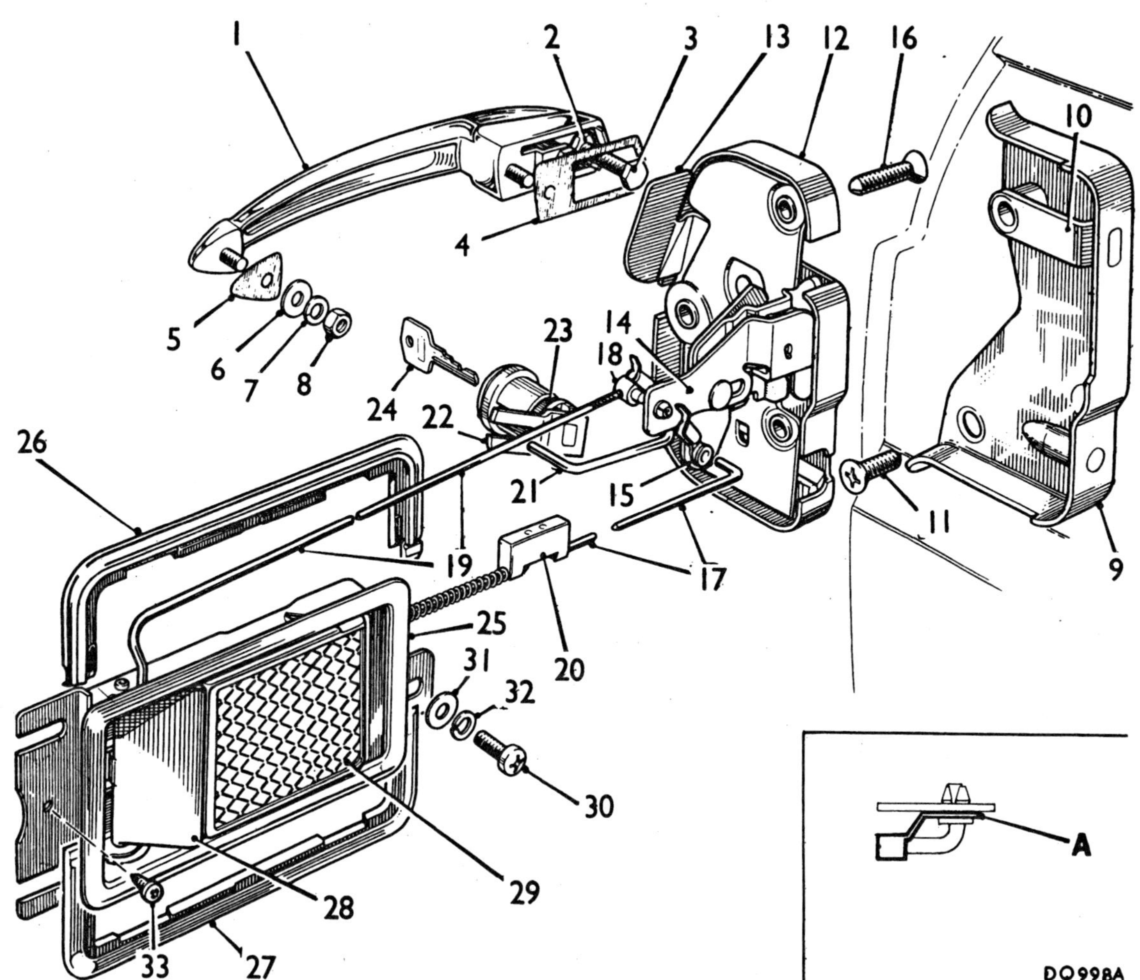

Fig. R.4
Exploded view of door lock mechanism

1. Push-button.
2. Locknut.
3. Push-button plunger bolt.
4. Sealing washer.
5. Sealing washer.
6. Plain washer.
7. Spring washer.
8. Nut.
9. Striker.
10. Anti-burst strap.
11. Striker screw.
12. Latch unit.
13. Latch contactor.
14. Locking slide.
15. Latch release lever.
16. Latch unit screw.
17. Latch release rod.
18. Screwed pivot.
19. Lock control rod.
20. Plastic clip.
21. Locking lever.
22. Lock operating fork.
23. Key operated lock.
24. Key.
25. Remote control unit.
26. Remote control bezel–upper.
27. Remote control bezel–lower.
28. Locking latch.
29. Inside door handle.
30. Remote control unit screw.
31. Plain washer.
32. Spring washer.
33. Self-tapping screw.

control unit screws. If the control unit adjustment is restricted by the securing screw slots, enlarge the slots by filing.

20. With the latch in the closed position, check the operation of the latch release handle. The striker should be released before the handle has reached the full extent of its movement. Fit self-tapping screw.
21. With the latch in the closed position set the locking latch rearwards to the locked position.
22. Adjust the position of the screwed pivot on the lock control rod so that the locking latch overlaps the latch release handle, the pivot pin fits freely into its bush in the locking slide, before being pressed into the spring clip.
23. Check the operation of the lock mechanism as described in Section R.11.

Lubrication

24. Smear the linkages inside the door with grease and add a few drops of thin oil into the key slots.
    IMPORTANT.–Key locks must not be lubricated with grease.

Section R.15

CONSOLE

Removing

1. Disconnect the battery.
2. Remove the change speed lever knob and locknut.
3. Unscrew the four screws securing the retaining ring.
4. Raise the hinged arm-rest, remove the retaining screw and withdraw the arm-rest assembly complete with the change speed lever gaiter and retaining ring.
5. Remove the four screws retaining the console.
6. Partially withdraw the console, disconnect the wiring from the back and then remove the console.

Refitting

7. Reverse the removing procedure in 1 to 6.

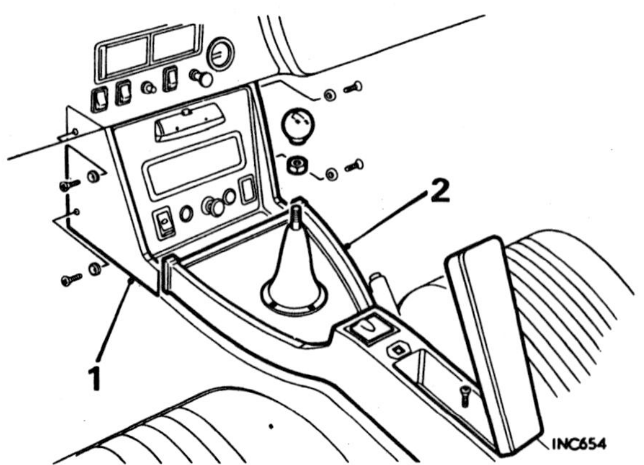

Fig. R.5
Removing the console
1. Console 2. Arm rest.

Section R.16

FASCIA

Removing

1. Disconnect the battery.
2. Unscrew the three retaining screws from the lower fascia cover panels and remove the panels.
3. Remove the heater air control knob, unscrew the control securing nut and disengage the control from its fixing bracket.
4. Remove the heater temperature control knob, unscrew the control securing nut and disengage the control from its fixing bracket.
5. Remove the two fixing screws from the lower edge of the fascia.
6. Unscrew the two knurled nuts retaining the tachometer, disconnect the earth wire, and remove the retaining brackets.
7. Disconnect the wiring from the tachometer and remove the instrument.
8. Remove the six nuts from the fascia upper edge fixing studs.
9. Remove the screws securing each end of the fascia trim piping from behind the fascia.
10. Unscrew the trip recorder reset knob retaining nut and disengage the reset from its bracket.
11. Disconnect the speedometer drive cable from the back of the instrument.
12. Ease the fascia assembly rearwards to disengage the top fixing studs from the body panel, then lift the assembly clear of the steering-column switch cowl.
13. Disconnect the wiring from the instruments and switches, withdraw the mixture control cable and remove the fascia complete with instruments and switches.

Refitting

14. Reverse the removing procedure in 1 to 13.

Section R.17

GLOVEBOX AND LID

Removing

GLOVEBOX ONLY

1. Remove the screw retaining the stay to the glovebox lid.
2. Remove the screws retaining the glovebox lid stay to the glovebox.
3. Remove the screws securing the glovebox lid catch.
4. Remove the screws retaining the glovebox.
5. Withdraw the glovebox.

GLOVEBOX LID

6. Carry out operations 1 to 5.

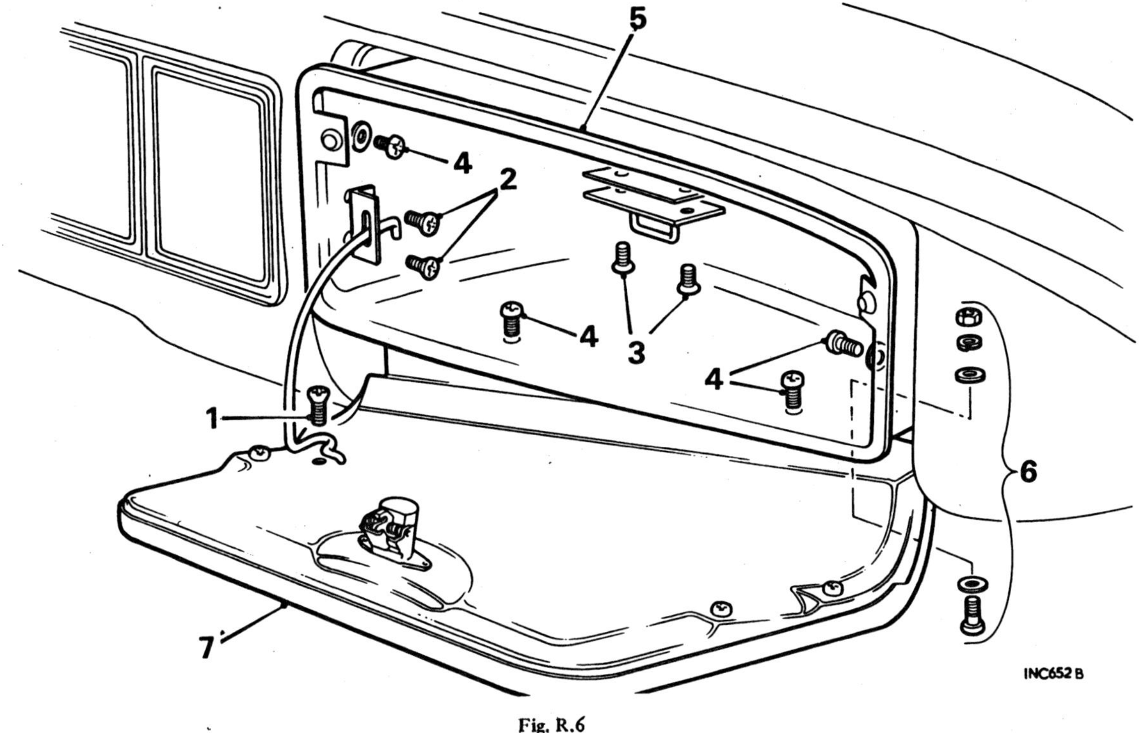

Fig. R.6
The glovebox and lid

1. Screws for glovebox lid stay.
2. Screws for glovebox lid stay.
3. Screws for catch.
4. Screws for glovebox.
5. Glovebox.
6. Screws for glovebox lid hinge.
7. Glovebox lid.

7. Remove the screws and nuts securing the glovebox lid and withdraw the lid.

Refitting

GLOVEBOX LID

8. Reverse the removing procedure in 6 to 7.

GLOVEBOX

9. Reverse the removing procedure in 1 to 5.

Section R.18

FACE-LEVEL VENTS

Removing

FACE-LEVEL VENTS AND ESCUTCHEON ASSEMBLY

1. Remove the glovebox–Section R.17.
2. Disconnect the air duct hoses from the back of the face-level vents.
3. Remove the two screws and retaining strap securing the escutcheon assembly to the fascia.
4. Withdraw the face-level vents and escutcheon assembly from the fascia.

FACE-LEVEL VENTS

5. Carry out operations 1 to 4.
6. In turn, ease each bottom locating tag of one vent inwards and slightly withdraw the vent until the tag rests on the lip of the escutcheon.
7. With the aid of a narrow blade tool, inserted from the back between the escutcheon and the vent, depress the two top locating tags.
8. Withdraw the vent from the escutcheon.
9. Repeat 6 to 8 for the remaining face-level vent.

Refitting

FACE-LEVEL VENTS

10. Push one only of the face-level vents into the escutcheon noting:
    a. Ensure that the rounded corners of the face-level vent adjacent to the serrated wheel registers in the recess of the escutcheon with the rounded corners.
    b. The vent assemblies are marked L.H. (left-hand) and R.H. (right-hand) on their flaps for correct assembly when viewing the fascia from inside the car.
11. Reverse the removing procedure in 3 to 4 ensuring that the escutcheon assembly is fitted with the serrated wheels uppermost.
12. Push in the remaining face-level vent into the escutcheon noting operation 10 a.
13. Reverse the removing procedure in 1 to 2.

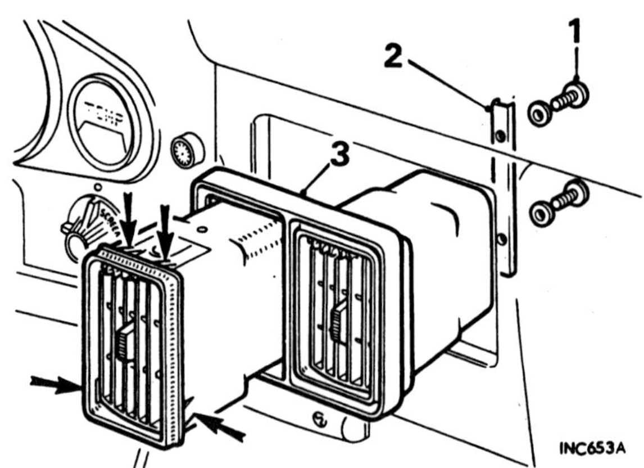

Fig. R.7
Removing the face-level vent showing the locating tags arrowed

1. Screw for retaining strap 2. Retaining strap. 3. Escutcheon.

FACE-LEVEL VENT AND ESCUTCHEON ASSEMBLY

14. Reverse the operations 6 to 8 to refit one of the face-level vents.
15. Carry out operations 11 to 13.

Section R.19

SEAT BELTS

Removing

SHORT BELT

1. Lift the carpet adjacent to the tunnel and disconnect the wiring from the seat belt.
2. Remove the bolt and spacer to release the belt.

LONG BELT AND REEL

3. Remove the bolt, waved washer and spacer to release the belt from the sill.
4. Remove the bolt and spring washer to release the reel from the rear wheel arch.

Refitting

LONG BELT AND REEL

5. Reverse the removing procedure in 3 to 4.

SHORT BELT

6. Reverse the removing procedure in 1 to 2.

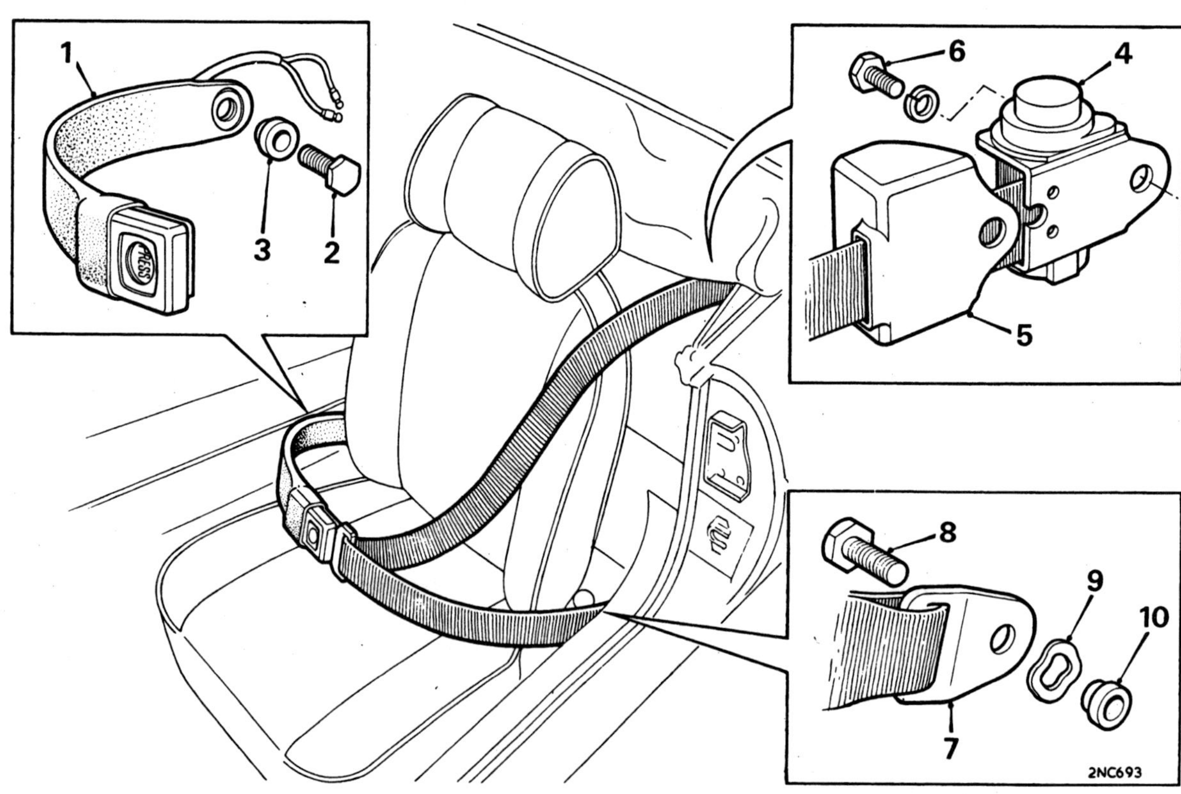

Fig. R.8
Seat belt fixings

1. Short belt.
2. Retaining bolt.
3. Spacer.
4. Seat belt reel
5. Cover for reel.
6. Retaining bolt.
7. Seat belt sill mounting.
8. Retaining bolt.
9. Anti-rattle washer.
10. Spacer.

Section R.20

ANTI-BURST DOOR UNITS

Removing

ANTI-BURST PLATE UNIT

1. Remove the two screws to release the plate from 'B' post.

ANTI-BURST PIN UNIT

2. Remove the door trim pad–Section R.12.
3. Unscrew the nut and remove the spring washer to release the pin unit from the door.

Refitting

ANTI-BURST PIN UNIT

4. Reverse the removing procedure in 2 to 3.

ANTI-BURST PLATE UNIT

5. Refit the plate unit to the 'B' post and retain in position with the two screws.

Section R.21

FRONT BUMPER ASSEMBLY

Removing

1. Disconnect the battery.
2. Disconnect the parking flasher lamp wiring at the connectors under the bonnet and pull the leads through the rubber grommet so they hang under the front wings.
3. Remove the four nuts and eight washers securing the bumper inner mountings to the longitudinal chassis members

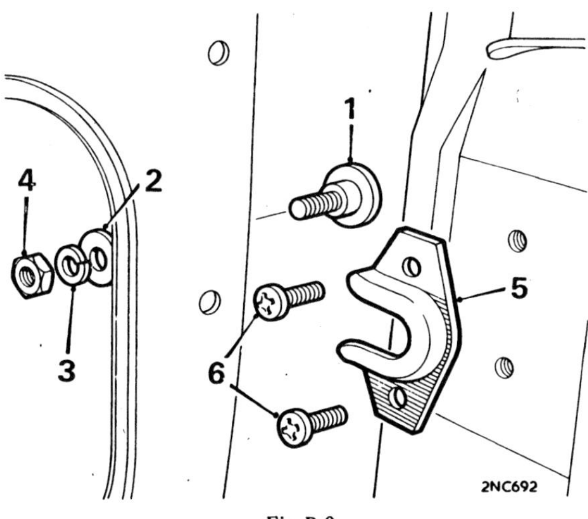

Fig. R.9
Anti-burst door unit

1. Door pin.
2. Plain washer.
3. Spring washer.
4. Retaining nut for pin.
5. Plate.
6. Retaining screws.

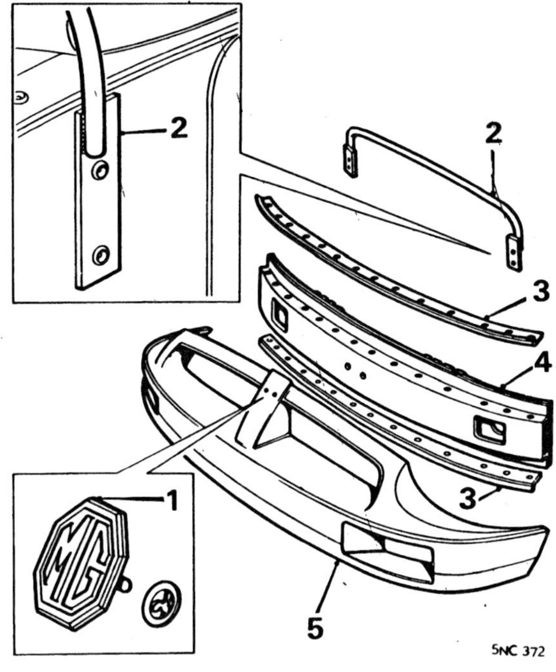

Fig. R.10

The front bumper components

1. 'MG' motif
2. Support tube
3. Clamping plate
4. Armature
5. Rubber bumper bar

4. Remove the four bolts and eight washers securing the bumper to the outer springs.
5. Remove the bumper assembly and collect the two towing eyes from the outer springs, and the spacer plates (if fitted) from the inner mountings, noting the quantity of spacer plates on each side.

Dismantling

6. Remove the two bolts and washers to release the number-plate assembly.
7. Remove the lamp lenses and lamp assemblies.
8. Remove the 'MG' motif.
9. Drill the heads of the four rivets and remove the support tube.
10. Drill the heads off the rivets securing the rubber bumper bar to the armature, levering the rubber clear of the top rivets as necessary.
11. Punch the rivets through into the armature and remove the clamping plates.
12. Remove the armature from the rubber.

Reassembling

13. Ensure that the new rivets fit all the holes in the rubber; if necessary clear the holes with a drill.
14. Fit the armature into the rubber, ensuring that the number-plate bracket holes are towards the bottom of the assembly.
15. Fit the bottom clamping plate and insert the centre rivet and both end rivets.

16. Secure the three fitted rivets.
17. Fit and secure the remainder of the bottom rivets.
18. Fit the top clamping plate and insert the centre rivet and both end rivets.
19. Clamp the rubber to the armature with 'G' clamps.
20. Lever back the rubber as necessary and secure the three fitted rivets.
21. Lever back the rubber as necessary and fit and secure the remainder of the top rivets.
    NOTE: It may be necessary to move the clamps so that they are close to the area being levered.
22. Rivet on the support tube.
23. Fit the 'MG' motif, the number-plate assembly and the lamp assemblies and lenses, noting that the drain slots in the lenses fit downwards.

Refitting

24. Reverse the procedure in 1 to 5.

Section R.22

REAR BUMPER ASSEMBLY

Removing

1. Remove the nut, washer and spacer securing the bumper to each rear wing.
2. Bend back the rubber from the rear wing and detach the side fixing bracket and spacer from each side of the bumper.
3. Remove, from inside the boot, the three nuts and six washers securing the bumper assembly to the L.H., R.H. and centre of the rear body panel.
4. Remove, from under the rear body panel, the two nuts and four washers securing the bumper assembly to the body.
5. Remove the bumper assembly.

Dismantling and reassembling

6. Follow as necessary the procedure for dismantling and reassembling the front bumper, see Section R.21. noting that the rear bumper is fitted with lashing brackets which should be refitted towards the bottom of the assembly

Refitting

7. Reverse the procedure in 1 to 5, ensuring that the bumper assembly is central about the body before tightening the five nuts securing the assembly to the rear body panel.

Section R.23

BODY ALIGNMENT DIMENSIONS

VERTICAL ALIGNMENT CHECK

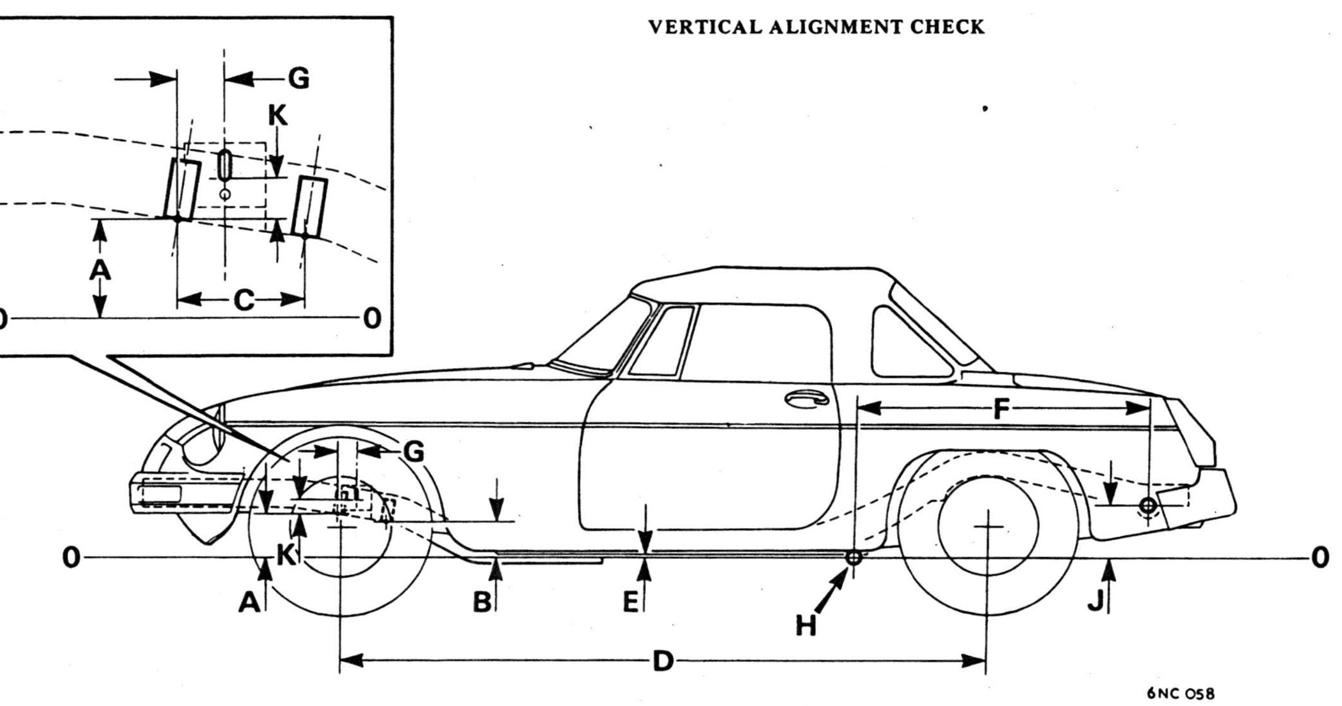

Code	Dimension		Location
O			Datum
A	$6\frac{31}{64}$ in	164.70 mm	Datum to front cross member – front mounting
B	$5\frac{41}{64}$ in	143.28 mm	Datum to front cross member – rear mounting
C	$6\frac{7}{16} \pm \frac{1}{32}$ in	163.51 ± 0.79 mm	Front cross member – front to rear mounting
D	$91\frac{1}{8}$ in	231.5 cm	Wheelbase
E	$\frac{31}{32}$ in	24.61 mm	Datum to bottom sill
F	$43\frac{1}{16} \pm \frac{1}{16}$ in	1093.79 ± 1.59	Rear spring centres – eye to eye
G	$2\frac{1}{8}$ in	53.97 mm.	Engine mounting to front cross member front mounting (rearward dimension)
H	$0 \pm \frac{1}{16}$ in	0 ± 1.59 mm	Datum to rear spring – front mounting
J	$5\frac{5}{8} \pm \frac{1}{32}$ in	142.87 ± 0.79 mm	Datum to rear spring – rear shackle mounting
K	$1\frac{13}{32} \pm \frac{1}{32}$ in	35.72 ± 0.79 mm	Engine mounting to front cross member front mounting (height)

HORIZONTAL ALIGNMENT CHECK

76.10.01

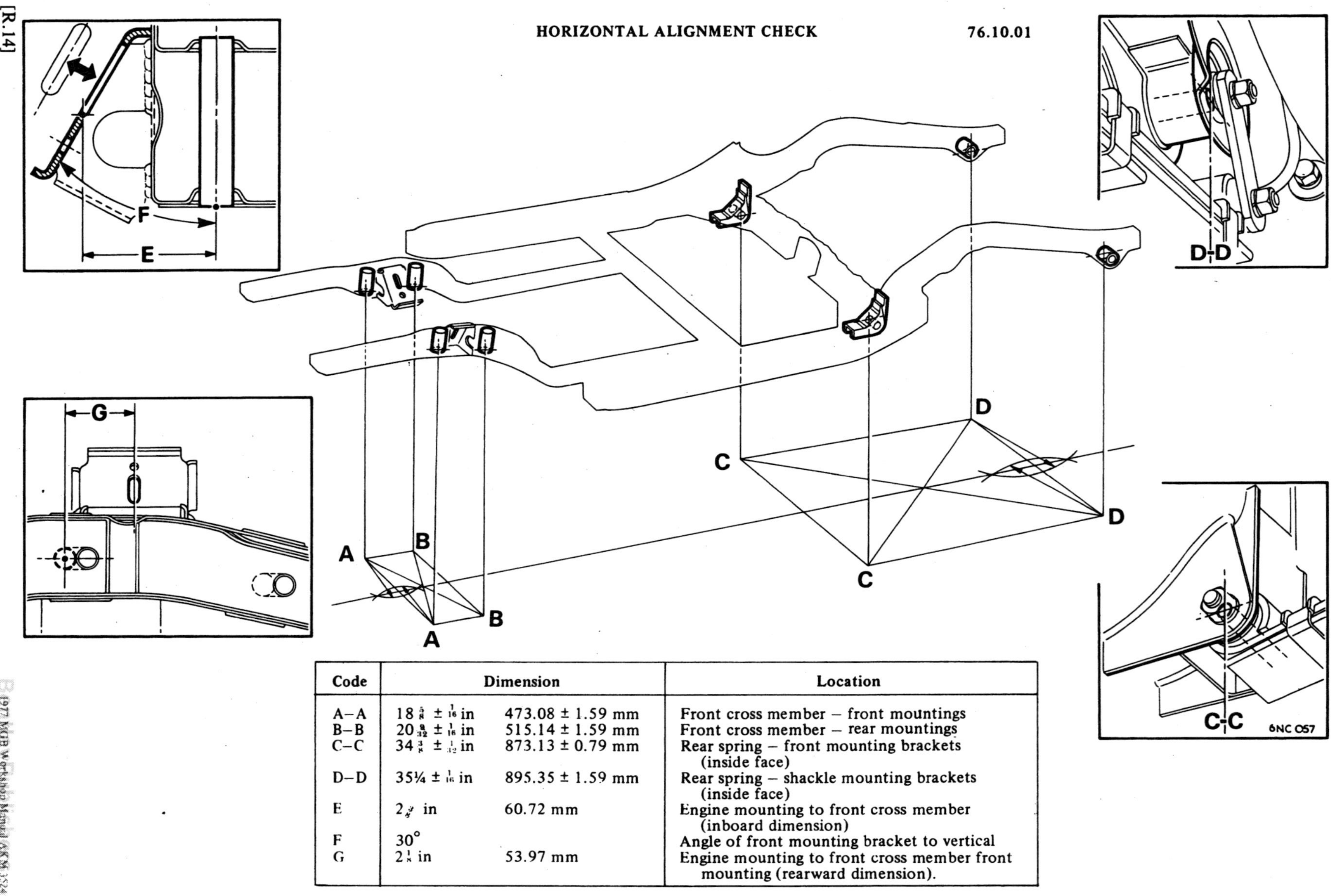

Code	Dimension		Location
A–A	18 5/8 ± 1/16 in	473.08 ± 1.59 mm	Front cross member – front mountings
B–B	20 9/32 ± 1/16 in	515.14 ± 1.59 mm	Front cross member – rear mountings
C–C	34 3/8 ± 1/32 in	873.13 ± 0.79 mm	Rear spring – front mounting brackets (inside face)
D–D	35¼ ± 1/16 in	895.35 ± 1.59 mm	Rear spring – shackle mounting brackets (inside face)
E	2 3/8 in	60.72 mm	Engine mounting to front cross member (inboard dimension)
F	30°		Angle of front mounting bracket to vertical
G	2 1/8 in	53.97 mm	Engine mounting to front cross member front mounting (rearward dimension).

[Section R.24]

REAR WINDOW

If the rear window becomes creased because it has been folded when the top was lowered or stored, you can roll out the crease with a plastic bottle filled with hot water. When rolling out the crease, place the rear window on a clean, soft cloth that has been spread on a smooth tabletop.

EDITOR'S NOTES

R. The Body

Windscreen — reassembling

A silicone sealant (such as G.E. 1200 slow setting) should be used in the glass groove of the glazing rubber — mainly at the bottom and the sides of the windscreen. The sealant should be allowed to cure for six hours with the top up.

Technical Service Bulletin 73-C-1
Technical Service Bulletin 76-C-1 of February, 1976

SECTION S

SERVICE TOOLS

All Service tools mentioned in this Manual are only obtainable from the tool manufacturer:

Messrs. V. L. Churchill & Co. Ltd.
P.O. Box No. 3,
London Road, Daventry,
Northants, England.

OPERATION	TOOL No.	PAGE No.
ENGINE		
Camshaft liner reaming	18G 123 A	S.7
	18G 123 B	S.7
	18G 123 E	S.7
	18G 123 F	S.8
	18G 123 L	S.8
	18G 123 T	S.8
	18G 123 AB	S.8
	18G 123 AC	S.8
	18G 123 AD	S.8
Camshaft liner removing and replacing	18G 124 A	S.8
	18G 124 B	S.8
	18G 124 C	S.8
	18G 124 F	S.8
	18G 124 H	S.8
Crankshaft gear and pulley removing	18G 2	S.5
Crankshaft oil seal replacing	18G 134 CQ	S.9
	18G 1108	S.16
Crankshaft pulley nut removing	18G 98 A	S.7
Crankshaft spigot bush removing and replacing	18G 284 H	S.12
	18G 284 L	S.12
	18G 1037	S.15
Gudgeon pin, removing and replacing	18G 1150	S.17
	18G 1150 D	S.17
Main bearing cap removing	18G 284	S.12
	18G 284 A	S.12
	18G 284 AC	S.12
Oil pump relief valve seat grinding	18G 69	S.7
Piston refitting	18G 55 A	S.7
Timing cover locating and oil seal replacing	18G 134	S.9
	18G 134 BD	S.9
Cover locating	18G 1046	S.15
Torque spanners	18G 372	S.13
	18G 536	S.13
	18G 537	S.14
Valve removing and refitting	18G 45	S.6

OPERATION	TOOL No.	PAGE No.
Valve seat cutting	18G 25	S.5
	18G 25 A	S.5
	18G 25 C	S.5
	18G 27	S.5
	18G 28	S.5
	18G 28 A	S.5
	18G 28 B	S.6
	18G 28 C	S.6
	18G 174 B	S.10
	18G 174 D	S.10
Valve seat grinding	18G 29	S.6
	18G 29 A	S.6
CLUTCH		
Refitting	18G 1027	S.15
(Involute spine clutch plates)	18G 680	S.14
GEARBOX		
Bevel pinion flange retaining	18G 34 A	S.6
First motion shaft assembling and replacing	18G 4	S.5
	18G 5	S.5
Layshaft replacing	18G 1138	S.16
Propeller shaft flange removing	18G 2	S.5
Rear oil seal removing and replacing	18G 389	S.13
	18G 389 B	S.13
	18G 134	S.9
	18G 134 BK	S.9
Selector fork and rod guiding	18G 41	S.6
Third motion shaft, synchromesh assembly	18G 262	S.11
	18G 1026	S.15
Laycock Overdrive, Type 'LH'		
Hydraulic pressure testing	18G 251	S.11
	18G 251 E	S.11
Mainshaft bearing removing and replacing	18G 185	S.10
	18G 186	S.10
	18G 391	S.13
	18G 1045	S.15
	18G 1024	S.15
Oil pump removing and replacing	18G 1117	S.16
	18G 1118	S.16
Rear oil seal removing and replacing	18G 389	S.13
	18G 389 D	S.13
	18G 177	S.10
Roller clutch assembling	18G 178	S.10

OPERATION	TOOL No.	PAGE No.
REAR SUSPENSION AND FINAL DRIVE		
Semi-floating Rear Axle		
Axle shaft assembly replacing	18G 1067	S.16
Bevel pinion bearing removing and replacing	18G 47 C 18G 47 AS 18G 191 18G 264	S.6 S.7 S.10 S.11
Bevel pinion flange wrench	18G 34 A	S.6
Bevel pinion outer race removing	18G 264 18G 264 AA 18G 264 AB 18G 264 AD	S.11 S.11 S.11 S.11
Differential bearing removing and replacing	18G 47 C 18G 47 AK 18G 134 18G 134 CM	S.6 S.6 S.9 S.9
Differential reassembling	18G 191 18G 191 F 18G 191 H 18G 191 J	S.10 S.10 S.11 S.11
Final drive and rear axle shaft nut	18G 586	S.14
Impulse extractor	18G 284	S.12
Propeller shaft flange removing	18G 2	S.5
Rear axle casing stretching	18G 131 C	S.9
Torque setting spanner	18G 592	S.14
FRONT SUSPENSION AND STEERING		
Spring compressing	18G 693	S.14
Steering-arm ball pin removing	18G 1063	S.16
Steering-wheel hub removing	18G 1181	S.17
Steering rack ball joint spanners	18G 706	S.15
Swivel axle bush removing, replacing, and reaming	18G 68 18G 596 18G 597 18G 1063	S.7 S.14 S.14 S.16

OPERATION		TOOL No.	PAGE No.
FRONT AND REAR HUBS			
Hub removing and replacing		18G 304	S.12
	Disc wheels	18G 304 A	S.12
		18G 304 J	S.12
	Wire wheels	18G 1032	S.15
		18G 363	S.13
Front hub bearing cup replacing		18G 1122	S.16
		18G 1122 A	S.16
Front hub oil seal replacing		18G 134	S.9
		18G 134 BH	S.9
Rear hub bearing removing		18G 134	S.9
		18G 134 P	S.9
Rear hub nut spanner		18G 152	S.10
BRAKING SYSTEM			
Brake adjusting (rear only)		18G 619 A	S.14
Disc brake piston re-setting		18G 590	S.14
MISCELLANEOUS			
Carburetter adjusting tool		S353	S.17
Petrol gauge tank attachment lock ring spanner		18G 1001	S.15
Remover; hydraulic version of 18G 304		18G 304 Z	S.13
Rocker type switch and bezel, removing		18G 1145	S.17

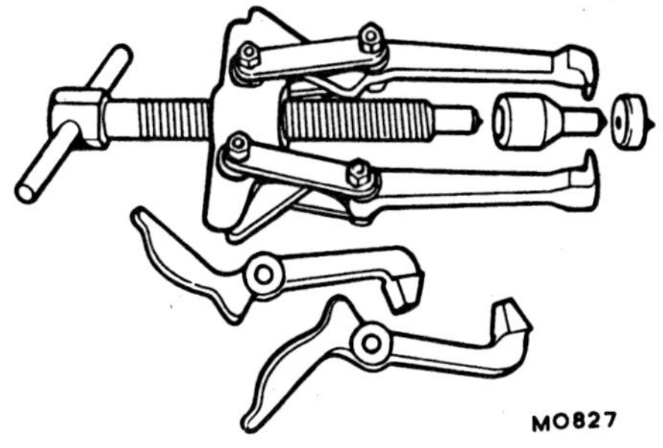

18G 2. Crankshaft Gear, Pulley, and Propeller shaft Flange Remover.

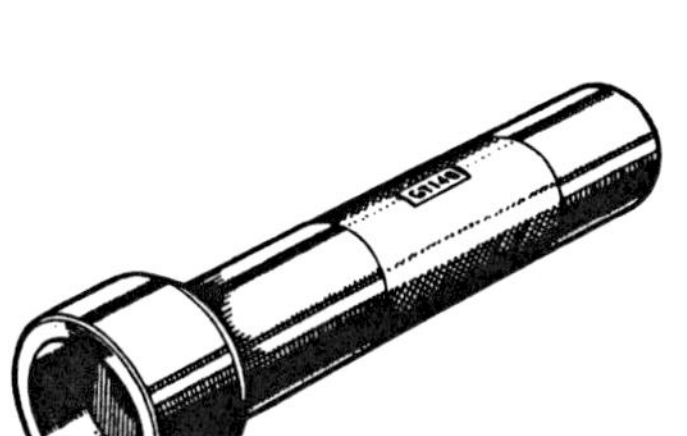

18G 4. First Motion Shaft Assembly Replacer.

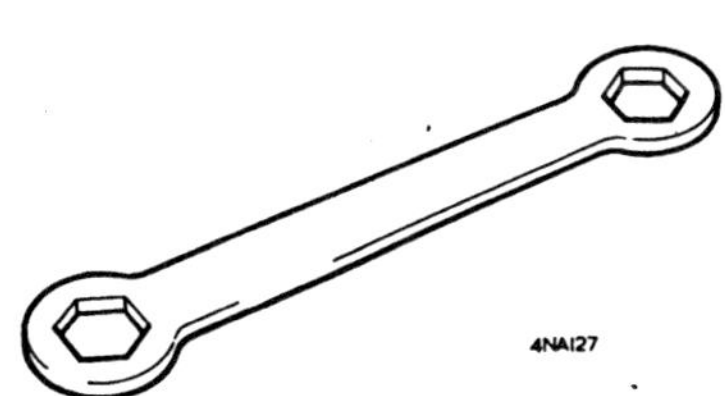

18G 5. First Motion Shaft Nut Spanner.

18G 25. Valve Seat Finishing Cutter (exhaust).

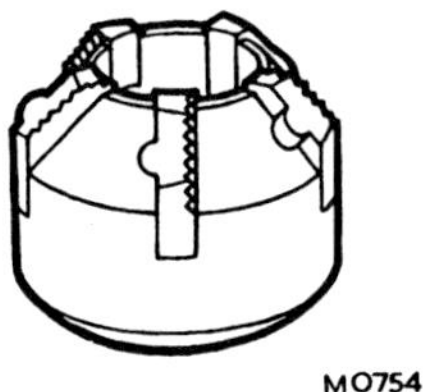

18G 25 A. Valve Seat Glaze Breaker (exhaust)

18G 25 C. Valve Seat Narrowing Cutter–Bottom (exhaust).

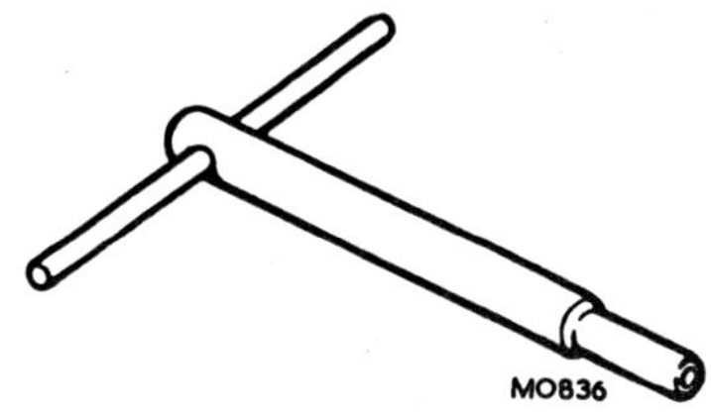

18G 27. Valve Seat Cutter and Pilot Handle.

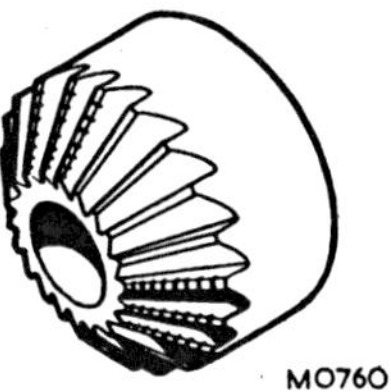

18G 28. Valve Seat Finishing Cutter (inlet).

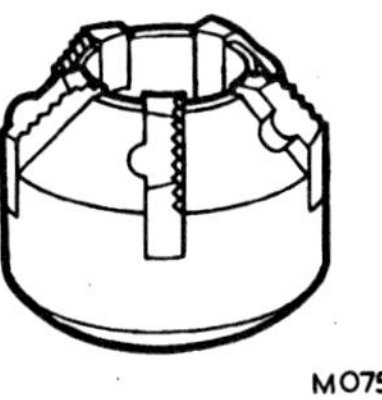

18G 28 A. Valve Seat Glaze Breaker (inlet).

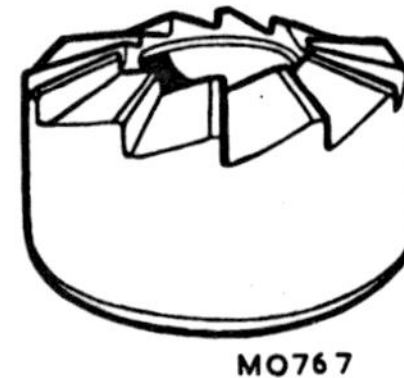

18G 28 B. Valve Seat Narrowing Cutter–Top (inlet).

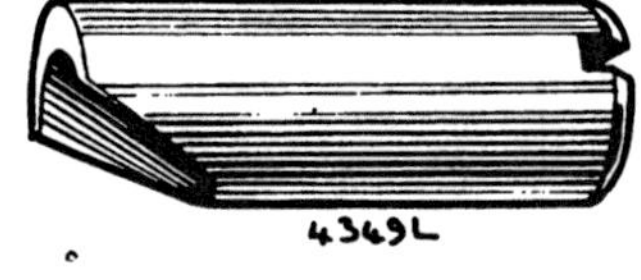

18G 41. Selector Fork and Rod Guide.

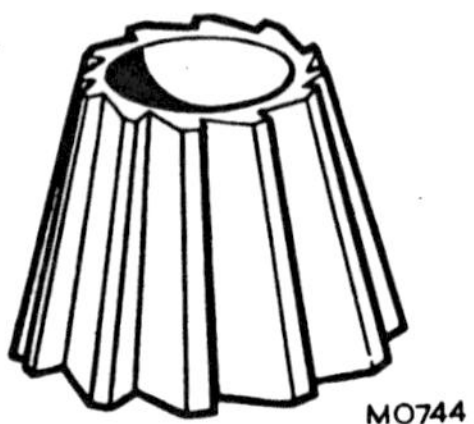

18G 28 C. Valve Seat Narrowing Cutter–Bottom (inlet).

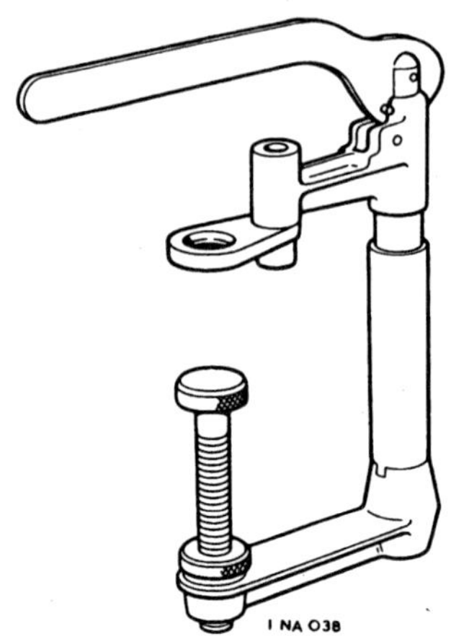

18G 45. Valve Spring Compressor.

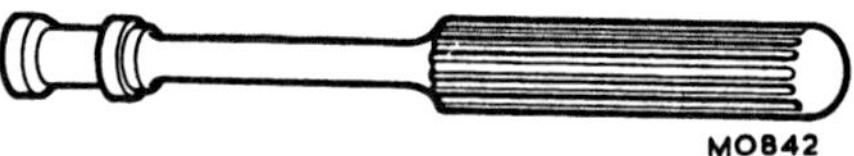

18G 29. Valve Grinding-in Tool.

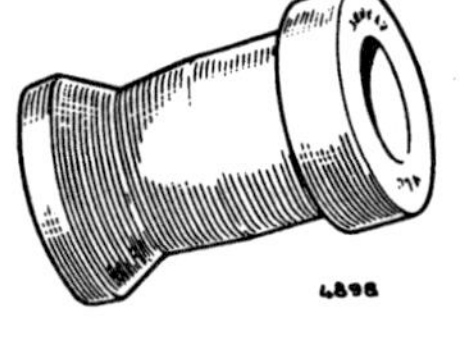

18G 29 A. Valve Grinding-in Tool Suction Pad.

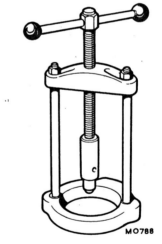

18G 47 C. Differential Bearing Remover (basic tool).

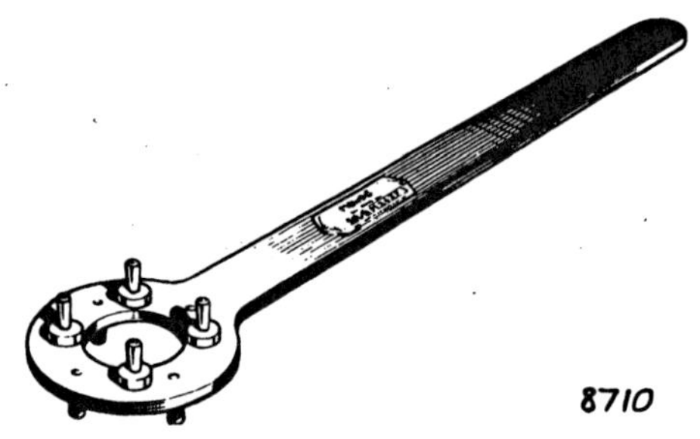

18G 34 A. Bevel Pinion Flange Wrench.

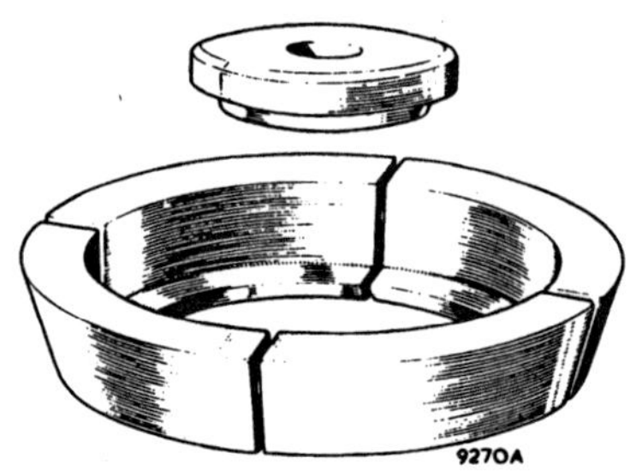

18G 47 AK. Differential Bearing Remover Adaptor.

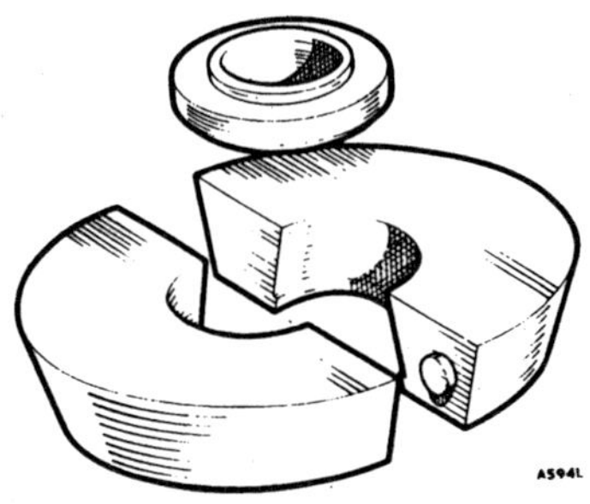

18G 47 AS. Bevel Pinion Bearing Remover and Replacer Adaptor.

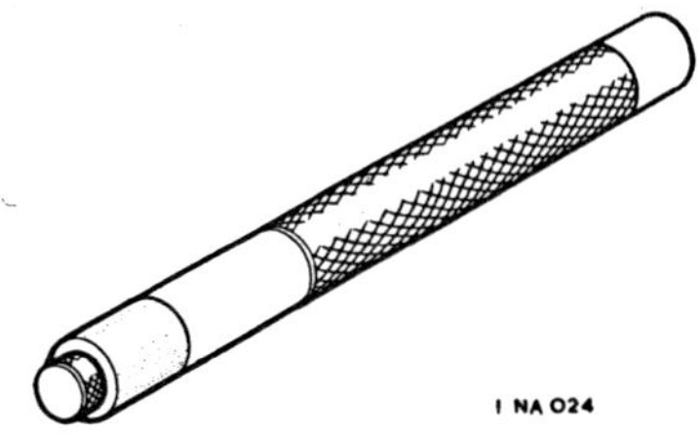

18G 69. Oil Pump Relief Valve Grinding-in Tool.

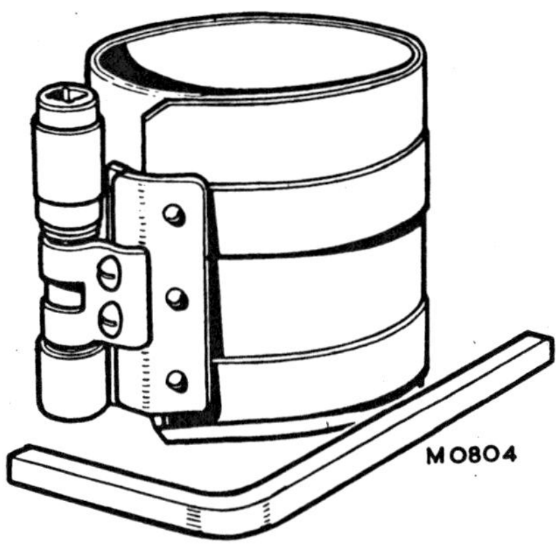

18G 55 A. Piston Ring Clamp.

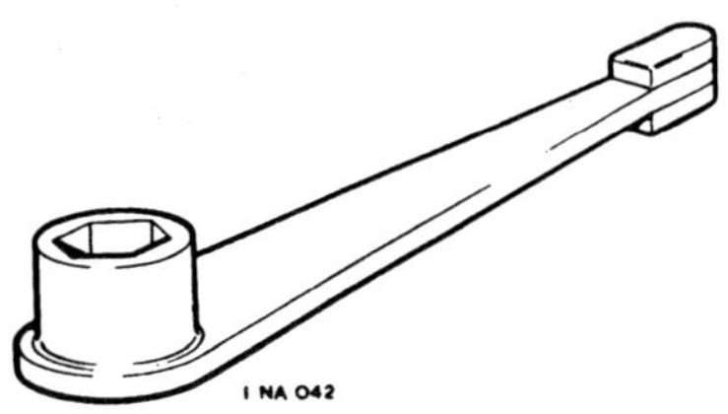

18G 98 A. Starting Nut Spanner.

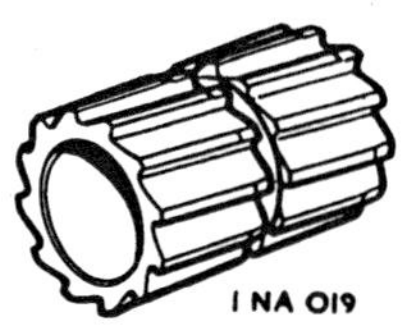

18G 123 B. Camshaft Liner Reamer Cutter–Rear.

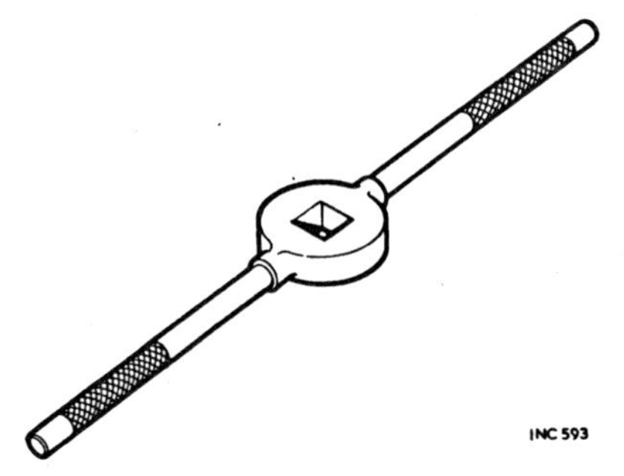

18G 68. Swivel Axle Bush Reamer Wrench.

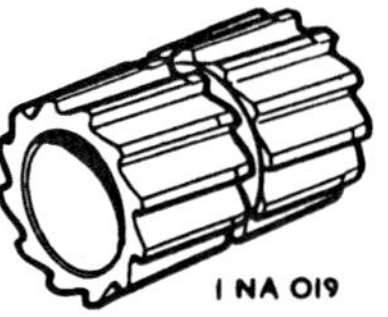

18G 123 E. Camshaft Liner Reamer Cutter–Front.

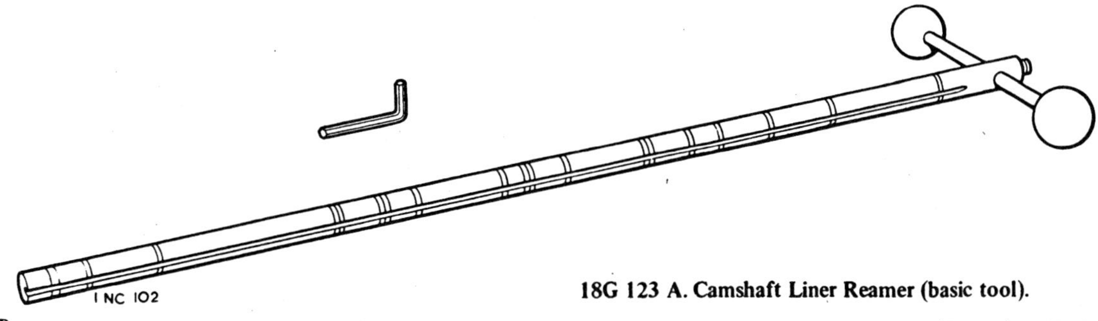

18G 123 A. Camshaft Liner Reamer (basic tool).

18G 123 F. Camshaft Liner Reamer Cutter–Centre.

18G 123 L. Camshaft Liner Reamer Pilot–Front.

18G 123 T. Camshaft Liner Reamer Pilot–Front.

18G 123 AB. Camshaft Liner Reamer Pilot–Centre.

18G 123 AC. Camshaft Liner Reamer Pilot–Rear.

18G 123 AD. Camshaft Liner Reamer Pilot–Rear.

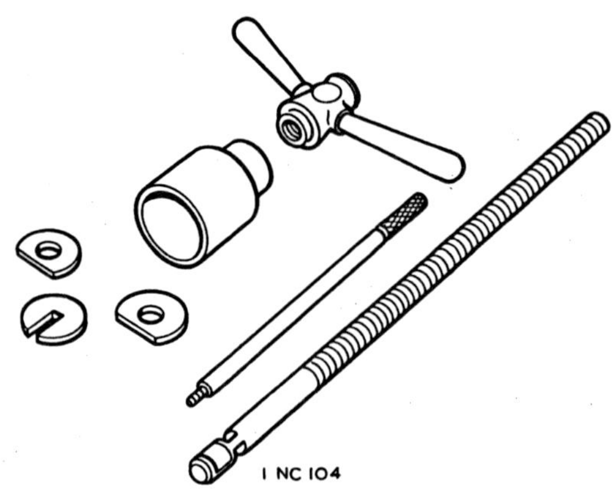

18G 124 A. Camshaft Liner Remover and Replacer (basic tool).

18G 124 B. Camshaft Liner Remover Adaptor.

18G 124 C. Camshaft Liner Remover Adaptor.

18G 124 F. Camshaft Liner Remover Adaptor.

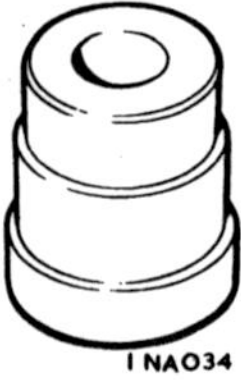

18G 124 H. Camshaft Liner Remover Adaptor.

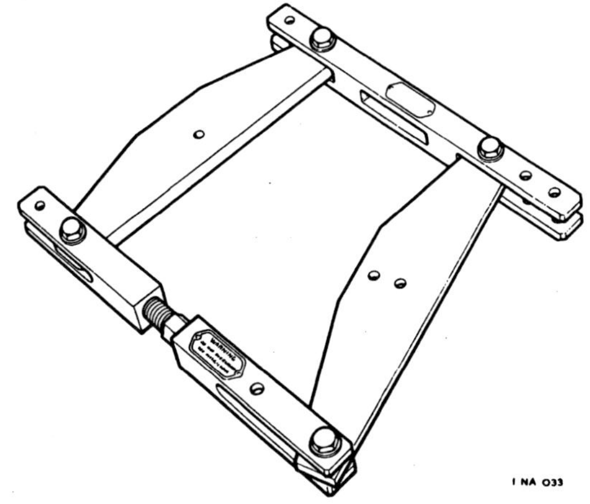

18G 131 C. Rear Axle Casing Stretcher.

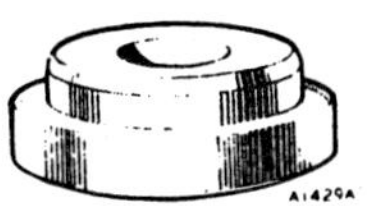

18G 134 BH. Flywheel and Front Hub Oil Seal Replacer Adaptor.

18G 134 BK. Gearbox Rear Oil Seal Replacer Adaptor.

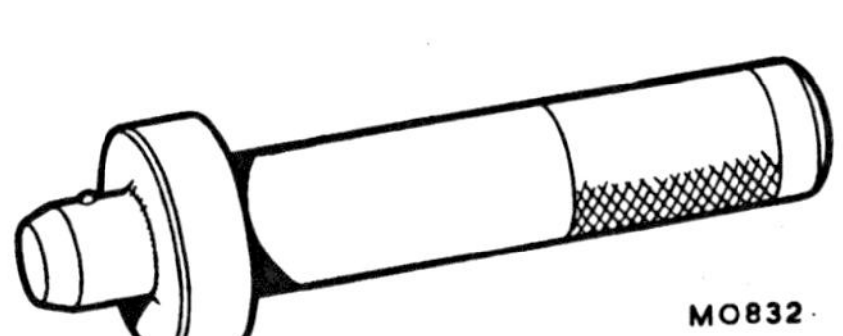

18G 134. Bearing and Oil Seal Replacer (basic tool).

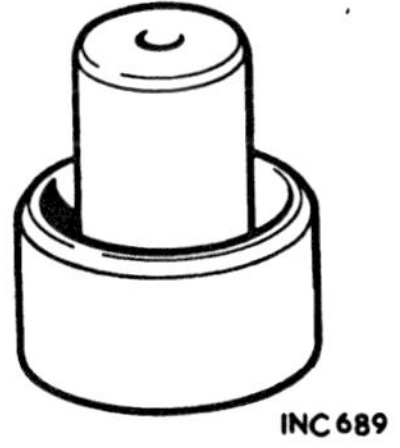

18G 134 P. Rear Hub Replacer Adaptor.

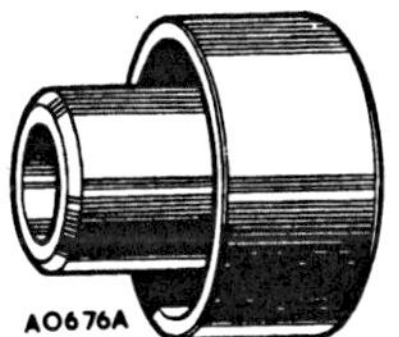

18G 134 CM. Differential Bearing Replacer Adaptor.

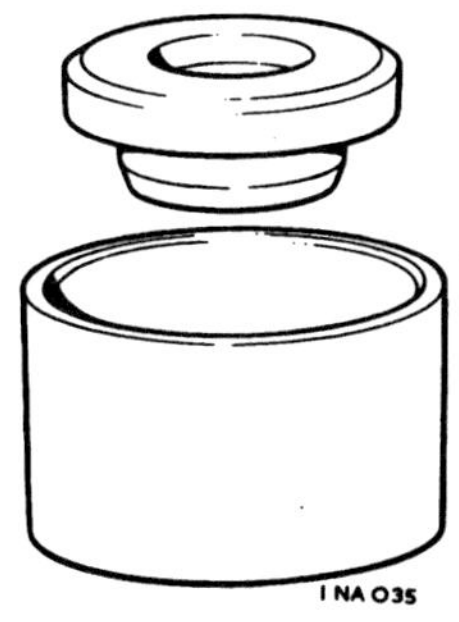

18G 134 BD. Timing Case Oil Seal Replacer Adaptor.

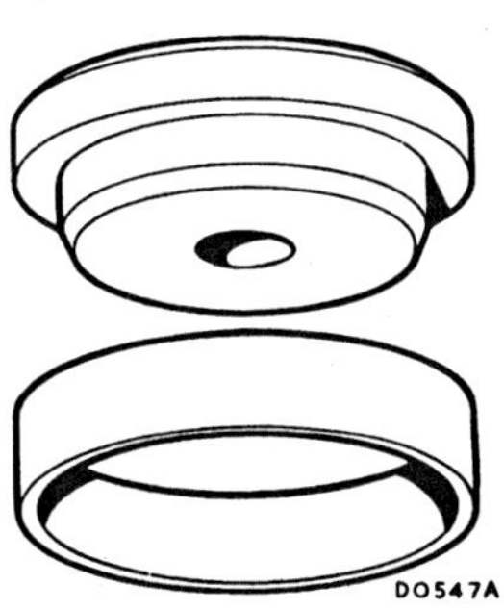

18G 134 CQ. Crankshaft Oil Seal Replacer Adaptor.

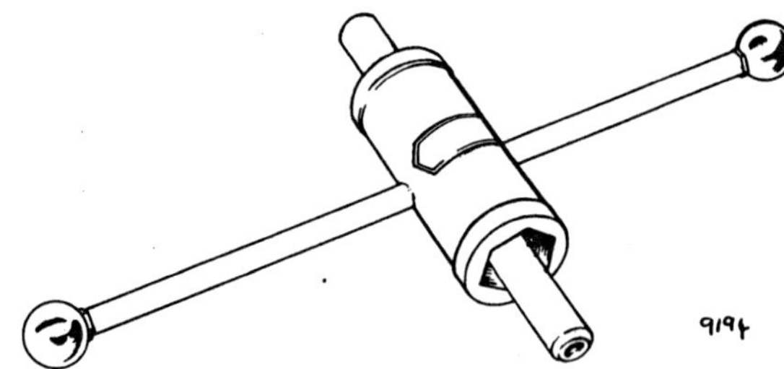

18G 152. Rear Hub Nut Spanner.

18G 174 B. Valve Seat Narrowing Cutter–Top (exhaust).

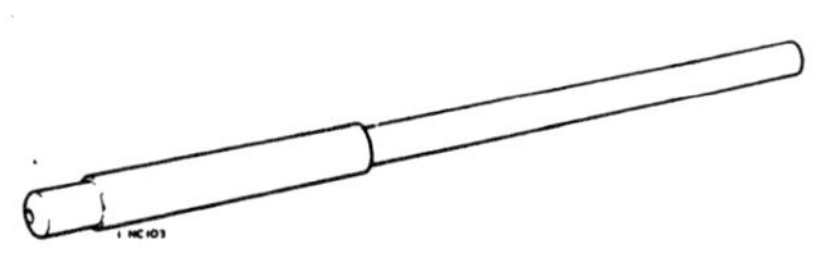

18G 174 D. Valve Seat Cutter Pilot.

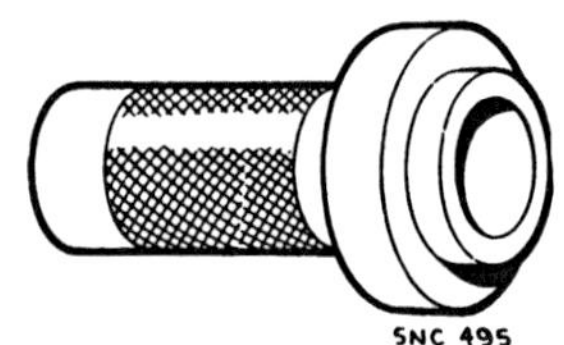

18G 177. Oil Seal Replacer.

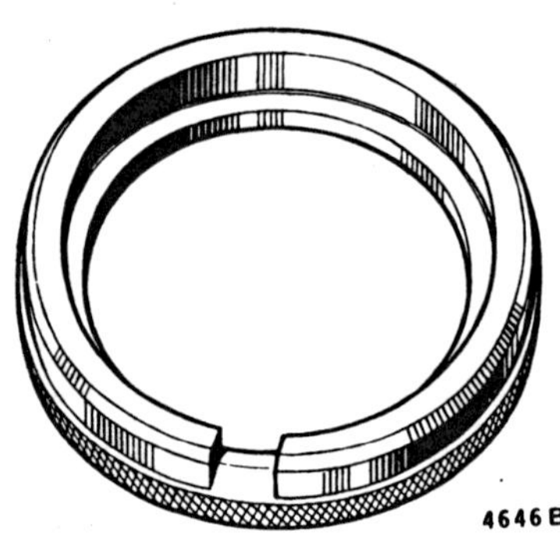

18G 178. Roller Clutch Assembly Ring.

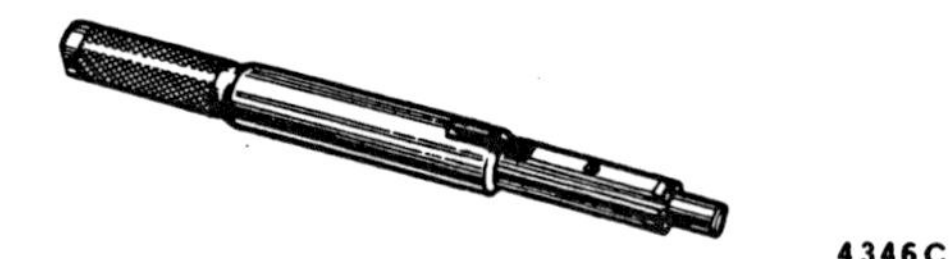

18G 185. Dummy Layshaft.

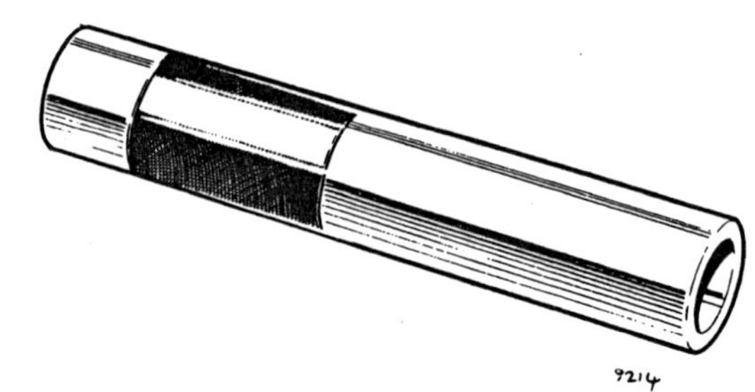

18G 186. Mainshaft Bearing Replacer.

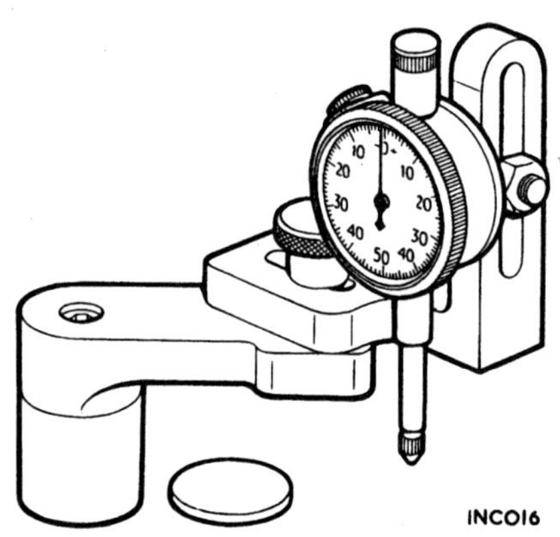

18G 191. Bevel Pinion Setting Gauge.

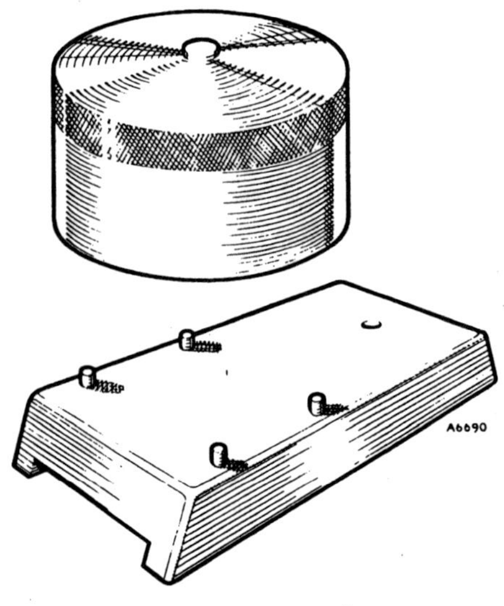

18G 191 F. Differential Case Assembly Gauge.

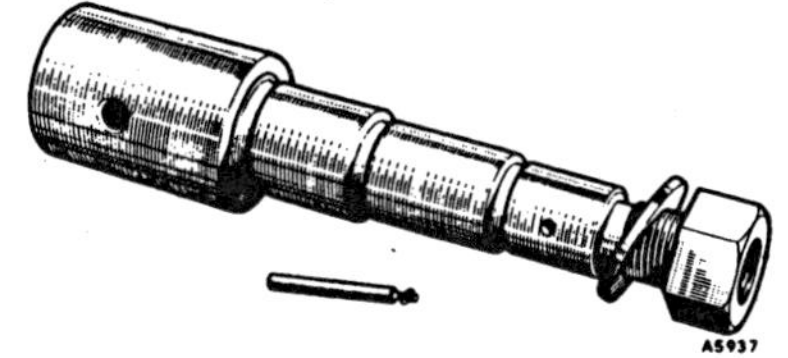

18G 191 H. Dummy Pinion.

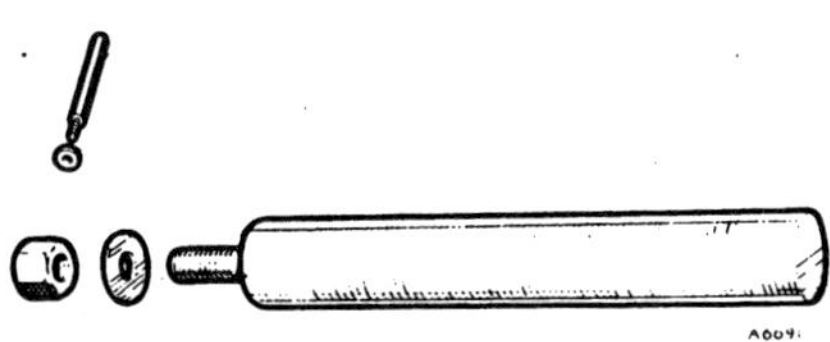

18G 191 J. Differential Case Assembly Gauge Pillar Adaptor.

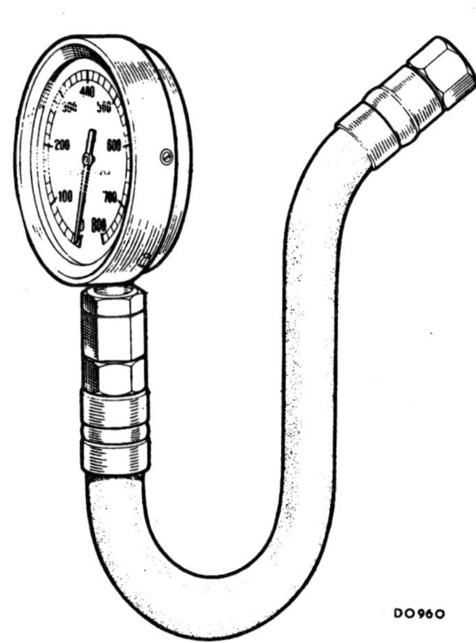

18G 251. Hydraulic Pressure Gauge.

18G 251 E. Pressure Test Adaptor.

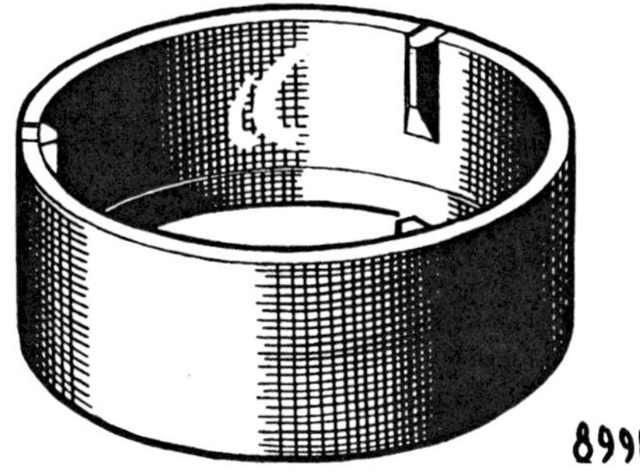

18G 262. Synchromesh Unit Assembly Ring (First and Second Speed).

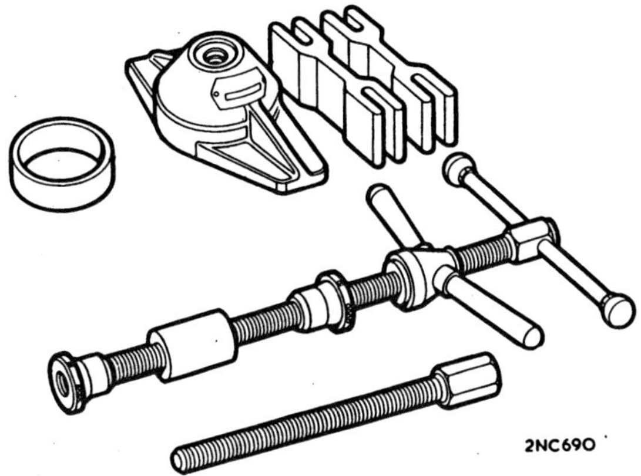

18G 264. Bevel Pinion Bearing Outer Race Remover (basic tool).

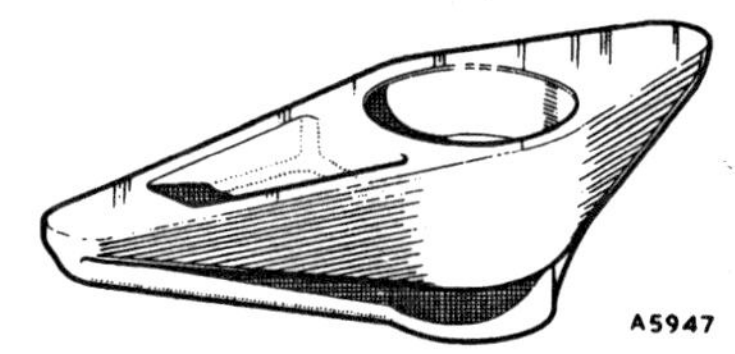

18G 264 AA. Bridge Piece Adaptor–Large.

18G 264 AB. Bevel Pinion Outer Race Remover and Replacer Adaptor (Rear).

18G 264 AD. Bevel Pinion Outer Race Remover and Replacer Adaptor (Front).

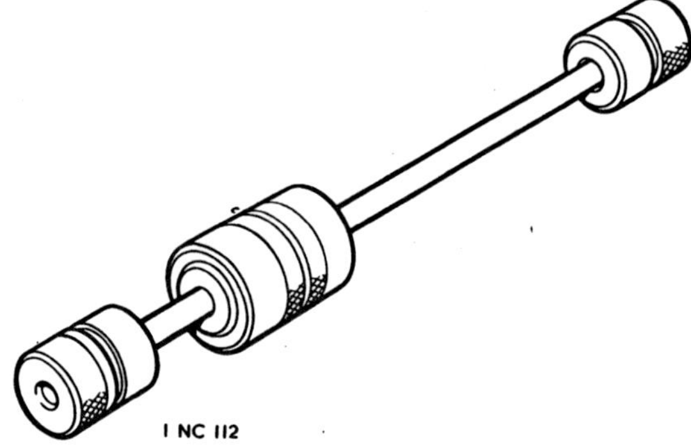

18G 284. Impulse Extractor–UNF. (basic tool).

18G 284 A. Main Bearing Cap Remover Adaptor.

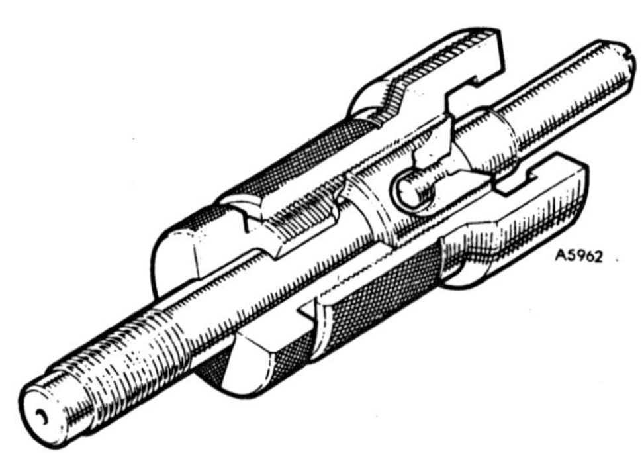

18G 284 H. Basic Bearing Remover Adaptor.

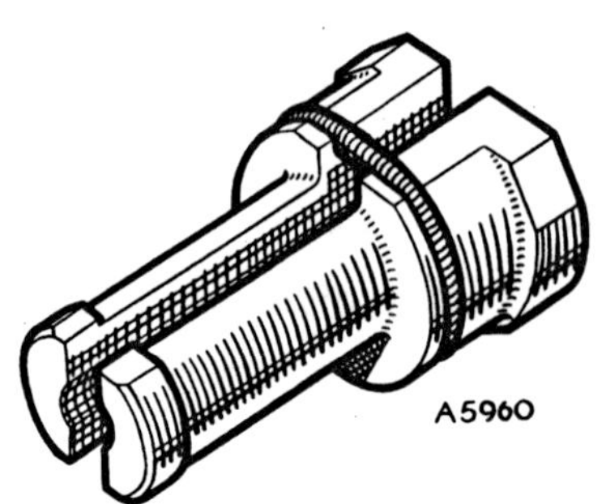

18G 284 L. Crankshaft Spigot Bush Remover Adaptor.

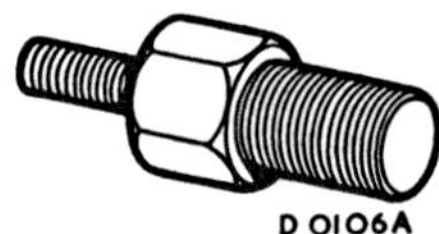

18G 284 AC. Main Bearing Cap Remover Adaptor.

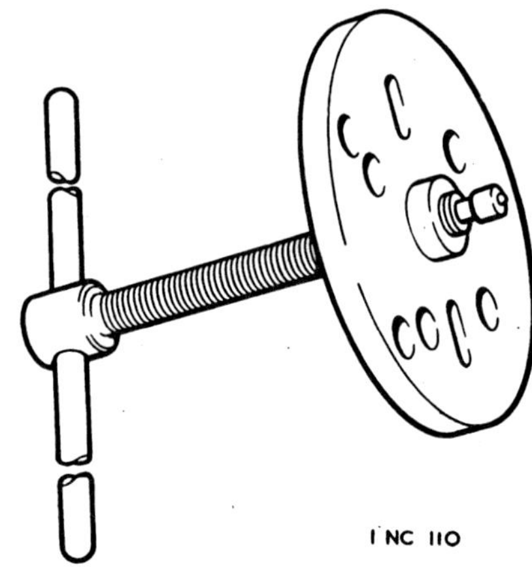

18G 304. Front and Rear Hub Remover (basic tool).

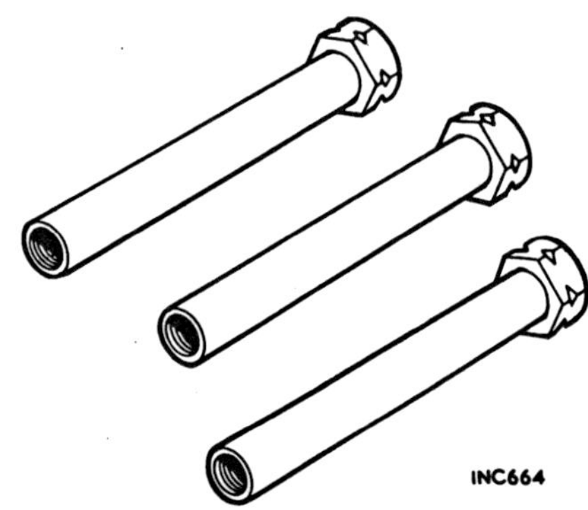

18G 304 A. Bolt Adaptor–½ in. UNF.

18G 304 J. Hub Remover Thrust Pad.

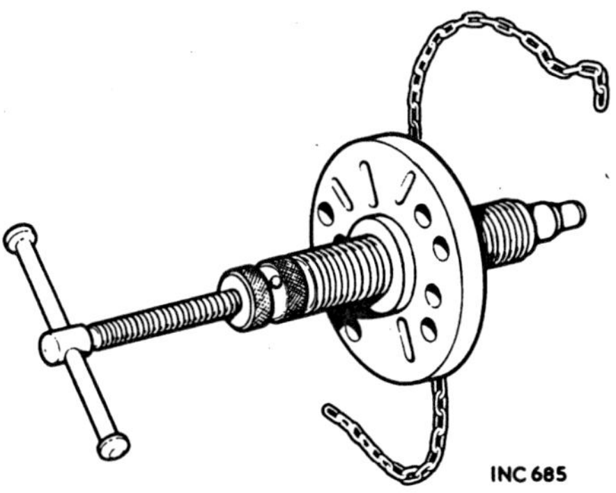

18G 304 Z. Hydraulic Hub Remover (basic tool).

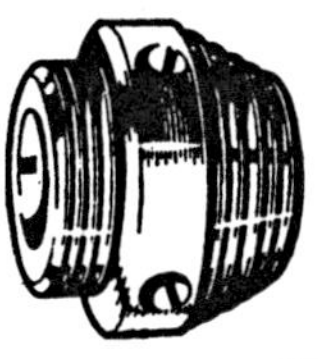

18G 389 B. Gearbox Rear Oil Seal Remover Adaptor.

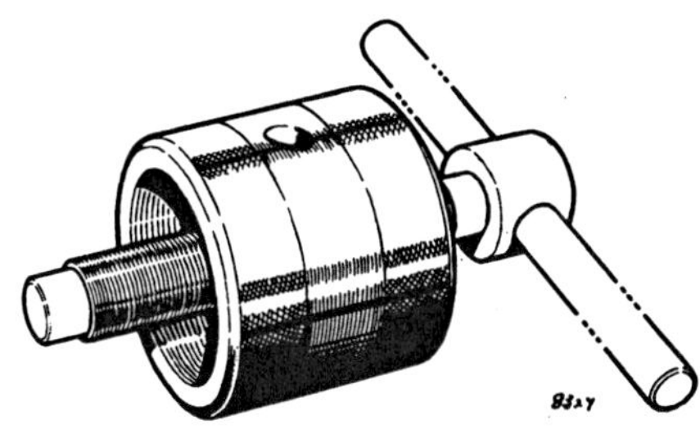

18G 363. Hub Remover Wire Wheels (12 T.P.I.).

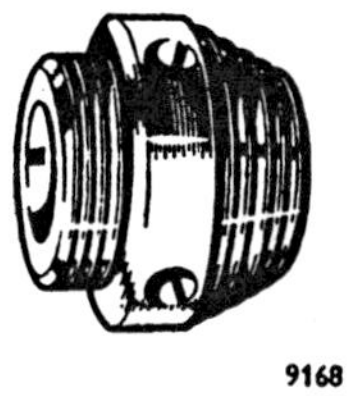

18G 389 D. Gearbox Rear Oil Seal Remover Adaptor.

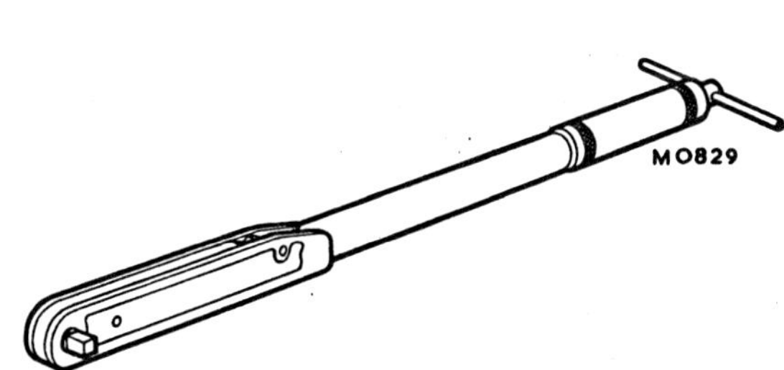

18G 372. Torque Wrench–30 to 140 lb. ft. (4.15 to 19.4 kg. m.).

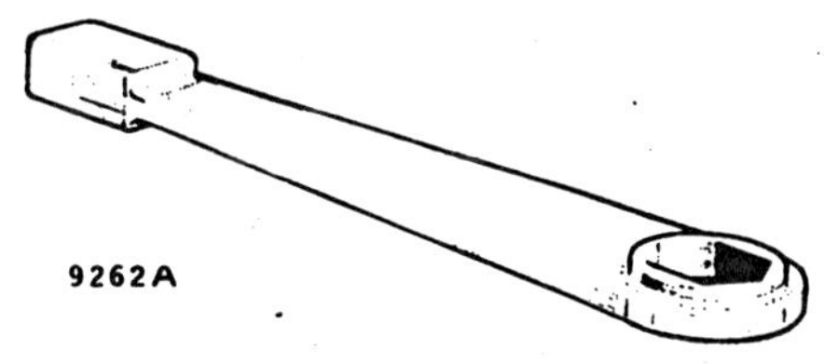

18G 391. Starting Dog Nut Spanner.

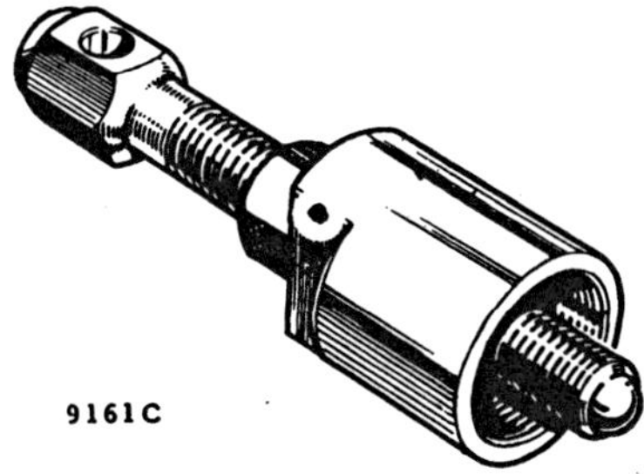

18G 389. Gearbox Rear Oil Seal Remover (basic tool).

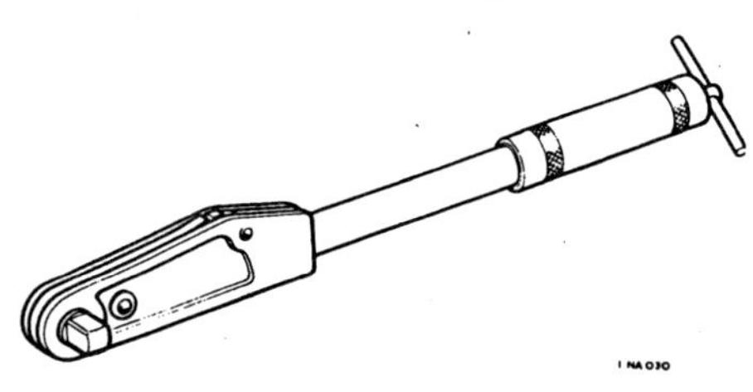

18G 536. Torque Wrench–20 to 100 lb. in.–2 to 8 lb. ft. (300 to 1200 gm. m.).

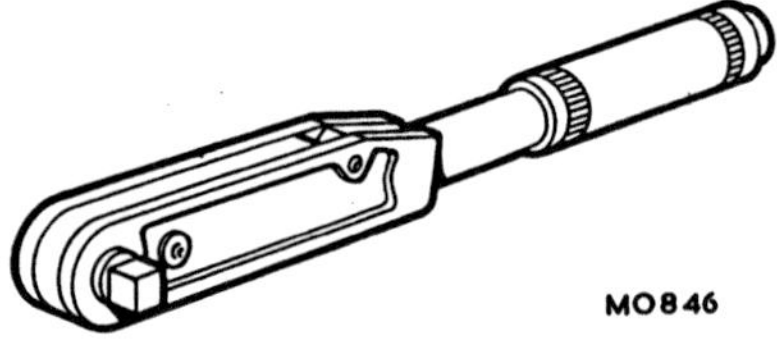

18G 537. Torque Wrench–10 to 50 lb. ft. (2 to 7 kg. m.).

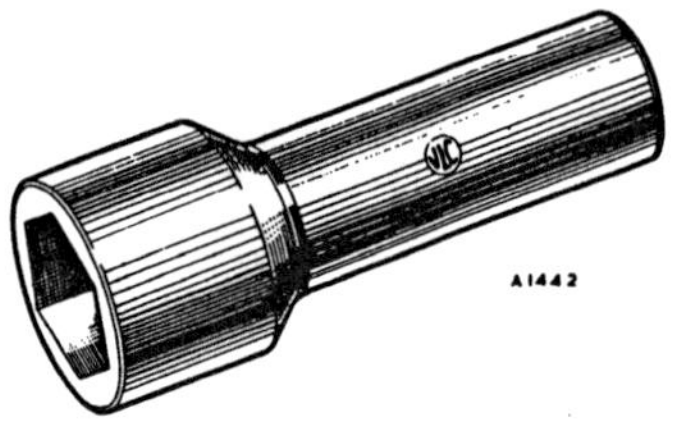

18G 586. Rear Axle Shaft Nut Spanner (Wire Wheel).

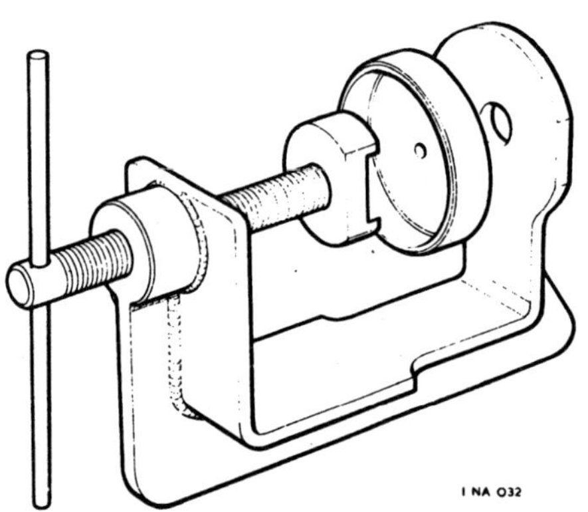

18G 590. Disc Brake Piston Resetting Tool.

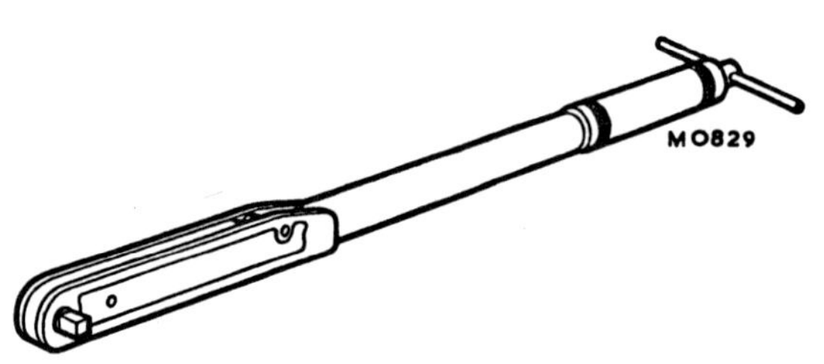

18G 592. Torque Wrench–35 to 225 lb. ft. (4.84 to 31.144 kg. m.).

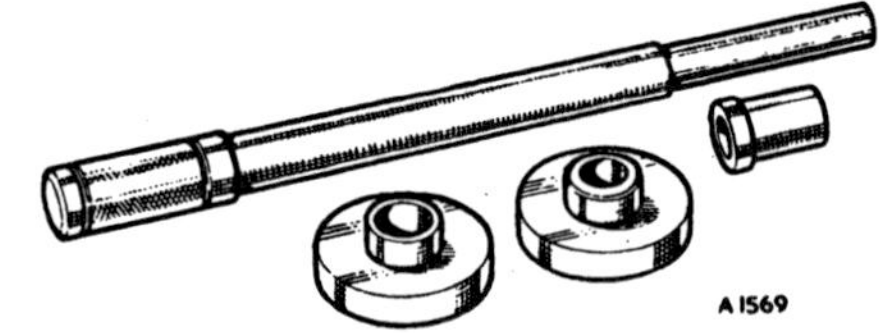

18G 596. Swivel Axle Bush Remover and Replacer.

18G 597. Swivel Axle Bush Reamer.

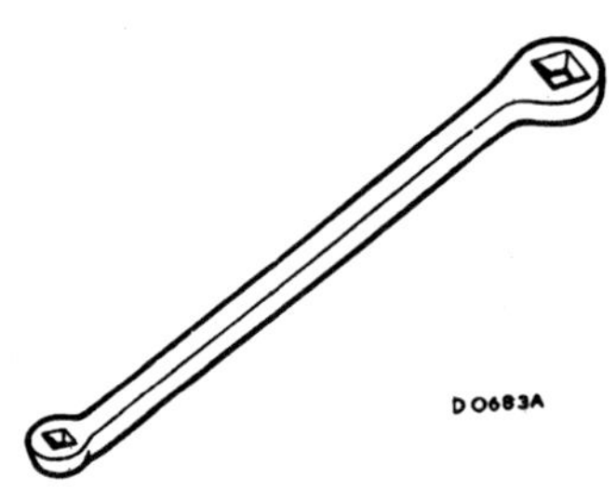

18G 619 A. Brake Adjusting Spanner.

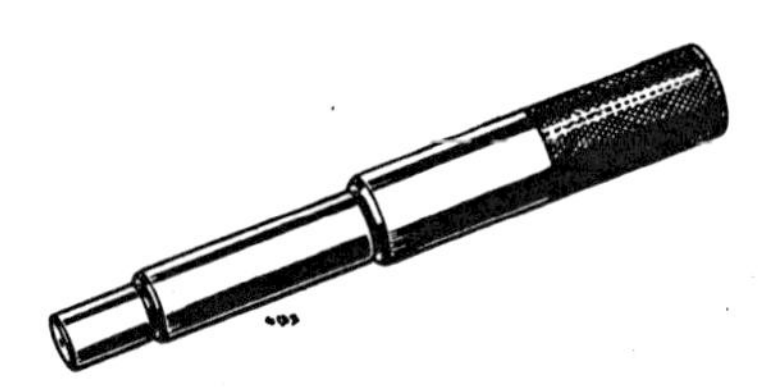

18G 680. Clutch Plate Centralizer.

18G 693. Coil Spring Compressor.

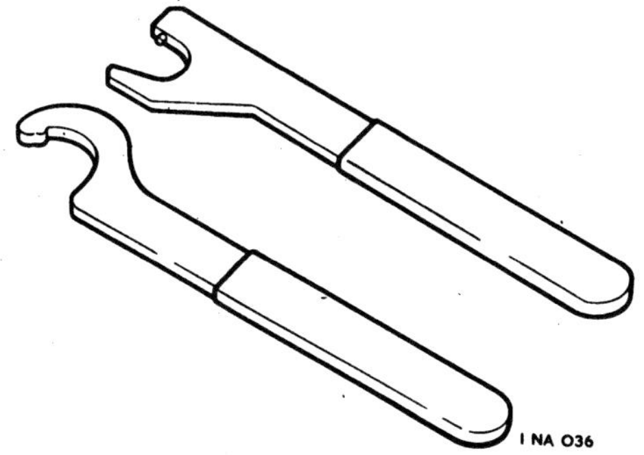

18G 706. Steering Rack Ball Joint Spanners.

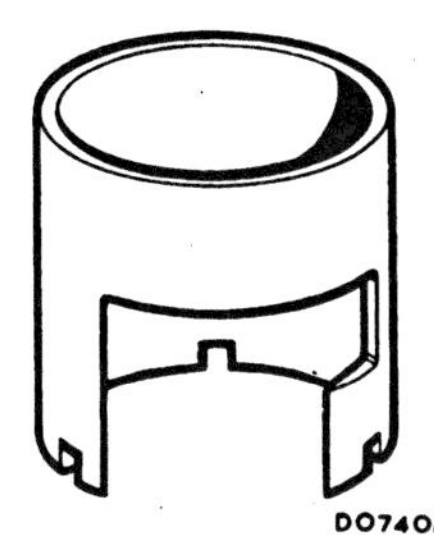

18G 1001. Gauge Locking Ring.

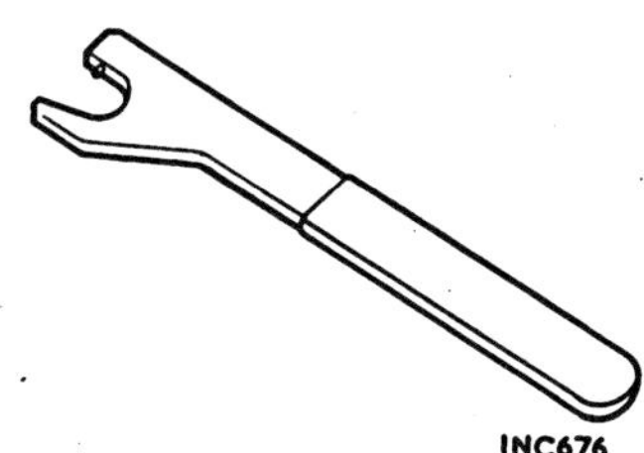

18G 1024. Mainshaft (Third Motion) Spanner.

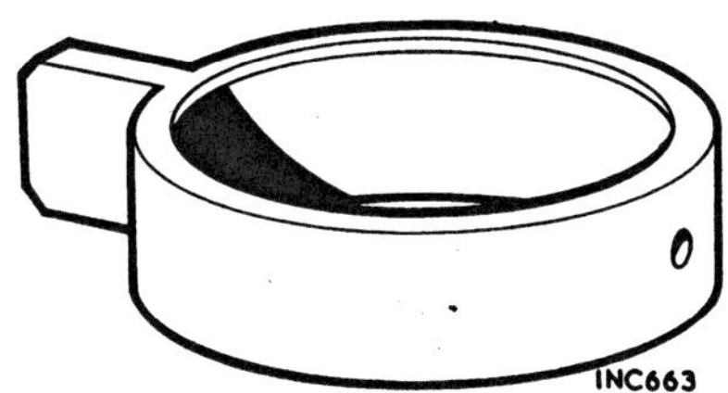

18G 1026. Synchromesh Assembly Ring.

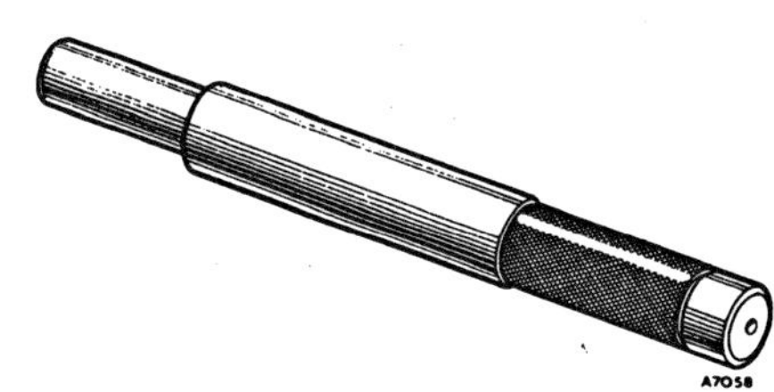

18G 1027. Clutch Centralizer (18GB).

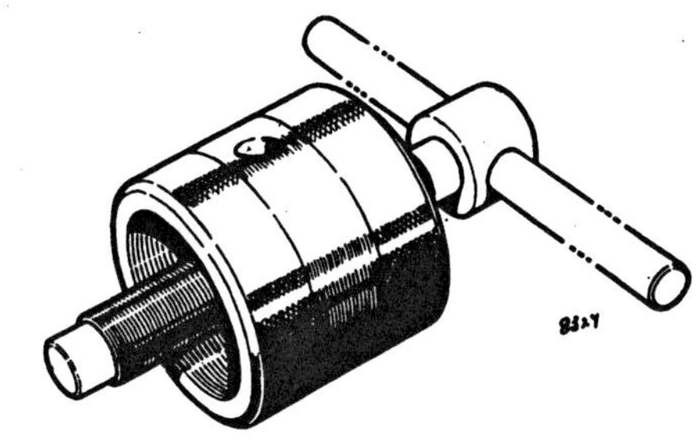

18G 1032. Wire Wheel Hub Remover (8 T.P.I.).

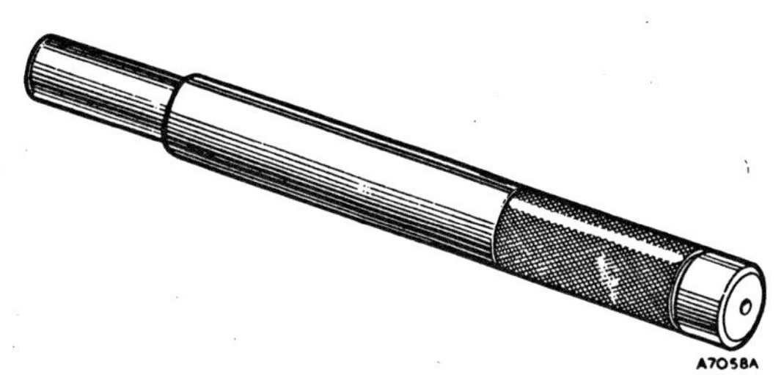

18G 1037. Crankshaft Spigot Bush Replacer.

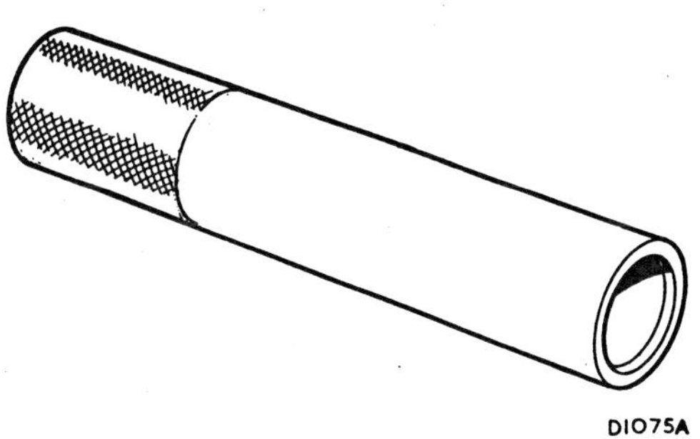

18G 1045. Mainshaft (Third Motion) Drift.

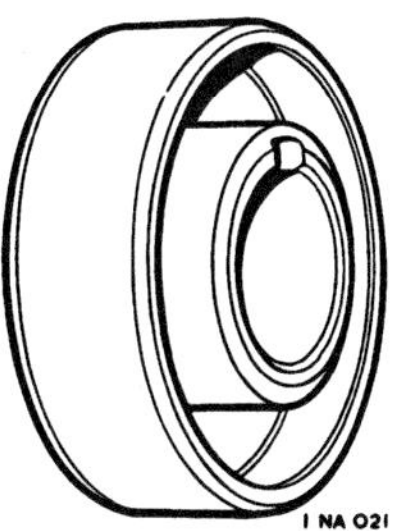

18G 1046. Engine Front Cover Centralizer.

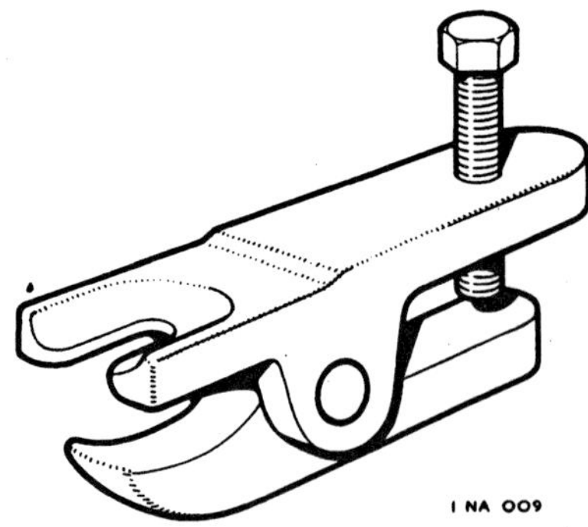

18G 1063. Steering Arm and Swivel Hub Ball Pin Remover.

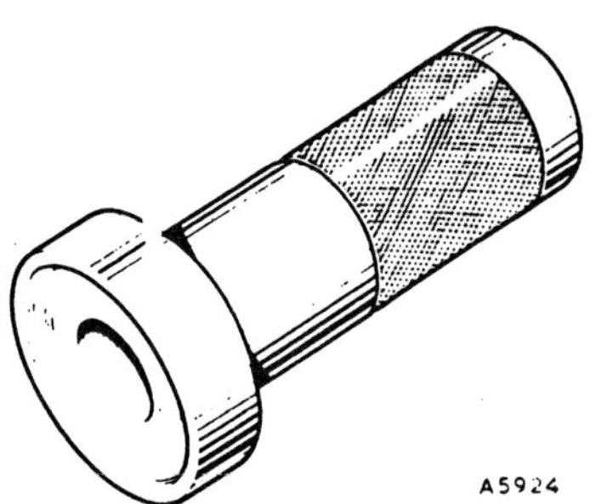

18G 1067. Rear Axle Shaft Assembly Replacer.

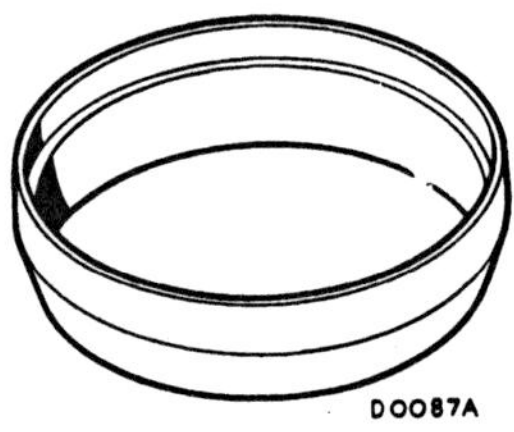

18G 1108. Crankshaft Oil Seal Protection Sleeve.

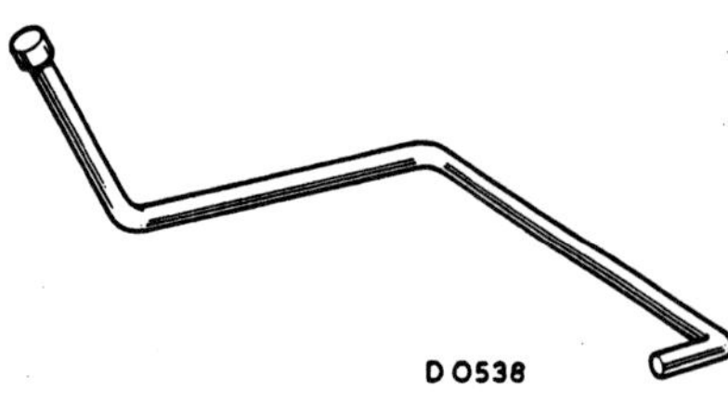

18G 1117. Pump Body Holder and Seat Remover.

18G 1118. Oil Pump Body Socket.

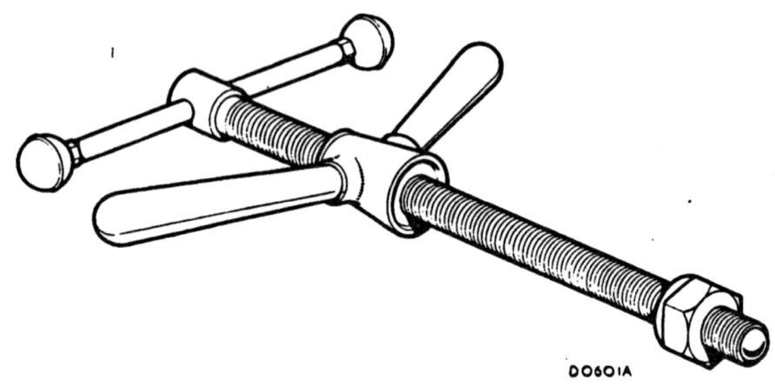

18G 1122. Bearing Cup Replacer (basic tool).

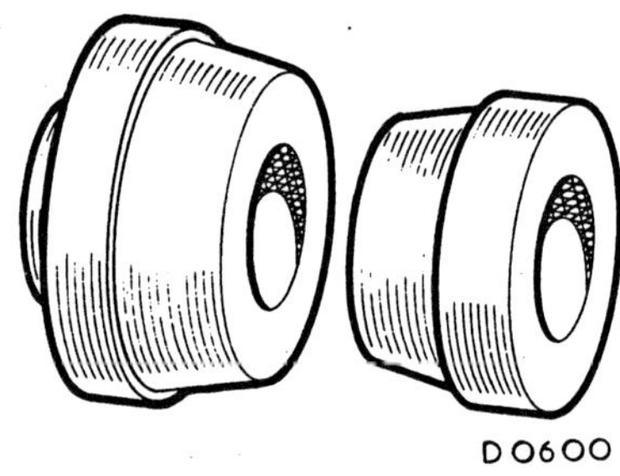

18G 1122 A. Front Hub Bearing Cups Replacing Adaptor.

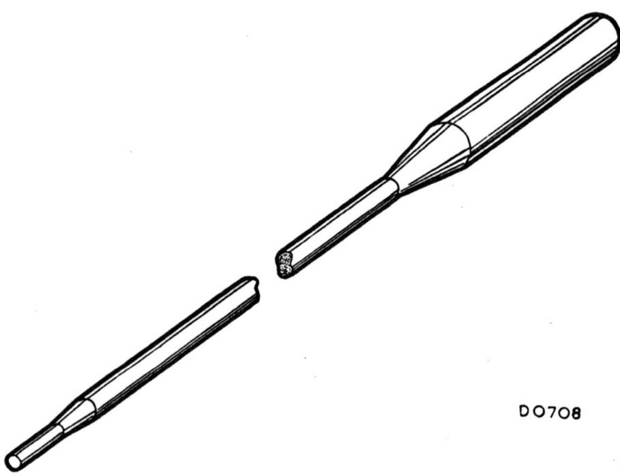

18G 1138. Dummy Layshaft.

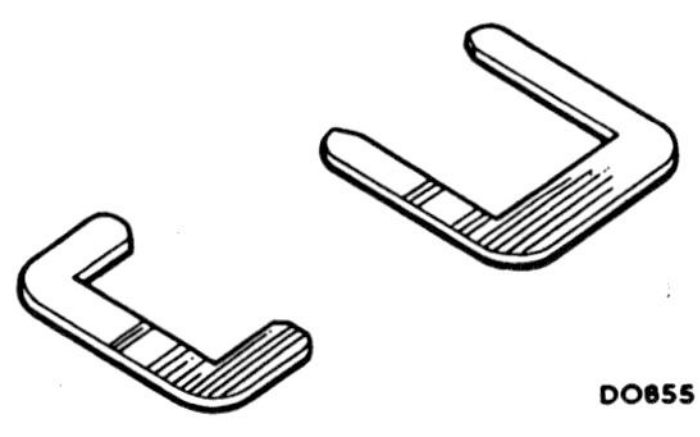

18G 1145. Rocker Type Switch and Bezel Remover.

S353. Carburetter Adjusting Tool.

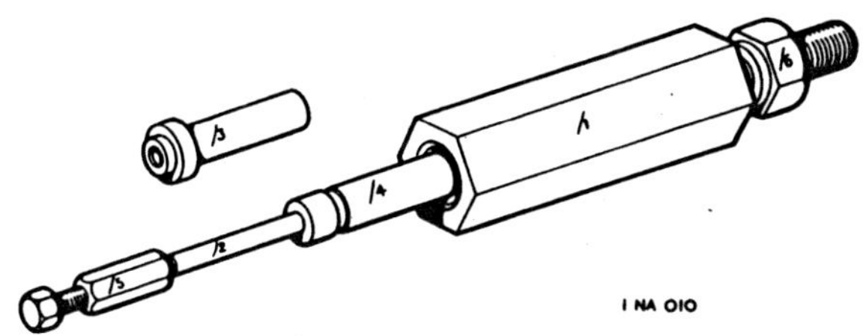

18G 1150. Basic Tool–Remover and Replacer–Gudgeon Pin.

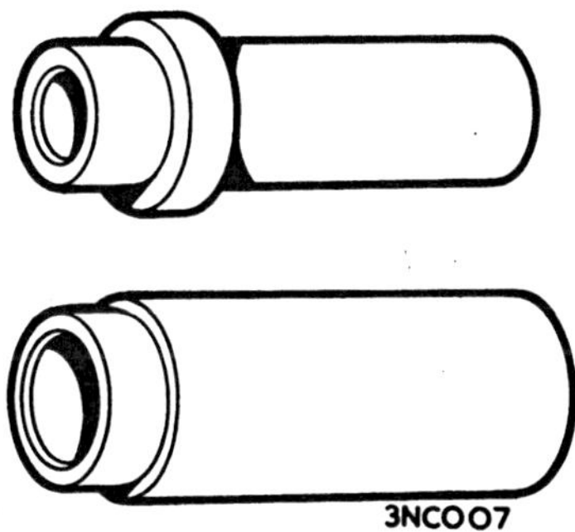

18G 1150 D. Adaptor Set–Remover and Replacer–Gudgeon Pin.

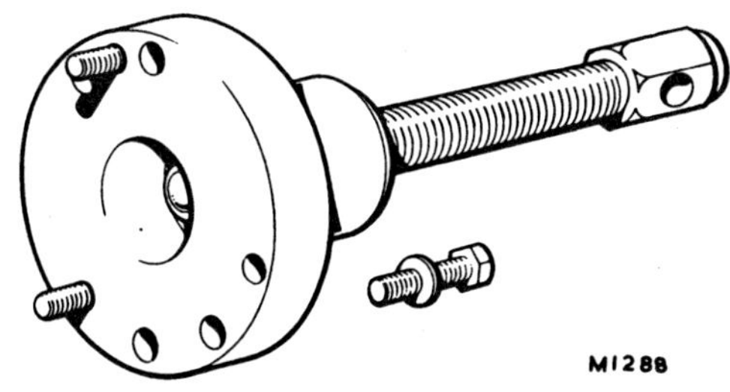

18G 1181. Steering Wheel Hub Remover.

SECTION T

EMISSION CONTROL

SECTION

† These operations must be followed by an exhaust emission check 

[**NOTE**: Additional tests and maintenance procedures for the various emission control systems can be found in the MAINTENANCE pages of this Workshop Manual. The data found in Section T is mainly useful in reinstalling emission control components after extensive engine repairs and for troubleshooting major components that are not routinely replaced as a part of normal maintenance.]

GENERAL DESCRIPTION

EXHAUST EMISSION CONTROL

Air is pressure-fed from an air pump via an injection manifold to the cylinder head exhaust port of each cylinder. A check valve in the air delivery pipe prevents blow-back from high pressure exhaust gases. The pump also supplies air through a gulp valve to the inlet manifold to provide air during conditions of deceleration and engine over-run.

IMPORTANT: The efficient operation of the system is dependent on the engine being correctly tuned. The ignition and spark plug settings, valve clearances, and carburetter adjustments given for a particular engine (see **'ENGINE TUNING DATA'**) must be strictly adhered to at all times.

Air pump

The rotary vane type air pump is mounted on the front of the cylinder head and is belt driven from the water pump pulley. Provision is made for tensioning the belt.

Air is drawn into the pump through a dry-type renewable element filter. A relief valve in the pump discharge port allows excessive air pressure at high engine speeds to discharge to the atmosphere.

Check valve

The check valve, fitted in the pump discharge line to the injection manifold, protects the pump from the backflow of exhaust gases.

The valve shuts if the air pressure ceases while the engine is running; for example, if the pump drive belt should break.

Gulp valve

The gulp valve, fitted in the pump discharge line to the inlet manifold, controls the flow of air for leaning-off the rich air/fuel mixture present in the inlet manifold immediately following throttle closure after running at full throttle opening (i.e. engine over-run).

A sensing pipe connected between the inlet manifold and the gulp valve maintains manifold depression directly to the underside of the diaphragm and through a bleed hole to the upper side. Sudden increases in manifold depression which occur immediately following throttle closure act on the underside of the diaphragm which opens the valve and admits air to the inlet manifold. The bleed hole allows the

[NOTE: For a diagram of the single-canister system used on earlier cars, see page 37.]

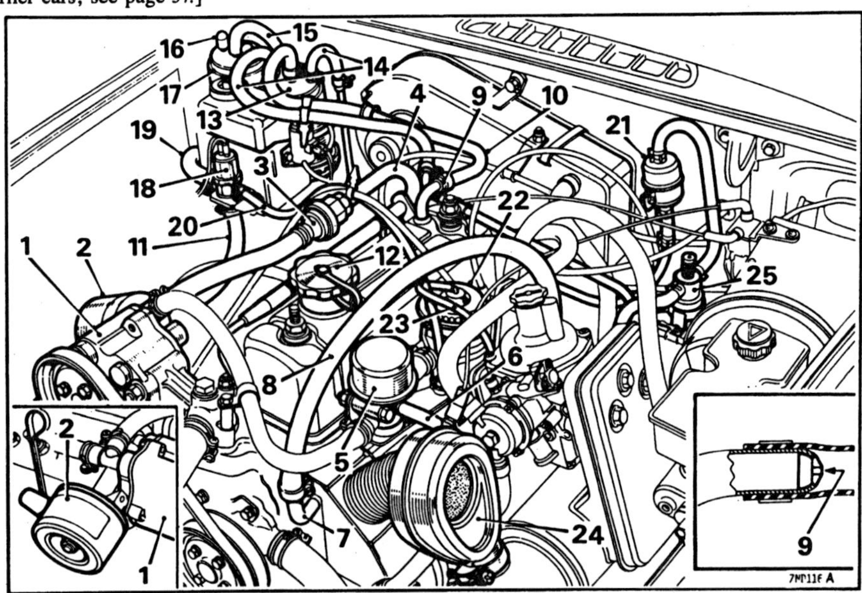

Fig. T.1
The emission control components—1979 and later

1. Air pump
2. Air pump air cleaner
3. Check valve
4. Air manifold
5. Gulp valve
6. Sensing pipe
7. Oil separator/flame trap
8. Breather pipe
9. Restricted connection
10. Purge line
11. Air vent pipe
12. Sealed oil filler cap
13. Primary charcoal adsorption canister
14. Vapour lines
15. Canister inter-connecting pipe
16. Sealing cap
17. Secondary charcoal adsorption canister
18. Running-on control valve
19. Running-on control hose
20. Running-on control pipe
21. Fuel filter
22. Exhaust gas recirculation (E.G.R.) valve
23. E.G.R. valve hose
24. Air temperature control valve
25. Fuel cut-off valve

differences in depression acting on the diaphragm to equalize and the valve closes.
A restrictor is fitted in the air pump discharge connection to the gulp valve, to prevent surging when the gulp valve is operating.

Carburetter

The carburetter is manufactured to a special exhaust emission control specification and is tuned to give optimum engine performance with maximum emission control.
To ensure consistency of fuel metering, the carburetter needle is spring loaded against the side of the jet.
A limit valve is incorporated in the carburetter throttle disc which limits the inlet manifold depression ensuring that under conditions of high inlet-manifold depression the mixture entering the cylinders is at a combustible ratio.

Running-on control valve

The solenoid-operated valve is connected by hoses between the adsorption canister ventilation connection of the evaporative loss control system and the inlet manifold. A third hose connected to the valve is open to atmosphere for canister ventilation while the engine is running normally.
The electrical circuit of the solenoid is connected through the ignition switch and an oil pressure operated switch.
The valve is fitted to prevent prolonged running-on (dieseling) which may occur when using low octane fuels.

Exhaust gas recirculation valve

The exhaust gas recirculation valve (E.G.R.) mounted on the engine manifold controls the circulation of exhaust gas into the inlet manifold. One side of the valve diaphragm operating chamber is connected to the carburetter inlet manifold, the other side is open to atmosphere. The amount of exhaust gas recirculation is dependent upon inlet manifold depression influencing the position of the diaphragm and therefore the manifold valve.

[**NOTE:** See page 38 for a diagram of the evaporative loss control system fitted to 1978 and later cars. On these cars, make the leak test described on page 284 at the canister with three hoses at the top.]

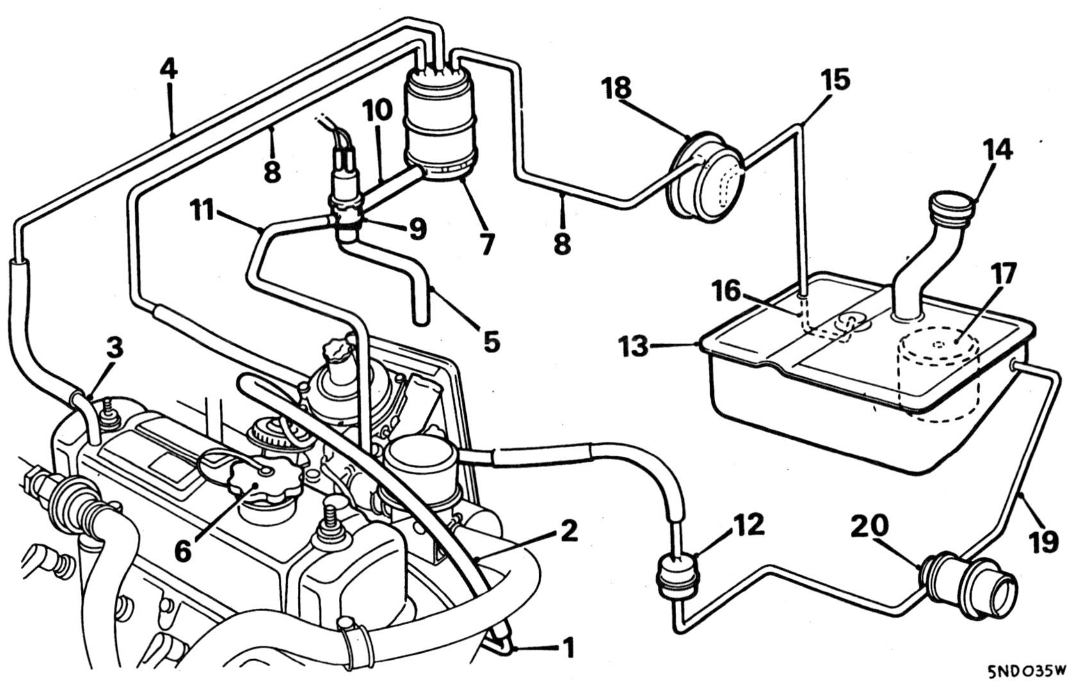

Fig. T.2
The evaporative loss control components

1. Oil separator/flame trap
2. Breather pipe
3. Restrictor connection
4. Purge line
5. Air vent pipe
6. Sealed oil filler cap
7. Charcoal adsorption canister
8. Vapour lines
9. Running-on control valve
10. Running-on control hose
11. Running-on control pipe
12. Fuel line filter
13. Fuel tank
14. Sealed fuel filler cap
15. Vapour line
16. Vapour tube
17. Capacity limiting tank
18. Separation tank
19. Fuel pipe
20. Fuel pump

EVAPORATIVE LOSS CONTROL

The system is designed to collect vapour from the fuel in the fuel tank. The vapour is stored in an adsorption canister while the engine is stopped, and then after the engine is restarted, passed through the crankcase emission control system to the combustion chambers. While the car is being driven the vapours are drawn directly to the crankcase emission control system.

Ventilation tubes on the fuel tank ensure that vapours are vented through the control system even when the car is parked on an inclined surface.

To prevent spillage of fuel by displacement due to expansion, sufficient capacity is available to accommodate the amount of fuel from a full tank which would be displaced by a high temperature rise.

The inclusion of a small separation tank in the vapour line prevents liquid fuel from being carried with the vapour to the storage canister.

IMPORTANT: The fuel and oil filler caps seal the system, and it is essential for its efficient function that they are correctly refitted after removal.

Adsorption canister

The adsorption or vapour storage canister mounted in the engine compartment contains activated charcoal (carbon) granules. Filter pads are fitted at both sides of the charcoal to filter incoming ventilating air and to prevent the granules from leaving the canister through the purge line. Vapour tubes from the fuel tank, carburetter, and the purge line from the engine breather system are connected to the ports on the top of the canister. The port on the bottom section provides a connection for the ventilating air tube.

Fuel vapour entering the canister through the vapour tubes is adsorbed and held by the charcoal. When the engine is started, air is drawn by the crankcase emission control system, through the ventilation tube and into the canister. As the air passes over the charcoal granules the vapours are given up and are carried with the air through the crankcase emission control system to the combustion chambers.

Fuel expansion

To ensure that sufficient space is available to accommodate fuel displaced by expansion due to high ambient temperatures an air lock chamber is incorporated in the tank which prevents the tank being completely filled with fuel, thereby ensuring that sufficient space is always available for expansion.

Fuel line filter

A renewable filter is fitted in the main fuel line as an added safeguard against foreign matter causing the setting of the carburetter float-chamber level to be exceeded.

Crankcase emission control

The engine breather outlet is connected by hoses to the controlled depression chamber; the chamber between the piston and the throttle disc valve, of the carburetter. Engine fumes and blow-by gases are drawn from the crankcase by the depression in this chamber, through an oil separator incorporated in the engine outlet connection, and from there to the inlet manifold. Air for engine breathing is drawn through the filtered adsorption canister of the evaporative loss control system into the engine valve rocker cover. A restrictor in the rocker cover connection reduces the air flow to ensure crankcase depression under all conditions.

Section T.1

EVAPORATIVE LOSS CONTROL 

NOTE: As a preliminary check for leaks on the induction and evaporative loss control systems when fitted with running-on control valves, temporarily block the air vent pipe of the valve while the engine is idling. If no air leaks exist in the systems the engine will stop almost immediately; if the engine continues to run on, an air leak is indicated.

If a fault in the operation of the system is suspected or components other than the filters or canister have been removed and refitted, the evaporative loss control system must be pressure-tested for leaks as follows.

Testing

1. Check that there is at least one gallon of fuel in the fuel tank.
2. Run the engine for one minute to prime the fuel system.
3. Stop the engine, slacken the clip and disconnect the fuel tank ventilation pipe at the canister.
4. Connect a 0 to 10 lbf/in^2 (0 to 0.7 kgf/cm^2) pressure gauge, a Schrader valve, and a low-pressure air supply (tyre pump) to the disconnected pipe.
5. Pressurize the system until 1 lbf/in^2 (0.07 kgf/cm^2) is registered on the gauge.
   WARNING: Do not exceed this pressure at any time.

Fig. T.3

Leak testing the evaporative loss control system

1. Adsorption canister
2. Fuel tank ventilation pipe
3. Pressure gauge

6. Check that the gauge is maintained for 10 seconds without falling more than 0.5 lbf/in² (0.03 kgf/cm²). If the reading is not maintained, check the system for leaks commencing with the fuel filler cap and seal.
7. Make a visual check for fuel leakage.
8. Remove the fuel tank filler cap and check that the gauge falls to zero.
9. Remove the test equipment.
10. Reconnect the fuel tank ventilation pipe to the canister.
11. Tighten the retaining clip.

Section T.2

AIR PUMP 

Testing

Faulty operation of the air pump is generally indicated by excessive noise from the pump.

1. Check the pump drive belt for correct tension; if incorrect, refer to 'MAINTENANCE'.
2. Connect a tachometer to the engine in accordance with the instrument maker's instructions.
3. Slacken the clip and disconnect the gulp valve air supply hose at the gulp valve.
4. Plug the air supply hose.
5. Slacken the clip and disconnect the air manifold supply hose at the check valve.
6. Connect a 0 to 10 lbf/in² (0 to 0.7 kgf/cm²) pressure gauge to the air manifold hose.
7. Run the engine at the air pump test speed as given in 'ENGINE TUNING DATA'. A gauge reading of not less than 2.75 lbf/in² (0.19 kgf/cm²) should be registered.

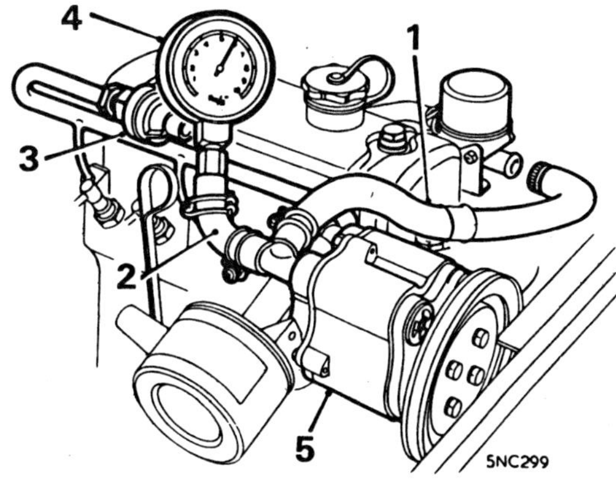

Fig. T.4
Testing the air pump

1. Gulp valve hose
2. Air manifold hose
3. Check valve
4. Pressure gauge
5. Air pump

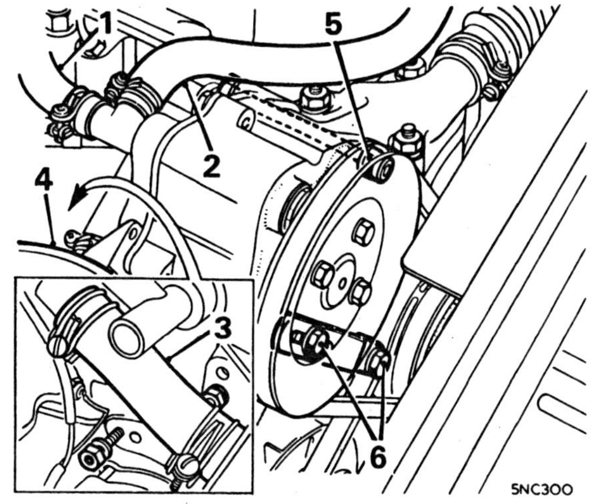

Fig. T.5
Removing the air pump

1. Air pump hose
2. Gulp valve hose
3. Air cleaner hose
4. Air cleaner
5. Mounting bolt
6. Adjusting link bolt

8. If the recommended air pump output pressure is not obtained, fit a new air pump air cleaner element, see 'MAINTENANCE'.
9. If the recommended pressure is still not obtained, temporarily blank off the relief valve and repeat 7; if the reading is as specified, renew the relief valve, see Section T.3.
10. If a satisfactory reading is still unobtainable, overhaul the air pump.

Removing

11. Disconnect the air manifold hose and the gulp valve hose from the air pump.
12. Slacken the clip securing the air pump air cleaner hose to the air pump.
13. Remove the two nuts and washer securing the air cleaner assembly to the air pump.
14. Detach the air cleaner assembly complete with hose from the air pump.
15. Slacken the mounting bolt and the adjusting link bolts and detach the drive belt.
16. Remove the mounting bolt, nut and washer.
17. Remove the adjusting link bolt and lift the air pump from the engine.

Dismantling

18. Remove the four screws with spring washers retaining the end cover and withdraw the cover.
19. Remove the four screws securing the rotor bearing end plate to the rotor and remove the end plate.
20. Lift out the vane assemblies.
21. Remove the carbon and spring assemblies from the rotor.

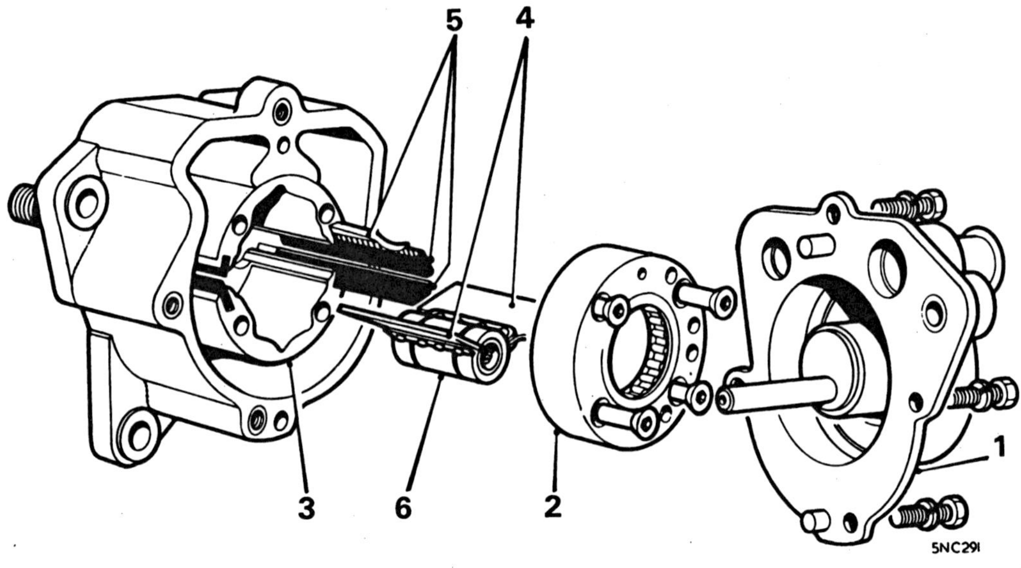

Fig. T.6

Air pump components

1. End cover
2. Rotor bearing end plate
3. Rotor
4. Vane assemblies
5. Carbon and spring assemblies
6. Vane carrier

Inspecting

22. Clean and inspect the vane assemblies for signs of having fouled the pump wall and for grooves. Replace worn or damaged vanes.
23. Clean and inspect the remaining components of the pump.

Reassembling

24. Pack the vane carrier and rotor end plate bearing with Esso Andok 260 lubricant or equivalent.
25. Fit new carbons, chamfered ends to the inside (the original springs may be re-used if serviceable). The slots which carry the carbon and springs are the deeper ones.
26. Reverse the procedure in 18 to 20.

Refitting

27. Reverse the procedure in 11 to 17 ensuring that the drive belt is correctly tensioned.

Section T.3

AIR PUMP RELIEF VALVE 

Testing

WARNING: Do not attempt to check air flow from the relief valve by placing a finger between the valve and the air pump driving pulley.

1. Fit a temporary air duct over the face of the relief valve by fixing a length of adhesive tape over the valve outlet forming a duct as illustrated.
2. Slacken the clip and disconnect the gulp valve air supply hose at the gulp valve.
3. Plug the air supply hose.
4. Slacken the clip and disconnect the air manifold supply hose at the check valve.
5. Connect a 0 to 10 lbf/in² (0 to 0.7 kgf/cm²) pressure gauge to the air manifold hose.
6. Start the engine and slowly increase the speed until air flow from the relief valve is detected. The pressure gauge should read 4.5 to 6.5 lbf/in² (0.32 to 0.45 kgf/cm²) at relief valve blow-off.
7. If the relief valve fails to operate correctly, fit a new relief valve.

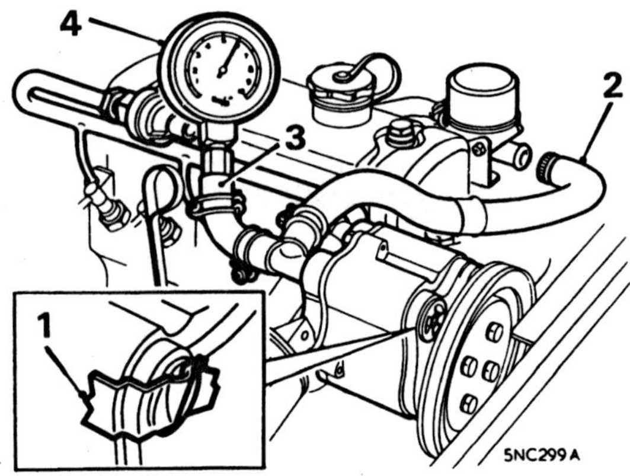

Fig. T.7

Testing the air pump relief valve

1. Temporary duct over relief valve face
2. Gulp valve hose
3. Air manifold hose
4. Pressure gauge

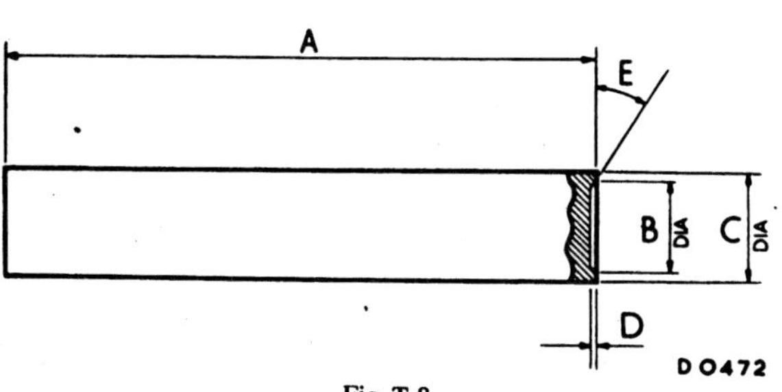

Fig. T.8

Air pump relief valve refitting tool

A. 5 in (127 mm)
B. 0.986 in (25 mm)
C. 1.062 in (27 mm)
D. 0.05 in (1.27 mm)
E. 30°

Removing

8. Remove the air pump.
9. Remove the four bolts and spring washers retaining the pump drive pulley.
10. Remove the pulley.
11. Pass a ½ in (12.7 mm) diameter soft metal drift through the pump discharge connection so that it registers against the relief valve. Drift the valve from the pump.

Refitting

12. Fit a new copper seating washer to the new relief valve and enter the valve into the pump body.
13. Using a tool made to the dimensions given, drive the valve into the pump until the copper seating washer is held firmly but not compressed between the valve and the pump.
14. Reverse the procedure in 8 to 10.

Section T.4

AIR MANIFOLD

Removing

1. Disconnect the air pump hose from the check valve.
2. Remove the rubber clip to release the running-on control pipe from the air manifold.
3. Remove the screw and spring washer securing the air manifold to the rear cylinder head nut.
4. Unscrew the four air manifold unions from the cylinder head and remove the air manifold assembly from the engine.
5. Hold the air manifold connection to prevent it twisting and unscrew the check valve from the air manifold.

Refitting

6. Reverse the procedure in 1 to 5, noting:
   a. Start the screw securing the air manifold to the rear cylinder head nut before tightening the four air manifold unions.
   b. Tighten the four unions evenly.

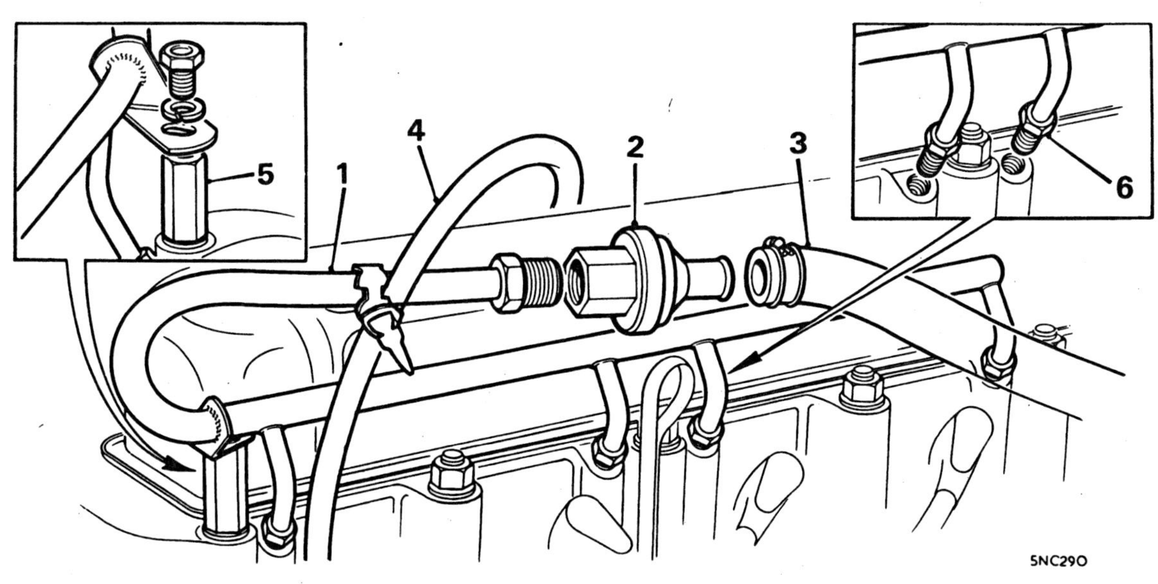

Fig. T.9

Removing the air manifold

1. Air manifold
2. Check valve
3. Air pump hose
4. Running-on control pipe
5. Rear cylinder head nut
6. Air manifold union

Section T.5

HOT AIR DUCT

Removing

1. Slacken the wing nut and pivot the air cleaner end cover and air temperature control assembly away from the engine, detaching the hot air hose from the hot air duct.
2. Remove the nut and washer and the bolt and washer securing the outer duct to the manifold.
3. Remove the outer duct.
4. Remove the nut and washer securing the inner duct to the manifold.
5. Remove the inner duct.

Refitting

6. Reverse the procedure in 1 to 5.

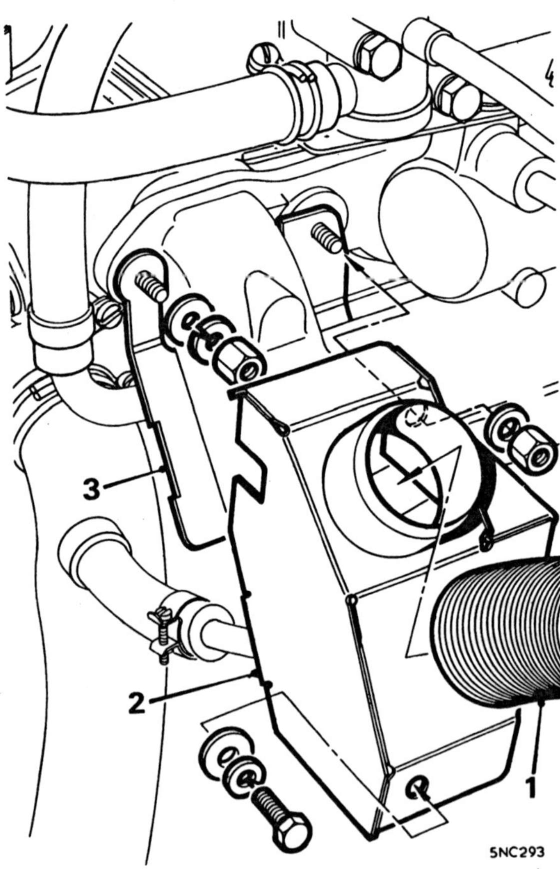

Fig. T.10

Removing the hot air duct

1. Hot air hose
2. Outer duct
3. Inner duct

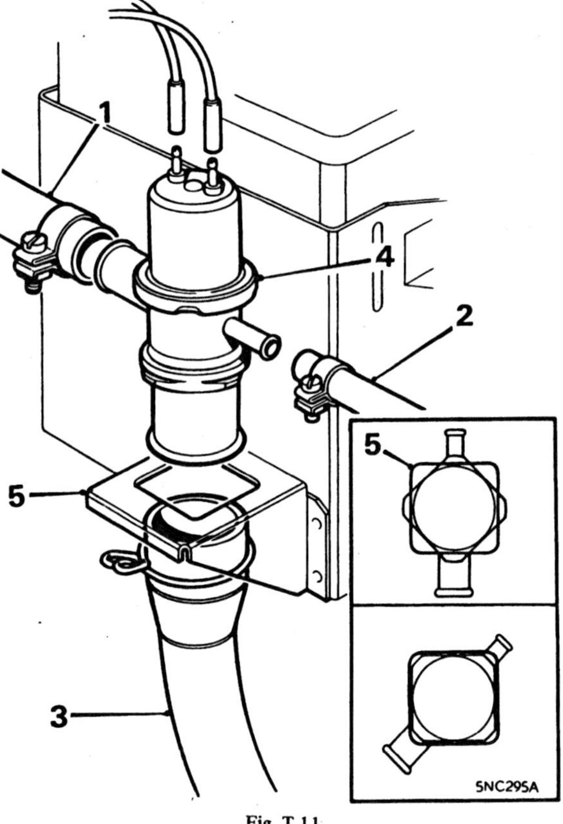

Fig. T.11

Removing the running-on control valve

1. Adsorption canister hose
2. Manifold pipe
3. Vent pipe
4. Running-on control valve
5. Mounting bracket

Section T.6

RUNNING-ON CONTROL VALVE

Testing

1. Check the control valve line fuse.
2. Disconnect the control valve electrical lead at the oil pressure switch.
3. Touch the disconnected lead against a good earth-point on the vehicle. If the electrical circuit and valve are satisfactory the valve will be heard to operate as the lead is earthed.

Removing

4. Disconnect the adsorption canister hose from the valve.
5. Disconnect the manifold pipe from the valve.
6. Squeeze the ends of the clip and disconnect the vent pipe from the valve.
7. Disconnect the electrical leads from the valve.
8. Turn the valve 45° to align the base with the bracket cut-out.
9. Remove the running-on control valve.

Refitting

10. Reverse the procedure in 4 to 9.

CPSIA information can be obtained
at www.ICGtesting.com
Printed in the USA
FSOW02n0957251114
3574FS

9 780837 601120